Lonergan's Quest

WILLIAM A. MATHEWS

LONERGAN'S QUEST
A Study of Desire in the
Authoring of *Insight*

UNIVERSITY OF TORONTO PRESS
Toronto Buffalo London

© University of Toronto Press 2005
Toronto Buffalo London
Printed in Canada

ISBN 0-8020-3875-1 (cloth)
ISBN 978-1-4426-1315-7 (paper)

∞

Printed on acid-free paper

Lonergan Studies

Library and Archives Canada Cataloguing in Publication

Mathews, William A
    Lonergan's quest : a study of desire in the authoring of
Insight / William A. Mathews.

(Lonergan studies)
Includes bibliographical references and index.
ISBN 0-8020-3875-1

1. Lonergan, Bernard J.F. (Bernard Joseph Francis), 1904–1984.
2. Lonergan, Bernard J.F. Insight.   3. Knowledge, Theory of.
I. Title.   II. Series.

B995.L654M385 2005   121   C2005-904230-3

University of Toronto Press acknowledges the financial assistance to
its publishing program of the Canada Council for the Arts and the
Ontario Arts Council.

University of Toronto Press acknowledges the financial support for
its publishing activities of the Government of Canada through the
Book Publishing Industry Development Program (BPIDP).

Contents

Preface / vii

1 Introduction: Desire and the Shaping of an Author / 3

I TRADITIONS AND THE EDUCATION OF DESIRE: THE
APPRENTICESHIP OF A PROBLEM SOLVER, 1904–1940 / 13

2 Quebec Origins: A Classics Student, an Illness, and a
Surprising Vocation / 15
3 Heythrop: Awakening to the Problem of Knowledge / 32
4 Puzzled in Montreal by the Depression and Plato's Ideas / 49
5 Struggling with History and Reality in Rome before
the War / 65
6 Postgraduate Studies in Theology: A New Road Taken / 86

II FINDING AND FOLLOWING THE GOLDEN CORD
OF THE HEART'S DESIRE / 107

7 Economics or Cognitional Theory: Towards Desire's
Decisions / 109
8 Insights into Phantasms as the Origins of Words / 131
9 Thought and Reality: Measuring the Kantian Bridge / 146
10 Aquinas on Cognition and Its Transcendence / 160
11 Toronto, the Operations of the Mind, and a
Creative Illness / 177
12 Human Insights as Reflections of the Divine Nature / 191

III COMPOSING INSIGHT: THE ARTISTRY OF DESIRE / 207

The Proto-Insight, 1949–1951 / 209

13 1949: The Vision of the First Beginning / 211
14 Experimenting with the Insights of Mathematicians
    and Scientists / 221
15 The Breakthrough to Cognitional Structure / 241
16 The Mind's Desire as the Key to the Relation of Thought
    and Reality / 251
17 Exploring the Real Known World: A Metaphysical
    Beginning / 267

The Autograph, 1951–1953 / 285

18 Finally Beginning in the Middle: Common Sense,
    Consciousness, and Self-Affirmation / 287
19 Insights into Emergent Probability / 310
20 Insights into the Dialectical Development of
    Common Sense / 328
21 Insights into the Irreducibility of Things / 346
22 Insights into Philosophical Method, Polymorphism,
    and Isomorphism / 363
23 Process Metaphysics: Finality, Development,
    the Human Image / 375
24 On Mythic and Philosophical Consciousness: Truth and
    Its Expression and Interpretation / 397
25 The Cognitional and the Ethical / 415
26 Questions and Insights in Religion / 429
27 Introduction, Epilogue, Prefaces, Publication / 452
28 Epilogue: Recollecting the Human Mystery / 470

Notes / 479
Bibliography / 533
Benard Lonergan Index / 543
General Index / 549

Preface

Every human life within the compass of its artistry and span is, in its own unique way, a distinct face of the human truth. But as with physical faces, so also with the faces of truth: we have to learn how to read them. Composing the present work has been such an experience. As it unfolded, I found myself drawn into two great human themes, desire and quest, central to the truth that takes shape and is waiting to be read in Lonergan's life.

That the human mind and heart at their core are constituted by a restless desire for truth and value is central in Lonergan's writings. Intellectual desire is for him the anonymous author of the creative solutions and their linguistic expression of the wide range of problems addressed by scientists in recent centuries. In response to life's existential problems, it is a well-spring of new insights and related communicative acts in the dramas of our daily lives. It is the driving force in mastering the plot in a life and articulating it in a biographical narrative. To overlook this desire dimension of mind is to lose sight of the meaning of ourselves as authors of our own knowledge and related language. Its strangeness begins to come to our attention with the discovery that it is nowhere present in its authored products. It invites us to discover that there is much more to human consciousness than perception and instinct. Collectively to take possession of the meaning of our intellectual desire would provide a basis for unifying the otherwise accelerating fragmentation of our knowledge of ourselves and of our worlds.

The quest dimension of desire, largely absent from Lonergan's writings, shows its presence in the artistry and span of his life. Through its incarnation and embodiment at a place and time in a human life it gives that life, in line with an insight of MacIntyre, the shape of a narrative quest.[1] Where

Ricoeur continued MacIntyre's line of inquiry in exploring the dimension of the emplotment of character,[2] the present study is concerned with probing and articulating the emplotment of desire in a life quest. This in turn raises questions concerning how and how well we can know the desire of another person. The presupposition of the biographical task is that the works in a life, as well as available and relevant autobiographical remarks, express its core desires, dreams, and limitations. Following the path of the unfolding of those works reveals the desire that has called for an exodus of the self from its ignorance in a past awakening. That exodus carries it to the creative tension of a present that, in turn, anticipates and strives towards a filling out of the strange present empty nothingness that is to be our future.

The present intellectual biography follows the successive transformations of Lonergan's intellectual desire up to the time of the composition and publication of *Insight*. The spring and summer of his intellectual life, this was a period of intense and vigorous intellectual vitality. It would in time become a part of the wider quest that eventually resulted in *Method in Theology*.[3] In those later years his intellectual desire had to struggle with issues of aging, illness, and mortality, themes present in his life but not in his philosophy.

I intend this work to be of interest both to students of Lonergan's writings and to those interested in the themes of narrative identity and the meaning of authorship. To the former it will provide a resource as well as a framework from within which to read and interpret as parts of an intellectual narrative such collected works of Lonergan as *Grace and Freedom*, *Verbum*, *Insight*, *Collection*, *Political Economy*, *Circulation Analysis*, *Topics in Education*, and *Understanding and Being*. I hope also to provide a valuable interpretative key and a form of commentary on *Insight*. Through narrating the story of the composition of *Insight*, I present that work as more like a travel journal of the mind of its author in his world than as a fortress of thought. I illuminate aspects of the structure of *Insight*, such as its order of composition and its remarkable rewriting of Kant's Copernican revolution in the light of Aristotle, Aquinas, and modern science, that are not easily accessible on a purely internal reading. Out of this an entirely new understanding of the structure of the subject-object relationship is forged. The need to relate Lonergan's thought in chapter 8 on genera and species of things and in chapter 15 on process metaphysics to parallel contemporary currents in order to make sense of the chapters' meaning also involves an element of commentary.[4]

This study also addresses a range of questions in the fields of personal identity and authorship. What Lonergan terms the 'pure desire to know' is just as much a key force in the authoring of a person's identity as it is in the composing of a text. There are, however, no shortcuts to appreciating the strange qualities of the intellectual desire of the human mind or of the manner in which it relates us to the universe and unifies otherwise fragmentary experiences in our lives. However one responds to his philosophical insights, the fact remains that Lonergan's own life is a striking instance and case study of the performance of that intellectual desire. Detailing and narrating his quest is a long and demanding undertaking. I offer this attempt in the conviction that an understanding of intellectual desire, in the manner in which it both relates us to the universe and directs the intellectual quests and authoring within our temporal lives, is an exercise of immense anthropological significance. It involves getting to grips with a quality and power that makes us humans truly unique within the universe.

In conclusion, I would like to acknowledge, with gratitude, the help and encouragement of many individuals in the course of the long years involved in the composition of this text:

In Montreal, Lynn Lonergan-Doyle and her family for their interest and support, Charlotte Tansey and members of the Thomas More Institute, and the hospitality of the then Loyola community.

In Toronto, Frederick Crowe, Robert Doran, Robert Croken, and Michael Shields for their support and for helping me to find my way around the archives; and the hospitality of the Arrupe community.

In Boston, Fred and Sue Lawrence, whose Lonergan Workshops enabled me to develop some of the ideas in this work; Joseph Flanagan for funding research during a summer; and the hospitality of the St Mary's Hall community.

On the West Coast, Mark Morelli and Elizabeth Murray, and the hospitality of the LMU community.

For help in different ways, Philip McShane, Conn O'Donovan, Michael Shute, Richard Liddy, Des O'Grady, Garrett Barden, Oliver Maloney, Leonard and Joan Ryan, and Peter Coghlan.

Ron Schoeffel of the University of Toronto Press for helpful comments and encouragement in the course of composition, and Terry Teskey for her editorial work.

For their help in the endgame, Noel Barber, Phil Huston, Brendan Duddy, and Kevin O'Higgins.

Lonergan's Quest

1

Introduction: Desire and the
Shaping of an Author

We can see horribly clear in the works of such a man his whole life, as if we were
God's spies.[5]

Desire

Biographers have to listen long and carefully to the experiences of their
subjects in order to disclose what, in the words of Pedro Arrupe, character-
izes those lives as most personal, as most uniquely them.[2] Only after they
have built up a level of familiarity with the cast of significant characters and
the creative works of the life do the properly biographical questions begin
to come into focus. At this point, certain events, relationships, and remarks
in the life can light up, stand out from the great multiplicity of known facts
as the signatures of the life as a whole.

One such remark is to be found in the opening chapter of *Insight*, written
early in the process of composition, possibly in 1951, Lonergan's forty-
seventh year. Reflecting on the disposition of mind that led Archimedes to
make his discoveries, he wrote:

> Deep within us all, emergent when the noise of other appetites is
> stilled, there is a drive to know, to understand, to see why, to dis-
> cover the reason, to find the cause, to explain. Just what is wanted,
> has many names. In precisely what it consists, is a matter of dispute.
> But the fact of inquiry is beyond all doubt. It can absorb a man. It
> can keep him for hours, day after day, year after year, in the narrow
> prison of his study or laboratory. It can send him on dangerous

voyages of exploration. It can withdraw him from other interests, other pursuits, other pleasures, other achievements. It can fill his waking thoughts, hide from him the world of ordinary affairs, invade the very fabric of his dreams. It can demand endless sacrifices that are made without regret though there is only the hope, never a certain promise, of success.[3]

Although not presented as a personal statement about Lonergan's own desire, the remark has an unmistakable autobiographical ring to it. It invites us to transpose it into the first person and listen to it as though it were Lonergan talking about himself. It then becomes a revelation of the unusual personal lifestyle and experiences involved in authoring *Insight*. Intellectual desire and passion were central to Lonergan's existence.

Further clues to the heart of the man are to be found in the preface, written last in 1954. There he acknowledged his debt to his teachers, who left their mark on him in the course of the twenty-eight years that had elapsed since he was introduced to philosophy. Much of his search during the ensuing years when he was thinking out *Insight* was a dark struggle with his own flight from understanding, a slow development characterized by dim light and detours. His later description of the intellectual pattern of experience again throws light on his experiences throughout those twenty-eight years:

> Still, even with talent, knowledge makes a slow, if not a bloody, entrance. To learn thoroughly is a vast undertaking that calls for relentless perseverance. To strike out on a new line and become more than a week-end celebrity calls for years in which one's living is more or less constantly absorbed in the effort to understand, in which one's understanding gradually works round and up a spiral of viewpoints with each complementing its predecessor and only the last embracing the whole field to be mastered.[4]

His remarks make clear that Lonergan's introduction to philosophy in 1926, when he was twenty-one years old, was the beginning of a twenty-eight-year quest whose eventual product was the book *Insight*. His initial challenge was formed in part by his early encounter with Kant's Copernican revolution and Mill's methodology. Through these and some later lights gleaned from Aquinas, Lonergan would find himself drawn into one of what he would term the big questions in his life: *what* is intellectual desire, how does it relate us to the world, how is it satisfied, and what sort of world does it make known? He would answer that it was a principle of cognition that structures consciousness in terms of levels. In response to it a rich variety of distinct types of scientific, common-sense, and philosophical insights emerge. Through them is made known the many different kinds of intelligibilities we find in our world.

The narrative that follows finds itself drawn into exploring that same desire and related insights, but from a complementary perspective. Its task, prompted by our long quotation from chapter 1 of *Insight,* will be to show how Lonergan's intellectual desire, as it unfolded in response to the emerging problems in his life, directed him both towards the decision to author *Insight* and in the subsequent work. It was a factor that shaped the emergent design of his life and of his personal identity. At the centre of his daily and yearly lifestyle over the twenty-eight years it took to think out and compose *Insight* was the solitary space and time in which he worked. The cast of persons in his life knew and respected this, knew not to trespass on that sacred space where his intellectual passion engaged with the problems that came to him and, when successful, authored his texts. It is in this work, complemented by teaching and seminars, that we find the heart of the man.

What follows is an effort to show that core desire in its awakenings, formative phases, struggles to grow, and creativity. The difficulty of narrating it, given Lonergan's reluctance to disclose the details of his struggle to distinguish his own intellectual desires from his senses, instinct, and imagination, should not be underestimated. But to fail to narrate it would rob him of his core.[5]

Desire as the Mover of a Narrative/Vision Quest

Complementing Lonergan's account of desire, MacIntyre suggests that the unity of a life is the unity of a narrative quest. He holds that when we set out on a quest we have only the vaguest notion of what it is that we are in search of:

> But secondly it is clear the medieval conception of a quest is not at all that of a search for something already adequately characterised, as miners search for gold or geologists for oil. It is in the course of a quest and only through encountering and coping with the various particular harms, dangers, temptations and distractions which provide any quest with its episodes and incidents that the goal of the quest is finally to be understood. A quest is always an education both as to the character of that which is sought and in self-knowledge.[6]

The remarks bring into sharp relief the quest dimension of our intellectual passion as a journey into an unknown. Like all quests, it is story structured in time. It moves from a now, past awakening, through an unresolved present towards an anticipated resolution in a future. Through many refigurations of its path, intellectual desire traces an unread story as it opens itself up to what Joseph Campbell would term its 'sought-for vision.'[7]

Insight was the product of a quest for an intellectual vision, the vision that was anticipated in the set of questions that emerged and formed the plot structure of the quest. In this context Paul Ricoeur's experiences are worth recalling. When asked about the authoring of his many books, he replied that each was determined by a fragmentary problem.[8] This was in line with his conviction that philosophy was a matter of addressing 'well-circum-scribed difficulties of thought.' Every time he finished a book he found himself confronted with something that had escaped beyond its orbit. After finishing *Time and Narrative* and *Oneself as Another*, he found it was the theme of memory. It was his experience as an author that such a theme would first prowl at the edges of his consciousness and then move towards the centre, eventually becoming an obsession out of which would grow the next work he would author. The theme of the new book would begin off-centre in relation to the previous one. Beginning as a fragment, it would grow into a totality. In this manner, through the transformations of his desire in the succession of his authored books, an intellectual vision opens up.

As the narrative that follows will elaborate, entering into Lonergan's vision quest involves tracking his emerging questions. How was the course of his intellectual desire awakened and shaped by the positive or negative encounter with the traditions that educated it? How, during his philosophical studies during 1926–7 in Heythrop, did Lonergan find his intellectual desire awakened and drawn into the major Kantian problem of the relation between thought and reality? What, this study asks, is the relation between the thought processes and thoughts that characterize our conscious life and living and the independent existence of the facts, situations, and things in our worlds that we think about? At least since Kant there has been a tendency to think about these so-called inner and outer realms as separated by an unbridgeable chasm. The issue requires us to ask probing questions about the nature and relational properties of our elusive and strange conscious mental processes. Whiteside, Lonergan's teacher at the time, impressed on him that there was currently no satisfactory answer to the problem.

After detailing his awakening to a path, the narrative will follow his progress during and after the 1930s. His subsequent first-hand experience of the Depression while teaching in Montreal in the 1930s drew him into an attempt to understand why the economic cycle had collapsed, again an unsolved problem. He would work on it in his spare time for fourteen years, and in its own way it would contribute to his world view of emergent probability in *Insight*. After moving to Rome in 1933 for his theology studies, he witnessed at close quarters the beginning of a further collapse of European history with the rise of Hitler and National Socialism and the fascism of Mussolini. Out of this he found himself drawn into the problem of progress and decline within a philosophy of history of which the collapse of the economic order was a part. His subsequent insights became the background for his analysis in *Insight* of the biases of common sense.

At the same time he was struggling with the contrast between materialist/ intuitive and Platonic and Kantian visions of understanding. The latter clearly would not reduce understanding to sensibility but did not have a satisfactory answer to the problem about the mind's relation to reality. A chance encounter with the thought of Maréchal and, through Leeming, Aquinas on the relation between judgment and existence began to open up for him an alternative solution. Central in those refigurations was the liberation of Lonergan's mind from what Cushman calls the bondage of the Platonic cave of the senses and instincts and the accompanying highly reductionist empiricist sense of reality.[9] That transition and the related liberated sense of reality were only attained by a highly disturbing *periagoge*, a turning around of his psyche in an intellectual conversion. Out of it came his use of the word 'insight' to designate certain irreducible qualities of the human mind. Lonergan clearly acknowledged that such a disturbing process had occurred in him on his journey, but was quite unable to describe and communicate in any depth how, precisely, he experienced it.

His interest in the philosophy of history continued through the mid-1930s, when he found himself unexpectedly moved by others from philosophy to theology. His subsequent postgraduate studies dealt with a highly disputed text in Aquinas on the problem of grace and human freedom. It was the beginning of his interest in the problem of the method of theology.

Although assigned to teach theology in Rome, he returned to Montreal in 1940 because of the war. Initially he continued his work on economics, but as it ran its course and petered out he found himself drawn back to the problem of the mind-world relation. In 1943, convinced that Aquinas had something significant to say about this matter, he embarked on a six-year study that was to become the *Verbum* articles. Far from reading Aquinas, as some have suggested, from a Kantian perspective, he was searching for clues to a solution to this central problem posed in Kantian philosophy. Although the search was an intense and desert-like experience, he was not disappointed by what he found. In his published articles we find him assembling the elements of the problem of levels of cognitional operations and the related meaning of consciousness.

In the middle of this research, in 1945 he gave a course entitled 'Thought and Reality,' a precursor to a later course entitled 'Intelligence and Reality.' Encouraged by the response, he made the decision to research and write *Insight*. The titles of the courses show the centrality of the mind-world relation for him and its significance for our understanding of *Insight*.

Soon after, in January 1947, he was moved to Toronto. After settling down and finishing the *Verbum* articles, he found in 1949 that the time had come to work out and compose *Insight*. Centrally, this involved working out his own highly original solution to the problem of the nature of the relation of the subject and object of knowledge, of thought and reality. From this perspective, he explored the relation between the knowing subject and the known world in the highly theoretical empirical sciences and in the field of common sense with its world of drama and history.

As in his earlier explorations, Lonergan had engaged with economics and history; now, in thinking out and authoring *Insight*, he was embarking on a massive engagement with the dominant scientific culture of the time. In the course of this research unusual insights emerged into world order as evolving in accordance with a problem-solving principle of finality and a related emergent probability. In the structure of the relation between different levels in consciousness he found clues on the manner of the relation between the distinct empirical sciences of physics, chemistry, biology, and so forth. Common-sense knowledge he came to identify as a specialization distinct from science. Its development was revealed to be inherently dialectical. He identified metaphysics as that philosophical discipline which has the task of unifying other disciplines in a world view, articulating a framework for collaborative creativity.

As the unique desires of a human being constitute an irreducible component in his or her human identity, to show them is to show who, irreducibly, the Other is. To show the emerging course and growth of intellectual desire in a lifetime is to bring into view that power of mind that in important ways unifies our existence, identity, and related vision quest. To lose sight of it is to be left with an inevitable fragmentation in our sense of how we exist in time. That power of mind, intellectual desire, is story structured in time. To reveal the manner in which, as it grows, it moves a vision quest is to reveal, in detail, what is meant by the narrative self. To show how an individual responds to and lives his or her emerging desires is also, in a sense, to show that individual's spirituality.

Desire as Author

If MacIntyre and Campbell are illuminating on desire as the mover of a vision quest, a remark in Bergman's autobiographical reflections invites us to focus on its role in authoring:

> Watching forty years of my work over the span of one year turned
> out to be unexpectedly upsetting, at times unbearable. I suddenly
> realized that my movies had mostly been conceived in the depths of
> my soul, in my heart, my brain, my nerves, my sex, and not least, in
> my guts. A nameless desire gave them birth. Another desire, which
> can perhaps be called 'the joy of the craftsman,' brought them that
> further step where they were displayed to the world.[10]

The desire in us to open up to an intellectual vision ultimately enlarges into
the desire to communicate that vision to others, in which communication it
finds its proper fulfilment. In this second dimension intellectual desire,
through the insights it calls forth, is revealed to be the source or wellspring
that causes the subsequent original language use of the author. Bergman
explicitly adverted to his desire as the author of his works but considered
that it was futile to try and understand it, a position at odds with MacIntyre.

Lonergan began composing the text of *Insight* in the summer of 1949,
finishing it in 1953. The question arises, what sort of an understanding can
we arrive at of this process of authoring? In his academic research Edgar
Schein found himself drawn into the problem of how individuals, be they
prisoners of war in China, trainee IBM salespersons, or seminarians in
the Maryknoll Seminary, struggle to retain their identity in the face of the
coercive forces in institutions. When he reviewed the way in which the
problems had formed for him, he concluded that in both their inspiration
and in their resolution the image presented of his mind at work was artistic:

> I see 'artistry' in my work at several levels. My insights into phenom-
> ena came unexpectedly and often at times when I was not thinking
> about that phenomenon at all. It was therefore always wise for me to
> juggle several intellectual domains at the same time instead of work-
> ing on one thing until it was finished. I see in my writing the same
> kinds of 'problems' of how to render something that artists talk
> about. I have creative bursts when everything seems to click and a
> paper or part of a chapter just flows in an uninterrupted way.[11]

In his memoir entitled 'The Academic as Artist' Schein argues that the
manner in which the desire and insights of an author move and accumulate
in the performance of authoring a text is inherently artistic. That artistry of
mind is just as much involved in scientific research and inquiry as in
searching for a storyline with its characters and twists and turns in authoring
a novel.

The implication of these assertions is that there is and must be a basic
artistry of mind, whether it is involved in dramatic intersubjective living or

in literary and scientific authoring. The basic performative nature of mind is artistic.[12] As it takes shape throughout a lifetime its form is more music-like than law-like. Through that artistry and the stream of insights it calls forth, the original verbal structure and meaning of the text comes to be composed.

The process of composition between 1949 and 1953 divides into four movements. In a first movement spanning the initial two years, inspired by his insights into Aquinas on the desire to know and its relation to the knowable world, Lonergan worked out in a proto-*Insight* some key elements of a solution to Kant's problem. He came to understand that from the standpoint of the mind's desire to know, facts, situations, and states of affairs in the world and the conscious activities of the knowing subject are both known in essentially the same way: through our questioning activity, insights, and judgments. This eliminates the myth of the chasm but leaves us with the task of determining how to distinguish, within what we know, between the subject and objects of knowledge and the nature of their relation.

The MSA autograph of *Insight* was composed between the summers of 1951 and 1953. It was a period of intense, explosive creativity in which we find expressed the depths of the desire moving his vision quest. He began the second movement by articulating in chapters 9–13 his breakthrough in the proto-*Insight*. The rest of the autograph, chapters 1–8 and 14–20, was written from the horizon of those foundations.

In a third movement, chapters 1–8 of *Insight*, written next, explore the nature of the subject-and-world relation in scientific and common-sense knowing. The scientific knower can be characterized by such distinctive types of questions and insights as the classical and the statistical, which are operative in the scientific community. The proportionate known world order of emergent probability is, for Lonergan, forged by the interplay in the world of classical and statistical laws. In order to be clear about what we know, the world order of an emergent probability, we must also be clear about how we come to know it, not by mere looking, picturing, or imagining but through a combination of classical and statistical questions and insights. In this, his analysis of the insights of scientists presupposes an existing mind-world relation that it sets out to understand.

Chapters 6 and 7 explore the relation between the common-sense subject and world. The consciousness of that subject can be patterned in many different ways, including the biological, the aesthetic, and the dramatic with its blind spots and related dramatic biases, of which the intellectual pattern is one. The knowing of the common-sense subject is not necessarily pure, but can be distorted by those further dimensions. The world of the common-sense subject is a community of others characterized by a dialectical tension between intellectual development and the inertia of the spontaneous sensitivity of individuals, groups, and humankind in general. From there spring the biases of common sense, individual, group, and general.

In composing chapter 8 Lonergan embarked on a massive analysis of the significance of his theory of insight into phantasm for our understanding of the different kinds of things in our world, elementary particles, elements, and compounds, genera and species of plants, animals, and humans. A thing or species is for him a distinct solution to the problem of living in an environment. As an insight and the solution it grasps cannot be reduced to the imaginative presentations of the problem, so a thing or species as a solution cannot be reduced to the materials that enter into its living. Hence the irreducibility of things or species.

A fourth and final movement in the composition runs from chapter 14 through to the end. No less than the agent of common sense, the philosopher is not a pure intellect and must come to terms with the fact that the many ways in which consciousness can pattern itself tend to mask or obscure the startlingly strange nature of the pure desire to know and the related insights into the world that it seeks. From this perspective, the earlier philosophical solution to the Kantian problem in chapters 9–13 is enlarged to include this dialectical dimension. There follows an outline sketch of an analysis of a related process metaphysics of the known world that involves a transformation of Aristotle in the light of Kant, modern science, and Henri Bergson's *Creative Evolution.*

The relation between interpreters of texts such as the classics in religion, literature, or philosophy and their audiences is offered as a further realm in which the relation between the subject and object of knowledge can be explored. The fact that a conflict of interpretations seems to be the norm again points towards a dialectical dimension in the relation. In this manner, Lonergan worked out the implications of his basic set of insights for our understanding of the subject and object of science, common sense, the irreducibility of the things we understand, a world order constituted by a process metaphysics, and the interpretation of the classics of a tradition for their current audience.

The final chapters of *Insight,* which deal with insights in the ethical and religious fields, must be considered somewhat exploratory. They contain many significant insights into the enlargement of consciousness into the ethical, the structure of the human good, and the enigmas of existence and evil. These, taken with Lonergan's remarks in the epilogue on interpersonal relations, point towards further possible developments of his analysis of the subject-world relationship in the realms of ethics, religion, and the self and the other.

In the artistry of an author there is also to be identified that individual's own particular voice and its related style and tone. Lonergan's style is heavily mathematical, the method of implicit definition developed by Hilbert, the mathematician, being constantly in the background. Numbers abound in his works: the three or four levels of consciousness and the eight functional specialties of theology. Mathematical terms are used analogically, such as differentiated and undifferentiated common sense and the differentials of history. His tone of voice leans towards the doctrinaire in that he tends to put his answers to questions before us rather than the questions themselves; 'Being, then, is the objective of the pure desire to know.'[13] But his style is also characterized by an almost superhuman patience. There are for him no quick fixes to the fundamentals in philosophy, the structure of the pure desire to know. Problem solving takes as long as it takes. This patience in the author requires a parallel patience in his interpreters.

Considerations of the manner in which the life and identity of an author are shaped by his or her desire ultimately lead us to the further question: how is the desire of Lonergan present in the text of *Insight*? A careful reading of a text might find no reference in it to the desire of the author and conclude that text and desire were unrelated. Against this is the fact that the author's absent desire is involved as an efficient cause in the shaping and crafting of every word that is to go into the text. In its totality the text is also an expression of the values that are desired by the author. By bringing Lonergan's desire as author out into the open, the narrative that follows will bring into focus the question about the presence of an author's desire in the text. The author's desire shapes the structure and style of the text just as much as it shapes the life of the author.

This introduction has articulated some elements of the heuristic structures of the question: who desired to think out and author the book *Insight*? The task of the narrative that follows will be to fill out details of the answers. On three fronts, assimilating the narrative that follows requires a patient commitment of time. Firstly, Lonergan's path to the summer of 1949 when he began to author the text was necessarily long and complex. Secondly, the technical content of his quest and of the related vision articulated in the book is highly complex. Thirdly, the vision of the human as author involved is largely unfamiliar and resolutely anti-reductionist.

PART ONE

Traditions and the Education of Desire: The Apprenticeship of a Problem Solver, 1904–1940

2

Quebec Origins: A Classics Student, an Illness, and a Surprising Vocation

Bernard Lonergan, the eldest of three boys, was born to Gerald and Josephine Lonergan on 17 December 1904 in Buckingham, Quebec, a small town on the Lièvre about eighteen miles east of Ottawa. About his origins he has remarked:

> My great grandfather, Timothy Lonergan, and his wife Bridget Casey emigrated from Ireland and settled at Ste-Thérèse-de-Blainville. When my grandfather, Mickey, saw that the Lonergans were all marrying French girls, he decided to move off to Buckingham where he found a red-headed Irish girl and married her.[1]

The girl's name was Frances Gorman. Michael, who was not a success at farming, became a butcher on Main Street. The two had a large family; Gerald, Bernard's father, their second, was born in 1871.

Present-day Buckingham is a neat and prosperous town with a population of around twelve thousand. Named after its English counterpart, it was first settled in 1827. By the turn of the century its population of three thousand was made up of a number of quite distinct cultural groupings. Two-thirds of the population at the time were French speaking. Of the remainder, roughly five hundred were Irish and half that number each English or Scottish. There was also a small German population. The French, Irish, and Germans were mainly Catholic, the English and Scottish mainly Presbyterian and Baptists. At the turn of the century they were rigidly demarcated groups with little intermarrying. According to Pierre Louis Lapointe, the golden age of Buckingham ran from 1891–1903. From 1903 until 1943 it underwent a difficult transition because of certain problems that arose between the different groups during those years.

James MacLaren (1818–92), an orthodox Presbyterian two of whose brothers were ministers and whose family came from Glasgow, was the local industrial giant. A banker and a lumber merchant, he and his family were to determine the fate of Buckingham in the first half of the twentieth century. The Calvinist principles imprinted on him by his father David made him 'a tireless worker who never counted hours or cowered before the obstacles he encountered on the road to success. He was stubborn and uncompromising.'[2]

His sons, in particular Alexander and Albert, who lived in Buckingham, were largely responsible for a notorious strike in 1906. Because of their monopoly, they paid lower wages than elsewhere in the region: to millwrights, forty cents an hour, the average in the region being closer to sixty cents. Bill Dobson, who was at school with Lonergan, left Buckingham because it was too difficult at the time to make enough money to get married. In the spring of 1906 the company cut its workforce, increasing the workload of every employee. Three meetings of the workers were held, the second and third in St Michael's College, where later Lonergan would attend school. A union executive was formed:

> The workers were asking for so little! They apologetically formed a union in order to demand equitable salaries but only for the poorest among them. They asked for a minimum wage, such as had been paid for several years before in the Ottawa-Hull region. What transpired goes beyond all understanding. The extreme measures employed by the MacLarens to crush the workers make sense only if the MacLarens truly believed that the workers threatened their very existence: their property, their business, and even their lives. If this was the case, it was only a question of perception and images, because the reality was a long way from being so bleak. Perceptions of reality, however, always motivate actions, rather than reality itself. The MacLarens were fully convinced that they were in serious danger and they prepared themselves accordingly.[3]

Two strikers were shot dead during the strike, and afterwards others were quite unjustly jailed.

The MacLarens, it seems, were ready to go to any lengths to preserve their monopolistic control of the lower Lièvre. After the strike they drew up a blacklist of some 262 names, the vast majority being French. Until 1943 those named on the list would not find employment in Buckingham. As a result, a quarter of the working population left the town.

Family Circle, Parish, and School

Lonergan's father studied at Ottawa University and, like his sister Mary, taught for a number of years in a school in Buckingham. After attending McGill University from 1890–4 and graduating as a civil engineer, Gerald was employed as a Dominion surveyor. His work involved leaving the family home as soon as the snows melted and travelling to distant parts of Canada to survey the territories. It was tough outdoor work that did not require the cultivation of the social graces. For much of the time it involved living in a tent. Ann Lonergan, the wife of his youngest son, Mark, smiled at the memory of a dishevelled racoon coat, much in need of repair, that he wore for one of his trips. Mark accompanied him once and remembered walking great distances, sometimes up to twenty-five miles a day. Gerald would not return home from his work until the late fall.

He married Josephine Wood on 16 February 1904, when both were approaching their mid-thirties. Given the antisocial nature of his work and its implications for family life, marriage was a matter he took seriously. As he was away for most of the year, their courtship was prolonged. Finally it became too much for Josephine; when, yet again, he was returning to the territories without setting a date for the wedding, she threw the ring he had given her back at him. This seems to have had the desired effect, and they were soon married. She accompanied him to the west, honeymooning in a tent. The following December Bernard was born.

To counteract the loneliness his wife would experience during his long periods of absence from the family home, he invited one of her sisters to come and live in their house, paying her the salary she was receiving from her work.[4] Mary Adelaide Wood, known as aunt Minnie, was at this time in her early forties, nine years older than her sister. Ann Lonergan was of the opinion that in her earlier years Mary had been in love but it was unrequited, possibly because of religious differences.

Gerald was gruff by temperament, almost to the point of being offputting, until, as Ann Lonergan remarked, you learned how to read him. He could also have a hot temper, but most recognized that behind his grave exterior lay a soft interior. His wife bore him three sons, but he would also have liked a daughter and was disappointed to learn, after Mark was born, that she had been advised not to have any more children.

Among his peers he had the reputation of being an honest man, a man of his word. Although not a pious Catholic, he had clear-cut norms about right and wrong. He treated the boys with equality, giving them the same pocket money. Bernard remembered his father teaching him some mathematics and how to swim in the river, but he usually had more to say about his mother. Gregory remembered Gerald insisting that children should have a childhood and not be forced to grow up too quickly. The boys were sorry to see him go to his work and glad to see him return. Who knows what impact this image of a father departing to map vast territories had on his first-born son, who would later set about mapping vast fields of knowledge. Being the eldest of the three boys, Bernard, in the absence of his father, became the man in the house, a matter in which he took much pride and that stamped itself on his adult personality.

Lonergan's mother, born Josephine Wood of English-German origins at Faran's Point Ontario, on 27 March 1869, was a devout Catholic. Her father was a millwright who moved to Buckingham, presumably to find work. The youngest of a family of four daughters and two sons, she worked in Thompson's General Store on Main Street before her marriage. In Buckingham she had a reputation for holiness, saying the rosary and going to Mass every day. Bill Dobson remembered her showing a real interest in children that she met on the street. She took the responsibility of the religious formation of her own children seriously.

At her convent school she had learned music and enjoyed playing the piano and painting. In his later years, hearing the Kreutzer Sonata reminded Bernard of sitting on the lawn as a child and listening as she played 'The Mockingbird' in the house.[5] By temperament Josephine's piety and holiness were combined with an aristocratic self-image, even to the extent of being proud, as Mary confided to Ann. As she cultivated the social graces, so she tried, not with much success, to cultivate them in her husband. She treated the boys equally and fairly, but Mark remembers that she always served Bernard first at table. He was her first born. She made him feel special, loved by God. Though gentle, she did not want the boys to be sissies. Despite her considerable fears, she let them bathe in the river, knowing that like other children they jumped across the logs that were floated down the river to the mill. This was extremely dangerous and from time to time resulted in fatalities.

Among his brothers Gregory, who like him would become a Jesuit, and Mark, he was the senior, the boss. Mark remarked, rather poignantly, that when their aunt Mary sent them a storybook about the three bears they immediately identified Bernie with the big bear, Greg with the middle, and Mark with the little bear. Bernard was close to Gregory throughout his life, holidaying with him many summers, and they would both spend their last days together in the Jesuit retirement home in Pickering, Ontario. But this did not exclude an element of sibling rivalry between them:

> The point is that all of us in childhood have to solve implicitly and pragmatically a whole series of questions in cognitional theory, epistemology and metaphysics. We have to distinguish dreaming and

waking, imagining and seeing, stories and what really happened; we have to discover the possibility and learn to suspect the occurrence of a sibling's joke, trick, fib.[6]

Later discussing Cicero's egoism (in getting the pattern of a man's mind fairly fast), Bernard said that 'the first time I read about Achilles crying, he wasn't a great hero to me. Only cry-babies cry!'[7] In the family games he was, at the expense of his brothers, out to win.

After Bernard was born in the Wood's family home, just off Main Street, in December 1904, Gerald bought Rosehurst as his family house. A sturdy brick house on Pine Avenue, it was later built on by the Knights of Columbus. With his father away most of the time, the young Bernard was brought up largely by his mother and his aunt Minnie, of whom he was fond. The family friends at the time included the Woods, Gormans, Vallillees, and Costelloes, and from the evidence available it seems that Bernard enjoyed birthday parties and family social gatherings. His older cousin Lucia, the daughter of his mother's sister, Jane Alice (Nellie) Wood and her husband, Charles de Villiers, was from early on a favourite friend of both Bernard and Gregory. In 1914 she married Rupert Vallilee. When Bernard returned to Buckingham he would visit her. A much loved person, she had the reputation of being a book-worm. All her family read books.

From the house it was a short walk down the street to the local parish church, St Gregory of Nazienzen,[8] named after one of the great fathers of the Trinity. The Lonergan children were obliged by their mother to visit it daily. The parish was initially bilingual, announcements being made in French and English at the Sunday masses and a sermon in French or English alternating at 7 and 9. It was not until 1939 that the English-speaking community built a Church of their own.[9]

Situated opposite the church, St Michael's College was founded in 1897 by Fr Francois Michel, the parish priest. It was planned as a grade school complemented with a business course rather than as a classical college. The parish invited the Brothers of Christian Instruction to run it. Most of the early teachers were unable to keep discipline and lacked pedagogical skills, a problem that was overcome by replacing them with new teachers. The business course, when first presented, was badly planned and failed. (It would be more successful a second time around.) There were also tensions between the French and Irish groups – the Irish wanting Irish brothers to teach them – that came to a head in 1903.[10]

Starting in 1910, Bernard attended the school from his sixth until his thirteenth year. During the summer before he began school the six-year-old Bernard was bored. Asking his cousin what he should do on a slow, hot summer day, he was told, 'Well, you read a book.' He immediately read *Treasure Island* as his first.[11] When his aunt Minnie moved into the house she brought with her the collected writings of Dickens, which he would read by the fire after the rest of the family had retired. From this point on reading became his passion. He was always reading something: Newman's *Grammar of Assent*, Christopher Dawson's *The Age of the Gods*, J.A. Stewart's *Plato's Doctrine of Ideas*, Shull's *Evolution*. In this manner he would experience how, through his engagement with the text, his sense of himself and of his world could be transformed quite beyond the realm of immediate experience. With hindsight, he described the manner in which certain books turned up at significant moments in his life and formed his questions as a form of providence.[12]

Bernard attended the small English-speaking stream of the school, which had three teachers until it too, in time, sought its separate identity. Dobson, who was in his class, remembers having occasionally to struggle through groups of French boys on his way to school. The different groups had quite distinct timetables and used the recreational facilities at different times. In 1914 Bernard's father inquired as to why Latin, a requirement for university entrance, was not being taught. The last two years of the program included commercial studies and could have stimulated Bernard's life-long interest in economics. It was probably at this time that he began to read the stock exchange page in the newspaper, the Ottawa *Journal*, an unusual boyhood trait. Many who knew him felt that he would have been good in business or finance.

His teachers, including Brother Michael O'Dea, his class teacher for three years, were careful about assigning and collecting work. O'Dea was a stern disciplinarian, to the extent of introducing a reign of terror.[13] When asked to describe his school days, Dobson used the word 'strict' repeatedly. Addressing the indiscipline of the earlier years, the brothers did not allow the pupils to get out of line. Despite this, Bernard was influenced by O'Dea: when the question of his religious vocation surfaced he thought, for a time, of joining the Brothers.

Bernard acknowledged that he developed good work habits at the school, for which he was grateful. He always had to work his hardest.[14] About those days he has remarked, 'In elementary school I liked math because you know what you had to *do* and could get an answer ... but mathematics helped a lot in clarifying what on earth you are doing when you are doing something.' English composition he found at first troublesome, until his last year when he was 'able, confident enough, to write good English composition ... When I had something to say I could write.'[15] He later became a competent linguist, fluent in many languages. His religious education in the elementary school would have come from one of the early editions of Butler's *Catechism*, with its emphasis on God, Creation, the Fall and the Incarnation, Church, Sacraments, and the commandments. The Brothers also used a simplified text of the four gospels and a book on apologetics. Bernard remembered being taught that they were not going to understand the Trinity.[16]

He was, on his own admission, a diligent rather than an imaginative or creative student. Once when doing a problem in mathematics he got a negative number as answer, his first encounter with that type of number. He was sure he was wrong until the concept was explained to him. A remark made in 1967 gives us a further window into his childhood:

> When I was a boy, I remember being surprised by a companion who assured me that air was real. Astounded, I said, 'No, it's just nothing.' He said, 'There's something there all right. Shake your hand and you will feel it.' So I shook my hand, felt something, and concluded to my amazement that air was real. [17]

In that lecture he draws a distinction between the mythical world of childhood and the world mediated by meaning into which as adults we enter.

He was always learning.[18] Dobson remembered him as studious, so much so that he skipped fourth grade. He was always well dressed at school and rarely stayed on in the playing field when classes were over. He could be shy, aloof, one day greeting you and the next walking by preoccupied with his thoughts. From a letter he wrote in 1946 it is clear that he had some respect for his early education, remarking that what he got from his parochial school in Buckingham was a work discipline.

The New Century

Lonergan was born at the start of a new century, a time when several currents of thought were building up that would eventually influence his own. Towards the end of the nineteenth century Albert Michelson made the celebrated remark that since all the basic laws of nature had been discovered, the end of physics was at hand. Future work would only be concerned with improving the precision of what was already known by adding a few more decimal points. Ironically, his own Michelson-Morley experiment undermined the status of the ether and opened up a whole new and unexpected chapter in physics.

The work of Planck (1901) and Einstein (1905 and later) undermined certainties that had held sway in the field of the natural sciences for several centuries. Planck found that in certain exchanges of energy discrete quantities (quanta), always multiples of a basic unit, were involved. This flew in the face of a tradition in the science of mechanics that held that energy was a continuum. In 1913 Niels Bohr used this concept of a quantum to explain, convincingly, the structure of the hydrogen atom. After that there was no going back. This unexpected development severely shocked the scientific mentality of the time and was resisted by many. Hence Planck's famous dictum, much quoted by Lonergan, that new ideas are not accepted on the basis of the clarity of their presentation or the rigour of the arguments, but rather by the retirement of the older generation of professors and their replacement by a new generation whose minds have not yet been fixed.[19]

Starting in 1905 Einstein, through his researches on special and general relativity theory, brought about the unthinkable: the elimination of Euclidean geometry as the basis of natural science. As Euclidean geometry was the cornerstone of Newtonian mechanics and of naive realist interpretations of space, again there was a major shock. In the 1920s statistics, chance, and randomness began seriously to challenge the deterministic world view of mainstream science. Through these developments, naive views that the realities studied by science could be simply imagined or pictured were undermined. The question of reality was restated anew.

As these surprises were emerging in the natural sciences, William Dilthey and others were searching for the categories and foundations of the human sciences. As the categories of Kant stood to the world of nature and natural science, these would stand to human experience and human history. The search involved a constant debate with the demands of the famous last chapter of Mill's *Logic* concerning the human sciences and their methodology.[20] In the last decades of the nineteenth century the new science of psychoanalysis was born. Breur maintained that his treatment of Anna O. in the 1880s contained the germ cell of that whole discipline.[21] From 1895 Freud embarked on his adventure of self-analysis, a project that reminds us that at the heart of Lonergan's work is a complementary adventure. Freud's *Interpretation of Dreams* appeared in 1900, and in 1910 the International Psychoanalytic Association was founded, with Jung as its president. These studies challenged conventional interpretations of the human person, underlining the fact that there is an extensive non-rational dimension to human existence.

Especially in Germany the new study of history was part of the academic landscape in the nineteenth century. Friedrich Wolf conceived classical philology to be the historical and philosophical study of human nature in antiquity. Boeckh, his pupil, considered it to be a matter of reconstructions of the constructions of the human spirit. Ancient languages were deciphered, sites excavated, artefacts of all kinds collected, and an ocean of monographs began to be written. The impact of the new history on religion at the time is well summed up in 1890 by the influence of Frazer's noted study of magic and religion, *The Golden Bough*. From his comparative stance, Christianity became one of a number of mystery religions competing with the Roman Empire. This historical and agnostic outlook on early Christian history constituted a new attitude at the start of the new century. It aimed at 'depriving Christian theology of any claim to absolute truth, and making Christianity one among many responses to the special pressures and circumstances of Roman imperial society – no more, no less.'[22] Frazer's book would be instrumental in the departure from Christianity of such figures as the young Toynbee and C.S. Lewis.

European humanism since the Renaissance had tacitly left Christian scriptures and doctrines to theologians, concentrating more on classical authors such as Cicero and Virgil. At the turn of the century this situation was at an end. According to McNeil, Toynbee's biographer:

> Theology was in retreat; biblical texts had long since been torn apart by German scholars using the tools of humanistic philology; now British anthropological study of 'primitive' peoples invited classicists of the humanistic tradition to extend their jurisdiction over popular and irrational aspects of ancient thinking as manifested both before and after the 'golden ages' upon which their predecessors had centred attention. Gilbert Murray, a lapsed Roman Catholic and aggressive agnostic in private life, was a leader of this assault on domains once left to theologians. His book *Four Stages of Greek Religion* (1912) made that clear. The chapter dealing with the rise of mystery religions was entitled 'The Failure of Nerve,' and Christianity, of course, was the most important of the new faiths that Murray characterized in this dismissive fashion.[23]

The young Toynbee, like many others, took to these currents like a duck to water. In contrast with adherents of the nineteenth century, he experienced almost no pain in abandoning his religious tradition. Heroic achievement in the sense of the Greeks now became his gospel. Only later in his life would he, like Lewis, return to his religious roots.

The Catholic world into which Lonergan was born was on the defence against this modernism, as expressed in the encyclicals *Aeterni Patris* (1879), mentioned as a source of inspiration in the epilogue to *Insight*, and *Pascendi* (1907). On 4 November 1904, Louis Martin SJ, the then Jesuit General, issued a letter to all the provincials of the Society of Jesus. Earlier, Straus's quest for the historical Jesus had attempted to destroy the foundation of all revealed religion. Now the same end was being pursued by the historical method. Each provincial was to warn his subjects of the dangers involved.

Martin's major target was Lagrange's *Methode Historique.* With rare exceptions, the theological education of the clergy took place outside of the state university context, in a self-contained seminary system whose universal language was Latin. Thus they were largely ill equipped to deal with these new historical methods emerging in the state universities. This was part of the developing context within which, on 4 August 1903, Pius X succeeded Leo XIII. Many serious questions were being raised about dogmas and their relation to religious living as well as the norms governing the interpretation of the scriptures. Whereas Leo XIII seemed to advocate the marriage of the old and the new, the *vetera* and the *nova,* Pius X was suspicious of the new. He placed many works on the index and in 1907 published the decree *Lamentabilii,* which condemned sixty-five propositions in the area of criticism and dogma. *Pascendi,* published in the same year, painted a portrait of modern theologians and philosophers as characterized by a radical intellectual pride in the face of divine revelation, and thus holding that the explanation of the religious form of life could be found in the human person. In so doing they emphasized personal religious experience and religious immanence: 'It is this *experience* which, when a person acquires it, makes him properly and truly a believer.'[24]

This was a position denounced by Pius X. Modernists who wished to explain the whole of religion by a combination of experience and symbolism undermined the importance of tradition and authority. By contrast, traditional theologians and philosophers were characterized by a humble acknowledgement of the church's teaching authority. There was really no middle ground between the two.

In 1909, by way of a response, Pius X founded the Biblical Institute in Rome and entrusted its management to the Jesuits. Its task was 'to prepare Catholics who would be able to evaluate at first hand the languages and manuscripts and excavations behind the new thinking.'[25] Leopold Fonck, a man not much taken with the new historical scholarship, was appointed rector. Immediately he began to critique Lagrange.[26] On the fifteenth centenary of the death of St Jerome the encyclical *Spiritus Paraclitus,* drafted by Fonck, was issued. It made clear that the Biblical Institute was not sympathetic towards the new trends.[27] The response to modernism and the promulgation of the code of canon law in 1917, which enshrined Thomism as the official theology and philosophy of the Catholic Church, were important events in defining the Catholic mentality and identity for much of the new century.

Jesuit Education and Vocation in Montreal

In 1918, just short of his fourteenth birthday, Bernard started four years of study as a boarder at the Jesuit-run Loyola College, Montreal. It was his first encounter with members of the Jesuit order that he would later join and in which he would spend the greater part of his life. Bernard opted for Loyola because Ottawa University, which his father attended for college studies, was now French speaking. He was also impressed by the fact that the boys wrote poetry in the *Loyola Review*. Loyola, which had moved out to its present site in Sherbrooke Street in 1916, had connections with Montreal going back to 1693. Its predecessor opened in September 1848 under the name St Mary's, announcing its goal of providing a complete classical and commercial course.[28] The classical ideal was dominant during Bernard's years and was not complemented by a full science faculty until 1943.

As one of 180 boarders, he would participate in much of the daily order followed by the Jesuit teachers. He would rise at 6:20; prayers and Mass were at 6:45 and breakfast at 7:30. Study began at 8:15 and classes at 9:00. The day was highly structured until lights-out at 9:45 pm. A review of the educational climate of the college during the first three decades of the century is given in chapter 14 of Slattery's *Loyola and Montreal: A History*. In the early years of the century the course was a poor translation from 'le college classique.'[29] Its ideal was to study the classics, the *philosophia perennis*, the immortal works of art in literature, architecture, statuary, laws, and customs – the depository of the prudence and wisdom of mankind. For Bernard his boarding school

> was organized pretty much along the same lines as Jesuit schools had been since the beginning of the Renaissance, with a few slight modifications. So that I can speak of classical culture as something I was brought up in and gradually learned to move *out of*. The Renaissance period was the period of the *uomo universale*, the man who could turn his hand to anything. The command of all that there was to be known at that time was not a fantastic notion. There was one culture, culture with a capital C: a normative notion of culture. That you could acquire it – a career opened to talent, and so on – was fairly well understood in various ways, and either you got it or did not. Communication fundamentally occurred *within* that one culture. You made slight adaptations to the people who were uncultured – and they were also not expected to understand things.[30]

In 1918, because of the effects of the First World War (a war that brought about the destruction of the nineteenth-century dream of progress as inevitable), the full course was not on offer.[31] Bernard registered as a Third Grammar student with Mr Keenan SJ as his class teacher and soon found himself in Special Latin. From morning to night one teacher taught nouns, another pronouns, and another verbs until a flu epidemic, during which Bernard returned home, put paid to it.[32] At the end of the first term he came first in the Third Grammar class exam with First Class Honours and was awarded a medal for good conduct. Bill Bryan, one of the teachers, recalled that he set the hardest exam he could think of, all the irregular verbs, but it presented Bernard with no difficulties.

As a result he was immediately promoted to Second Grammar, effectively skipping a year and coming second to Brian Hammond in the end-of-year exam. In Joe Keating and Bill Bryan, both Jesuits and born teachers, he had extremely good and dedicated teachers of the classics. John Keenan was more a pastoral person, the sort that influences vocations to the religious life. John Holland taught him maths for a while and felt Lonergan knew more maths than he himself did. The class chronicle from the *Loyola Review* for the year described Bernard as 'so justly surnamed "brains."'[33]

In 1919, at the start of his second year of study, he registered for First Grammar. During the first term the question of a religious vocation had surfaced and was disturbing him. His mother sent him to see Charbonneau, who was the curate at St Gregory's from October 1919 to January 1920 and who later became the Archbishop of Montreal, to talk it over.[34]

Early in February 1920 as he was playing hockey on an outdoor rink, his ears froze, his jugular became blocked, and he developed mastoids. The consequences were severe. He was in the Royal Victoria hospital for a month, his weight fell to seventy-three pounds, and he was anointed, but then recovered. He spent the rest of the school year convalescing in Buckingham. His mother stayed with him during his time in hospital and impressed the visiting Jesuit teachers from Loyola with her holiness.[35] On the basis of her care, he later remarked that when a person was so loved by his mother he never felt lonely. In his later years, however, a certain kind of loneliness would surround him.

The illness and its consequences made him think that he did not have the health for the religious life, which he found a relief. It even raised questions about his continuing at Loyola, but one of his teachers wrote to his mother that he ought to come back in September. When Bernard returned the teacher raised the question of vocation again with him and got the reply: 'There won't be any question of that. I'm ill.' His teacher replied: 'There's nothing organically wrong with you; you had some operations but you recovered.' So the question was raised again.[36] Bernard considered joining the Brothers for a time, but his father decided against that. Another possible road at the time was a career in economics or finance (which were to remain life-long interests).

Later Bernard set off on a two-hour journey across Montreal to the Sault to make a retreat to help him address the decision. Before he arrived he had decided, 'on the street car on the way out,' to join the Jesuits.[37] It was one of the most significant decisions of his life. The experience of God's intervention in his life inviting him to pursue a religious vocation generated in him a certain amount of disturbance, resistance, and even dread. One is reminded here of C.S. Lewis's remarks on his resistance to conversion: 'feeling, whenever my mind lifted even for a second from my work, the steady, unrelenting approach of Him whom I so earnestly desired not to meet.'[38] For Bernard, endowed with a strong sense of honouring his commitments, his vocational decision was a major road taken, one that would set directions in his life and make possible his work on *Insight* and later on the question of method in theology. I have no doubt that he later interpreted those works as integral to the living out of his religious vocation.

Bernard did not have to repeat the school year because of his illness, registering in 1920 as a First Arts student. In his final two years in English he studied, among other works, *The Deserted Village* and *The Merchant of Venice*; in mathematics he read Hall and Knight's *Algebra* and *Trigonometry* and Hall and Stephens's *Euclid* and *Solid Geometry*. For three successive years he studied Betten's two-volume history. The first, *The Ancient World*, dealt with history up to 800 A.D. Here he was introduced to Greek art and intellectual culture, to the Roman genius at making and ruling an empire, and through it all to the need for a Christian perspective on history. The second volume, *The Modern World*,[39] co-authored by Kaufmann, spanned from 800 A.D. to the First World War. It dealt initially with the era of religious unity from Charlemagne through the Crusades up to the Renaissance, followed by the disruption of religious unity in the Reformation, the French Revolution, the Industrial Revolution, and the outbreak of the First World War. Both volumes were presented as a contribution to a true Christian education.

His high school religious education was based on Deharbe's *Full Catechism*,[40] the preface of which draws attention to Augustine's assertion that unless the experience of the love of God in the catechist visibly animates the teaching, that teaching will not bear fruit. The Catechism opens with a condensed history of revealed religion, from Adam through Moses to Christ. The relation of the Catholic Church to Protestantism also figures strongly. After a brief discussion of faith, its object, and mysteries, the Catechism explores the contents of the Apostles' Creed and the commandments. In dealing with the third article of the creed, it introduces the mystery of the incarnation and the doctrine of one divine person consisting of two natures. It defines actual grace as a grace of assistance that acts transiently on the soul. Sanctifying grace remains habitually in the soul. In Bernard's college years the text used was Devivier-Sasia's *Christian Apologetics*.[41] It is astonishing to open it and find as the opening phrase 'Idea or notion of God.' In these texts he would have been introduced to the language of doctrines and of apologetics.[42]

Through Mr Keating, his first arts teacher, he heard about *quid sit*, 'but no one ever explained what was meant by it.'[43] Henry Smeaton, two years his senior, was the star pupil of the school, each year winning almost all the class awards. Like Bernard, Smeaton was later to become a Jesuit, and for a time became one of the few persons with whom Bernard could talk, intellectually, as a peer. Bernard's first adult friend, Smeaton would later preserve for us some of his earliest letters.

When asked by Charlotte Tansey, of the Thomas More Institute in Montreal, if he had any idea of what he would like to study when leaving Loyola, Bernard said that he did not.[44] But he did admit that during his years at Loyola he was interested in understanding:

> Well I had my idea of what understanding was.
> How early?
> I had some idea of it going through Loyola. I acquired great respect
>   for intelligence. [45]

At the end of his high school and college years, Bernard would have been considered quite a gifted student who did not have a specific intellectual direction in his life. But he had made the decision to test a fundamental option, that of becoming a Jesuit.

On 29 July 1922 Bernard entered the Jesuit Noviciate. Situated on a farm on the outskirts of Guelph, it had provided the two-year noviciate programme for English-speaking Canadian Jesuits since 1913. In 1923 a further two-year study programme in the classics was added. In 1924 the Canadian Province, then comprising of 551 members, was divided into the French-speaking Province of Lower Canada and the English-speaking Vice-Province of Upper Canada, the latter with 137 members. Bernard was joining a Society in which, during his training, there would occur a progressive separation of the French- and the English-speaking groups. Up to 1930 the English-speaking students studied philosophy in England, in Jersey and Heythrop College, Oxfordshire. In 1930 they moved to the newly founded Regis College in Toronto. It is in this building, at 403 Wellington Street, that Lonergan would write *Insight.* For theology studies, English-speaking Jesuits were scattered in the United States, England, Ireland, and elsewhere. Many studied at the Collège de l'Immaculée-Conception in Montreal until 1943, when they began to move to Regis College. After 1946 the separation was complete.

Fr Arthur McCaffray from the New York Province, who had just spent a year as dean of Boston College, was the novice master, and a man who made a considerable impression on his novices.[46] It was said of him that he had always said yes to whatever it was God asked of him.[47] His style was

pious, dramatic, ascetical, immediate, and charismatic rather than systematic and orderly. He communicated a sense of Ignatian detachment with
respect to the fateful twists of life, a sense of the human foolishness of the
call to follow Christ and of the need to trust in providence.

The spirituality of the time focused almost exclusively on the persona
rather than on the ego. Learning a set of habits related to the community
rules and customs through which one participated in the public religious
order of the community was central. The guiding spirituality also viewed
with suspicion any aspirations of the ego, which were bound to be self-
centred.[48] Its emphasis on rules and on the Latin language in liturgy,
education, and conversation made it a world constituted by a religious form
of classical culture. It valued silence, discouraged exclusive friendships among
peer groups, and attached significance to grades, order, and seniority. The
novices alone worked on the farm – famous for its apples – at certain times.
The inner life was nourished through prayer and devotions, but it was not a
time when individuals were encouraged to communicate their inner experiences of God's directing presence in their lives and prayer. Personal difficulties in those realms were matters that one did not talk about.

The most significant event in Bernard's first year was the thirty-day
retreat based on the spiritual exercises of Ignatius of Loyola. After Ignatius
suffered a serious injury in a battle at Pamplona, his worldly youthful life
came to an end. During his recovery at the family castle in Loyola, God
intervened in his life, and over a period of time he underwent a religious
conversion, recounted in his autobiography. His particular genius was his
ability to listen to and own what was happening in the process, to analyze
his own religious psyche. So it was that he came to grasp the difference
between the feelings that accompany the exercise of evil behaviour and the
efforts to shake off such behaviour. Equally he realized that when Christ,
after releasing him from his unfreedoms, was calling him to decisions about
discipleship or about advancing in discipleship, there were quite different
feelings, patterns of consolation and desolation, involved in responding to
that call. The focus of his exercises is on freeing oneself from unfreedoms
in order responsibly to make certain key personal decisions.

Out of this listening Ignatius came to formulate his own spiritual exercises related to decision making and divided into four movements or weeks.
The exercises of the first movement work with our unfreedoms; the second
with our response to our project in Christ, our Christian vocation; the third
with the suffering or passion involved in that vocation; and the fourth with
the joy or resurrection involved. Lonergan would meditate on the text of
the exercises, both disliked and admired by many,[49] each year in his annual
retreat.

Bernard's long retreat started on Saturday, 30 September 1922. Detailed notes made by one of the participants show that the input for the first week was reminiscent of Joyce's famous hellfire sermon. Meditations follow on the gospels and on the tension in us between good and evil. A concluding contemplation on discovering the love of God in all created things balances the dramatics of the first week.

Ignatian meditation invites us to make extensive use of our imagination in recreating the elements of the scenes in the Gospels and of our senses in their contemplation. Called the composition of place, it is a method that inspired the poet Gerard Manley Hopkins. Soon Bernard would begin to affirm that the starting point of knowledge is not self-evident logically first propositions, but what is given to our senses and imagination. On one occasion in the 1930s he would refer to the Ignatian method as an example of disposing the phantasm.

The cultivation of a spirit of personal detachment from the contingencies and vagaries of fate in one's life journey, from good or ill health, from persons and situations, desires, good or bad fortune, is central to Ignatian spirituality.[50] Such a detachment is for him a condition of love in that enables us to give others their true freedom. Lonergan's position that our knowledge, if it is to be objective, must be the product of a detached, disinterested spirit of inquiry rather than of attachment suggests an Ignatian influence.

In his later years Bernard remarked that the Ignatian inspiration was cut off by Roothaan, whose influential commentary on the exercises emphasized memory and reasoning. It was 'a stone that was offered when he was looking for bread.'[51] Bernard seems to have returned to the Ignatian position through Voegelin's treatment of the golden cord in Plato's *Laws*: 'The pull of the golden cord doesn't force you; you have to agree, make the decision. But the jerk of the steel chain, that's what upsets you. That viewpoint is Ignatius and it is the whole ascetic tradition of the discernment of spirits.'[52]

Bernard took his vows on the Feast of St Ignatius on 31 July 1924. In his later reflections he referred to the religious vocation as both a gift and an obvious symbol of transcendence.[53]

After the novitiate he spent a further two years of study of Latin, Greek, English, and mathematics in the Juniorate at Guelph. Joseph Bergin SJ, considered by many to be an unusually gifted teacher, taught him Latin for a year. In the first year Bernard read and presented his ideas on the Greek text of Plato's *Crito*. In letters to Henry Smeaton in August 1925 he talks about reading Homer's *The Illiad*, with great zeal, interest, and satisfaction. In November he read *Historia Thucydio*. A mathematics class started in February of the next year. During the vacations he read Thackeray to enlarge his vocabulary.[54]

When later questioned by Stanley Machnik about aesthetic wonder and awe, he summed up what exactly he got from these years:

> The aesthetic side was my formation at Loyola and within the Juniorate which was all literary, pre-philosophic. I had that formation, but my ability to say things came with my study of philosophy. I remember Bolland asking me if I had any interest in philosophy. I said: I'm very interested in Butcher's *The Theory of Art.* 'Oh! That's not philosophy!', he said … that was the opening, eh? That had a fuller development later on.[55]

When he was in Weston in his last years, Joe Flanagan asked him how he got onto the phenomenon of insight. In his response he referred to the process of translating involved in his classical education. In translating one and the same insight, one has to find different expressions for it in different languages. But the insight and its meaning are not to be identified with any of these instrumental expressions.

Philosophy, he had remarked in his letters to Smeaton, was bad for one's imagination.[56] On 30 August 1926, in the company of MacGilvray and Phelan, Lonergan left to study that dangerous subject in Heythrop College, Oxfordshire, England.

3

Heythrop: Awakening to the Problem of Knowledge

On 5 August 1926 the Jesuit faculties of philosophy and theology moved from St Mary's Hall, Stonyhurst, and St Buenos, respectively, to Heythrop College, Chipping Norton, Oxfordshire, a very large and remote estate situated in the countryside about eighteen miles north of the City of Oxford. The drive from the front entrance along a narrow twisting road to the faculty buildings and residence was close to a mile. Geoffrey Holt, a Province archivist, thought the move was motivated by the desire to establish in one place, near a university such as Oxford, joint faculties of theology and philosophy.[1] It was to this newly established but remote location that, providentially, Lonergan was assigned for his study of philosophy.

The entry in the philosophy beadle's log of Heythrop for Tuesday, 14 September 1926, informs us that Fr Whiteside 'arrived with three first year Canadians, Mr McGilvray, Mr Phelan and Mr Lonergan.' Lonergan was one of twenty-four first-year students of philosophy in an academic community that included sixty-five students of philosophy and eighty-two of theology. It was a large and highly structured rule-governed community with considerable demarcation between the different groups. The daily order began early in the morning with meditation. On working days there were lectures in the mornings and late afternoons. Thursdays, on which there were no lectures, was a so-called Blandyke day on which from time to time the students could take a bus to Oxford. Entertainment was largely homespun in those days before television. The community boasted an orchestra, which performed from time to time. A highly active drama and musical society hosted the inevitable *Gondoliers* and Sherlock Holmes–based dramas. Sporting facilities abounded, but not for ice hockey. The

Canadians attempted to overcome this by imagining that the marble corridors were an ice rink.

As the community, so also did the philosophy faculty have its lifestyle and world. Lonergan's teachers included Whiteside, Bolland, Moncel, Watt, O'Hara, Irwin, and Waddington. He considered them honest men who did not try to claim credit for skills and wisdom they did not have.[2] They had to accept that their students were being significantly influenced by their overlapping studies at London University, which were preparing them for professional qualifications as teachers.

Following roughly the division of philosophy given in Frick, *Logica*,[3] the major courses Lonergan took were taught in the following order:

Year 1 Logic, epistemology, and ontology (Whiteside and Bolland)

Year 2 Psychology and cosmology (Moncel and Bolland)

Year 3 Ethics and natural theology (Watt and Bolland)

The textbooks, which he recalled 'were German in origin and Suarezian in conviction,' included works by Frick, Hahn, and Boedder.[4] The tone of the scholastic agenda was set more by Scotus and Suarez than Aquinas. It was also critical of Kant. Watt's ethics course had an unusually enlightened bibliography covering the social questions of the time. Background courses were taught in subjects such as history of philosophy, chemistry, biology, and mathematics, where Lonergan would later encounter O'Hara.

According to fellow student Leo McCauley, Lonergan spent a lot of his time in his room reading and was referred to as 'the brain.' He came across as someone who had mastered the philosophical issues at a deeper level than the rest of the students. John Foley remembered him as a master of the one-liner. In conversation he would come out with a single phrase that would deftly encapsulate the matter, would chuckle at it, and that was it.

The Awakening of the Heart's Desire

The man who introduced Lonergan to philosophy and who, somewhat against Lonergan's natural inclinations at the time, succeeded in awakening his heart's desire was Philip Whiteside.[5] The class, Lonergan included, were quite fond of him. Nassan, Foley, and McCauley remembered him as having a great sense of humour. With a deadpan face he could slip in humorous remarks in his lectures, including some about 'The Silent Woman,' a local pub.

According to Paul Kennedy, Whiteside used Frick's *Logica* as his text for his course on logic and epistemology. Part 1 of the book, 'Dialectic,' opens with nominal and real definitions of logic and then addresses the three operations of the mind, apprehension, judgment, and reasoning. Ideas, notions, concepts, and *verbum mentis* are listed as names of objects of apprehension. An idea is a similitude of an object expressed in the perceiving mind. It is not to be confused with phantasms, which involve acts of the sensitive faculty and are restricted to concrete sensible objects. Ideas are apprehended by a spiritual faculty that deals with intelligibilities and universals. Genera and species and Porphyry's tree with its distinction of the inorganic, organic, sensitive, and rational are addressed in the analysis that follows. A judgment is defined as an act of the mind by means of which we unite two objective ideas through affirmation or separate them through negation. The treatment of judgment involves a detailed analysis of the structure of propositions. Under reasoning the syllogism enters.

Part 2, entitled 'Critica,' addresses the question of truth. Containing a refutation of scepticism, nominalism, and conceptualism, it also included references to universal doubt and clear and distinct ideas in Descartes. Under its critique of idealism we find a treatment of points in Kant, Fichte, Schelling, and Hegel. An introduction to Scotus and his theory of universals is given in paragraph 60. Paragraph 86 of Frick's other work, *Ontologia*, elaborated the Suarezian thesis that essence and existence are not to be distinguished in any physical entity.

According to Lonergan, Whiteside spent months on logic and the rest of the year on epistemology, the division possibly related to the two parts of the book. His method was to put questions, enabling the students to ask their own questions and challenge the accepted positions.[6] For instance, the houses in England had fireplaces but at Heythrop they had steel pipes and radiators, 'so the epistemological problem there was: what are these steel pipes?'[7] Lonergan also remembered Whiteside talking at length on a topic that he would then sum up in a little dictation. When discussing Kant, presumably following the critical section in Frick, he warned the class not to think he had offered a refutation. He was just offering a few pinpricks, but Lonergan felt whatever he said was absolutely true.

Paragraphs 390–402 of Frick's *Logica* are a critique of Kant's transcendental idealism as presented in the *Critique of Pure Reason*. They discuss synthetic *a priori* judgments; the three cognitive faculties, sensibility, intellect, and reason; the thing in itself; the Copernican revolution; and the rejection of immanentism as a modernist error in the encyclical *Pascendi* by Pius X in 1907. Given that Frick highlights the passage on the Copernican revolution, it does not seem unreasonable to assume that at some point Lonergan would have read it and been struck by its challenge to make metaphysics a science. Centrally, that revolution brings into sharp focus the problem of the relation between our thought processes and the realities that we think about.

Whiteside sold his students the idea that 'there is a problem of knowledge,' but Lonergan did not think that Whiteside had any solutions. Being a potential problem solver, he found this exposure through Frick and Kant to a major unsolved problem a core formative experience. According to Richard Liddy, the Catholic scholastic tradition of philosophy feared that if the Kantian turn was taken in analysing our minds, the subjective would eliminate the objective.[8] Liddy remembered quite vividly being told that the only answer to the bridge between subject and object of knowledge was dogmatically to assert that our knowledge does cross from in here to out there, from within the subject to the world. Supporting Liddy, T.Z. Lavine in his *From Socrates to Sartre: The Philosophic Quest* remarks that for Kant, 'the order which Newtonian laws establish is not in nature but comes from the universal and necessary concepts of the human mind.'[9]

Closer to Lonergan's own time, Bradley in his *Appearance and Reality* in a chapter entitled 'Thought and Reality,' illustrates the problem as it engaged him:

> There is an erroneous idea that, if reality is more than thought, thought itself is at least quite unable to say so. To assert the existence of anything in any sense beyond thought suggests, to some minds, the doctrine of the Thing-in-itself. And of the Thing-in-itself we know that if it existed we could not know of it; ... I dissent wholly from the corollary that nothing more than thought exists. But to think that anything can exist quite outside of thought I agree is impossible ... Thought desires for its content the character which makes reality. These features, if realized, would destroy mere thought; and hence they are an Other beyond thought. But thought, nevertheless, can desire them because its content has them already in an incomplete form.[10]

In response to the accusation that we can only desire what we know, Bradley explores the relation between thought's desire and the Other of thought. Thought's desires, he suggests, contain what it does not know in an incomplete form. This leads to a discussion of the relation between the Other and an anticipated self-transcendence.

Thus, behind the student's quaint discussion of radiators were probing questions: what is the nature of our thought processes, of the thoughts we think and of their relation to the independent existence outside our minds of what it is that we can think about, be it radiators or other minds? The unsolved Kantian epistemological problem entered into Lonergan's intellectual horizon. It will become our constant companion later in this narrative.

In January 1927 Lonergan sat for his matriculation examination for London University.[11] An entry in the beadle's log for 16 February 1927 reads:

'Sermon Mr Lonergan.' In a manner that he could never have anticipated at the time, the sermon was to become the source and inspiration of a further question that would puzzle him throughout his life. About the experience Lonergan remarked:

> In the same year at Heythrop I had to preach to two hundred and fifty students during supper. I took as my text 'You may hear and hear but you will never understand. You may look and look but you will never see' (Acts 28:26). Our superior advised that, while my doctrine was true, it would be better not to preach it, and I never have but the idea remained fruitful. It became, in *Insight*, 'inverse insight,' understanding there is nothing to be understood ... In *Method in Theology* that idea became 'dialectic' ... In *Grace and Freedom*, sin is a surd, an irrational ... I knew there was something there, but what it was took me years to figure out. I haven't exhausted the issue yet.[12]

The surd sermon posed for him the question: what happens when we avoid or fail to understand something of significance for the course of our lives? It became not a fleeting interest for examination purposes, but his very own question, containing within it the seeds of the problem of dialectic. In these experiences, focal directions of his interests were being established.

In a letter written to Henry Smeaton on 20 June 1927 Lonergan gives us an insight into the impact of his first year of philosophy:

> I am afraid I must lapse into philosophy. I have been stung with that monomania now and then but I am little scholastic though as far as I know a good Catholic. Still modern logic is fair. The theory of knowledge is what is going to interest me most of all. I have read Aristotle his *peri psuches* and am of strong nominalist tendency.

Stung by the challenge of the problem of knowledge, he found his passion for philosophy awakened. The twenty-eight-year quest that would result in *Insight* had begun.[13]

Modern logic, as we shall see, refers to the work of John Stuart Mill and a related school of authors who would engage Lonergan in his second year. In his reading of the Greek text of Aristotle's *De Anima* he does not yet seem to have picked up the remark on Book III, chapter 7 on understanding the forms in the phantasms.

Nominalism, conceptualism, and realism were three strands of logic broadly concerned with the referent of thought.[14] Conceptualists held that logic was concerned with abstract and universal concepts or forms of thought, but made no claims as to whether such mental objects had an existence outside of our minds. According to Joseph, we think and reason about things through concepts but are not directly acquainted with those things:

> And a concept may be said to differ from a thing in being universal, not individual: an object of thought and not of sense: fixed and not changing: completely knowable and not partially ... It may be asked, is a concept merely an object of thought, with no existence in things (as it is put, outside our minds)? or does it exist in things?[15]

For realists the universal concepts – such as man, colour, shape – refer to parallel universals in nature. Sceptically, nominalists denied the existence of abstract and universal concepts and of parallel universal attributes in nature. Logic, for them, dealt simply with the common names of things and their attributes, such as man and reason or circle and roundness. They denied the real identity of anything universal in different individuals or attributes bearing the same name. Conceptualism, realism, and nominalism are particular responses to questions about the relation between our concepts, thoughts, language use, and reality, the Other of thought. Later Lonergan held that his nominalism was really a reaction against the then prevalent conceptualism with its emphasis on the importance of universal concepts.

Classics or Methodology: A Road Not Yet Taken

Lonergan's first year of philosophy ended with a half-hour oral examination on Monday, 11 July, from 6:00 to 6:30 p.m. His second year began the following September with courses on psychology, taught by Moncel,[16] and ontology, taught by Bolland, a Suarezian who was highly critical of Aquinas.[17] At this time he had also to register for a parallel external bachelor of arts degree at London University. Before registering, he studied the Prospectus for External Degrees of London University and noticed the regular recurrence of the terms 'methodology' and 'logic and methodology.' As a result, he was troubled by the question, which course should he register for?

> B.L. – 'I was very much attracted by one of the degrees in the London Syllabus: Methodology. I felt there was absolutely no method to the philosophy I had been taught; it wasn't going anywhere. I was interested in method and I wrote to Father Fillion: "Instead of classics, what about methodology?" He said, "No, do classics." ...'
> P.L. – 'So your interest in methodology was early?'

B.L. – 'Oh yes. What on earth are they doing? The same thing in theology: what on earth are they doing?'[18]

He was later to remark: 'The only time I had an idea of what I'd like to study, I wanted to do methodology. Now I'm glad they wouldn't let me.'[19] With hindsight, he came to recognize that at the time he was not ready for the problem.

There is no course in the London University Regulations for External Degrees for the time entitled General Methodology. He could have taken a BSc with a major in logic and methodology, as well as two other scientific subjects such as physics or chemistry or biology. The methodology syllabus was largely shaped by Mill's *A System of Logic*, the history of scientific method and discovery being an added item. On the BA honours philosophy paper on logic and methodology, Bradley's *Principles of Logic*, Venn's *Empirical Logic*, and Russell's *Introduction to Mathematical Philosophy* featured.

On the Logic and Methodology exam papers in philosophy we find questions such as: 'Consider how far the concept of law involves that of determinism' and 'Is a judgment of probability a judgment concerning frequency?' Variations on these themes, which appear in chapters 2 and 4 of *Insight*, also occur. The question, 'What is scientific explanation?' featured strongly and was considered to involve a quite different form of understanding from that of natural history with its descriptive categories. When the provincial's reply came back, Lonergan registered for a BA in classics, taking Latin with Roman history, Greek with Greek history, French, and mathematics.

The written examinations for his London degree were structured in two parts, an intermediate and a final. In the last week of November and first week of December he would sit for the intermediate part, taking eight three-hour papers, two in each subject.[20] In those exams he would have to show his skill at translating to and from Latin, Greek, and French. He would have to deal with questions about Gracchi and the Senate, the coalition between Pompey, Caesar and Crassus, and Caesar's legislation as dictator. On the Greek paper we find the following questions: 'Give the main outline of Greek economic development to the end of the sixth century B.C.' and 'Give a brief account of the history of Athens from 560–495 B.C.'

Significantly the regulations allowed him to take the intermediate examination in logic and methodology rather than mathematics. Almost all of the headings on the syllabus derive from the table of contents of Mill's *A System of Logic, Ratiocinative and Inductive (Being a Connected View of the Principles of Evidence and the Methods of Scientific Investigation)*.[21] The range of Mill's interest in methodology was vast, spanning the sciences of the mind, personality, economics, sociology, and history as well as the natural sciences. Of particular significance was his introduction, following Bacon, of a distinction between formal and applied logic or methodology. Like Kant's general and applied logic, the former dealt with the universal operations of the mind, the latter with the details of their applications to particular fields or disciplines.

Lonergan sat his intermediate logic examination in London for the first time on 30 November 1927. The opening question on the first or general methodology paper was about the cause or grounds of judgment and the relation of a proposition to a judgment or assertion.[22] The eighth question asked about the meaning of a law of thought and how it differed from a law of nature. The second or special methodology paper posed questions about Mill's methods, multiple causes, the probability that improbable things should happen, and the nature of circumstantial evidence.

Inspired by the last chapter of Mill's *Logic* with its questions about social progress, the final question on the second paper was usually concerned with method in the social sciences, history, and economics. Mill suggests that there might be laws of history that relate the different stages in historical progress in a manner that parallels the way in which Newtonian mechanics explains successive stages in the movement of a projectile. According to Gadamer, Dilthey's arduous work, spanning decades, on the question of history and the human sciences 'was a constant debate with the logical demand that Mill's famous last chapter made on the human sciences.'[23]

The story goes that when answering the two three-hour logic papers, Lonergan felt he knew the answers that were expected but thought they were wrong. Being too stubborn to compromise, he gave the examiners his own ideas, and was referred. This meant he had to resit the logic paper. John Foley remembered him boasting to the group that this had happened because he challenged the ideas of his examiners. Foley did not think he felt humiliated, but it must have left its mark on him. Bolland discussed his referral with Ray Phelan, one of the other Canadian students, and simply decided to let it be. Lonergan resat the examination on 4 July 1928 and found himself invited to discuss the sentence, 'The laws of chance are not applicable to individual cases.' He was successful this time, and had no further problems with the London BA.

In preparing for his examinations Lonergan had to read Joseph, *An Introduction to Logic* (1906), Joyce, *Principles of Logic* (1908), and Coffey, *The Science of Logic* (1912). The contents of Joseph, Coffey, and Joyce were largely defined by Mill's *Logic*, Coffey and Joyce at the time being textbooks for the London and other examinations on logic. All of them are quoted in some essays Lonergan would shortly write. Some of the problems they raised would influence the shape of his longer term thought.

Mill wonders whether logic is the science of reasoning or of the process of advancing from known to unknown truth by the operations of the understanding.[24] For Joyce, logic is the science that directs the operations of the mind in the attainment of truth rather than the science of the operations themselves, that is, conceiving, judging, reasoning. Logic treats largely of things as they exist in the conceptual order, which warns us against reading Lonergan's later meaning of the word 'judgment' back into these authors.[25] For Joyce and Joseph, judgments are largely concerned with propositions, their subject, predicate, and 'is' or copula of predication. Both Joseph and Joyce distinguish between judgment as the assertion of a relation between a subject and a predicate in a proposition, and the affirmation of a fact or of existence.

The great diversity of fields of inquiry in the natural sciences posed for Mill the question, what is the general definition of a method? For Joseph, different enquiries have their own peculiar difficulties arising out of the nature of their subject matter and of the problems they set. Rules of method, which fall under the domain of applied logic or methodology, are concerned with how to address those differences.[26] In this context Joseph considers, in rather vague terms, such realms as cause and effect, multiple causes, human laws and history, statistics (which are treated briefly), historical method and, on the very last page, natural selection. For Coffey, methodology or applied logic is concerned with the manner in which we coordinate the mental operations of conception, judgment, and reasoning when exploring different aspects of the universe.[27]

In these authors formal logic was concerned with the manner in which the human mind attained the truth in every discipline. Applied logic or methodology was concerned with particular departments of knowledge. What their writings would have impressed on Lonergan is that there is not a single type of scientific inquiry or insight, but a multiplicity.

Chance and probability also merit discussion. For Joyce, chance is defined as the negation of causality; for Lonergan, randomness as the absence of system.[28] An unplanned meeting with someone in a city for Joyce is casual, for Coffey a coincidence. Although the meeting can be attributed to chance, this does not mean that chance is a positive entity that causes meetings. Rather, it signifies that 'the event was a coincidence, that it was outside the scope of either of the two causal series needed to bring it about.'[29] Joyce goes on to remark that what seems to happen by chance, coincidentally, from one standpoint could be planned from another viewpoint. By way of an example, he considers a master despatching two servants on different errands to the city, where they meet by chance.[30]

In his discussion of species, genus, differentia, property, and accident, Joyce underlines the fact that the Porphyrian account of the Predicables 'depends on a fact strongly emphasized by Aristotle (*Categ., cc.* 2,5) that the ultimate subject of all predication is the individual.'[31] The constitutive notes by which an individual is what it is, its essence (*ousia*) or quiddity (*to ti en einai*), answers the question, what is it? (*quid sit?*). As an alternative for 'essence' we find 'species' (*eidos*), or characterizing form.[32] Joseph, following Aristotle rather than Porphyry, replaces the term 'species' with 'definition.' In him the relation of the question, 'what is it?' with the definition and substance or species is made clear: 'We may ask the question *ti esti?* – what is it? – of an attribute (like momentum) as well as a substance (like a man or a lobster); and the answer will be a definition.'[33]

On Conceptual and Sensible Inference

As he was preparing for his resit of the logic examination in January and February of 1928, Lonergan published his first two essays in an in-house journal called *The Blandyke Papers*. Entitled 'The Form of Mathematical Inference' and 'The Syllogism,' both were concerned with inference. In the first paper, noting Coffey's hypothesis that the expository syllogism is a sensible demonstration or resolution of the facts to the senses, he divides inferences into conceptual and sensible. Conceptual inference goes from one set of concepts to another. Sensible inference goes from some particular sense data, diagrams, or situations to some inferred understanding.

The paper sets forth a series of images from which sensible inferences can be made and 'axioms' framed: 'An egg is in a dish, the dish is in a warmer, therefore, the egg is in the warmer.' This leads to the axiom, 'Whatever contains a container, contains what is contained in the container,' which, he remarks, Kant might have called a synthetic *a priori* judgment. This, he suggests, demonstrates how axioms are present in sense data, using the phrase *resolutio ad phantasma*. Geographically, 'London is east of Bristol, Bristol is south of Liverpool, therefore it can be inferred that London is south-east of Liverpool.' We can draw a parallel with a right-angle triangle: 'If we say A is east of B, B is south of C, therefore A is south-east of C.' In order to prove that the sum of the two internal non-adjacent angles in a triangle is equal to the external angle, we need a kinetic image in which the vertex of the triangle is rotated around its base. This leads to the prophetic remark that 'the fallacy of the pseudographma shows that the diagram is more important than it is ordinarily believed.'[34]

Lonergan's interest in the problem of the nature of the sensory origins of our knowledge is first given expression here. That all knowledge originates on the level of our senses would later become for him a fixed point of reference. On the basis of his examples he formulates a hypothesis:

> It would seem that axiom and concrete inference are on the same level of thought, that both depend directly upon an intuition of the *vis cogitativa* and therefore both are equally and *per se* valid. In no real sense then is the truth of a particular a consequence of the truth of the general: there seems to be the same relation between them – or at least a similar one – as is found between the scientific law and a fact of experience.[35]

The use of the terms 'intuition' and 'fact of experience' here are significant. Only in writing *Insight* will he clarify the distinction between brute and cognitional facts. The paper ends with a teasing remark: 'I do not think Card. Newman's illative sense is specifically the same as these concrete inferences but that question requires separate treatment.'[36]

Following Moncel, in Lonergan's second paper, 'The Syllogism,'[37] he talks about the act of inference as a judgment in which the mind intuitively knows the implications of a premise. His analysis of predication, which expresses the identity of object and attribute and of logical whole and part, marks his first grapplings with the notion of the thing. Predication expresses the identity of object and attribute. An object is for him 'a unity in a sensational continuum,' a unification of attributes that can involve the *per accidens*. In response to the question, 'What do I mean by manhood or triangularity?' he answers, 'no more than the more notable characteristics of a "man" or the properties of a "triangle."'[38]

In his revised conclusion to the paper, he talks about God knowing the thing in itself – a yellow flower – but of our knowing it through its phenomena. Perceptively, Liddy identifies in this an agnosticism, to be found in both British empiricism and Newman, with regard to our knowledge of things in themselves.[39] Notable also is Lonergan's first use of the word 'insight' in a quotation from Joseph: 'The subsumption in syllogism belongs to thinking which has not full insight into all its premises at once.'[40] At this point I do not believe the word was significant for him.

In his third and final year of philosophy, natural theology was taught by Bolland and ethics by Lewis Watt. Bolland claimed that the First Vatican Council had defined the possibility of proving the existence of God, but he would not tell the class which was the proof that held. In response to Francis Courtney's review of Fr Hontheim's 'Creation from Eternity' in the *Blandyke Papers* at Easter of 1929, Lonergan wrote 'that the action of God is one, eternal and not successive.' There is no temporal succession in God's activity. All events, whenever they happen in history, are simultaneously present to God, whatever that means.

According to Leo McCauley, Lewis Watt, the professor of ethics, was a gentle soul. He was always telling the students to be good to the poor, even if it turned out that the beggars were fakers. The workmen at Heythrop were paid thirty shillings per week because it was the regular pay, but this, Watt pointed out, was not a sufficient family wage. Hence his analysis of wages was existential. Watt's course is unusual in that we have a set of notes for it taken by Maurice Nassan. The first part covered the questions of special ethics, dealing with suicide, self-defence, property rights, usury, and so forth. The second part covered topics in social philosophy, socialism, Marx and Marxism, the living wage, the family (referring to a work by Miss Rathlene, *The Disinherited Family*), marriage, civil society (Hobbes, Locke, and Rousseau), fascism, Leninism, and church and state.

In 1928 Watt published the book *Capitalism and Morality* at a time when, noted Lonergan, 'the laws of economics were iron – not just necessary but *iron* ... It would have been sinful to interfere with the Irish famine; that was supply and demand! So I was interested from that viewpoint.'[41] Watt challenged Lonergan: 'How can you get economic moral precepts that are based on the economy itself? That was my question.' The family needs a living wage, yet employers cannot afford to pay it. They are obliged in charity but not in justice to pay it. A question was posed that echoed the dispute with the MacLarens in Buckingham.

In his course Watt gave an account of Marx and of the main characteristics of the materialist concept of history that would sit well in a contemporary introductory course. He also discussed the distinction between use value and exchange value:

> The exchange value of an object is its price. This may be different from its utility. Use value means that it has the power of satisfying some need or demand. Some objects have no exchange value though they have utility, e.g. the air, the sun's rays, etc. [42]

These points would be taken up in Lonergan's 1942 text on economics. Watt's discussion of socialism brought into sharp focus questions about the control of ownership of capital, of producer rather than consumer goods. The considerations of usury would have raised questions about finance.

Lonergan's Discovery of Newman

> I was taught philosophy on an intuitive basis – naive realism – and I took refuge in Newman's *Grammar of Assent.*[43]

A sense of dissatisfaction and confusion brought about by, among other things, the Scotist and Suarezian influences on the philosophy he was being taught drove Lonergan to pick up Newman's *Grammar of Assent,* not a set text, from the library shelf.[44] He was, he remarked, looking for someone who had some common sense and knew what he was talking about. Newman's opening remark that he is only interested in propositions that bear on concrete matters immediately sets him apart in tone and content from the works of Frick, Joseph, Joyce, and Coffey. His opening chapter is entitled 'Modes of Holding Propositions.' As propositions can be interrogative, conditional, or categorical in form, our holding of them can be by way of doubt, inference, or assent. Newman's main concern in the *Grammar* is with real and notional assent, by which he means the personal act of judgment.

Newman's approach to the question, how do we determine the truth about something? is highly imaginative. After introducing the notion of reasoning in the concrete, he offers three illustrations of the process: how do we infer that Great Britain is an island, that Hardouin's theory that the works of Horace and Livy and Tacitus were thirteenth-century forgeries is or is not satisfactory, and that I will die? A discussion of the term 'evidence' leads to three further illustrations of inference from the field of physics, a criminal trial, and a problem of authorship.[45]

Newman provides a profound insight into the way or method of the human mind. Against those who hold that only formal inference is knowledge, he writes:

> It is plain that formal logical sequence is not in fact the method by which we are enabled to become certain of what is concrete; and it is equally plain, from what has already been suggested, what the real and necessary method is. It is the cumulation of probabilities, independent of each other, arising out of the nature and circumstances of the particular case which is under review; probabilities too fine to avail separately, too subtle and circuitous to be conversable into syllogisms, too numerous and various for such conversion, even were they convertible. As a man's portrait differs from a sketch of him, in having, not merely a continuous outline, but all its details filled in, and shades and colours laid on and harmonized together, such is the multiform and intricate process of ratiocination, necessary for our reaching him as a concrete fact, compared with the rude operation of syllogistic treatment. (p. 288)

That knowledge of what is concrete should model itself on the scientific ideal of the logic of formal inference is rejected.

In this manner the question about the relation between inference, formal or informal, and assent arises. Newman relates them in the following way:

> As apprehension is a concomitant, so inference is ordinarily the antecedent of assent; ... but neither apprehension nor inference interferes with the unconditional character of the assent, viewed in itself ... Assent is in its nature absolute and unconditional, though it cannot be given except under certain conditions ... how is it that a conditional acceptance of a proposition, – such as an act of inference, – is able to lead as it does, to an unconditional acceptance of it, such as is assent? (pp. 157–8)

Newman's assertion that assent to a proposition entails the transition from conditional to unconditional acceptance brought into focus for Lonergan the problem of the virtually unconditioned. The question now arises, What, according to Newman, effects the transition from inference to unconditional assent?

Newman's impact on Lonergan was such that on 3 February 1929 he read a paper entitled 'The Illative Sense' to the philosophical society, later published as 'True Judgment and Science' in the *Blandyke Papers*. Central for Newman in the transition from inference to assent, and thus true judgment, was the operation of the illative sense, which Lonergan describes in the opening of his essay as follows:

> That judgment may be consciously true is the contention of the *Essay in Aid of a Grammar of Assent*, and the principle of reflex knowledge is the Illative sense. On the analogy of the names 'moral sense' 'sense of the beautiful' which designate the mind judging morality or beauty, the name illative sense was given to designate mind in the function of judging inferences. According to logic which is the form of demonstrative science, the only certain conclusions are deductions from self-evident propositions; hypotheses, theories, views may have any degree of probability but cannot be certainties, for absolute verification is logically impossible. The Illative Sense is just such an absolute verification.[46]

The magnitude of the claim in the final sentence is startling.

To make science the only criterion of certitude in the pursuit of truth is wantonly to tempt humans to give up the quest for wisdom. The alternative criterion is the mind itself, which is wider and subtler than logical inference. For Newman, within the mind the illative sense, that is, the reasoning faculty, as exercised by gifted, or by educated or otherwise well prepared minds, has its function in the beginning, middle and end of all verbal discussion and inquiry, and in every step of the process. It is a rule to itself, and appeals to no judgment beyond its own; and attends upon the whole course of thought from antecedents to consequents, with a minute diligence and unwearied presence, which is impossible to a cumbrous apparatus of verbal reasoning, though, in communicating with others, words are the only instrument we possess, and a serviceable, though imperfect instrument.[47]

Newman's claims for the illative sense are uncompromising: 'the sole and final judgment of the validity on an inference in concrete matters is committed to the personal act of the ratiocinative faculty, the perfection or virtue of which I have called the Illative Sense.'[48]

When Lonergan read Newman's account of the illative sense he recognized a basic truth about human mental processes: 'I wanted something I did know, eh? And this I knew was right. I put the illative sense as reflective understanding which is an important point.'[49]

It was Lonergan's later view that Fichte, Schelling, and Hegel wrote their enormous systems because in order for judgment to be possible you had to know everything about everything: 'that was the only possible unconditioned. They didn't have the idea of the virtually unconditioned.'[50] Newman provided him an answer to their problem. The illative sense, reflective understanding, can grasp the virtually unconditioned without having to understand everything about everything. This influence came to be somewhat concealed in Lonergan's writings because, as he says, 'I don't mention Newman in *Insight* either because I would have had to explain what Newman said, and that's another task.'[51]

This insight now became a stepping stone, a fixed point of reference in Lonergan's intellectual history. There is in this a certain dramatic fitness: that Newman, of whom, Mark Pattison said, 'all the grand developments of human reason from Aristotle down to Hegel were a closed book,'[52] should enable Lonergan to get clear on such a fundamental point about the human mind.

If the illative sense and assent bring us to the truth, Newman does not seem to address directly the question of the relation between assent to propositions as true and facts or existence. Liddy, drawing on Cameron and Sillem, notes an agnosticism in Newman about our knowledge of things:

At what period of his life he arrived at the doctrine which he held firmly in later life, namely, that the material world is a world of things or substances of which we can know nothing, because what we perceive of them are merely their sensible phenomena, it is difficult to say with precision. One thing, however, is quite certain: he did not take his doctrine from Locke.[53]

Although for Newman we live in a world of facts, the relation between judgment, facts, and existence, and between brute and cognitional facts, were points that Lonergan would work out later.[54] We should not read Lonergan's later viewpoint on judgment into his essay on Newman at this time.

Lonergan's fourth and final year of study at Heythrop was devoted totally to preparation for the final examinations of his London BA in June 1930. During the first term of that academic year, between Saturday, 26 October, and Tuesday, 29 October, the Wall Street stock market crashed. Because of the economic context of the time, with its absence of welfare, the consequences of the crash were ruinous. But only when Lonergan returned to Montreal in 1930 would the consequent Depression really affect him and awaken his intellectual desire to the problem of explaining the collapse of the economic order.[55]

Lonergan's fourth year also involved an intensive study of mathematics. Charles O'Hara, the mathematics teacher, whose sayings were famous and who succeeded in getting the class interested in astronomy and reading star charts, made a deep impression on Lonergan. He also, it appears, exerted some influence on Wittgenstein.[56] O'Hara taught Lonergan coordinate and projective geometry and was an unusually brilliant pedagogue:

> One of his methods was: flag the diagram. Draw a diagram; mark all the values you know on it. You should be able then to see an equation or two equations – whatever you need – and get the solution. Don't learn the trigonometrical formula by heart; just flag the diagram and read off the formula ... Well, with O'Hara it was always insights. He didn't talk about them but that was what he was giving you.[57]

With Dudley Ward, O'Hara later authored a book entitled *An Introduction to Projective Geometry* (Oxford: Clarendon Press, 1937). Based on the material of his lectures, it contained a short section on relativity theory but nothing on Hilbert or quantum theory. Lonergan's powers of retention are illustrated by the fact that he would draw on O'Hara's statement of the relations between points, lines, planes, and surfaces of projective geometry in his work on economics in 1944.[58]

Hingston, the Canadian provincial, who would be responsible for decisions about Lonergan's work and studies for the next three years, visited Heythrop on 10 June. He would have talked to Bolland, the director of studies, about the qualities of the Canadian students. Bolland had singled out Lonergan as a prospect for work in philosophy or theology, and it is most likely that he made this known to Hingston. Before Lonergan left Heythrop on 19 June he went to Bolland to ask his advice about his future:

> It was on leaving Heythrop that I was encouraged to think I might work in philosophy. I was bidding Fr. Joseph Bolland farewell ... I left Heythrop a votary of Newman's and a nominalist. On my departure I had been to see Fr. Bolland to ask him whether I best devote my future efforts to mathematics or classics. I had done both for an external pass at London; I was obviously cut out to be a student; I could not keep at both. He raised the question that I might be wanted to teach philosophy or theology; I put the obvious objection of my nominalism, while admitting philosophy to be my fine frenzy. He said no one could remain a nominalist for long.[59]

As with his religious vocation, so also with his philosophical there was involved a certain amount of resistance. Although he admitted that philosophy was his 'fine frenzy,' he was seeking advice about a future academic life in classics or mathematics. Despite his protests the damage had been done: his passion for the subject had been awakened.

Lonergan left Heythrop on June 19, the day before his mathematics examination in London University. The next morning he took the wrong train from his residence in London and was twenty minutes late for the examination. Given that, as the paper rather quaintly says, 'Full marks may be obtained for about EIGHT questions,' a twenty-minute loss was serious. Lonergan commented: 'I read the paper, picked a question, had it out in three minutes and began to feel I was all right! It was a tricky question but I saw one of O'Hara's tricks to solve it, using the square root of minus one.'[60]

4

Puzzled in Montreal by the Depression and Plato's Ideas

Soon after his London University examinations for his BA were over Lonergan returned to Canada, where he found that the rich had become poor and the poor were out of work.[1] In 1930 the industrial world was in the throes of the Depression, a prelude to the Second World War. That summer the incoming Canadian government faced a situation in which two hundred thousand people were unemployed. As welfare did not exist, unemployment was ruinous and became a major political issue. The government's first move was to introduce legislation to make twenty million dollars available for relief work. In October a world economic conference took place in London, and a further one was planned for 1933. Late in 1931 Britain went off the gold standard, American banks were failing, and five and a half million were out of work in Germany. By 1932 American production was 53 per cent of its pre-Depression level, Italian 67 per cent.

Daily, Lonergan would have read about the Depression and observed its effects around him. As a result, he began to question the causes of the breakdown of the economic order. Along with the demands posed by his Jesuit life, this concern would play a part in defining the road on which his awakened intellectual vocation would now travel. He became one of nine young Jesuits in the Loyola teaching community, where the daily order had hardly changed since his student days. So he knew the ropes: 'I was busy you know. My first year at Loyola I taught Latin, Greek, French and English and had the College debating society, the newsletter and the annual review.'[2] As he faced the new decade, he could have had no idea where it would lead him.

One of his pupils during those years was Eric Kierans, later to become a lifelong friend and a cabinet member in the Trudeau government. He found Lonergan an inspiring teacher, but something of a loner until Eric O'Connor came on the scene in the 1940s. Kierans also remembered Lonergan turning out with his fellow teachers at 5:00 p.m. to play ice hockey against the students. On two occasions in 1932 Lonergan discussed with Kierans the possibility that the latter might have a call. Kierans' considered response was that he had no call but had a duty to his family, who were suffering greatly from the Depression. To Lonergan's reply that God would look after them Kierans responded, 'I will look after them.'3

Christopher Dawson's *The Age of the Gods*

In spite of the pressures of teaching, one of the providential books Lonergan read in 1930 was Christopher Dawson's *The Age of the Gods*. In a February 1973 discussion at Regis College with academics from McMaster University, Lonergan was asked about the adaptation of religion to culture. He replied that he was brought up in a classicist culture where mathematics and Greek were considered the major subjects. Reading Christopher Dawson's *The Age of the Gods* was his 'first introduction to an opposed view ... an anthropological notion of culture'4 whereby Eskimos, who are discussed in the introduction to Dawson's book, have a culture, just like everyone else. In large part the book addressed the emergence of Sumerian culture, with its religion of the mother goddess, and related city-states in Mesopotamia. It then traced the dawn of higher civilisations in Europe.

To the question, what is a culture? Dawson responds that it is 'a common way of life – a particular adjustment of man to his natural surroundings and his *economic* needs. In its use and modification it resembles the development of a biological species' (italics mine).5 Reflections on race, environment, economics, and mind, the main influences that shape a culture, lead Dawson to ask, what is progress? He is concerned with understanding the world order by means of which, empirically, a succession of cultures emerge, flourish, atrophy, and decay into extinction or are reborn. Mill's question about progress is being further embellished.

Progress for Dawson does not follow a single uniform law, but rather a series of possible types of social and cultural change. A people can develop their life in their original environment without outside influence, they can change their geographical environment, they can be the agents or objects of conquest, or they can adopt some element of the technology of their neighbours. Their vision of reality, central for Dawson to a culture, can change: 'For the history of the earth is not a simple uniform development. It has proceeded by a series of vast cyclic revolutions, true world-ages in which the stages of geological, climatic, and biological change are co-ordinated and dependent on one another.'6 There is a suggestion of cyclic processes with reference to the Aristotelian theory of the Great Summer and the Great Winter.[7]

An attitude to life and a conception of reality are embodied in every religion. When they change, so too does the whole character of the culture, as happened in the transformation of ancient civilisation by Christianity or of the society of pagan Arabia by Islam. Later Lonergan will be deeply concerned with the realism implicit in Christianity, his approach being more epistemological than that of Dawson.

Since the dawn of agricultural civilisation, the economic production of a standard of living has been a constant of history and culture. It can be witnessed in the lifestyles of the early primitive fruit gatherers, hunters, and fishers along Egypt's Nile valley and Babylon's Euphrates.[8] Lonergan's 1942 economics text (the typescript 'For a New Political Economy') describes how in the European expansion one finds everywhere the pulsating flow, the rhythmic series, of the economic activities of man. His concern in that work was with untying a knot in the mechanics of economic production so that the higher processes of culture and civilisation could be liberated. Significant for Dawson are major epochal changes such as the transition from a hoe to an ox economy. For him these, and their related forms of life, can be defined just as much by new discoveries – how to domesticate the ox or cultivate wheat or barley – as by significant changes in the social relations within the workforce.[9] The banking role of the temple in early civilisations is also discussed. The business centre of the social world, the temple lent money at interest and made advances to farmers on the security of their crops.

In his brief essay on Chesterton in the *Loyola College Review* in 1931, Lonergan refers to the Marxist conception of history as 'outrageous' and of value as 'wild.'[10] In contrast, Chesterton was putting forward a theory of distributism rather than of capitalism or communism. His somewhat grotesque insistence on standing on one's head to see things properly and on enjoying the mysteriousness of even the most obvious things clearly attracted Lonergan. Cocksure, certain minds eliminate mystery and put an end to thought. Chesterton felt that the human mind resembled the nose with its poor sense of smell.

The Causes of the Depression

If Dawson's book posed questions about economic and cultural progress, other works were addressing the more pragmatic question of how to get the stalled production process of the economy back into movement. In an exchange economy, movement requires that money circulate continuously. In Alberta, William Aberhart was convinced that Major C.H. Douglas'

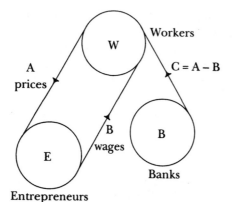

Workers

C = A – B

Banks

Entrepreneurs

Fig. 1. The System of Social Credit

doctrine of Social Credit could bring this about. Its proponents argued that in order to make a cyclical profit, entrepreneurs must always charge more for their products, amount A, than they pay in wages, amount B. As a result, there is always a differential, C, between the available income that the community has to spend on commodities and the price of those commodities. That differential is defined by the simple equation $C = A – B$ (fig. 1). Unless it is made available to consumers, there will be a permanent brake on the economy because a community can never purchase what it produces. Some schools of economics have claimed that the differential C has been at the heart of the succession of inflationary cycles that we have witnessed throughout the last century.

Social Credit argued that in order to offset this differential, it was necessary for the banks or community to balance the flows by injecting finance equal to C into the economy. The workers were to be paid an extra twenty-five dollars each payday, which led to the policy's being described as the politics of 'funny money.' The hope was that making up the differential would cause the flow of money and of economic activity to resume. It is important to note that the wages B, payments A, and the injection C are not lump sums but circulating flows.

It was clear to Lonergan that such an intervention by the banks would be inflationary. Still, he asked, 'what was wrong with the argument, the theory; why would it be inflationary?'[11] In this puzzlement we find the genesis of the question, are there healthy and unhealthy ways in which money can both be introduced to and circulate in an economy? According to Eric Kierans, in response to this new awakening and engagement of his wonder Lonergan read Valere Fallon's *Principles of Social Economy*.[12] Containing significant methodological reflections, it addressed questions such as: Are there economic laws and, given that men are free, are they the same or different from those of chemistry? For Fallon economics is a social science, a science of the economic relations of exchanges and other economic activities in society. The laws are more flexible than those of chemistry and are verified in large numbers of economic transactions. The discipline will involve inductive, deductive, and statistical methods.

The book divides the economy into production, distribution, exchange, and consumption, each being discussed in detail. Through the economic force, production is concerned with transforming nature to meet human needs, something akin to what Lonergan will later term 'producing a standard of living.' Part 3 contains a detailed analysis of exchange covering exchange value, wages, incomes, and prices. Fallon's analysis of credit and banking echoes Lonergan's interest in finance. Production and exchange are the main categories in Mill, of whom Fallon had a low opinion.

In his spare time Lonergan would spend fourteen years trying to soften up the problem, producing a difficult typescript of 126 pages. Few, to date, have made sense of it.

In his second year Lonergan taught courses on mathematics and mechanics, using as his mathematics text Silvanus Thompson's *Calculus Made Easy*.[13] As we shall see, the theoretical horizon opened up by these courses would later influence his work on both economics and history. Thompson illustrates the meaning of a differential with reference to economics: if y stands for the amount of money and t for time, then dy/dt stands for the rate of spending or saving (p. 46). Thompson concluded that because of sudden changes in saving or expenditure, economics was not an apt field for illustrating differentials. Lonergan and most macroeconomists would disagree, but the mathematical symbolism of Thompson seems to have influenced Lonergan's first economics text.

According to Ed Sheridan, Lonergan's mechanics course was low-key. Although no textbook was used, it is likely that he was influenced by Kimball's *Elements of Physics*, which was in general use at the time.[14] In it he would have read again about the methods of the empirical sciences, empirical verification, and the definition of such terms as 'mass', 'force.' and 'acceleration'. He would have discussed how, by discovering a differential equation among those variables, Newton could explain almost any kind of physical movement, including the movement of the planets, a cannonball, a projectile, or an object in free fall.

From Newton Lonergan acquired an appreciation of the horizon of theory. That theoretical attitude and orientation would be translated, analogously, into his work on both economics and history. The descriptions of production and exchange offered by Fallon invite a theoretical explanation. The aggregate prices A and wages B, respectively charged by and paid by entrepreneurs, are not once-off quantities of money but velocities of the form of X dollars per month. If one thinks of exchanges as characterized by velocity-like properties and is at the same time studying Newtonian mechanics, the key importance of accelerations becomes manifest. Thinking of accelerations and decelerations in prices and wages opens up a line of analysis relevant to the explanation of cycles in an economy. Over a long period of time Lonergan wondered if there exists a system of relations among a number of economic variables. Identifying those variables and their relations would enable one to predict under what circumstances an economy would grow, boom, slump into a recession, or even crash.

History was another field that he would explore and in which he would extend, by way of analogy, the categories of direction and force. Unless forces disrupt it, a projectile moves in a straight line. Without the disturbing forces of the sun, a planet would move in a straight line. History, by analogy, can be thought of as moving in an ideal line except to the extent that human ignorance and prejudice disrupt it. In this sense intellect is a basic variable in history. Lonergan's discussion of progress and decline will ask about the differentials between two historical situations. This will lead him to wonder if there is something analogous to a differential equation for history that would explain all the historical variations historians describe and discuss.[15]

Reading Stewart's Plato

During his first two years of teaching Lonergan also read Stewart's *Plato's Doctrine of Ideas,* even admitting that he was rather high on it. The book came out of a school of Platonic studies influenced by Kant, a point that has been explored in detail by Mark Morelli.[16] Lonergan later recalled:

> It contained much that later I was to work out for myself in a somewhat different context, but at that time it was a great release. My nominalism had been an opposition, not to intelligence and understanding, but to the central role ascribed to universal concepts. From Stewart I learnt that Plato was a methodologist, that his ideas were what the scientist seeks to discover, that the scientific or philosophic process towards discovery was one of question and answer. My apprehension, at that time, was not that precise. It was something vaguer that made me devote my free time to reading Plato's early dialogues (Stewart followed Lutoslawski's order) and then moving on to Augustine's early dialogues written at Cassiciacum near Milan. Augustine was so concerned with understanding, so unmindful of universal concepts, that I began a long period of trying to write an intelligible account of my convictions.[17]

What, Stewart asked, did Plato mean by 'ideas'? He was opposed to a positivist exegetical approach that, in response to the question, demanded that the text, and the text alone, be allowed to speak for itself. What Plato means by an idea was some experience that he and his friends had in common and that we too can have today. Plato's challenge becomes: 'Tell us in the language, vernacular or philosophical, of today what that experience is.'[18] Lacking that familiarity, we will lose our way in the dark and walk ourselves into a labyrinth. Acknowledging that that familiarity does not guarantee infallibility, Stewart singles out Kant's categories and scientific laws as relevant to what Plato had in mind.

From this perspective he explores the range of Plato's ideas. The early dialogues discussed mainly moral ideas such as piety and justice. By *Parmenides* five classes of ideas have been discussed: logical, ethical, biological (life and health), elements (fire, air, water, earth), and matter. These are divided into logical or general and specific ideas. General ideas, such as substance or same, which we have implicitly from the start, are not confined to special departments.[19] The extension of ideas to all departments of scientific inquiry is shown by *Parmenides* to be absolutely necessary.

Ideas, for Stewart, are acquired by means of the method of question and answer, by 'anamnesis,' abstraction from the sensible, measurement, and by the use of the *a priori* notions or categories of the mind. That we discover the idea of justice (or of life or air) by letting just and unjust situations (or their equivalents for life and air) provoke us into raising and answering the corresponding question, What is the definition or idea of justice? is for Stewart a constant of the dialogues. The slave in *Meno* is led by the questioning of Socrates to discover in the diagram that a square of two, three, and four units of length encloses four, nine, and sixteen times the area of a square of one unit of length. From this standpoint it could be suggested that the whole corpus is an exploration of the many faces of the What is it? question. The range and meaning of the ideas are related to the range of the question.

For Stewart the *Phaedo* concludes that the intelligible order of being is known through the sensible. The *intelligibilia* have the 'function of making the *sensibilia* intelligible.'[20] Without the senses, Plato's ideas and Kant's categories are empty. This poses the question of the relation between intelligence and reality. From the viewpoint of logic or methodology, the ideas are ways in which the understanding interprets the sensible world. For Plato, clearness or *safeneia* is the test of truth.[21] For Stewart, this test of truth is the same as that which we find in the clear and distinct ideas of Descartes and Spinoza, and in Kant's ultimate proof of the categories that we cannot think them away.

Understanding what Plato meant by an idea was for Stewart a central problem in working out what is meant by scientific method. The *Timaeus* suggests that ideas are the patterns according to which God, figured for the imagination as an artificer, makes sensible things. The absolute separation of these ideas from sensible things is maintained.[22] Despite this, Stewart holds that the Platonic *eidos* is really what the scientist is trying to discover by his inquiries: 'This is the law which explains the facts.'[23] By *Laches* Stewart maintains that a great advance has been made towards Plato's later methodological standpoint:

> The Doctrine set forth is that of the Idea as scientific point of view – point of view, not uncritically assumed after observation of a few particulars, but critically fixed, as the only right point of view, after a survey of the whole system of classes to which the class of particulars observed belongs.[24]

Also included are the native categories that human understanding cannot but employ in scientific discovery. Stewart's account of how Plato develops his general theories of ideas or, in the second part of his study, of the good as the dialogues unfold bears some resemblance to the emergence of a higher viewpoint.

As well as generally influencing Lonergan's attitude to scientific method, Stewart's book had a more specific impact. For Plato, as read by Stewart, the relation between an idea and its related particulars is similar to that between a mathematical equation and instances of the curve of which it is the equation. Give specific numerical values to the coefficients in the equation and you can then trace the curve:

> The Idea of the circle, as defined by its equation in the general form, is not itself properly speaking a curve ... Such an equation, like the ideal number, is at once many, as synthesising an indefinite plurality of positions, and one, as synthesising them in accord with a definite law.[25]

An idea is a unity that synthesises a multitude of relations.

The impact of this point on Lonergan was such that on four different occasions in his later life he referred to it: firstly, in 1973 in *Philosophy of God, and Theology*; secondly, in a question session in Boston College on 19 June 1979; thirdly, in *Caring about Meaning* in 1981; and fourthly, in his essay 'Myth, Symbol and Reality.' Reviewing his intellectual history in that question session at Boston College, he remarked:

> Aristotle and Thomas held that you abstracted from phantasm the *eidos*, the *species*, the *idea*. *And my first clue into the idea* was when I was

reading a book by an Oxford don by the name of J.A. Stewart who in 1905 had written on Plato's myths and in 1909 on Plato's doctrine of ideas. And he explained the doctrine of ideas by contending that for Plato an idea was something like the Cartesian formula for a circle, i.e. $(x^2 + y^2) = r^2$ and that exemplified the act of understanding for me, and the idea was getting what's in behind the formula for the circle. So you have something in between the concept and the datum or phantasm. And that is the sort of thing that you can't hold and be a naive realist. (italics mine)[26]

His use of the phrase 'I was home' in *Caring About Meaning* is strong but has to be balanced by his caution that his apprehension was not that precise at the time. In a letter to his provincial in January 1935, he commented that reading Plato gave him a theory of intellect but left his nominalism intact. This suggests that Stewart's Plato cured him of his naive realism of the intellect but left the question of the relation between intelligence and reality unresolved.

What Lonergan picked up at this point was a first clue in a major problem centring on ideas and their relation to understanding and reality. It was a problem that would occupy him until the end of the *Verbum* articles and after. He later changed their book title to *Word and Idea in Aquinas*, published after *Insight* in 1967. At the end of his journey it will become clear that what Stewart, Descartes, and Kant meant by 'ideas' differs hugely from what Aristotle, Aquinas, and Lonergan meant.

As he was reading Stewart during his second year of teaching, Lonergan had a fairly serious row with the rector, Thomas MacMahon. MacMahon was a well-known disciplinarian who set an example of regularity to his community and was feared rather than liked. He could also be lacking in sympathy. The exchange was heated, as Lonergan could fly off the handle when provoked. The precise cause of the conflict remains obscure, but is thought to have involved Lonergan's refusal to follow elements of the daily order, possibly the time of rising. MacMahon was at the time one of the four consultors to the provincial, and so, as a result of the episode, Lonergan's departure to theology was delayed a year, until the fall of 1933.

The consequences – having to stay on and teach for another year at Loyola and a related sense of being disciplined – were unpleasant. Later Lonergan remarked that it was during this time that he learned to pray. Crowe has referred to it as a time of fairly severe crisis in his religious vocation. The departure from the Society of two friends as well as his bad relationship with the rector provided 'the occasion for him to rethink his vocation and commit himself anew to the life he had chosen eleven years earlier.'[27] In a letter in January 1935 he would refer to the period as one of painful introversion. In later years he used to joke with Eliott McGuigan that at the time the question was not Are we leaving? but rather When are we leaving? Both remained and celebrated their golden jubilees, but the incident left scars. Later in his life Lonergan would complain about superiors and the way in which they had never given him his head.

Reading Augustine's Early Writings

Despite the setback, the seed of his later work was germinating. During the summer of 1933, before his theology studies began, he read St Augustine's early Cassiciacum dialogues, which he found to be psychologically exact.

After the trauma of his conversion in August 386, Augustine, in poor health, retired from his teaching job. While he waited for his baptism the following Easter, his friend Verecundus offered him the use of the latter's villa at Cassiciacum, just outside Milan. There Augustine went with his mother Monica, his son Adeodatus, his best friend Alypius, his brother Navigius, two cousins, Lastidianus and Rusticus, and two pupils, Licentius and Trygetius. In the course of their short stay in the villa, they engaged in a number of dialogues. In this manner there came to be composed the *Contra Academicos (Answer to Skeptics*, started first but not finished until later), *De Beata Vita (The Happy Life*, finished first), *De Ordine (Divine Providence and the Problem of Evil)*, and finally his *Soliloquies*.[28] Lonergan read these works during the summer of 1933. In the course of his reading it became clear that Augustine's religious conversion, far from damping down his intellect, had awakened in him a new passion for understanding. Involving an element of intellectual conversion, it had, as Augustine told a friend, 'broken the most hateful bonds that had held me away from the breast of Philosophy – the despair of finding Truth, Truth which is the nourishing food of the soul.'[29]

The *Answer to Skeptics* opens with the question, Does wisdom consist in the lifelong pursuit of the truth, or rather in its possession? The sceptics claimed that all things are uncertain. In order to avoid commitment to truth, they introduced the notion of 'truth-like,' or probability. Augustine is as convinced that the truth can be discovered as the sceptics are that it cannot.[30] According to Brown, he puts forward as a central educational thesis that students 'should learn, thereby, to prize their own powers of thought, their *ingenium*,' an indication of his great respect for the faculty of sheer and hard ratiocination.[31] Although the question of truth is everywhere present in this work, it is in part 2 of his later work, *Soliloquies*, that he gives more shape to his understanding of it.

The dialogue *The Happy Life*, begun on Augustine's thirty-second birthday, discusses human happiness. In it he recalls that since reading Cicero's

Hortentius at the age of nineteen, he has been inflamed with a love of philosophy. In the intervening years he was confused and led astray by what he refers to as the mists. Then, through his conversion, some twelve years later he found the land where he learned to know the North Star. He continues:

> For I have noticed frequently in the sermons of our priest [Ambrose, Bishop of Milan] and sometimes in yours, that, when speaking of God, no one should think of Him as something corporeal; nor yet of the soul, for of all things the soul is nearest to God.[32]

This passage inspired Lonergan to write in the introduction to *Insight* that it took Augustine years to discover that the word 'real' might have different connotations from the word 'body.' This discovery involved a break with corporeal thinking, a topic well discussed by Richard Liddy.[33]

It is at this point in Lonergan's intellectual journey that the problem of intellectual conversion, that is to say, of something akin to the journey out of Plato's cave, enters the story. Later in his life he critiqued the validity of 'an intuition of what exists and is present' as found in fourteenth-century scholasticism. Acknowledging that his readers may not hold perception as a valid criterion of objective knowledge, he continued:

> But at least in all probability you did at one time take a percept-ualism for granted. And if, by some lucky chance, you succeeded in freeing yourself completely from that assumption, then your experience would have been quite similar to that of the prisoner who struggled might and main against his release from the darkness of Plato's cave.[34]

Lonergan, as we shall see, was himself undergoing his own intellectual conversion. A first move was his acknowledgment that you cannot both be a naive realist and accept Plato's account of the equation of the circle. Human understanding cannot be reduced to the imagination. Such conversion does not involve eliminating the role that the senses, imagination, and instinct have in objective knowing. Rather, it involves breaking their dominant grip on our notion of knowledge and of reality. For Augustine and Plato, recognizing that there is more to mind or consciousness than the senses involved a radical change in their self-understanding and in their interpretation of the known world.

Divine Providence and the Problem of Evil is prefaced with observations about God's providence and the occurrence of evil. There is a wish in the human heart to understand how God cares for human affairs. Still, the extensiveness of perversity makes us wonder if evil must be beyond God's providence or else committed by God's will.[35] Augustine censures those who, by magnifying a particular disorder, conclude that the whole universe is disordered.

Book 2 poses the question, what is unwisdom? It concludes that unwisdom cannot be understood, for it alone is called the 'darkness of the mind.' On account of unwisdom, one cannot understand things that otherwise can be understood. If there is no order in the things done by the unwise man, will there then be something that the order by which God governs all does not embrace? Ought evil activities to be excluded from the order in the universe? Are the hangman or the prostitute necessary evils within the social order? Viewed narrowly, they seem evil, but perhaps are not so in the whole scheme of things.[36]

The question of the relation between God's justice and good and evil is now raised. Augustine will not accept that evil had its origins in God, but Monica puts things in perspective:

> I think that nothing could have been done aside from the order of God, because evil itself, which has had an origin, in no way originated by the order of God; but that divine justice permitted it not to be beyond the limits of order, and has brought it back and confined it to an order befitting it.[37]

There are, it seems, certain parallels in the problem of evil and in the consequences of the flight from understanding.

Book 2, chapter 9 addresses the order of the development of mind or reason. Only after one's mind had developed from articulating sounds for the alphabet, through syllables and words, grammar, literature, and history to geometry will one be able to raise the question about the soul. Without that preparation, one will fall into every possible error.

Chapter 17 introduces a definition of philosophy. Repeated in the *Soliloquies* it states: 'To philosophy pertains a two fold question: the first treats of the soul; the second of God. The first makes us know ourselves, the second, our origin.'[38] On the next page Augustine continues: 'By some kind of inner and hidden activity of mind, I am able to analyse and synthesise the things that ought to be learned.' Reason, which it is the task of philosophy to understand, measures the universe. To know one's soul will, for Augustine, involve knowing this power. His concern is to outline an educational order by means of which this might be achieved.

The *Soliloquies*, a work in two books, is a conversation or dialogue with his own mind rather than with his friends. Something of a new genre, it was a work in which Augustine's position on faith and reason began to take shape. The first book was largely concerned with the knowledge of God and underlines the significance of faith. Reason is the eye of the mind but, just like the physical eye, its sight might not be healthy. In order for it to see clearly, faith is needed. The mind recognizes its need for healing, and out of this need hope arises. Without love, faith, and hope the mind's pursuit of truth will not endure. So in order to see God the human soul needs faith, hope, and charity.

It is in book 2 of the *Soliloquies*, concerned largely with truth and false-hood, that Augustine's notion of truth, which had an impact on Lonergan, is developed. The basic thesis is stated in chapter 2 and repeated in chapter 15: 'Truth, therefore, in no way will cease to exist.'[39] Truth cannot perish because if the whole world, including truth itself, were to perish it would still be true that the world and truth had perished.

When asked to define 'true' by Reason, his partner in the conversation, Augustine replies, 'That is true which is in reality as it is seen by one perceiving, if he wishes and is able to perceive.'[40] In response to objections by Reason concerning unperceived realities, he adds a second definition: 'The true is that which exists.' Nothing will then be false, Reason responds. Augustine is perplexed but replies: 'Though I am unwilling to be taught in any other way than by this questioning, I nevertheless fear to be ques-tioned.' The questioning focuses on the meaning of 'false', it being recog-nized that truth cannot be better pursued other than by question and answer.[41]

In 1933 Lonergan spent his summer vacation at Loyola Island, Kingston. According to John Swain, 'The area was marshy, the mosquitoes bad, so lights did not go on in the evening. But Bernie could be heard night after night typing through the twilight and into the dark.'[42] He was writing an account of his growing convictions: 'I then put together a 25,000 word essay on the act of faith and gave it with a challenge to Fr Smeaton now at Amiens.'[43] Smeaton was quite positive in his response. Gerald McGugian, a Montreal Jesuit, told me that Lonergan also gave it to his teacher, William Bryan, to read. Bryan told him to put it in his drawer until after he was ordained.

Theological Studies and the Impact of Hoenen

In September 1933 Lonergan started his theology studies at L'Immaculée in Montreal. Some months earlier Hoenen had published an article, 'On the Origins of the First Principles of Knowledge,' in *Gregorianum*.[44] About it Lonergan remarked that he had been 'much struck' by its argument that 'intellect abstracted from phantasm not only terms but also the nexus between them. [Hoenen] held that that was certainly the view of Cajetan and probably of Aquinas.'[45]

For Hoenen, scholastic authors such as Frick and Pasch had in recent times appealed to Kant's distinction between analytic and synthetic judgments in explaining the origins of such indemonstrable first principles as 'the whole is greater than the part.' As a result the true scholastic explanation of such origins had been lost. Early in his paper he states what he considers it to be: 'the first principles of mathematics, *hence the universal judgments* themselves (*not only the notions* of the subject and predicate) are derived *by immediate abstraction* from the phantasm.'[46] Intellect abstracts not just the terms, 'whole' and 'part' or 'Socrates' and 'man,' but a nexus of terms and relations; Socrates is a man or snub-nosed. In this it reflects an objective nexus between a substance and its attributes in the real order.[47] Hoenen's task in the first paper was to explore scholastic textual sources that support or oppose his thesis. In favour he finds Cajetan with support from Aquinas, in opposition Scotus and his disciple, Antonious Andreas.

According to Cajetan, for Andreas experience is necessary in order to know the terms in a first principle but not the nexus. This he considers to be contrary to both reason and Aristotle. Experientially, for Aristotle, we come to know that a particular herb is useful for a particular illness. Knowledge proceeds from such a particular to a complex universal: 'every herb of this kind cures this kind of disease.' Cajetan then goes on to argue that Andreas' position originated with Scotus, his teacher. Where Scotus talks about the nexus between terms, Aquinas talks about *ratio*, about understanding something. Lonergan finds Scotist presuppositions in Kant's analytic and synthetic propositions and the notion that judgment, in certain respects, is a matter of comparing concepts.[48]

Scotus held that the intellect employs the senses in conceiving the simple terms but not their nexus:

> The latter (the possible intellect) therefore, having conceived the simple terms, can by its own power compose and divide them: such complex concepts, if they belong to the first principles, are known to be true by the natural light of the intellect.[49]

The natural light of the intellect works out the nexus between the terms independently of the phantasm.

In section 4 Hoenen addresses the question, did the doctrine of Cajetan derive from Aquinas himself? In response, he assembles a huge conglomeration of texts that address Aquinas' thought on such matters as agent and possible intellect, the imagination, the manner in which species actuate the possible intellect, and understanding. First conceptions of the intellect, such as one and being, or principles such as 'Every whole is greater than its parts' are the foundations on which all demonstrations of the speculative sciences proceed. About their origins he concludes:

> *But these principles known by nature become manifest (evident) to man from*
> *the light of the agent intellect, which is part of man's nature: by this light,*
> *indeed, nothing becomes evident to us except insofar as, through it, the*
> *phantasmata are rendered intelligible in act. For this is the act of the agent*
> *intellect, as is said in 3 De Anima.* (italic in original)[50]

The fundamental expression of what is called the agent intellect is the performance of raising questions, so central to Socratic philosophy and the unending interrogation of parents by their young children.

In his disputed questions Aquinas argued that the agent intellect, the capacity to question, must exist prior to and be the cause of both the habit and the act of the first principles in the possible intellect.[51] The principles are like an instrument that the agent intellect uses. He opens up the question of the intellect being informed by the 'species,' and operating through such a form in the formation of the quiddities of things in composing and dividing. Through composing and dividing the intellect arrives at the knowledge of external reality, a second factor by means of which understanding is realized.

The *Posterior Analytics* holds that induction is necessary to know first principles, but does not describe the process.[52] The imagination is indicated as the ultimate ground of any judgment in mathematical questions. Having articulated Aquinas' position on the agent intellect and the imagination in deriving first principles, Hoenen raises the key question: 'How does cognition of principles arise from phantasm?'[53] He ducks it for two pages before arriving at a threefold conclusion. It is the possible intellect, the understanding, that performs the abstraction:

> The human possible intellect does not therefore only require the
> phantasm to acquire the intelligible species, but also so that it may
> *as it were behold them in the phantasms* ... and so the intellectual power
> *understands* the species *in the phantasms* ... And so its proper opera-
> tion is to understand the *intelligibles in the phantasms.*[54]

The species, that is to say Aristotle's *eidos*, are understood in the phantasms. This leads into a discussion of the counterpart in Aquinas of the phrase from Aristotle's *De Anima* (III, 7, 431b2) that Lonergan used on the title page of *Insight*:

> Anyone can verify this in his own experience, that when someone is
> trying to understand something, he forms some *phantasms* (images)

for himself by way of examples, and in these he, in a manner, looks at what he wants to understand.[55]

Crowe is of the opinion that at the time this text interested Lonergan but did not yet tower for him: 'Later it became almost a focal text, the single text in Thomas Aquinas that stands for what he wants to say about insight into phantasm.'[56]

Repeatedly Hoenen states in the article that the intellect knows by simple intuition, which suggests a possible reason as to why Lonergan replaced that term by 'insight.' Judgment, the second of what Boyer calls the two operations of the mind, is mentioned. It involves reflection on the apprehensions of the understanding, the first operation, in order to determine knowledge of the conformity of the simple apprehension with its object.

Through his reading of Hoenen, Lonergan must have recognized that what was being said about the sensory origins of knowledge and about *species* and *eidos* being understood in the images was sufficiently different from the views of Stewart and Plato to cause puzzlement. Only through a thorough personal investigation of the text of Aquinas would Lonergan's curiosity be satisfied.

Despite this further awakening of his intellectual desire, when asked if he had some project in mind at the start of his theology studies, Lonergan answered no.[57] Less than two years later he would write about himself at that time: 'You see I had regarded myself as one condemned to sacrifice his real interests and, in general, to be suspected and to get into trouble for things I could not help and could not explain.'[58] Some creative work was trying to unfold in him, but he felt he was being called to sacrifice it.

5

Struggling with History and Reality in Rome before the War

In early September 1933 John Swain and Charles Bathurst, Canadian Jesuits, were sent for their theology studies to the Gregorian University in Rome, the first-ever members of the Province to study theology there. Some time later the rector in Rome announced to Swain that three Slav students, for whom places were being reserved, had cancelled. As Hingston, the Canadian provincial, had requested places for five students in Rome, the rector advised Swain that these places were now available for Canadians. Swain wrote immediately to Hingston informing him of the development. After taking advice, Hingston accepted the offer by telegram. In his interview with Lonergan in Montreal he put to him the question, was he orthodox? Lonergan replied that he was but that he thought a lot about things. The outcome of the interview was that Lonergan was to go immediately to Rome for his theological studies. Had his passage to theological studies not been delayed for a year because of his conflict with MacMahon, this opportunity would not have arisen. By means of this series of accidents, in November 1933 he arrived in Rome.[1]

Before moving, he visited his family in Buckingham and asked his mother to play for him her favourite piece, 'The Mockingbird.' Sadly, she exclaimed that her fingers were not up to it.[2] Although he could not have known it, it was to be the last time he would see her alive.

There now began his long involvement with the Gregorian University. He took up residence in a room with a view of the roofs of Rome, in the Bellarmino, a building steeped in Jesuit history and situated on the narrow via del Seminario. With his background in Roman history, he must have found the City fascinating. Turn right at the front door and walk for less than a minute and you are at the Forum. Continue across the decorative

Piazza Navone and you are soon at St Peter's and the Vatican. Turn left at the front door and almost immediately you are at the Church of St Ignatius where, for the cost of a small coin, a spotlight lights up the words over the high altar, *Romae Vobis Propitius Ero* (I will be well disposed to you in Rome), words that Lonergan, as Ignatuis, felt were a good omen. Continue along the via del Seminario a short distance to the via del Corso, turn right, walk for about a minute and you are in the Piazza Venezia. There, from the balcony of the Palazza Venezia, Mussolini would address the crowds with his microphone. Phillip Donnelley, a friend in Rome, recalled that he and Lonergan used to use code names when they talked about Hitler and Mussolini. According to Paul Shaugnessey, Donnelley said that he and Lonergan were just across the street from Hitler during one of his visits.[3]

Mussolini's campaign to establish an empire in Africa opened in March 1934. In 1936 he entered the Spanish civil war on the side of the nationalists. War was now becoming an addiction for him. But the cost of the Spanish intervention bled the Italian economy dry. It began to falter, and from 1937 Mussolini lost the support of the Italian people.

In Germany Hitler's Nazi party, fuelled by rising unemployment, bankruptcies, and bank failures, had made its breakthrough in the elections of September 1930. The Weimar Republic was gone by January 1933, the year of Hitler's appointment as chancellor. The totalitarian wave was rising. Jews, excluded from membership in the German *Volk*, began to leave the country. In April 1933 Heidegger was elected rector of the University of Freiburg and, during his fateful year as rector, promoted National Socialism and anti-Semitism, events whose mark on the history of twentieth-century philosophy will be permanent.[4] On 10 May 1933 in the public squares of cities and university towns there was a book-burning ceremony of works by Einstein, Freud, the Manns, Kafka, and other Jewish intellectuals. In the autumn of 1933 Heidegger took a public vow to support Hitler and, in a later lecture in Heidelberg, abused those who did not follow suit.[5] A cycle of decline and disintegration had begun.

One has only to read Overy and Wheatcroft's *The Road to War* to appreciate the stranglehold of the Versailles Treaty and the Depression. In 1933 eight million Germans were unemployed. To the citizenry, caught between the collapse of the parliamentary system, economic misery, and social overthrow, between Soviet communism and Western capitalism, Hitler's radically conservative National Socialism must have appeared an alluring way out. What the conservatives got in return has been described as follows:

> In 1933 the young men of the Party, brought up on street violence, suddenly found the law on their side. They took revenge on all the enemies of the 'new Germany'; on trade union officials and commu-

nists; on moderate sociologists and Catholics; on artists and writers of the avant garde; and on the Jews. By the end of the summer Germany was a one-party state, the trade unions were destroyed, democratic government replaced by the authority of the *Fuhrer*, the leader. The conservatives had powerfully misjudged Hitler; he could not be tamed.[6]

In contrast with the philosopher kings of the *Republic,* Europe was now being led astray by predator hunters. Hitler, Stalin, and Mussolini were leading it into a movement of the absurd.

The Theological World

In 1929 the Gregorian University embarked on a period of expansion, uniting with the Biblical and Oriental Institutes in Rome, an association that has since ceased. In the years that followed, the staff expanded to over three hundred. New faculties were added, including a faculty of church history in 1932, joined by the influential Robert Lieber, who had previously taught Church history at Valkenburg from 1923–9.

In 1931 the Constitution, *Deus Scientiarum Dominus* (God, the Lord of the Sciences), whose drafting commission included Bea and Lanzarini, was issued by the Vatican. The problem it addressed was that of locating what was then considered the heart of Catholic theology, dogmatic theology, within the context of the growth of positive and human sciences. The various disciplines involved were considered to be constituted by a logical, psychological, and didactic coherence rather than a merely a material conglomeration. At the summit stands the main field of study, the '*disciplina praecipua.*' In theology it is dogma with the fundamental and the speculative parts of moral theology. In philosophy it is the universal scholastic philosophy with all its divisions, logic, ontology, cosmology, and so forth.[7]

There was, nonetheless, a recognition that dogmatic theology taught in an inadequate context is impoverished. Doctors of theology, even though thoroughly schooled in dogma, must also be schooled in those positive sciences that are now necessary for all theologians. An ignorance of the methods of study and scientific work in those fields will render theologians defenceless in the face of attacks on religion. The Pontifical Biblical Commission and the Pontifical Institutes – Biblical, Oriental, and Archaeological – were put in place to improve the academic standards of biblical studies.[8]

Deus Scientiarum Dominus, with its emphasis on dogmatic theology, was a part of a wider paradigm of manual theology, largely inspired by Melchior Cano (1509–60). Whereas earlier the term 'dogmatic theology' was used to differentiate that field from moral or historical theology, for Cano it was used to differentiate it from scholastic theology. Dogmatic theology, as Lonergan later put it,

> replaced the inquiry of the *quaestio* by the pedagogy of the thesis. It demoted the quest of faith for understanding to a desirable, but secondary, and indeed optional goal. It gave basic and central significance to the certitudes of faith, their presuppositions, and their consequences. It owed its mode of proof to Melchior Cano and, as that theologian was also a bishop and inquisitor, so the new dogmatic theology not only proved its theses, but was also supported by the teaching authority and sanctions of the Church.[9]

Its sense that there could be no new and surprising insights in theology was in contrast with Aquinas' intellectualism and the exhortation of Vatican I to understand the revealed mysteries.

In his first year Lonergan found himself in a class of just over three hundred students. About it he has commented:

> 'Fundamental theology' was a traditional term in scholastic theology. In the first year of theology you learned 'On the true religion' – you settled that – and then 'The true church,' and then 'The inspiration of the Scripture' – and you were off to the races. It settled the premises from which you were going to deduce the rest of theology: the 'basic truths.'[10]

The third part of the church history course taught by Robert Lieber addressed modern political questions such as the relation of the church to revolution, liberalism, nationalism, socialism, and bolshevism. Its influence can be traced in a text Lonergan wrote soon after, 'An Essay in Fundamental Sociology.'

In a long letter to Henry Smeaton dated 9 May 1934, Lonergan recounts his experience of the year, describing his view of the rooftops, the noise of the traffic, and the villa Borghese. He writes amusingly about the lecturers, the difficulty of attending a morning of lectures on an empty stomach and of recovering from a soporific dinner in time for a 4 p.m. lecture. On Thursdays they had to relax outside the house, so the only time he had for some form of study was on Sunday afternoon. The lifestyle was not suited to private study, and *Deus Scientiarum Dominus* had simply added worry to a reposeful way of life. On examinations he complained about the need to have a memory like Macauley, to be familiar with the synoptic problem, the 28th Canon of Chalcedon, the significance of Osius being head man at

Nicea, and 'far from having a chance to display your knowledge, coming a cropper over the long speeches in St John.' The dogma exam was a half-hour affair in which the students were asked two subjects out of four but, 'unfortunately[,] one never knows which two.'

The year of study successfully completed, Lonergan spent fifty days of his summer vacation in 1934 learning German in the villa of the German College in Rome. Despite feeling the strain of being made to feel a guest, he felt there were good ideas to be found among the Germans. He would request permission to repeat the experience the following year, assuming his provincial did not mind 'my offending the extraordinary susceptabilities of some of the local nationalists.'[11]

In his second year the main dogma courses dealt with God as unity and trinity. The text for the former was volume 1 of the *Summa*, supplemented by *De Deo Uno* and *De Novissimis* by Lennerz, a German theologian of whom Lonergan had a high opinion. Topics included the existence, knowledge, and will of God. In Lonergan's second semester Filograssi introduced him to the classical theology of the Trinity, which he himself would teach in his years as a professor in Toronto and later Rome. The course was structured around theses on the processions of a Word and of Love in God, and on the relations defining the Divine persons and missions. The text was the *Summa Theologica*, I, qqs. 27–43, complemented by Billot, *De Deo Uno et Trino*. Later Lonergan was to remark: 'But I mean the tradition like Billot, who said that we get the Trinitarian procession far more clearly in the imagination than in the intellect – missing the whole point of the Trinitarian processions.'[12]

Following His Own Questions: Idealism, Realism, and History

Lonergan was further encouraged in his intellectual vocation by Leo Keeler, an American professor of the history of philosophy at the Gregorian. As at the time Lonergan felt his future was in teaching philosophy, he took the unusual step of trying out his ideas on Keeler in the form of a thirty-thousand-word essay on Newman.[13] This must have made an impression, because when Keeler's doctoral thesis, *The Problem of Error from Plato to Kant*, was published in 1934 he invited Lonergan, a student, to review it for the journal *Gregorianum*. Lonergan's essay for Keeler is notable in that Crowe finds in it a scorn of Aristotle and a favouring of Plato.[14] Liddy considers that it gives us valuable insights into Lonergan's statement in *Insight* that the halfway house between materialism and critical realism is idealism.[15]

The remaining fragments of the essay for Keeler open with Hume's conclusion of his study of perception that causes cannot be seen. This famously stimulated Kant and posed for Lonergan the question; what exactly does understanding apprehend? A related recurring question concerns the reality of substances that can be of different kinds. A common noun denotes an intellectual grouping of phenomena, our understanding of a single unit, thing in itself, substance plus accidents. Substance not only unifies the different appearances and makes a thing in itself distinct from other things; it is also the cause of the appearances. As these are the substance manifested to us sensibly, so there is no real distinction between substance and appearance or accidents. Substance is the cause of appearances and the explanation of action and reaction according to intelligible law:

> 4. Hence, the idea of substance has become the trial case, the experimentum crucis, between the dogmatic and the critical schools. For if understanding is ultimately apprehensive, then 'substance', what lies beneath or stands beneath the appearances, must be had by apprehension: this is the scholastic position. On the critical theory, the substance is known by an immanent activity and so is not apprehended but merely understood to be there; clearly, this corresponds exactly with our knowledge of substance: we do not know what it is – as we would, if we had ever apprehended it; all we know is that it is there.[16]

Lonergan was critical of the scholastics' spiritual apprehension of substance, and set out to explore the extent to which the critical account can be verified in philosophical inquiry. Remarks such as 'And while on the point, one may mention how well the theory of intellection as an immanent act fits in with a philosophy of mysticism' suggest that, at this point, understanding was for him an immanent activity.[17]

Linguistically, he continues, the words *entendement* in French, *verstand* in German, the medieval *intus-legere*, and *epistemi* in Greek (but not yet 'insight') suggest that by understanding we know something not sensibly presented. As light makes visible but does not add new features to what is presented, understanding makes intelligible the sensible features. It is preceded by wonder, which he distinguishes from the more aesthetic curiosity. Both are conspicuous in children, with their 'Let-me-see-it' and passion to know 'why' and 'what for' and 'how it works.' Curiosity desires the aesthetic pleasure 'attributed by Keats to Cortez when he describes him as gazing fixedly, eagle-eyed, at the Pacific.'[18] The joy and pleasure of the light of understanding are found in students who have discovered connections in the drama of history, glimpsed the mysteries of mathematics, made sense of a bleak and insignificant plurality in philosophy, or who are blessed with 'lights' in mental prayer.

Truth is not the conformity of perception to things but of the way of understanding. Against Kant, Lonergan holds that a contingent being must have a cause, otherwise its existence could not be understood: 'We must be able to understand, else reality is not *per se* intelligible.'[19] He is critical of Kant's position that understanding is concerned with the dull business of life rather than with theory. Hegel's positing of an identity of *intelligence and reality*, the title of a course he would later give, contained the germ of a solution. He adds that this identity, central to Plato, need not be verified in the actual world: 'Strip the imagery off Plato's myth of anamnesis and we are left with an assertion of the ultimate identify of intelligence and reality.'[20] In the later *Verbum* articles he would consider Plato's position a misguided intellectualism.

Knowledge, Lonergan suggests, consists in a conjunction of presentation and understanding into one whole:

> The law of the object is distinct from the fact that the object exists. This distinctness is due to the nature of our knowledge. For the fact of existence is known by the apprehension; the law of the object is known by understanding. Knowledge consists of a conjunction of presentation and understanding into one whole: the pure presentation of experience and the pure intellection (abstract idea) are the *entio quibus* of knowledge (human). This distinction the scholastic theory objectifies by a real distinction between essence and existence; it puts the composition, not in the mind, but, in some very obscure way, in the object. Whether the critical metaphysician will assert such a real distinction or not, I shall discuss presently. But if he does, it will not be due to the distinction in the mind but only on the analogy of this distinction and as a theory to explain definite facts.[21]

The contrast with his later position in *Insight* on the relation between facts and judgment is startling. In 1935 his position on the real distinction between essence and existence will change significantly.

There are also explorations of the relation between the image, understanding, and idea involved in arriving at knowledge of the unseen.[22] Illustrations include diagrams in geometry, experiments in physics, images in oratory, parable, analogy, the use of the imagination in the spiritual exercises of Ignatius – which is considered a thorough-going use of the principle – and the incarnation as phantasm. Comments follow on the idea of space and time in critical theory.

Critical metaphysics is a science of sciences grounded in induction. In developing its theory of reality it will draw on all human understanding through science of the objective world. Each science discovers its particular empirical laws or relationships, Tycho Brahe, Kepler, and Newton being mentioned. There follows the visionary punchline: 'Critical metaphysics takes the explanations arrived at in every field of science – physics, chemistry, biology, psychology, history, ethics, etc. – and frames a unified view of reality in its totality.'[23] The approach is in contrast with the straitjacket of Kant's categories, in which, Lonergan comments, no one believes.

The world religions and philosophies bear witness to different human types. The mystic Socrates and the spectacular Plato glimpsed a vision of religion that foreshadows the new man, the *aner pneumatikos*. This is the one who is to assimilate 'the man born not of the blood (the human animal), nor of the will of the flesh (*aner sarkhikos*) nor of the will of men (*aner psychikos*), but of God.'[24] Within the context of Stoic humanism Lonergan explores different human shapes: the lower unstable and incomplete *aner psykhikos* and the higher *aner pneumatikos*, which influences the lower. The inadequacy of humanism (stoicism and Buddhism being mentioned) results in cold relationships and an indifference to humanity, even indolence. The life of the spirit is above the life of the human soul as intellect and influences the *aner psyhikos*. Within this fragmentary framework Lonergan brings things into focus with the remark, 'Such then is the "Whole I planned," the general scheme of human life into which the acts of assent and certitude must be fitted and of which they form parts.'

Drawing their inspiration from Newman, the fragments now explore assent and consent, which differ not in themselves but in their objects. A hypothesis is not a mere guess but a possible or even a plausible explanation, 'It is an act of understanding, an idea that has to be evident in the object. Thus there is an intelligible relation between the hypothesis and the facts; ... Certitude is therefore an assent to an idea, to a theory, as the sole possible explanation of the facts.'[25] The doctrine of assent goes to the heart of the Christian drama, that the truth will set you free.

Although irritatingly fragmentary, the Keeler essay on Newman is a major text in the realm of Lonergan studies. Unlike many other texts, it shows him in process, struggling towards a destination in his problem solving that is not yet in sight. Noteworthy is the suggestion that facts are directly experienced. It is difficult not to conclude from his analysis of the scholastic and the critical that at the time he was flirting with idealism. Still, his engagement with the question of intelligence and reality shows him trying to find a way out of it. In this sense, the text gives meaning to his later remark that idealism was the halfway house between materialism and critical realism. It also provides evidence that that remark was autobiographical.

That Lonergan was also actively pursuing his dream of a critical metaphysics will be made clear in the course of a letter he will write shortly, in

January 1935, to his provincial. In it he stated that he had a draft of an essay on the metaphysics of history, a topic that Joseph Komonchak has established was at the time being explored by Peter Wust and others.[26] In his letter Lonergan remarks that his projected essay

> will throw Hegel and Marx, despite the enormity of their influence on this very account, into the shade. ... It takes the 'objective and inevitable laws' of economics, of psychology (environment, tradition) and of progress (material, intellectual; automatic up to a point, then either deliberate and planned or the end of a civilisation) to find the higher synthesis of these laws in the mystical Body.

Clearly economics was for him a significant component in such a metaphysics of history. Some insights into that work can be gleaned from the surviving chapter of his 'Essay in Fundamental Sociology' entitled 'Philosophy of History.'[27] This can be dated as prior to the January 1935 letter but after his first-year course by Lieber on church history, close to the time when Heidegger was transferring his allegiance from Hitler to Hölderlin and reshaping his metaphysics of history, politics, and the nation.[28]

The essay is prefaced by a hand-written quotation in Greek of the passage from the *Republic* on the need for philosophers to rule. The surviving text takes as its theme the question of the human control of history. The successful emergence of liberalism since the Middle Ages poses again not only the question of who controls the power in history, but also whether that assumption of power is for progress or extinction. The text goes on to discuss philosophical foundations with reference to persons, social acts, and the notion of progress. It then explores the phases of history from the viewpoint of a philosophy of society and history whose goal is to master the process. It concludes with the problems of dialectic, of meaning, and of God's presence in history.

At the time a philosophy of history for Lonergan was to be a pure theory of what he calls external human action. In the action of the individual there are three things: a physico-sensitive flow of change, the intellectual forms with respect to the phantasmal flux, and the power of imposing intellectual forms upon the flow of change that comes from the will. The three elements, which Michael Shute has remarked do not distinguish understanding from judgment, constitute a single action. The end of the individual is to accept the intellectual forms: assent to the true and consent to the good. In this way the individual's personality is energized.[29] Human nature can be both rational and irrational, sin being the failure to obey reason. The original creative individual is an agent of social change, but the intellects of most are determined by their upbringing and experience. The nineteenth century was for Lonergan a time of good wills and bad intellects, a fatal combination.

The problem about the meaning or purpose of the flow of history leads him, with echoes of Mill and Dawson, to the question, what is progress? In order to work out a metaphysic of history, a differential calculus of progress, one must examine the differentials separating off one epoch from another. The fluctuations of history will stand to 'the differential equation of history' as the aggregate of values of a mathematical curve stand to its differential equation:

> But what is progress?
> It is a matter of intellect. Intellect is understanding of sensible data. It is the guiding form, statistically effective, of human action transforming the sensible data of life. Finally, it is a fresh intellectual synthesis understanding the new situation created by the old intellectual form and providing a statistically effective form for the next cycle of human action that will bring forth in reality the incompleteness of the later act of intellect by setting it new problems.[30]

Human understanding is for Lonergan the basic variable of history. The human intellect is intellect in potency. Its development is gradual and not the achievement of the individual, but rather of the race. It can operate in three kinds of situations. Firstly, there is the ordinary action in which an individual lives as did his or her ancestors. Secondly, there is the change that follows from the emergence of new ideas – scientific or economic – that understand the objective world, ideas vitiated by the existence of sin or elevated by the influence of divine revelation. Thirdly, there is the change that follows from the emergence of systems of ideas, philosophies, or world views.

Reflections on philosophy itself and the form of philosophical knowledge lead Lonergan to his first metaphysical category, matter.[31] Related is the cyclical and statistical role of the intellect in social processes. There is the recurring cycle of situation, new understanding generating new forms or rules, effective action resulting in a new situation and leading to further new understanding. The process unfolds in accordance with statistical laws. Consciousness for him at this point will always be consciousness of actions of something – the self – acting. That acting is contingent, contingence being the ultimate empirical in the order of consciousness as matter is in the order of sense. His final metaphysical category is truth. The project of setting up a theory of life with these categories is another day's work, but what he does assert is the possibility of philosophy as a universal science that masters the form of all science because it rests on the forms, the outer edges, the frames, of all possible human knowledge.

There follows a review of the stages through which philosophy has passed in relation to social and historical process. Firstly, there was the world before philosophy and revelation. In it there can be identified the shift from the primitive cultures of hunters and fruit gatherers through Temple states and their economy to empire with its bureaucratic rule. Each enlargement of culture requires a wider and stricter social bond and solidarity. Needless to say, the Temple states and their gods resist the expansion:

> A bureaucracy cannot integrate the individual differential forces that would make for change and advancement; it suppresses them; it rules by rule of thumb which, however excellent at the beginning of the rule becomes more and more antiquated, more and more the understanding of a situation that is anything but the existing situation. Hence, when there is no tendency to advance, a bureaucracy merely encases a mummy, ... On the other hand, given a fundamentally new idea, the bureaucracy passes away in a bath of blood.[32]

He would remain a life-long critic of bureaucracy.

Secondly, in the time of Plato philosophy emerges and asserts its social significance. The function of the state is to teach virtue, but as only philosophers know what virtue is, there arises a need for a higher-order control. Involved is the problem of the shift from symbols to concepts, which illustrates at the time the impotence of philosophy. Plato's greatness for Lonergan lies in his fidelity to the problem of social control in its most acute form. He posed a perfect question but failed to answer it.

After Plato the situation involves both progress and decline. Through the feudal period, the Renaissance, and the wars of religion there emerged the modern liberal state, which Lonergan holds to be the villain of the piece. Its modernist thrust desires to leave the whole of history without any higher control. Modern states are not conducted according to any intelligible principles – bolshevism attempting to reduce man to an animal level. Social theory cannot justify their pretended rights to making absolute decisions, as they are neither economically nor politically independent. Their actions are immoral and cannot but be immoral, as witnessed in the perversion of the newspaper and school and in armament manufacture and almost everything else. Nationalism is the setting up of a tribal god, and not merely in the case of Germany – at whom the whole world smiles mockingly for its self-idolatry – but in every case.

At the heart of the final analysis is the comparison, based on Pauline teaching, of humankind in the image of Adam and of Christ. It is from these themes, treated in Bernard Leeming's second-year course on creation and redemption, that the fundamental meaning of history is derived. For Lonergan 'the greatest evil in the world is the evil that is concretized in the historic flow, the capital of injustice that hangs like a pall over every brilliant thing.'[33] The Christian antidote to this is Christ's victory over sin and the exercise of charity. Still, the crucifixion of Christ, the scandal of the anti-popes, the Reformation and its aftermath show that a religious solution to the problem of the control of human history will not eliminate the dialectic that arises from sin. Catholics, for Lonergan, have not grasped the significance for history of intellectual development and of the need to relate their social thinking to it.

Error, Apprehension, and Judgment

Sometime after its publication in 1934 Keeler invited Lonergan to review his *The Problem of Error from Plato to Kant*, the review appearing in Latin in *Gregorianum* in 1935. Lonergan's review of Keeler's book has been extensively analysed by Liddy, on whom I am drawing,[34] and who directs our attention to the phrase 'halfway house' and to the term 'judgment.'

The problem of error forces cognitional theorists to acknowledge that there is more to cognition than an apprehension of terms or a nexus between them. Many who err claim that their opinion is supported by the evidence. Descartes developed epistemology as the scientific discipline concerned with the criteria of truth, but his reduction of judgment to will blocked a solution. For Hume to explain error the phenomena would have to contradict themselves. Kant's immutable laws of the mind also encounter problems when faced with contradictions. In the *Sophists* Plato anticipated Aristotle on terms, propositions, and error in judgment. Aristotle did not, however, see the thing through. Later debate centred on judgment as free and voluntary. In the debate that raged in the scholastic age the Thomists and Scotists were too intellectualist and the nominalists too voluntarist. Liddy translates Lonergan's account of the aftermath in Spain:

> The question formerly raised by Scotus was raised again after the re-birth of philosophical studies in Spain: whether the mental process should be divided into both apprehension and judgment. To which question Suarez, among others, responded to the effect that judgment is the apprehension of the nexus; but this happens in such a way that in a false judgment a nexus that does not exist is apprehended – something that not even the will can command.[35]

That judgment consists in the apprehension of a nexus cannot, for Keeler, be carried over to false judgment. When we err, we certainly do not perceive the nexus we affirm, that nexus being non-existent.

Keeler, according to Lonergan, approaches Aquinas in order to see what light he can shed on the problem:

He especially tries to show that for St. Thomas the apprehension of a nexus is one thing, the act of assent is another; the former dwelling in the purely intelligible world, the latter affirming the objective existence of the intellectual content. ... when a proposition is present to the mind without full evidence, the way is open for the undue influence of the will.[36]

Liddy notes Keeler's reading of the discursive activity of the mind in Plato's *Theatetus*, which leads to the conclusion that judgment, affirming or denying, concludes such interior discourse. For Liddy it is clear that at this point knowledge of existence, for Lonergan, cannot be achieved by simple apprehension or intuition. Breaking with such intuitionism will be a painful and difficult option.

A further providential accident in Lonergan's years in Rome was the manner in which a Greek student with whom he revised for his examinations, Stephanos Stephanou, introduced Lonergan, around the time he was in dialogue with Keeler, to the thought of Maréchal. Their informal conversations on the matter saved him from the labour of pouring over endless volumes.[37] Maréchal held that the questions about mind that had surfaced in the *Critique of Pure Reason* could only find their proper answers with the help of Aquinas. In opposition to the static mind described by Kant in the *Critique of Pure Reason*, Maréchal put at the heart of the human mind its dynamic and discursive nature. Through its dynamism the mind culminated in objective judgments of existence. In this manner Aquinas held a key to Kant's immanentism. These notions, communicated informally in conversation rather than through a scholarly reading of the text, convinced Lonergan that Aquinas had something to offer on the problem. Later Lonergan remarked that the unusual emphasis placed on judgment in cognition was unique to the then Catholic tradition in philosophy. For many, however, it involved an intuition of being, to which he was totally opposed.[38]

The 1935 Letter to His Provincial

Around this time, on 22 January 1935, Lonergan wrote a significant personal letter to his provincial, Henry Keane. It was a letter he had great difficulty writing, discarding a number of versions and completing the final version as a last measure. Given his reluctance to open up about his innner life, he clearly found it hard to write what amounts to a confessional statement of where he stood on his life's work at that time. There was also the difficulty of articulating what was going on inside him, because as of yet in a sense he did not know. Before a creative work has actually been performed it is vulnerable and insecure. It is all in the bud, and we don't in the bud know the kind of flower we are going to get. Before he left Montreal for Rome, Lonergan did not have a sense of direction. This being the case, the letter illuminates for us something of the ferment that was going on in his inner life during his first two years in Rome. The very fact that he was there and destined for further studies was allowing him to dream.

The core of the letter centres on some problems that his projected future as a teacher of philosophy has aroused in him. In response, he firstly traces the elements of his own personal intellectual history. Starting with his philosophical formation at Heythrop, the letter recalls his nominalism, the influence of Newman, the Cartesian *cogito*, agent intellect, his later reading of Stewart, Christopher Dawson, Augustine, and Maréchal, and 'seeing the nexus.' It was his earliest communication of the nature of the sources and circumstances that inspired his intellectual development to this point.

Secondly, the manner in which he finds himself so out of sympathy with the consistent misinterpretations, even the traditions of misinterpretation, that pass for commentary on Aquinas amounts to something like a crisis of conscience for him. The issue had already been raised by Maréchal, whose views find favour in Louvain but not in Rome:

> in a word it is that, what the current Thomists call intellectual knowl-edge is really sense knowledge: of intellectual knowledge they have nothing to say: intellectual knowledge is for example, the 'seeing the nexus' between subject and predicate in an universal judgment: this seeing the nexus is an operation they never explain.[39]

Clearly he feels the need to be open with his superior about this conflict of interpretations. He further develops his arguments for his position by discussing the relations between Augustine and Aquinas on intellect and faith.

After Aquinas there came Scotus, the nominalists, and the conceptual-ists: 'then Suarez and the Spaniards with their naive realism (substance is "something there").' There follow remarks on the brilliance of Descartes, the antithesis of Spinoza and Hume, Kant, knowledge of the singular and the thing in itself. They sum up in a few sentences much of the history of Lonergan's struggle with the problem of cognition. Through his recent reading of Aquinas he was beginning to find a way out. He comments about going into his own experience on intellect and will to identify what Aquinas had meant. The letter makes clear that Lonergan was now starting to read and explore Aquinas, but his own interpretation was incomplete and, on the problem of the nexus, not beyond criticism. Later he would refer to it as Scotist terminology.

Thirdly, he outlined his dream, already mentioned, of developing a metaphysics of history as an exercise in the application of his ideas. This will draw on all the stages of his education in history, Loyola, London, Dawson, and the courses on church history in the Gregorian. The synthesizing viewpoint will be the theology of the mystical body of Christ and the role of understanding in social and historical processes. It seems clear that in January 1935 this was Lonergan's focal interest. Significantly, the question of method in theology is not yet on his agenda.

The letter ended by posing to his superior a question about the unfolding of his life's work: ought it be left simply to providence, or ought the involvement of his superiors, as agents of providence, be recognized? It was a problem that occupied him throughout the 1930s and on which he would seek advice in 1938, the time when, as we shall see, decisions were to be made about his future work. Its significance ought not to be underestimated. The thirty-one-year old Lonergan had a dream, and in its pursuit felt deeply the dialectic of hope and anxiety.[40] It was an unfolding life dream that involved elements of ambiguity, uncertainty, and daring. To the extent that such dreams are daring, for fear of misunderstanding and ridicule we are reluctant to reveal them even to those to whom we are close. In this sense, the letter is a wonderful clarification of the projected content and personal experience of his quest at this difficult and vulnerable time. The conditions of its success at the time lay largely in the hands of others.

Despite his protests in his letter to Keane that he had to learn 'tons of stuff' off by heart for his exams, by June 1935 he had completed a further essay running to 25 pages of typescript on the theory (metaphysics) of human solidarity. Subtitled 'A Theology for the Social Order,' it addressed the drawing of all things up into a new head, a *pantôn anakephalaiôsis*.[41] The encyclical *Aeterni Patris* affirmed the need for a social philosophy of fallen man with his tendency to sensism and nominalism. In line with this, Pius XI commanded that all candidates for the priesthood be adequately prepared by the intense study of social matters, a command not yet put into effect.[42] The church needed to develop a *Summa Sociologica* in order to challenge the Marxist materialist conception of history and its realization in Bolshevism. (National Socialism is here conspicuous by its absence.) At the heart of such a view will be the understanding of the contrasting place and role of Christ and Adam in the social and historical process. Adam set up a reign of disharmony and maladjustment of the corporate unity of man. Christ set up a new motion to harmonize, readjust, and reintegrate a humanity that had reached the peak of disintegration and death described in the first chapter of the Romans. This process Lonergan calls *anakephalaiôsis*.

The social and historical presence of Christ in the world is in the Christian community, his mystical body. That dogma needs to be developed so as to include 'a conscious body of social science illuminated by supernatural light.' Until such a *Summa Sociologica* is in place, we will continue to flounder about in the blundering and false science that has created the current problems in the world.

The analysis ranges over six elements. Firstly, there is freedom of the human will, which is a natural appetite following intellectual forms.

Secondly, there is the historical determination of the human intellect and, through it, of the forms presented to the will. A change in the flow of operations follows from the emergence of one new idea. The form of a flow of changes follows from a flow of new ideas. Truth unifies, but there is also a dialectic of fact, sin, and thought.

Thirdly, there results the unity of all human operation because all can participate in the discoveries of the past.

Fourthly, there is the synthesis of all historical human operations in God who is the principle cause of all operation.

Fifthly, there is the unity of humankind and of human operations. Why, Lonergan asks, are there economic forces making it impossible for industrialists to pay workers a family wage and political forces holding the world in the unstable equilibrium of a balance of power secured by realpolitik? In this he is clearly acknowledging both an economic and a political dimension to the problem of progress and decline in history.

The intellect and will are, for him, the defining human features. An infant is actually an individual but only potentially a personality. Actual personality is the ultimate difference of intellectual pattern and habit of will called character that results from the operation of the intellect and will in a material individual. Moral personality emerges from the flux of birth and change and death. It involves the relational orientation of all human beings toward each other. The sensate are orientated towards sensible satisfaction; the *psychikos* are orientated towards the true, the good, and the beautiful; and the *pneumatikos* are orientated towards God in his transcendence of the transcendentals and as he is known only by faith through revelation.

Sixthly, there is the Pauline conception of the role of Christ in creation as the *pantôn anakephalaiôsis*, the one who draws all things together in a new head. Dogma should unite humanity, but the dogma of communism unites by terrorism to destroy. The dogma of race unites to protect but is not a big enough idea to act as a principle of human unity. Out of the bankruptcy of philosophy there came the supernatural revelation in Christ, which involved not merely a content but also a living and developing mind, the mind of the mystical body (1 Cor. 2:16). There results in the community the development of an absolute *Geist* from the primitive tradition of dogma that must eventually come to include consciously a body of social science illuminated by the light of faith. There follows some rich reflections on the role of Christ in human history.

The essay was completed just a month after Husserl's Vienna lecture on 7 May entitled 'Philosophy in the Crisis of European Mankind.'[43] In response to the crisis Husserl proposed to explore the notion of European humanity, which, he maintained, was characterized by a unity of spiritual life. Along these lines he worked out a '*concept of Europe as the historical teleology of the infinite goals of reason.*'[44] This left him with the task of explaining the success of reason in the realm of the natural sciences and its failure in the realm of spirit and culture. That failure was, for him, a result of reason being rendered superficial by its entanglement with naturalism. As a result, it became incapable of grasping the true spiritual problems of the time. Husserl was groping towards an understanding of the pathologies of reason, of the illnesses of the political and cultural mind, but without the redemptive categories of Lonergan. Astonishing in his lecture, perhaps for political reasons, is the absence of any reference to the Jewish situation. Husserl's lecture is an expression of a profound malaise among the educated, who in an hour of extreme need had nothing to say to the European crisis.

This was also the time when Heidegger was giving his summer semester lecture entitled 'An Introduction to Metaphysics' in Freiburg.[45] In it he maintained that the questions of metaphysics are 'historical questions through and through.' The task of philosophy is, for him, to pursue that knowledge by means of which a people fulfils itself historically and culturally. He maintained that from a metaphysical viewpoint Russia and America are the 'the same dreary technological frenzy, the same unrestricted organisation of the average man.' Caught in a pincers and endangered because of the number of its neighbours, Germany is the most metaphysical of nations. Ironic, in the light of later developments, was his assertion that it was the vocation and destiny of the German Nation to regenerate Europe, to become the centre from which new spiritual energies would unfold. There was for Heidegger an inner truth and greatness in National Socialism, especially in its encounter between modern humanity and global technology.

The Realism of the Incarnation: His Intellectual Conversion

In the autumn semester of 1935 Lonergan took a course on the Incarnate Word by Bernard Leeming, a course he himself would teach in Toronto and Rome. Topics addressed included Christ's knowledge and consciousness, about which he would later write. The central question concerned the mode of union of the eternal word of God with a temporal human nature, Jesus of Nazareth. The Christian tradition of the patristic era teaches that Christ is a divine person in whom, through the incarnation, there are hypostatically united divine and human natures. By a person, divine or human, is not meant a personality but an ontologically distinct, non-fictional, existing, indivisible unity. This means that in Christ, considered as a divine person, there can be a human nature but not an ontologically distinct human person. The human nature cannot enjoy an existence separate from the divine person. The Christian doctrine that Jesus of Nazareth who was born in Bethlehem is not an ontologically distinct, existing, indivisible human person is a position that, like the reality of the air, brings us up short in our tracks. It challenges us to clarify what kind of a reality we are talking about when we talk about Christ.[46]

Clearly the doctrine implies a realism, a stance on the ontological reality of the being of persons and their natures:

> Can you have one person who has two natures? The argument given me by a good Thomist, Father Bernard Leeming, was that if you have a real distinction between *esse* (existence) and essence, the *esse* can be the ground of the person and of the essence too. If the *esse* is relevant to two essences, then you can have one person in two natures. On that basis I solved the problem of Christ's consciousness: one subject and two subjectivities. It wasn't the divine subjectivity that was crucified but the human subjectivity; it was the human subjectivity that died and rose again, not the divine person.[47]

Much of the difficulty centres on the meaning of the phrase 'real distinction,' which can be major between things and minor within things. Is Peter really distinct from his arm, his sight, his mind, his existence, from Paul? What does it mean to say that the nature of sight or of hearing or of questioning is different from the existential act or operation or exercise of sight or hearing or questioning? What is the difference between the nature of sight or questioning and the nature of a human person? As Aristotle put it, Why are these flesh and blood a human being? Would the nature of a human person somehow within its *unity* encompass the nature of sight and of hearing and questioning? (If so, it seems close to the central form of *Insight.*) What does it mean to say that human nature is distinct from human existence? What is the difference between the nature and the (act of) existence of a human person? What does it mean to say that they are really distinct? If they are really distinct, how does this allow a human nature in Christ but not a human act of existence? Leeming's answer seemed to be that the *unicum esse*, the single act of existence, indivisibly united the two natures.

The above questions address distinctions between natures and existence in the object of our knowledge. What happened late in 1935 for the thirty-one-year old Lonergan was that he realized some of these questions were related to parallel distinctions in our cognitional powers or operations. In a letter to Bernard Tyrrell in October 1967, he remembered picking up the notion of the constitutive role of judgment in human knowledge from Stefanu at the time when Leeming was teaching about the *unicum esse*, the single existence of being in Christ. By a providential accident during the academic year in which he took Leeming's course he was also revising for his final examination with Stefanu. In '*Insight* Revisited' he described what happened:

> It was through Stefanu ... that I learnt to speak of human knowledge as not intuitive but discursive with the decisive component in judgment. This view was confirmed by my familiarity with Augustine's key notion, *veritas*, and the whole was rounded out by Bernard Leeming's course on the Incarnate Word, which convinced me that there could not be a hypostatic union without a real distinction between essence and existence. This, of course was all the more acceptable, since Aquinas' *esse* corresponded to Augustine's *veritas* and both harmonised with Maréchal's view of judgment.[48]

Through Stefanu and Maréchal Lonergan was beginning to make the break with knowledge as intuitive that was a strong element in the tradition that formed him. Involved in the break was a grasp that being, existence, is known not by intuition but by judgment at the term of the discursive process of knowing. This was in line with Augustine's Cassiciacum experience, after his religious conversion, of his passion for the truth and of truth as a matter of affirming the real. One of the pillars of Lonergan's later philosophy was now falling into place. In this, judgment makes known existence rather than the 'is' of predication, which is a relation or nexus that can be thought.

Lonergan later described this development in him as an intellectual conversion:

> I had the intellectual conversion myself when in doing theology I saw that you can't have one person in two natures in Christ unless there is a real distinction between the nature and something else that is one. But that is the long way around.[49]

A significant passage in *Caring about Meaning* illuminates, to some extent, what was involved. The way to answer Aristotle's *what is it?* question is to change the 'what' to a 'why,' change 'what is a human being?' to 'Why are these flesh and bones a human being?' The answer to the latter is: because of the form or soul and the common matter. Lonergan continues: 'This is Aristotelian essentialism. But Augustine spoke of *veritas* and corresponding to *veritas*, Thomas added *esse*.'[50] What this is making clear is that judgment does not answer the What? or Why? question about the nature or essence of man. Through judgment we come to know, not the common matter or the essence or nature, but the existence of such natures. That Newman's notion of the illative sense and of assent did not feature in Lonergan's account is puzzling. What the breakthrough would make possible for him in time was the task of explaining the relation between assent or judgment and cognitional facts.

Giovanni Sala's description of a parallel personal experience helps us to make sense of what Lonergan means by an intellectual conversion and the shift from one philosophical paradigm to another that is involved in it.[51] In the early 1960s Sala studied with Lonergan at the Gregorian. Given his Kantian background, he was amazed and confused when Lonergan spoke repeatedly about the force of existential judgment by which the existent is known. Sala's principle of realism based on Kantian intuition was called into question. After a long personal journey through *Insight, Verbum,* and Lonergan's seminar on method in theology in 1962, Sala slowly came to understand what was involved in Lonergan's principle of realism. About his breakthrough he has commented: 'The surprising thing about this insight, which came to me at the end of a long search in which the scales of intuitionism fell from my eyes, was that in spite of all the complex particular forms and instances of human knowledge in all its various branches, the core of the doctrine proved to have a disarming simplicity.'[52]

Through Lonergan's providential encounter with Stefanu and Leeming, something definitive for his quest clicked into place. The obscure distinctions raised by the Christological doctrines forced Lonergan to come to terms with the manner in which through judgment, rather than through sensing or understanding, we come to know what exists, existence, what there is, being. In this difficult territory, for the first time Lonergan got to some extent clear in his mind that what exists, being, becomes know to us not through an intuition but through the process of judgment.

Occurring in the middle of his theology studies, this was an experience whose implications for his life and work would have to remain on hold for the moment. After Leeming, Lennertz taught him a course on grace and the theological virtues of faith, hope, and charity that Lonergan would later teach in Montreal and Toronto. At the end of his third year of studies he was ordained to the priesthood, in Rome on 25 July 1936 in the Church of St Ignatius. Later he remarked that he added the final chapter of *Insight* to explain what his thought might have to do with the meaning of the priesthood.[53]

In his fourth year of theology studies, Boyer, who was soon to play an important role in Lonergan's life, taught him a course on Augustine. In March of that year Pius XI published two encyclicals, *Mit Brennender Sorge* (With Burning Dismay) and *Divini Redemptoris*, the former condemning Nazi neo-paganism.[54] The latter, in whose drafting Gustave Desbuquois was highly influential, contained a condemnation of aetheistic communism. Desbuquois will cross Lonergan's path the following Easter. It was in this tragic world that Lonergan took his final theology examination in dogma on 28 June 1937. At the age of thirty-two he was no doubt pleased at last to be finished with undergraduate study.

6

Postgraduate Studies in Theology: A New Road Taken

In the summer of 1937 Lonergan took a holiday, visiting the Pitti Palace in Florence, where he enjoyed the Raphaels. At the beginning of September he went to the Abbaye St-Acheul in Amiens for his final year of prayer and formation as a Jesuit, his Tertianship. The town, through which the Somme flows and which boasts a magnificent gothic cathedral dating back to 1220, is seventy-five minutes north of Paris by rail. Within the cathedral walls are plaques from Australia, Canada, England, Ireland, New Zealand, and South Africa commemorating the dead of the Battle of the Somme. The French in the locality had been expecting a war since 1932. With the question of Czechoslovakia on the agenda, in 1937 war must have seemed near. The Tertian instructor, Pere Leontius Aurel, gave the Tertians information about the political developments during his conferences. In May 1940 the town would be invaded, the cathedral alone escaping the bombs.

The group of twenty-three Tertians included the later well-known Tertian director Paul Kennedy. A casual reading of the small custom book for the Tertianship evokes in the modern reader a deep sense of austerity. In the group photograph Aurel emanates a certain sadness, but Kennedy found him admirable.

As in the noviciate, the thirty-day retreat was the major event. It began two weeks after arrival and involved three and sometimes four conferences each day. Lonergan must have been impressed by the experience because his notebook survives. Central was the fundamental reality of God's invitation to both the religious life and the priesthood, and our response in faith. In the Old Testament, humility, submission, and obedience were central; in the New Testament, love not of the law but of the invitation 'follow me' is central. As well as invitation there is also the element of mission. No doubt all of this provoked in Lonergan the question, what will my mission in the church be, what will I be invited to do? At this point it was for him a matter of faith.

The final exercise was concerned with finding the love of God in all things. Love consists in deeds rather than in words, in mutual communication of good. God's love is his desire to find himself in us. He inhabits, transforms, and finds in us the image of himself. God's love expresses itself in history.[1]

In the two thirty-day retreats Lonergan did, here and in the noviciate, the retreat conferences were largely preached or lectured. At the time there was not spiritual direction in the modern sense as outlined by Barry and Connelly and others.[2] Such spiritual direction does not set out to lecture or tell the retreatant what to do, but strives to enable them to listen to and discern the subtle prompting of God's movements in their own hearts. In this sense, to a certain extent Lonergan's spirituality was formed by a tradition of misinterpretation. In its own way, it was at the time just as much out of contact with its sources and their inspiration as was the case in cognitional theory and the theology of the Trinity.

As well as the exercises, he studied the constitutions of the Society of Jesus and worked for a week in a local hospital. Starting on Sunday, 28 November, Aurel held a series of ten weekly conferences.[3] His second lecture contains an interesting passage on the psychology and conscious-ness of Christ. The fourth lecture deals with the grace of sanctification and merit. The seventh was largely concerned with our cooperation with God's grace, instrumentality, and the divine movement within the soul. These would be major categories in Lonergan's doctoral thesis. Charity or love excludes egoism, *l'orgeuil*, and *envie*. The tension between love and egoism will recur in his writings on the analytic concept of history and in 'Finality, Love and Marriage.'[4]

The group also had a certain amount of external input, including a visit from de Lubac. After Easter 1938 Lonergan was sent for a week to the École Sociale Populaire in Paris to listen to four leaders each day speaking about specialized movements in Catholic action. It was here that he met Gustave Desbuquois, whom he considered to be a charming man. Desbuquois had been captured in the war, was an expert on poverty, spoke four languages, and his personal initiatives had resulted in remarkable achievements.

> He was a man I felt I must consult, for I had little hope of explain-
> ing to my superiors what I wished to do and of persuading them to
> allow me to do it. So I obtained an appointment, and when the time
> came, I asked him how one reconciled obedience with initiative in
> the Society. He looked me over and said: 'Go ahead and do it. If
> superiors do not stop you, that is obedience. If they do stop you,

stop and that is obedience.' The advice is hardly very exciting today but at the time it was for me a great relief.[5]

Here we find him again asking for advice on the same personal problem that he had expressed in his concluding remarks to his provincial, Henry Keane, in his letter of January 1935. The problem of the providential role of his superiors in the unfolding of his academic vocation was now acute for Lonergan. It was clear to him that major decisions about the future of his life and work were about be made, and this was disturbing him.

His colleagues on the Tertianship compiled a character profile of him, which he kept. They considered him obviously an academic although probably more suited for writing than teaching. Kennedy remembered walking on the banks of the Somme with him as he tried to explain the three degrees of humility in terms of symbolic logic. He felt that Lonergan was extremely perceptive and intelligent but at the time liked to let everyone know it. He was to an extent shy, at times not an easy person to talk to, and could have a rough sense of humour. He could say something hurtful without being sensitive to it and did not suffer fools gladly. Kennedy sensed that Lonergan himself felt he could be rough or lack sensitivity in his dealings with people. He did not trust himself and could react very strongly when questioned or attacked about something.

Analytic Concept of History

In his essay '*Insight* Revisited,' Lonergan refers to work he did during his Tertianship year on the philosophy of history. The extant texts from the time comprise three files of typewritten notes of seventeen, eighteen, and nineteen pages, each with slightly different titles. The contents are summed up under eight brief headings, which in the three documents show slight variations:[6]

1. Analytic Concept
2. History
3. Human Solidarity
4. The Three Categories
5. The Ideal Line
6. Decline
7. Renaissance
8. The Multiple Dialectic

By an 'analytic concept' Lonergan means analyzing history, not into genus and difference as in botany, but into its constitutive elements. Through apprehensive concepts, which correspond to his later nominal definition, we know what an object – a chemical, flower, circle, or the movement of a planet – is like. But we do not know the explanation or the why of it, why it is what it is rather than something else. Synthetic acts of understanding are concerned with a synthesis of a concrete multiplicity that would be somewhat narrative in form, Christopher Dawson's historical essays being given as an illustration.

Analytic concepts are concerned with the why, the manner in which the compound is made up of elements, the movement of forces and accelerations, the circle of spatial relations. An analytic concept of history will prescind from accidental causes such as plagues and race. It will attend to the why, the essential cause or explanation of history, what makes it what it is rather than something else, the action of human wills in the framework of solidarity.

Lonergan begins with an analogy from Newtonian mechanics that conceives planetary motion as the resultant of a uniform velocity, an acceleration towards the sun, and minor accelerations towards the other planets. Newton's law that bodies move in a straight line with constant velocity holds unless some force intervenes. The question arises: what if anything stands to the multiplicity of historical data as Newton's laws stand to the data of movement? By analogy, Lonergan's first approximation in his theology of history was the assumption that human beings always do what is intelligent and reasonable. This would result in progress. Add to this the inverse insight that persons can be biased and therefore unintelligent and unreasonable in their choices and you get a brake on progress. Finally, the resulting social surd needs to be redeemed by God's gift of his grace.

Human action divides into three categories of acts according to nature, acts contrary to nature, and acts above nature. As intelligence is central to humanity's nature, the three metaphysically ultimate categories that will figure in the dialectic can be described as human actions intelligible to humankind, as unintelligible, and as too intelligible.[7] The categories relate to the New Testament on light and darkness and to Lonergan's surd sermon on the flight from insight. Light is too intelligible; darkness is unintelligible. The course of history can be analysed as the resultant of an ideal line of progress from acts according to nature, of decline from acts contrary to nature, and of renaissance from the exercise of the supernatural virtues. Acts of will and freedom are then central. He concludes that the whole can be viewed as a multiple dialectic, a difficult term to explain. By an analysis of the dialectic, Lonergan hopes to arrive at an analytic concept of history.

Under the heading of solidarity we find an emphasis on the pronoun 'we,' in contrast with later existentialist emphasis on 'I.' Economic development liberates humanity from physical needs only to impose upon it social dependence. In proportion as economic development proceeds, the social unity is of necessity enlarged. As the power of intellect becomes greater, its higher specialization requires a broader basis.[8] At all times in every social community there is a body of thought (in his earlier writings, *Geist*) that is socially dominant and effective. Though it may change over time, at each moment it is the rule, dominant. Other thought is the exception. This dominant thought is subject to a dialectical process:

> Taking the matter more largely, we observe that the dominant thought at any time arose from the situation that preceded it; that its tendency is to transform the situation; that the transformed situation will give rise to new thought, and this not merely to suggest it but to impose it.
>
> By the dialectic, then, we mean the succession (within a social channel of mutual influence) of situation, thought, action, new situation, new thought, and so forth.[9]

The dialectic is really an inverted experiment in which reality continuously strives to mould the outlook of humankind into conformity with itself by revealing the evil arising from human errors. Because of the transference of ideas across frontiers and of reaction to them, we find in culture a multiple dialectic.

The ideal line of history would result if humankind lived perfectly according to its nature. Since the instrument of progress is the intellect, it follows that the form of progress is a projection in history of the form of intellectual development. Such development is involved in a cycle of fact, antithesis, and higher synthesis. In the discussion Lonergan refers to Belloc on science as the enemy of truth, to Newman on real apprehension, and uses the term, 'apperceptive unity' in a manner reminiscent of Kant.[10] Because of the spontaneous and reflexive character of intellect, there will be spontaneous and 'reflex' history.

Decline is a deviation from the ideal. It can be minor, major, or compound. Social tension arises because it is not clear that new economic or political ideas are better than the old, again linking economics with the dialectic of history. But what really brings about decline is sin, the irrational. In this section we find some of Lonergan's earliest thought on the surd and individual and group bias. Self-interest is not enlightened because it is not objective. It centres the world in the ego of the individual or class, and neither is the centre:

> Second, by reason of their advantages, the favoured are able to solve the antitheses that stand against their own progressive well-being. By

reason of their ego-centricity, they barely think of solving any others. The bourgeois is full of the milk of human kindness: but this bias in outlook makes him pronounce non-existent or insoluble the antitheses that do not directly affect him.[11]

There results a distinction between the privileged and the depressed, who are degraded by a set of palliatives to ease the bourgeois conscience. The result is an objective disorder that contains the irrational. It cannot be understood in the same manner as intelligible progress from one situation to another: 'Objective disorder sets problems that have no solution in the intellectual field. Acknowledge the "fait accompli" and you perpetuate injustice; refuse to acknowledge it and you are but fashioning an imaginary world in which you cannot live.'[12]

There follows an accumulation of surds in the social situation and structure that handicaps the progress of the people. Conscience is deformed. Social evils pass from being exceptions to being rules, until the critical stage is reached and decline itself becomes a principle with the assertion that morality can be revised. There results, in stark contrast with development, a succession of social syntheses that are actually decreasing in intelligible content. Each of the stages in the succession of lower syntheses calls forth a human mysticism,

> the organised lie of a society defending what it was and, for the moment, preventing it from being worse than it will be. Thus we have the mysticisms of Protestantism and the nation, the mysticism of rationalism and free-masonry, the mysticism of naturalism and progress, the mysticism of the revolution in Russia, the race in Germany, traditional glory in Italy...
>
> Protestantism based itself on the mysticism of righteousness; Nationalism Socialism on the mysticism of race; Communism on the mysticism of revolution; as each of these falls short of a whole view of human nature, in that measure it is a lie and its mysticism drug-like in its effects.[13]

Elsewhere in the notes Lonergan quotes Christopher Hollis to the effect that 'when in travelling across the world you meet a new lie, you know you are in contact with another culture.'[14]

Decline sets a problem that has no internal human solution. Revolutionaries transform tensions into rage and tear down what was better and replace it with what is worse. The solution will be a renaissance that must come from without, from a higher order, the genesis of Lonergan's later thought that religion is basically a good of order. His concern is to specify some of the characteristics of that higher order.

The new order, though it will be transcendent, will be knowable and will work with human nature as it is. It will be individualist, rational, obligatory, mystical, social, and authoritarian. It will be a higher synthesis of progress and decline, overcoming major decline by penance, charity, and faith. It will set up model societies in which the individual wills only to obey, a position that clearly needs to be carefully interpreted. Minor decline would be overcome by the spirit of poverty, chastity, and obedience. The new order will arrest decline and establish ordered freedom. There follows an analysis of the role of the church as the mystical body.

It is Lonergan's view that major decline is excluded from the church by providential guidance. There is a deposit of faith that is called the development of dogma. There is the development of Christian spirituality, of works of charity, and of Catholic action. Here the text stops abruptly, and with it his writings on the philosophy of history for the foreseeable future. Chapters 7 and 20 of *Insight* will presuppose and build on these writings.

In June 1938 Pius XI invited John Le Farge, an American Jesuit from Fordham University, to prepare a preliminary draft for an encyclical condemning anti-Semitism and racism. Overwhelmed, Le Farge looked for assistance. Ledochowski, the general, assigned the Jesuits Gustav Gundlach, Heinrich Bacht, and Gustave Desbuquois to assist him. By the end of the summer the four had produced a draft entitled 'The Unity of the Human Race,' written in French, English and German.[15]

Assigned to Teach Theology in the Gregorian

In June 1938 the consultors of the Canadian Province, this time without MacMahon, advised the provincial, Henry Keane, that Lonergan was a suitable candidate for further studies in Rome. The consultors also agreed that when Lonergan had completed his studies he could teach there for a while, adding that the Canadian Province should pay for his studies in case he was recalled to Canada at a later date. Around this time the Jesuit general was holding a special congregation in Rome. He invited the assembled provincials to donate men to the Gregorian University. Keane donated Lonergan: 'I was informed of this at the end of the Tertianship and told to do a biennium in philosophy.'[16]

On 20 July Vincent McCormick, the rector of the Gregorian, wrote to Keane thanking him for the Canadian Province's donation of Lonergan to the work of the Gregorian. The letter continued:

> Fr. Lonergan has left a splendid record behind him here; and we shall be happy to see him back for further studies. I would suggest – supposing his own preferences are not too strong for one field

rather than the other – that he devote himself to Theology. In that Faculty there are hundreds of English-speaking students, who will be needing his help in the future. At present there is only one English-speaking professor in the Faculty.

The provincial would clearly fall in with his request.

After his Tertianship Lonergan moved to Milltown Park, Dublin, to prepare his notes for his first retreat, which he would give at the Loretto Convent in Wexford. On 10 August he wrote a letter to his provincial that reveals how much he was still engrossed in his reflections on history:

> As philosophy of history is as yet not recognized as the essential branch of philosophy that it is, I hardly expect to have it assigned me as my subject during the biennium. I wish to ask your approval for maintaining my interest in it, profiting by such opportunities as may crop up, and in general devoting to it such time as I prudently judge can be spared.

Clearly, the work he had done in Amiens in his spare time was still exciting him. At this time, given his head, he would have written his PhD on the philosophy of history rather than epistemology. The letter ends: 'I had a splendid letter from my mother the other day, and that pulls a cloud out of the sky.' Sadly, none of the letters between mother and son survived.

In September Lonergan himself received a letter from Fr McCormick informing him that he was to do a biennium in theology. Since January 1935 Lonergan had wondered about the providential role of his superiors in his unfolding quest. He was now getting his answer. The shift from a career in philosophy to one in theology effectively, at a moment's notice, removed him from one major road and placed him on another, a road on which the problem of method in theology lay in waiting.

Lonergan spent the last three weeks of September in Heythrop before returning to Rome just as the Munich Conference, with its promise of peace, was taking place. That prospect was devastated on 5 October when Hitler invaded Czechoslovakia. Living in the room next to Lonergan at the time was Michael Connolley, an Irish-Province Jesuit who remembered Lonergan's typewriter incessantly on the go. Shortly after the invasion, the two went for a walk up to the gardens. Lonergan was agitated by the event and remarked to Connolley that war was coming and that he wanted to get out of Europe as quickly as possible. It was Connolley's impression that Lonergan was well informed and understood the significance of what was happening. This was the time of Kristallnacht: on 9 November 1938 the murder of a third secretary in Paris, Ernst von Rath, by a teenaged Polish Jew, Hersche Grynszpan, sparked off a reaction in which 191 synagogues were set on fire, one thousand shops destroyed, and forty thousand Jews arrested in Germany and Austria and sent to camps.

Despite these distressing events, Lonergan's main task was to find a thesis director. When he was in France Boyer had been suggested to him. Boyer was intelligent and contra Suarez, had changed his view on the real distinction between essence and existence. About his thesis topic Lonergan has said:

> I had a good thesis because Charles Boyer said to me: 'There's this article in *the Summa* and I don't think the Molinists interpret it correctly; and I don't think the Banesians interpret it correctly. Find out what it means ... Study the *loco parallela* and the historical sources. See what light you can shed on the question.[17]

Just as Vincent McCormick and Henry Keane decided he should change to theology, Boyer chose his thesis topic and issued quite focused directions. None of these men could have foreseen the fateful significance of their choices for the direction of his life. The topic was approved on 6 December 1938 under the title 'A history of St. Thomas' Thought on Operative Grace.'

The question, Q111, in the I–IIae, is about the divisions of grace into sanctifying (*gratiae gratum faciens*) and actual grace (a word never used by Aquinas, who used terms such as *auxilium* or *inclinatio*), operative and cooperative, prevenient and subsequent. The second article of the question, which is the significant one, is on the division of grace into operative and cooperative:

> As was said above, grace can be understood in two senses. Firstly, as the divine assistance by which God moves us to will and do good; secondly, as the habitual gift implanted in us by God. In both these senses grace is satisfactorily divided into operative and cooperative grace.

The basic question Boyer put to Lonergan was, what is the meaning of this article? As such, the task he set was not concerned directly with theological dogmas, but with charting the history of a *speculative movement* in systematic theology. An abbreviated version of the thesis later published under the title *Grace and Freedom* outlined a question related to the development on operative grace: how does divine grace as operative and cooperative respect and preserve the freedom of the human will?

One aspect of the background to the interpretation of the article was a rancorous dispute between the theologians Bañez and Molina, and between Dominicans and Jesuits from 1582 to 1598.[18] In 1582 the Jesuit Montemayor defended the thesis that through his obedience Christ died neither freely nor meritoriously. The ensuing dispute was brought before the Inquisition, which in 1584 condemned, among others, the following propositions of Bañez:

[•] God is not the cause of the free operation but only causes the cause to be
[•] The providence of God does not determine the human will or any other particular cause to operate well, but rather the particular cause determines the act of divine providence
[•] The impious man in his justification determines the sufficient help of God to actual use by his own will.[19]

The conversion of Saul is a classic illustration of a grace, yet does it not have all the hallmarks of coercion? Many of the Old Testament prophets affirm that God chose them before they were in their mother's womb. Their lives in this sense were determined. In modern terms, small children can be educated with the help of imaginative computers. Adults with behaviour disorders approach psychoanalysts. This poses questions such as: Should the computer determine the child or the child the computer, the analysis determine the patient or the patient the analysis? Does God totally determine us, leaving us in no way free to determine ourselves?

Molina's central doctrinal assertion was that God's graces are rendered efficacious by the actual consent of the human will. God's infallible foreknowledge is safeguarded by recourse to Molina's hypothesis that there is in God a middle knowledge (*scientia media*) whereby God foreknows what every person will choose in varying circumstances before the will determines itself, and independently of any divine predetermination. It follows that God predestines those whom he foresees as consenting to his grace. Bañez took exception to this, affirming the 'traditional' teaching that grace is intrinsically efficacious in effecting the will's free consent. As a result, predestination is ultimately gratuitous rather than depending on foreseen merits. In turn, Bañez's reading of Aquinas on these topics and on premotion was criticized as his own innovation. At the heart of the controversy is the problem of reconciling two distinct Christian doctrines, of human freedom on the one hand and the infallibility of God's providence on the other.

The Methodological and Theological Content of His Thesis

In discussing the passage, Lonergan drew attention to the notorious fact that for several centuries Molinists have uniformly concluded that Aquinas was a Molinist and Bañezians that he was a Bañezian. Each started from their dogmatic presuppositions and built up their arguments accordingly. This methodological impasse Lonergan considers would not be broken 'unless a writer can assign a method that of itself tends to greater objectivity than those hitherto employed.'[20] And so the first part of his thesis is devoted to the problem of theological method. The method that Lonergan will suggest involves the use of a theory of the history of theological speculation:

> A study of St. Thomas's thought on *gratia operans* cannot but be historical ... Because the inquiry is historical, it does not open with the *a priori* scheme of current systematic theology with its point of view, its definitions, its interests, and its problems. That would be simply to ask St. Thomas a series of questions which he did not explicitly consider ... Patently such a procedure would be fallacious: 'it would be deducing an extrapolation from the thought of St. Thomas before taking the trouble to find out what St. Thomas was really thinking about.'[21]

Though historical, the inquiry will make no concessions to positivism:

> It remains that history can follow a middle course, neither projecting into the past the categories of the present, nor pretending that historical inquiry is conducted without a use of human intelligence. The middle course consists in constructing an *a priori* scheme that is capable of synthesising any possible set of historical data irrespective of their place and time, just as the science of mathematics constructs a generic scheme capable of synthesising any possible set of quantitative phenomena. In the present work this generic scheme is attained by an analysis of the idea of development in speculative theology.[22]

Understanding the development of theological ideas by means of a genetic method was central to the problem. Boyer had dealt Lonergan an unusually good hand containing an unsolved problem in the method of theology.

In 1252 at the age of twenty-seven, Aquinas, feeling, it is said, somewhat inadequate to the job, began his theological lectures in the University of Paris. Previously schooled in Aristotle's thought by Peter of Ireland and Albert the Great, he began by lecturing for four years on the Sentences of Lombard. His *Commentary on the Sentences*, completed in 1256, was a medieval equivalent of a modern doctorate.[23] In 1256, now thirty-one, he was incepted as a master of theology at a time of severe conflict between the mendicants and the secular masters of the university. According to

Mandonnet, he composed the *De Veritate* during this time, between 1259 and 1263, roughly eighty articles each year (Miethe dates it as 1256–9). Composition of the *Contra Gentiles* was begun towards the end of his time in Paris and completed around the same time as *De Potentia* in 1264 in Orvieto, Italy. The *Pars Prima* of the *Summa* was written in Rome and Viterbo between 1266 and 1268, overlapping with the *De Malo*. The *Prima Secundae*, written in Paris, followed. After finishing most of the *Tertia Pars*, Aquinas stopped writing on 6 December 1273, with only one further letter, composed during 1274, being attributed to him.

It is in the phantasm of the chronological sequence of these texts, all of which are mentioned in Lonergan's thesis,[24] that we find the locus of the problem.

> If Thomas treats the same question several times, compare the passages. My dissertation was on operative grace, a topic Thomas treated three times explicitly and each time he changed. Operative grace was only sanctifying grace in the *Sentences*. It was sanctifying grace and help, *auxilium,* in the *De Veritate*. ('Lead us not into temptation,' eh? and 'We must pray for perseverance.') So sanctifying grace was both *operans* and *cooperans* – but for perseverance, *cooperans.* In the *Summa* he had actual grace (though he never used that expression) but he also had *motus divinus* or *motio divina* and both were sanctifying grace, and the *motiones divinae* were *operans* and *cooperans.* To arrive at his final position he was changing his mind on liberty and he was developing his notions on operation. How could God change the will, pluck out the heart of stone and put in the heart of flesh? That is God operating on the will. Well, what's that operation?' He was working on things like that.[25]

In this, Lonergan's work is reminiscent of that of J.A. Stewart, who, after ordering the Platonic writings, studied in them the development of Plato's understanding of the term 'idea.' When Lonergan was asked what put him onto the fact that Aquinas changed his mind on the topic, he replied that he just read the texts and it clicked. After about a month he dropped the Molinist ideas he had been taught in theology, as they had no contribution to make to an understanding of Aquinas. In contrast, he considered that 'Garrigou-Lagrange's *Dieu déterminate ou déterminé* (his argument with the Jesuit D'Alès) was right on the ball.'[26]

Under the heading of 'the phases of a development' he is exploring, not any *a priori* form of history, but sets of abstract categories that have a special reference to the historical process. These include the initial, intermediate, and final phases of the development. Theology does not explain but rather isolates mystery. In the initial phase, mystery is not distinguished from related philosophical problems and the connections between the different mysteries are not appreciated. Part of the development can be philosophical and involves the clarification of natural elements appropriate for isolating and bringing into focus the mystery of faith. As in his explorations of analytic concepts of history, so here Lonergan is trying to articulate the why of intellectual development in theology.

Although the text is speculative and technically difficult, in the opening chapter of his dissertation what is clear is that Lonergan had begun to reflect on theological method. Involved was a break with the method and paradigm of Melchior Cano and the whole manual tradition, then the custodian of Thomism. That Aquinas changed his mind a number of times on specific topics was a view at odds with the manual tradition. Through the providential interference of McCormick and Boyer, the big question in Lonergan's life now made its entry. If *Insight* began during Whiteside's course in Heythrop, *Method in Theology* began while thinking out the methodological dimension of his dissertation in Rome.

Lonergan's theological analysis begins, not with the text from Aquinas, the master of technical theology, but with Augustine's more psychologically penetrating *On Grace and Free Will.* Some of the monks at Adrumentum, to whom that work was addressed, valued grace at the expense of freedom. Others valued freedom at the expense of grace. Augustine quotes from John XV:22 and Romans 1:18–20 to prove the fact of human freedom. He continues that men and not God are responsible for sin and evil and the resulting necessity of grace. Chapter 10 holds that free will and grace together are the basis of the Christian life. Later chapters probe God's activity of removing or converting the stony heart, and assert that both freedom and grace are involved in a conversion. In chapter 33 for the first time the terms 'operative' and 'cooperative' grace emerge together, themes that are not unrelated to the movement of the first two weeks or movements of the Ignatian exercises. Later chapters affirm that the wills of men, both good and evil, are utterly in the hands of God, who can do with them what he likes. Chapter 45 suggests that the reason why one person is assisted by grace and another is not must be referred to the secret judgments of God.

At the heart of Augustine's text is an early effort to reconcile two apparently irreconcilable realities, the gift of God's grace and human freedom. How can statements that God is more in control of the will than the will itself be reconciled with those that affirm that human willing is inherently free, that at the heart of freedom is some element of autonomy, noncoercion, and personal responsibility? For philosophers, liberty is freedom from necessity, from constraint or coercion. To be free is to be self-moving and autonomous like the romance heroes rather than the saints. For theologians, we are free because of the gift of God's grace.

Related to Augustine's subtle handling of the problem of predestination was his distinction between 'free from justice' (that meant being in sin) and 'liberation from sin' – the freedom of the sons of God, a different kind of liberation.[27] There follows the dialectical statements:

> Grace is necessary; but the will is also free. Scripture asserts both; Scripture is the word of God; therefore both are true.

> The will of man is always free but not always good: either it is free from justice, and then it is evil; or it is liberated from sin, and then it is good.[28]

Real freedom of the will is a consequence of human goodness.

After Augustine came Anselm. An earlier era had prized freedom as the basis of virtue. Now there were many who feared the responsibilities it demanded.[29] For Anselm the real issue was not directly the problem of freedom but the value and possibility of theological speculation itself.[30] Since God's grace is a mysterious gift, does it make sense to try and understand it in a human way? Does that not inevitably involve erasing the mystery?

Anselm raised, speculatively, all the deepest theological questions. But according to Lonergan he did not yet recognize the two standards for understanding: 'natural truths can be reduced eventually to perfect coherence, but the truths of faith have the apex of their intelligibility hidden in the transcendence of God.'[31] Without a clear understanding of this duality and of the way of analogy, intellectual speculation may reduce mystery to the level of natural truth or elevate natural problems to the order of mystery. Anselm, who held that freedom was an effect of grace and grace was what makes freedom free, tended to mystify the human will. In his speculations he challenged Lonergan to think about the nature of theological understanding.

Lombard next introduced the four states of human liberty: the earthly paradise, fallen man, man redeemed, and heaven. Grace as operative and cooperative is what makes the difference between the second and third states. This in turn gave rise to the question, what is natural and what is gratuitous? In the work of Philip the Chancellor, around 1218–30, there was formulated the theorem of the supernatural:

> [He] reaffirmed William of Auxerre's affirmation of a natural *amor amicitiae erga Deum*, quite distinct from charity, the meritorious love

of God. He then presented the theory of two orders, entitatively disproportionate: not only was there the familiar series of grace, faith, charity and merit, but also nature, reason, and the natural love of God.[32]

In Philip's explorations there is emerging a profound insight into the nature of theology itself. Before Newton, mechanics was in a state of confusion. Before Philip, there was a nascent confusion about the nature of faith and reason and grace and freedom. As late as 1959 Lonergan put it as follows:

> The discovery of the supernatural order was the discovery of a do-main of intelligible relations proper to theology. Just as Newton discovered that the natural laws reduced to a system of their own, mechanics, and not as Galileo had thought to a pre-existing system, geometry, just as Mendeleev, by discovering an order to which chemical entities reduced defined the field of chemistry, so too when Aquinas was still a boy, theology found itself. The meaning of the supernatural is that Christian theology has to deal with the gift of God, where not only is the gift from God but more basically the gift is God ... Knowing it is a faith that is above reason, possessing it is a grace that is above nature, acting on it is a charity that is above good will, with a merit that is above human deserts. Christian fellow-ship is a bond, transcending family and state.[33]

With Philip theology begins to move from a pre-paradigm to a paradigm phase. The necessity of grace now came to be defined, not in terms of the liberation of liberty, but rather in terms of human finality. This reorientated the four states of Lombard. Philip and later Albert developed the notion of sanctifying grace.

As well as the reorientation, some confusions arose. Initially Albert and Aquinas rejected the notion of *non posse non peccare*, both in the name of the supernatural and in terms of a coherent idea of freedom:

> For example, Thomas, treating the question 'Can a man in the state of sin avoid further sin?' says in his *Sentences*, 'Certainly; otherwise he wouldn't be free.' In the *De Veritate* he has twenty-two objections (negative, eleven; positive, eleven) and a solution that runs over about nine columns in the Marietti edition. He answers both the affirmative and the negative, but he has a theory of moral impotence there. To handle that, you have to know about the surd. 'Why did Adam sin?' If there were a reason, it wouldn't have been a sin, eh?[34]

(The modern equivalent would be couched in terms of the freedom to change from bad will to good will.) The dogmatic datum forced Aquinas to revise his initial position. Out of this confusion there began to emerge the notion of actual grace. The question arose, are there graces that are not habitual but that presumably could change our habitual state?

Aquinas was searching for a theological understanding of the manner in which God operates on the human heart of stone, removes it, cooperates with good will to give it good performance, and yet respects human freedom. This was a theological project with considerable bearing on the Ignatian exercises that Lonergan followed each year in his annual retreat and in the previous year had taken in their thirty-day form. During the academic year of 1975/6 Harvey Egan gave a lecture in St Mary's, Boston College, that addressed the theme of consolation without a previous cause. Only then did Lonergan link the exercises with his thesis:

> I was hearing that my own work on operative grace in St Thomas brought to life a positive expression of what was meant by Ignatius when [he] spoke of 'consolation without a previous cause.' In Aquinas grace is operative when the mind is not a mover but only moved; in Ignatius consolation is from God alone when there is no conscious antecedent to account for consolation.[35]

The remark shows the extent of the chasm between spirituality and theology at the time.

A first step in Aquinas' project was to think out in the most general terms the meaning of operation. Operating and being operated on are phenomena that occur at all levels in our universe, physical, chemical, biological, and human. Our answers to the question, what does an agent do and what can be done to it? will be in terms of operations. To operate is to enter into a relation with an entity on which one operates. To be operated on is to enter into a relation of patienthood or dependence on an operator. When an agent operates, its operation produces an effect. So the question arises, does the production of an effect result in a change in the agent? It was Aquinas' position that when the fire heats the meat or the musician makes music or the teacher teaches that all the change was in the object operated on; no change occurs in the operator.

Causes act in time. But for a cause to act effectively, that on which it operates must be predisposed to the operation of the cause at that particular point in time. So the wood must be brought to the axe, the hair to the scissors, a disposition to learn to the pedagogy of the teacher. What brings the object into the right relation or disposition with the cause is termed 'premotion' by Aristotle and 'application' by Aquinas. As the influence of

Aquinas, so that of Aristotle would now begin to grow for Lonergan, and that of Plato diminish.

How then does God premove or apply the subject so that his operation can produce a required effect at a given point in time? For Molina God would tailor his operation to the situation, so the individual determined God's providence. For Aquinas the answer was through providence and fate. He acknowledged Aristotle's assertion of the *per accidens* and that there could be no science for us of the accidental.[36] The divine plan has a twofold existence: it exists in the mind of God and there it is termed 'providence'; it exists in the created universe and there it is termed 'fate.' God in his eternal providence understands exactly all the myriad of situations and circumstances an individual will encounter in the course of his or her life. It is through those circumstances as providentially ordained that God premoves the individual. Later Acquinas will divide premotion into external and internal. According to Lonergan, God, for Aquinas, was a transcendental artisan planning history.[37]

An instrument is a lower cause moved by a higher so as to produce an effect within the categories proportionate to the higher. So the computer or the electronic technologies used by the media are instruments through which properly human meaning is communicated. As the universe is hierarchical, so also are causality and instrumentality. The highest cause is unmoved or uncaused. It follows that all causes except the highest are instruments: 'if the instrument is to operate beyond its proper proportion and within the category of the higher cause, it must receive some participation of the latter's special productive capacity.'[38] If providence is the art of the divine artisan, then fate is the *virtus artis* in his tools. Divine ideas correspond to the essence of creatures, but providence corresponds to fate. Fate impresses itself upon things and is unfolded in the course of events. Thus a distinction has to be drawn between the natural forms of things and the divine design that was impressed upon them as they entered into the dynamic order of events, their fate.

In the *Summa*, Aquinas affirmed that by fate things are ordained to produce given effects. Fate is a cause in conjunction with natural causes. It is the disposition, arrangement, seriation of the order of secondary causes. It is not a quality and much less a substance, but belongs to the category of relation: 'Together such relations give a single fate for the universe; taken singly, they give the many fates of Virgil's line, *Te tua fata trahunt*.[39] Application is then the causal certitude of providence terminating in the right disposition, relation, proximity between the mover and moved: without it, motion cannot now take place; with it, motion automatically results. Fate is the dynamic pattern of relations through which the design of the divine artisan unfolds in natural and human history. Without fate things cannot act. With it they do. Thus fate and application and instrumental virtue all reduce to the divine plan. It is interesting to consider in this context the set of fateful circumstances in Lonergan's life that moved him to decide to write the *Verbum* articles in 1943 and *Insight* in 1946.

How then did Aquinas conceive the analogy between the causation of the creator and that of the creature? God acts by his substance. Creatures act by an accidental form or act such as knowing or willing. God causes the causation of all creatures, makes every procession proceed, operates the operation of every creature by application, instrumentality, and finality because he is creator and conserver. What is involved here is an analogous understanding of a mystery. Once operation in natural instances is apprehended, one extrapolates to the infinite.

After such general considerations are worked out, the task becomes that of applying them to the human will and freedom. The operation of God on the operation of the human will is but a particular instance of a general law. First, then, there is the question, what do we mean by human freedom? For Aquinas it entails a field of action in which more than one course of action is possible, an intellect that is able to work out many courses of action, a will that is not determined by the first course of action that occurs to the mind, and a will that moves itself.

What is the manner of divine action on the human will? Through all his various writings Aquinas affirmed a divine intervention in the will. In virtue of the theorem of the analogy of operation, for him God was more a cause of the will's act of choice than the will itself. But does God operate the choice or the antecedent orientation? By infusing a new habit or by substituting one inclination for another, does God heal and change the powerlessness of our wills?

There remain questions about contingency and sin. If God's providence is infallible, how can anything be contingent? If God knows the future infallibly, must not the future be necessary rather than contingent? Must not the creation necessarily be what it is? Aquinas' answer has to do with time and eternity. To say that God is eternal is to say, negatively, that he has no past and future but is always present, always now. Nothing is future or past to God. God does not know future events as future. And what God's providence intends to be contingent will inevitably be contingent.

Does God in any sense cause sin? Bañez and Molina offered various explanations of the possibility of sin in terms of two- and four-lane highways. For Bañez there is one lane for what God effects, another for what he can never effect. For Molina there are two hypothetical lanes in the order of futurabilia in which God knows what James would do or not do under given circumstances. Two more lanes are in the real order in which God provides or does not provide the situations in which James sins or not. For

Aquinas there were three lanes: what God wills, does not will, and permits but does not will. The point holds not only for willing but also for knowing. In the order of being, as well as the truth about what is and the truth about what is not, there is also objective falsity. God does not cause but permits errors in our knowing.

The Death of Lonergan's Mother

In February 1939 Piux XI died, his encyclical on racism unfinished. On 2 March, as the European situation was worsening, the new Pope, Pius XII, took up office. In April in the middle of his work on the thesis, Lonergan communicated to his provincial his desire to return to Canada for the summer. He had been promised a trip to Canada before he took up his appointment as a lecturer in the Gregorian. He was now asking that the trip be brought forward. The provincial wrote to the general in Rome and communicated the request. He added that Lonergan had been away for six years, was somewhat tired and unwell, and felt that a trip to his native parts would refresh him. He made it clear that Lonergan was finding his exile hard, but did not mention that his mother was seriously ill, surely a strange and unusual omission.

The reply came in May, refusing the request for the trip. It added that Lonergan was to return to Canada after finishing his thesis and teach there for a number of years before taking up his appointment in the Gregorian. Lonergan spent part of the summer in England. On 15 August in Stonyhurst College, near Blackburn, he made his final solemn vows as a Jesuit. On 1 September Hitler invaded Poland; two days later Britain and France declared war. As Lonergan was giving a retreat in Worthing, Hitler began the bombardment of Danzig (now Gdansk).

At Christmas 1939 Lonergan's father wrote concerning his mother's illness. She was suffering from cancer and there was talk of an operation. Lonergan wrote back advising against an operation, at least locally. By the time his letter arrived the situation had changed: the operation had taken place but was unsuccessful. So far away his mother, the one who had made him feel special, loved by God, died. Later he described the impact of the experience on him in a letter to Crowe of 21 December 1976, at the time of the death of Crowe's mother:

> The death of your mother keeps reminding me of the death of mine. It was in February 1940. I had been in Europe since November 1933. Fr Vincent McCormick, Rector of the Gregorian broke the news to me. He did it very nicely, but I did not speak for three days. I guess I was in a minor state of shock.

His brother Mark wrote a moving letter to Gregory about the death. At the end their mother wanted to die, and he felt that the only thing keeping her alive was the thought of welcoming Bernard back from Rome. When asked in her last moments if she had any message for Bernard and Gregory, she simply smiled. Mark's letter also mentions the existence of letters to his mother from Bernard and Gregory. Unfortunately, no trace of them has ever been found.

Just three months later, on 1 May, Lonergan's thesis was handed in to the secretariat; after suddenly being switched from epistemology to theology, he wrote his thesis in roughly eighteen months. On 10 May, just as Churchill came to power in Great Britain, Germany invaded the Netherlands and Belgium. After a flurry of consultations involving the Jesuit curia, Lonergan was assigned an early date for his defence. As things turned out, two days before that date he was forced to take the last boat leaving from Genoa for New York, the Conti di Savoi, his thesis undefended.

With hindsight, we can identify a series of accidents that landed Lonergan in Rome in 1933, that exposed him to Keeler and Leeming, and that moved him at a moment's notice from a career in philosophy to theology and related doctoral studies. The intervention of a tragic war frustrated his inauguration as a professor of theology in Rome and returned him to Montreal. In these accidents, which in their own way will shape the decisions that Lonergan would make about his life's work in the next two decades, can we see at work in his life what Aquinas meant by 'application'?

PART TWO

Finding and Following the Golden Cord of the Heart's Desire

7

Economics or Cognitional Theory: Towards Desire's Decisions

Lonergan arrived in New York on 24 May 1940. On the voyage he must have found himself pondering the madness of the world he had left, as it disintegrated into war. He was also sailing towards a world that would present him with the personal challenge of coming to terms with the death of his mother. Soon after his return he made his way to Buckingham to meet the family, his father, brothers, and aunt, and grieve with them in the aftermath of her recent death. Its effect on his father was such that on 14 November 1940 he himself died of a heart attack.

All of this left Aunt Minnie alone in the large house with her memories. The loss of her younger sister and brother-in-law took its toll, and soon after, in March of the following year, she too died. By the middle of 1941, less than a year after he returned from Europe, a whole emotional continent that had formed and supported his early years had passed away. What his reactions to the losses were at the time we do not know. As his three days of silence in Rome reveals, in personal matters he was a deeply private individual, which made it difficult for him to talk about and deal with the death of loved ones.[1] I have no doubt that he felt these losses deeply. One of his ways of coping was simply to continue in his chosen life, to keep working at his intellectual projects.

The educational work of the Imaculée in Montreal, where he would now begin teaching, continued quietly in the climate of the war, which America entered in January 1942. For most of the next thirteen years he had a light teaching load, which gave him a chance to read, think, and generally allow his desires and interests to expand. Almost for the first time in his life, Lonergan had considerable leisure time to pursue his own interests, to browse. There would follow over the next six years a time of letting the emerging themes in his polyphonic consciousness play their melodies until, eventually, the dominant ones became established, those indicating the direction of pull of the golden cord in his life. After a decade of Lonergan's having decisions made for him, it is interesting to follow the unfolding of his own emerging agenda and decisions.

At this time Eric O'Connor began teaching mathematics at Loyola Montreal, and was having difficulties. He and Lonergan met and discussed them,[2] initiating a life-long friendship that was to be extremely fertile and supportive. Later O'Connor recalled one of his discussions with Lonergan in the early 1940s:

> He came to my room to ask me a simple question in mathematics that he was working on in his book on philosophy. Well, it was a subject that I knew well, the area that I knew very well. I learned more from a few questions of his, just because he was asking the questions, not being an expert, but asking the question in the right way. I learned more about how one proved things in that area of mathematics than I had in getting my PhD.[3]

In different ways O'Connor and Lonergan were both highly gifted individuals, Lonergan a problem solver and writer, O'Connor a midwife of the questions of others and the visionary inspiration of an institute of adult education. A great respecter of the mathematical mind, Lonergan felt at home with him.

The editor of the recently founded journal *Theological Studies* communicated through a friend to Lonergan that there was interest in publishing sections from his dissertation. He immediately set to work, with the result that one article was published in 1941 and three in 1942.[4]

In the summer of 1941, during one of the few retreats Lonergan gave to the Jesuit students of philosophy, he met Frederick Crowe for the first time. Crowe remembered the occasion as a preached retreat, four talks a day plus a conference, following the Ignatian format. Lonergan stayed on after the retreat and engaged in an informal discussion about the value of a classical education. He argued that in a manner different from learning French and German, which are similar, learning Latin and Greek made you think, get hold of ideas that were wordless. Sometime after the retreat Crowe tried to read the first paragraph of *Gratia Operans* but gave up. His interest in Lonergan's work began when he attended the latter's theology classes six years later, in the spring of 1947 in Toronto.

According to Jack Belair, Lonergan read Toynbee's *A Study of History* in the long winter evenings of 1940–1, borrowing the set from McGill. He bought his own set a year later, as well as four volumes of Sorokin.[5] At this dark time in human history, Toynbee's books raised the question, what is a civilization? They went on to explore the genesis, development, expansion, disintegration, collapse, and breakdown of the civilizations of the world. Volumes 1 and 2 explored the nature of challenge to and response of a host of civilizations to their specific environment. Volume 3 introduced the notion of withdrawal and return as a creative force. In volumes 1–5 the problem of disintegration was explored, using such notions as 'schism' and 'palingenesia.' In volume 6 the 'rhythm of disintegration' makes an entry and is explored in a variety of cultures. This notion of rhythm, of both growth and disintegration, will be taken up by Lonergan in his economics.

For Toynbee, creativity on the civilizational level requires a creative minority who are prepared to withdraw from the immediate issues of day-to-day living to think out the longer term issues. Their later return will transform the social and civilizational world. This theme of withdrawal and return is given expression in Lonergan's *Topics in Education* and 'Healing and Creating in History.'[6] It was also an image with personal significance for him, in that he recognized in it the shape of his own life's work. But he would write nothing directly on history in the 1940s.

Important in the light of his preoccupation with economics are four untitled and undated pages of notes he drafted around this time on the ideas of progress and decline.[7] They open with the remark that until a decade earlier the naturalism of Rousseau, the mechanistic framework of the old political economists, and the evolutionary ideas of Darwin had made progress the dominant idea in the modern world. Now:

> The political economists are utterly discredited: no economist to-day believes in the old theories; no thinking man who has lived through the Depression can accept the view that the greatest happiness of the greatest number results automatically from the laws of supply and demand.

Even if aspects of the doctrine of progress are discredited, Lonergan still addresses the question, does humanity progress? for he can agree with neither unqualified affirmations nor rejections of the idea of progress, seeing a need to distinguish between the principle and the cause of both progress and decline.

There is progress, he affirms, because humankind has an intellectual potential that can be educated up to the level of civilization and then go on to engage with its problems. He reviews the economic progress of humanity in outline, tracing a line from horticulture through agriculture, commerce, art, and literature to philosophy and science. Finally, he attempts to sketch the lines of decline that are based on the falsification of the intellect to be found in rationalism (Descartes to Kant), naturalism (Rousseau and modern education, democratic government by public opinion), communism (Marx, Lenin, and Stalin), and racialism and the Nazis. The lines of both progress and decline are not separate tracks, but mixed and interacting forces. The notes make clear that we should read his work on economics that is to follow within the context of the problem of progress and decline within a philosophy of history.

The Problem of Explaining the Economic Cycle

From 1930 to about 1944 I spent a great deal of my free time on economic theory, eventually producing a 120 page manuscript which was, it seemed, either an aberration or, at best, ahead of its time.[8]

Since he had been provoked by the suggestion of Major Douglas, Lonergan had been working away behind the scenes on the economic problem. In 1981 he offered a helpful clarification of what, precisely, was the problem he was addressing at the time:

There is a problem in explaining the cycle but at least you have a datum there, something to explain; you know what you are trying to explain. When my father spoke about 'the hard times in 1890,' people wanted to refer to earlier hard times. But they didn't talk about a cycle ... The point is that you are not understanding your economy until you understand the cycles. It isn't the whole of economics, but it is the sort of thing that sticks out like a sore thumb, a really sore thumb.[9]

It was commonplace in the newspapers during the 1930s to talk about the economy oscillating between periods of prosperity and periods of hardship. Are we, in economic history, locked into trade cycles with their booms and slumps and, ultimately, full depressions? Are these the result of the iron laws of nature or of human mismanagement? If the latter, might it be possible to manage an economy in history in a way that avoided the collapse of the standard of living into a slump or depression? The basic tangle to be unravelled and understood was that of the unknown causes of cycles of booms and slumps through which a desirable standard of living gives way to an impoverished one.

A clue to the enormous intellectual engagement involved is given in the preface to his 1944 text:

To discover such terms is a lengthy and painful process of trial and error. *Experto crede.* To justify them, one cannot reproduce the tedious blind efforts that led to them; one can appeal only to the success, be it great or small, with which they serve to account systematically for the phenomena under investigation. Hence it is only fair to issue at once a warning that the reader will have to work through pages, in which parts gradually are assembled, before he will be able to see a whole and pass an equitable judgment upon it.[10]

His analytic approach differs from both statistical and descriptive ones in that it aims at discovering the significant functional interrelations.[11] His typescript was the product of sustained intellectual wrestling with the problem, but leaves us in the dark about the moments of insight and the shape and artistry of the intellectual journey involved.

The problem solving finds its first public expression in a 133-page typescript completed, according to Crowe, between mid-1942 and mid-1943.[12] Entitled 'For a New Political Economy,' its opening pages rank as some of Lonergan's most political.[13] In the nineteenth century democracy was the successful political form, he wrote, but times have changed and modern economics aims at replacing democracy with the totalitarian state. The regimenting of the Russians by the Soviets, of the Germans by the Nazis, and of the Italians by the Fascists are moves towards making the whole world conform. In contrast, the power of the old political economists was solely that of argument, the aim to release the creativity that resides in human beings rather than in ideologies or parties or bureaucracies.

What is needed in economic thinking is a 'scientific generalization of the old political economy and of modern economics that will yield the new political economy we need.'[14] It will be a new point of departure, not unlike that established by Newton in relation to the science of mechanics. It will seek to understand most generally the patterns of relations among certain human activities that make up an economy. This Lonergan will break down into questions about production, exchange, and finance.

Production, Exchange, and Finance

The first part of the investigation explores the functional relations that constitute the production process. In order to enter into the problem of production we have to ask ourselves, how would one go about producing a certain amount of consumer commodities such as shirts or dresses or corn or milk each day, week, month, or year? What is to be produced is not a once-off quantity but a flow, a so-much-per-so-often, or even, as Philip

McShane suggests, a surge.[15] A basic requirement would be a supply velocity of so-much-per-so-often of cloth and sewing machines, usable land, cattle, and tractors. In order to maintain a flow of consumer items like clothes, there is needed a parallel flow of producer items like sewing machines and cloth.

Challenging is the further question, how could a flow of consumer commodities be increased from one level, X, to another, Y? This in turn leads to the question, how is the production of producer goods related to that of consumer goods? While producer goods are being manufactured, financial capital will have to move in their direction and will not be available for paying wages to manufacture or purchase consumer goods. There will result a delay before the flow of consumer goods can be increased. Once a flow of producer goods comes on-stream, it stands in a multiplier relation with the flow of consumer goods. In this way there arises the possibility of accelerating the flow of consumer goods from a lower to a higher velocity. Within the overall economic cycle there is a phased multiplier relation between the production of flows or velocities of producer and consumer goods.

For Lonergan this points to the basic rhythm or cycle of the production process. To the total rhythm of production he assigns the rather opaque symbol DA, the D being replaced by f in 1944 to suggest a flow. A velocity or flow, DA is a so-much-every-so-often of both producer and consumer goods, of sewing machines and cloth and of shirts and dresses. Within DA there is a primary rhythm that relates to the production of a flow of consumer goods DA', such as shirts and dresses; and a secondary that relates to the production of producer goods DA'' such as sewing machines. Four phases are identified in the relations between DA'' and DA', a static, capitalist, materialist, and cultural phase.[16]

In an economy where DA'' is zero no new producer goods are coming on stream. There results the static phase in which DA', the level of consumer output, remains constant. In the capitalist phase, illustrated by nineteenth-century capitalism, there occurs a massive investment in capital. As a result new producer goods such as machines and factories are manufactured. In this phase DA'' increases but does not yet result in an increase in consumer output, DA'. In the materialist phase DA'', having increased to a magnitude greater than zero, begins to have an impact on the material standard of living, resulting in a rapid increase in consumer goods, DA'.

The new fields that have been prepared for their crops begin to produce, the new factories and their machines for manufacturing begin to operate. In the cultural phase DA'' is a constant above zero, but it devotes its surplus to overhead DA'. This Lonergan illustrates by reference to the medieval emergence of monasteries, churches, schools, universities, guild halls, and, ironically at the time of writing, to armaments. It is characterized by investment without any direct expectation of profit.

The identification of four phases in the basic economic rhythm leads through brief reflections on economic progress and decline (which Lonergan considers the result of human blunders) into the analysis of *a pure economic process of production*. In the pure process DA' and DA'' can be constant or increasing, but they never decrease. The emerging standard of living never falls:

> Significantly different combinations of DA' and DA'' as constant or increasing yield the four cyclic phases of this ebb and flow: a capitalist phase that transforms the means of production; a materialist phase that exploits new ideas to raise the standard of living; a cultural phase that turns material well-being and power to equipping the developing cultural pursuits; a static phase in which the process lies fallow and non-economic activity develops independently of material conditions ... This cycle never implies retrogression, a drop in the existing rates as a whole. It leaves them constant or it increases them.[17]

In this remark Lonergan is setting forth and expressing his major insight into a pure cycle or wave in the production process that effectively raises the standard of living tide-like. Different economic theories are adapted to different phases in the cycle.[18] Few, if any, deal with the totality of relations that constitute the whole of an economy in history. The alternative trade cycle, in which booms and slumps recur, is but one possibility brought on largely by human oversight of the processes of production and exchange.

Economic production is also for Lonergan a series of conditioned emergences, the emergent component of what he will later call emergent probability: 'In making a coat of mail each new link has to be added to previous links, and similarly the successive stages of economic progress presuppose the previous stages and arise from them.'[19] Each stage having emerged, there is the challenge of survival, and so in time the stagecoach gives way to the train, clipper ships to steamers, money changers give way to brokers who in turn give way to banks and financiers.[20]

In a modern economy production is for exchange. Goods such as food or cars are exchanged for money, for dollars, euros, yen. A coincidence of decisions between producers and consumers is involved in an exchange. The actual exchange value is the ratio at which different categories of property exchange.[21] Money is a bridging dummy, exchange ratios being represented by a quantity of the dummy, a price. The dummy must have a constant exchange value; otherwise we get inflation or deflation, the famous twins of which 'inflation swindles those with cash to enrich those with property or debts, while deflation swindles those with property or debts to enrich those with cash.'[22]

Exchanges take place in markets, which tend to adjust ratios to variations in supply and demand. Markets also integrate large numbers of decisions to exchange and not to exchange, to settle on an exchange ratio at which supply and demand equate. They have a dark side as well, tending towards 'wholesale deception, to fraud, to sharp practice, to ruthlessness, they tend to exploit the snobbery of the rich, the ignorance of the masses, the impotence of the poor, the passions of human nature, the gullibility of the world's endless supply of fools.'[23] There follows a preliminary definition of an exchange economy as

> an attempt to give a continuously satisfactory answer to the continuously shifting question, *Who*, among millions of persons, is to perform *which*, among millions of tasks, in return for *what*, among millions of possible rewards?[24]

The exchange economy is concerned only with what the members of a population do for a proportionate remuneration. It directs goods and services to local, regional, and national markets, which control contributions and apportion rewards. Because individuals are unequal in ability and opportunity, the exchange economy as it currently exists can tend to favour the few who have intimate knowledge and control of it. It creates two classes, the successful and the failures. It has no place for those who are willing to contribute for little or no return, even though what they contribute might be of considerable human value.

As the goal of production is a linked flow of producer and consumer goods, it has to be matched by parallel flows in the circulation of money if the exchange economy is to function successfully. Dysfunctions in that circulation and related exchanges give rise to the core problem of slumps and depressions. Lonergan articulates his second and critical economic insight as follows: 'for the economic process that sets us problems is not the pure process of primary and secondary rhythms but the exchange process in which the cyclic phases tend to become alternations of prosperity and misery.'[25] The slumps or depressions result, not from the inevitable nature of things, but from money flows in the exchange structure that are out of tune with the structure of the flows of the production process. There arises the need to master and critique these possible dysfunctions.

Identifying the Flow Circuits of Money

Graham: Where did you get the original diagram?
Lonergan: That's my own, my baseball diamond.
Graham: It is a funny diamond. Do you remember the day you
    got it?
Lonergan: No. I did all sorts of diagrams before I got that one.[26]

A scientific economics demands that we go beyond a common-sense apprehension of money and examine theoretically and critically its functions and
circulation in an economy. For money does not do just a single thing, like
buying a particular kind of car over and over. Like language, it has many
functions, buying consumer and producer goods, paying wages, paying
taxes, investing in stocks, saving. Whereas production involves transforming the potentialities of nature into an emergent standard of living, a key
point about the way money functions in the macroeconomy is that it
circulates. Recurrently, manufacturers pay their employees wages and their
employees purchase manufactured goods. In aggregate, a large percentage
of the money in an exchange economy money circulates between the two.

Whereas Harvey set out to understand the circulation of the blood in the
human body and ecologists the circulation of water on the earth's surface,
Lonergan wondered: what might be the theoretically significant manners
in which money, in aggregate, can circulate and function in a macroeconomy? The question assumes that at any point in time in an exchange
economy there is a total aggregate quantity of money in circulation, an
aggregate that can vary over time. It asks if there are significantly different
functions that different fractions of that total ought to address and related
circuits in which they ought to circulate.

The question, where does my money come from and go to? can be
enlarged to extend to the whole economic community. Some of my money
is paid to me in wages by my employer. Some of it is spent on consumer
goods such as clothes, food, houses, cars, books, and computers, a percentage of which makes its way back through the distribution process to employers and manufacturers. I may work for a car manufacturer, but much of the
money I am paid could go for food and clothes and books as well as for a
car. From the standpoint of circulation, this is not significant for Lonergan.
Such movements of money are all within the one aggregate circuit from the
prices paid by the aggregate of consumers of consumer goods to the
aggregate of producers of such goods and back in the wages the latter pay
(see fig. 2).

If, however, as well as being a consumer of food and clothes and a home
I am also a manufacturer of cars or clothes or food or electronic products,

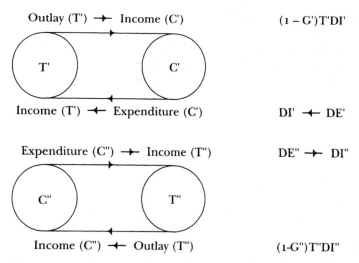

Outlay (T') → Income (C') $(1-G')T'DI'$

Income (T') ← Expenditure (C') $DI' ← DE'$

Expenditure (C") → Income (T") $DE" → DI"$

Income (C") ← Outlay (T") $(1-G")T"DI"$

Fig. 2. Partial circuits
T' = primary trader (of consumer goods) – basic supply
C' = primary consumer (of consumer goods) – basic demand
T" = secondary trader (of producer goods) – surplus supply
C" = secondary consumer (of producer goods) – surplus demand

then I will also be a consumer of producer goods. Inhabiting and furnishing manufacturing plants and factories, these are the goods such as sewing machines, assembly lines, tractors, and robots that are used in the production of basic consumer goods. The manufacturers of producer goods will create a supply, their consumers a demand. Money, in aggregate, will move from the demand or consumer side to the manufacturers as consumer expenditure. Money will move from the manufacturing side to the demand side in terms of outlay, including wages. The circulation of money involved in the manufacture and sale of such producer goods belongs, for Lonergan, to a significantly different aggregate circuit in the exchange economy.

If the two circuits are distinct in terms of the circulation and function of money in each, it does not follow that they are isolated. A first mode of interconnection is in terms of what Lonergan calls the 'crossovers' (see fig. 3). The operators of producer goods in the basic circuit will need to maintain their equipment, replace obsolete machinery, and invest in new equipment for start-up projects. Accordingly, a quantity of money, $G'T'DI'$, will cross over from the primary traders/supply side of the basic consumer circuit to the producer circuit as such operators purchase producer goods.

In the same way, not all the income in the secondary or surplus circuit,

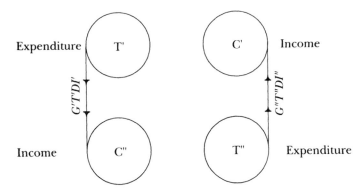

Fig. 3. Crossovers

DI″, will be spent on producer goods. Wage earners will spend a fraction for basic consumer goods, clothes and food and so forth; owners will spend some of their profits in the same way. A fraction of *DI″*, *G″T″DI″*, will make its way across to the basic demand side and be spent on such commodities. In this manner two basic circuits and related crossovers come to be defined. Should the economy contain higher levels of production of, for instance, machine tools and robots to make producer goods, then further related circuits can be added.

Identifying a series of consumer and producer circuits and related crossovers does not exhaust all the possibilities. Governments tax wages and consumer items, banks loan money for the acquisition of consumer and producer goods and require repayment. There results a redistributive function and its related circuits that redirects taxes and so forth between the primary and secondary production circuits. Defining the redistributive circuits and functions enables one to calculate under what circumstances money, in aggregate, could either be drained from or injected into the basic/primary or the surplus/secondary circuits. In this manner the possibility of the redistributive function enabling or disrupting the phased relations between the circulation of money in the primary and surplus levels in the production process can be explored.

On page 82 of the original typescript (64 of *CWL 21 Political Economy*), Lonergan drew up one of his earliest 'circulation' diagrams, reproduced here as fig. 4. (I have broken this down into its parts in figs. 2 and 3 to clarify its meaning.) It was the expression of his response to the challenge of identifying all the economically significant circuits in which money flows, and their functional relations (see fig. 4). What is unusual and difficult about the diagram is that it is defining money in terms of its functional relations rather than in terms of interpersonal relations.

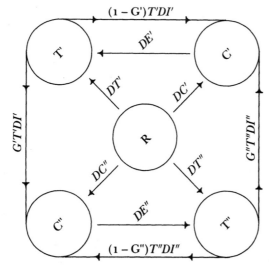

Arrows indicate the flows of money.

Fig. 4. 1942 circulation diagram

Having offered a definition of the production process and introduced the notion of significant money circuits and functions, Lonergan focused in his subsequent analysis on exploring the relation between the two:

> Our immediate task is to work out the correlations that exist between the velocity and accelerator rhythms of production and the corresponding rhythms of income and expenditure. The set of such correlations constitutes a mechanical structure, a pattern of laws that stand to economic activity as the laws of mechanics stand to buildings and machines.[27]

Within the total circulation there is a distinct rhythm of circulation in the consumer circuit and in the producer circuit. In the initial phase of a pure cycle there will be a need for an acceleration of the quantity of money circulating within the producer circuit. In the final phase the same will be true in the consumer circuit. In their budgeting, governments can frequently disrupt the rhythm of one in order to deal with short-term problems in the other. At a crucial time in the productive cycle, they can rob money from the producer circuit in order to meet short-term demands in the consumer circuit, with devastating consequences. The autonomy of the different circuits in the process must be respected. One of Lonergan's insights was that as the rhythms of the phases of the productive process change, the manner in which money circulates in its distinctive circuits has to adjust to those changes. The phased relation between producing producer and consumer goods in the pure cycle needs to be reflected in a phased relation between the monetary flows in the distinct circuits.

Understanding the relations between those velocity and accelerator rhythms in production and exchange will amount to a scientific explanation of the 'why' of an exchange economy. Those velocities, accelerations, and rhythms can act in harmony or in opposition. Mastering these possibilities will enable the human community to replace the dysfunctional trade cycle, with its booms and slumps, with a pure cycle in which the standard of living never drops.

Lonergan's final question asks about the manner in which an expansion in an exchange economy is to be financed:

> There is the fact that the economic process runs through a series of transformations and exploitations; the real flow varies, and the dummy flow has to vary concomitantly or else suffer inflation or deflation; moreover, the real flow attains volumes that greatly exceed previous maxima, and these peaks can be scaled only if the dummy has a noticeable elasticity. By finance we understand the effort made to solve these problems.[28]

There immediately arises the question, what is the correspondence between the financial phases and the phases of the real flows? Does a real expansion, such as the capitalist and materialist phases, necessitate a real expansion of the total quantity of money in an economy? Does the real static phase, when goods and services are produced and sold at constant rates, postulate monetary continuity? Does economic decline, when production and sales are dropping, postulate real monetary contraction?

> Essentially the financial problem consists in finding a stable and permanent solution for the monetary requirements of a long-term expansion. We may begin by enumerating what certainly are unsatisfactory solutions.[29]

The problem is not and cannot be solved by an increase in the rate of gold production, mercantilism, systematic deflation, or merely greater efficiency in the use of money. In section 30 Lonergan offers a retrospect. It has been his goal to show the existence 'of an objective mechanical structure in economic activity, of something independent of human psychology, of something to which human psychology must adapt itself if economic activity is not to become a matter of standing in a tub and trying to lift it.'[30]

The 1942 typescript may be less technical than his 1944 *Essay on Circulation Analysis,* but its strength is in the manner in which it articulates the basic questions. In the long run, economic theory will be as good as the questions it attempts to answer. Economic theory for Lonergan has the task of understanding production, exchange, and finance, not in isolation from each other, but in the fullness of their interrelatedness.

As Lonergan was working on his economics text, the editor of the journal *Thought* approached him for a contribution. The story goes that he reached into his drawer and pulled out an essay entitled 'The Form of Inference.' Published in the June 1943 edition of *Thought,* it gives some interesting insights into his thoughts on cognition at the time. In certain respects an amalgamation of his Heythrop essays, it was notable in that it gave public expression to his dependence on Newman's illative sense. It opens with a statement of his problem:

> Is the human mind a Noah's arc of irreducible inferential forms? Is there no general form of all inference, no highest common factor, that reveals the nature of the mind no matter how diverse the materials on which it operates? Is everything subject to measure and order and law except the mind which through measurement and comparison seeks to order everything with laws?[31]

An indication of his intellectual dream at the time is given in the last paragraph of the essay, where he talks about 'taking a first step in working out an empirical theory of human understanding and knowledge.' Although the cognitional question had been on hold for some eight years in his public writings, it had not gone away, but was biding its time.

The essay also contains two of his earliest uses of the word 'insight.' In the first he describes classroom drill as a method that teaches students how to arrive at mathematical results like calculating machines without any intellectual insight into the arithmetical operations that define numbers. In a second, the phrases 'intuition of the moment' and 'insights of experienced judgment,' occur in the same sentence.[32] Does this suggest that, despite his intellectual conversion of 1935, there were still traces of the ghost of intuitionism in his thought at this time? It is my view that the word 'insight' was not of central significance in the essay.

If the essay in a large part relates to his *Blandyke* papers, there is, however, a sting in the tail:

> We have not considered inductive conclusions. To correlate the movement from data through hypothesis to verified theory with the

movement from implier through implication to implied, and both of these with the more ultimate process from sensa through intellection to judgment, is indeed a legitimate inquiry; but it is more general than the present and presupposes it.[33]

The advances here in his understanding of cognition, drawing on his intellectual conversion on judgment in 1935, are considerable. The emphasis on movement squares with the fact that around this time Lonergan was thinking of cognition as a process, the term 'levels' being absent from the essay.

Finality, Love, Marriage: A Surprising New Question

In the *Canadian Register* for 23 May 1942, Lonergan published a review of von Hildebrand's book *Marriage*, his conclusion being that the values were sound but the doctrine vague. He also compared von Hildebrand with Doms on the ends of marriage. In the academic year 1942/3 he taught a course on the sacraments that included marriage. In the September 1942 issue of *Theological Studies*, which included one of Lonergan's 'Gratia Operations' articles, John Ford also published an article entitled 'Marriage, Its Meaning and Purpose' that centrally was a critique of Doms' book *The Meaning of Marriage*. Traditional Catholic teaching held that there are three ends in marriage: procreation and education of children, healing from concupiscence, and mutual help. It firmly emphasized that procreation is the primary end. Doms took issue with this, suggesting that this terminology be dropped from the debate. Ford critiqued Doms, but in doing so could not help raising questions about the relation between the primary and secondary ends of marriage.

In this way, as he was articulating his economic insights, Lonergan found himself challenged and stimulated by the problem of explaining the relation between the different ends of marriage. He invited his class to study on their own the positive part on marriage in the moral books, a proposal that was not universally welcome. He then concentrated on the ideas that appeared in his speculative essay 'Finality, Love, Marriage,' published in the December 1943 issue of *Theological Studies* and presented as a discussion paper. This is, I believe, one of Lonergan's most visionary pieces of writing, opening up a cosmic and interpersonal religious horizon that in ways would influence but in other ways take us beyond the horizon of *Insight*.

The paper opens with some wide-ranging reflections on the question of ends or 'finality.' The latter, a term with a background in Bergson, involves the response of appetites to motives or of processes to terms. By means of it Lonergan hoped to establish a cosmic framework within which the question of the relation of the different ends could be explored. The concept of finality assumed that the universe is hierarchical, embracing the levels or grades of physics, chemistry, biology, human psychology, and grace. Mainstream scholastic thought had distinguished between horizontal finality, which occurs on a particular level of being, and the absolute finality of every level to its creator and final destiny. Each level has its defining essence, the resulting universe being a series of horizontal strata or levels.[34] In this sense 'levels' is one of the central categories of the essay. The manner in which oxygen combines to form compounds, in which biological organisms reproduce, and in which the mind solves its problems are illustrations of horizontal finality on the different levels.

What has not been clearly examined in the tradition, but is central in modern science, is what Lonergan terms 'vertical finality.' This is the finality that relates processes on one level or grade of being to those on another:

> So it is most conspicuous to one who looks at the universe with the eyes of modern science, who sees sub-atoms uniting into atoms, atoms into compounds, compounds into organisms, who finds in the patterns of genes in reproductive cells shifting, *ut in minori parte*, to give organic evolution within limited ranges, who attributes the rise of cultures and civilizations to the interplay of human plurality, who observes that only when and where the higher rational culture emerged did God acknowledge the fullness of time permitting the Word to become flesh.[35]

As well as the horizontal manner in which oxygen forms compounds, there is also the vertical manner in which it can work within the respiratory system of a higher life form. In this manner it contributes to and sustains that higher life form and its goals.

The influence of Shull, whom Lonergan read and footnoted in the essay, is evident in the following quotation. On page 281 of his brilliantly clear textbook *Evolution*, we find Shull wondering:

> Assuming that once upon a time the elements did not exist (which the psychologist McDougall, in discussing emergent evolution, declines to admit), the electrons and protons must have come together in new relations which resulted in the elements. The properties of these elements were wholly different from those of the component charged particles; their origin was an example of emergence. More complicated illustrations have likewise been used. Proteins, or perhaps better, their properties, emerged out of carbon, hydrogen, oxygen, nitrogen, sulphur and phosphorus, none of

which had any of the qualities of proteins. Protoplasm with the quality of life emerged out of proteins, carbohydrates, fats, salts, enzymes and water, with properties which none of the components had before they entered into the new relation. Sentience emerged from new relations within living protoplasm, and mind emerged from sentience.[36]

There was a time when chemical elements, sentience, and mind did not exist. In order for them to come into existence, there must have occurred some form of emergence. This poses the question, what is new in emergences? – a question that weaves its way through Lonergan's thought. Shull's response was: new relations. His series of emergences are instances of vertical finality. They in turn pose the question of the manner of the relation between the horizontal and vertical processes.

Lonergan attempts to explain the relation between horizontal and vertical finality in terms of four properties: instrumental, dispositive, material, and obediential. By 'instrumental' he refers to the many acts of the chisel of the sculptor by means of which the statue is generated. By 'dispositive finality' he means that a concrete plurality of acts on one level may be dispositive to a higher end in the same agent. He offers by way of illustration 'the many sensitive experiences of research [that] lead to the act of understanding that is scientific discovery.'[37] An extremely prophetic remark, this provides a first glimpse of a possible insight into the explanation of vertical emergences that he will offer in *Insight*. The levels in the universe are not autonomous; the higher emerge from and interact with the lower. Vertical finality results, not from isolated single incidences or acts on the lower levels, but from an accidental conjunction of a concrete plurality.

It is within this analysis of horizontal and vertical finality that the term 'levels,' makes its entry in his thought. Central is the sense of different levels of reality or of life. The universe for him 'is not an aggregate of isolated objects hierarchically arranged on isolated levels, but a dynamic whole in which instrumentally, dispositively, materially, obedientially, one level of being or activity subserves another.'[38] There is involved an upthrust to the higher from the lower levels, God being the divine artisan who works through the medium of both horizontal and vertical finality in this hierarchical universe. Once we acknowledge both horizontal and vertical finality on each level, the question as to the manner of their relation arises. Lonergan's insight is that while horizontal ends might be more essential, vertical ends are more excellent. Can such an insight illuminate the relation between the different ends of marriage? Might the horizontal goals of procreation be more essential but the vertical personalist goals more excellent?

Lonergan now has to explain how love relates to his considerations of horizontal and vertical finality. Love is introduced as a basic form of appetition and as the first principle of a process. It is the ground of union of different subjects both in their pursuit of a common end and in its consummation.[39] It is thus subject to the general laws of finality, although there is no specification at this point of the end.

Many appetites are involved in love: hunger for food, maternal instinct for the good of the child, rational appetite for the reasonable good. Because of tensions between the multiplicity, disorder can result. The unreasonable is what suits mistaken self-love. The fundamental opposition is not between egoism and altruism, but virtue and vice. Only by being attuned correctly to the absolute good that is God will egoism and altruism be transcended and virtue loved. Selfishness stands in a dialectical relationship with love. There follows a passage right out of his Rome writings on dialectic, but this time focused on the family within a social and historical context of solidarity in either sin or grace. If, initially, failures in the field of love are recognized as failures and repented, there can come a time when they are not repented but rather rationalized. There results a solidarity in sin and unloving with a 'dialectical descent deforming knowledge and perverting will,' and a counter solidarity in grace.[40]

As through the dialectic love can find itself caught in a descent, so also through grace it can find itself involved in an ascent. The nature of that ascent, involving the relationship between love and finality in human relations, is given in a passage that can only be quoted:

> He can love God only in an ascent through participated to absolute excellence. Thus love of others is proof of love of God ... Hatred of others is proof of hatred of God ... Now towards this high goal of charity it is no small beginning in the weak and imperfect heart of fallen man to be startled by a beauty that shifts the centre of appetition out of self; and such a shift is effected on the level of sensitive spontaneity by *erôs* leaping in through delighted eyes and establishing itself as unrest in absence and an imperious demand for company. Next, company may reveal deeper qualities of mind and character to shift again the centre from the merely organistic tendencies of nature to the rational level of friendship with its enduring basis in the excellence of a good person. Finally, grace inserts into charity the love that nature gives and reason approves. Thus we have a dispositive upward tendency from *erôs* to friendship, and from friendship to a special order of charity.[41]

Love, in its dialectical ascent from *erôs* through friendship to charity, involves the interplay of both horizontal and vertical finality.

Husband and wife are made for one another by their differing sexuality. Their coming together through sexual attraction also involves the full realization of the other self, a distinctive use of the term 'self' from what we find in *Insight*.[42] On the level of spontaneity and reason marriage is the full expression of union with another self. Active love seeks its own self-perpetuation and the formation of a community of friendship and mutual support. The encyclical *Castii Conubii*, for Lonergan, speaks of a process of development through conjugal love to the very summit of Christian perfection. In this context marriage is to be understood 'not strictly as an institution for the proper rearing of children, but broadly as two lives at one till death, lived in intimacy, lived in pursuit of a common goal.'[43] This process itself is to be considered an end of Christian marriage.

Lonergan next analyses love into three levels: the appetitive, a level lower than reason; the level of reason; and the level of grace.[44] The three levels are realized in the living of the one subject, the lower disposing itself to the higher and the higher perfecting the lower. The hierarchy of ends in marriage are a special case of the most general ends of the human person:

> Corresponding to the three human ends – life, the good life, and eternal life – are three levels of human activity: there is the level of 'nature' understood in the current restricted sense of physical, vital, sensitive spontaneity; there is the level of reason and rational appetite; and there is the level of divine grace.[45]

In this context 'levels' refers to levels of life, 'level of reason' to the life of the mind as a whole. It is within this framework of different levels of life and their horizontal, vertical, and absolute finality that Lonergan explores the different ends of the marriage relationship.

Within the marriage context Lonergan holds that there is a natural, vital, organistic, sensitive spontaneity operative between the masculine and feminine whose horizontal goal is the production of offspring. Through it there occurs the automatic correlation of the activities of the many individuals within the family unit. Equally, there is a level of intellect and reason whose spontaneous tendency within the interhuman is the pursuit of friendship and commitment. For his analysis of friendship Lonergan draws largely on Aristotle, for whom friendship could be based on utility, pleasure, or the pursuit of the good of the other in a life of virtue. But the pursuit of friendship of the last type is always a struggle with selfishness and egoism. And so it is that there is a need for our natural desire for friendship and intimacy to be augmented by the infused desire for charity and the life of grace.

In the December 1944 issue of *Theological Studies* John C. Ford SJ included his usual review of notes on moral theology for the year. On page

530 he referred to the discussion of Doms' views on the ends of marriage and to Lonergan's response in 'Finality, Love, Marriage.' Lonergan's paper, he remarked, does not desert the traditional terminology on ends. Being speculative, it explores them in terms of more and less essential ends and the somewhat unusual terminology of 'vertical and horizontal finality.'

According to Crowe, some years later Lonergan urged him to read Ford's comments, which Lonergan considered a 'stricture,' in order to make up his own mind. Ford recommends Lonergan's article to those studying the issue, and goes on to point out that the Holy Office has reasserted in the traditional terminology the essential subordination of the secondary ends to the primary end of marriage. In English translation, the Latin text, reprinted on page 531 by Ford, concluded:

> The Fathers of this Supreme Congregation who are chosen to protect matters of faith and morals, in a plenary session held on Wednesday 29 March 1944 considered the proposition put to them: 'Can the opinion of some recent authors be admitted who either deny that the primary end of matrimony is the generation of off-spring and their education, or teach that the secondary ends are not essentially subordinated to the primary end but are an equal principle and independent.' We reply, negative.

The decree 'explains' why Lonergan dropped the subject:

> I never went back to the controversy centred on the primary and secondary ends of marriage. Anyone can understand that in an agricultural society, the procreation and education of children is extremely important because it means cheap labour. In the eighteenth century, agriculture was the key thing in the economy. When you get into the complexities of modern life and modern marriage, you're living in a different world and the success of agriculture is not a primary interest of the marriage.[46]

After this, Lonergan has stated, he became more interested in the *Verbum* articles.

There remained the unfinished business of the defence of his dissertation on Aquinas. Because of the war, his thesis could not be defended in Rome. The authorities were anxious that it be completed and his academic status established. By agreement, on 6 June 1943 he was examined by Bleau, Bouvier, Brunet, and Pellard of his own faculty in Montreal. For this defence he prepared an elaborate set of notes running to twenty-two pages of single-spaced typing. After an introduction, they described the topic of the dissertation and the state of the question when Aquinas began writing. This was followed by an account of the principal stages in the evolution of his thought on divine providence, on the principal elements in the theory of operation, and the main stages in the evolution of the notion of liberty. An account the development of his thought on both habitual and actual grace as operative and cooperative brought into focus the aim of the dissertation, with its origin in Boyer's to him puzzling remark on the text in the *Summa*. His aggregate mark turned out to be a nine, Bleau's eight being the lowest awarded him. To meet the publication requirement in December 1946 he forwarded to the Gregorian the required number of offprints of the final article from *Theological Studies*. The degree was awarded in the year 1946–7.

A significant stage in Lonergan's economic quest was reached with the completion of a typescript in 1944 entitled 'An Essay in Circulation Analysis.' There is evidence in it of further work in progress, of the self-correcting process of learning and a related rewriting of the 1942 text. Keynes and Schumpeter are mentioned, as well as the cycles associated with Juggler, Kitchin, and Kondratieff and a theory of history.[47] Lonergan, like Marx, clearly wished his economics to be understood in a historical context. Schumpeter's *Business Cycles*, subtitled 'A Theoretical, Historical, and Statistical Analysis of the Capitalist Process,' may be significant here. His headings include 'How Economics Generates Evolution' and 'The Contours of Economic Evolution,' and in these sections he develops his cycle theory. He insists that the economic order is part of the evolutionary process and raises questions about the occurrence of economic cycles in history. Whether, after recently reading Shull on emergent evolution, Lonergan took Schumpeter's work as a signpost on his road to emergent probability is an open and important question.

In the 1944 text, references to politics, to democracy and its opponents, or to the economic liberation of culture are dropped, the terms 'democracy' and 'culture' being absent from the index of *CWL 15 Circulation Analysis*. The problem is narrowed down to the technical, mechanical issue as set forth in the 1942 text that has to be overcome in order to liberate culture. The account of the production process is more technically developed and nuanced. The vocabulary of an emergent standard of living is evidence of Lonergan's growing awareness of emergent process but not yet emergent probability.[48] Primary and secondary rhythms give way to the basic and surplus stages in the production process. In Heythrop he was introduced by O'Hara to the relations from projective geometry of point to line, plane, and surface. He now draws on them to suggest the multiplier relations between the basic and surplus stages of production in an economy.[49] He will use, throughout, Hilbert's technique of implicit definition. Few descriptive definitions are offered. He concentrates, relentlessly, on working out in the most general terms possible the relations between production, exchange, and finance.

What has not changed in the 1944 text is his fundamental insight into the possibility of a pure cycle of the production process:

> The (wave or) cycle that is inherent in the very nature of a long-term acceleration of the productive process is not to be confused with the familiar trade cycle. The latter is a succession of booms and slumps, of positive and then negative accelerations of the process. But the cycle with which we are here concerned is a pure cycle. It includes no slump, no negative acceleration. It is entirely a forward movement.[50]

It is Lonergan's contention that with correct financial management such a pure cycle can be realized.

Between 1930 and 1944 Lonergan devoted a great deal of his time to the problem of mastering the rhythms of an economy. His analysis opened up the possibility of defining the ethical aims of an economy in terms of progressively raising the standard of living of the entire community. He found, to his disappointment, that economists at the time could make no sense of his account.[51] Given the depth of his commitment to the problem, he must have been severely disappointed by the response. Perhaps he recognized at the time that circumstances were not favourable, and to an extent this softened the blow. The road was not taken: soon his desires would be redirected elsewhere.

8

Insights into Phantasms as the Origins of Words

Sometime during the autumn semester of 1935, while taking Leeming's course, Lonergan made a breakthrough, had what amounted to an intellectual conversion, on the cognitional question. Involved was a new understanding of the relation between judgment (Augustine's *veritas*) and what exists, Aquinas' *esse*. If it is through our understanding that we grasp the what or why or nature of a thing, it is through our judgment that we come to know that it exists. For the next eight years Lonergan's writings are largely silent on matters that are directly cognitional.[1] To an extent this can be understood in terms of existential issues in his life. He was, unexpectedly, diverted from philosophy to theology. This intimated a quite different future from what he had had in mind throughout the early 1930s. Because of this he found himself writing a thesis, not on philosophy, but on the theology of grace and freedom. The outbreak of the war resulted in his teaching assignment being changed from Rome to Montreal. It took time to assimilate these zigzags in his life. In Montreal he had to publish and defend his dissertation while finding himself drawn into questions about the economic cycle and the ends of marriage.

As his passion for the economic problem ran its course, the cognitional problem made its re-entry. It was, he admitted, Hoenen's essays, published in 1933 and 1938, that brought him back to it:

> Later (1938) he returned to the topic, arguing first that Scholastic philosophy was in need of a theory of geometrical knowledge, and secondly producing various geometrical illustrations such as the Moebius strip that fitted in very well with his view that not only terms but also nexus were abstracted from phantasm. So about 1943

I began collecting materials for an account of Aquinas' views on understanding and the inner word ... The basic point was that Aquinas attributed the key role in cognitional theory not to inner words, concepts, but to acts of understanding. Hoenen's point that intellect abstracted both terms and nexus from the phantasm was regarded as Scotist language, both terms and nexus belong to the conceptual order; what Aristotle and Aquinas held was that intellect abstracted from phantasm a preconceptual form or species of *quod quid erat esse*, whence both terms and nexus were inwardly spoken.[2]

Hoenen's second article, entitled 'On the Scholastic Philosophy of Geometrical Knowledge,' explored the possibility that even the most exact and abstract mathematical concepts could arise from our senses and imagination. Neither of these faculties perceives points without extension, and only with great difficulty can we identify the point at which three fine lines intersect. A draughtsman can draw a fine line ten units long, each unit of length being marked, yet none of those units are exactly equal. Hoenen helped Lonergan to appreciate that it is through *supposing* the otherwise bumpy image of a cartwheel is exactly round that mathematical insights grasp necessity and impossibility.

In their analysis of the concept of numbers, counting, and the continuum, mathematicians pose questions such as, what fraction comes after $1/3000$ or what number comes after the square root of two? Hoenen wonders how mathematicians get from inexactly drawn lines and points to mathematical questions of such exactitude. Because of that exactitude, Poincaré's analysis of intuitions of the senses, imagination, induction, and pure number was not convincing.[3] Strangely, Hoenen does not address Cantor's famous proof, with its diagonal image, that the infinite decimals or real numbers cannot be counted. In an unpublished passage from the original autograph of *Insight* Lonergan poses the question, how many points are there on a straight line one inch long? Drawing on Cantor's proof, he concludes that there is no answer. His insight into that mistaken expectation became for Lonergan an illustration of an inverse insight, the details of which he removed from the book just prior to publication.[4]

In his final paper, 'On the Origin of Necessity in Geometry,' Hoenen wondered how it can be proved that of necessity Plato's number 5,040 can be divided in no more and no fewer than fifty-nine ways. He considers mathematical approaches as well as simply empirically playing with 5,040 pebbles.[5] Further questions follow: can it be proved that of necessity there are twenty-five prime numbers below one hundred, or that $7 + 5 = 12$ follows of necessity from the first principles of arithmetic? The latter, drawing on Leibnitz's definition of the integers, influences the section on the homogeneous expansion in chapter 1 of *Insight*.

For Hoenen, 'The ball is white' is an example of a material nexus; 'The ball is round,' 'the line is divisible,' '5040 can be divided into two, three, etc.,' are examples of a formal nexus. The nexus is mastered by means of intuitions yielding necessary conclusions: 'In each of these examples we intuitively grasp the necessity of the nexus between the subject and the predicate of the judgment by which we affirm; it is necessarily so.'[6] Hoenen distinguishes intuitions of the senses and the imagination from those of the intellect, which intuits the nexus between the terms and their relations. In general, it is implied that intuition is related to the image or phantasm. When Lonergan was later questioned about his attitude to the word 'intuition' he replied: 'for me, intuition is the same as seeing and that is why I am against the use of the word.'[7] In line with this, after reading Hoenen's articles Lonergan began to focus on the preconceptual nature of understanding rather than intuition as the source of conceptualization.[8]

Hoenen's three articles had a twofold impact on Lonergan. The first, with its assembly of texts from Aquinas, made it clear that his possible contribution to the problem of knowledge merited study. What was provoking and stimulating about the second and third was the manner in which they attempted to explore new problems in mathematical knowledge by drawing on the old insights of Aquinas.

The force of circumstances of Lonergan's life, beginning with his awakening to the problem of knowledge in 1926, brought him at the relatively late age of thirty-eight to the decision to study what Aquinas had to offer on cognitional theory. One of the major decisions he would make for himself in his life, it would result in the six years of intensive research involved in authoring the *Verbum* articles, two years longer than it took to compose *Insight*.[9] He was now firmly on the path of his true agenda.

His interest reawakened, in 1943 Lonergan began his study, which he entitled 'The Concept of *Verbum* in the Writings of St. Thomas Aquinas.'[10] Centrally it involved an analysis of the relation between what the scholastics called *verbum mentis*, which can be of two kinds, and understanding or insight. By a first kind of *verbum mentis* is meant concepts, definitions, propositions, objects of thought: the meaning of the written or spoken linguistic expression of the concepts, definitions, or propositions. Without *verbum mentis* such expressions are so many arbitrary sounds or shapes. Concepts or definitions such as those of the triangle, number, mass, element, species, human nature, friendship, and even love do not come to exist in our minds uncaused. There was a time before which we could not think the concept or definition of DNA. More generally, in all unsolved problems we cannot yet think or say a solution. The *Verbum* articles will explore the manner in which, through understanding, we make the transition from the unthinkable to the thinkable and sayable.

By a second and distinct kind of *verbum mentis* is meant judgment: the meaning in whatever language of the written or spoken words 'yes, it is so' or 'no, it is not.' Again, without the *verbum mentis* of assent such linguistic expressions are just so many arbitrary sounds or shapes, but not without their social significance.

Hoenen's assembled texts in his 1933 article inspired Lonergan to ask, what exactly did Aquinas have to offer on the question of the origins of knowledge in sense data? His experience with Leeming in 1935 opened up the question about Aquinas' understanding of the distinctive properties of judgment. Lonergan would now find himself drawn into questions about how Aquinas' thought developed on the distinction and relation between the *verbum*, understanding, and judgment. That development ran from the *Sentences* (1256), where Aquinas had not yet distinguished concepts and understanding, through the brilliant treatment in the *De Veritate* (1259–63) where he had, to the detailed treatment in the *Contra Gentiles* (1259–64) and the mastery in the *Summa* (1266f).[11] Lonergan would also find himself drawn into metaphysical questions about the agenthood and patienthood of mental acts as well as the influence of Trinitarian theology on the philosophy of mind. In his researches, his desire will awaken to each of these themes and follow them through the texts of Aquinas. The author of the *Verbum* articles came to desire to understand this dynamic development in Aquinas.

As with his doctoral thesis, Lonergan began by reading the texts and creating a still extant card index system of significant terms. A biographical passage in *Insight* indicates what was involved:

> To penetrate the mind of a medieval thinker is to go beyond his
> words and phrases. It is to effect an advance in depth that is propor-
> tionate to the broadening influence of historical research. It is to
> grasp questions as once they were grasped. It is to take the *Opera
> Omnia* of such a writer as St.Thomas Aquinas and to follow through
> successive works the variations and developments of his views. It is to
> study the concomitance of such variations and developments and to
> arrive at a grasp of their motives and causes. It is to discover for
> oneself that the intellect of Aquinas, more rapidly on some points,
> more slowly on others, reached a position of dynamic equilibrium
> without ever ceasing to drive towards fuller and more nuanced
> synthesis, without ever halting complacently in some finished mental

edifice, as though his mind had become dull, or his brain exhausted, or his judgment had lapsed into the error of those that forget man to be potency in the realm of intelligence.[12]

Although focused on Aquinas, the quote also draws back the veil on the kind of personal experience involved in Lonergan's six-year encounter. Significant is the element of mastering a development, of spontaneously employing a genetic method.

Behind the *Verbum* articles was an intense intellectual experience of engaging with the mind and works of a classical author on a particular problem over a long period of time. Those who have had a parallel experience of trying to master in depth an equivalent problem in the thought of a major writer will recognize in it the kind of experience involved. It was an exercise that required great discipline, not least in that it involved leaving behind the apparently more pressing and exciting questions of economics and history. During this time his mind would journey in the desert. The insights sought by his awakened intellectual desire would only be attained after a long and patient non-linear detective-like inquiry. He would return from the desert quite transformed by the experience.

Early Work on *Verbum* – Insight into Phantasm

Pages 1, 16–22, 60–77 (which may be a distinct draft), and 90–102 of early work on the *Verbum* articles are extant.[13] On page 20, in addition to three other uses of the word 'insight,' we read: 'Thirdly, the first terminus in this intellectual drive is insight into phantasm.' Reminiscent of Aristotle's remarks on thinking the forms in the images, it is the first known use in Lonergan's writings of the phrase, unique to him, 'insight into phantasm.'[14] For Aristotle the phantasms or images – diagrams or even, it might be added, word patterns and the like – serve as though they were contents of perception, and thought cannot take place without them.

Lonergan's choice of the word 'insight,' a Middle English word possibly of Scandinavian and Low German origins, in contrast with the *intuitio* of Late Latin, is hugely significant.[15] It is not a word to be found in Aristotle, Aquinas, or the scholastic tradition, but it does occur frequently in the writings of Kant, in particular his *Critique of Pure Reason.* In its selection and conjunction with 'into phantasm,' a use original to him, Lonergan is defining his position on understanding in opposition to both Kant and the scholastic tradition. Contra that tradition, understanding is not to be confused with intuition. For Lonergan it rises above the level of the senses and the imagination. At the same time, to hold that insights are always into something in the images or phantasms asserts that there is an interactive relation between the understanding and the imagination that can never be severed. That the content of what we imagine could be a partial cause of our understanding is contrary to Kant's view of their relation. The use of 'insight into phantasm' is suggestive of a new development in Lonergan's intellectual quest. The question about the relation between the understanding and the imagination – in particular about what, precisely, insights are into in phantasms – is now up. The related quote from Aristotle's *De Anima* on the title page of *Insight* suggests that in a sense Lonergan sees that whole work as an opening up and exploration of the relation.

The second terminus of thought is the critical understanding that necessitates and grounds judgment. The third terminus is the contemplative understanding that regards reality through the medium of intelligible truth. The remaining uses of 'insight' on the page are in the sentence:

> Fourthly, intellect as act is insight, critical understanding, contemplative understanding; but intellect as a process through inquiry to insight, from insight to critical understanding, from critical to contemplative understanding is reason, rational consciousness, thought, consideration, method, logic, dialectic – any name will do, as long as one grasps the idea of process from one act of intellect to another.[16]

Insight into phantasm is intellect in act. But there is also intellect as process, as a process through inquiry to insight, and from insight to critical understanding and judgment. Before Lonergan thought of knowing as a structure, he thought of it as a process. Significant is the fact that he here uses the term 'rational consciousness' to refer to that process in its totality. The concept of being, of what is, is related to the teleological anticipation of the judgment.

Judgment, Realism, *Compositio*

Pages 16–22, employing an earlier terminology, deal with judgment. In virtue of a direct insight all we can say is that 'it may be so.'[17] The activity of defining is followed by the critical activity of evaluation involving such elements as resolution into principles, into the data of sense, or, in the case of Euclidean geometry, into the imagination. There follows a reflex act of understanding that apprehends the evidence as a whole and as a sufficient ground for the anticipated judgment. From this critical act of understanding will proceed the rational utterance of assent, the yes or no, the affirmation or negation. The judgment stands to question or hypothesis or definition as act to potency. Judgments can be absolute or modal, probable or possible. Between the initial infinite potentiality of inquiry that ranges without bounds, what Lonergan would later term the 'pure desire to know,' and the ultimate unqualified determination, the gap is absolute.

A judgment is true because a reflex act of critical understanding sees a necessary consequence linking first principles of thought or data of sense and of internal experience (imagination) to the projected judgment. The ultimate validation of judgment is not something we know, but something that we are. There is something in us that is in inner harmony with the ground of the universe and is attuned to the absolute of truth. The essence of truth lies in the nature of its emergence in us, in its procession from the infinite potentiality of unbounded inquiry: 'It spans an infinite gap, consciously, intelligibly, rationally, and there is no possibility of assigning any meaning to the term, merely subjective, except by setting that term in opposition to what spans an infinite gap.' Judgment, promoted by the infinite potential of unbounded inquiry, bridges the gap between the mind and the world.

Echoing his intellectual conversion of 1935, on page 19 Lonergan writes; 'In true judgment, as in a medium, we contemplate reality.' In itself the real is prior to the true. But for us the true is prior to the real because we can only know reality as reality through the medium of judgment:

> Realism is immediate, not by a process of self-stultification that supposes a comparison between the real as known and the real as unknown, not by sheer force of assertion that realism is obvious and anything else is idealism or materialism, but because we know that the real cannot be other than what is affirmed in true judgment. To posit any other as real is to posit the unknowable as the real – and that is gratuitous nonsense – and further it is to posit the impossible as the real, for true judgment can affirm anything possible.[18]

The intellect, he continues, is not to be thought of as a principle of empirical knowledge by means of which 'we know without knowing why but merely as a matter of brute fact.' Through the senses and instincts we 'know' without knowing why. Does this shed light on his use of the term 'facts' in the Keeler essay on Newman? Lonergan is clearly separating off the intellect proper from the senses, imagination, and instinct. The active principle of intellect is inquiry, the drive to know causes. Agreeing with Aquinas, he holds that it can only be satisfied by the vision of God, the first and last cause of all.

Pages 68 to 75 and 77, also, dealing with judgment, are clearly an earlier draft of the opening section of the second *Verbum* article. It is in the *compositio et divisio* of Aristotle that Aquinas recognized how truth and falsity are to be found. Our knowledge begins with sense. It develops through understanding and finds its perfection in judgment. The reasoning that leads up to an insight has to be distinguished from the insight itself. Similarly, an insight has to be distinguished from a concept. In the same way, preparatory thinking has to be distinguished from the assent of judgment.

There are two meanings of the word 'composition.' Firstly, there is the ontological composition of the real thing, of form in matter or of accidents in a substance. Secondly, there is the conceptual composition of true judgment, which affirms and is caused by the ontological composition. That causation is mediated by our senses, memory, cogitation, phantasms, our insights and reasoning. Reasoning plays a twofold role. It helps us to understand, but it also prepares the way for a particular understanding that is the coalescence into a particular view of previously distinct insights. There follows a third meaning of 'composition,' distinct from the previous two, 'an intellectual composition in developing understanding.'[19] When Aristotle discussed the twofold operation of the intellect in the *De Anima*, the composition and division that was foremost in his mind was, for Lonergan, that of developing understanding.

Compounded insights are not yet an assent. Judgment can follow both simple and compound insights. Its ground is neither of these, but what Lonergan now names a 'critical act of understanding.' Later renamed by him a 'reflective act,' this stands to judgment as Newman's illative sense stands to Newman's assent. He argues that Aquinas' acknowledgment of this critical act is implicit rather than explicit in his writings.

Judgment is constituted by a content, a true and a false. But it is also an act of a subject that involves a personal commitment. Judgment as assent is divided into scientific certitude, opinion, and belief. The different kinds of assent are related to motives and grounds. These come into play in the process of assembling and weighing the evidence. Aquinas refers to this activity, which is prior to judgment and the cause of it, as a *resolution in principia*. If a conclusion clearly follows from principles, then to deny that conclusion would result in intellectual suicide. The resolution does not just involve principles, but also concrete sensible data.

So Lonergan concludes that Aquinas was fully aware that a marshalling and weighing of all of the relevant evidence precedes the act of judgment. But precisely what does this mean? To grasp a necessary nexus between the evidence and the anticipated judgment involves a reflective act of understanding. It is a critical act in the sense that a failure to grasp the necessity of the judgment will demand that judgment be withheld. It is distinct from the act of assent.

Cajetan's Intellectual Conversion

The final part of the fragment, running through pages 90–102, addresses issues behind the various theories of *verbum* to be found in Scotus, Cajetan, John of St Thomas, and Aquinas, all of whom are named in the final *Verbum* article. It begins in the middle of a critique of Scotus by Cajetan, the opening pages of which are unfortunately missing. In listing opinions on the nature of the beatific vision, Cajetan names a common Scotist opinion on the cooperation of the faculty and the object in producing the act, which he himself once held, taught, and even included in his writings. To break out of his Scotism Cajetan had to undergo an intellectual conversion, one of the earliest occurrences of the phrase in Lonergan's writings. Two things were involved.

Firstly, Cajetan had to grasp the true nature of the Aristotelian theory of knowledge by identity. This, Lonergan adds, had its origin in the *Physics*, which considered motion in the agent as action, in the patient as passion, the one act uniting the agent and patient. An extension of this analysis leads to the conclusion that the intelligible in act is the intellect in act. In immaterial reception the agent acts by its form, reproducing not its matter but form. The actuation of the *intellectus* by the *intellectum* does not yield a third; rather, the *intellectus* becomes the *intellectum*. Hence Aristotle's affirmation that '*anima est quodammodo omnia.*' [20]

Turning to the text of Aristotle's *De Anima*, we find: 'The thinking part of the soul must therefore be, while impassible, capable of receiving the form of an object; that is must be potentially identical in character with its object without being the object ... Actual knowledge is identical with its object.'[21] Learning is a matter of becoming each of the possible objects involved in the exercises. The suggestion is that the mind or understanding must be such that it can be acted on and receive the form of what it understands. When in the given sensible presentations we understand the relations that constitute a circle, the law of gravity, DNA, or the plot in a life, the mind is acted on by those intelligible qualities of what it understands. The implications of this doctrine for Lonergan's thesis of insight into phantasm, especially on what it receives from the phantasm and on the implied passive nature of the insight, are substantial.

Secondly, Cajetan had to master Aquinas on knowledge by intentionality because of different ways in which the knower can relate to the known. Ontologically, as is the case with God who knows all things by what he is, the knower may in fact be the known. For humans, knowledge of our own being is not sufficient to generate knowledge of the other. There is needed a species: 'Species are intentional reality, the reality of the known in a knower who is not knowing in virtue of his own natural, ontological perfection.'[22] Cajetan, for Lonergan, had grasped the theorems of both intentionality and immaterial identity, points that will surface in the second *Verbum* article. Still on page 93, Lonergan is critical of Cajetan for thinking out the analogy of being 'without recalling the twofold *verbum* of definition regarding *natura rei* and judgment regarding *esse rei.*'

Despite acknowledging that it would be anachronistic to find an epistemologist in Cajetan, on pages 93–5 Lonergan is reading Cajetan, Scotus, and John of St Thomas from the standpoint of their tacit epistemology. This he distinguished from gnoseology: 'For the practical role of epistemology is not to inquire into mind as mind but to bring my mind to a grasp of the manner in which really I do know, to purge it from illusions about knowledge that too easily I may entertain.'[23] His comment that a metaphysical account of knowledge is not helpful links with his conclusion to the first *Verbum* article on the cognitional rather than the metaphysical as the starting point. Still, in this passage the gnoseological, epistemological, and metaphysical make an early entry.

Three final themes play out in the concluding pages of the fragment. Firstly, there is the genesis of a recognition of the theme of animal knowledge and realism. The animal mentality deals with immediate and vital objects rather than with real things. This, Lonergan considers, 'may do for animal faith, but it hardly does justice to the *verbum* of rational consciousness, or Cajetan himself.'[24] There follows a puzzling remark: 'For common sense knowing is identical with knowing an object, contacting an object, being in the presence of an object, being confronted with an object, standing opposite an object.'[25] Is he equating common sense with animal knowledge or referring to a common-sense notion of cognition? The problem of the two realisms was being thought out.

Secondly, running through the epistemological considerations is the question of the subject and object of knowledge

Thirdly, there was his contrast of Scotus and John of St Thomas on the origin of the *verbum*. Does it precede, or not, insight into phantasm? Lonergan's conclusion on this point is central to his entire project and to the reading of the articles: 'According to the interpretation we wish to put forward the *verbum* is an act of rational consciousness proceeding from an act of understanding.'[26] Miss this in the *Verbum* articles and you have missed everything. To show that in Aquinas the *verbum*, that is to say the definition, proposition, or thought, is the product and expression of what insight has apprehended in the phantasm, and is caused by such insight, is the main motivation behind the articles. Understanding plays a causal role in the thoughts we think and in the language we use to express them.

Of the six uses of 'rational consciousness,' the following best captures his meaning:

Secondly, there is the point that the Thomist *verbum* is an act of rational consciousness; for it is a definition or a judgment; both are acts of rational consciousness; both suppose and proceed from understanding.'[27]

Rational consciousness here includes both insight into phantasm and reflection leading to judgment. The term 'level' occurs once in the draft text in a non-cognitional context.

On 7 May 1945, as Lonergan was engaged in this exercise of recovery, Germany surrendered unconditionally. Through the newspapers the tragic details of the concentration camps now became public. The Japanese surrender would follow shortly, on 14 August, but not before atom bombs were dropped on Hiroshima and Nagasaki. After the political settlements worked out between Churchill, Roosevelt, and Stalin at Potsdam and Yalta, the map of Europe was yet again redrawn, leaving it with a difficult legacy.

At the end of May in Wildenstein Castle above the now-occupied Freiburg, Heidegger was holding a seminar on Kant's *Critique of Pure Reason*, medieval history, and above all, Hölderlin. It concluded on 24 June with a party at a time when the French authorities were preparing to requisition his house. Heidegger's denazification hearing began on 23 July, Jaspers drafting his famous letter at Christmas 1945. As a result the authorities resolved in January 1946 that Heidegger be deprived of his teaching licence for five years.

The reconstruction of Europe began and went forward on many levels, practical – the rebuilding of villages and towns and cities – as well as economic and cultural. A significant event at the time was Sartre's lecture 'Existentialism is a Humanism,' which he delivered in Paris on Monday, 29 October 1945, shortly after the publication of two volumes of his *Roads to Freedom*. The era of post-war existentialism had begun.[28] According to James Miller, existentialism was under attack from Catholicism for its indifference to morality and from communism for its nihilism. Its atheistic strand would find disapproval in *Humani Generis* in 1951. At the time, Sartre's lecture was of the form of a statement of defiance. The thought of Martin Heidegger began to be promoted by Sartre and other French intellectuals at a time when in Germany he was under a cloud for his Nazi sympathies.[29] A post-war consciousness was beginning to emerge.

In Cambridge, during the Micklemas and Lent terms of 1945–6, Wittgenstein, depressed by what he considered the darkness of the time, with considerable difficulty was finishing the text of his *Philosophical Investigations*. In August 1945 Rahner was called to Berchmann's College in Pullach, near Munster, where the Jesuits were again opening their theological faculties. He would return to the re-established Innsbruck faculty in 1948. In many cases the reconstruction went hand in hand with a forgetfulness of the immediate past, as illustrated in Steiner's strictures on Eliot's *Notes Towards a Definition of Culture*. Steiner was amazed that they contained no references to the war.[30] Similarly, Metz would criticize Rahner's theology for its forgetfulness of the war experience.

The Procession of a Word in God

From September to January 1945–6 Lonergan taught his first course on the Trinity. Clearly, his preparatory work for it overlapped with that on the *Verbum* articles. No notes of the course remain, but it is likely he based it on Bleau's 1942 Trinity codex, two personally annotated copies of which he retained. In them we find the traditional manual order of the questions:

What is the evidence for the doctrine of the Trinity in the New Testament?

What is the evidence for the doctrine of the Trinity in tradition?

What constitutes a theological understanding of processions, relations, and persons in God?

What does it mean to hold that the doctrine is a mystery?

A long history of theological speculation lies behind this ordering. The first two are concerned with the positive theology of the Trinity, which addresses the sources of the doctrine and related questions in the New Testament and the Patristic Era. Later Lonergan referred to this as the *via inventionis*, the way of discovery of the doctrine, and devoted the second of his two volumes on the Trinity to it.

Central in that historical movement is a significant shift in the meaning of the term 'Father' as a name of God. In the New Testament God, considered as a unity, whole and entire, is commonly referred to as Father. By the time of Augustine progress had been made in articulating the Trinitarian doctrine of the Christian God. That doctrine states that in God there are three divine persons, really distinct but equal in all ways, distinctively named Father, Son, and Holy Spirit. 'Father' now came to be used as the name of a particular divine person rather than as the name of the unity of God.

As the patristic era came to differentiate the Divine Persons, questions began to emerge about their origins and relations. In St John's Gospel the Son is also named the Word. This gave rise to a deep current of theological speculation concerned with the manner in which a Word or Son originates from an origin and source, the Father, in God. What precisely does the Word of God express? What sort of complex self-expression would be involved in God's Word? At this point Trinitarian theology, largely in

Augustine and Aquinas, found itself drawn into speculations about the cause and origin of mental words in our human minds. It was Lonergan's position that the later tradition, which, following Billot, held that we can understand the Trinitarian procession of a Word far more clearly in the imagination than in the intellect, had missed the whole point.[31]

In this movement Augustine played a pivotal role. Books X to XVI of his *On The Trinity* are concerned with human and divine words. Book XVI opens up the question of the Holy Spirit. In book XV, chapter x Augustine draws a distinction between the mouth of the body, which body utters sounds, and the mouth of the heart, which utters thoughts, inner words:

> Whoever, then, is able to understand a word, not only before it is uttered in sound, but also before the images of its sounds are considered in thought – for this it is which belongs to no tongue, to wit, of those which are called the tongues of nations, of which our Latin tongue is one – whoever, I say, is able to understand this, is able now to see through this glass and in this enigma some likeness of that Word of whom it is said, 'In the beginning was the Word, and the Word was with God, and the Word was God.' For of necessity, when we speak what is true, i.e. speak what we know, there is born from the knowledge itself which the memory retains, a word that is altogether of the same kind with the knowledge from which it is born. For the thought that is formed by the thing which we know, is the word which we speak in the heart; which word is neither Greek nor Latin, nor of any other tongue. But when it is needful to convey this to the knowledge of those to whom we speak, then some sign is assumed whereby to signify it.

The meaning of the thought or inner word of the mind finds its expression in the familiar sign dimension of language, from which it is strangely different. He goes on:

> For the word is then most like to the thing known, from which also its image is begotten, since the sight of thinking arises from the sight of knowledge.[32]

Augustine found a likeness in this linguistic process for the manner in which an eternal word proceeds from an origin in God, which it perfectly reflects.

Drawing on this movement, Aquinas will begin his later systematic treatment, not with God as Father, but with the unity of God. Within that unity there are the processions of a Word and of the Spirit of love. What is meant by the 'Word in God' clearly differs from human words and meaning in that it is unrestricted, infinite, all powerful and encompassing, complete, eternal, permanently mysterious, and beyond our understanding.

This proceeding Word in God, as the Prologue to St John's Gospel puts before us, is the creator of all things. For God things do not, as for us, first exist and then become known. They only exist because God knows them. Words and language are both communicative and efficient. As communicative they express what we have understood by way of a proposition or definition or a conversation. As well as communicating, they also make things. Before an existing house came to exist in fact it existed in thought and came into existence through such thought. The meaning of the universe as a whole as disclosed by science and history is the most complete expression available to us in which we glimpse something of the Word's mystery. Its meaning is a part of, within the meaning of, that Word.

For Bleau, etymologically and properly, a procession involves an ordered transition of a body from one place to another. Universally it designates the manner in which there is a certain order of one thing from another or after another. One thing emanates or originates from another, a ray of light from the sun, an operation from an operator, offspring from a parent, an artwork from an artist. As God has neither a body nor a past and future, obviously many kinds of temporal procession will not be candidates for the theological analogy. In some senses 'procession,' as normally understood with its inherent sense of temporality, is a rather inappropriate term for the theologians to have chosen.

In created reality theologians focus on two kinds of processions. Firstly, there is procession of an operation or the activation of a power or potency such as is involved when we understand and will. Secondly, there is the *processio operati*, the procession of the thing operated or as operated. In the former the operation consists in the actualizing of a power or virtue that otherwise remains in potency. When, existentially, we act courageously, there is the procession in us from potency to act of courage. When we understand or will something, there is the procession in us from potency to act of understanding and willing. Considered as *intelligere*, understanding is then a basic illustration of a *processio operationis*, the procession or emergence of an operation of a faculty. Considered as the *dicere* of the *verbum*, the understanding is the basic illustration of a *processio operati*, the procession of the thing operated.

God is omnipotent, but because there is no unactivated potency in God, the processions of an operation cannot provide us with a created likeness of processions in God.[33] When we understand something, according to Aquinas, there is a speaking, *dicere*, of an inner word of meaning. That inner word proceeds within the understanding and is a unique kind of created procession, *processio operati*. Aquinas singled this out as a created likeness of the procession of a Word in God.

As human words have origins in time, so the Word in God has an origin in eternity. As proceeding, it emanates from, proceeds from an origin, a source, a Father, God's understanding, which it perfectly reflects and expresses. As expressive, that eternal Word is distinct from but related to its origin. It is in this attribute of relationality of a word to its origin that theologians seek to understand, by way of analogy, the relations that define the divine persons. The Word, as proceeding, stands in a particular kind of relation with its source or origin. Theologians search for analogies in order to understand, in human ways, the revealed mysteries. One of the fundamental likenesses of God in us, in this respect, is the manner in which the meaning of language emerges in us from an origin, insight into phantasm, and in so doing reflects and gives expression to its origin.

9

Thought and Reality: Measuring the Kantian Bridge

In 1945 Loyola College in Montreal discontinued its adult education or extension courses. Given the interest in further education among teachers, the closure created a vacuum. Out of this felt need the Thomas More Institute was born. The challenge was to set up an intellectual ambience in which adults could pursue their questions in a community. With almost no time for planning, the institute began suddenly to operate in the autumn. Emmett Carter was its first president, Eric O'Connor the director of studies. With little notice, Lonergan was invited to lecture in the first year:

> I gave a course there on *Thought and Reality*. In September there were about forty-five students coming; at Easter there were still forty-one. It seemed clear that I had a marketable product not only because of the notable perseverance of the class but also from the interest that lit up their faces and from such more palpable incidents as a girl marching in at the beginning of class, giving my desk a resounding whack with her hand, and saying, 'I've got it.' Those that have struggled with *Insight* will know what she meant.[1]

The course title, the same as that of chapter 15 of Bradley's *Appearance and Reality*, points to a focal concern of his, the mind-world problem.[2] His later solution to the problem of the relation of thought to reality would provide him with the foundations of *Insight*. The experience of the course itself was also a significant event for him. In contrast with the negative responses to his 'Finality, Love, Marriage' and his work on economics, the very positive response he now received convinced him that there was a demand, a market, for a book such as *Insight*. Out of the historical accident that brought the Thomas More Institute into being, around Easter 1946, three years after the *Verbum* decision, he arrived at his major decision to compose *Insight*.[3]

The Animal and Human Mentalities and Realisms

Access to the contents of the course comes from notes taken by Martin O'Hara, a participant.[4] After posing the question, what is reality? Lonergan asks, Does a dog know real things or phenomena? His answer is: a few. Later he puts it that dogs know things non-intellectually. What on earth does he mean by this 'non-intellectual' knowledge and realism? It seems to resemble knowing a matter of brute fact rather than knowing the why of something of the *Verbum* fragment. There the measure of reality was judgment alone. Here there seems to be a suggestion of two realisms, an animal and a human. The notes now chart a movement from animal knowledge to real human knowledge, in which the process of cognition as a whole is involved.[5] This would include questioning, having insights, and making judgments. This process, and its related realism, is for Lonergan unique to the human species. But as well as being constituted by the attribute of thought, humans, he holds, also share in their own way an animal mentality and a related animal realism.

Because of the veiled manner in which he deals with it, this problem of the two realisms haunts interpreters of his thought. Its centrality in his journey is made clear in the following passage from *Insight*:

> For unless one breaks that duality in one's knowing, one doubts that understanding correctly is knowing. Under pressure from that doubt, either one will sink into a bog of knowing that is without understanding, or else one will cling to understanding but sacrifice knowing on the altar of an immanentism, an idealism, a relativism. From the horns of that dilemma one escapes only through the discovery (and one has not made it yet if one has no clear memory of its startling strangeness) that there are two quite different realisms, that there is an incoherent realism, half animal and half human, that poses as a half-way house between *materialism* and *idealism* and, on the other hand, that there is an intelligent and reasonable *realism* between which and materialism the half-way house is idealism. (italics mine)[6]

Lonergan is here diagnosing a radical dualism in the knowing of the human person. There is involved an instinctive way of knowing that is highly intelligible but devoid of understanding the what or why, and a contrasting intellectual way that is not so lacking. Mastering this dualism as a project within philosophical self-analysis involves a massive personal struggle.[7]

A parallel recognition of a basic dualism in the human condition is to be found in Simone de Beauvoir's *Ethics of Ambiguity*. Although mind can rise above the fact that we are rooted in the earth, it can never escape it. According to Kristana Arp, de Beauvoir's interpreter, materialists reduce mind to matter, idealists reduce matter to mind. Dualists settle for a stand-off with both poles co-existing in the individual human being, in Francis Heanson's words, 'like eternal strangers.'[8] Lonergan's analysis invites us to address the estrangement of the eternal strangers.

Some remarks in Lonergan's 'Finality, Love, Marriage' help to clarify his distinction between the non-rational and rational components in human behaviour:

> There is also a contrast between the organistic spontaneity of nature and the deliberate friendships of reason. By 'organistic' spontaneity I would denote the mutual adaptation and automatic correlation of the activities of many individuals as though they were parts of a larger organic unit: this phenomenon may be illustrated by the ant heap or the bee hive; but its more general appearance lies in the unity of the family.[9]

Organistic spontaneity is largely the fruit of human instinct, of stimulus and response, rather than of human understanding. Clearly differentiating them in human behaviour is the basic challenge.

It is within the field of interpersonal relations, of mother and child, brothers and sisters, husband and wife, that such organistic spontaneity resides in greater or lesser harmony with the friendships of reason. In the realm of adult male-female relationships these two realisms, and their related tensions, are experienced and lived out in their most dramatic manner. On one level there is the spontaneous awakening of eros by its attraction to the Other as an object of erotic desire. To the extent that erotic desire becomes dominant, there arises the possibility of a 'knowing' of the Other that is without understanding or friendship. On another level there is the awakening of the desire for friendship, with its elements of conversation and understanding, in the light of the attractiveness of the Other. These two desires and related orientations stand in a dialectical tension. An excessive emphasis on one reveals in time the consequences of the neglect of the other.

In every field of life, including philosophy, this dualism makes its presence felt. There is in all of us the spontaneous extroversion of the hunter and food gatherer seeking satisfaction of our instinctive desires in the already-out-there-now real. In startling contrast is the march of modern science, with its counterintuitive discoveries about the same things that primitive consciousness 'knows' and hunts. Empirical scientists know the world through their intellectual desire and insights. Yet when they come to describe that known world, a failure clearly to distinguish between the two orientations can result in confusion. Elementary particles, chemical atoms, plants are pictured and imagined as 'out there' rather than as intelligible species of things made known through insight. For Lonergan the philosophical task will be clearly to differentiate the two orientations in human consciousness and their proportionate realities.

Thought

Having, in his direct but veiled fashion, introduced the problem of the dualism in our self-awareness and sense of reality, Lonergan addresses its intellectual wing. As in the interpersonal, the desire of the mind is for friendship, so more generally understanding the world is its goal. Scientific understanding gives us access to the strange nature of that goal. Scientific activity, from the design of experiments to significant discoveries, is characterized by understanding. Reflection on the scientific experience will open a window on a realism based on understanding.

The starting point of science is, for Lonergan, the questioning spirit of wonder. That spirit finds vital expression in the robust and tireless questions of children. There is in all of us what he referred to in the *Verbum* fragment as an infinite potential to question and to learn. The task of the educator is to awaken and cultivate this potential. In modern times, by which Lonergan means the 1940s, the empirical sciences are the great expression of questioning and learning in action. What is it that gives science its dynamism and its coherence? Lonergan divides his response into five headings:

1. Science in action – products in industry, etc.
2. Science as talk – textbooks and periodicals, the spiral staircase of progress
3. Science as data, the given – brute facts mentioned
4. Science as inquiry, an expression of wonder
5. Science as understanding

The first four points would not be controversial in a modern discussion. But what precisely does he mean by science as understanding, insight, discovery?

This opens up the problem of recognizing insights and insightful persons. As Lonergan remarks:

Like an interpretation, there is understanding the object. You will not get much out of *Insight* unless you have had experience of insight of your own.[10]

In the *Verbum* draft, rejecting the word 'intuition,' for the first time Lonergan started to write about insights into phantasms. Now, in the 'Thought and Reality' lectures, for the first time in public he explains what he means by 'insight.' On page 4 of the notes taken he lists different kinds of insights: direct, judicial, contemplative, methodical. On page 9 he refers to anticipatory and concealed insights, and on 19 to mystical insights, which are not restricted to Christians. In the lectures he does not distinguish mathematical, classical, and statistical insights, as in the later book.

All insights manifest themselves psychologically. They cannot be controlled, but emerge suddenly in response to the tantalizing problem on which one has been stuck. Insights cannot be interrupted or broken up. They are simple and indivisible. They can be pleasurable, even explosive when they bring about a major change in viewpoint. They are luminous in that they add to knowledge. They accumulate; insights add to insights. They become habitual and can be reproduced at will. They are communicative – if you have had an insight into a point in mathematics or grammar or a computer software routine, you can teach it. They are the expression and accompaniment of intelligence. The greater a person's intelligence, the greater the facility that person will possess for having insights. Insights can have different degrees of synthetic power or ability to take in all the parts in a single view. Cognitionally, an insight 'supervenes on sense and experiential experience and consciousness (Brute Fact),'[11] this being one of the rare mentions of the term 'consciousness' in the notes.

There is freshness, even excitement, in the tone. Lonergan has settled on the word 'insight' and here, for the first time in public, is explaining what he means by it, what it is that it names. The sweep is comprehensive, but there are few details in the notes. Significantly, there is no reference to the dramatic eureka experience of Archimedes. (Later Lonergan will choose that anecdote to open his 1951 lectures 'Intelligence and Reality' and the book *Insight*.) Still, there is a sense of a beginning.

In the fifth *Verbum* article Lonergan listed five aspects of understanding: grasping the point, grasping the implications, reflecting, grasping what is to be done, and finally, mastering how to do it.[12] Understanding is the act 'which, if frequent, gains a man a reputation for intelligence and, if rare, gains him a reputation for stupidity.'[13] In contrast, the sergeant major who knows and applies his manual-at-arms purely by rote is not what is meant by a man of insight. Intellectual habit is not slavery to the book, but freedom from it. A further image in *Insight* is of the ideal detective who picks up all the clues and works out the murder mystery. In a discussion in *Understand-*

ing and Being Lonergan suggests a correlation between emotional disturbance and the impeding of insights.[14]

It is important that, at this beginning, we as interpreters try to recognize
in ourselves what Lonergan is talking about. Otherwise we will not be able
to begin, will fail to gain an entry into his journey and path. When would we
say of something someone had done that it was insightful? What do we
mean by an insightful person? Is it through skilful insights into the patient's
verbal account of the symptoms, into the X-ray photographs and the
laboratory tests, that medical diagnosticians recognize a condition? Does
the thoughtful psychiatrist, through insights into the symptoms, recognise
the psychological disorder of the patient? Are the insights of common
sense involved in quickly sizing up the character of the other and assessing
its possible strengths and weaknesses in certain situations? Do trouble-
shooters have insights into the malfunctioning of equipment or into how to
deal with a disaster? Can an insightful jury person probe the deceits of the
witnesses, the rhetorical persuasiveness of the arguments, even his or her
own biases? Do insights cause and express themselves in the intelligent
behaviour, both verbal and practical, of the good counsellor, interviewer,
arguer, computer user, taxi driver, technician, financier, jury person,
politician?

Many affirm that they have sensations, perceptions, and thoughts but not
insights. It is one thing to list the psychological properties of an insight,
quite another to recognize and become interested in them in one's own
experiences. We should not underestimate the difficulty of appreciating
what it is like to have an insight and what they do. About this difficulty
Lonergan has remarked:

> You have an empirical basis, not in the sense of what is out there
> now, that you can put your paw on, but in the sense of something in
> here now that clicks inside you. But it has to click because if you
> haven't had the click you are not going to get anywhere with *In-
> sight.*[15]

In his *Surprised by Joy* C.S. Lewis recounted three episodes from his life in
order to explain what he meant by joy.[16] He went on to say that those who
could not identify with such episodes or who were not interested in them
need read no more. The same is true about the study of insights. What
Lonergan refers to and means by 'insight' should never be taken for
granted.

Insights, as the early *Verbum* fragment made clear, are moments in the
cognitional process, in thought. The cognitional question asks, what is the
significant pattern of activities and relations of which they are a part?

Insights are intrinsically related to inquiry, to the questions that ask about the why of a thing or a situation. Those questions presuppose a given empirical situation or datum on which insights supervene, which poses the problem, how can insights at the same time be both supervening and into phantasm, even caused by phantasm? Transcending phantasm, insights add something additional and unexpected, even surprising. Lonergan asserts that insights cannot misunderstand an image and that error arises from wrong data or incomplete sensible presentations. This seems to presuppose that the image can pose only a single, unique question.

What insights grasp in images and data finds expression in the definitions or laws that scientists talk about. Until Watson and Crick had their final insights, they could not define the law of DNA. Understanding how an insight is involved in working out the definition of the circle was, as we have seen, a turning point in Lonergan's own intellectual history. He now uses it in order to illustrate some of the points he has been making. The point is to explain why a particular given shape is uniformly round. Start with a rough wheel with a bumpy rim, uneven spokes, and a thick hub. Because of the bumps in the rim and the differences in the spokes, the circumference of the wheel will not be uniformly round. In one's imagination, allow the number of spokes to multiply, their lengths to become uniform, the rim to gain in roundness, and the hub to shrink towards a point. If there are no bumps and dents, if the centre is a point and the radii are all equal, then, of necessity, the curve must be uniformly round. It cannot be other.

When through insight one has grasped why the curve is uniformly round, one can define the circle as the locus of coplanar points equidistant from a fixed centre:

> We get to language through 'insights.'
> Sensations ... Then Insights ... Then Language.
> If you have insight you are able to define.[17]

Mathematical definitions and scientific laws do not emerge at random. They are caused by insights into phantasms.

Why two wheels differ is not explained by two different definitions of roundness. Rather, they are two instances of individual matter as alike as two peas in a pod. The make of the wheel, colour, size, and so forth are also irrelevant to the definition of roundness. Such attributes are termed 'accidental matter.' The common matter is the shared roundness, which differs from both the individual and the accidental.

Lonergan continues with a discussion of the empirical and the intelligible in knowledge. The empirical is what we know by our senses, memory, imagination, instinctive valuation, and consciousness, before we understand. By our senses we *know* the place and duration, colour and texture of two wheels before we understand why they are round. The intelligible is what we *know* when we understand uniform roundness. It can involve necessary internal relations of a unity. It can grasp the merely possible – can be but isn't; the contingent – is but might not be; or the necessary – can be, must be; all of which point towards the idea of being. Interesting is the distinction, which Lonergan will later elaborate, between a knowing by the senses and a knowing by the intellect.

When we understand we can act, go on intelligently with the situations that arise in our lives. At this point in time Lonergan holds that understanding or insight is the *main* control in regard to action. The will follows the intellect. Without the understanding, action is blind or based on guesswork. Through understanding, the rules for action are shaped or alternatively thrown out and replaced by new rules. In this sense they are not *a priori*. He distinguishes between the theoretician who understands the why of the rules – why doing this repairs a fault in the car – and the technician who knows how to follow the rules without understanding why they work.

Containing a reference to Mill's method of agreement and difference, the opening section concludes with the question, how do insights accumulate? For insights are not isolated mental atoms, but elements in the journey of the mind. It is Lonergan's suggestion that scientific insights accumulate after the manner of a spiral staircase. There is firstly a cross-dialectic. It works through the repetitive process of the formulations of insights into data, returning the inquiry to the data in search of further insights and formulations. But there is also an upward dialectic arising out of the cross-dialectic. As insights grow there emerges an upward trend, number concepts being specifically named. Although the term 'viewpoint' is not used, the section anticipates *Insight* on the definition and redefinition of numbers through the emergence of higher viewpoints. The cross-dialectic is akin to a development within a viewpoint, the upward dialectic like the emergence of a higher viewpoint within which a process of redefinition occurs. No details of the manner in which number concepts develop are given.

Methodological and Analytical Concepts of Reality

Having made some progress with the concept of insight, Lonergan now uses it to explore the problem of reality. His question is 'not whether there is reality, [but] what is reality?'[18] Again he affirms the knowledge that is without understanding by means of which dogs 'know' bones, their master, and so forth. As an animal knows, we 'know' real objects sensibly before and after we understand and think about them. Lonergan's remark that scientifically understanding something is a different kind of knowledge than common sense is again puzzling.

Naive realism is a first step in philosophy that results from an articulation of the animal fact that we 'know' real objects sensibly before we understand or speak about them. It is a realism that excludes the insights of understanding. Later Lonergan will refer to it in terms of the distinction between the world of immediacy and the world mediated by meaning. From naive realism there results phenomenalism – the position that experience contacts things. Because phenomena are all disconnected, the thing in itself cannot be known. 'Phenomenalism' and 'Things in Themselves' are the titles of chapters 11 and 12 of Bradley's *Appearance and Reality*. The general stance of Kant, with his system of *a priori* categories, and of idealism is that things in themselves are unknowable. The conclusion of idealism must be that there are no real things, after which we find the name of Hegel and a related reference to A. Bremond's *Story of Philosophy*. Pragmatism concentrates on data and thinking, not on the question of the real. For Dirac, a set of formulae connects to the data. In contrast, in Platonism sensible things are just shadows of reality. The real is conceptual, what you know when you think. Conceptual knowledge is of the intelligible, necessary, eternal. At the end of Lonergan's list comes Aristotle, for whom reality is what corresponds to true judgment.

Reality itself is the condition of true propositions being true. Methodological concepts of reality are linked through propositions to Aristotle's list of the categories and predicaments, substance, quantity, quality, etc., a listing that is repeated in great detail on page 23. Greatly influenced by books 7 and 8 of Aristotle's *Metaphysics*, Lonergan devoted the bulk of his analysis to the analytic concept of reality. At the very centre of the project is the analysis of substance. Clearly, he is out to refute the thesis of idealism that there are no real things.

Potency is defined by its relation to be acted on and act and by its relation to form. There is the potential or power of sight, which is an essential potency in the embryo. In the formed but closed eye there is the potency and the form of sight, but not the act of seeing. Form is the condition of truth of all propositions that affirm laws of nature, illustrations being the laws of seeing or hearing. Lonergan's equating of the metaphysical category of form with both the laws of nature and the referent of propositions or thoughts involves a significant insight. Those laws are not seen or pictured, they are understood and thought. Hence the need to understand what is involved in understanding and thinking a law of nature in order to understand what a law is. Similarly, his remark that 'all events occur according to some law'[19] involves a significant insight into aspects of the relation between what he will later term 'classical' and 'statistical' laws. The events of statistical science correspond to the metaphysical category of act.

On page 13 substantial form is defined as 'Intelligible Unity of a concrete pattern of events – higher unities that make one thing one thing.'[20] The emphasis on intelligible rather than sensible unity is central but not illustrated or explained. As intelligible unities are apprehended through understanding, Lonergan is groping towards a realism of substances based on understanding.

Interesting is his schematic summary on page 15 of his analysis of form in relation to things, their existence, scientific laws, and related events:

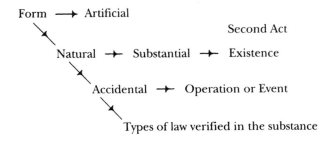

Form ⟶ Artificial

Second Act

Natural ⟶ Substantial ⟶ Existence

Accidental ⟶ Operation or Event

Types of law verified in the substance

His treatment on page 16 of the notes of the questions, What is man? and Why are the sensible data a man? points towards a growing influence of Aristotle's analysis of the relation between being and substance at the start of book 7 of his *Metaphysics*. A primary sense of what it means for a thing to be is its substance, what it is. In chapter 17 of book 7 Aristotle asks specifically, Why is this body having this form a man? Later Lonergan would state that for him the greatness of the mind of Aristotle shines forth in books 7 and 8 of the *Metaphysics* and book 3 of the *De Anima*.[21] On page 24 of the notes he states that form, being intelligible in itself, is what is known by an act of understanding. Also of interest is his recognition of the problem of differentiating substances into genera and species.[22]

Truth and the Relation of Thought to Reality

A discussion of definition and meaning, which repeats matters treated in the *Verbum* fragment and first article, opens up questions about truth. In response, Lonergan's separate considerations so far of thought and reality now, between pages 19 and 25 of the notes, give way to an exploration of their relation. As the notion of truth is at the heart of this issue, there follows a long probing of tests of the criteria for truth.

For pragmatists the criterion of truth is utility, so they will argue that it is sometimes useful to tell a lie. Alternatively, as different authorities might disagree on a specific claim, the reasons why you accept a particular authority are the real test. But what about mystical insights, where no reasons are given? Here you have to test the reasons but not the message. For common sense, truth involves a correspondence between what one thinks and reality. This, it is suggested, belongs to the nature of truth rather than to procedures for testing the truth. Would self-evidence or coherence provide us with such procedures? The latter makes clear that reality is not shoved on us by sensations.

Objective truth is the object of subjective necessity, the necessity that holds that it would be irrational to say anything else. If such subjective necessity is the test for truth, how does it arise and what is its object? Involved are the laws of thought, identity, non-contradiction, excluded middle, and sufficient reason. To reject the laws of thought is to reject your rationality. If you have not sufficient reason, then say, 'I don't know.' To reject a judgment is to judge. If you can't reject judgment you can't reject understanding. Something must be understood. This is the plight of the universal sceptic, and for this reason scepticism is not a problem for Lonergan.

There follows on page 21 an illuminating digression, reminiscent of Porphyry's tree, into what in *Insight*[23] he calls the hierarchy of grades of being, the reality that is proportionate to our thought and reason:

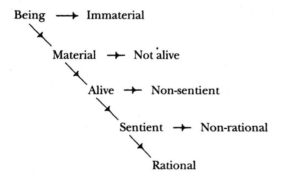

Being ⟶ Immaterial

Material ⟶ Not alive

Alive ⟶ Non-sentient

Sentient ⟶ Non-rational

Rational

Included, we find the remark that there are more complex judgments where the evidence is not readily seen, one of only two uses of the word 'evidence' in the notes. 'Sentient' is a term that occurs in Shull, whom he had recently read and quoted in his 'Finality, Love, Marriage.'

Lonergan's conclusion of this experimental exploration of the criteria for truth is directly out of Newman:

> There is no mechanical test for truth. It is the mind – It is the intelligence. A man's ability to judge is the test of truth in the last analysis. Judgments are sometimes wrong. Cure is not to throw out judgments. It means you have to be careful.[24]

An analysis follows of three senses of 'What I cannot help judging to be so.' The first examines the thesis that our judgment will be subjective if we let our emotions and desires, love and hate, and irrationality rather than rationality influence us. A second has to do with self-reflection, through which the quality of our judgment moves onto another level. The third way, influenced by Augustine, presupposes the existence of God. Truth is not merely within us, it is also above us. We know the truth from our obscure vision of God. For Thomas we know because of what we are – intellectual. We want to know the why. We start from boundless inquiry, which can address the whole range of reality. God knows things in himself, not in themselves. In what way are our intellects like God? We are in potency, we don't know but can ask, why? As God has the whole range of reality in act, we have it in potency. We know the real through judgments. The fundamental idea of reality is that what is intelligible can be, what is unintelligible can't be. Being can't be known by someone who has not understood anything. Being is predicated of everything intelligible.

After his introduction on the two realisms, Lonergan went on to explore the elements of thought. His subsequent explorations of reality focused on species and genera of substances and their related attributes. Such substances are for him entities that come to be known by us through our thought processes. There follow his efforts to understand how we 'effect the transition from subjective necessity that exists in our minds to the certainty that it is so (To an objective truth.)'[25] In this manner he has assembled the elements of the problem of the relation of thought and reality. The challenge is to work out the relation between our talk about cognition and our talk about known things, facts, situations, states of affairs.

What most impressed Eric O'Connor about the course was not so much the problem Lonergan was grappling with – What does one mean by 'reality' and how does one come to know it – as the manner in which he went about it:

> What came through from him was that all questions could be asked and should be asked, that in fact one didn't begin to learn until one began asking questions. This was a shock to anyone educated before 1945 ... Having those lectures didn't become important as a theory. That is definite. It became important as an experience: the way you learned anything was by slow questioning ... In those early lectures, he somehow gave us the sense that the world is open to explore – because he is curious himself about anything, and explores it. Slowly, in the lectures, he gave us a little glimmer about the obvious next level of questioning: You ask whether you have understood a thing correctly or not.[26]

Lonergan's questioning of the economic process, of the texts of Aquinas on grace, of the ends of marriage and the problem of 'Thought and Reality' show his questioning mind at work. By way of contrast, O'Connor referred to his own training in mathematics. He had first learned the definitions in topology without understanding the questions behind them. He didn't know that the way to learn topology was to play with the shapes, listen to the questions they posed, and then try to define them. He found that he was not asking the questions that were answered by what he was learning.[27]

The 'Thought and Reality' course notes are fragmentary, difficult, and irritating. Like the fragments of the 'Essay on Newman' he wrote for Keeler, they show Lonergan grappling with a problem that fascinated him, the relation between cognition and reality. Although at this point he had some ideas, specifically on the significance of judgment, he had no overall solution. That would come in the course of composing the *Verbum* articles and *Insight*. With hindsight, his position in those later works will illuminate just what it was he was searching for in the pressent lectures. Thought or cognition at this point was for Lonergan a process. Interesting is the mention of facts and brute facts, and the almost complete lack of attention to the elements and levels of consciousness is notable.[28] These aspects of the problem had yet to find their place in his thinking.

Eric Kierans, Lonergan's former student from Montreal, attended the lectures and, in conversation, asked him what he considered to be the most important thing in life. Lonergan's response was, to get clear about one's relationship with Christ; after that, other things fell into their place. Kierans remembered an occasion on which doubts about faith were being discussed. Lonergan commented that for him it was foundational that there was a Jesus Christ and that he did in historical fact say, 'Thou art Peter and on this rock I will found my Church.' Lonergan, Kierans believed, had a very deep faith but could not talk about it: he came to his own beliefs and that was that. Kierans felt that Lonergan at the time tended to keep what he was thinking about to himself. If something came up in conversation that interested and challenged him, he would go away on his own and think about it; when he had got the matter clear in his own mind he would discuss it. Kierans had no recollection of Lonergan discussing his own personal insights.

During the course Lonergan met Patricia Coonan, a mathematics teacher in Montreal, who enjoyed Lonergan's style of analysis with its mathematical undercurrent. Although Lonergan would shortly leave Montreal, she became a life-long friend. He would write her some letters in response to her questions about faith, and when in his later years he visited Montreal she was a helpful presence, driving him around and the like.

Shortly after the course was over, Stanley Machnik introduced him to Beatrice Kelly, a friend of Machnik's fiancée Roberta Soden. Beatrice and many of those associated with the Thomas More Institute were at the Machnik-Soden wedding, at which Lonergan was the celebrant, and later at the reception in the Soden home.[29] According to Charlotte Tansey, Beatrice was tall, attractive, red-haired, bright, and had an 'Irish' temperament. Between 1949 and 1953 she would type up the text of *Insight* for publication, and later the text of *Method in Theology*. Ann Lonergan, Mark's wife, remembered Bernard inviting her once to a meal with them, adding that it was clear that he thought the world of her. In 1956 she married Peter White, Lonergan staying with them for two or three days in Montreal in 1957. His introduction to her was an important event. As well as making a significant contribution to his work through her typing, Beatrice would also become a valued friend to him.[30]

10

Aquinas on Cognition and Its Transcendence

'Do you see that book on the table?'

'Yes.'

'After I had finished all my research and checked all my references how long do you think it took me to write the first chapter?'

'A month?'

'One year! I'd write a few pages, and the next day I'd throw all of them away and start over. It took me a full year before I discovered a way to make everything hang together.'

'Wow!'

'And how long do you think it took me to write the second chapter?'

'Six months?'

'Three weeks! So take heart: once it comes, then it really goes.'[1]

Verbum 1: Understanding and Defining

The first *Verbum* article opens with Penido's observation in his *Glosses on the Procession of Love in the Trinity* that most theologians acknowledged that the issue was beyond them. Those who did claim to understand it were not convincing. Billot in his account of the procession of the Word in his *On God, Unity and Trinity* proposes that the likeness is in the imagination. Lonergan was certain that this was not the mind of Aquinas. It is with the intellect that we must begin. When we are clear about how Aquinas understood a word to proceed in our minds from our understanding, we can move on to the procession of the spirit of love in God. The search to find created likenesses of the two processions in God is a challenge to the philosophy of mind and heart. The revelation invites us to search more deeply into our meaning as human.

That search begins with reflections on the relation between inner words or concepts and their expression in spoken or written words. When I wish to communicate some point to you, what is the causal relation between the thoughts I wish to communicate and the physical spoken or written words I employ? Clearly, that meaning would not be communicated if I chose the spoken or written words of an unfamiliar language. But it can also be the case that the words of the language are familiar but the meaning they are intended to convey is strange or original and difficult to grasp.

For Aquinas the mental word can be the efficient cause of the physical. The meaning of the thought that we entertain causes us to express it in a particular combination of spoken words. That combination can cause the other to think the meaning of the original thought. Early in the first article Lonergan puts it as follows:

> But commonly he asked what outer words meant and answered that, in the first instance, they meant inner words. The proof was quite simple. We discourse on 'man' and on 'triangle.' What are we talk-ing about? Certainly, we are not talking about real things directly, else we should all be Platonists. Directly, we are talking about objects of thought, inner words, and only indirectly, only in so far as our inner words have an objective reference, are we talking about real things.[2]

Although inner words or thoughts can be caused by outer, the outer mean the inner. Remove that meaning and they are just brute sounds.

This affirmation of a distinction between meaningful objects of thought and their verbal expression, spoken, written, or signed, is central to all that follows. In his article 'The Mother Tongue,' the linguist William Allman points out the dramatic sound changes in words as the English language, for instance, evolves from the eighth-century Old English of *Beowulf* through Chaucer's fourteenth-century Middle English to Shakespeare and after.[3] He suggests that, with some onomatopoeic exceptions (like 'sizzle'), the sound of a word or its symbolic expression, such as 'dog,' has no direct connection to its related thought meaning, the concept of a dog, and reference, a real dog in the world. Any number of sounds or symbolic expressions will do. Despite the fact that an obvious correlation exists between the use of word patterns and such meaning, thoughts are strangely different from their verbal expressions.

Lonergan's main interest is in the manner of the correspondence of our thoughts, not with outer words, but with reality.[4] In their objective reference such thoughts, unlike the sounds that express them, entail for him a realism that stands in stark contrast with that of our senses and instinctive appetites. Repeating 'Thought and Reality,' he holds that dogs know not merely appearances but bones, other dogs, and their masters:

> Now this sensitive integration of sensible data also exists in the human animal and even in the human philosopher. Take it as knowledge of reality, and there results the secular contrast between the solid sense of reality and the bloodless categories of the mind. Accept the sense of reality as the criterion of reality, and you are a *materialist*, sensist, positivist, pragmatist, sentimentalist, and so on, as you please. Accept reason as a criterion but retain the sense of reality as what gives meaning to the term 'real,' and you are an *idealist*; for, like the sense of reality, the reality defined by it is non-rational. In so far as I grasp it, the Thomist position is the clear-headed third position: reason is the criterion and, as well, it is reason – not the sense of reality – that gives meaning to the term 'real.' The real is, what is; and 'what is,' is known in the rational act, *judgment*. (italics mine)[5]

This remarkable statement develops our earlier quotation from the *Verbum* fragment (p. 137) with its use of the terms 'idealism' and 'materialism.' Autobiographically, I believe it is articulating Lonergan's efforts to make sense of his intellectual conversion during and after Leeming's course.

Having opened up the question about the difference between the sounds of words and their meaning and the confusion of realisms, Lonergan articulates his main thesis:

> that we must begin by grasping the nature of the act of understanding, that thence we shall come to a grasp of the nature of inner words, their relation to language, and their role in our knowledge of reality.[6]

What is meant by 'understanding' is illustrated with a fleeting reference to the eureka of Archimedes, in which the mind clicks. Without the insight one can repeat, like a parrot, the spoken words that make up the sentence whose meaning is the proposition, definition, rule, thought, or law. But in so doing one does not know what one is talking about. The thought or inner word of human meaning emerges at the end of a process of thoughtful cognitional inquiry. Until it emerges we are questioning in order to understand. It emerges simultaneously with the act of understanding, although it is distinct from it. Lonergan now affirms that the processes he has been talking about are accessible to introspection, but does not elaborate on what that means.[7] Throughout the article there is again a strong emphasis on cognition as a process, but not one that is purely subjective. His goal, as the previous quote makes abundantly clear, is to understand how in and through that process subjects come to a knowledge of reality, of something beyond themselves. Implicitly, the Kantian problem of the relation of the subject and object of knowledge, of thought and reality, is being addressed.

The second section of the article is entitled 'Definition.' Later, in the book version, he would retitle the whole article 'Definition and Understanding.' This indicates that, focally, this was a study of the manner in which the understanding directs and controls the terms that are to go into the concept or definition of, for instance, a circle, of mass, or of life. Acknowledging that the use of concepts and related spoken or written words in a definition is not arbitrary, what precisely controls their selection and the way they relate? The clue to the meaning of the definition is in the meaning of the question it answers, the What is it? (or Why?) question.[8] In his zeal to prick complacent bubbles of ignorance, Socrates 'made it a practice to ask people just what things are. What is virtue? What is moderation, courage, justice? What is science?'[9] He discovered that most could not answer his questions. This suggested that questions, formulated or unformulated, precede definitions or propositions that they anticipate as their answers.

In the *Posterior Analytics* Aristotle concluded that the *what* question could have four meanings. We can ask, what is X or why X is Y – what is justice or why is this justice? What is refraction and why does light refract are for him not two but one and the same question. (He does not seem at this point, as in the later 'Natural Desire to see God,' to distinguish between nominal and explanatory definitions, the former being concerned with the use of names.)[10] How, he asks, can one translate the question, what is a man into the *why* form? Two further meanings arise because we can ask, is there an X or whether X is Y – is there justice, or whether this is justice?

The most convoluted section in the first article, concerned with the expectations of the *what* question, is entitled '*quod quid est.*' The questioning of the detective works with the expectation that some unknown person committed a criminal offense. In the same way it can be asked, What precisely does the 'what' or the 'why is this an X?' question anticipate or expect? What is the 'whatness' or 'whyness,' the rule, so to speak, of courage, of a circle, a movement, hydrogen, a fruit fly, or a human being?

As forms of human behaviour, virtue differs from vice, prudence from courage, wisdom from ignorance, bias from openness. As experienced shapes, circles differ from triangles and ellipses. Why is this so? As the behaviour patterns or spatial shapes differ, so also, we might expect, do their corresponding definitions. The questions can be extended to the explanation of differences among things on all grades of being, inorganic, organic, sensate, and intellectual.

Aristotle answers the What? question in terms of four causes: material, efficient, formal, and final. The form or *morphe* is not revealed by the appearance or shape or colour. Extending Empedocles, Aristotle argued that it means proportion and becomes known only through understanding.[11] What is known by intellect is a partial constituent of the realities first known by sense. Building on this, Aquinas affirmed that intellect penetrates the inwardness of things.

As we cannot answer challenging questions at will, conceptualization, another name for defining, is neither automatic nor unconscious but intelligent. We have to think out the answer, and that can be a twisting and winding process. The search for the definition that expresses the *why* of courage, prudence, virtue, vice, a triangle, or helix cannot be successful without appropriate imaginative presentations: 'Insight into phantasm is the first part of the process that moves from sense through understanding to essential definition.'[12] Aristotle maintained that intelligible objects do not exist apart from concrete extensions but are in sensible forms and mathematical diagrams. Images, taken in conjunction with the questioning activity, are the movers of our understanding.

So hand in hand with the search for understanding goes the search for an image suitably disposed and appropriate for the question involved. It is because of this that Euclid introduced lines of construction into his proofs and mathematicians play with diagrams:

> In the first instance, phantasm has to produce the act of insight whereas, in subsequent instances, informed intellect guides the production of an appropriate phantasm; in other words, in the first instance we are at the mercy of fortune, the subconscious, or a teacher's skill, for the emergence of an appropriate phantasm; we are in a ferment of trying to grasp we know not what; but once we have understood, then we can operate on our own, marshalling images to a habitually known end.[13]

At the heart of that ferment is the desire to know, which, in *Insight*, he acknowledges can influence the fabric of our dreams. Elsewhere, with a reference to his 'Finality, Love, Marriage,' he acknowledged that in that context the unconscious can be the source of relevant images, points that are well illustrated by the experiences of Mendelevey and Kekulé.[14] In early February 1869, in the throes of his problem, Mendeleyev wrote down the details of all of the known elements on a set of cards, with which he played a game of chemical patience in order to discover their law. The insight eluded him until he fell asleep. In his subsequent dream the proper disposed image or phantasm presented itself, in which he grasped through insight the law of the elements. Some years earlier Kekulé was pondering a problem related to the chemical structure of benzene. Having made no progress, he relaxed by the fire and dozed. In his dream the rows of atoms formed and moved snake-like until eventually one of the snakes bit its own tail. The required disposed phantasm for the insight was a ring structure rather than a linear one. As some disposed images release the insight, others can imprison it. In *Insight* Lonergan will remark that it is very difficult to work out the square root of MDCCLXVII.

A distinction is emerging between the way we relate to images and diagrams by means of our senses and imagination, and our intellect. It is through our senses and our senses alone that we 'know' the image as an image of two distinct intersecting circles or identify that a certain curve, because of bumps in it, is not uniformly round. When our intellectual desire to understand is awakened by some puzzling features of what is imaginatively presented, that relation is quite transformed. Now we are out to understand some strange attribute of the image, illuminated and made interesting by the light of intellectual desire, that cannot be known by our senses and imagination. Starting with an initially bumpy wheel, it is through our understanding that we grasp that if the equal radii increase in number, the hub becomes thinner, and the centre becomes a point, there will result uniform roundness. It is through our understanding alone of a suitable diagram that we grasp the definition of a triangle in terms of three intersecting lines, the sum of whose interior angles is equal to two right angles.[15]

Although Lonergan holds that insights cannot be reduced to the senses or imagination, what is extraordinary and alien to those of a Kantian or Cartesian way of thinking is the unusual intimacy between them that he is advocating. The intellect, even when it is understanding entities remote from our senses – the existence of God for instance – needs phantasms. The phantasm, the content of the imaginative presentations, produces, that is to say, is at least a partial but necessary cause of the emergence of, the act of understanding. Towards the end of the process of composing *Insight*, this will pose for Lonergan the question, what sort of phantasms are necessary in order to understand the unimaginable data of consciousness?

In an explicit reference to Kant at this point Lonergan states that, for him, the intellect according to Kant is purely discursive and not in any direct way causally related to the senses or imagination.[16] By way of contrast, in the third and fourth *Verbum* articles he will hold that for Aquinas the understanding in the learning mode is passive and operated on by its object in the phantasm. A startling development of the cosmic implications of this relation between image and insight will take place in chapter 8 of *Insight*. On this point the cognitional theories of Kant and Lonergan diverge irreconcilably.

What insight apprehends in the sensibly or imaginatively given – the *quiditty* – is articulated and expressed in a definition whose content expresses what the insight has grasped in the image:

> For human understanding, though it has its object in the phantasm and knows it in the phantasm, yet is not content with an object in this state. It pivots on itself to produce for itself another object which is the inner word as *ratio, intentio, definitio, quod quid est.* And this pivoting and production is no mere matter of some metaphysical sausage-machine, at one end slicing species off phantasm, and at the other popping out concepts; it is an operation of rational consciousness.[17]

The pattern of spatial relations that is understood in a supposed uniformly round image cannot be pictured or imagined. It is made present to the insight in the phantasm. Later Lonergan will hold that the insight grasps how the relations between the centre, radii, plane curve, and uniform roundness fix the terms and their relations that are to go into the definition.[18]

Verbum 2: The Standard of Judgment Is Not Found in a Comparison

The second *Verbum* article, published in March 1947, was written in two or three weeks and soon after the first. The four-point plan in the opening paragraph makes it clear that, at least from this point and possibly earlier, Lonergan had a plan of most of the articles:

> The plan of our inquiry has been, first, to determine the introspective psychological data involved in the Thomist concept of a *verbum mentis* or inner word; secondly, to review the metaphysical categories and theorems in which these introspective data were expressed by Aquinas; thirdly, to follow the extrapolation from the analysis of the human mind to the account of the divine intellect as known naturally; fourthly, to study the theory of the procession of the divine Word.[19]

Its elements quickly clicked and fell into place for him because it continued the theme of the first article. As the first article focused on insight into phantasm as the source and cause of definition, the second focuses on reflective understanding, which he considers 'not unlike Newman's illative sense,'[20] as the cause of judgment. Under what circumstances do we reasonably and correctly, rationally or irrationally say yes, it is so, assent to some definition/proposition or some complex of propositions? Just as insights and related definitions cannot emerge without some suitable imaginative presentations, so also the movement towards judgment cannot begin without some suitable propositions.

To discuss single questions, insights, and related definitions is to abstract from a much wider cognitional context. Aquinas was fully familiar with the psychological fact that insights are not unrelated atoms. He acknowledged that they develop, coalesce, and form higher unities:

> Insight into phantasm expresses itself in a definition. Such an expression *per se* is neither true nor false. Next, many insights into many phantasms express themselves severally in many definitions; none of these singly is true or false; nor are all together true or false, for as yet they are not together. Third, what brings definitions together is not some change in the definitions; it is a change in the insights whence they proceed. Insights coalesce and develop; they grow into apprehensions of intelligibility on a deeper level and with a wider sweep; and these profounder insights are expressed at times indeed by the invention of such baffling abstractions as classicism or romanticism, education, evolution or the *philosophia perennis*, but more commonly and more satisfactorily by the combination, as combination, of simple concepts ... but man has to reason it; his intellect is discursive. Still it is not pure discourse. Without initial and natural acts of understanding, reasoning would never begin; ... Fifthly, reasoning in its essence is simply the development of insight ... Aquinas refused to take as reason the formal affair that modern logicians invent machines to perform. He defined reason as development in understanding; and to that, formal reasoning is but an aid.[21]

Through the development of understanding there emerges a linguistic and mental synthesis. For a Kantian or a Cartesian such a mental synthesis must be a purely internal construction of the mind. For Aquinas it involves the interaction of insight into phantasm and the related theorem of identity. The act of judgment involves *positing* a real synthesis in which there emerges knowledge of the truth. What does this mean?

Lonergan acknowledges that 'there is the real composition in things in themselves; there is the composition of inner words in the mind; there is the composition of outer words in speech and writing.'[22] The printed text of the book *The Double Helix* is a linguistic synthesis. It could be linguistically translated and printed in many languages. As composed in the mind of the author or received in the mind of the reader, it constitutes a mental synthesis of meaning. Related is one's position on how the mental synthesis is formed in our minds in the first place. For a Kantian the mental synthesis must in some sense form in one's mind independently of the situation in the world. For Lonergan and Aquinas that synthesis can only form through an interaction with the situation in the world of one's questions for intelligence, one's insights into the relevant imaginative presentations of the situation and the resulting thoughts and language. The mental synthesis is in a sense derived from the world situation.

Distinct from the linguistic and the mental is the real synthesis, the sequence of events in the world by means of which, for instance, Crick and Watson discovered the chemical structure of DNA. Judgment, which includes knowledge of the truth, takes us beyond a presupposed mental synthesis. Truth is not a subjective synthesis. It is the correspondence between the mental synthesis of concepts and the real synthesis of things and their relations.[23]

Two questions arise. Firstly, how do we make the transition from the mental synthesis in the realm of thought to the real synthesis in the realm of things, of being? If judgment always presupposes some proposition or definition or mental synthesis, there is no path to what is real except through it and such mental constructs, for judgment cannot short-circuit the insights and formulations of intelligence. Neither does it add to their content. Given that there might be a plurality of conflicting mental syntheses, how does one determine the one that corresponds to the real? The second question, which addresses the meaning of the correspondence of the mental and the real synthesis, opens up, in its own way, the Kantian problem of the relation of the subject and object of knowledge, of thought and reality.

In making a judgment, Lonergan states, 'the intellect not merely attains similitude to its object but also reflects upon and judges that similitude.'[24] This, he acknowledges, presents a familiar problem. Does determining the correspondence entail that knowing involves a comparison between some possible item of knowledge and some standard? If the standard is known, then is one not simply comparing two possible instances of knowledge?

Aquinas recognized the need for a standard, but his standard was not the thing in itself as thing in itself, and so unknown. Nor was it some inner representation of the thing in itself coming to aid the process. His standard lay in the principles of intellect itself. This poses the problem, what does Aquinas mean by intellect measuring things by its own principles? Given the subjective necessity of some judgments, how does the mind proceed from such immanent coercion to objective truth and knowledge of reality?

The question of the standard of judgment only begins to bite when one has mastered the fact that judging is not a matter of a comparison of outer presentations with some inner representation of an object. The theorem of identity as applied to the understanding calls that duality into question. But if the correspondence between the mental or conceptual and the real synthesis is not based on some form of comparison, what might it mean?

Lonergan then adds some brief remarks on assent, certitude, and the related fact that subjectively, whether rightly or wrongly, in certain circumstances individuals feel a need to pass judgment. There is a quiet emphasis on the coercive nature of the evidence here that we do not find in his later writings. As an understanding of the relations presented in a phantasm moves the understanding to produce the inner word of definition, the reflective understanding of the evidence coerces or moves the judgment, the inner word of assent to the mental synthesis. Assent, echoing Newman, is contrasted with consent, which is an act of will. Assent is judgment considered as a personal act, committing a person to a responsible act based on his or her apprehension of the evidence.

On the criteriological level, judgment or assent is the result of a resolution into principles. Invention has to do largely with the historical accumulation of insights in, for instance, chemistry or biology. Composition has to do with the selection, at a particular point in the history, of the first principles of the science from which demonstrations follow. Demonstration, in the sense of resolution to principles, is a matter of deducing a conclusion from the selected first principles. Actual thinking oscillates dialectically between the two. Still, there is a second meaning in Aquinas of the phrase, 'resolution into principles' that has to do with the *via judicii*. This involves the reflective activity of the mind in understanding the link between demonstrations and conclusions. When such resolution is reached, 'the mind is coerced by its own natural acceptance of the principles to accept the conclusion as well.'[25]

Judgment involves an accumulation of understanding. But it is also a reflective activity of reason that involves the whole person. As the proposition proceeds from an act of understanding, so also does the judgment. To judge without understanding a sufficient reason would be to lapse in one's rationality, 'for clearly judgment arises only from at least supposed sufficient ground.'[26] Probabilities, however strong, are not a sufficient determination for reason. They do not coerce assent. In *Insight* Lonergan will allow probable judgments where the evidence points in one direction but is not conclusive.

The section ends with a summary of Aquinas' cognitional theory: 'There are two levels of activity, the direct and the reflective.'[27] Levels of cognitional activity slip in for the first time, but what is meant by the phrase is not explained. Both acts of understanding have human questioning as their principal cause. The direct act has the appropriate phantasm as its proximate cause or mover, but the reflective act is moved by the data of sense and imagination and the hypothetical products of direct understanding. Reflective questions are answered by a *resolutio in principia*, a return to sources in which a necessary connection between the sources and the hypothetical synthesis is grasped. Judgment proceeds from this grasp.

Thought's Transcendence: Wisdom, Self-knowledge, and Intellectual Light

It is one thing to explore the activity of judgment; it is another to inquire into the role of the inner words of definition and judgment in our knowledge of reality. How in the emergence of the inner word of judgment is there effected the transition from forming a mental synthesis to positing a real synthesis? In the sections that follow we find Lonergan grappling with what he will later term 'the epistemological question,' as he finds it treated in Aquinas. How, and through what standard, does judgment transcend itself?

If it is in true judgment that we know reality, then wisdom, defined as the virtue of right judgment, has to do with knowledge of the real as real. If the habit of intellect regards the first principles of demonstration, the habit of wisdom regards the first principles of reality:

> On the other hand, the habit of wisdom has a dual role. Principally, it regards the objective order of reality; but in some fashion it also has to do with the transition from the order of thought to the order of reality. Principally, it regards the objective order of reality; for the wise man contemplates the universal scheme of things and sees each in the perspective of its causes right up to the ultimate cause.[28]

Because wisdom is concerned with reality it has the task of validating not just particular inferences or conclusions, but the very first principles of the sciences, such as physics or chemistry or economics. Where science explores the link between conclusions and first principles, 'wisdom passes judgment upon that connection. Where Aquinas spoke of the habits of intellect, science, and wisdom, we are led to distinguish between direct understanding, the development of direct understanding, and reflective understanding.'[29] Direct understanding grasps the point in imaginative presentations, developing understanding establishes logical links in the scientific network. It is in reflective understanding and its judgments on the validity of direct and developing understanding that 'the transition is effected from mental construction on an imagined basis to knowledge through truth and reality.'[30]

The *Metaphysics* of Aristotle acknowledges an epistemological element in the habit of wisdom, for the first philosophy is really a wisdom just as much as a love of wisdom. In books 2–5 Lonergan identifies what he terms a gnoseological and an almost epistemological dimension. On pages 80–1 (69) of the *Verbum* articles we find articulated the names of what Lonergan considers the three basic disciplines, gnoseology, epistemology, and metaphysics. The relation between these disciplines will come to define his foundations.[31]

Aristotle's wise man knows the difference between appearance and reality. He is ready to refute sophistries that would confound the two, 'but he is not prepared to discuss how our immanent activities also contain a transcendence.'[32] Knowledge is by identity. The sounding of the bell is in the agent action, in the recipient passion, the one act uniting the agent and the patient. By extension, the agent object of understanding acts on the understanding as patient. When I understand and apply a rule in using my word processor, the rule and what I understand are identical, suggesting that in some sense the correspondence between knowing and known is a form of identity.

But a problem arises when the notion of identity is applied to judgment out of which arises knowledge of the other as other. Our knowledge of essence and of existence has to have different grounds: 'But the act of the thing as real is the *esse natural* of the thing and, except in divine self-knowledge, that *esse* is not identical with knowing it.'[33] The theorem of identity will not get us to knowledge of the other as other. Reflection is needed, and since reflection is not identity, the theory of knowledge by identity is incomplete. Aquinas added the further theorem of knowledge by intentionality. Rational reflection has to bear the weight of the transition from knowledge as perfection to knowledge as knowledge of the other. Lonergan concludes that Aquinas came to the boundary of the modern epistemological problem but did not cross it.[34]

If wisdom is one line on the problem of self-transcendence, self-knowledge, knowing how we know what we know, is another.

> Or is one to say that, since we know by what we are, so also we know that we know by knowing what we are? ... to know truth we have to know ourselves and the nature of our knowledge.[35]

Lonergan concludes that the critical or epistemological problem will only be solved by self-knowledge. There follows a section entitled 'Self-Knowledge of Soul.' Its opening section prefigures the chapter on self-appropriation in *Insight*, which *precedes* the raising of the epistemological question proper. At this point some of Lonergan's earliest remarks on the data of consciousness and the method of self-appropriation are articulated, but by reading the *Verbum* articles alone it is difficult to enter into them.

How then might we go about knowing ourselves as knowers? After defining '*psyche*' in general, Aristotle in the second book of the *De Anima* raised the problem of differentiating different kinds of psyches or souls. For him what has life has psyche, so there is the psyche of the plant, of the animal, and of the human. The question arises, how do you study life or psyche? This is a question about method, and in response Aristotle had an extraordinarily brilliant insight: you begin not with the agent but with the object with which the agent interacts. Organic life, with its appetites, has food as its object, sensory life the world of senses and imagination, intellect the intelligible. Begin with the object. Study how the organism interacts with the object. From the acts involved identify the powers or potencies.

In order to study the mind do not begin, like Descartes, with navel-gazing introspection. Begin, rather, with a problem situation in one's world: 'It was by scrutinizing both the object understood and the understanding intellect that Aristotle investigated the nature of the possible intellect.'[36] Allow the problem to unfold through its various phases towards resolution. In that performance identify the various mental activities involved through a process of self-analysis that Lonergan terms 'introspection.' Given our current emphasis on intersubjectivity, there is no reason in principle why the 'object' of intellect with which one begins could not be another subject or person whom one is attempting to understand.

Aristotle's procedure was accepted and taken over by Aquinas and, in his own way, Lonergan. But as it is advocating a form of psychoanalysis with respect to the intellect, there arises the difficult question about the sense in which mental processes are conscious. In his writings apart from his *Commentary of Aristotle's the De Anima*, Aquinas makes a further fundamental distinction between

> an empirical awareness of our inner acts and a scientific grasp of their nature. The scientific grasp is in terms of objects, acts, potencies, essence of soul. It is reached only by study; it is a matter of which many are ignorant, on which many have erred ... On the other hand, empirical knowledge of our own souls is knowledge of the existence of their acts, knowledge of what is proper to the individual, knowledge of the inner movements of the heart.[37]

The empirical awareness or 'knowledge' is the basis of the scientific knowledge. In his later work Lonergan would draw a distinction between experiencing one's knowing as conscious and knowledge of one's knowing.

Many people experience their intellectual desire through the expression of their questions. They experience their insights through the manner in which they resolve the tension of inquiry and make answers known. But that does not mean that they advert to these conscious activities or find them significantly interesting or important. For Lonergan it is in a grasp of the nature of our acts of understanding that we obtain the key to Aristotelian psychology.[38]

The remarks on wisdom and self-knowledge of soul preface a long and demanding reflection on the intellectual light of our souls as a measure of reality.[39] Lonergan suggests that by that light Aquinas meant the desire to know that, when operative, lights up and makes interesting, even fascinating, the elements of a field of investigation. In this way intellectual light prepares the way for understanding and is the principle of inquiry and discourse, the source of the search for causes. There is present within it in potential the whole of science, and through its operation first principles are established. It is the principle cause of understanding. As agent intellect it subconsciously orders the phantasm to bring about the appropriate image for the insight, standing to the imagination as artist to materials. It can be taught by both a human and the divine teacher. No less than understanding or thinking, intellectual light itself can come within the field of introspective psychology. We can wonder about our wonder, question our questioning.

Aristotle acknowledged an agent intellect, an active principle of mind, but did not, according to Lonergan, succeed in relating it to judgment. Neither did Aquinas make that move in the course of his *Commentary on the De Anima*, but he affirmed it repeatedly and clearly in his independent writings.[40] What agent intellect, the light of the human mind, desires to know in any instance is made known, present, through a true judgment. If in 1935 Lonergan grasped the link between judgment and what exists, now he is relating both to the agent intellect, the light of the mind. Understanding that link was a major development in Lonergan's thought, and it would become foundational to his epistemology in both 'Intelligence and Reality' and *Insight*. Our understanding is perfected in two manners, 'by intelligible species and by intellectual light; in virtue of the former we have our apprehension of things; but in virtue of the latter we pass judgment on our apprehensions.'[41] Knowing truth is an outcome of the operation of intellectual light as witnessed by the judgments of Joseph and the dream, and Solomon and the moral dilemma. Because of this,

> in particular, there is a relevance of intellectual light to the critical problem, for it is by intellectual light that we can get beyond mere relativity to immutable truth and that we can discern appearance from reality.[42]

Earlier the question was posed, how does the mind effect the transition from its mental synthesis to the real synthesis? Aquinas suggested that it was by means of a standard that resided in the principles of the intellect itself. That standard of self-transcendence and objectivity was for him intellectual light, the light of the mind that expresses itself in questioning. If we understand that intellectual desire, we will understand 'how it is that our minds are proportionate to knowledge of reality.'[43]

According to Lonergan, Aquinas also stresses that the native infinity of the mind can be grasped:

> But the native infinity of intellect as intellect is a datum of rational consciousness. It appears in that restless spirit of inquiry, that endless search for causes which, Aquinas argued, can rest and end only in a supernatural vision of God. It appears in the absolute exigence of reflective thought which will assent only if the possibility of contradictory proposition is excluded.[44]

Problematic again is the meaning of consciousness, and in particular of rational consciousness, which occurs here and a number of times later in the second article. Although the notion of levels of operations in cognition has slipped into Lonergan's thinking he has not, at this point, extended it to levels in consciousness. 'Rational consciousness' is a blanket term for thought or cognition.

Problematic also is the assertion that we as finite limited temporal and mortal historical beings can natively understand and affirm the infinity of our intellectual desire.[45] In his later 'Openness and Religious Experience,' Lonergan talked about openness as an achievement and as a gift, suggesting that God is the one who awakens in us an awareness of the infinity of our desires.[46] I believe that it was by the grace of God that when Lonergan read in Aquinas about the infinity of intellectual light, he recognized the unrestricted questing of his own intellectual desire.

Because of its infinite range, the object of intellect must be being. Being is not unknown. It is known *per se* and naturally. It is through understanding understanding itself as *potens omnia et fieri* that we become capable of grasping the analogous concept of being:

> For the concept of *ens* is not just another concept, another *quod quid est*, another but most general essence; the concept of *ens* is any concept, any *quod quid est*, any essence, when considered not as some highest common factor not again simply in itself but in relation to its own *actus essendi* ... Only on the condition that the human intellect is a *potens omnia facere et fieri* is the concept of all concepts really commensurate with reality – really the concept of *ens*.[47]

Although the phrase 'concept of being' occurs frequently in *Verbum*, the notion of being is not to be found, although the extent to which it is implicit in the above passages is a good question.[48] The movement had now begun in Lonergan's thought that will result in his insight into the pure desire to know as a notion of being.

Towards a Solution: Intellectual Light and Duplication

The general principle of the conaturality of being with intellectual light or wonder in Aquinas suggests a solution to the epistemological problem posed by the mental and real synthesis. Lonergan now adds his own comment on its implications for our understanding of the self-transcendence of knowing and the problem of the relation between the subject and object of knowledge.

We know the real before we know how we know it or before we know such a significant difference within the real as the distinction between a knowing subject and a known object. Understanding the self-transcendence of knowing and the distinction between the subject and object of knowledge – the knower and the known –

> is not a problem of moving from within outwards, of moving from a subject to an object outside the subject. It is a problem of moving from above downwards, of moving from an infinite potentiality commensurate with the universe towards a rational apprehension that seizes the difference of subject and object in essentially the same way that it seizes any other real distinction.[49]

Separating metaphysics and epistemology creates a violent duality of subject and object, thought and reality. Reality, by which is meant nothing less than the universe in the multiplicity and individuality of its members and in the interrelation of all, is the basic framework.

Within that framework there is the distinction between the knower and the known. Where earlier Lonergan talked about intellectual light applying itself to itself to know itself, now he adds to his earlier remark the notion that self-knowledge involves *a duplication in ourselves*:

> We know by what we are; we know we know by knowing what we are; and since even the knowing in 'knowing what we are' is by what we are, rational reflection on ourselves is a duplication of ourselves. [50]

In it the processes that we are verifying duplicate themselves. Only later will he add that in that duplication the subject of knowledge becomes known in effectively the same way as any object of knowledge, through intellectual light. What is perhaps clearer here than in *Insight* is that both modes of knowledge are the outcome of the operation of intellectual light, the desire to know. Key elements to the solution to Kant's problem of the subject and object of knowledge are beginning to fall into place. In particular, his problematic perspective on the in-here subject and the out-there world is being dismantled.

The wisdom that is sought by our intellectual light, 'the most convincing sample in us of the stuff of which the Author of the universe and of our minds consists,' is acquired gradually.[51] Ontologically, the uncreated light that is God is first. Epistemologically, we first experience our own immanent intellectual light in our search for insights into our world. The journey of our desire oscillates dialectically between the two, advances on one level throwing light on the other. If for Augustine our hearts are restless, for Aquinas, Lonergan asserts, it was his mind that was restless until it rested in God. There is a profound spirituality in the authentic living of one's intellectual desire. Beyond the wisdom that we can attain by the natural light of our intellects, there is that attained through the supernatural light of faith 'when the humble surrender of our own light to the self-revealing uncreated Light makes the latter the loved law of all our assents.'[52] Aquinas' remark that the presence of God in the mind is the memory of God in the mind has for Lonergan a mystical ring.

The concluding pages of the second *Verbum* article deal with the relation between mystical experience and the cognitional analogy for the Trinity. Having articulated some of the basic operations of the mind, Lonergan now asks, how is God present in the human mind? His remarks there on Aquinas and Teresa anticipate his position in *Method in Theology* that theology is the expression of the love of God in the life of the theologian.

11

Toronto, the Operations of the Mind, and a Creative Illness

In January 1947 Lonergan was moved from L'Immaculée, Montreal, to Regis College, then at 403 Wellington Street, Toronto. This had been a house of studies in philosophy since 1930 for English-speaking Canadian Jesuits. Between 1943 and 1946 theology programmes were added. At that time the Basilians were responsible for Catholic theology in the university, and it was Lonergan's view that the Jesuits should not compete with them. Rather, they should respond to Charbonneau's invitation to set up a bilingual university in Montreal.[1] When he moved to 403, the Jesuit presence and the theological tradition and library in Toronto were not as well established as in Montreal, although they would grow considerably in the second half of the century.[2] The academic community was smaller than the one he had left in Montreal, with ninety-three members, including fifty-one students. Robert Nunan was the rector and Elliot McGuigan, a contemporary, was the prefect of studies. With his roots well established in Montreal, Lonergan had difficulties in adjusting to the new situation.

Before it was bought in 1867 by the Loretto Abbey, 403 Wellington Street was a fashionable residence occupied by government officials. Onto this they built a rather dark baroque-like convent and chapel, the building in which Lonergan would complete the *Verbum* articles and compose *Insight*. By the time the Jesuits purchased it in 1930 it was surrounded on three sides by factories and at the rear by the main rail yard of Union Station. Freight trains spent the night shunting to build up their cargo for their journey the next day. The house, photographs of which convey a sense of a dismal dark building, was constantly showered with soot and grime from the coal fires of the steam engines. In the estimation of many, it was a health hazard. It was also a poor and austere environment, the heating system frequently being in a state of disrepair. In winter it could be cold, in summer uncomfortably hot. Despite all of these hardships, those who resided there at the time asserted that there was a good spirit in the community.

Culturally, Toronto at the time was in transition from its Scottish Presbyterian origins to one broadened by post-war immigration. There was no sign of the present CN tower or the Skydome, later built right next to the site of the building. After the building was demolished in 1961, the site became the home of the *Globe and Mail* newspaper. A satellite dish scans the sky, gathering news for the newspaper close to the space in which *Insight* was written. As is frequent in the ways of the world, the site is now at the centre of prestigious upmarket developments.

Among Lonergan's students in Toronto for the next number of years were Frederick Crowe and William Stewart. Crowe first met Lonergan in 1941, but it was during these later years as a student of theology that he began to form some sense of Lonergan's potential as a major thinker. He found him to be extremely vigorous in class, pacing the room with energy, 'but his lectures were up and down. He would read the text book, pages 31, 32 ... Then he would come to his own explanation. A dullness at times, but when he came to a question he was interested in he came alive.'[3] He enjoyed questions he was interested in, but he could deal abruptly with those who posed questions that did not interest him or that he felt were trying to trap him.

During Crowe's time at 403 Gilson, mentioned in the Introduction to *Insight*, gave a lecture on existentialism that Lonergan attended. Gilson remarked that we should study and understand authors such as Marcel but not refute them, for that was not pertinent to what they were doing.

Shortly after his move, Lonergan was invited to give a series of weekly lectures in the Theological Faculty of the Pontifical Institute of Medieval Studies of St Michael's College. The previous May Marshall McLuhan had joined the faculty at St Michael's[4] and, possibly as a result of meeting Lonergan there, gave a lecture at 403. According to Crowe, Lonergan and McLuhan had difficulty getting on each other's intellectual wavelength when they met over a drink after the lecture.

The title of his lecture course, 'The Divine Processions,' was directly related to that of the third *Verbum* article, published in September 1947. Books mentioned included Arnou's *De Deo Trino* and Prestige's *God in Patristic Thought*, but he worked mainly with the texts of Aquinas. Walter Principe CSB, one of the five students who attended the course, remembered it as his first real exposure to serious textually based historical scholarship, and initially found it overwhelming. Lonergan struck him as having a computer-like mind.

His first two *Verbum* articles, Lonergan explained, were concerned with the psychological aspects of the procession of an inner word. But St Thomas uses metaphysical categories to express the psychological data. Accordingly, the project would be to explore this use in dealing with the question of operation or act and related processions in the human mind and in God.

Principe's notes give us a glimpse of the process of composition of the third and parts of the fifth of the *Verbum* articles. The introduction attempted to explain how questions about processions in God and in the human mind arose. The New Testament refers to the Father as God, but the precise divine status of the Son and Spirit is ambiguous. In the Arian heresy the notion of person and related questions began to emerge. There followed in Basil and the two Gregories questions about the relations of origin of Father, Son, and Spirit. It is out of the question of the relations of origin that the problem of processions in God arises. This issue was developed by Augustine and later Aquinas, and, for Lonergan, distorted by Scotus.

In this context the term paper that Lonergan set Principe is interesting: 'Problem: Is the act of love a *processio operationis* with respect to the will but a *processio operati* with respect to the *verbum*?'[5] Lonergan invited him to discuss how Aquinas distinguished the processions and how his thought changed on the matter. Are the intellect and will autonomous and parallel faculties, as Scotus held, or is Aquinas right to hold that they are interdependent? Does the act of love emerge in the will independently of what Lonergan would refer to on page 209 (201) of the articles as the 'judgment of value'? He himself would not resolve the problem of the relation between the judgment of value and willing during the composition of the *Verbum* articles and *Insight*.

Verbum 3: The Metaphysics of Act or Operation

At its heart the third *Verbum* article is an exploration of the meaning of act(ivity) or its equivalent, operation, most generally and as applied to mind. The task is to establish if Aquinas' metaphysical analysis of mind in terms of such categories is consistent with the psychological account given in the first two articles. In line with Principe's essay, the third article opens by reviewing the development of Aquinas' thought on processions.[6] It then addresses the claim that the *De Veritate* denied there was a *processio operati* in the will. This Lonergan finds doubtful on the basis that for Aquinas the intellect and the will are not parallel faculties. The inner word in the will proceeds not autonomously from the will but from the inner word of the intellect.

There follows a general discussion of activity. The activity of running in a race is distinct from its end. Some activities, such as sensation, understanding, and willing, are considered to be coincident with their ends. A movement can become in time but not, it appears, an operation that endures in time and is coincident with its end. Aquinas made a basic distinction between the form of sight, which is given in a definition, and the act of seeing. The question now arises, in what sense can an act be considered a *pati*, a received perfection, something that can be caused in us?

> The difficulty here, in so far as I have been able to grasp it, lies in distinguishing between the grammatical subject of a transitive verb in the active voice and, on the other hand, the ontological subject of the exercise of efficient causality. When it is true that 'I see,' it is also true that 'I' is the grammatical subject of a transitive verb in the active voice. But it is mere confusion to conclude immediately that 'I' also denotes the ontological subject of the exercise of efficient causality.[7]

Almost apologetically Lonergan wonders if it makes sense to talk about sensing in act and mean by it that sensing is a matter of undergoing change and being moved. Is not sensing in act just the opposite of being changed and being moved, namely, acting? Or can we talk about an acting or operating that is simply being in act, and not opposed to being changed and being moved? Are some activities such that they require a separate agent, others a separate patient in order to occur? Are there activities that require neither an agent nor patient in order for them to occur? From this standpoint how are we to interpret understanding, human and divine, as an activity?

Potency is the principle of activity in the agent or patient. The term, according to Avicenna, initially referred to powerful men. It means power to act but also entails immunity from suffering. It was then transferred to natural things. On page 123 (114) Lonergan lists a range of meanings of the term as used by Avicenna: a disposition, a possibility of receiving, and a principle of action.

How, he wonders, do such general considerations of act or operation and potency apply specifically to the human intellect? When we hear a bell ringing, there are the linked activities of sounding and of hearing. Could it be said that our sense of hearing is a receptive potency to the activity of sounding? The sound that we hear acts on the receptive potency that is our hearing and calls it into act. Significant in this context is one of Lonergan's first references to *the operation* of sensation.[8] The same line of questioning can be applied to the agent and possible intellect, to the intellect as understanding and as speaking an inner word of thought, and finally, to reflective understanding and judging. In what sense can these activities be considered as active and passive?

The goal of the complex analysis is brought into focus into lengthy but helpful summary statement:

> The distinction between agent and possible intellect is the distinction between an efficient potency that produces and a natural potency that receives. The distinction between the possible intellect of one that is learning and the possible intellect of one in possession of a science is a distinction between the *De Potentia's* passive potency to the reception of a form and its active potency to the exercise of operation in virtue of form. The distinction between *intelligere* and *dicere* is a distinction between the two meanings of action, operation: *intelligere* is action in the sense of act; *dicere* is action in the sense of operating an effect. The distinction between agent object and terminal object is to be applied twice. On the level of intellectual apprehension the agent object is the *quidditas rei materialis*, not *to ti estin* but *to ti en einai*, known in and through a phantasm illuminated by agent intellect; this agent object is the *objectum proprium intellectua humani*; it is the object of insight. Corresponding to this agent object there is the terminal object of the inner word; this is the concept, and the first of the concepts is *ens*, the *objectum commune intellectus*.[9]

It is worthwhile to continue with the quotation in order to see the parallels he draws for the level of judgment:

> Again, on the level of judgment the agent object is the objective evidence provided by sense and/or empirical consciousness, ordered conceptually and logically in a *reductio ad principia*, and moving to the critical act of understanding. Corresponding to this agent object, there is the other terminal object, the inner word of judgment, the *verbum*, in and through which is known the final object, the *ens reale*.

Just as the object of understanding, *quidditas rei materialis*, is strangely different from the phantasm as perceived or imagined, so also the object of judgment, existence, differs from the *quidditas* that is understood.

The early occurrence of the phrase 'empirical consciousness,' a phrase to be found in Kant's *Critique of Pure Reason,* is significant. Later on the same page the words 'rationally conscious' are used again as a blanket term for the process of thought. In the quotes we again find reference to two levels of activity or operation, the intellectual and the level of judgment, but at this point I don't think Lonergan grasped their significance. The elements of the problem of cognition as conscious are being assembled.

Little metaphysical analysis of the will is offered in terms of action, passion, causality, agent, and terminal object. In his summing up Lonergan simply states that 'the act of love with respect to an end is, as proceeding from the will, "*processio operationis*," but as proceeding from the inner word, "*processio operati.*"'[10] His main emphasis is on a detailed analysis of the mind rather than of the will in Aquinas.

O'Connell's Attack on the First Verbum Article

> My first article on *Verbum* was greeted by a scholastic, speaking for his professor, saying: 'That is just a mosaic of texts. It doesn't mean anything.'[11]

In May 1947, after the second article had been published, Matthew J. O'Connell, then a Jesuit student of philosophy from St. Louis University, wrote a highly critical review of the first *Verbum* article. Entitled 'St. Thomas and the *Verbum*: An Interpretation,' it was published in *The Modern Schoolman*. O'Connell's teacher, Henri Renard, was a professor of philosophy in the Gregorian during Lonergan's student years, and was said to be of the impression that Lonergan was an idealist. Later Lonergan will make clear that distinguishing his position from idealism is the critical problem in philosophy. O'Connell's article opened:

> In a recent issue of *Theological Studies*, there appeared an article concerning St. Thomas's doctrine on the *verbum*. It is of interest to Thomistic philosophers as an example of how easily a concatenation of texts from St. Thomas can be made to support a theory he could never have accepted.[12]

O'Connell acknowledged that Lonergan was translating *intelligere* by 'to understand.' This point, which Lauer, Kenny, Clark, and many others saw as centrally problematic, did not concern him.[13] In *Verbum* 1 Lonergan acknowledged a dozen senses of *intellectus* in Aquinas, but held that the principal meaning of *intelligere* is 'understanding.'[14] What does bother O'Connell is that the subsequent interpretation of Aquinas on understanding as psychological undergoes a strange transformation.

On the basis of the first article alone O'Connell accused Lonergan of radically misrepresenting Aquinas on insight into phantasm, on knowledge of the singular, on conceptualization, on abstraction, and on the concept of being. The role of phantasm poses questions for him about knowledge of the singular and the universal. Remarking that it is difficult to understand how Lonergan could have so misinterpreted Aquinas on insight into phantasm, he concludes:

> His treatment makes it clear that any discussion of the genesis of ideas in St. Thomas which does not stress the role of the agent intellect and the passivity of the possible intellect is bound to lead to misapprehensions. The further effects of these omissions shall be noted shortly.[15]

Although Stanley Machnik remembers discussing the agent intellect with Lonergan around this time, it is mentioned only in two footnotes in the first *Verbum* article, notes 52 (48) and 126 (122). Although the What? question, which is a form of its expression, is discussed, the agent intellect does not feature significantly. It is mentioned only once by name in the course 'Thought and Reality,' but also tacitly as the spirit of inquiry in science. It begins to make its entry in the second article in the discussion of intellectual light and then grows in importance in Lonergan's later work.

O'Connell further accuses Lonergan of confusing abstraction with conceptualization. He quotes Lonergan to the effect that in the first act of intellect 'one knows not the thing, but only the idea of the thing, because as yet one is in the purely logical order,' adding, 'need we remark that such a statement, with its logical implications, contains all the requisites for idealism?'[16]

In his fourth *Verbum* article Lonergan will make reply to the accusation that he is an idealist.[17] Firstly, he holds, the content of the object of thought is not subjective, but objective. Secondly, if one overlooks insight into phantasm then some form of idealism seems inevitable. At the end of the article he is more explicit on the significance for his case of what insight grasps in the phantasm. As one allows the number of radii to increase, insight grasps in the imagined equal radii in a curve on a plane surface uniform roundness. In this instance imagination presents the terms, the insight the intelligible relations. In an endnote he adds:

> This is the critical point in philosophy. For a materialist the terms are real, the intelligible unification subjective; for an idealist the terms cannot be reality and the intelligible unification is not objective; for the Platonist the terms are not reality but the intelligible unifications are objective in another world; for the Aristotelian both are objective in this world; Thomism adds a third category, existence, to Aristotelian matter and form.[18]

O'Connell goes on to quote a confused and self-contradictory passage from the unauthentic *De Natura Verbi Intellectus*, on the priority of the *verbum* over the understanding. (It is a point Lonergan will explicitly refute in the fourth article.)[19] O'Connell, with the author of that text, seems to want the 'word,' 'proposition,' or 'thought' to be both subsequent to understanding and prior to knowing. On abstraction he again warns about the danger of overlooking the agent intellect, concluding that abstraction is a preconscious rather than a conscious process, the exception being the third mode.[20] He is also critical of Lonergan's reference to the concept of being as the first concept.

O'Connell concluded that those who knew their Thomas would see through Lonergan's thesis, adding:

> Any philosopher has the right to speculate – no one can deny him that; but he has not the right to speculate in the name of St. Thomas Aquinas, unless he accepts and follows the basic principles that guided St. Thomas's own thought.[21]

Lonergan would list O'Connell in a footnote in the third article as one of his adversaries.

Lonergan remarked to Crowe that he could see the hand of Renard in O'Connell's article. Although Crowe felt Lonergan seemed calm when making his comments, the article upset him. As Crowe put it: 'He came up to villa that summer, 1947. He did not do much work. He had a long rest. George McInerney, a close friend, spoke about how downcast he was all summer.'[22]

Breaking Out of the Philosophy of Immanence

In the fall Lonergan started teaching two courses, the first on faith and the virtues, the second on grace.[23] Interesting are his comments on dialectical theology, containing references to Barth, Emile Brunner, Gogarthen, Bultmann, and Ferre. Against the immanentism of Schleiermacher and Kant, religion cannot have its origin and source within the individual alone.

On the second page of Crowe's notes for the faith course, Lonergan contrasts his own critical realism with the philosophy of immanence, dogmatic, and naive realism. Cryptically he makes his point: 'If we make the three judgments, I'm real; You're real; I'm not you; then we are out of immanence.' In *Insight* he varies the content: I am a knower, this is a typewriter, I am not this typewriter.[24] There is involved in this a significant advance beyond his insight in 1935 that the object of judgment is that which exists. Now he recognizes that if we make a plurality of such judgments, in this case three, we will in fact be affirming the existence of more than a single reality. If I am one of the judged existences and you or something else is another, then I am not the one and only existent or reality. The foundations of Lonergan's critical realism will require us to make not just a single but rather a plurality of judgments. We find here the genesis of what in *Insight* he will term the 'principal notion of objectivity,' which he affirms solves the problem of transcendence. It takes a plurality of judgments to define, distinguish, and relate the object and subject of knowledge.

Science and faith have different motives. Empirical faith is belief in another who through his or her senses has witnessed what you cannot witness through your senses, be it in science, detective work, or miracles. There is also the intellectual faith of a student who eventually hopes to understand as the teacher; of a disciple of, for instance, St Thomas who knows he or she will never understand as Aquinas did; and there is the faith of a believer, where the revealed object, being supernatural, can't be understood, irrespective of that believer's hopes. In religion the authority of God moves us to faith, but such faith is obscure because of the nature of its evidence. Following Lennertz, Lonergan's reflections now cover the freedom, infallibility, rationality, and light of faith that illuminates and makes interesting the things of God that are above our natures.

The last ten pages of the notes contain some of his earliest reflections on the love of God and on the good.[25] The good is that which satisfies our appetites. Love is the willing of the good, the will being defined as a spiritual appetite following reason. What is important for morality is the dictate of right reason, whether this is concerned with what is good for me or what is good for the other. The intellect, by its ordering, relates the whole to its parts, the husband and wife being parts of the family. At times it is easier to love the part rather than the whole, for us humans to love one another than to love God.

Effective love is directed to a particular person or situation. Affective love 'makes the man, directs his attention to and observation of reality, controls the series of phantasms, thoughts, counsels, judgments, makes almost the whole man and this spontaneously and in a hidden way.'[26] The fruit of prayer or meditation is not directly clear practical decisions. It is, rather, the transformation of the person's will 'so that affective love may be formed.' Lonergan concludes with some reflections on the difficulty of friendship.

An Epiphany and a Creative Illness

The course on grace opened by reviewing many of the familiar terms in Lonergan's doctoral thesis. According to Crowe, at the conclusion of the treatment of the grace of justification Lonergan attempted to develop a systematic approach to the material. Pages 31–48 of William Stewart's course notes are, at this point, full of surprises.[27] Attempting to explain the meaning of a system of primitive terms and relations, they are of the form of an unexpected epiphany of the ferment in Lonergan's inner life at the time.

Primitive notions cannot be reduced to anything else. A system, for example, a machine, consists of a set of members in which each part is determined by its relations to all others. Systems can be closed, open, direct, analogous, or universal. The number system is instanced as an open system in that it can admit an indefinite number of members, $N_1, N_2, N_3, \ldots$ defined by their operations, $O_1, O_2, O_3, \ldots$ It is also analogous in that members have relations within themselves: $N_1:O_1::N_2:O_2$. Lonergan illustrates this with reference to the integers and the decimals: Let $x = 0.9999\cdot$. $10x = 9.999\cdot$. By subtraction, $9x = 9.000$. It follows that $x = 1$, an illustration we find in the first chapter of *Insight*.

Peter is not his body but has some reality in common with it. Peter and Paul have no reality in common but both share the concept 'real.' It follows that being (Ens) is an open, universal, and analogous system. Other concepts connote certain aspects of a thing and prescind from others. Being (Ens) in certain respects includes every aspect of every thing because all such aspects are parts of the universal system of Being.

In the section on Cajetan of the early *Verbum* draft and in the second *Verbum* article, we found Lonergan using the terms 'gnoseology,' 'epistemology,' and 'metaphysics.' On page 32 of Stewart's notes there is recorded one of his clearest statements about the three related disciplines, their defining questions and relations.[28] Metaphysics is the science of being, of universal reality. In this sense it links to Lonergan's remarks about his aspirations for metaphysics in the Keeler essay on Newman and the letter in 1935 to his provincial. As a science of universal reality it relates to the term 'reality' in his courses 'Thought and Reality' and the later 'Intelligence and Reality.'

Gnoseology or cognitional theory (in which he had been interested since his Heythrop days) treats of knowing as knowing and clearly links to the terms 'thought' and 'intelligence' in those courses, the first *Verbum* article, and the opening sections of the second.

Epistemology treats of knowledge inasmuch as through knowledge intellect reaches out to reality, transcends its subjectivity contra Kant's separation of understanding and object. Accordingly, it is concerned with the relation between thought and reality in those courses. Central to the second article was the task of understanding how reality became known through the inner words of definition and true judgment. There Lonergan addresses the task in his discussion of wisdom, self-knowledge, and intellectual light.

In the hiddenness of these notes, as in an epiphany, he is articulating the basic questions that are motivating his whole research programme. That programme will find expression in the *Verbum* articles, in 'Thought and Reality,' and later in 'Intelligence and Reality' and the book *Insight*. As there are the foundations of mathematics and of economics, so also for Lonergan there are foundations for philosophy, and he is probing them.

The necessary and sufficient criteria of the real are our true judgments. His fifth point is to the effect that there is harmony between his philosophical definition of the real and Catholic dogma, the propositions established by the church. It seems to confirm that his concern with realism is not peripheral but central to the question of method in theology. He then goes on to consider a number of mistaken criteria of the real, including common sense: '[Something] is real if common sense says so.' Decisively, on the question of the flat earth science made a fool of common sense. Only the true judgments of science and common sense, then, are a criterion of the real. He is also critical of empiricism as a criterion. But it puts to us the question, how are we to understand theological realism in which the light of faith will illuminate the light of natural wonder?

On page 34 of William Stewart's notes Lonergan addresses the question of the relations that will hold the system together, and specifically the role of understanding in making relations known. There are two kinds of relations, empirical and intelligible. The empirical are known by 'taking a look at them.' Intelligible relations are known when you know the why, the because, the therefore, the if–then. A key relation is the formal cause. As it becomes known by understanding, understanding is the key to the system of reality. Materialists, idealists such as Hegel, and transcendental empiricists, the chief of whom for him is Kant, fail to grasp the key role of understanding the formal cause in the system of reality.

Understanding always presupposes a residue, some given that in certain respects it explains and in others it can never explain. This residue belongs to the same family of terms as 'matter' and 'potency' and is 'known,' not by understanding, but by the senses. Not explained by understanding, it poses questions about the limits of explanation. Lonergan cites as illustrations of the empirical residue the existence of material things, material particularity, space-time, accidental conjunction, the contingence of operations, and probability. With some modifications, all of these will make their appearance in *Insight*. Chemistry explains the why of hydrogen, but not why two different instances of hydrogen atoms differ. The physics of space and time orders places and their times but does not explain why one place and time differs from another.[29] At this point the notes could be read as a draft of the section on the empirical residue in the first chapter of *Insight*.

His treatment of the contingency of operations leads to a short but significant section on probability. Absent from his 'Thought and Reality' course, probability is the measured ratio of actual occurrences of an event to the number of possible occurrences. It is objective because determinism is false. The universe for him is not a closed but an open system because of the contingency of operations and free will. Objective probability is a central feature of the thinking of modern science, but also squares with key points in Aristotle and Aquinas. As *Insight* was composed, probability would come to constitute a key component of world order as he understood it. Pages 31–8 of Stewart's notes are a major source of insight into how Lonergan thought out and composed the book.

This unusual excursion of his thought ended when Lonergan became unwell. As a result he had to take a break of three or four weeks from teaching. According to Crowe:

> He had come to a point where he was trying, as it were, a systematic approach to the question. He was dictating and we were writing furiously. Proposition 1, 2, 3, ... in thesis form. He called them theses. He got up to 19 or 20. You could see he was struggling. It wasn't at all anything like a breakdown. Fatigue, yes. He went away for 2 or 3 or 4 weeks. Later he came back and started again, but the series was different now. I can't remember if he started from no. 1 but could tell from my notes. So it was a tough time. It followed pretty directly on the *Modern Schoolman* review.[30]

It is clear from a number of sources that Lonergan went through some kind of crisis in the summer of 1947 and during the following year. He was forty-three at the time, an age when many have to come to terms with the beginning of the second half of the life cycle. He was disturbed by the attack in *Modern Schoolman*, and was also disturbed by the move to Toronto and the new environment. He had left a well-established circle of friends and a supportive environment in Montreal. In Toronto he would have to start over again. The bleakness and isolation of the house posed difficulties for him. Coming two years before he would begin to compose *Insight*, the disturbance presents itself as a creative illness similar to those suffered by Freud and Jung.[31]

Henri Samson, a Jesuit, was a professionally trained psychotherapist in Montreal. As well as having a private practice, he was a resource person for Jesuits who needed counselling. Lonergan consulted him, meeting with him on about three occasions. Samson had been a pupil of his in theology and admitted that he found it awkward that his former professor should seek his help. Indeed, that Lonergan should seek help from a former student is unusual. According to Samson, he was suffering from a form of nervousness, depression, and was feeling very lonesome. He had difficulty adjusting to people and the group and he was not as clear-minded as normal. There was also a suggestion that the problem related to the integration of his affective side with his intellectual side, and with facing again the implications of a celibate vocation.

After three meetings Lonergan decided against therapy. Our understanding of these events in Lonergan's life is incomplete, in terms of both the details and their significance. What is clear, however, is that whatever experience he underwent, he came back from it in a state of readiness to finish the *Verbum* articles and begin the ascent of *Insight*. Not unrelated is a remark that he made in a letter to Louis Roy, OP in 1977: 'After twenty four years of aridity in religious life, I moved into that happier state and have enjoyed it now for over thirty one-years.' This arithmetic would place him in the joyful state in 1946, surely a year too soon. What Lonergan is saying in this communication is that after his creative illness a radical change took place in his religious interiority. The problems that were disturbing him faded and were replaced by an inner peace and joy. His writing project and the demands for solitude it would make now became central. He became more detached. As after his Sicilian illness there burst forth a flood of new ideas in Newman, so after his transitional illness in Toronto there would begin in Lonergan the creative process whose product would be *Insight*. He had settled into what Julia Cameron refers to as his vein of gold.

He returned and resumed the course.[32] In pages 51–4 of Stewart's notes, entitled 'The Natural Desire to See God,' Lonergan directly addresses some of the questions raised by de Lubac's *Surnaturel*, which was published in 1946 and had created something of a stir. De Lubac wants to argue that the supernatural order is an intrinsic component of the order in the universe as a whole rather than something gratuitously added. The concept of a state of pure nature in which man could achieve a natural fulfilment, short of participation in the life of God, would then be ruled out. He argues that there is no mention of pure nature in the scripture and the Fathers. Self-transcendence is natural to man. Biological species evolve. In the same way, the human person had an innate tendency to rise to a higher state. There are echoes here of what Lonergan means by finality. Finally God is Love and could not create rational creatures without also raising them to the level of mutual love and friendship. The thrust of his argument was to soften the then radical distinction between nature and grace. This was at the time controversial and not well received in Rome.

Lonergan began by acknowledging that the nature of grace is not well understood. Some think that the desire for the vision of God can be proved from St Thomas. Still, in paragraph 1518 of *Denzinger*, the theological handbook of Catholic sources, we find condemned the assertion that by purely natural powers a man can actually desire the end promised by Christ. But what is that end, and in what sense is it proportionate to our natures or beyond our natures? Lonergan suggests that whereas it is known from revelation that the destiny of the intellect is the beatific vision, the destiny of the human will is neither specific nor determinate. He concludes his introduction with remarks echoing 'On The Supernatural,' about one and the same intellectual potency being natural and obediential. It is obediential if God activates it.

Lonergan takes up each of De Lubac's points in turn. Against the objection that the human person has a desire for the vision of God in himself and that such a desire is absolutely supernatural, Lonergan replies by conceding that man desires the most perfect vision of God. That the desired vision is the same as what is known as the beatific vision, the vision of God as he is in himself, is denied. The transcendental tendency does not place man in a transcendental order. But the supernatural order really places human beings in a higher order.

The argument from love has a certain probability. But love or friendship is between equals, and so for a human being to be admitted into God's friendship would involve elevation to a supernatural order. It is Lonergan's conclusion that the possibility of a state of pure nature has not been disproved by De Lubac.

The question raised by de Lubac was given further treatment by Lonergan in an important essay, 'The Natural Desire to See God,' published in 1949.[33] His central thesis there is that human intellectual desire is a natural rather than an acquired desire or skill like playing the violin. Under normal circumstances it finds its fulfilment in proper rather than in analogical knowledge. So we want to know, properly, what is the nature of the chemical elements, what it is that happened on an occasion, and so forth. Analogies help but are ultimately frustrating. But the question arises; do we have a natural desire to understand God? The philosopher and the theologian, for Lonergan, have different perspectives. The theologian can affirm such a desire, but the philosopher is faced with a paradox.

12

Human Insights as Reflections of the Divine Nature

In May 1948 Quentin Lauer, then a student of theology at Woodstock College, wrote a defense of Lonergan entitled 'Comment on "An Interpretation"' in *The Modern Schoolman.* Responding to O'Connell point by point, he ended with the question 'whether *intelligere* does mean precisely understanding,' a question O'Connell avoided.[1] This, for Lauer, was the most disputed aspect of the first article. In order to appreciate how new that interpretation was, Lonergan invited Crowe to read both of the articles by O'Connell and Lauer. As a result, Lonergan came to focus on the distinction between intellectualist and conceptualist interpretations of Aquinas, a theme that runs through the fourth and fifth articles. In the fourth, published in March 1949, he explored the implications of those different readings of Aquinas for the formation of concepts. The fifth, published in September, examined their different responses to Aquinas's understanding of God. In both he threw down the gauntlet to conceptualist interpreters of Aquinas.

The fourth *Verbum* article opened with a review of Lonergan's findings so far. There is the inner word of definition or conceptualization and there is the inner word of judgment. Both are caused by and originate in understanding. Reality becomes known in judgment. This Lonergan names the intellectualist interpretation of Aquinas, which, for him,

> runs counter throughout to the currently accepted conceptualist view, but the point of most apparent conflict lies in the issue to which conceptualists attend almost exclusively, the abstraction of concepts. To this issue we may now direct our attention, asking: first, what is the matter from which intellect abstracts; secondly, what is

the immateriality by which it knows; thirdly, what is the formative abstraction of the concept; fourthly, what is the prior apprehensive abstraction of insight into phantasm; and fifthly, what is the intellectual knowledge of the singular.[2]

Intellectualists are those who are aware of the difference between their questioning and insights, on the one hand, and their thoughts, propositions, and linguistic expression, on the other. Conceptualists overlook the preconceptual activities of questioning and understanding in the problem-solving experience. The focus of their attention is on the conceptualized solutions. To recognize one's intellectual desire and related insights requires a fine sense of attunement to the data of one's consciousness. The challenge for Lonergan was to show on the basis of his writings that Aquinas was an intellectualist rather than a conceptualist. In reading the article it is good to have the problem-solving experience in mind.

In their experiments physicists, chemists, and biologists operate not simply on language, but also on material entities, particles, atoms, the genes of biological organisms. Matter at particular places and times is an ultimate source or given of the problem solving of the sciences. So the question arises, what is meant by matter that is the inspiration of understanding and concept formation in the sciences?

Tables and chairs, weights and measures are obviously material. But can weights and measures themselves be divided endlessly, or do we arrive ultimately at some elementary and indivisible units? Is everything made of some primal matter? If so, what is it like? Where can it be identified? How does the obvious matter of tables and chairs, of heavy things and even of living things, relate to prime matter? The old naturalists, Lonergan remarks, from their observations of tables and chairs, wood and bones inferred the existence of an element, earth. Similarly, from the melting of gold and bronze to an element, water. The ultimate subject of change is for them some sensible body, the stuff of the universe, substantial and permanent. All the rest is mutable and accidental. The bottom line is that it is our senses that have the last word in establishing the reality of matter.

Because Aristotle held that everything changed, he concluded that there could be no ultimate unchanging subject of change. In order to define matter he had to have recourse to analogy. Matter is primarily proportionate to form, which Lonergan interprets as scientific law, be it physical, chemical, or biological. So prime matter for him is what is proportionate to the form or law of the lowest science. Between Aristotle and the old and the new materialists there is a terrible chasm. For where the old materialists defined matter in terms of its sensibility and its immutable indivisibility, Aristotle defined it in relation to its capacity to take on intelligible forms.

Intelligible properties or forms are not known by the senses, but rather by the understanding. Accordingly, Aristotle completely undermines the view of the old materialists that reality is sensible by placing 'in the most material of assignable things an intelligible component known by our intellects and identifiable in our knowledge.'[3] Aristotle also corrects the misguided intellectualism of Plato, for whom the real was intelligible but not in this world.

Beside the question of prime matter arising out of the givenness of objects in our world, there are also questions about the parts of the matter and about material and individual conditions. What these mean 'is simple if one grasps that natural form stands to natural matter as the object of insight (*forma intelligibilis*) stands to the object of sense (*materia sensibilis*).'[4] Sight, the intelligible form of the eye, does not arise out of an arbitrary conjunction of matter. Rather, it requires a unique and precise conjunction of material elements. The same is true of all other objects in the world.[5]

In the intellectualist account matter is proportionate to form or intelligibility. Forms, species, or quiddities are known directly by the intellect. But these knowns 'have antecedent suppositions, simultaneous suppositions, and consequents, all of which, as such are indirectly known,'[6] a remark that has to do with the empirical residue in *Insight*. There is a huge divide between this intellectualist account of matter and the opposed empiricist one in which the senses have the last word.

Knowing as an Immaterial Assimilation of a Material Object

The third article opened up the question of the causal relation between the knower and the known. The analysis offered left one wondering whether the human mind in its patienthood and agenthood, in the way it moves and is moved by its object, is no different from anything else. The next section of *Verbum* 4 on the immateriality of knowing explores the uniqueness of the agenthood and patienthood of the mind. It is one thing to experience a falling body, it is another to investigate the nature of the fall, to measure directly the relations involved and arrive at some understanding of its law. Through the agency of the mind, what is understood becomes detached from the given place and time of the matter.

In order for our minds to be able to understand gravity or the life of a cell or something about the plot in another person's life, they must share some kind of affinity with what it is they understand. When we know something, the form of the thing and the form of the knowing must be similar.[7] It is because of this that Aristotle defined the mind as the form of the forms rather than a specific form. If this is so, how is it that we can understand gravity without our minds becoming gravity? How is it we can understand another person without our minds becoming that person? How is it that our understanding of a particular material object or person can be detached from its specific place and time and communicated to others across space and time? This in turn points to something different about the human mind as contrasted with the material objects it can come to know.

In coming to understand gravity, DNA, or a person's life history, what precisely is the nature of the intimate relation between the knower and the known? Aristotle held that it was of the form of an identity. When I see the ball falling because of the force of gravity, what is falling and what I see are identical. Nothing comes between them. Similarly, when I make my measurements and correctly understand the nature of the acceleration, the acceleration and what I understand are identical.

Understanding involves an assimilation of some attributes of the thing understood. When we understand gravity we assimilate something of how masses relate. When we understand the plot in a life we assimilate some attribute of the person. What we do not assimilate in each instance is the matter, the materiality of the object. In response to this problem, Aquinas worked out the theorem of the immaterial assimilation of the known by the knower.

So the senses and the intellect assimilate different properties of the object in different ways. The senses are receptive of the sensible forms without the natural matter in much the same fashion as the wax is receptive of the imprint of a seal without receiving the metal of the seal. When the string vibrates my senses receive the sound, not the vibrating string. The senses are, however, material organs. Sight is the form of the material organ that is the eye. By way of contrast, 'the possible intellect is not the form of any organ; it has no other nature but ability to receive; it stands to all intelligible forms as prime matter stands to all sensible forms.'[8]

The understanding, unlike sight, touch, taste, and smell, is not the form of any sense organ. Nonetheless, as Aristotle insisted and the blind, deaf, and dumb Hellen Keller discovered, without our imagination and some sense operations we cannot understand. The questions in this section are puzzling and provocative, leaving the impression that the conclusions come too quick.

Critiquing the Conceptualist Account of Problem Solving

The intellectualist account of matter and of the immateriality of knowing leads into an analysis of the formation of concepts. The problem is best grasped by addressing the question, How, in solving an initially unsolved problem, do new concepts and a related language use form and emerge in us? In the initial stages of the problem solving we cannot think or speak or write out an answer. We are stuck. For Lonergan the conceptualists hold that solutions arrive in our minds unconsciously; how they get there is of no importance. The intellectualists hold that solutions are produced by the preconceptual activities of questioning and understanding. Lonergan's discussion of the abstraction of concepts addresses the problem of correctly or incorrectly understanding the problem-solving process. It could be argued that it was, in part, inspired by the criticisms of O'Connell and the response of Lauer.

As in the first *Verbum* article, so also here Lonergan begins his analysis with propositions and their expressions, the more obvious products of the process of abstracting a solution to a problem. From this perspective he will work back to the questioning and understanding that form the propositions. Abstraction can be considered by reflecting on common names. Names are signs of meaning. They refer to things through the concepts we think. It follows that reflection on names or, more generally, linguistic structures leads immediately into reflection on knowledge or science. Scientific understanding is of the necessary and universal, but things are particular and contingent. Still 'intellect can define universally and deduce with necessity on the basis of the changeless forms of changing things.'[9] But what is the changeless form or *ratio* of the thing? It is that aspect of it which can be understood apart from its assigned matter and its determinate place and time. It is not some empirical replica, but the constitutive relations of the given. Abstraction, for Lonergan, involves the grasp of those objective relations. Modern illustrations that come to mind would be scientific laws, categories, or rules such as the gas laws or the periodic system of the elements. In this way science considers the thing apart from its matter.

At this point Lonergan, commenting that he has been accused of being an idealist (an accusation levelled in O'Connell's article), goes on to defend himself:

> First, the universal *ratio* or object of thought known by means of the inner word is not subjective but objective; it is not the thinking, meaning, defining, but the thought, meant, defined; but though it is objective, still it is universal and all reality is particular.[10]

It is a position he will repeat many times. In *Insight* he will draw a distinction between *pensée pensée* and *pensée pensante*, between the thinking and the thought. On page 169 n.96 (159, n.97) of *Verbum* he clearly states that *quidditas* and *esse*, which are objects of mental acts or operations, are not to be thought of as attributes of our cognitional activities or minds, but of the object or thing known. It is Lonergan's conclusion that, without an appreciation of the prior apprehensive abstraction, the application of universal *rationes,* for which we could read modern rules or scientific laws, to particular things must be blind.

Three Kinds of Abstraction in Problem Solving

Lonergan's main argument is that for Aquinas formative abstraction or concept formation is the outcome of the prior stages of objective and apprehensive abstraction. In objective abstraction our questioning selects some datum out of the entire world of sense or of consciousness and becomes interested in it:

> In the *Contra Gentiles* the actual intelligibility of phantasm is clarified: in the dark colours are visible in potency; in daylight they are visible in act but seen in potency; they are seen in act only inasmuch as sight is in act; similarly, prior to the illumination of agent intellect, phantasms are intelligible in potency; by illumination they become intelligible in act but only understood in potency.[11]

Subjectively, this constitutes the awakening of our mind's desire to a problem in the world. Objectively, it involves a particular realm in the universe being selected out as interesting or even fascinating by our minds. In the initial stages of the opening up of a problem there is no question of our being able to understand it in depth or converse about it. Until the problem is solved we will not have the concepts and words with which to explain it.

In the intellectualist reading of Aquinas, it is through apprehensive abstraction, which Lonergan equates with insight into phantasm, that the unsolved problem comes to be resolved and the solution, the *ratio* with its concepts, comes to be formed. There follows a probing analysis of Aquinas' thought on the relation between understanding and its proper object. Present in but distinct from the phantasm as seen or imagined, the object of understanding is variously named *quiddity, species, eidos, forma intelligibilis, species intelligibilis, quidditas rei materialis.* In footnote 96 (97) Lonergan acknowledges a development in his understanding since writing the first article in relation to *quidditas,* conversion to phantasm, and reflection on phantasm. Footnotes 111–12 (112–13) point to a similar deepening in his understanding of the relation between insight and phantasm. The significance of the section derives from the fact that it constitutes a sort of crucial experiment between intellectualists, who affirm that understanding is preconceptual and directly related to images and phantasms, and conceptualists, who deny this.

What did Aquinas take to be the object of insight, of understanding in the phantasm? How the question is answered separates off whole philosophies and related realisms. Aquinas' mature position that it is the *quidditas rei materialis*, the 'what it is' of material things, is given in the treatise on the human intellect in the *Pars Prima*. On his way to that position there were earlier ways of putting it:

> In the incessantly quoted third book of Aristotle's *De Anima* there is recalled the distinction of *Metaphysics* Z, 6 between water and the quiddity of water, magnitude and the quiddity of magnitude, Socrates and the quiddity of Socrates; then it is advanced that directly by sense we know water, magnitude, flesh, that directly by intellect we know the quiddities of water, magnitude, flesh, and that indirectly by intellect we know what directly we know by sense. From this passage Aquinas drew three conclusions and of them the first regarded the proper object of human intellect. That object is the *quidditas rei* which is not separate from the thing, as the Platonists held, nor apart from sensible things, even though intellect apprehends it without apprehending the individual conditions it possesses in sensible things.[12]

A variety of terms are used to specify the preconceptual object of understanding: *forma intelligibilis*, *quidditas rei*, object of intellect, species, eidos, form. It can be called both *forma intelligibilis* and *species intelligibilis*.[13]

Before the position in the *Pars Prima* was worked out, a dualism in the Aristotelian inheritance that suggested the object of intellect might be phantasm or the *quidditas rei materialis* had to be overcome. The *Pars Prima*, with its thesis that the proper object of intellect is the *quidditas rei materialis*, resolves the tension between these positions. That object is made potentially intelligible by the illumination of the phantasm by the agent intellect, the spirit of inquiry. It is apprehended in the phantasm by the possible intellect. What Aquinas is saying is that the proper object of our understanding is not something in our minds, but something in our worlds that is made present in sensible or imaginative presentations: 'for sense directly knows the sensible object, but intellect directly knows not phantasm but the thing that phantasm represents; accordingly, insight into phantasm is like looking *in*, not looking *at*, a mirror.'[14] In this context we find occurring the phrases 'on the sensitive level' and 'on the level of intellect.'[15]

The questioning activity of our wonder illuminates and makes the image interesting. But what, it can be asked, is meant by the abstraction of species from phantasm? By way of response Lonergan continues:

The principle meaning clearly is that there is produced in the possible intellect a similitude of the thing presented by phantasm; this similitude is similar to the thing, not in all respects, but with regard only to its specific nature; it is to be identified with the 'species qua.'[16]

Conceptualization or formative abstraction entails the formation and speaking of an inner word or object of thought. The intelligible structure of that word or thought reflects the intelligible structure of what the insight has apprehended in the image. Once the insight into the phantasm has occurred, we can conceptualize a solution to our problem.

At this point Lonergan's odyssey on the meaning of ideas, awakened by his reading of Stewart's *Plato's Doctrine of Ideas*, had reached its term. Involved was a change in his loyalties from Plato to Aristotle. It was a journey that brings into sharp focus the meaning of an earlier quote that ended as follows:

what Aristotle and Aquinas held was that intellect abstracted from phantasm a preconceptual form or species of *quod quid erat esse*, whence both terms and nexus were inwardly spoken.[17]

Those preconceptual forms, which can find their articulation in scientific laws, cannot be imagined or pictured in the phantasm. It is from this point and context in the *Verbum* text that the word 'idea,' used in the later title of the book version, *Word and Idea*, derives its meaning. Lonergan, when composing *Insight*, will be left with the challenge of translating this insight into the context of the modern empirical sciences. What do the insights of the modern sciences abstract from their sensible and imaginative presentations?

Finally, there is the distinction between conceptualist and intellectualist accounts of the application of solutions and their concepts to particular instances. For the conceptualist there is a chasm between our thoughts and situations in the world. Precisely how our minds apply abstract rules and their concepts to concrete particulars is a puzzle. The intellectualist acknowledges that the meaning of our thoughts originate in insights into phantasms or situations in the world. Our understanding natively recognizes the phantasms or situations relevant to a given proposition. This is acknowledged by John McDowell in his 'Wittgenstein on Following a Rule.' Understanding how to apply a rule to a situation involved a cottoning on, a leap or inspired guess at the pattern of applications, the leap of insight.[18] In this context we find Lonergan beginning to use phrases such as 'to a merely sensitive consciousness' and 'the imagined object as present to intelligent consciousness as something-to-be-understood.'[19] How at this point 'intelligent consciousness' relates to his earlier blanket usage of 'rational consciousness' is an interesting question, bearing in mind that in the fifth article he will refer to the two operations of the intellect.

Writing the fourth article was a significant factor in getting Lonergan through his earlier difficulties. When he had finished writing it, presumably sometime towards the end of 1948, he felt that it was the pure mind of Aquinas and beyond criticism. After he sent it off to the publisher he remarked to Fred Crowe: 'It's good. They'll have to say it's Aquinas. They cannot say it is Lonergan because it's too good.'[20] Writing it was for him the best form of therapy.

Insight and the Nature of God

The fifth and final *Verbum* article addresses the question, to what extent for Aquinas is there in the human mind a divine likeness? In the second *Verbum* article Lonergan remarked that it was a problem for Aquinas that God should know anything distinct from the divine essence. A comparison of the views of Plato and Aristotle followed. In his discussion of activity and passivity in *Sophistes*, Plato concluded that absolute being, if it was to know, must be moved by what it knows. For him knowledge is not an identity but a form of confrontation or spiritual contact with the known. Lonergan repeats his earlier contrast between the two positions, noted by Aquinas in the *Contra Gentiles*, in the fifth article:

> Such are the basic positions. The Platonist conceives knowing as primarily confrontation, but the Aristotelian conceives knowing as primarily perfection, act, identity; again, the conceptualist knows the human intellect only by what it does, but the intellectualist knows and analyzes not only what intelligence in act does but also what it is.[21]

To the conceptualist/intellectualist stances on understanding of the fourth article, the fifth adds this distinction between Platonic and Aristotelian notions of knowing. If knowledge is a confrontation between a knower and a knowable, Plato's 'subsistent idea of Being would have to sacrifice immobility to have knowledge.' Aristotle, because he conceived knowing as identity in act rather than confrontation, 'was able to affirm the intelligence in act of his immovable mover.'[22] A finite intelligence, for him, could be moved by an agent object.

If knowledge is a confrontation with another then God cannot be a knower, because God can exist and understand and know without another existing and being the cause of God's knowledge. If knowledge is a perfection and an identity then God can exist and understand and know himself. There is no need for him to be moved by an object of knowledge other than himself. His status as an unmoved mover is retained.

The two opposed views on knowing lead to two equally opposed views of the human intellect:

> All men are aware of their sensations. All educated men, at least, are aware of their thoughts and so of the division of thoughts into concepts, judgments, and inferences. But only Aristotelians are sufficiently aware of their intellects to turn this awareness to philosophic account. Between the activities of sense and, on the other hand, the concepts, judgments, and inferences that constitute thought, there stands the intellect itself.[23]

There follows an attempt by Lonergan to illustrate what conceptualists overlook in their analysis of mind. Intellectually, mind is the light of intelligence within us, the spirit of inquiry that moves us to wonder, the wonder that is the source of all science and philosophy. Intelligence grasps the point, its implications, reflects, understands what is to be done, and grasps how to do it. Intellectual habit is freedom from the book, which enables us to rework definitions and scrutinize arguments. From such habits of understanding there results, with pleasure and ease, the act of understanding.

In this there is to be discerned the building up of the elements of the phantasm or data that poses the question, how are all these different elements related in human knowing? The pieces of *the problem* of cognitional structure with its elements of operations, levels and consciousness are slowly emerging throughout the *Verbum* articles. But Lonergan's discussion of two radically opposed views of knowing with reference to Plato and Aristotle suggests that his insight into cognitional structure would come at a later date.

Aristotle, no less than Aquinas, Lonergan continues, did not escape the conceptualist interpreters:

> Aristotle did not anticipate Hegel to posit Absolute thinking relative thought. He extrapolated from insight into phantasm to posit pure understanding unlimited by sensible presentation. If you object that modern interpreters translate *noesis noeseos* as 'thinking thought,' I readily grant that this implies, namely, that modern interpreters suppose Aristotle to have been a conceptualist. But I also retort that medieval translators did not write 'cogitatio cogitationis' but

PF 3640
W53
1938x

Lon B 995 L.

sich zu etwas gedrängt fühlen – to
impelled to do sth.

STAFF INITIALS:

STAFF are to exit together.

...ON and do not set alarm unless instruct...

...keys in fabric bag and drop in false draw...

...ent clears 4th floor, electronic classroom...
/student completes clearing of lower flo...

...RWARDING on front telephone.

...r count on daily question sheet.

...s, turn off photocopiers.

...doors to verify they are locked.

...akes final closing announcement at 12:...

false drawer. *Make sure bag falls into s...*

'intelligentia intelligentiae.' It seems that medieval translators did not regard Aristotle as a conceptualist.[24]

Aquinas accepted Aristotle on agent and possible intellect, but Augustine's speculations on the inner word helped him to distinguish between understanding and its products of definition and judgment. Conceptualists are unaware of this distinction.

In the light of his intellectualist reading of Aquinas, Lonergan concludes in the fifth article that God, for Aquinas, is unrestricted understanding:

> When Aquinas spoke of God as *ipsum intelligere*, did he mean that God was a pure act of understanding? To that conclusion we have been working through four articles ... Either *ipsum intelligere* is analogous to sensation, or it is analogous to understanding, or it is analogous to conception, or it is analogous to nothing we know. No one will affirm that *ipsum intelligere* is analogous to sensation. But it cannot be analogous to conception; for it is the *dicens, dicere, verbum* of trinitarian theory that is analogous to conception; ... Further in trinitarian theory, *intelligere* is essential act common to Father, Son, and Spirit, while *dicere* is notional act and proper to the Father.[25]

To make sense of this position requires a fine attunement to the data of consciousness and a related ability to discriminate between insights and thoughts.

The *Verbum* articles began with the observation that because the tradition had lost sight of Aquinas' theory of understanding it could make no sense of his thought on processions in God. Having spent nearly six years recovering that theory, Lonergan now concludes that his interpretation does make sense of the processions. That the Word and Spirit are not caused but have the same status as the Father is acknowledged.

Lonergan responds to Penido's perplexity about the procession of the Holy Spirit at the opening of the first *Verbum* article with a remarkable statement about the relation between the intellect and the will: 'from understanding's self-expression in a judgment of value there is an intelligible procession of love in the will.'[26] Possibly the only occurrence of the phrase 'judgment of value' in the articles, it is significant by its absence from his chapter on the possibility of ethics in *Insight*. Only when he came to write *Method in Theology* in the mid-1960s did Lonergan finally come to terms with the notion or pursuit of value and, related to it, judgments of value.

The will, which is contrasted with our sensitive and natural appetites, is a rational appetite: 'Natural appetite is blind; sensitive appetite is spontaneous; but rational appetite can be moved only by the good that reason pronounces to be good.'[27] There follow reflections on Aquinas' thought on the procession of the spirit, the basic text being *Contra Gentiles*, IV, 19. What is willed is loved. But there is a fundamental difference between the presence of the beloved in the intellect and in the will. The object is in the intellect in terms of a similitude or similarity. But the object of love in the will is not a reproduction, but like a goal in a tendency to a goal. Willing to become a doctor or to create a constitution is not willing something that exists, but something that will come to be in place at the term of a process.

The articles end with some probing reflections on the two orders of understanding in theology, the way of discovery and the way of synthesis, which will turn out to be central in Lonergan's *Method in Theology*.

Eugene Burke, in his struggles to master Lonergan's articles on *gratia operans* and *verbum*, recognized that they were opening up quite new horizons for those teaching the theology of grace and of the Trinity.[28] His recommendation led to the Spellman medal being awarded to Lonergan in the fall of 1949, an event that helped the latter complete his recovery from his depression of 1947–8. He received the award at a special dinner. When he returned to class, Crowe celebrated the event with a little speech in which he spoke of the 'odyssey of the intellect from *quod quid erat esse* to its final goal in the *verbum complexum*.'[29] Lonergan was delighted with the award, which he felt was a vindication.

The Transformative Value of the Encounter with Aquinas

As late as March 1980 Lonergan wrote to Crowe stating that his book *Method in Theology* did not place sufficient emphasis on the place and role of research in theology. He commented that he himself had done eleven years of research on *gratia operans* and *verbum* in Aquinas. He added, 'It is from the mind set of research that one most easily learns what *Method* is about, surmounting differences in historicity.'[30] Firstly, there is the interpretative experience itself as a process, the experience of reading Aquinas on various themes in the texts of the *Sentences, Contra Gentiles, Summa, De Veritate,* and *De Malo*. Through that reading one comes to grasp the questions of Aquinas and their development in his writings. This highly creative transformative experience brought about in Lonergan by his modern hermeneutical reading of the texts was in complete contrast with the manual approach of the Thomism inspired by Melchior Cano.

That interpretative process also shows what, in *Method in Theology*, Lonergan refers to as normative theological achievements of the past. Among them he lists Aquinas' thought on grace and freedom, on cognitional theory and on the Trinity. Those achievements have a permanence of their own that history does not make redundant. Obviously they can be improved on and inserted into larger and richer contexts, 'but unless its substance is incorporated in subsequent work, the subsequent work will be a substantially poorer affair.'[31]

Researching and thinking out the *Verbum* articles opened up and brought about a decisive transformative development in Lonergan's questioning that made the projects of *Insight* and *Method in Theology* possible. He himself has remarked on the significance of the experience for his later work:

> Nor is this labour of penetration enough, for I have tried it. After spending years reaching up to the mind of Aquinas, I came to a twofold conclusion. On the one hand, that reaching had changed me profoundly. On the other hand, that change was the essential benefit. For not only did it make me capable of grasping what, in the light of my conclusions, the *vetera* really were, but also it opened challenging vistas on what the *nova* could be.[32]

Although the elements of the problem of his later theory of knowledge with its three levels of operation and related qualities of consciousness are emerging and present in the *Verbum* articles, the insight has not yet occurred. His tendency to associate the term 'rational consciousness' with the two operations of the intellect shows that he had some way to go to work out the understanding of consciousness that we find in *Insight*. The articles have also brought him to the door of the notion of being and a solution to the Kantian problem of the subject and object of knowledge. When these further steps are taken he will have in place the foundations out of which *Insight* will be forged. Through them a transformed encounter with the meaning of modern empirical science, the *nova*, will result. It takes time and patience for the interpreter to appreciate the depths of this change in him and the vastness of the process that brought it about.

Between September and January 1948–9 Lonergan taught a course on Christology using D'Alès' *De Verbo Incarnato* as his text. Crowe again was a student at the course and has kept the notes he took. The first part of *De Verbo Incarnato* deals with Christ as God and man, emphasizing the Christ of the New Testament as the fulfilment of the prophesies of the Old. The second part deals with Christ as God-man, the hypostatic union of two natures and two operations unconfused in one person. The third part deals with the reasons why God became man, including a long section on the redemption that was not addressed in the course.

Lonergan prefaces his discussion of the early theses on Christ in the Bible with some brief comments on faith, on our knowledge of God, and on modernism. Between the traditional and the modernist believer are different perspectives on religion, revelation, faith, and science. For the modernist, religion is immanent. A universal phenomenon, its explanation must be within. The religious sense flowers in the mystics and corresponds to the philosophical unknowable. Faith is a vital adaptation between this subjective experience and an objective unknowable. It does not involve God revealing and the human person responding believingly. Faith becomes the adaptation of the human to the unknowable. The modernist as believer affirms divine reality not because of philosophical proof but because of personal religious experience. The faith of believers transfigures historical events. The scientific analysis of modernists reduces the study of religion to that of history. There is involved a disfiguration of what happened.

Lonergan's reflections on the thesis on the Divinity of Christ in the New Testament remark pointedly: 'Radical philosophical difficulties surround "God-Man"' (*Radicalis difficultas philosophica circa 'Deus Homo'*).[33] Reminiscent of his philosophical conversion while taking this course with Leeming in 1935, realism is at the heart of those difficulties. For naive realism, 'what's out there' is real. It follows that what I don't see, hear, and so forth, are not real. It results in an empiricism of the self. I feel myself. Therefore I too am real. Idealism begins by acknowledging that to say the real is what you sense is absurd (the conjunction of these remarks with those in the fourth article on idealism being notable). Affirmations are made for reasons. What is 'known' by the senses is simply a brute fact, a further occurrence of a phrase Lonergan used previously in the *Verbum* fragments. But the problem is that there is no possibility of an absolute judgment in general human opinions, which are always opposed, or in the positive sciences. Science involves a series of approximations that never arrive at the goal. It is true from a point of view. Similarly, philosophy never attains an absolute. It too is a point of view. The real cannot be known by the senses. And by judgment we never arrive at an absolute. Knowledge is a process tending towards an ideal goal. It follows that not only are all judgments relative, even the distinction between subject and object is relative.

In critical realism, reality is what is affirmed in a true judgment: 'I know there is a real table out there when my judgment affirming the table to be out there is true.' I know it then and not before. The senses do not in themselves give knowledge. My acts of judging are constitutive of my knowledge of the real. Thinking is a thinking towards knowing an object. It is not merely subjective. There is in me something that is the cause of my knowledge of all things, the agent intellect. But what does not seem to be adequately treated is the relation between faith, the agent intellect, and theological realism. How are faith and natural inquiry involved in coming to know the reality of Christ as incarnate God? Is there a theological realism based on understanding by way of analogy of the mystery of Christ?

Theses 12 and 13 affirmed that in Christ there are two natures and two operations, divine and human. It follows that there is in Christ, through whom all things were made, divine and human knowledge.[34] Christ as God does not know things because they exist, but rather they exist because he knows them. As human and as divine, what sort of knowledge does Christ have of himself and of the world? No doubt many will wonder what sense is to be made of the question.

After discussing some relevant church pronouncements, Lonergan turns to the experience of the mystics, with Crowe's notes referring to *Mystik als sealische Wirklichkeit*, by Alois Mager OSB.[35] The classic example of the mystical life is the dark night of the soul that leaves its subject without any sensible consolation. In this condition the mystic can come to look on himself as a sheer pagan, an outcast from God. The effect of grace is simply perseverance, because without it perseverance through such a condition would not be possible. According to Mager, Lonergan comments, when the *Geist-seele* begins to deal alone with God without any intervention of *phantasms* from the *Leit-seele*, then the mystical life has begun. The discussion moves on to consider the relation between what Lonergan terms higher and lower levels in consciousness. Health and prayer can mutually interact although there is no necessary law connecting them. John of the Cross describes the dark night of the soul as being in a spiritual stage that is much more advanced than the sensitive state of the person who has yet to adapt to it.

The mystic is involved in awful enlargement of consciousness, which he or she cannot express in terms of lower levels, of intellectual consciousness. Those different levels, Lonergan suggests, do not conflict or interfere with one another. By way of analogy of three- and n-dimensional geometry, he suggests that the beatific vision in Christ adds a new dimension. The higher levels in Christ enlarge his vision but do not rule out the lower. The parallel question, is Christ's humanity during his lifetime on earth slowly in time in the process of adapting to his divinity? is 'hovering' but not strongly focused. In the course of these lectures, on 5 January 1949 there occurs on page 70 of the notes one of his earliest uses of the phrase 'levels of consciousness.' It is not clear at this point that he was applying this phrase to levels within cognition or a level of life. But the process had started.

Work on *Insight* began during the summer of 1949, a development that will be taken up in the next chapter. In the fall semester of that year Lonergan taught the Trinity for the second time. Crowe again attended and has retained his notes, which conclude with the question: how does the natural life of the human adapt to the supernatural life of God? Lonergan comments: 'Grace operates and mod[ifies] nature slowly. Why? Because of the terrific process of adaptation required. It took St Theresa 13 years to move through the stages of the mystical life – for adaptation of the nervous system, whole personality. Adapt[ation] on the moral side is spiritual life, on the intellectual side – it is theology.'[36] Reflections on the question, What is theology? follow.

PART THREE

Composing Insight:
The Artistry of Desire

The Proto-Insight, 1949–1951

13

1949: The Vision of the First Beginning

For instance, you want to write a book. And before you have it written, you do not know exactly what is going to be in it, but you are totally dedicated to it ... And it is only in writing and rewriting that you find out what you wanted to do ... You slowly work out what is in your inspiration.

When I was writing *Insight* I was also listening to Beethoven ... he gave me a lift. He is known as being 'titanic.'[1]

Creativity has its phases and moods, its tempo and rhythm, variables of temperament and topic. In simpler problem solving we can identify times when, although the question we are interested in is clear to us, we are stuck and cannot work out an answer. In complex problem solving there are times when we don't really understand the problem itself and have to labour to clarify it. In the summer of 1949 the time for Lonergan's creative desire to compose the new vision of *Insight* had arrived.[2] The questions of his awakened desire having matured through the desert experience of thinking out the *Verbum* articles, he now had the perspective and power to begin to work out answers.

Understanding and authoring for Lonergan involved an indefinite process of rewriting. He rewrote all of *Insight* very many times. Jean Marc Laporte and John Wickham talked about hearing the constant sound of a typewriter coming from his room during those four years. When in September 1953 the text was effectively finished and he moved to Rome, Michael Lapierre moved into his vacated room. There on the floor and in the bureau desk he found the residue of the process of composing, several feet of draftings. Over the years he used the blank sides for his own notes, paper being scarce. By 1961, when the faculties moved to Willowdale, only a few pages remained. On them we see paragraphs crossed out, sections discarded and started again, new versions started, this on quite a large scale. In their own way these few pages are a fragment of the textual phantasm of the process of composing *Insight*.[3] Although fragments, they do show us something about what went on in the totality. We can have insights into where and when they were composed, into what they mean, and through them into the authorial insights they express.

The wider sequence of textual drafts is the expression of the life and movement of Lonergan's mind involved in the intense problem-solving process. His insights into the problems he was addressing and into possible ways of verbally expressing them guide the process that moves through those texts to the final version. This interaction of the moving viewpoint of the author with the moving viewpoint that is being written about does not expand indefinitely. At different speeds on different topics it reaches the term of its development. Integral to the process of composition were the books he read for inspiration. Significantly, there was a strong emphasis in them on Kant.[4] What is surprising is how many of the insights necessary in order to compose the book had yet to emerge when he began.

A First Vision Statement

Between the summer of 1949 and May 1951, in the first movement of the process of composition, Lonergan puzzled out a proto-*Insight*. What can we know about his mindset when, around the time when Schilpp's *The Philosophy of Ernst Cassirer* was published, he began to compose?[5] That that book made an impact on him is clear from his remark to McShane that he worked very hard reading the Cassirer volumes in German during the process of composition. Where did he begin?

Two significant transitional texts, a review and an essay, both published in the January 1950 issue of the *Modern Schoolman*, give us some entry into his mindset in the period between *Verbum* and *Insight*. Firstly, there is his review of Dom Illtyd Trethowan's *Certainty: Philosophical and Theological*.[6] Knowledge for Trethowan must be certain rather than incomplete or doubtful. Reminiscent of Sebastian Day's view in *Intuitive Cognition*, this certain knowledge through apprehension and affirmation is intuitive. Platonic confrontation is identified with the Aristotelian identity of knower and known in act. Critical of a sharp distinction between sense and intellect, he affirms the intellectual intuition of bodies.

For Lonergan the real weakness of the work lies in the notion of intuition and related self-evident intuitions of reality. For him such intuitions, which eliminate the need for evidence, simply do not exist. In the last paragraph of the review he continues: 'In its first moment on each level, knowledge seems to be act, perfection, identity.' In its second moment, perception, conception, and judgment, it involves a derived confrontation. Here we find one of Lonergan's earliest references to three levels in knowing. He concludes that breaking with intuitionism and identifying knowledge as primarily act, perfection, and identity is a momentous basic philosophic option. Writing *Insight* will, for him, involve working out that difficult option.

Secondly, there is his essay 'A Note on Geometrical Possibility.' At face value it seems to have been provoked by Hoenen's remark that 'only Euclidean three-dimensional extension is known as possible.'[7] This pointed him towards the question of possibility and world order. Related is the problem of the integration of philosophical and scientific issues.[8] Around September 1950 Lonergan will draft a number of texts exploring the problems of integration and of possibility, central themes in *Insight*.

The second section of the essay, entitled 'The Division of Definitions,' illuminates how he began to think out the translation of the *Verbum* articles on insight and definition into the context of modern mathematics and science. In continuity with those articles he framed what I will call his first vision statement for *Insight*:

> Our basic assumption is that science primarily is understanding, that only secondarily in virtue of self-scrutiny and self-appraisal is scientific understanding expressed in definitions, postulates and deductions.[9]

The definitions and theorems of geometry and the laws of the sciences are the expressions not of intuition but of understanding. Until Crick and Watson had their final insights into the chemical structure of DNA in terms of a double helix, they could not frame their definition. That definition is the expression of what they had understood in the data. The same is true for Wiles' articulation of the proof for Fermat's Theorem, which has been so dramatically narrated.[10] Until Wiles had the final insight, which took years to emerge, he could not yet frame the proof.

Rothstein illustrates the point in terms of the years of puzzling it takes to resolve a mathematical problem:

> I was always amazed that the steady accumulation of theorems and proofs in the books I studied bore little relation to the way I thought about mathematics when attempting to solve a problem or prove a theorem on my own. This seemed to me a purely personal eccentric-

ity (like my impatience with the descriptive power of standard musical analysis) until I realized that a three-line proof of a subtle theorem is the distillation of years of activity. It is not a picture of thinking; it is its final 'formalized' draft. So understanding mathematics's inner life means understanding more than just the rules governing its formal systems.[11]

His example from Gauss' school days beautifully illustrates the point. When Gauss was ten his school teacher, presumably at his wits' end, asked the class to add up all the numbers between 1 and 100. Gauss thought for a moment and then wrote down the correct answer. Clearly he did not arrive at it by tediously adding up all the numbers but rather by means of an insight into a trick.

If definitions or laws are expressions of insight, then significant differences in understanding will be reflected in different kinds of definitions or laws. One type of insight grasps the way in which the language of a science is to be used. A second understands the things investigated in that science: 'Hence, definitions will be of at least two kinds, namely, nominal and essential.'[12]

The nominal definitions of geometry are the expressions of insights into what geometrical shapes in the world, words such as 'cone,' 'sphere,' 'cube,' and 'cylinder,' refer to. From this perspective, a sphere could be defined as a uniformly round volume, a cube as an enclosed volume with six identical square planar sides, and so forth. Mastering a nominal definition involves knowing the common matter in the world to be associated with those names. In this sense it is not a purely linguistic process but entails some knowledge of reality: 'Clearly common matter is an element in realities and not merely a name. The paradox is resolved quite easily by the distinction between the empirical and the intelligible.'[13]

This identification of the material object associated with the name Lonergan dubs 'empirical knowledge of reality':

Now, nominal definitions involve no understanding of reality, but it does not follow that they involve no knowledge of reality; they do involve empirical knowledge of reality; and we have such empirical knowledge precisely because, besides strictly intelligible forms, there is also common matter to be known.[14]

This empirical knowledge of the reality of the common matter of essences is prior to scientific understanding proper.[15] Involved in the use of a nominal definition is not merely an ability to link certain words with certain objects in the world, but also a pre-intellectual 'knowing' of the common matter of the named object. As he puts it: 'It seems to follow that nominal definitions have the function of determining the residual common matter involved in essential definition.'[16]

Essential or what he later terms explanatory definitions are the expression of insights into the relational properties of what become known empirically in a nominal definition. Each distinct geometrical shape has its own point or character, its own peculiar relational spatial qualities and explanation. Like the details of a crime scene, the shape brings its question to us, invites us to discover its secret. What set of spatial relations make a circle a circle, an ellipse an ellipse, a helix a helix, a triangle a triangle, and so forth?

Why is a circle a circle, uniformly round rather than oval or boxed shape? Consider a much-used cartwheel with its uneven rim, unequal spokes, and slightly out-of-centre hub. What needs to happen to it in order to make it more uniformly round? In your imagination allow the spokes to become identical and numerous, the rim to become thinner and thinner and the hub to become a centre point. In the limiting image one understands the meaning of uniform roundness in terms of a plane structure of spatial relations such that the distance from the centre to the rim is always the same.

What is discovered in the image finds its self-expression in the definition: a circle is the locus of a co-planar curve such that the distance of any point on its surface from a fixed point, its centre, is a constant. The single insight unifies a multiplicity or even an infinity of concepts. The structure of the definition, which emerges from the insight, mirrors the complexity of the relations of the object. Further questions arise, such as the nature of the relation between the area of the shape and its circumference and diameter. They make the point that a single question and a related definition do not exhaust the character or relational properties of the uniformly round shape. It is equally important not to confine the analysis to the definition of a single geometrical object such as a circle.

Geometrical insights are into spatially structured images. They are what Kant had in mind when he wrote in Bxi of the *Critique of Pure Reason*: 'A new light flashed upon the mind of the first man (be he Thales or some other) who demonstrated the properties of the isosceles triangle.' In this perspective the image is a partial cause of the insight or understanding. What an insight grasps in an image finds its expression in the geometrical definitions:

> Finally, from the understanding of sensible data, there results the
> definition: without understanding one can repeat the definition
> like a parrot; but one cannot discover the definition, grasp what it

means, without understanding equality of radii as the ground of circularity.[17]

As Lonergan will put it in the first chapter of *Insight*, in the insight into the phantasm there is grasped 'a circle of terms and relations such that the terms fix the relations, the relations fix the terms and the insight fixes both.'[18]

The analysis of definitions leads to a section addressing questions of possibility. In a true judgment '*X* is,' we know the actuality of *X*. In a true judgment, '*X* is possible,' we know the possibility of X. Antecedently, the unintelligible is impossible and the intelligible possible, 'as possibility is ontologically antecedent to being, so intelligibility is cognitionally antecedent to true judgment; for true judgment is rational, and one cannot rationally affirm the unintelligible.'[19] What is possible is what can be understood. As an illustration he turns to Aristotle's substance, the understanding of which entails a grasp of unity in an empirical multiplicity. A thing is said to be possible if it involves a unity of a multiplicity.

Although Lonergan admitted the essay was obscure, themes that make their appearance in *Insight* are being opened up in it. The section on the analysis of mathematical definitions, taken in conjunction with his later lecture notes 'Intelligence and Reality,' makes clear that this is where he began drafting the text of *Insight*, at chapter 1. Although it does not yet use the term 'levels,' the essay is moving towards the recognition of levels in knowing. There is an empirical knowledge of things involving the use of our senses. There is an intellectual understanding of their essential definitions. In the true judgment '*X* is,' we know the actuality of *X*. Clearly cognition as structure is in the air, but the language of cognitional structure has not yet emerged.

A parallel can be noted at the time in his analysis of the human good. In the fifth *Verbum* article Lonergan concluded that for Aquinas God was essentially infinite understanding and love. In *Insight* he attempted to structure an argument to prove the existence of such infinite understanding. Between those two poles, in March 1950 he composed a set of notes for his course on the unity of God entitled 'On God's Knowledge and Will.' Addressing Aquinas' thought on eternity and on God's knowledge and will, it amounts to a major theological tract on the unity of God. The section in chapter 19 in *Insight* on the notion of God would draw substantially on these notes.

Of interest for our understanding of the development of Lonergan's insights at this point are some remarks he made in the notes about the human good.[20] The basic good is the divine goodness. All created goods are good by participation. Within such created goods he distinguishes between the general good and particular goods. The general good is the good of the greater whole. The particular good is the good of a smaller whole that is part of a greater whole. Such would be the good for a man in terms of a home, food, work, and a salary. Far more excellent for Lonergan is the general good of a perfectly operating economic system from which all men have work, homes, a salary, and food. The greatest good among created goods is the order of the universe, which includes within itself all other possible orders.

As well as the true good there is also the apparent good, which easily deceives us. Evil is a privation of the good, moral evil a defect in the human will itself. Section (d) of chapter 14 of the notes takes up physical evils, which he seems to suggest can be explained. Divine love involves willing the good for someone. Finally, when discussing the divine will, he again talks about the common good and the personal good. Within a year, in his treatment of the human good in the essay 'The Role,' his vocabulary and approach will undergo a sea change. Central in that new treatment will be a significant new insight into the notion of levels in the good.

Deepening the Vision: On Understanding World Order

In the course notes taken by William Stewart, Lonergan affirmed that probability was objective because determinism was wrong. Related is the emerging theme in his thought of questions about possible world orders. Further clues come from a related set of unpublished notes he composed with the header 'Notes on Integration' and with section headings entitled 'The Meaning of Possibility,' 'Absolute Possibility,' and 'Order' (by which is meant world orders).[1] Lonergan opens his discussion of possibility with the question whether hens could croak and frogs cluck, a phrase that rings of Buckingham in the summer. In the next section his basic theorem on possibility is that anything is possible and nothing is impossible. The background here is the remark on God's omnipotence in the Creed.

To enter into Lonergan's emerging understanding of world order we must engage with the problem of the possible, the probable, and the actual. How are the possibilities in the universe realized? Are all or only some of them realized? If only some, why X rather than Y? Are there more possibilities in the universe than are realized? Do the possibilities that might be realized at a later stage depend on those that have been realized at an earlier stage? Does this mean that at every stage of its unfolding some possibilities are realized and others not? On the basis of the possibilities realized some future possibilities become achievable and others not. Clearly there is a difference here from determinism, in which all the possibilities in the universe are determined in accordance with a fixed law.

We can consider possible world orders. We can also consider a world order that contains within itself different possibilities, in which at any historical point many different possibilities, ways of going on with things, are possible.

A further set of unpublished notes that illuminate the early stages of the composition of *Insight* emerged in 1950 in the wake of Pius XII's encyclical *Humani Generis* of 12 August 1950.[22] Central to that encyclical was a concern to address some of the dangers that the Pope thought evolution, communism, existentialism, and historicism posed to the then dominant scholastic school of Catholic theology and philosophy. Lonergan's response had to do with the problem of world views and world order.

His remarks on world order are prefaced with comments on the problem of the integration of the multiplicity of the sciences. The differences among the sciences, philosophy, and theology create a human need for understanding and integration. All of those disciplines have something to say about the human being. Mathematics for him constitutes a clue for the integration of the positive sciences. But, in an echo of a passage from the later 'Intelligence and Reality,' as one proceeds from physics through chemistry to the higher sciences of biology and psychology, the role of mathematics seems to decrease. At this point does philosophy have a distinctive role? Lonergan goes on to suggest that the ultimate principle of integration is God himself. It will be given by revelation and faith and articulated by theology.

In 1950 Lonergan claimed that the problem of integration has a certain novelty. The Renaissance started a new trend; science established its distinctive methods. The emergence of the empirical sciences of the human gave birth to a new situation:

> There is a radically new method of answering the old question, What is man? Biologists, palaeontologists, anthropologists are concerned with his origins. Economists are concerned with the material conditions of his life. Psychologists and sociologists are busy with the inner and outer manifestations of his mind. Historians are busy with everything that is past, and historical theorists collect and analyse the facts relevant to the origins, developments, crises, break-downs, and disintegrations of man's cultural patterns, his religions, and his civilizations.[23]

Through the unifying work of philosophy Lonergan sees this situation as a core challenge to modern theology.

Still, how can any particular individual master the totality of disciplines? There will be those who know a particular department at first hand and in detail and other departments at second and third hand. Can even a rare few enjoy sufficient leisure and sufficient intelligence to work towards a synthesis? How can any individual be erudite in the totality of the modern sciences as well as in philosophy? Such are the modern dimensions of the problem of integration. The remarks here echo those in the Introduction to *Insight* to the effect that it is not an erudite work.

The problem of integration is at heart a problem of understanding the order in the world. Aquinas occupied a middle ground between the extremes that, on the one hand, denied the intelligibility of the world order, and, on the other, affirmed its necessity: 'World order is intelligible for it is the product of wisdom. World order is contingent, for it is the product of freedom.'[24] For Lonergan, in opposition to Scotus, Aquinas held that knowledge of world order would be the product of insights into sensible images. [25] By means of this we grasp the intelligibility of a concrete multiplicity: 'We understand the master builder erecting the particular cathedral by directing the several workmen each to his proper task. We can have a notion of the intelligibility of world order. But while we can, Scotus cannot.'[26] This more communicative image of the metaphysician as a master builder would later be replaced by the notion of an integral heuristic structure. In these notes we find articulated a second vision statement, his dream of working out a world order based on integrating all the different kinds of insights we find in modern empirical science. Significant is the recognition that world order is not known by a single type but by many irreducibly distinct types of insight.

The Beginning of the Book

Between March and May 1951 Lonergan gave a course at the Thomas More Institute entitled 'Intelligence and Reality.' In the brochure it was initially scheduled for January and entitled 'Reality and Thought.' Its aim was to propose a theory of knowledge that would satisfy the modern thinker. Based on the ideas of Aristotle and Aquinas as well as the Western experience of science and philosophy, its goal was 'to give an awareness of how we come to know.' In the notes he prepared for this course, the movement of Lonergan's mind over the first two years of composition starts to emerge from the dark. They enable us to assess the questions that were up for him during those years and the advances he had made on them. They also clarify points he was grappling with and points from the final text of *Insight* that were beyond his vision at this time.

Out of the ferment of his mind Lonergan now chose to begin his book with an account of Archimedes' eureka experience. In the notes for the course he uses this account to pose the question, What is it like to experience an act of understanding or insight? – a question that attempts to part the veil on the conscious workings of the human mind. Although both in these notes and in the book the story of Archimedes' discovery is prefaced by a paragraph or two, *Insight* begins with this story. Out of many possible options Lonergan has chosen to begin his work with this story, chosen it as the place where he wants the reader to begin. As beginnings can signal the course of the journey on which we are embarking, even convey a sense of the destination, it is important that the point of this beginning of the story is clearly grasped. Archimedes pondered the problem, How can I discover if the crown is made of pure gold or contains baser materials mixed in?[27] While reclining in his bath, he noticed how his body displaced the water and suddenly hit on the solution: weigh the crown in water. The experience was such a release of his tension of inquiry that, according to the story he jumped out of the baths and rushed about naked shouting, 'Eureka, I've got it!' Clearly Archimedes was aware of an experience in his self-consciousness through which the conscious tension of his inquiry was resolved. In this dimension the story illustrates dramatically what it is like to have an insight.

Drawing on it in the 'Intelligence and Reality' notes, Lonergan provides a detailed list of headings involved in describing an insight. Insights can be delightful, unexpected, internally conditioned. In the opening chapter of *Insight* he will later identify five aspects of the personal experience of having an insight:

1. It comes as a release of the tension of inquiry.
2. It comes suddenly and unexpectedly.
3. It is a function not of outer circumstances but of inner conditions.
4. It pivots between the concrete and the abstract, and
5. It passes into the habitual texture of one's mind.[28]

Lonergan deliberately begins his book by drawing to our attention a certain kind of elusive but nonetheless verifiable human experience. It is the experience of adult persons finding themselves with a significant personal problem. That problem occupies them centrally in their living, but they are stuck and there is no way forward. They are frustrated and even downcast. They seek solace in a bath and, quite unexpectedly, in this unusual and unscholarly situation, suddenly the insight comes and they can shout, 'I've got it.' In Boston on 19 June 1979, in a long and illuminating response to a question about his own intellectual development, Lonergan remarked that his cognitional theory requires something to click inside one.[29] When this highly elusive experience has clicked and been identified, the journey can begin.

14

Experimenting with the Insights of Mathematicians and Scientists

Direct und[erstanding] : sensible data :: introspective und[erstanding] : data of consc[iousness] No difference qua understanding; Begin from experience of understanding; relate to inquiry, presentations, concepts, in process of maths, class[ical] phase, statist[ical] phase ... identity of experimenter, experimented on, experimentation.[1]

You have to become accustomed to insights by setting yourself problems. For example: why does taking a square root work? When you see why it works you'll have an insight.[2]

Understanding a world order would, for Lonergan, result from an integration of all of the different kinds of insights that can be identified in the empirical sciences. Earlier in 1943, in his 'Forms of Inference,' he articulated his dream of an empirical science of the mind itself. In the early draft of chapters 1, 2, and 8 of *Insight* that follow in the notes for 'Intelligence and Reality,' these two approaches are united. Involved was a first move in exploring the possibility of developing an experimental method for the study of insights as conscious with the eventual aim of integrating them in a world-view. We should not underestimate the diffculties involved in learning that method.

The statement that there is an identity of experimenter, experimented on, and experimentation rings strange. In one sense it is related to Aristotle's method for the study of the psyche: begin not with the activity of mind but with its objects, the problems of mathematics or science or the more concrete problems that our lives in the world throw up. Engage directly with them and, as they open out, begin to reflect on the experience. Lonergan is now suggesting that the direct mode of engagement of mind can be of the form of an experiment that the introspective mode attempts to understand. In the latter we are the experimenter, in the former the experimented on. The two modes of operation are not unrelated to his earlier remark in *Verbum* on duplication in self-knowledge. Many modern empirical studies of 'mind' remove the subject of those studies, the inquiring mind of the philosopher or scientist and what he or she does and says, entirely from the equation. This form of experimental study of the mind and its insights, being an unfamiliar project in modern education, presents its own difficulties for both author and reader. Missing in the methodology is the requirement of keeping a record of what happens and intersubjectively discussing such records.

In the notes that follow Lonergan begins his experimental analysis of different kinds of insights with nominal and explanatory, already rehearsed in 'A Note on Geometrical Possibility.' He expands it into an analysis of insights into the emergence of higher viewpoints in mathematics, into the conjugates or relational laws of classical empirical science and the probabilities of statistical science. This leads to a significant discussion of insights into the data of consciousness as it is experienced in the direct mode of cognitional activity in mathematics or science. He ends with a brief section on insights into the intelligible unity of things.

At this point each example is treated briefly, more suggestively than pedagogically. Lonergan is not concerned with a detailed descriptive account of the inner life of the mathematicians and scientists within which these insights emerge. No biographical or historical details are offered. He limits his focus to an experimental exploration of the link between the sensible data or their symbolic representations of an unsolved problem and the solutions that arise in the form of objects of thought or propositions. Insights provide and constitute that link. Before their emergence we are stuck and can neither think nor speak a solution. The point of the experiment is to identify how the emergence of the insight gives birth to the thought and spoken solution.

Experimenting with Accumulating Mathematical Insight

After some simple examples of the pivotal role of insights in elementary geometry and arithmetic, the analysis expands to address the more difficult question of the development of mathematical understanding. That development for Lonergan is not linear and logical, but rather progresses through a sequence of what he terms 'ever higher' viewpoints. Mathematical activities and operations on a lower viewpoint can become the source of problems that cannot be answered internally. The challenge now becomes that of understanding the pivotal role of insight between the images and problems posed by the lower-viewpoint operations and the emergence of the formulations of the understanding of the higher viewpoint. As a succession of higher viewpoints is a possibility, that pivotal role will repeat itself at each new stage in the development. If correct, it will call into question the sufficiency of an analysis of mathematics in terms of logical deductions from first principles. Although problematic for the non-mathematically minded, in *Insight* it will enable him to offer a possible explanation of the relation between the laws of the higher and lower sciences.

The experiment begins with the recognition that in the course of our lives we are constantly learning new questioning skills and acquiring new related insights. The human mind is dynamic. As its questions and insights accumulate in any field, there emerges a viewpoint. This poses the question, how would we characterize the intellectual viewpoint or horizon of a teacher of elementary mathematics, a language teacher, a medical doctor, a taxi driver, and a software programmer as they go about their business?

Intellectual viewpoints involve an acquired mastery of certain types of questions and related insights. Unlike a fixed perspective, they involve a dynamic skill of being open to raising and answering further related questions. The taxi driver has to be able to ask and answer questions about the geographical location of every street in the city in which he conducts business. He or she also has to ask questions about the character of prospective customers and the risks involved in taking them to certain parts of the city. The driver's viewpoint is not static, but constantly expanding as he adds to his knowledge street locations previously unknown and qualities of character to be avoided.

Similar considerations can be applied to the viewpoint of a teacher of elementary mathematics or language. Within their domain these will have developed the skill of working with a set of questions. The one will teach the arithmetical tables and related mathematical skills, the other the alphabet and the skill of forming sentences. All such viewpoints are limited. The taxi driver will not have the skills necessary to drive in an unknown city, the language teacher to teach an unknown language.

In order to open up the notion of an elementary viewpoint in mathematics, consider, initially, the viewpoint of a man who lives in a world taken up simply with sheep. Involved would be the management of their conception, birth, rearing, and sales and of the units of currency employed in their exchange. Let us also suppose that the sheep pens and fields were multiples of a basic unit of area. Central to that person's world would be the notion of counting, of adding and subtracting, multiplying and dividing numbers of sheep.[3] When new lambs are born he will add that number to the flock, when they are sold in the market he will subtract the number. Such counting will also extend to the units of the currency.

In his thought experiment Lonergan effectively allows for an unlimited number of sheep.[4] Addition arises when sheep are added through purchase or birth, subtraction when they are sold or die. On this simple level the concept of a negative number of sheep does not exist. Multiplication arises when we have to add a certain number on a regular basis. We multiply the addition. Inverse to multiplication, we have division, which involves the repeated subtraction of a certain number of sheep. In this way we can become familiar with adding, subtracting, multiplying, and dividing. This entails learning how many sheep will be left if we subtract 20, add 12, divide the number by 10.

It is Lonergan's thesis that on this basis we can develop the addition, multiplication, subtraction, and division tables as they apply to positive integers. This he terms the 'homogeneous' expansion within which, he suggests, we can detect certain primitive terms and relations that he names as 'one,' 'plus,' and 'equals.' All later developments within the homogeneous expansion presuppose those common notions.

Neither a live sheep nor the basic unit of currency can be divided into fractions. The same is not true of fields. At some point the primal farmer might find himself faced with the question of measuring a number of new fields, and in so doing discover that they did not quite relate as units. In this way the question of fractions, $\frac{1}{3}$, $\frac{1}{4}$, etc., and the manner in which they are to be added, subtracted, multiplied, and divided would come to be posed. As defined, subtraction can only bring us back to our starting point, so the notion of subtracting 20 sheep from 10 does not make sense. It is a question that has no answer in the sheep man's world-view. As for fractions, so also there arises the puzzle of negative numbers, −1, −2, −3, etc., and the manner in which they are to be manipulated.

Multiplication and division as so defined work only for integers and not for fractions. We can multiply the number of the sheep by 7 but not by 3.5. We can divide by 3 but not by $3\frac{1}{3}$. At this point we still cannot address questions about the square root of two or of −1. Starting from the simple viewpoint of elementary school arithmetic, a host of further questions about arithmetical operations and their outcomes can emerge that in turn cannot find answers within the initial, limited viewpoint. As Cassirer notes in his book *Substance and Function*, which Lonergan had read, the new questions call for an extension of the concept of number.[5] The insights that answer those questions bring about horizontal enlargements of the initial arithmetical viewpoint in which new types of numbers come to be introduced, but not yet to the emergence of a higher viewpoint.

As the image of the circle is the source of the geometrical question, Why is a circle uniformly round? so the expanding performance of doing arithmetic is the image that poses the algebraic question, What is the definition of an arithmetical number? On the arithmetical level the particular numbers, 1, 2, 3, etc., are defined relationally in and through the various tables that govern their use. At this point the solutions to problems concerning numbers and operations that emerge on the arithmetical level become the source of questions on the algebraic level. Faced with the expanding field of arithmetical numbers, the algebraic question does not ask, What is the definition of 1, of π, of the square root of 2 or of –1? Rather than asking about the definition of any specific number, it asks, What is the definition of any and every number? What are the rules that govern the operations involved in the generation and manipulation of all numbers? The source of the question is not a static image, but the performance of playing the game of arithmetic.

> For the image of the cart-wheel one substitutes the image of what may be named 'doing arithmetic'; it is a large dynamic virtual image that includes writing down, adding, multiplying, subtracting and dividing numbers in accord with the precepts of the homogeneous expansion. Not all of this image will be present at once, but any part of it can be present and, when one is on the alert, any part that happens to be relevant will pop into view. In this large and virtual image, then, there is grasped a new set of rules governing operations. The new rules will not be exactly the same as the old rules. They will be more symmetrical. They will be more exact. They will be more general. In brief they will differ from the old much as the highly exact and symmetrical circle differs from the cart-wheel.[b]

The imaginative performance and expression of doing mathematics at a particular level or viewpoint now becomes the source and inspiration of the questions that are going to move the development of mathematical understanding to a higher level.

Before one can master the definition of the circle, one has to allow the question, What are the spatial properties of this shape? to take root. In the present instance one has to become engaged by the algebraic question in relation to the operations of arithmetic. If this move is missed, permanent confusion about what is happening in the shift from arithmetic to algebra will result. Using his dot symbolism, the mathematician Lanczos helps us to understand how insights into the laws of algebra arise in response to questions about arithmetical operations.[7] As we follow the analysis we should keep in mind the question, posed in the fourth *Verbum* article, What precisely is insight into in the images or phantasms?

Insights into the Laws/Rules of Elementary Algebra

The Commutative Law of Addition

A first question that arises about the operations has to do with the order of addition. If we add two numbers, does the outcome depend on the order in which we add them? Lanczos writes out the numerical symbols and below them adds the equivalent in dots:

$$7 + 5 = 5 + 7$$

. . . .

Through insight we can grasp that whichever way we add them, there is involved the same number of dots. The image can be expanded by drawing in other lines of dots for other numbers. Clearly the same holds true for all numbers, not just for 7 and 5 or 6 and 8. In the disposed image the insight into the first law of algebra can be grasped:

$$a + b = b + a$$

What is interesting about Lanczos' treatment is the use of the dot image or phantasm in order to evoke the algebraic insight. This is to be contrasted with learning the laws by rote.

The Associative Law of Addition

Given the task of adding three successive numbers, the question again arises, Does the result depend on the order in which we add them?

$$(9 + 7) + 5 = 9 + (7 + 5)$$

In dot form:

. . . .

In this form we can, through insight into the image of the dots, grasp that the outcome of the sum is the same whatever the order in which it is performed:

$$(a + b) + c = a + (b + c)$$

Sheep traders are only interested in trading the particular sheep they have in the pen. They deal with integers. By way of contrast, land surveyors deal with fractions of units, bankers with negative numbers, the Greeks with the number π. In the development of the higher viewpoint, mathematicians become interested in the rules defining the numerical operations that generate the different kinds of arithmetical numbers. In the algebraic insight into the definition of a number, the above laws are understood as applying to fractions and negative, irrational, complex (with some modifications), and transcendental numbers, but not to vectors.

Through the formulation of the above set of insights all the different kinds of arithmetical numbers – integers, fractions, negative, complex, irrational, and transcendental – now come to be redefined from the higher viewpoint in terms of the basic laws of algebra. What the insights grasp in the images are the rules that specify the operations that define numbers:

$$a + b = b + a$$
$$(a + b) + c = a + (b + c)$$
$$a \times b = b \times a$$
$$a \times (b + c) = a \times b + a \times c$$
$$a \times (b \times c) = (a \times b) \times c$$
$$a - b - a + (-b)$$
$$1/a \text{ is defined such that } a \times 1/a = 1.$$
$$a/b = a \times (1/b)$$
$$(a/b) \times (c/d) = (a \times c)/(b \times d)$$
$$a + 0 = a$$
$$a \times 0 = 0$$
$$a/0 \text{ is not allowed in the rules.}$$
etc.

What has happened is that numbers are now being defined in terms of a set of operations, each operation in turn being specified by its particular rules. Those rules take into account the new insights into the way in which negative, irrational, and, with some modifications, complex and other numbers function. In response to the algebraic questions about the rules and operations that define and constitute numbers, the algebraic insights enable us to think and speak a solution. They grasp the relations between the rules that specify the operations that generate the numbers. As a result, one now has a new understanding of numbers that takes one quite beyond the horizon and viewpoint of arithmetic.

Needless to say, algebra at this point has only begun. It too undergoes an operational expansion. Questions arise about the solution, the numbers x, that satisfy the equation $ax^2 + bx + c = 0$. Solutions are sought in terms of the coefficients, a, b, and c. The quadratic equation is found to be just one of a series:

$$ax^2 + bx + c = 0$$
$$ax^3 + bx^2 + cx + d = 0$$
$$ax^4 + bx^3 + cx^2 + dx + e = 0$$
etc.

Again, the question arises, Can solutions be found in terms of the coefficients, a, b, c, d, e, etc.? Galois made the significant discovery that these equations cannot be resolved in terms of their coefficients, a, b, c, d, e, for a power greater than 4. In order to prove this, he had to move to the higher viewpoint of group theory, which, as Cassirer points out, is a general theory of operations and their rules.[8] Group theorists are interested in the operations of arithmetic, of algebra or whatever. Their questions and insights take us to a viewpoint beyond elementary algebra. But those further questions and insights arise with respect to the operational image of the algebraic expansion. The cycle of images, questions, insights, and formulations repeats itself at the emergence of each successive higher viewpoint in the development of mathematical understanding.

Based on this, Lonergan represents the development of mathematical understanding schematically as:

4   A resulting new higher level of symbolic images and operational context, which in turn are the sources of further questions that lead to group theory, its definitions, operations, and rules

↑

3   The formulation of the content of those insights into objects of thought – rules defining operations and related symbols (a, b, c, +, –, x, /, etc.)

↑

2   New questions about the rules, operations, and symbols (numbers) on that level, leading to related insights

↑

1   Lower context of performing arithmetical operations (arithmetic, 1, 2, 3, +1, +2, +3)

The successive viewpoints, for Lonergan, are not logically related. Algebra cannot be logically deduced from within the viewpoint of elementary arithmetic; it is simply not an internal expansion. The same holds true for the relation between the algebraic expansion and group theory: the link between them is cognitional rather than logical. Images, operations, questions, and insights and their expression in definitions and symbols emerge on a particular level. That dynamic virtual image becomes the source of the questions, insights, definitions, and their expressions on the level of the higher viewpoint. The link between the viewpoints is the link between images, questions, insights, and definitions.

In the opening section of these notes Lonergan is rehearsing chapter 1 of *Insight*. It seems that in the final act of composition, started around the following January, a section on inverse insights was added.

Sights, sounds, textures, sense data generally are the contents of acts of seeing, hearing, touching, and so forth. Images are the content of acts of imagining. But what is the corresponding content or object for human understanding? Maintaining continuity with the fourth *Verbum* article, Lonergan now names it as an idea, by which he means a 'pre-conceptual, intelligible form emergent in sensible data.'[9] Crucial to understanding is an exact grasp of idea or intelligible form in the data.

Abstraction is a matter of giving conceptual and verbal expression to the idea made present through the insight: the spatial relations of the geometrical object, or the operations, rules and definitions of algebra. Through the activity of conceiving, formulating, defining, thinking, considering, supposing, what is understood in the idea comes to be conceptualized. The structure of the relation between the concepts in the definition is identical with those between the elements of the idea of the object.

Simple abstraction is concerned with formulating a particular idea such as that of a circle or of a mathematical series in a definition. We write down the first five terms and add, and so forth. To understand the meaning of the 'and so forth' is to understand the idea or intelligible form of the series that finds its expression in a formulated rule such as $1 + 2n^2$.

Systematic abstraction is concerned with the conceptualization of the first principles of a science as a whole. In the history of the empirical sciences it has been the work of such creative minds as Euclid, Newton, Einstein, and Bohr. Lonergan's own effort to articulate a basic system of terms and relations relating production, exchange, and finance in his *Essay on Circulation Analysis* would be an illustration of such a development of understanding. Later in the notes Lonergan will again address the question of the system of primitive terms and relations that might constitute philosophy itself as a science.[10]

Lonergan is here talking about the massive development of understanding that takes place when a science shifts from a pre-paradigm to a paradigm phase or undergoes a further paradigm shift. Involved is a set of strategic insights by means of which the foundations of the whole science are established. The system of definitions is the expression of the set of insights. From those primitive terms and relations, derived solutions to a vast range of problems can be deduced.

This line of analysis leads naturally to the question, How are the primitive terms and relations of a multiplicity of sciences such as physics, chemistry, biology, and sensitive and rational psychology related? With an eye on the problem of integration, Lonergan asks whether those primitive terms must, in every instance, be mathematical. It is a problem that Cassirer, whom Lonergan read, reminds us goes back to Kant:

> In his *Metaphysical Elements of Natural Science* (1786) he declared that the scientific and the mathematical views of nature were one, and that in any particular theory there was only as much real science as there was mathematics. A few years later, however, he attained a different orientation. The *Critique of Judgment* (1790) marked a decisive break when it asserted the autonomy and the methodological independence of biology without giving up its connection with mathematical physics. Herewith there was posed a new question, which biological research, no matter what its school or trend, could not in future neglect.[11]

Kant clearly acknowledged a tension between causality and purpose in the biological sciences. Purpose had to do with the structure of the living organisms and cannot be explained within the framework of mathematics and physics. Cassirer, following Kant, makes it clear that biology is a quite distinctive discipline from physics or chemistry. Around the time that Crick and Watson were discovering in DNA the chemical basis of heredity, Lonergan was deeply preoccupied by the problem of explanation in the higher sciences but did not, it seems, at this point link the problem with higher viewpoints.

Experimenting with the Insights of Classical Science

As mathematics, so also empirical science is a theatre of inquiry and insights and thus can be become a domain of cognitional experimentation. Empirical scientists pose their own distinctive questions about the nature and laws of movement, of electricity, of a gas, of light, sound, colour, of a chemical element, and various forms of life. In *Insight* Lonergan will appeal to Lenzen's account of the genetic nature of the experimental method in his *Nature of Physical Theory*. This begins with experiential contents of force, heat, and so forth. From them it moves through an experimental process towards the discovery of a pattern of relations that amounts to an implicit definition. Like mathematical definitions, the formulated laws of the empirical sciences are the expression of understanding.

Helpful in grasping this point is the description, in Dava Sobel's *Galileo's Daughter*, of the untold Paduan hours 'Galileo spent tracking the course of a small bronze ball down the groove of an inclined plane to probe the mystery of acceleration.'[12] His experiment was a response to his puzzlement about how the ball speeds up from rest as it moves down the slope. Well, how does it speed up? As the image of an approximately round wheel was a necessary starting point for the question about the definition of a circle, so this experimental set-up is a necessary starting point for resolving the question of acceleration. A first *aha!* experience suggests a correlation between the measured distance x, moved along the inclined plane, and the measured time t taken to move that distance. Under the guidance of that intellectual illumination there results, through experimentation and measurement, a table of measurements of distance against time. Through insights into the correlation (relation) of the numbers (terms) in that table, the law or definition of the movement is given: $x = kt^2$. In the light of that insight into the table of measurements, a solution to the initially unresolved problem of acceleration can now be thought and spoken.

Again, the question arises, What is it that insight is into in the sensible presentations or phantasms? Can it, no less than the circle of terms and relations fixed by insight into the definition of the circle, be pictured?

Galileo's formulated discovery that the measured distance x was proportionate to the square of the measured time t taken to travel that distance is the expression of an insight. From it there can be worked out the position x, the velocity v, and the acceleration of the ball at a time t. In this simple illustration we can gain insight into the nature of scientific insight and its expression in a formulated law or rule. For the nature of acceleration we can substitute that of red or colour, of sounds, mass, of a gas, of electromagnetism. The 'nature of' is a heuristic notion, a notion of something to be found through insights into measured correlations and expressed in an appropriate definition or law.

In the course of some comments on the revision of insights in science, with little by way of introduction, Lonergan slips in the term 'conjugates.' It is not a mainstream term in the philosophy of science, and is not to be found in Cassirer, or Lindsay and Margenau's *Foundations of Physics*, which he had not read at this point.[13] Occurring in Dewey, it will feature centrally from now on in Lonergan's writings, especially in chapters 8 and 15 of *Insight*. On page 6 of his course notes he elaborates: 'Terms are conjugate when they are defined by their relations. Conjugates terms are empirical when their defining relations admit experimental proof.' In this sense the variables x and t in Galileo's law or the variables P, V, and T in Boyle's gas law are conjugate terms.

In some pages he typed between 'Intelligence and Reality' and *Insight* he elaborates as follows:

> To meet this issue let us say that basic terms are conjugate when 1) they are fixed by their mutual relations and 2) these relations are

established through the techniques of the second phase, that is, through observation, experiment when possible, and verification. Thus it is that in mechanics one begins from ordinary notions, such as 'light' and 'heavy,' advances to the notion of 'weight,' to arrive at a coefficient of inertia named 'mass'; once it is reached 'weight' becomes a derived term defined by the product of 'mass' and the 'acceleration of gravity' while 'light' and 'heavy' denote relative weights. But the point to be grasped is that a similar transposition takes place all along the line. There may or may not emerge new names, but there do emerge new concepts. The 'distance' and 'time' of ordinary speech are one thing; the 'distance' and 'time' of Newtonian mechanics are another; and the 'distance' and 'time' of relativity mechanics are a third. Basic terms are conjugate; they form a system in which the determinate factor is the pattern of relations between the terms; and this pattern is modelled on the correlations and laws that are reached by observation, experiment, and verification.[14]

Dewey in his *Logic: The Theory of Inquiry* identifies the variables time (t), length (x), and mass (m) as conjugate terms, where by 'conjugates' he means not efficient causality but some form of correlation.[15]

The introduction of the technical term 'conjugates' reminds us that scientific laws are not made up of the homely terms of drama and story. Instead of familiar proper names and place names, or specific dates and places, we find in those laws abstruse technical terms such as 'force,' 'mass,' 'acceleration,' various quantum numbers, chemical symbols. Physics is full of equations such as $w = mg$, $f = m.d^2x/dt^2$; $PV = kT$, $V = RI$, $F = q_1q_2/r^2$, as well as the more complex electromagnetic equations of Maxwell. Those terms can be defined by the most complex of equations. Chemistry is full of symbols for compounds: H_2O, CH_4, and the like. In biology we find the bewildering complexity of DNA base sequences made up of the units C, T, A, G, whose founding insight is so well described by James Watson.[16] Every one of these terms, from the simplest $w = mg$ to the most complex, is the formulation of an insight or set of insights similar to those of Galileo's into varieties of relational properties in the data. Before they emerge the scientific problem is found to be baffling and a solution cannot be framed. When they have occurred the scientist understands the kind of experiment necessary in order to determine and verify the relations. Unless we in turn make those insights our own, the equations or symbols we read in the scientific texts are just so many meaningless marks on a page. In *Insight* Lonergan will state that it is up to scientists to determine specific conjugate forms, it is up to philosophers to clarify what such conjugate forms mean.[17]

Involved will be an identification of the understanding that the scientific laws with their conjugate terms express. In this move Lonergan is replacing the medieval terminology of *quidditas rei materialis* by conjugates.

Scientific insights grasp a possibility rather than a necessity in the data. Heuristic abstraction, the effort 'to find an explanation of the nature of *X*,' can direct a succession of revisions. There can emerge new conjugate terms, but the anticipation of conjugates or systems of relations as such is constant, a point surely illustrated in the history of the sciences.[18] Like an anonymous teacher, the heuristic notions guide us towards our unknown destination through a series of revisions.

In line with this, Lonergan now sees scientific explanation operating in two modes like the two blades of a scissors. A first mode, the theoretical, entails a free intellectual exploration of possible conjugates and of systems of conjugates. It would be best illustrated by the minds of Newton, Einstein, Bohr, and Heisenberg. A second mode, the experimental, which is focused on by Lenzen, is concerned with the empirical verification of those conjugates in experimental situations. Kepler, Galileo, and Rutherford would exemplify it.

Clearly, there is no limit to the possible explanatory systems that the human mind can think up. This poses the question, how do we select an appropriate system of explanation from such a multiplicity? Lonergan's answer is in terms of the principles of exclusion and relevance. Conjugates, as noted, are empirical when experimental proof can verify their defining relations, so a system that does not admit of any experimental verification is to be excluded. Systems that are open to verification can be excluded on the basis of disagreement with experiments.

Under his somewhat obscure treatment of the principle of relevance, we find Lonergan yet again puzzling over whether the conjugates of the higher sciences are necessarily mathematical. The question, what is the nature of the conjugate or relational forms of biology, psychology and cognitional theory? is there, but not developed. In *Insight* he will remark:

> Thirdly, while we affirm forms both in atoms and in organisms, while we do so for the same reason in both cases, still we do not affirm that biology deals with the same type of conjugate forms as does chemistry or physics.[19]

How the primitive terms and relations of the higher disciplines such as biology and psychology and, by implication, cognitional theory, transcend mathematics was at this stage deeply problematic for him.

At this point the question arises, to what extent would a complete understanding of classical scientific laws and their synthesis in an explanatory system allow us to explain and predict the course of future events in the world? A parallel in analytical philosophy is that of applying rules to situations. In this it links with Lonergan's reflections in *Verbum* IV on knowledge of the abstract and of the singular. The laws of classical science are abstract. They do not contain any dates, places, or proper names. So there arises the problem of how they apply to datable and nameable situations and events in the world. The determinist holds that if you know all the laws and all the data on the initial conditions you can predict the future with certitude. There now begins a critique of determinism that Lonergan will continue in *Insight.*

Events, a major category in his world view, are defined by their laws or conjugates but are known by judgment. The laws of motion, being abstract, say nothing about the concrete initial conditions necessary, for instance, for the event of a particular solar eclipse or of a particular outcome of a coin toss. Those laws apply to particular events assuming certain initial conditions and assuming other things are equal. We can predict events such as a solar eclipse or a sequence of chemical reactions as long as the stipulation 'other things being equal' is honoured in relation to the appropriate initial and sustaining conditions. This effectively requires that certain controllable initial conditions be fulfilled. Only if those initial conditions are controlled will the future, up to a point, be determinate or predictable. His critique of determinism focuses on the question of the control of the initial conditions of events.

For Lonergan, although the initial conditions of the events of world order might be controlled in certain limited ways, they cannot be controlled in any absolute manner. It is this inability to make systematic the initial conditions of an event that illuminates the inevitable non-systematic element in the order of events in the world. Knowledge of all classical laws does not exclude the occurrence of coincidences: coincidences are inevitable. Thus, determinist dogma is utterly fanciful, a misconception of science and of the application of science. At the heart of the argument is the problem of the transition between laws, which are abstract, and events, which are concrete.

His conclusion I believe to be sound. But although he has the basis for a significant argument in its favour, that argument is obscurely presented in the headings in the notes. He does not yet have the clearer notion of a diverging series of conditions involved in fulfilling any particular set of initial conditions, and thus resulting inevitably in statistical residues, that will feature in *Insight.* Here we can see the genesis of the problem of statistical residues. It is in this context that Lonergan introduces his analysis of statistical insights and probabilities.

In his repeat examination at London University on 4 July 1928, one of the questions set invited the student to discuss the sentence 'The laws of chance are not applicable to individual cases.' It is interesting to bear this in mind as we follow Lonergan's introduction of the term 'coincidences,' in his course. Inevitably it opens up the question, what is a chance aggregate?[20] In *Insight* he will rename it a 'coincidental aggregate.' You could have a slow-motion picture of a dice in motion and predict its movement. But could you predict a succession of such movements? His answer is that the succession of such tosses is a chance aggregate. To it Lonergan here applies the term 'non-systematic': as a whole it cannot be explained in systematic terms. Later he will argue that the sequence of initial conditions of each coin toss of such an aggregate is non-systematic. There arises at this point the statistical phase of empirical method, which invites us to acknowledge the contrast between systematic and the non-systematic processes.

Experimenting with Statistical Insights into Probabilities

Determinists hold that the data of science are systematic, chaoticists that they are purely non-systematic or random. In contrast with each of these, Lonergan now affirms that scientific data are both systematic and non-systematic.[21] Concrete individual events are governed by more than law, by which presumably he means their initial conditions. Aggregates of events, conditioned by non-systematic initial conditions, are a non-systematic or chance aggregate. The question arises, can some understanding other than the systematic be reached of a random aggregate of events?

Lonergan's account of probability insights is at this point somewhat obscure: 'a probability aggregate is a chance aggregate that has been understood.' He then poses the question, what sort of insight is involved in understanding probability? It will be the same form of cognitional event as that involved in the definition of the circle. But because the data differ radically, the content of the insight will be different. Those data are not a supposed uniformly round curve but a field of successive events. The closest he comes in the notes to defining probability is in the phrase 'Probability = divergence of concrete from systematic must be non-systematic.'[22] This leaves us with the question: by 'systematic' does he here mean 'frequencies'? The terms '*a posteriori* frequencies' occurs at the end of page 8 of the notes, 'ideal frequencies' only much later, on page 26. In his attempt to locate the insight involved in probability, Lonergan does not begin with a set of frequencies but with a random aggregate of events that poses a quite new type of question to us. In response to those data and question, he works towards an insight into a set of frequencies of occurrences.

An illustration is offered in which the question is posed, what reasonable expectations might we have concerning the combined outcomes, 2, 3, ... 12, of the tossing of two dice? The statistical analysis assumes that there can be no systematic influence favouring any of the thirty-six possible outcomes or events. Statistically there is involved an 'aha!' experience as a result of which it is seen as reasonable to expect that no one of the thirty-six possible outcomes is more likely than any of the others. Statistical analysis assumes that there can be no systematic influence favouring any of the possible outcomes. Lonergan continues on page 8, 'there cannot be systematic divergence for any one of 36 so that regularly it occurs oftener than 1 in 36 throws.' The key word here is 'regularly.' Understanding probability invites us to grasp through an 'aha!' experience that in a large enough sample of throws none of the rates of occurrence of the thirty-six outcomes can diverge regularly from the ratio of 1 in thirty-six. If, over a long period of tosses, one and six came up regularly in a patterned and predictable way in the series, further questions would be asked about the dice. On this basis the reasonable expectations of the different combined outcomes can be calculated. Again it is intimated that any divergence of the measured frequencies of the events from the reasonable expectation or probability must be non-systematic. The statistical insight is into the reasonable expectations of the outcomes of aggregates of events.

As in the classical so also in the statistical phase there is a lower-blade movement from empirical data to insights and an upper-blade theoretical enlargement as exemplified by the work of Laplace, Poisson, and Gauss, whom Lonergan names. As the section on probability began with the question of the application of classical laws to events and situations, it would have been interesting to end it by discussing the difficult question of the application of statistical laws to aggregates of events and situations. In *Insight* he will make it quite clear that probabilities do not relate directly to individual events, but rather to rates or frequencies of occurrence of events. Although not directly stated, it is intimated that probabilities disclose to us an understanding of the frequencies of occurrence in the universe of the initial and sustaining conditions necessary for the occurrence of particular events in populations that come under classical laws. There is involved in this a highly distinctive type of scientific insight.

Puzzling Over the Data of Consciousness and Things

Page 9, which follows the statistical analysis, is entitled 'Data, Images, Percepts,' a title that we shall see later has a significant bearing on how the autograph, the final text, of *Insight* was composed. Although the new section opens by addressing the data of sense, it expands to address the data of consciousness. There has to be a component in knowing that is presupposed by inquiry and insight: 'Ergo, definition of data, images, percepts by relation of presupposition and complementation to inquiry and insight.'[23] When, two pages later, Lonergan comes to articulate cognitional structure, the levels will be related in terms of presupposition and complementation.

Mathematicians imagine circles and other geometrical figures but suppose their lines are of no thickness. Empirical scientists have to deal with the data of sense and verify concepts not just in their imagination, but in the world made present by the senses. Free images can be produced more or less at will, but perceptual images involve the integration of sensible presentations with memories and anticipations. Such perceptual images are not experienced individually but as parts of a flow, as in listening to music or speech, following a movie, or dreaming, suggestive of Lonergan's later category, patterns of experience. Empirical science is not concerned with the scientists' flow of percepts; the 'spontaneously integrated animal or man has to recede' and the desire to understand emerge and take charge. It is this that makes science so difficult. There follows a puzzling remark that a datum is 'the residual presentation when all memories and anticipations are removed.'[24]

Paragraph 5 on page 9 of the notes enlarges the analysis to include the data of consciousness: 'Data of consciousness: acts of seeing, hearing, imagining, desiring, fearing, inquiring, understanding, conceiving, reflecting, judging, choosing.' This is one of the rare occurrences of the word 'consciousness' in the notes. If Lonergan is to achieve his 1943 dream of developing an empirical science of consciousness, he has to explain what it is the word 'consciousness' refers to. Although largely cognitional in its designation, it also includes non-cognitional desires and fears and ethical choices, but stops short of including remembering. Here Lonergan is beginning to designate the referent, for him, at this point, of the word 'consciousness,' which poses very difficult questions about the way in which nominal definitions operate for such conscious events or activities. In the final write-up elements of this section will be relocated within chapter 9 of *Insight*. Here, located directly within the experiments with insight of chapters 1, 2 and 8, the analysis invites us to situate the referent of the term 'consciousness' and its associated activities within that experimental context, to relate consciousness in the direct mode with the introspective mode of analysis. Only when we are engaged in such direct-mode cognitional performances as attending to, puzzling over, and understanding imaginative presentations in mathematics or the data of sense in classical or statistical science or other direct-mode realms do we experience the conscious activities Lonergan is naming. We cannot find them in ourselves or name and define them apart from that direct-mode activity. In contrast with his usage in the *Verbum* articles, 'consciousness' now becomes a blanket term for a whole host of human acts.

A critic might say that Lonergan does not seem to address the many difficulties and misunderstandings associated with the word. The imaginative content of the problems of mathematics and the empirical content of science are readily and publicly accessible. The conscious experience of having an insight in the direct mode is extremely elusive. Although its emergence does make the enormous difference of grounding a solution to one's once-perplexing problem, it does not have anything like the same self-evident and accessible nature as the data and world of the senses. At this point Lonergan glosses over differences in their givenness. If our 'aha!' experiences are occasionally noticed they are, as time goes by, largely forgotten or ignored. The answer to the problem is our focal concern, not the conscious process that produces it. The tension of inquiry and the related insights it seeks, as experienced, are characterized by a given and recognizable conscious awareness. When we attempt to describe that awareness we discover that it is strangely unimaginable. It simply cannot be described in terms of sensory or imaginative contents. It is strangely elusive. For many this is a startling discovery, a wake-up call. This strangeness will leave Lonergan at a later stage with the question of the phantasms, derivative of the direct mode of cognitional performance, necessary in order to understand cognition.

The elusive data of consciousness, no less than the more accessible data of sense, are the sources and loci of questions and related insights. The latter will be understood by direct, the former by introspective insights. Such insights for Lonergan differ only in their object or content, in what they understand. As in understanding the data of sense the challenge is to discover the relations among the elements in the field, so also in the data of consciousness. Here one begins, not with the experience of repeatedly tossing two dice or rolling a ball down an inclined plane or a geometrical shape, but with the accompanying conscious experiences of attending to and puzzling about those direct experiences. Once the ineffable insight event in the problem solving has been identified, the challenge becomes that of discovering the pattern of conscious operations within which it fits: imagining and sensing, questioning, conceptualizing, and judging. As Galileo repeatedly experimented with the movement of spheres on slopes, so cognitional experimenters have repeatedly to devise cognitional experiments with their experiences of mathematical and scientific insights in which those elements and their relations can be identified. What also needs to be included in the cognitional experimentation, following the example of Galileo, Mendel, Mendeleyev, and Darwin, is the dimension of making a record of the data or even a journal of the mental journey. No less than the movement on the inclined plane, the conscious experiences involved in the cognitional experiment need quickly to be carefully described and recorded before the passage of time erases them from our memory.

The goal of that analysis will be the determination of a system of primitive terms and relations constitutive of knowing and its relation to reality. As the sciences of the empirical world of sense head towards primitive terms and relations, so also does the science of the data of consciousness, a trend that will be further developed in the third section of the notes. In chapters 6 and 7 of *Insight*, after the introduction of patterns of experience or self-awareness, Lonergan's notion of consciousness will take another significant turn. His remarks at the end of chapter 7 on generalized empirical method will continue to flesh out his dream in 'The Form of Inference' of an empirical science of consciousness and mind. All of these developments will pose the questions, How might the terms and relations of a science of consciousness differ from those of mathematics, physics, or biology? How do the laws of the mind differ in content and form from those of nature? How do they relate to the more historical and hermeneutical attitude to consciousness adopted by the autobiographer and biographer?

On page 10 of the notes, under five headings, Lonergan sketches the elements of a brief and dense analysis of the manner of our understanding of things. By way of illustrations he refers to chemical elements and compounds, plants, animals, and men as, in the technical sense, things. He acknowledges that in history mistakes were made as to the number of chemical elements. Although not mentioned, I would take it for granted that at this point he had read the section on Boltzmann on the problem of the unity and identity of atoms through change in Cassirer's *Substance and Function*.[25] Classical philosophy since Aristotle dealt with this topic under the heading of substantial form. In paragraph five Lonergan refers to Aristotle's treatment of substance in the *Metaphysics* Z, cumulative up to chapter 17. There the question, What is man? is restructured in the form, Why are these data a man? We see Lonergan now beginning to make the transition in his thinking from the classical notion of substance to the modern explanatory notion of species.

Substances, for Lonergan, are understood not by looking or picturing, but by a distinctive type of insight different from the classical and statistical. In that insight there is grasped what it is that makes a thing one and identical. In paragraph 4 he uses the phrase 'Unity and identity (idea) to something (concept).' That unity and identity of idea is differentiated by its descriptive and conjugate terms and by its probabilities. Different things, elements, plants, animals, and humans will be differentiated by their different descriptive and explanatory relations and their probabilities. To the descriptive categories of Aristotle he adds the explanatory categories of modern science. Scientific inquiry presupposes the unity and identity of the things it investigates. Change in their qualities does not annihilate them. That notion of a unity can be verified and applied.

He concludes paragraph 4 with the comment: '3 invariants: identity, conjugate, frequency.' What Lonergan is doing here is linking his analysis of conjugates or relations and probabilities in the chapter so far to the Aristotelian notion of substantial form. In *Insight* he will rename it as central form and have a slightly more advanced notion of intelligible unity. That being said, the intelligible unity of the thing for Lonergan is an open or heuristic notion that needs to be filled out. There is the intelligible unity of a chess game, which begins when the clock is started and ends at a later time. All the legally acceptable chess moves are parts of that intelligible unity. The same is true of a recipe or a rule: it involves an intelligible unity characterized by specific activities or parts. The intelligible unity of a human being differs from that of a game or a rule. Certain activities belong to that unity; others have no part in it. But how the conjugates and probabilities are parts of that intelligible unity and whether the intelligible unity is a unity for something is a puzzle.

Galileo, among others, pioneered the introduction of an experimental method into empirical science. In these pages Lonergan is tentatively taking the first steps in introducing an experimental method into his empirical science of mind. Significant in it is the distinction between what he will later term the 'direct' and 'introspective' modes of operation of the mind. The direct mode is constituted by spontaneous mental activity in the empirical sciences with its classical and statistical insights, in common sense, and in mathematics with its successive viewpoints. Through the understanding that results from that activity our minds come to know and relate us to our worlds. The introspective mode takes the emergent mind-world relations established in the direct mode as a datum to be understood. Those relations cannot be understood except through this experimental and analytical interaction between the two modes. Notable also in his experimenting is his openness to a range of different types of insights, into geometrical definitions, higher viewpoints, classical and statistical laws, the data of consciousness and cognition, intelligible unities. When later in the notes he begins to articulate his world view, all of them will be brought to bear on its contours.

15

The Breakthrough to
Cognitional Structure

In 1983 Lonergan remarked to Tom Daly that 'he had to work very hard on the question of self-knowledge before he got his notion of consciousness. It can't be clarified until you realize that there are levels in knowing.'[1]

Cognitional Structure: From Question to Insight

As early as 1926/7 the unsolved problem of cognition, of how we come to know something in the world, fatefully emerged as a central interest in Lonergan's intellectual narrative. Initially he was frustrated by the naive realism and intuitionism of Suarez and others, but found inspiration in Newman. Later he was challenged by J.A. Stewart and Hoenen, but it was not until 1935 that he made a significant breakthrough on the relation between judgment and what exists. Despite this, in 1943 he was still asking whether everything in the world was subject to law other than the human mind.

Significant in the light of what is to follow are remarks in his 1943 essay 'Finality, Love, Marriage' whose basic thesis was that the universe is comprised of levels of being, a physical, chemical, biological, and so forth. Those levels are related in terms of vertical finality, which has four properties: instrumental, dispositive, material, and obediential. By 'dispositive' he means that a concrete plurality of acts may be dispositive to a higher end in the same agent, his illustration being 'the many sensitive experiences of research lead to the act of understanding that is scientific discovery.'[2] This is suggestive of a living and emergent structure, of the emergence of the insight out of the chaos of sensory experiences.

In the *Verbum* articles there emerged the acknowledgement that we know by what we are. Knowing how we know entails knowing what we are. There followed the hard grind in which, slowly, the strange operations or activities of our thought as a process came to be identified and differentiated. That two levels of operation were involved was faintly recognized, but both were referred to as rational consciousness.

After the *Verbum* articles Lonergan began to take the analysis a stage further. As he was composing his course notes he was also reading Kant, who acknowledged that human knowing, being complex, was made up of more than a single power, element, or operation.[3] The senses and their role in knowledge are to be distinguished from the understanding, and both from reason. As understanding is a faculty of rules, so the highest faculty, reason, is a faculty of principles that relates to the understanding but never to objects.[4] This clearly implies levels in mind.

It is a difficult enough thing to identify and differentiate the elements of cognition, to identify and become familiar with the referent of the words 'spirit of inquiry', 'insight,' 'judgment'; it is quite another to understand the law of their relations. How, precisely, are sensing, imagining, questioning, understanding, thinking, and judging related? Given the strangeness of our desire to know and related insights and thoughts, it is a question that we should not take for granted. We need to be puzzled by it and make it our own if we are to follow the movement of Lonergan's mind.

On 20 December 1948 we find Lonergan, in his Christology class, using the phrase 'levels of consciousness', but not in a directly cognitional context. In his review of Trethowan in January 1950 he referred to three levels in knowing: perception, conception, judgment. In March 1950 in his course notes 'On God's Knowledge and Will' he was writing about the particular and the general good, but not yet levels in the good. In the previous chapter we have seen how in his March 1951 notes for his course 'Intelligence and Reality,' he considered consciousness as a datum of cognition to be understood in much the same way as the empirical sciences understand the data of sense. What kind of understanding can we aspire to of the data of consciousness, what sort of insight are we seeking?

Sometime between January 1949 and, at the latest, March 1951 Lonergan made his initial breakthrough to cognitional structure. His first public articulation of the insight comes in the brief preface to his analysis of judgment that follows on pages 11–13 of the March course notes. The impression is almost given that it is the analysis of judgment, viewed as the operation that in any inquiry completes the cognitional process, that is significant. What direct insights grasp is articulated in propositions that can be either true or false. With respect to them we can adopt two attitudes: we can think and consider them or we can judge their truth or falsity. It is not the direct insights of intelligence but judgment that terminates an inquiry.

After some introductory remarks, reminiscent of Newman on utterance, sentence, and proposition, Lonergan locates judgment within what he calls the 'structure of knowing as a whole.' The text of the passage in which he communicated his discovery follows.

> 4. Questions for intelligence and questions for reflection.
> Structure of Knowing
> 1. Level of experience, of intelligence, of reflection.
> 2. Introspection and reflection; former a generalization.
> 3. Levels related by presupposition and complementation.
> 4. Total and partial increments of knowing.

It is his insight that the questions for intelligence and for reflection structure human knowing into three levels of experience, intelligence, and reflection. The different levels and their elements in cognition are related in terms of presupposition and complementation. Lonergan's affirmation of the equal status of the senses with both understanding and judgment suggests Kant's influence on the involvement of both the senses and understanding in knowing something. How, precisely, the level of the operation of the understanding presupposes, complements, and emerges from the operation of the senses is left an open question. As a result, at this point Lonergan does not seem to offer much clarification of the intractable problem of the manner of the relation between the mental and the physical. The distinction between the direct and the introspective modes of operation is also somewhat obscure in the headings. In the parallel final text of *Insight* it will be crystal clear – the direct mode of cognitional performance provides the data for the introspective mode.

Clearly this insight into cognitional structure would have predated the course and notes by some time. The word 'introspection' links the account with his earlier discussion of the data of sense and of consciousness in the notes, and through it with the experiment with the insights of mathematicians and scientists. There he also talked about understanding presupposing and complementing the data of sense. Nowhere in the notes does the phrase 'levels of consciousness' occur.

As his course notes are largely of the form of topic headings for his lectures, it is clear at this point that chapter 9 of the autograph MSA of *Insight*, written soon after, was well advanced. Accordingly, the text of that chapter gives us a fairly good indication of how he might have elaborated on the headings in his notes. In the opening four pages of the *Insight* text the emphasis is on levels in cognition. Although the phrase 'introspective process' is used, only after articulating the three levels of cognitional process does he, on the fourth page of the chapter, introduce the notion of consciousness. Data of sense include colours, shapes, sounds, and so forth. Data of consciousness consist of acts of seeing, inquiring, understanding, and judging. He continues: 'Thus, the three levels of the direct mode of cognitional process provide the data for the introspective mode.'[5] To sever this connection and attempt to analyse consciousness independently of the direct mode of cognitional activity is to find oneself in a cul-de-sac. This crucial remark is also, I believe, as close as he gets to 'levels of consciousness,' a phase that does not occur in the chapter. By contrast, the term 'level(s)' occurs eight times, 'consciousness' twice.

What his account understates is the radical differences in the qualities of the activities or operations on the different levels. Struck by the huge qualitative chasm that exists between unconscious neural activities in the brain and the conscious sensory level of activity, many are presently baffled at the nature of their relation and interaction. Some go so far as to suggest that it is beyond our comprehension. It is my belief that there is an even greater chasm between the qualities of our imaginative and empirical sensory activities and those of wondering, suddenly understanding, and thinking. A still greater chasm exists between the qualities of the intellectual and the rational, between inference and assent, whose term is knowledge of what is so, what exists. How our imagination and senses are involved in causing activities such as insight that, qualitatively, are so different from them, is hugely baffling. The same is true about the manner in which our imagination, senses, and understanding, through assembling the evidence, partially cause our judgments.

Significant in the notes and in chapter 9 of *Insight* is the absence of the notion found in *Verbum* of duplication. In the direct mode of cognitional activity, we can experience cognitional structure but not know it. Initially we know by what we are but don't know what we are. Actually understanding cognitional structure involves a duplication in us of the structure. The same structure that knows objects in the world applies itself to itself. This is a point that is too important to be left implicit. Also implicit is the fact that knowing cognitional structure involves an intellectual conversion par excellence, a notion Lonergan will introduce shortly in the notes. Involved is a clear-cut breaking out of and decentring of the dominant role of our senses, imagination, and instincts in our knowledge of the world.

The fifth point on page 11 of the course notes explores the relations between total increments in knowledge in terms of logic and dialectic. The sixth point comments on the influence of former judgments on present judgment. Former judgments 'elucidate, clarify, qualify, substantiate, prove, persuade to present judgment.' It is one of his few remarks on how earlier knowing might influence a current judgment, and clearly it poses questions about memory in cognition. The emphasis on the levels of the structure as articulated tend to mask the process or temporal dimension of the creative process of cognition and the manner in which the unusual tense structure of the desire to know unites a past with a present and a future. What is clear is that he considers his structure as defining both a unit of knowing and a unit of knowledge. Equally, he considers his theory as applying to all and every instance or increment of knowing. It is a general theory of knowing.

When, precisely, in the time interval he had the insight we do not know, but in this seminar he shared it in public for the first time with the group at the Thomas More Institute. The language of knowing as a three-level structure is not to be found in 'Thought and Reality,' in the notes William Stewart took in 1947, in the review of Trethowan, or 'A Note on Geometrical Possibility.' Although *Verbum* talks about two levels of operation of the intellect and, separately, about the operation of the senses, nowhere does it talk about three levels or structure, the term 'levels' rarely occurring in the text. What stands out within his structure of knowing is that it gives the experiential level the same status or standing as the levels of understanding and judging. After the 'Intelligence and Reality' notes that structure becomes foundational in his thought, to such an extent that as late as 1964, when asked to write an essay on some of the essentials of his thought, he chose the topic 'Cognitional Structure.' Sadly, his account omitted all autobiographical details of the insight. Although he will fill out and deepen his viewpoint on knowing, it will not be revised.[6]

Page 9 of the notes would suggest that the pattern of relations between the elements of cognition bears a resemblance to that between the conjugates in a scientific law: $PV = krT$, $f = ma$, or a mathematical definition. Only later will it become clear that the emergent pattern of relations that comprises the structure of cognition is such that they can measure and reflect all other patterns of relations in the universe. There is involved an unusual use of the terms 'levels' and 'structure.'

Cognitional structure, as articulated, amounts to a possible understanding of a pattern of relations among the cognitional dimension of consciousness as a whole. That cognitional dimension should never be equated with the entire field of consciousness. Later, in chapter 6 of *Insight*, Lonergan will enlarge his notion of consciousness to include a biological, aesthetic, intellectual, and dramatic dimension. Even this will not be exhaustive.

Biographically we are dealing here with a most significant event in Lonergan's life, in the journey or quest of his mind. It is an event comparable in its significance to his later discovery of the functional specialties in theology in February 1965. Watson's childhood interest in the nature of a gene had to wait long years before it found its destination in the discovery, significant for him, of DNA in 1951. Lonergan's awakened passion to discover the nature of human cognition in 1926/7 also had to wait long years before it found its destination in this discovery somewhere between January 1949 and March 1951. Before the insight came he was like any problem solver in a long process of intellectual striving, the desire of his mind unsatisfied. His life moves through the stepping stones of the problem towards this moment of resolution. In this sense it unites all the elements of the problem that were developing through those elements in his life. In this biographical sense, insights, which result in theories such as Lonergan's of cognition, are emergences within stories. As well as disclosing, in this case, possible intelligible properties of the mind, they are also defining moments in a person's intellectual story and identity.

Without this emergence *Insight* could not have been written, containing as it does the seed of the book. As *Method in Theology* grew out of his later insight into the functional specialties in February 1965, so the book *Insight* grew out of this insight, which is first expressed in chapter 9. The event was both an end and a beginning. Lonergan's intellectual biography moves towards and forward from the discovery. Once the theory has fallen into place, a whole range of further possibilities open up. The moment of the discovery and its expression is like a centre point or focus in Lonergan's philosophical quest whose influence radiates out. The narrative so far has shown how he journeyed to this event. As it continues, the challenge will be to explore the role of that event in the further chapters of his story. How does this moment of insight and its public communication enter into the life story of his mind from this point forward, become a central element in his intellectual identity, in who Lonergan is?

Reflective Understanding and Judgment

> I was looking for someone who had some common sense, and knew what he was talking about. And what was Newman talking about? About judgment as assent; about real apprehension and notional apprehension, notional assent and real assent. He was answering the liberal view that all judgments are more or less probable but nothing is certain ... I wanted something I did know, eh? And this I knew was right. I put the illative sense as reflective understanding, which is an important point.[7]

There follows in the course notes a section with the heading 'Analysis of Judgment,' notable for the inspiration it draws from Newman and Kant. Although their names were written out of the parallel sections in the final text of *Insight*, here the positive influence of Newman and the dialectical influence of Kant on Lonergan shine forth.

His analysis opens, as in chapter 9 of *Insight,* by distinguishing between sentences, utterances, and propositions. Just as the movement towards direct insights cannot begin without imaginative presentations, the pursuit of judgment cannot begin without a proposition, the formulation of an insight. Propositions, the mental synthesis or composition of the *Verbum* articles, can be considered or entertained. Judgment, the act of assent to a proposition, takes us beyond such an attitude and completes the cognitional process. As we know from the performance of juries, some judgments can be made rationally and responsibly, others not so. So the question arises, what are the grounds, the causes of a rational judgment? This leads into the further question, what does a judgment do, in the sense of 'make known'?

Between the question for reflection – Is what is held in the proposition the case? – and the judgment is the reflective act of understanding. Distinct from assenting or judging, its job is to understand and master the sufficiency of the evidence. That understanding enables or causes us to make the judgment. In response to the question, what is sufficient evidence? Lonergan writes the equation: 'Sufficient evidence = virtually unconditioned.' This he distinguishes from the absolutely unconditioned, which brings to mind Kant's supreme being who, in its unconditioned completeness, conditions reality.[8] In contrast, our knowledge of the existence of a virtually unconditioned being is dependent on the sufficiency of the evidence for its contingent existence. For Lonergan its existence is not unconditioned, but virtually unconditioned in the light of the sufficiency of the evidence. Accordingly, to understand the sufficiency of the evidence is to understand the virtually unconditioned.[9] The evidence is an attribute of the fact to be determined, not of the reflective act of understanding.

Significant from a cognitional point of view is Kant's analysis of the conditioned relation between the major and the minor premise in a syllogism.[10] The goal of reason is to reduce the varieties of understanding and knowledge to the smallest number of principles or universal conditions. Reason, in its logical stance, searches for the universal conditions of its judgments or conclusions. But any rule of reason is subject to the same requirement of reason, namely, that its conditions must be sought. In this process the notion of the unconditioned arises:

> But this logical maxim can only become a principle of *pure reason* through our assuming that if the conditioned is given, the whole series of conditions, subordinated to one another – a series which is therefore itself unconditioned – is likewise given, that is, is contained in the object and its connection.[11]

Kant goes on to consider this notion of a series of conditions extending to the unconditioned. For Lonergan this suggests that in order to know anything you have to know everything, get involved in an infinite regress. Following Newman, he will disagree.

Contrasting with Kant's use of the terms 'conditioned' and 'unconditioned' is that of Newman. The matter is complex, but in outline inference holds propositions conditionally, assent unconditionally. Real assents are to things, notional to the creations of our minds. The unconditioned acceptance of a proposition can be the result of its conditional verification. Newman is all the while grappling with the question, how is the conditional acceptance of a proposition in an inference able to lead to an unconditional acceptance of it? It is his conclusion that 'the sole and final judgment on the validity of an inference in concrete matter is committed to the personal action of the ratiocinative faculty, the perfection of virtue of which I have called the Illative Sense.'[12] This makes clear why Lonergan identified his reflective understanding with Newman's illative sense.

Out of his reading of Newman and Kant, Lonergan came to frame his own distinctive theory in terms of the virtually unconditioned: 'All judgments have ultimately the same basis; virtually unconditioned. Kinds of evidence vary; possibility of expressing evidence varies. Act and criterion invariant.'[13] It is his project to illustrate the meaning of sufficient evidence, which he equates with the virtually unconditioned, in syllogistic inference, analytic propositions, concrete judgments of facts (Newman), and empirical generalizations. Newman's illative sense seems to have rescued Lonergan from the impossible demands of the Kantian unconditioned. There are occasions in which the evidence is sufficient and compelling. On the basis of that sufficient and compelling evidence it would be irrational and irresponsible not to judge. We do not have to know everything about everything in order to attain the absolute. Once the evidence is sufficient, in virtue of that evidence we are dealing with a virtually unconditioned. Our knowledge then takes on the property that Kant was searching for in the unconditioned.

It can be assumed that under the heading 'syllogistic inference' in the notes, he discussed as in *Insight* the manner in which the deduction 'If *A*, then *B*; But *A*; Therefore *B*' illustrates the conditioned nature of the conclusion. *A* expresses the conditions of *B*. If *A* is fulfilled then *B* follows. The syllogism is not the starting point for an infinite regress, for there are analytic propositions and judgments of fact of equal validity. What breaks the infinite regress are reflective acts of understanding that grasp the sufficiency of the evidence. In this we should read that passage in *Insight* as a direct critique of Kant's infinite regress. In the headings in the notes Lonergan distinguishes between inference as a rule-governed process on propositions that could be done by a calculating machine and inference as involving the materials necessary for reflective understanding and judgment. For him judgments are not something that can be reduced to the rules of logic or method. Judgments are ultimately something we each do, an activity for which each of us has to take responsibility.[14]

His treatment of sufficient evidence in relation to analytic propositions is explicitly related to Kant. His brief cryptic remarks in which he sharply distinguishes his position from that of Kant are challenging. He refers to Kant's analytic *a priori* (all bodies are extended – B11) and synthetic (the quantity of matter in the material world remains unchanged, action and reaction are equal and opposite – B 17) as covert insights.

As terms may be defined and analytic propositions set up at will, the real issue is the existence theorem. In *Verbum* II Lonergan had discussed wisdom as the ability to discern reality, and in particular, those first principles that were appropriate for reality. Here, 'wisdom' is defined as a habitual cluster of reflective insights with respect to ultimate principles. The heading 'existence theorem' is subdivided into mathematics, empirical science, and philosophy. In these areas he probes the relation between the thesis on wisdom and the first principles of mathematics, empirical science, and later, philosophy. The section provides a background for his discussion of the judgments of mathematics and the natural sciences in chapter 10 of *Insight*.

There follows a series of headings critiquing Kant. Lonergan is highly critical of Kant's criterion for the valid use of the categories involving the schematism of the imagination. It excludes theories such as relativity and quantum theory, which are not rules for constructing images. Kant's mistake was his oversight of the virtually unconditioned, which, for Lonergan, he assumed was subsequent to judgment. There resulted the system of Hegelianism, the first of two references to Hegel in the notes. In the contrast with Kant, here and in *Insight* Lonergan is articulating a quite distinct cognitional paradigm. There are involved two quite different and in a sense incompatible universes of discourse about the world, rather than a difference in detail within a common universe of discourse.

Concrete Judgments of Facts

The heading of the eleventh and final section on page 13 is 'The Fundamental Importance of Newman'; its first subheading is entitled 'Concrete Matters of Fact.' The terms 'matter of fact' occur twice on the opening page of chapter 9 of the *Grammar of Assent*, entitled 'The Illative Sense.' The first subsection, entitled 'The Sanction of the Illative Sense,' opens with the highly significant phrase, 'We are in a world of facts.'[15] In contrast, the term 'fact' does not occur in the index to Kemp Smith's translation of Kant's *Critique of Pure Reason* or in Crowe's index to the *Verbum* articles.[16]

Reflecting Newman's influence on Lonergan, we find the phrase 'concrete judgments of fact' occurring twice in the three pages and 'judgments of fact' once, the former I believe to be unique to Lonergan.[17] In its own way it reflects as cognitionally significant an advance in Lonergan's thinking as his first usage of 'insight into phantasm.' Direct insights are not inner, private, subjective. They are relational, relating us to certain properties of phantasms and situations in our world. Reflective insights also relate us directly to the evidence, which is public. The judgments that they cause directly relate us not only to existence, as he came to acknowledge in 1935, but now to facts, which again are public. This poses a question about the ontological status of what I will term cognitional facts, which come to be known in true judgments. The status of such facts, which need to be sharply distinguished from brute facts, will be resolved at a later stage in the composition of *Insight*.

The headings suggest that he was here discussing the sections in *Insight* entitled 'Concrete Judgments of Fact' and 'Concrete Analogies and Generalizations.' What we do not find yet is any mention of common sense or treatment of common-sense judgments. The subheading, 'Concrete Judgment of Fact,' is followed on the same line, the last line in the section, by 'key to knowing existence, being in act.' This leaves us with the question, what precise properties of our known world are made known in a judgment, something we can imagine or picture, something we can think about, or something different from either of these? Significant for what is to follow is the fact that neither in the 'Intelligence and Reality' notes nor in chapter 9 of *Insight* on judgment does Lonergan invite the reader to make a judgment about a matter of fact in the world.

16

The Mind's Desire as the Key to the Relation of Thought and Reality

Epistemology treats of knowledge in as much as through knowledge intellect reaches out to reality.

At no point is this feature so significant as in the old question as to the relation of thought and being, of the subject and object of knowledge. If once 'things' and the 'mind' become conceptually separated, they fall into two separate spatial spheres, into an inner and an outer world, between which there is no intelligible causal connection. And the conflict constantly grows sharper.[1]

In his insight into cognitional structure, Lonergan has worked out his answer to one of the three related questions and disciplines he articulated in the notes taken by his student, William Stewart, in 1947: the gnoseological. At this point he now has to face the accusation that what he has articulated is a mental structure between which and the world of things there is no intelligible connection. Pages 15–17 and 18–19 of the course notes for 'Intelligence and Reality' that follow, addressing what he terms the episte-mological question, take up that accusation. Entitled respectively 'The Notion of Being' and 'Objectivity,' they densely rehearse the chapters with those same titles in *Insight* and give expression to a number of further significant breakthroughs.

Lonergan's opening sentence on page 15, 'Being is the objective of the pure and unrestricted desire to know,' is one such experience. It gives expression to his core insight, his 'aha!' experience, that potentially, intellectual desire is an anticipation or notion of being, of everything there is. This establishes in the most general manner the nature of the mind-world relation, but does not yet directly resolve the problem of thought/intelligence and reality. A somewhat cryptic breakthrough on the elements of this further longstanding problem is given expression within his treatment of objectivity. At this point the significance of the title he had chosen for the course begins to come into focus.

Reflections on the Desire to Know

In the normal experience of problem solving, our interests and concerns are focused on the content of the problem and desired solution rather than on the desire that seeks it. It takes an unusual effort to enlarge the field of one's interest and attention to include both the problem content and the desire of the mind through which one engages with it. Lonergan's opening points are of the form of an invitation to make that enlargement and engage with the question, what sort of a desire is this desire to know that is at the heart of our mental nature? What sort of desire is it that attempts to understand, for instance, the economic cycle, the mind of Aquinas on *verbum* or intellectual light, the insights and function of insights in mathematics, with its viewpoints and higher viewpoints, and in the sciences as they set about determining the classical and statistical laws of the universe? What sort of desire attempts to understand how we know and the manner of the relation between the knowing subject and known object? How does the self-awareness that accompanies the tension of inquiry differ from the awareness involved in hearing the phone ring or seeing the sun set? Is it something that we can look inside ourselves and see? The reflections that follow should not be read in isolation from problem-solving experiences and contexts such as those mentioned above.

Challenging is the suggestion that intellectual desire can exist and operate before putting its questions into words. In his *Autobiography* Collingwood held that only when he was a long way into a problem could he put words to it. Teachers experience this fact in the reverse order when they discover that teaching a student a familiarity with the words of a question does not necessarily engage them with the question. What precisely does it mean to engage with a problem? It seems that to put a question into words is to erect a signpost for desire.

In the operation of that desire, Lonergan suggests there is a core dialectical tension between, on the one hand, a pure and disinterested orientation and, on the other, an inhibited, reinforced, and interested one. Only the headings are given, leaving us in the dark as to how he developed them.

When intellectual desire is inhibited by other desires, there results a lessening of interest in understanding and truth. When reinforced by them, truth and understanding are pursued up to a point for the sake of something else that calls it into operation. When interested, by which, presumably, Lonergan means influenced by vested interests, intellectual desire is caught up in the flow of percepts that are consciously experienced.[2] Ideally in science it emerges as a pure and detached and disinterested desire for understanding, an idealization, as there might be interested but mentally unfree scientists and detached lawyers or journalists. The use of the term 'disinterested' brings to mind the Ignatian notion of spiritual detachment in the face of life's twists and turns.[3] In order to become mentally authentic we have to rise above our inhibitions, interests, and anxieties and become detached investigators. The unfolding of our desire will result in objective knowledge when it is purified of subjective distortions or interferences, will achieve the openness that later Lonergan would equate with normative objectivity.

The recognition that our intellectual desire can extend its operations to questions we can ask but not yet answer or even, in the future, to questions we cannot currently ask leads Lonergan to the question, reminiscent of Newman's illative sense: what is the range of intellectual desire? We can conceive the unknown and the unknowable, affirm that A is unknown and B is unknowable. Conceiving and affirming the unknown would involve conceiving all of those questions that we can frame but cannot answer. This brief and problematic section ends by Lonergan asking, is there something so alien to our modes of knowledge that we cannot conceive of it in any fashion? The fact that we can pose that question proves for him that the range of intellectual desire is unrestricted, but the extent to which this is predicated of an individual or of the species is not addressed. Based more on analytic than on experiential arguments, it is a problematic conclusion.

Even if ontologically our intellectual desire might be an infinite potential to question, there is also the question of the openness and range it has actually achieved within our finite lifetimes up to this point. The dialectical tensions in which it is involved in conflict situations or disputes reveal the need for the liberation of our desire in order to open us up to all the relevant questions. The actual openness to the universe that our intellectual desire can naturally achieve seems inherently limited and is achieved only with difficulty. Despite Kant's recognition that there is something illimitable in the human mind, existentially we have to struggle with the limitations of our finitude and counter our desire to remain in the dark. [4]

This poses the question, is it the case that the deeper infinities of our desire are manifest on the religious level? Is God the ultimate source of all questions, the one who, indirectly and subtly, through created reality awakens and unlocks our minds? More directly, it was through his conversion experience that Augustine came to recognize the deeper infinities of his desire, a possibility Lonergan later recognised in his unusual essay 'Openness and Religious Experience,' when he wrote about openness as gift.[5]

Intellectual Conversion: A Journey Out of Plato's Cave

Having invited the pure desire to know to step out of its usual anonymity in its management of the growth of knowledge in our lives, and opened up questions about its dialectical unfolding and range, Lonergan next introduces the notion of an intellectual conversion:

> The Starting Point of Philosophy
> 1. Radical intellectual conversion: takes anyone anywhere and advances towards whatever is intelligently grasped and reasonably affirmed.[6]

Reminiscent of the journey out of the cave, this process of intellectual conversion is for him the starting point of philosophy. Differing from Cartesian doubting, it can begin at any time.[7] We don't have to wait for something else to happen first. In this sense, the process of Lonergan's intellectual conversion began with his philosophical awakening in Heythrop to the problem of knowledge. It continued in Montreal with his engagement with J.A. Stewart's *Plato's Doctrine of Ideas*. Its destination was signalled in Rome in 1935 when he came to realize that what exists is not known by intuition but by judgment. Later he named this episode an 'intellectual conversion.' In the *Verbum* articles Aquinas helped him to relate judgments to intellectual light. What exists will become known through the pure desire to know and its pursuit of the totality of true judgments. With this history behind him he now adds: 'Function of radical conversion ... pull out of attitude that world of sense is criterion of reality.'[8]

In some draft notes made shortly after his 'Intelligence and Reality' course he elaborated on the roots of the problem:

> Man is born an animal and, as an animal, he develops without taking thought. It is not by asking and answering questions that he learns to function vitally and sensitively. On those levels development is spontaneous ... By a squatter's right, more ancient than any *contrat social*, we are in the world of sense and our immediate concern is to solve the particular problems that arise, to take things as they are, and to make the best of them.[9]

In those notes he states forcefully that becoming a philosopher involves breaking with a spontaneous orientation to an alternative that accepts what is true despite its strangeness. The desire to know should not be dislodged from its dominant position nor stripped of its unrestricted range. If one is to explore the meaning of the universe, one will need to leave behind the being of the transparent egotist without suspicion of reproach attached to unfettered self-seeking: he has no questions to ask about what truly is good and he is no longer in a position to settle what is true.

Cushman's diagnosis of the same problem from a Platonic perspective makes similar points. Because the mind is dominated by the senses and instincts, 'inversion of reality, as the character both of man's individual and of his social life, is Plato's picture of the "natural man."'[10] According to Callicles, the normal life which human beings live is one turned upside down.[11] Following John Wild's diagnosis, Cushman holds that for Plato the misapprehension of the hierarchical arrangement of human activities was central to the human condition.[12] Because that condition was self-confirming, the efforts of education and dialectic to awaken us to our plight encounter heavy weather. In our natural condition we need to be persuaded that we need to be persuaded that we have things upside down.

Lonergan's invitation in his lectures to engage with the problems and insights of mathematics and of classical and statistical science are of the form of an invitation to identify, in and through them, one's desire to understand. To acknowledge and become interested in one's intellectual desire and its role in problem solving in mathematics, empirical science, common sense, and philosophy is to begin a journey whose goal is to invert our spontaneous upside-down orientation. It is to identify a human attribute that is strangely and even disturbingly different from sensory or imaginative or instinctive activities. By an 'intellectual conversion' Lonergan means that personal transformation whose goal is to liberate us from the domination our senses and instincts have in shaping our sense of ourselves as knowers and of the reality that we know. Again and again in some notes he made after 'Intelligence and Reality' he emphasizes the inherent strangeness of the personal transformation involved.[13] As one begins to recognize and acknowledge the unusual strangeness of the desire of one's mind, such familiarity cannot but challenge the bondage of the status quo of uncritical lived experience.

With little reference to the intense struggle involved in the process, he moves almost immediately to its destination. Although intellectual desire is a desire of the subject of knowledge, it has an objective that quite transcends our subjectivity:

Intellectual conversion: turning from what seems to what is.
Incidental: from a particular error to a particular truth.
Radical: making explicit and deliberate the pure desire, acknowledg-

ing existence and influence of inhib[iting and] reinfor[cing desires], effecting transition from spontaneous to explicit, deliberate, effectively combative pure desire.[14]

An intellectual conversion is in this sense anything but something personal or subjective. Rather, it involves a radical transformation in our understanding of how we are related to the entire universe. An incidental conversion will correct particular errors and result in the surprising discoveries that the earth is not flat, the sun is not the size of a cart wheel and does not rise and set, liquids and solids are not continuous, and gases have weight.[15] An explicit or what he will later term a 'systematic' conversion will correct an error in the whole intellectual orientation of the person or group.

The prominence of the theme in the notes, his earliest public exploration of its meaning, suggests that at the time it was a significant personal preoccupation. Strangely, Charlotte Tansey and Stanley Machnik, who were at the lectures, had no recollection of Lonergan using the vocabulary of conversion in them. Also strange is the fact that when he came to write the final text of *Insight* he dropped the term 'intellectual conversion,' replacing it by the language of pedagogic strategy.[16] The whole book is an invitation to what at this point he is referring to as intellectual conversion.

Involved is a process that, since Plato's account of the philosopher's journey out of the cave of the senses and Augustine's discovery that reality was not simply bodily or corporeal, has had disturbing philosophical implications.[17] A comparison of Lonergan's account with that with that of Cushmann on Plato is illuminating:

> Throughout the centuries there has rested upon Plato a heavy burden of proof. Most men presume they are wide awake to the realities of their world. For them, seeing is believing. But Socrates' teaching concerning the *psyche* had loosed Plato forever from the tyranny of the obvious. For him there is an 'organ of knowledge the value of which outweighs ten thousand eyes,' because only by it is true Being discerned. He knew that those who shared his viewpoint would agree, but he was fully aware, as he stated in the *Republic* (527e), that those who had no first hand acquaintance with the powers of *nous* would necessarily regard his sketch of reality as incredible. Plato's task, therefore, was that of bringing men to the point of acknowledging that they were, in fact, asleep to the real nature of their world.[18]

For Plato, according to Cushman, conversion or *periagoge* meant a turning around of the whole psyche from a day whose light is darkness to the veritable day. He also contrasts Anaxagorus' and Socrates' versions of mind as the measure. For Anaxagorus mind as measure was equated with the senses, for Socrates with intellectual desire. For Socrates and Augustine intellectual desire is not a kind of super-sensing. Although it can be operated on and operate on the data of the sciences made present by the senses, it is nothing at all like the operations of our senses. The discovery and related identification of the manner in which it is not reducible to the activities of the senses and instincts are startlingly strange

The Breakthrough to Intellectual Desire as a Notion of Being

The outcome of the intellectual conversion is the recognition that our senses, imagination, and instincts are not the ultimate measure of knowledge and reality. Such is the task of the strange desire of the mind. To be in such desire is to stand in a relation of anticipation with something that is absent, be it an unresolved problem in mathematics, science, common sense, or philosophy. This opens up the question, what is the largely absent anticipation of intellectual desire? What is it that it desires? It is a question that begins to bring into the focus the goal of intellectual conversion in philosophy. No less than in the paradigm shifts in the empirical sciences, the destination of the intellectual conversion that Lonergan is talking about is a new understanding, in this case of the desire of the mind and its relation to reality. For the first time in public, on pages 15 and 16 of the notes he presents the basis of his answer to that question, his insight into the mind-world relation. Typical of his doctrinaire fashion, he presents it assertively and minimally. Being, what there is, universe, 'is (a) the objective of the pure and unrestricted desire to know and (b) what is known through the totality of true judgments.'[19] In contrast with Plato's realism, Lonergan's, with its emphasis on judgments, is of this world.

Lonergan is also defining his position in opposition to Kant, for whom 'our nature is so constituted that our *intuition* can never be other than sensible. That is, it contains the only mode in which we are affected by objects.'[20] By implication, human intellectual desire has by way of its potential the ability to relate us with the totality of what there is, of reality. A purely relational quality of mind, it is a notion or anticipation of being. Human intellectual powers are not locked up inside us, cut off from the world, as Kant would lead us to believe. In harmony with advances in the sciences from astronomy to archaeology, Lonergan is affirming that our desire to know can ponder and relate us to the big-bang singularity, the smallest elementary particles, the evolution of species, and the writings of every historical civilization. Nothing can escape its scrutiny. It is a desire is to come to know the facts in the world, not to invent them. Those facts become known through the true judgments that still the desire in a particular inquiry. Not only that: human intellectual desire can also ponder itself and, though insights and judgments, affirm its existence and relational properties.

As the desire for joyfulness and enchantment was an artery in C.S. Lewis's life, so also was the desire to understand in the life of Lonergan. Only late in the day, some twenty years after the initial awakening of that desire, did Lewis recognize something important about it, recognize that the form of the desired was in the desire itself.[21] The same is true of Lonergan. Although he was intellectually bright in his early years, it was in Heythrop that his intellectual desire found its direction and path. Still, he has stated that as late as 1946 'I may have had the "concept of being," not "the notion of being."'[22] Behind the words 'Being is the objective of the pure desire to know' is a significant moment of insight, an 'aha!' experience of 'suddenly it all fell into place.' In that experience, which enlarged his breakthrough in 1935, he came to recognize that the form of the desired is in the desire itself. A much richer understanding of the human being than can be found in empiricist and idealist epistemologies is emerging.

When and how he experienced this insight will never be known, but here, for the first time, he is sharing in public with the group in Montreal what in Robert Doran's opinion is one of the great insights of Western philosophy. When Lonergan states that our intellectual desire is a notion of being, he is saying that it is a totally relational potential through whose unfolding we are drawn out of ourselves and into ever deepening mind-world relations with the universe. It defines the mind-world relation in a manner that is totally beyond the horizon of Kantian philosophy. Lonergan's insight into the manner in which the desire to know promotes our mind-world relations now provides him with a framework from which to work out a solution to the problem of the subject and object of knowledge.

A significant distinction emerges in the notes (15, 6) between a pure uniform and a composite/protean notion of being. 'Pure' and 'uniform' connote that the pure desire to know, with its unrestricted range, is one and the same desire in all. In this sense it affirms a universal in all humans whether male or female, Jew or Greek or Gentile. In Greek mythology Proteus was a sea god who could change his form at will. The composite or Protean notion of being points towards variability and suggests that it can play as many parts as there are distinctive quests or questions that different individuals pursue in their lives. Philosophy Lonergan now defines as a strategic set of judgments related to the general character of the universe. His definition of being in terms of the objective of the pure desire to know would count as one such statement. Being is the universe.[23]

Lonergan's analysis of knowing being leads into the problem of the relation between the terms 'being,' 'knowing,' 'known' and 'meaning' in section 8 of page 16 of the notes. Involved is the difficult question of the relation between a theory of knowing and its known objects and a theory of meaning. For Lonergan it is not simply language, but what is known – being – that is meaningful. A particular full term of meaning is what becomes known in a true judgment in a particular investigation. A formal term of meaning would be what is considered or thought. A potential term of meaning would be the data of an investigation. It follows that if being is known through the totality of true judgments, being itself must be what in *Insight* he calls the 'all-inclusive term' of meaning. Contrast this with his second and final reference to Hegel (at the end of page 16), for whom, influenced by Kant's error on reason, 'being is an object of thought without determinate content.'

Important are his remarks that the pure desire 'is not a concept but the root of all inquiry, insight, formulation, reflection and judgment.'[24] It is pre-conceptual, pre-linguistic, the generator in us of all concepts and language. Intellectual desire, through its explorations in mathematics, science, and common sense of the meaning of being, of what there is, of the universe, is the source, origin, and cause of the conceptualizations, judgments, and related language that subsequently emerge. How far a mature understanding of human wonder, of its relation to the world of experience and its role in concept and language formation would go towards explaining the emergence, growth, structure, and function of language is a challenging question. But any effort to explain the relation between thought or concepts and language and their relation to the world that overlooks the pure desire to know would surely be out of focus. Intellectual desire is, for Lonergan, pivotal in a theory of meaning.

In *Insight* he will add the category of acts of meaning to that of terms, dividing them into full, formal, and instrumental. The full act of meaning is the act of judging, the formal the act of conceiving or defining, the instrumental the act of expressing the thought in words. Significantly, the pure desire to know, the notion of being, is the core of all acts of meaning, the cornerstone of his theory of language and meaning.

Objectivity and the Subject and Object of Knowledge

Subjectivity – interference with working of pure desire
Objectivity – pure desire unfolds without subjective bias.[25]

Theories of knowledge have to take a stance on what they consider to be the properties of objective knowledge proper and the subjective factors that can promote or hinder its attainment. Lonergan's earlier reflections on how the human desire to know can be pulled between the polarities of detachment and vested interests provide a basis for distinguishing between subjectivity and objectivity. In the latter the subjective prejudices of the agent came into play and inhibit the proper unfolding of their desire. The former relates to the analysis of normative objectivity in *Insight*. On page 17 of the notes, to some extent influenced by Cassirer's *Substance and Function*, a book that Lonergan read while composing *Insight*, he enlarges the analysis.[26] Chapter 6 of that work, entitled 'The Concept of Reality,' explores the development of the concepts of subjectivity and objectivity and of degrees of objectivity. In his course notes, in contrast with the treatment in *Insight*, Lonergan begins by considering four theories of knowledge: realism, his own position; relativism; empiricism; and obscurantism. What stances do the realist, the relativist, the empiricist, and the obscurantist adopt on the problem of objective knowledge?

For Lonergan, relativist theories of knowledge hold that there are no true judgments. Truth and falsity are not absolutes but relatives. Some opinions are more or less true than others. Knowing is the process by means of which we move towards the ideal of a full understanding of everything. The object, knowledge, is comprehensive coherence. Relativism for him misses the notion of the virtually unconditioned that he got from Newman. The answer must be that correct concrete judgments of fact actually occur frequently in practice.

In empiricist theories of knowing, both understanding and judging are subjective activities that follow knowing. They give one a subsequent intellectual mastery over what one previously knows. Rigorous empiricism confines our knowing entirely to the level of sense, Bergson's *durée pure* being mentioned to make the point. Concepts are either a falsification or a simplification of the real, which is the flow of experience. Empiricists argue that understanding and reasoning are subjective, to which Lonergan replies that they are constitutive of the knowing subject. By 'subjective' he would mean an interference with the pure desire to know.

For the obscurantist, whom he considers a confused empiricist, experiencing itself as well as understanding and judgment, being activities of the subject, are subjective. An object of knowledge is what is independent of the subject, 'it is "really real" "out there" whether or not it is known.'[27] It is what is left over when knowing is subtracted from the known, the thing in itself: 'Obscurantist confuses *a* property of object, namely that it is reached through unconditioned, affirmed absolutely with universal validity, and *b* question what is object.'[28] There is a distinction between the question about objective knowing and the objects that become known through such objective knowing. Only later will Lonergan address the question of the known objects.

His own position on objective knowledge is that the object or being (the terminology of facts having been dropped for the moment) is what becomes known in a true judgment. This position is a consequence of the intellectual conversion out of which intellectual desire and its relation with an object of knowledge in a true judgment come to be acknowledged by the philosopher of mind. Because being is the objective of the pure desire to know, realist objectivity is absolute. Although he does not expand the meaning 'objectivity,' his treatment of it here foreshadows that of absolute objectivity in *Insight*. The conditions of the conditioned judgment are independent of the knower. It follows that what becomes known in a true judgment is a public fact. Every theory of objectivity has to explain this property of what we know, its public nature.

In the treatment of objectivity on page 18, 3e, of the notes, anticipating the principal notion of objectivity in *Insight*, the summit of the mountain Lonergan has been scaling comes into view. In a few paragraphs he begins his direct engagement with the problem of explaining the relation between thought and reality, between the subject and object of knowledge. Cassirer's focused presentation of the Kantian view in the course of his treatment of degrees of objectivity in his *Substance and Function* sets the stage:

> The problem of transcendence ... it is the presentations in us,
> which alone are given to us in the beginning, and from them we
> gain access to the world of objects only with difficulty. The history
> of philosophy shows, however, how all attempts of this sort fail. If
> we have once enclosed ourselves in the circle of 'self-consciousness,'
> no labor on the part of thought (which itself belongs wholly to this
> circle) can lead us out again. On the other hand, the criticism of
> knowledge reverses the problem; for it, the problem is not how we
> go from the 'subjective' to the 'objective,' but how we go from the
> 'objective' to the 'subjective.'[29]

In this view, which Cassirer also seems to be attempting to deconstruct, the spheres of thought and reality, of subject and object, are separated by an almost unbridgeable gap. Mental processes are inner and immanent in us. Things in themselves belong to the distinct sphere of the outer world and are unknowable.

Lonergan's response will be to respect profoundly the problem but also to deconstruct entirely the above viewpoint and replace it with a surprisingly different one. In opposition to Kant he will argue that, in a specific sense, there is no gap between the spheres and that the things of our world are knowable.[30] His insights into cognitional structure, into the pure desire to know as a notion of being, into being as what becomes known through the totality of true judgments, and into the nature of objectivity are of the form of a preface to his response to the problem.

So far, his treatment of the problem of objectivity states that if the subjectivity of the questioner is transcended in relation to any problem, then in a true judgment, some being, some existing object of knowledge, will become known. A preliminary step in response to the above problem, this allows for the possibility that the universe contains only a single subject and no distinct objects, or many distinct subjects and objects. This poses the questions: what, within his framework, does Lonergan mean by an object of knowledge, what does he mean by a subject of knowledge, what is the manner of their distinction and their relation? 'Subject/object of knowledge' are terms that for him will replace 'thought' and 'reality,' 'reality' in turn being replaced by the term 'being.'

To enter into this problem, a first requirement is to engage with a question about a situation or fact or event in the world: is it the case that X is so? An ideal situation would be to find oneself on a jury panel in a complex court case and directed by the judge to take responsibility for determining a fact in the world. Alternatively, one might find oneself puzzled by and struggling to understand the unusual behaviour of a friend. Spontaneously there arises the question of correctly interpreting that behaviour. Is he or she suffering from stress or an illness such as depression, or perhaps being blackmailed? Various insights can emerge and be put to the test of the available evidence. When the question is resolved one takes responsibility for one's judgments in either the trial or the interpersonal situation, and affirms that, say, one's friend is stressed. In this way, without knowing what we are doing, we come to know facts, events, states of affairs, situations, or objects of knowledge in our world. It seems to be Lonergan's position that we could spend most of our cognitional lives coming to know such facts without ever, in a technical sense, knowing how we know them. Recall his remark from the second *Verbum* article that 'we know by what we are.'

During or after one's jury duty or engagement with the puzzle of one's friend's behaviour, one might find oneself being drawn into the further question, just what was I doing when I was problem solving on the jury or in my world? For the Kantian there can be no question about exploring a connection between facts in the world and my inner cognitional activities. If one understands what Lonergan means by the 'pure desire to know,' then such a question is inevitable and the mythical chasm between the object and subject of knowledge is deconstructed. Through becoming questioningly interested in how we come to know such facts in the world, we begin the process of coming to know ourselves as cognitional subjects. Such self-knowledge presupposes the direct mode of cognitional activity as its field of investigation, and cannot emerge without it. About it Lonergan now remarks:

> Startling because potential, formal and actual knowing: self as conscious, intelligent, reflective in potential knowing affirms self actually; only latter object in present sense because only latter is actually knowing being.[31]

The discovery that the cognitional subject may perform and come to know a vast variety of facts in the world and yet, in a technical sense, remain unknown seems to have startled Lonergan. Although the above quote is difficult to decipher, what does stand out in it is that the cognitional self only becomes an object of knowledge through an affirmation. Although not stated, that affirmation will, for him, be of one's cognitional structure. In it, to continue the above *Verbum* phrase, 'we know we know by knowing what we are.'

In the judgments 'X committed the offence' or 'My friend is stressed,' previously unknown facts in my social world become known. In the judgment of self-affirmation the previously unknown activities of myself as a cognitional subject become known in exactly the same manner as anything else, in response to the probing of the desire to know. On the realist view of objectivity all objects of knowledge, including the cognitional subject, are known in the same way. As they are different objects in the same universe of being, in this sense there is no chasm between them. What becomes known in the cognitional judgment, the cognitional structure of the subject of knowledge, is different from what becomes known in the direct judgment 'My friend is stressed.' There follows the judgment 'I as a cognitional subject am not my stressed friend.' The cognitional subject and the stressed friend are both known in the same way, through the proper, undisturbed unfolding of the pure desire to know its object. The known object and subject are distinctions within that object.

A further significant insight into the problem, not addressed in the notes, was implicit in the final part of the *Verbum* phrase, 'and since even the knowing in "knowing what we are" is by what we are, rational reflection on ourselves is a duplication of ourselves.' Uniquely in and through the duplication of ourselves we come to know ourselves, this not being the case for our knowledge of objects in our world. Not only is there no unbridgeable chasm between the subject and object, knowledge of the cognitional subject is conditioned by knowledge of objects in the world. I have introduced the theorem of duplication at this point because in his subsequent analysis Lonergan puts forward the judgment of self-affirmation as the first judgment. It is my own view that that judgment has to presuppose instances of other judgments concerning facts in our world. The theorem of duplication would also seem to have some bearing on Lonergan's later theorem of the isomorphism of the known and the knowing.

The preceding reflections have been offered in the hope that they will shed light on Lonergan's brief and cryptic explanation of the problem of thought and reality, of the subject and object of knowledge, given on page 18 of the notes. The matter is brought into focus for him in terms of four judgments, the first and second of which have been switched to underline the genetic sequence. Involved is the definition of the subject and object of knowledge:

> It is [a fact, situation, state of affairs, object of knowledge]
> I am [a knower]
> I am not it
> I make these judgments.[32] [One part knows others]

In these we can see taking shape what in *Insight* he terms the 'principal notion of objectivity.' To the judgments 'My friend is stressed,' and 'I am a knower' there had to be added the further judgment 'I am not my stressed friend.' This in turn leads to the judgment 'My friend is stressed, I am a knower, I am not my stressed friend, I make these judgments, I am the part that knows the others.' Analysis is no substitute for the existential performance of raising and following the questions through to their term. Through that plurality of judgments we come to know distinctions within being, the objective of the desire of our minds, between known objects and the distinct knowing subject. The foundations of Lonergan's philosophy invite us to make and identify ourselves making such a plurality of related judgments. In all of this the foundations from which he would write the autograph of *Insight* were beginning to come into focus.

In response to Cassirer, Lonergan makes the following cryptic remarks: 'nothing left over from which to cross; no possibility of immanence.'[33] In *Insight* he will state that 'sixthly, the principle notion of objectivity solves the problem of transcendence.'[34] The theorem of duplication, I believe, provides a significant clue to the interpretation of these brief cryptic remarks.

His concluding paragraph on objectivity raises a question about a path in his inquiry through the dependent existence disclosed in the virtually unconditioned to the unconditioned existence of the absolute. The light of our minds is a participation in the uncreated light of God. In this sense, the analysis of judgment and the virtually unconditioned has implications for the question of God. Lonergan at this point does not relate the virtually unconditioned with the contingent and dependent. That will come later.

Knowing, for Lonergan, is a perfection that rises on successive levels from potential to formal to actual and objective. In pages 19–22 of the notes he develops the contrast between his own view of knowing and objectivity with an opposed view, confrontationism, first discussed in the fifth *Verbum* article, and the mechanical model, a topic to be found in Cassirer.[35] For the confrontationist, knowing is a matter of taking some kind of look at an object out there to be seen, be it the look of perception or even intellectual intuition. Involving a dualistic confrontation in which an object becomes present to a subject with judgment a matter of rubber-stamping what is already known in the confrontation, this analysis is at odds with Lonergan's account of knowing and objectivity. In contrast to the difficult analysis of intellectual desire, insight, and judgment, it is easy to assert that knowledge is a form of confrontation.

The sources of confrontationism are identified in a dualism in one and the same human individual of animal spontaneity on the one hand, and intelligence and reason on the other:

> (a) Man is born an animal; integrates as animal spontaneously; prone to make intelligence and reason another organ at service of animal.
> Two orientations: universe of being by pure desire to know and radical intellectual conversion; world of sense by flow of precepts, successful living.
> Significance of Platonist flight from sense, Pythagorean five years of silence, relativity and quantum mechanics. [36]

There results two orientations that come to be confused. There is the orientation within the world of sense by a flow of percepts; and there is an orientation within a universe of being by the pure desire to know, its related questioning, insights, formulations, and judgments. From the former it is extremely easy to conclude that objective knowing is a matter of taking a look. Lonergan repeats his conviction that the latter invites a difficult and prolonged analysis of the intellectual desire. The confrontationist will simply not accept the call to a radical intellectual conversion, which is considered superfluous.

In some brief remarks that suggest elements of confrontationism in a list of philosophers, we can see, in seed, Lonergan's dialectic of positions and counterpositions in chapter 14 of *Insight*. What elements, if any, of Galileo's primary and secondary qualities and Descartes' dualism of the *cogito ergo sum* and the *res extens* are compatible with Lonergan's notion of being and objectivity? Similarly for Newton's account of true motion, Kant's subjectiv-

ism or phenomenalism and failure to grasp the significance of the unconditioned for judgment, and Scotus' oversight of insight into phantasm.
Lonergan's remark that Scotus assumed knowing presupposes an object
present to a subject invites us to think out how his own account of the
relation of the subject and object of knowledge differs. What sort of an
object, for instance, becomes present to us in and through a judgment?

17

Exploring the Real Known World:
A Metaphysical Beginning

The Third Question: What Is the Object of Knowledge?

In the domains of mathematics, of the natural and human sciences, and, as we shall see later, of common sense, the intellectual desires of communities of individuals and their related mental powers engage with their worlds. In the mathematical community the desires of those individuals can engage with the problems of geometry or of numbers and number theory. In the scientific community they can embark on the cognitional process of coming to explain the great diversity of species of things that are to be found in our universe, seek an understanding of the laws of their emergence, behaviour, and survival. In the common-sense community they are concerned with understanding the facts of their common-sense situations and the related tensions between progress and decline that need to be addressed in the worlds of the family, society, and history. In this primary field the strange activities of questioning, understanding and formulating, reflecting and judging engage with and come to know our world, but can go unnoticed. The focus of attention is on the product of cognition, not on the process. Although we know that we know certain things, it follows that we can be confused about what that means.

Philosophy is no substitute for this primary existential exercise of mind, what in *Insight* Lonergan will term the 'direct mode,' through which there emerges spontaneously in the lives of individuals the formation of varieties of mind-world relations. It is the givenness of that direct mode that is the source and origin and inspiration of the meaning of the philosophical questions with which are associated the terms 'cognitional theory,' 'epistemology,' and 'metaphysics.' Sever the connection with it, and those disciplines have nothing left to understand. Through engaging with it their aim is to understand and clarify emergent direct mode mind-world relations. For strategic reasons Lonergan begins with the cognitional question, but ultimately all three and their interrelatedness must be addressed. Because, in this, the philosophical mode is taking the mind-world relations of the direct mode as its data to be understood, his analysis is invulnerable to all accusations of psychologism.

The question of the known, present but bracketed in the preceding analysis, now becomes the focus of attention. Metaphysics for Lonergan is the science of being, of the objective, not of our sensing and picturing but of our pure desire to know. As has been made clear, being for him encompasses a hierarchy of grades: the inorganic, organic, sentient, and rational. Directly those domains become known through the intellectual creativity of physicists, chemists, biologists, and varieties of psychologists. Metaphysics is no substitute for those disciplines nor, as we shall see later, for common sense. Its aim is not to replace those presupposed realms of cognitive striving but to eliminate certain confusions concerning what it is that we claim to know through them about our world.

At this point the common-sense pragmatist will exclaim, how on earth could there be any confusion concerning what we know? Why is there this need to tell physicists and chemists and biologists and psychologists what it is that they know? Surely they are the experts. A response is that if, imprisoned by the bondage of their senses and instincts, they are mistaken about how they know anything, that mistake will weave itself throughout the whole fabric of what they claim to know. The metaphysician invites the experts in those fields to discover and work out how intellectual conversion brings with it enormous clarifications of what we know. The known, for Lonergan, could never be reduced to the content of what we imagine, picture, or intuit. To introduce the strange desire of the mind, the insights it seeks and the judgments that still its restlessness, into knowing poses the further question, what precisely do we come to know through these operations? The tone is set at the start:

> (a) Adequate object: any being whatever.
> Proportionate object: the range of beings with a structure that corresponds to our knowing. Cf. Kant: object of possible experience.
> Cf. Protean character of notion of 'being.'[1]

The range of beings that we can come to know is defined by the protean character of our desire to know, the range of distinctive questions that can form in it, the insights it seeks and judgments it makes.

Significant is the assertion that the structure of an object of our knowledge must be such that it corresponds to the cognitional structure of the knowing of the subject. This presupposes the definition of the subject and object of knowledge in Lonergan's treatment of objectivity, but goes beyond it. It invites us to determine what it is he means by the correspondence of objects of knowledge to our knowing. Substituting 'facts' or 'events' or 'states of affairs' for the scholastic and Kantian term 'object' is not unhelpful.

One occurrence of the Kantian phrase 'object of possible experience' is found in the B Preface to the *Critique of Pure Reason* (Bxxx). Worth recalling, because of its present relevance, is the preceding passage on Kant's Copernican revolution:

> We should then be proceeding precisely on the lines of Copernicus' primary hypothesis. Failing of satisfactory progress in explaining the movements of the heavenly bodies on the supposition that they all revolved round the spectator, he tried whether he might not have better success if he made the spectator to revolve and the stars remain at rest. A similar experiment can be tried in metaphysics, as regards the *intuition* of objects. If intuition must conform to the constitution of the objects, I do not see how we could know anything of the latter *a priori*; but if the object (as object of the senses) must conform to the constitution of our faculty of intuition, I have no difficulty in conceiving such a possibility.[2]

The Copernican revolution takes a particular stance on the manner of the relation of the subject to what is known. For Kant there is involved the categories of mind and the intuiting subject and intuited object, but the only manner in which the subject of knowledge relates directly to what is known is through sensible intuition. Accordingly, the order that Newton's or Darwin's or Mendel's laws establish is not something known in the world, but something conceptual in our minds. The laws have no counterpart in the known world.

Lonergan will be inspired by the question he finds at the heart of Kant's Copernican revolution but will, on three fronts, define his answer in opposition to Kant. Firstly, he will replace Kant's cognitional subject by the subject of cognitional structure at whose heart lies the pure desire to know, the notion of being. Secondly, he will assert that it is through the pure desire to know and the judgments it seeks rather than Kantian sensible intuition that our minds are related directly to what can be known. The form of the desired conforms to the form of the desire, not to sensible intuition. Thirdly, far from trying to derive the categories by which the mind interprets the world from the cognitional subject, he will hold that it is through operating cognitionally on all levels in the direct mode that we come to know those properties of the known. Through our sensing and perceiving we know an empirical dimension of reality, through our understanding a formal or intelligible component. In a true judgment a full, proper cognitional relation is established with a known object or fact in the world; we come to affirm the existence of a fact, situation, state of affairs. Although the two are quite distinct, there is no chasm between thought and reality; they are innately related to each other. The metaphysical question now explores a further aspect of that relation. The transformed Copernican revolution implies that what we say about what we know must be consistent with how we know it.

The Categories of the Known: Terminal, Heuristic, Dialectical

From this perspective, categories are introduced as differentiations in what is known, 'general lines of cleavage, division, ordering of the universe of being ... the ultimates in terms of which "being" can be described and analyzed.'[3] Holding that categories are attributes of the things and situations that we investigate in our world, Lonergan's approach contrasts with that of Kant, for whom they are purely mental. There is a need at this point to move the focus of one's attention from the linguistic to the real attributes of things and situations in one's world in order to enter into the analysis of descriptive, heuristic, terminal, and dialectical categories that follows.

In continuity with his course on 'Thought and Reality,' Lonergan's starting point is again Aristotle's categories: substance, quantity, quality, relation, action, passion, place, time, posture, habit. Aristotle's *Categories* draws on modes of speech; his *Metaphysics* Z investigates substance in detail. The *Physics* discusses place and time, action and passion, and offers a form of explanation of changes of quality and quantity, generation and corruption. Despite this, Lonergan considers the categories in these works to be largely descriptive of what we know and the analysis best suited to natural history rather than the explanatory thrust of the modern sciences. This does not mean that the descriptive categories are to be rendered redundant; quite the contrary.

Because of the modern sciences there arises a need to add both heuristic and terminal categories. Heuristic categories relate us as potential knowers to the unknowns that we seek to understand in the world of our scientific investigations. Those involved in a criminal investigation would work with the heuristic notion that some unknown person X committed a known crime. In this sense, being would be the ultimate heuristic category that is anticipated in the totality of questions for reflection and related judgments.

In *Insight* metaphysics will have the task of articulating the integral heuristic structure that the empirical sciences and common sense strive to fill out.

Building on his analysis of the questions for intelligence he has examined in his experiment with mathematics and the empirical sciences, Lonergan identifies and sketches three heuristic categories. The question, What is it? anticipates instances of concrete unities and identities such as an element, plant, or animal or, more generally, substance or species. The question, Why is it an *X*? – a circle, acceleration, element, plant, animal, etc. – anticipates data as similar, admitting systematization or law. In response to the questions, How often? What is to be expected? there are data not admitting systematization, a reference to the data and expectations of statistics. The different questions and related heuristic categories point to the fact that being, the objective of the desire to know, is differentiated into instances of intelligible unities, (things, species, or substances), of relational properties or laws, and of expectations concerning events or occurrences. Implicit is the notion that different aspects of the relevant data in our world form significantly different questions in us. Later in the notes Lonergan will remark: 'What are the substances, what are the laws, what are ideal frequencies, subject to possible revision. But these questions are not.'[4] Heuristic categories, being constants of revision, point towards invariants in what it is we seek to know. His remarks on the heuristic role of the imagination and the elimination of representative images by relativity and quantum theory need to be puzzled out. It is not the representative image that is verified, but what is the case.

The source and inspiration of Lonergan's detailed engagement with the terminal categories of potency, form, and act is again Aristotle. With a reference to *Metaphysics* 9 he remarks on the relation between potency, form, and act and eyes, sight, and seeing. With a reference to *De Anima* II he adds that the soul stands to the animal as the sight to the eyes, adding that Aquinas' position on existence needs to be added to that of Aristotle.

The terminal categories are defined by him in relation to our knowing as a structure, operating on different levels, indicating the influence of his revision of Kant's Copernican revolution. Here he classifies them as explanatory; in *Insight* his challenge will be to relate them to the distinct explanatory categories of modern science. He begins in paragraph 5 on page 23 with a general definition:

> Form presupposes and complements potency.
> Act presupposes and complements form.
> Potency, form, and act constitute a unity.
> Potency, form, and act share a common definition.

Cp. Level of experience, intelligence, reflection.
Second presupposes and complements first; third presupposes and
    complements second.

Potency, form, and act and their relations constitute the ontological structure of objects of knowledge in our world and are, in a sense, independent
of how, descriptively, we relate to them. Because of his intervening insight
into cognitional structure, this definition involves a considerable development from his approach in 'Thought and Reality.' It is as though he had
moved from a pre-paradigm to a paradigm phase.

There is a great need to imaginatively illustrate the definition. Consider
in this context the relation of an eye surgeon to the eyes of the patient
being examined. The eye surgeon 'knows' the potency, the matter of the
eye of the patient, not with the understanding but with the senses. Such is
not abstract knowledge, but empirical knowledge of this eye of this patient
at this time in this place. In the examination the surgeon illuminates and
examines the elements of the matter of the outer and inner eye. Through
his mastery of the descriptive categories, he could describe in detail what he
sees when he examines the eye. Similarly the ear surgeon, with his instruments, illuminates and looks at the matter of the inner ear of his patient.

As well as the matter, there is also the form of sight or of hearing. As the
insight grasps the form or idea of the circle in the image of uniform
roundness, so the form of sight becomes present through understanding,
in the matter of the eye, the interrelatedness of the relevant laws of optics,
of the nerve connections between the retina and the cerebral cortex, and
conscious visual processes. For hearing this involves understanding, in the
matter of the ear, the relation between the relevant laws of acoustics, the
corresponding neural networks, and an awareness of sounds. Form is known
not by the senses, but by the understanding of the eye and ear surgeons,
through their insights into the sensibly presented matter of the eye and ear.
It is because of this that they have to spend years studying the laws of physics
and the neural and psychic properties of the eye and ear. In the light of that
understanding the eye or ear surgeon brings certain questions to the
matter of the eye or ear, or even, in some cases, finds that the matter poses
its own questions. It is in this subtle engagement of mind with matter that
the distinction between potency and form can be acknowledged.

The eye surgeon could also adopt the role of an optician or opthometrist
and test the sight of the patient, invite her to read the letters on a distant
chart; the ear surgeon could invite her, in a hearing test, to listen to sounds
of varying degrees of loudness. In the patient's responses to these tests,
the optician or ear surgeon will affirm that the patient clearly saw/heard

certain letters/sounds and mistook others. In each instance there is identified specific activities of sight and hearing. Finally, there is the distinction between seeing and not seeing a letter, between hearing and not hearing a sound. Whether the eye is active and seeing something is known, not by our senses or our understanding, but in a correct judgment, it is the case that the patient is seeing X. The doctor has to grasp that the conditions necessary for the occurrence of the specific act or acts occur. In many instances such a grasp will be so obvious that the role of the reflective insight can be obscured, but it is the case that every act as such is conditioned.

We know the matter empirically by the use of our senses. We know the proportionate forms intellectually by the questions we put to that matter and it puts to us. We judge that acts of seeing have occurred on the basis of the answers to our request to read out the sequence of letters on the third line of the chart. Potency, form, and act are not attributes of the cognition of the surgeon but of the eyes and related consciousness of the patient. They transcend the surgeon's subjectivity and in a certain sense are independent of it. Only from this perspective will we be able to make sense of Lonergan's countercultural remark in the notes: 'Terminal categories: conditions of true propositions as true.'5 The illustrations need to be multiplied. We need to ask ourselves how the matter or potency of the eye differs from that of the ear, how both differ from that of a human being with its lifelong dimension of bodily continuity and of which they are parts. How might the matter or potency of a movement on an inclined plane differ from the chemical crystal DNA; of the wing of a bird from the branches of a tree or of a bird from a tree? How does the matter or potency of a population of pea plants or of coin tosses differ from that of an individual in the population, of world order as a whole from the matter of its constituent parts?

The term 'form' can in a sense be read as the name of the various laws of the sciences. In this sense, it is the general name of the laws of movement, of the chemical elements and their defining equation, of biology and psychology. Those laws are known not by the senses but by the understanding. 'Act' is the general name of events that come under those laws, and is known, not by the senses and understanding, but by judgment.

In this imaginative expansion the role and significance of the descriptive categories ought not to be downplayed. There is a descriptive function of both the understanding and judgment through which we come to describe and affirm how we relate, experientially, to the matter, that is to say, the bodily appearance of the animal, (species, thing, Aristotelian substance), its place and time, habitat, movements, behavioural activities, and social status. Such descriptive knowledge needs to be valued. Later in the notes

Lonergan will argue that both descriptive and terminal categories are necessary, a possible source for his later distinction between description and explanation in *Insight*.

On one level potency, form, and act can be defined in terms of what we know or identify by our senses and imagination, by our insights and by our judgments. Lonergan's analysis takes the matter a step further. The phrase 'presupposes and complements' occurred on two previous occasions in the notes. The second occurrence related to the levels in knowing of experiencing, understanding, and judging. What Lonergan is now implying in his new insight is that the relations between the terminal categories of the known objects – potency, form, and act – are the same as those between the different levels of cognitional operation of the knowing of the agent. Taken with his earlier phrase 'the range of beings with a structure that corresponds to our knowing,' we find here the theorem of isomorphism of *Insight* in the making. It is the defining insight, the key to his approach to metaphysics, to his response to the problems posed to Aristotle by Kant's Copernican revolution.

As with levels in cognitional structure, to say that act presupposes and complements form says very little at this point about the ontological constitution of the object. What we have here are the first, stumbling words of a new beginning. In the process of composing chapters 8 and 15 of *Insight* further insights into the nature of that relation will emerge.

As significant differences within what we know come to be identified, there arises the challenge of understanding the world order of which they are the parts. If there is a type of question that is concerned with understanding the intelligible unity of species of things such as particles, atoms, plants, animals, and humans, there will be a proportionate potency, form, and act. If there is a type of question concerned with understanding the conjugates or relations or scientific laws that define those things, there will be a distinctive, proportionate, conjugate potency, form, and act. If there is a type of question concerned with understanding the intelligible manner in which things and their laws emerge and relate within the cosmic process, there will be a further distinctive, proportionate potency, form, and act. A second movement in Lonergan's metaphysical searching is concerned with integrating differences into a world order constituted by an emergent probability. In it we see the genesis of his definition of 'metaphysics' in *Insight* as a discipline concerned with articulating the integral heuristic structure in terms of which being becomes known.

Classical insights are into conjugate forms, the laws governing the movement, chemistry, etc., of things. Such relations are for Lonergan properties of things or individuals (substantial forms) that are understood through insights into intelligible unities. The suggestion here that sight is a conjugate form seems to imply that in the higher sciences such forms transcend the mathematical. Some light will be shed on this question when he is writing *Insight*.

At this point something surprising emerges in the notes. Instead of dealing, as in the earlier section, with straightforward probabilities, we find Lonergan claiming that:

> group form is emergent probability (probability, because actual occurrence is governed by probability; emergent probability because events that actually occur affect the expectations of what is to occur).[6]

Two pages later in the notes he will comment on the parallels between Aristotle's substance, accident, and world theory and his group, conjugate, and substantial potency, form, and act.[7] Lonergan's transformation of Aristotle is drawing on both Kant and the modern empirical sciences.

Significant in the quote is the distinction between his usages of the terms 'probability' and 'emergent probability.' In the former, probability governs the actual occurrence of events, and the basic supposition is that the outcome of an event is in no way determined by the outcome of previous events. In the latter, the events that have occurred govern the subsequent probabilities, almost a reversal of the classical notion. This development approach does, however, connect with his earlier thoughts on the notion of possibility.

We find here one of the earliest occurrences of the terms 'emergent probability,' at this point identified as a group form, in Lonergan's writings. Shull's frequent use of the term 'group' in the context of genera and species of things in the opening pages of his book *Evolution* provides a possible context for the meaning of the phrase 'group form.' Lonergan is considering intelligible unities (Aristotelian substances) or things as members of groups defined by emergent processes. The word 'emergent' also occurs in Shull's final chapter.

Lonergan's approach to emergent probability differs at this point from what we find in chapter 4 of *Insight* in that it includes substances, later renamed 'things' in *Insight*, in its field. Nowhere in the notes are schemes of recurrence mentioned, the emphasis being on the events that have occurred in world order affecting our expectations of what is to occur. At this point emergent probability comes across as an enlargement of statistical theory. The process of questioning is underway that will find its resting place in his theory of emergent probability in *Insight*.

Having acknowledged three kinds of forms, conjugate, substantial, and group, in brief, cryptic headings Lonergan outlines something about the corresponding acts and potencies. Substantial act, which he names 'existence,' is the act that corresponds to the intelligible unity of the form of the individual. It is what becomes known when we make the judgment 'The intelligible unity that is X exists.'

Events, occurrences, performances, or operations he names 'conjugate acts.' They become known when we make the judgment 'Y occurred.' The remarks provide an important context for our reading of the meaning of the term 'event' in chapters 2–4 of *Insight*. Events or occurrences 'are according to law; presuppose law; complement law with actuality.'[8] There is the matter of the event of a coin toss, which differs from that of a pair of dice. There are the laws of motion that define the way the coin moves. There is the outcome, which is known not by our understanding, but by our judgment.

Group potency is the minimum set of substantial and conjugate potencies, forms, and acts that has to be postulated to account for functioning through emergent probability. Emergent probability necessitates such a basis. Significant are his remarks that group act – the totality of actual occurrences – presupposes and complements probability, the latter not featuring as a category itself. Important in the light of later developments in *Insight* is the suggestion that things and events on one level could be the potency or matter for forms on a higher level.

An outcome of the analysis of the distinction between substantial, conjugate, and group potency, form, and act is that the same data in the world are to be understood in three complementary manners. Distinct but complementary insights are involved in understanding the intelligible unity of a substance, its conjugates, and the world order of which it is a part. The three distinct types of form are relevant to an understanding of the proportionate universe. More forceful is Lonergan's affirmation that they are sufficient. How, it could be asked, could these categories be applied in a metaphysics of history with its dialectical conflicts or in a study of development in which the conjugate forms of the substance change? Problematic in his account is the relation between group form and classical probability and its fixed frequencies.

In these explorations we see the genesis of chapter 4 of *Insight*, where he will develop in detail the notion of two complementary types of questions and insights, the classical and the statistical. Emergent probability, the result of their interaction, will not be reducible to either, and in this sense it goes beyond classical probability. At this point he will bracket things, discussing only intelligible unities and applying emergent probability to things in chapter 8. The 'Intelligence and Reality' notes show us the close link in his thought between chapters 4 and 8 of *Insight*.

In his treatment of the metaphysical elements in chapter 15 of *Insight* only two types of forms, central and conjugate, are discussed. The omission of group form or emergent probability raises the question, is this to be interpreted as a change of mind or simply an oversight because of the pressures of composition? Does it suggest that in the final write-up of the book certain lines of exploration are left dangling?

Although the terminology of things is not used in the notes, in this metaphysical beginning we can see the genesis of the metaphysics of *Insight.* Involved will be a transition in which Aristotelian substance and accidents and scholastic *quiddity* will be replaced by the modern terms 'things' and 'conjugates,' potency by the opaque term 'empirical residue.' To them he will add the events and ideal frequencies of statistics and the emergent processes of evolution. Lonergan's attempt to translate Aristotle into the explanatory categories of the modern empirical sciences in the light of Kant's Copernican revolution had begun.

Lonergan's seventh and final section is on dialectical categories. The points, occupying two thin lines of text, might at first reading seem an afterthought in relation to his main emphasis on the terminal categories. The paragraph numbering also poses the question whether he saw them as distinct from or falling within the terminal categories. But what is here is the seed of a hugely significant later development.

Under point (a) we find the headings 'Person with Person' and 'I and Thou,' a rare reference to Buber or Marcel. As a footnote in the epilogue of *Insight* will make clear, Lonergan viewed that work as a preface to a later one on interpersonal relations. The main emphasis of his analysis in it is on the subject-object rather than on what Simone de Beauvoir calls the me-other relationship.[9] The present remarks acknowledge that the me-other relationship is a part of the wider subject-object relationship. They also inquire into the manner of our descriptive, heuristic, terminal, and dialectical knowledge of a particular Thou in our world. What more, if anything, would be involved in the dialectical rather than the terminal knowledge of the other?

Under point (b) we find the heading 'Situation, Understanding, Policy, Action, New Situation,' which links him to his thinking in the 1930s on a metaphysics of history. The term 'dialectical' points us back to his work in the 1930s on the dialectic of history that addressed the tensions between human progress and decline, a point that he will soon develop in an essay, 'The Role of the Catholic University.'

As a project, Lonergan envisages metaphysics as addressing interpersonal and historical realities. This brief section signals that out of that wider agenda he will select the dialectical dimension of those realms as his focus.

In these few lines of text we find hints of what will appear in chapter 7 of *Insight* under the title 'Common Sense and Its Object.' These lines suggest that although the roots of the chapter on common sense go back to his earlier work on history, they were thought out and written after chapters 9–13. Initially Lonergan treated both emergent probability and the dialectic of common sense within metaphysics proper. In the writing of *Insight* they were relocated, and take on the status of a preparation for metaphysics.

In terms of the further movement of Lonergan's thought, some points stand out. Firstly, despite his insight into higher viewpoints in mathematics at the start of the notes, there is no reference to development and genetic method. Despite his puzzling over the mathematics and the primitive terms and relations of the higher life sciences, he does not at this point differentiate different kinds of conjugate forms. Relatedly, there is no reference to the question of interactive levels of activity or operation in things. Thirdly, there is no reference to space and time. Finally, his remarks on the descriptive and dialectical categories will prepare the way for aspects of his later work on common sense.

The Aims of Philosophy

Lonergan's starting point for philosophy, as noted, involves the personal transformation of an intellectual conversion. Now, responding to Kant's challenge, he poses the question, can philosophy become a science, arrive at a defining moment when the overall shape of that science falls into place?[10] How, it will be asked, could something like the journey out of Plato's cave become an integral part of a scientific philosophy and lead to such a definition?

The starting point of that conversion is the present intellectual context of an individual. From that beginning it advances towards a position on knowing and reality. As conversion, philosophy would seem a way, a journey, an art work, rather than a theory. Without seeing any contradiction between the scientific and the conversion elements in his philosophy, Lonergan now asserts that philosophy is a science. The term of the journey that is the conversion process is an understanding, as in other sciences, of a basic set of primitive terms and their relations. There are echoes here of his remarks on primitive terms and relations of the science of reality in William Stewart's notes on grace. In this sense, conversion is not to be understood as some kind of psychological and emotional disturbance with no intellectual goal or content. Through the considerable disturbance involved, an unexpected intellectual clarity emerges. The points or headings here are clearer than in *Insight* and deal with philosophy rather than metaphysics as a science.

Can philosophy arrive at such a position? Reviewing his progress, Lonergan grasps in the movement of his thought precisely that possibility. The basic set of terms and relations of philosophy are supplied by an analysis of knowing, what he will later term 'self-affirmation,' and of the descriptive and terminal categories. Problematic is the place and significance of his position on objectivity and the subject and object of knowledge in this account. Is he collapsing the distinct epistemological question into the cognitional? In his consequent remarks on the structured relations of human knowing and of their verification in experience, the notion of self-affirmation tacitly makes its second appearance on the notes. It is through self-affirmation that elements of the terms and relations of philosophy as a science are established.

The analysis of knowing begins from a descriptive identification of the insight experience. That description is followed by an analysis of the set of relations within which insights occur. They are related to images, questioning, conceiving and formulating, to questions for reflection, a grasp of the unconditioned, and judgment. These relations are given in experience. They are universally accessible. Everyone knows the difference between understanding and not understanding something, between a guess, story, make-believe, and reasonable affirmation. Clearly we have a source here for the later invitation to the judgment of self-affirmation. The relations, he continues, are inevitable.

Although he does not directly set up the personal invitation to self-affirmation, this section concludes:

> One cannot intelligently repudiate intelligence; and one is committed by being what one is to reject unintelligent repudiation.
> One cannot reasonably repudiate reasonableness; and one is committed by being what one is to reject unreasonable rejection.[11]

The primitive terms and relations are experiential, universally accessible, and inevitable. They are defined implicitly on the analogy of Hilbert's procedure, and are beyond radical revision.[12] In Lonergan's claim that our knowing and the known universe, of which our knowing is a part, are correlatives, the later question of the isomorphism of mind and reality is present. There follows the possibility of articulating a set of primitive terms that define the structure of knowing, the structure of the known, and the relations between them.

The remark provides us with a crucial interpretative clue as to the plan of *Insight.* The point of the early chapters of that book is not to learn mathematics or empirical science or advance our common sense. The point of engaging in the intellectual performance of doing mathematics or with classical or statistical-type questions is to awaken an interest in one's intellectual desire, one's own pure desire to know. From that beginning the reader is invited to embark on a long journey of self-analysis whose term will be the discovery that his or her pure desire to know is the key to human knowing and its relation with the world. Prior to the intellectual conversion, an individual will engage in those activities but not have recognized them or their significance. The conversion involved is not something subjective. It involves coming to recognize the kind of object sought by the mind's desire, reality rather than appearances. There is involved in the journey a reinterpretation both of oneself and of one's world.

> Philosophy = Strategic set of judgments determining the general character of universe.[13]
> The goal is serene and objective apprehension of universe, of self in universe and of role of the self in universe.[14]

Earlier in his course notes Lonergan had remarked that 'Philosophy = Strategic set of judgments determining the general character of universe.' Now, in his concluding section he turns to the question of the good of philosophy: 'The goal is serene and objective apprehension of universe, of self in universe and of role of the self in universe. Its consequence is agape, love of intelligible order of whole.' Given Lonergan's stress on the cognitional at the expense of the ethical, this is an interesting question. To make the unrestricted desire to know thematic is to introduce the infinite into human life. That desire makes knowledge of the universe possible, as well as plans for promoting its good. It reveals the source of vast human energies in the execution of such plans. It throws into human desires, fears, loves a component that can make them terrifying, horrible, and disastrous for the individual and society.

The good that philosophy aims at arises, for Lonergan, on the level of self-understanding. Without successful philosophy, actual and objective self-knowledge is extremely precarious. The subject is thrown back on the experience of the self as a self-regarding centre or as capable of ecstatic devotion to a cause or person, and can oscillate violently between these extremes. Appropriating the pure desire to know involves a transcendence of stupid self-centred selfishness and blind ecstatic devotion, an oblique reference to National Socialism. the goal of overcoming these disorders of the self is serene and objective apprehension of the universe, of self in universe, and of the role of the self in universe. Here we find echoes of Lonergan's contrast between mythic consciousness and self-knowledge in chapter 17 of *Insight*.

In his final paragraph in these lectures Lonergan raises some questions about the effectiveness and limits of philosophy. Philosophy might express an ideal for individuals and society, but in the real world it can never attain it. It does not provide the final answer. There is a need to live by divine revelation and divine grace. There is need for a new knowledge centred on Christ and for a new love poured forth into our hearts by the Holy Spirit. This paragraph points towards elements of the epilogue of *Insight*. There, rather than directly referring to the need for a knowledge of Christ, he will be more heuristic.

Reading 'Intelligence and Reality' is like watching a portrait artist beginning to sketch the outline of a face. In his outline of cognitional theory, epistemology, and metaphysics Lonergan could be said to have drawn in the eyes of the portrait. Other sections of the canvas in relation to common sense, space and time, and development are blank. Further creative leaps will be involved in the final act of composition. But what we should not overlook is that 'Intelligence and Reality' articulates the horizon out of which Lonergan began to compose the final text of *Insight*. Until he had articulated its viewpoint he could not yet begin. In this sense it is a key to that later work.

As he was concluding his lectures on 'Intelligence and Reality,' Lonergan was invited by the editor of *Relations*, a Jesuit monthly in Montreal, to contribute a leading article to an issue dealing with Catholic university education.[15] His 'The Role of a Catholic University in the Modern World' was published in October 1951.

In order to relate the terms 'modern world' and 'Catholic university,' he felt it necessary to explore the meaning of different levels of the good. This suggests a possible link with his thinking in 'Intelligence and Reality' about levels and the good of philosophy itself. In his treatment of the good in his March 1950 course 'On God's Knowledge and Will,' there was no mention of levels. Now, a year later, clearly influenced by his insight into levels in knowing, he is exploring for the first time the possibility of parallel levels in the good: the particular good, the good of order, and values. Notable is his use of the phrase 'judgments of value,' which critique and appreciate possible goods.

Corresponding to the different levels of the good are different kinds of societies. Intersubjective community corresponds to experience and desire. Its nucleus is the family, its expansion the clan, tribe, or nation. Civil community corresponds to intellectual insights and the good of order. As it develops it sets a group off from primitive societies. Cultural community or cosmopolis corresponds to judgments of value and transcends state boundaries and historical epochs. These three types of community and social order are the presumed background for Lonergan's analysis of dialectic and bias in chapter 7 of *Insight*. Those communities and the individuals who make them up can be involved in progress or decline. As philosophers can get lost in a labyrinth, so also can culture. Because progress and decline are ambiguous, decline can in fact be mistaken for progress, and then instead of a succession of higher syntheses in cultural process we get a succession of lower syntheses, the hallmark of social decline.[16] A dialectic can be discerned in the history of philosophy and in the development and decline of intersubjective, civil, and cultural communities.

Taken with the brief paragraph on dialectic in 'Intelligence and Reality,' this is one of his earliest comments on dialectic in the period before he wrote the final text of *Insight*. Its treatment of bias and dialectic in an ethical context suggests that this, rather than the intellectual context in *Insight*, is the proper one.

He is now beginning to open up again the question of dialectic that had been with him since his surd sermon at Heythrop and during his reflections on history in the 1930s. Significant developments in his thought on it and on levels of consciousness will soon emerge. Against decline, there is the liberation of human reason through divine faith, 'for men of faith are not shifted about with every wind of doctrine.'[17] There are echoes here of his reflections on the limitations of philosophy in 'Intelligence and Reality.' His explorations around July 1951 of moral impotence, the ambiguity of progress and decline, and the theological virtues of faith, hope, and charity show that Lonergan was thinking about topics that would eventually emerge in chapters 7 ('Common Sense and Its Object'), 18 ('The Possibility of Ethics'), and 20 ('General Transcendent Knowledge') in *Insight*. Challenging is his concluding remark in 'The Role' to the effect that an integration of the sciences that deal with humankind concretely has to be sought not in a philosophy but in a theology. Taken with his remark in the epilogue about the poverty of his treatment of personal relations, *Insight* could be thought of as a preface to that study.

At this point in time, in his notes for his 'Intelligence and Reality' course and his essay 'The Role,' Lonergan had in place a proto-*Insight*. With the exception of the chapters on space and time and common sense, that proto-*Insight* sketched the broad outline of the first 15 chapters as well as points from chapter 18, and provides us with clues as to how he thought out the final text of *Insight*.

Two remarks in 'The Role' are of biographical and personal interest.[18] Firstly, there is his remark that a second-rate Catholic university is not any more acceptable than the sacrifice of a maimed beast in the Old Law. Lonergan was personally after excellence in Catholic education, and throughout his life was consistently critical of his own Jesuit Catholic education. Secondly, there are his remarks about the ambiguity of Catholic intellectuals, of the fact that through history they have been viewed by the Church as a mixed blessing. (In particular, he mentions the condemnations of Aquinas.) In spite of this, their task is not to wrap their talents in a napkin and bury it in the ground, but rather to use their intelligence to the limit.

In November 1951 Lonergan gave a domestic exhortation to the staff and students of Regis College, Toronto, entitled 'The Mystical Body of Christ.' It was a topic that he would link with his analysis of genetic method in the epilogue of *Insight.* The central point of his exhortation was love. Within God there is the love of Father for Son that finds its perfect expression in the Holy Spirit. But as the Son became incarnate, there is the love of the Father for the Son as God and as man:

> Because the Son has two natures, we might conclude that the Father
> has two loves, an infinite love that is the Holy Ghost for the Son
> as God, and a lesser love for the Son as man. On the other hand,
> because the Son is the same person in both his divine and human
> natures, one might argue that the Father has but a single love, the
> Holy Ghost, for the Son whether as God or as man.[19]

And so it is that at the baptism, as the dove descends, a voice is heard saying, 'This is my beloved Son in whom I am well pleased.' Because God became human, the love of God for God became the love of God for humankind. In the Incarnation, divine love broke out of the confines of the divinity.

Related is the love of Christ for humankind. Self-sacrificing, it is a love that is faced inevitably with incomprehension. Because the Father loves Christ and Christ loves us, there results the love of the Father for us as his adopted sons. That sonship is not lived in isolation. Christ is the vine, we are the branches. In response to the question, what does it mean to say that Christ lives in us? Lonergan answers that 'it means more than I can know or say.'

The Autograph, 1951–1953

18

Finally Beginning in the Middle: Common Sense, Consciousness, and Self-Affirmation

You slowly work out what is in your inspiration ... You write, and you read, and you see something is wrong. You perhaps go and have a little walk and come back and find a phrase that will twist the thing around more to what you want, and so on. An indefinite process of rewriting can be involved in it.[1]

Sometime after 'The Role' was written, Lonergan began to compose the autograph, the final text, of *Insight*.[2] His assembly, as noted, of a proto-*Insight* made it possible for him now to envisage sections of the finished work. The earliest known of the several outlines he would sketch of the book's table of contents follows.[3]

The Notion of Judgment	7	
Reflective Understanding	33	40
(nine headings as in *Insight*)		
Self-affirmation	24	64
Notion of Being	23	87
Notion of Objectivity	8	95
Forms of Experience	11	106
Critical enlightenment	12	118 + 92 = 180

The texts of chapters 9–13, which are filed with the table of contents, are identical with what we find in the book.[4] Containing a chapter on self-affirmation and a much more orderly treatment of reflective understanding, they show clear post–'Intelligence and Reality' developments.

This early table of contents and the related chapter texts pose the question, where did Lonergan start the composition of his final manu-script, or what is referred to by the editors of the *Collected Works* edition of *Insight* as the autograph MSA? Of the various possible options they discuss, my own research on the way Lonergan's ideas developed during the pro-cess of composition has led me to agree strongly with their first and main option.[5] The second movement in the performance of composing *Insight* between 1949 and 1953 began, not by reworking chapters 1, 2, and 8, but in the middle. This would be a shorter movement whose product would be the text of chapters 9–13 of the published book. In it Lonergan articulated his solution to the problem of thought/intelligence and reality. His break-through insights into cognitional structure and the notions of being and objectivity give chapters 9–13 their thematic unity. Early in chapter 9, more sharply than in the 'Intelligence and Reality' notes, Lonergan distinguishes between two interdependent modes, the direct and an introspective, in which our cognitional structure can operate. The performance of the direct mode, which is concerned with coming to know objects in the world in the realms of science and common sense, generates the data of the introspective mode. Reminiscent of what he termed 'duplication' in the second *Verbum* article (a term that does not occur in *Insight*), the introspec-tive mode is concerned with coming to know cognitional structure itself. Clearly, the introspective mode cannot emerge and operate in the absence of the direct mode.

In the middle of chapter 9 Lonergan wrote that at that point he was 'unprepared to answer the Kantian question that regards the constitution of the relation of knowing subject and known object,'[6] this despite the fact that the essentials of a solution to that problem are to be found in the manner of the relation between the two modes of operation. Through the performance of the direct mode, objects of knowledge in the scientific and common-sense worlds become known and related instances of the mind-world relation come into existence. The related introspective mode is concerned with understanding, not just cognition, but those emergent mind-world relations. In his discussion of these relations Lonergan initially concentrates on coming to know the knowing subject, a decision that, given the vastness of the known and the recurrence and regularity of the process of knowing, is strategic. One can only answer questions one at a time. Later, in his analysis of the principal notion of objectivity and subsequent meta-physics, he will take up the further questions. In what follows it is good to bear these points in mind. In chapter 13 he concluded, 'Sixthly, the princi-pal notion of objectivity solves the problem of transcendence. How does the knower get beyond himself to a known?' This signals the fact that the Kantian problem runs through and gives chapters 9–13 their programmatic unity.

Against this reading no doubt there will be those who question how on earth it can be squared with the remark in chapter 9 that 'this prior level was described in the chapter on common sense.'[7] On this the MSA typescript and the editors of the *Collected Works* come to my assistance, for in fact this phrase was not in the original typescript. Lonergan later inserted it by hand, presumably after he had written the chapters on common sense, replacing the original phrase 'data, percepts, images.' As this was a significant phrase in a parallel location in 'Intelligence and Reality,' the implication is that the first chapter of the autograph, chapter 9, was composed very soon after his notes on 'Intelligence and Reality.' There was no reference in chapter 9 of the MSA autograph at this point to a chapter or chapters on common sense, his first engagement with that topic occurring in chapter 10.

In the analysis of judgment that follows in chapter 10, the virtually unconditioned is now related to vulnerable and invulnerable insights and the totality of relevant questions in an inquiry. As Lonergan develops his thought on concrete judgments of facts, the new and major theme of common sense makes its entry in the process of composition.[8] The question of facts and an emphasis on the concrete, which had its origin in Newman, forced him to address the question, into what are the insights of common sense that concrete judgments of facts presuppose? His response will be the field of ordinary descriptions whose viewpoint is how the things in our world relate to us and enter into our concerns: 'Its object is what is to be known by concrete judgments of fact, by judgments on the correctness of insights into concrete situations.'[9] The phrase 'concrete judgments of facts' now makes its entry. Influenced by the problem in Newman, whose name does not appear in the text, it is a phrase that expresses as significant a development in Lonergan's thought as his earlier phrase 'insight into phantasm.' The insights of common sense are insights into concrete situations, the judgments of common sense are concrete judgments of fact.

Lonergan's illustration of a concrete judgment of fact involves a man returning home to find his house full of smoke, the windows smashed and water on the floor. He makes the extremely restrained judgment of fact, 'Something has happened.' What, Lonergan asks, is involved in reaching this affirmation? Basically, the evidence for the judgment is provided in the *memory* of the house as left and the contrasting experience of it now, a rare reference to memory in his cognitional analysis.[10] A strength of the illustration is that, against the sceptics, it makes it clear that in this situation it would be quite irrational to dither over the problem and not to make the judgment. Its weakness is its self-evident nature, because of which it does not draw the reader into the discernment process of the juror. In many jury trials a vastly complex weave of circumstantial evidence is presented. After the defence and prosecution have presented their arguments, the juror, sometimes agonizingly, has to deliberate at length to discern between them. He or she has to identify the significant relevant questions, identify witnesses who may not tell the truth, and recognize that in the judgment there could be involved his or her personal responsibility for the life of another person.

The discernment process that occurs prior to the judgment Lonergan refers to as a self-correcting process of learning, a sort of *compositio*:

> So it is the process of learning that breaks the vicious circle. Judgment on the correctness of insights supposes the prior acquisition of a large number of correct insights. But the prior insights are not correct because we judge them correct. They occur within a self-correcting process of learning in which the shortcomings of each insight provoke further questions to yield complementary insights. Moreover, this self correcting process of learning tends to a limit.[11]

The collaboration he names 'common sense' is, however, a mixed blessing. It offers enormous benefits and advantages but is also involved in deviation and aberration. As well as intellectual curiosity, there are also earthy passions and prejudices. The tensions between the two can result in deviation from the pure product of intelligence. Each tribe and nation, each group and class is prone to develop its own brand of common sense and strengthen its convictions by pouring ridicule upon the common nonsense of others. Nor do we ourselves stand outside this collaboration as spectators, we are born into it: 'But it is only in so far as I myself share in those mixed motives that my understanding and my judgment will suffer the same bias and fall in line with the same deviations and aberrations.'[12] The notion of mental bias has made its entry.

Further points about judgment in science and mathematics are opened up. Judgments about things, about correlations, and about probability expectations may be certain and may be probable. The possibility of the isomorphism between mathematical relations and the relations of the empirical sciences is suggested. In adding common-sense knowing to the explanatory knowing of science, Lonergan has taken a path that will lead him to his later insights into the differentiations of consciousness. Significantly, nowhere in the chapter is an invitation offered to make either a scientific or a common-sense judgment.

The Conscious Cognitional Self

In a major departure from the sequence and structure of 'Intelligence and Reality,' Lonergan now adds a new chapter entitled 'Self-Affirmation of the

Knower.' In it three new themes are played in: the question of the self, of consciousness, and of philosophical judgments. In chapters 9 and 10 he had analysed common-sense and scientific judgments. Chapter 11 will invite and challenge the reader to make a philosophical judgment.

Prior to this Lonergan's use of the term 'self' was infrequent and cautious. In 'Finality, Love, Marriage,' he wrote briefly about the self and other selves. In *Verbum* he discussed the distinction in the *De Veritate* between empirical and scientific or analytic self-knowledge.[13] In his analysis of objectivity in 'Intelligence and Reality' he made clear that it is only in the judgment 'I am' that the self becomes known. Prior to that judgment we may perform but do not know ourselves as cognitional beings. He also asked what the referent is of the 'I' of *cogito, ergo sum* and contrasted Kant's transcendental ego, a logical condition of possibility of experience, with the empirical self. The Kantian unity of apperception, the 'I think' that accompanies all our mental acts, was also acknowledged. Discussing the good of philosophy, he considers that without self-knowledge the subject may be thrown back on an experience of self as a self-regarding centre capable of ecstatic devotion to a cause or person.[14] In the chapter on ethics in *Insight* and in his more ethical-centred post-*Insight* writings he will tend to favour the terms 'subject' and 'world/horizon' rather than the 'self.'[15]

In his doctrinaire style Lonergan now defines the self as 'a concrete and intelligible unity-identity-whole. By "self-affirmation" is meant that the self both affirms and is affirmed.'[16] A first distinguishing point about what is to be affirmed about the self is that it is characterized by cognitional activities such as perceiving, imagining, inquiring, understanding, verbally expressing, and eventually judging.

A second distinguishing point to be acknowledged about the self is that it is the intelligible unity of which the concrete totality of those to-be-affirmed cognitional activities are parts:

> What is meant is that a single agent is involved in many acts, that it is an abstraction to speak of the acts as conscious, that, concretely, consciousness pertains to the acting agent.[17]

There follow remarks such as 'It is not that an individual performing ...' and 'I perform them ...,' where 'perform' refers to cognitional activity. This is suggestive of the unity in a single agent, past, present, and future, of a totality of cognitional activities, sensing and perceiving, questioning, understanding, thinking, judging. Later in the chapter Lonergan will ask:

> What do I mean by 'I'? The answer is difficult to formulate, but strangely, in some obscure fashion, I know very well what it means without formulation, and by that obscure yet familiar awareness,

> I find fault with the various formulations of what is meant by 'I'. In other words, 'I' has a rudimentary meaning from consciousness and it envisages neither the multiplicity nor the diversity of contents and conscious acts but rather the unity that goes along with them.[18]

The referent of 'I' is for him at this point an existential unity that is given prior to our efforts to understand and formulate it. Lonergan simply invites his readers to acknowledge that prior given as the locus of the crucial evidence for the basic philosophical judgment under consideration; to acknowledge that certain cognitional activities are parts of the irreducibly given unity of the self. That is about as far as he is going to pursue the issue of the unity just now.

In accordance with what he later terms a 'moving viewpoint,' as the remainder of the book unfolds he will begin to develop a wider notion of the unity of the acting self through his treatment of the subjects of common sense, things, genetic method, ethics, and religion. This in turn will open up the question, how does Lonergan relate his notion of the self to the wider notion of the human being? To argue that the cognitional self is an intelligible unity in its own right rather than a part of the wider unity of the human being is suspect.

Some of Lonergan's most sustained reflections on the meaning of 'I' and consciousness come in his 'On the Ontological and Psychological Constitution of Christ,' written in 1955–6 after *Insight* was completed but before it was published. There he holds that the human person is the ultimate subject of attribution. 'I' may refer to this person who I am and be filled out in terms of events I experience in the world with little reference to consciousness. Or 'I' may be taken to refer to conscious experiences of this person who I am and may be filled out with little reference to situations in the world.[19]

The present narrative shows that self-affirmation was a cognitional event and moment in the unity of Lonergan's intellectual life-story. Certain cognitional events and developments moved him towards it, others followed from it. It is in line with the thinking of Hannah Arendt, MacIntyre, and Stephen Crites that the intelligible unity of consciousness of the agent of activity has a narrative form. For Simone de Beauvoir the unity of the self, as contrasted with its cognitional operations, only becomes affirmed and known through composing an autobiography. Lonergan's later writings on the theme of historicity will make a small move in that direction.

A third distinguishing point about the meaning of the self is that its unity is to be discovered in the data not of sense but of consciousness. Although his remark that 'I do not think only cognitional acts are conscious'[20] shows that he is open in principle to the emotional and wider dimensions of the self, one gets the impression that *here* cognition is central to his notion of the self. The absence of any reference to the patterns of experience worked out in chapter 6, the first of the chapters on common sense and suggestive of multiple shapes of the self, suggests that it was written after chapter 11.

Conscious Awareness: Emperical, Intellectual, and Rational

As early as 1943 Lonergan articulated his dream of working out an empirical theory of human knowing as conscious. In the *Verbum* articles and 'Intelligence and Reality,' reflections on the meaning of consciousness, although clearly crucial to his whole enterprise, were marginal. All the cognitional activities constitutive of the self that have been the focus of his attention are conscious. Late in the day he now begins to address the question, what is meant and not meant by the word 'consciousness' as it applies to our senses, imagination, our spirit of inquiry or desire to know, insights, reflections and judgments, and our related notion of the self? What does it mean to say that these cognitional operations are conscious? The magnitude of the problem should not be underestimated.

Lonergan begins by making clear that by 'consciousness' he does not mean taking some form of an inward look. Elsewhere in 1956 he articulated the point as follows:

> Some take consciousness to be a type of perception in which the 'I' and all other interior data are directly and immediately perceived as objects, while others understand consciousness as experience in the strict sense, as we have defined it above.[21]

Consciousness is not an inner perception but a datum, a kind of awareness we experience when we perform the different operations involved in cognition.

The quality of consciousness or self-awareness associated with the awakening of an inquiry or with the event of having a dramatic insight or, as a jury member, discerning the evidence in relation to a difficult judgment differs from that associated with hearing the phone ring or a dog bark. Three questions follow. Firstly, assuming there are different operations in cognition, sensing, imagining, inquiring, understanding, reflecting and judging, in what sense does the word 'consciousness' have a common meaning that applies to them all? Secondly, how does that meaning differentiate conscious from unconscious activities? Thirdly, what is unique about the conscious qualities of the distinctive mental operations?

Lonergan makes clear that not every kind of awareness is, for him, conscious. He would be happy to say he was aware of the doorbell ringing, of the sun setting, of a problem, and so forth, but unlike Cassirer he would not refer to that kind of awareness as object consciousness. He would never say, 'I was conscious of the doorbell ringing, of the sun setting, of a problem, or of a resolution.' This denial of what for many is the self-evident meaning of 'consciousness' generates much confusion. What possible referent and meaning is left for the word? How does nominal definition operate in relation to the data of consciousness?

By 'consciousness' Lonergan means a second kind of awareness, given in all cognitional activity, but not necessarily restricted to such activity. He would be happy to say: 'I was aware of, conscious of, *myself* seeing the sun setting, hearing the doorbell ring, puzzling over or resolving a problem.' Consciousness for him is an awareness of the self seeing, hearing, puzzling over and resolving a problem: 'But one cannot deny that, within the cognitional act as it occurs, there is a factor or element or component over and above its content, and that this factor is what differentiates cognitional acts from unconscious occurrences.'[22] It is not an awareness of what is seen, heard, puzzled about, of the solution. Where Cassirer talks about an ego consciousness and a correlative object consciousness,[23] Lonergan will only use 'consciousness' for self-awareness, not for object awareness. Neural and other organic processes are unconscious in the sense that they are not characterized by this kind of self-awareness. Although he does not state it, that awareness is also in a sense private. The sound that you and I hear is public, but our awareness of ourselves hearing the sound is not.

In 1956 he developed this meaning of consciousness as an experienced awareness as follows:

> In the very act of seeing a colour, I become aware not only of that colour on the side of the object but also, on the side of the subject, I become aware of the one who sees and the act of seeing. In the very act of understanding an essence, I come to know not only that essence in an objective way but I also come to know in a subjective way the one who understands and the act of understanding. In the very act of judging that a certain thing exists, I not only know the existence of that thing objectively but also am subjectively aware of myself as judging and of my act of judging.[24]

His comment here on *knowing* the one who understands contrasts with his later approach. In the above work he added: 'This preliminary and unstructured sort of knowledge is what we call experience in the strict sense of the word ... Firstly, consciousness is not any kind of knowledge of oneself and one's acts, but only that which is preliminary and unstructured.'[25] In contrast, in his letter to Harper and Row concerning the 1977 edition of *Insight* he writes that the data of consciousness are the raw materials of knowledge but not yet knowledge.[26] Psychoanalysts are familiar with the fact that a person may have certain feelings that are clearly conscious, but not be in touch with them, not yet know them. Similarly in the cognitional domain, a person might engage passionately in questioning, frequently have significant insights, yet again not notice what was happening and the kinds of conscious awareness involved in the activities.

Lonergan's above remarks on the distinction between object and subject awareness bring out the unbreakable relation linking the object and conscious awareness, of colour and seeing, of solution and insight. One is only aware of oneself imagining a presentation, asking a question, understanding and judging when in fact imaginative presentations, the given of a question, the object of an insight and of a judgment are present. It follows that the conscious awareness of the imaginative or intellectual or rational activities of the self cannot be identified at will, but only when an appropriate object is present. Deny the existence of that conscious awareness and one has denied the self. Deny the intentional or object awareness of one and the same act, and mental acts are locked up inside the agent or subject. As the data of cognitional activity as a conscious process are not present all at once, they have to be remembered, a dimension that Lonergan tends to neglect.

In and through the conscious dimension of the operations there arises an awareness of the self or subject, a self-awareness. In and through the inseparable intentional dimension there arises an awareness of objects of knowledge or, as he will later put it, a horizon. It follows that the conscious awareness of the self, empirical, intellectual, and rational, is by its nature absent from and can never be found or identified anywhere in its world or horizon that becomes known through the direct mode. Our access to the unimaginable data of consciousness for the purpose of analysis is, accordingly, indirect, derivative of the direct mode performance.

Although the two kinds of awareness are inseparably linked, it seems that they could not possibly be less alike. There is a self-evident quality to our awareness of the sound of the dog barking, the sight of the sun rising, the problem to be solved, the judgment that the jury member is mandated to make. There is a highly unsettling strangeness about the correlative awareness of ourselves listening, seeing, imagining, wondering, understanding, reflecting, and judging. In order to begin to identify and describe the data of consciousness, a disturbing enlargement of one's questioning attentiveness is needed, to open it up to the realm of self-awareness. Startlingly strange in comparison with our more self-evident awareness of colours and sounds and solutions and judgments, it is a realm that our culture largely goes out of its way to ignore or even deny.

The difficulties involved in that enlargement should not be underestimated. In trying to come to terms with the meaning of the word 'insight,' Liddy found himself asking the question, where is this act of insight? After much frustration and disorientation, there emerged an inverse insight through which he grasped that he was asking a question that could not be answered:

> Asking 'where' is an attempt to visualise what can't be visualized. You're attempting to imagine what of its nature goes beyond imagination, that is insight! Indeed, you can be aware of the act of insight, understand it in its relationships with other cognitional acts, but you can't see it![27]

Initially, Liddy was trying to look inside himself in order to locate where an insight was. In this he was approaching the data of consciousness on the analogy of the manner in which we approach the data of sense. At that point what is needed is a general inverse insight that grasps that the data of consciousness are not in any sense like the data of sense. Consciousness as a real given self-awareness in cognitional activity cannot be visualized. The resulting sense of its strangeness does not arise without a certain amount of confusion and disorientation. Through that experience the transition is made from a notional to a real sense of problem. Although from Aquinas Lonergan learned that insights are always into images or phantasms, only later will he begin to recognize the problems this poses in terms of the largely linguistic images or phantasms necessary in order to understand the unimaginable data of consciousness.

There remains our third question about different qualities of consciousness. The self-awareness involved in listening to a sound is quite different from that involved in being puzzled by a problem or acting as a jury person determining whether or not X did Y. Lonergan's insight into the different conscious qualities of cognitional activities followed from the recognition that there were levels of operation in knowing.

In response, in his chapter on self-affirmation, for the first time Lonergan suggests that as cognitional acts can be grouped on three different levels, an empirical, intellectual, and rational level, so also can their related conscious qualities. Empirical consciousness is a quality of sensing, perceiving, and imagining; intelligent consciousness of inquiry, insight, and formulation. He continues, 'Finally, on the third level of reflection, grasp of the unconditioned, and judgment, there is rational consciousness.'[28] The meaning of the phrase 'rational consciousness,' used as a blanket term for thought throughout the *Verbum* articles, has been redefined. It is now the name of the distinctive conscious qualities of the third level of cognitional operations. This redefinition involves a considerable development of his position in the *Verbum* articles.

The different levels of cognitional operations have different qualities of conscious awareness. As the conscious awareness constitutive of a cognitional act cannot be perceived or imagined by an inner look, neither can the different levels of such activity. We cannot look into ourselves and see three levels of cognitional activity. This does not mean that different levels of conscious awareness cannot be experienced, discerned, identified, described, related, and affirmed.

There is a level of consciousness or self-awareness characteristic of the operation of the level of the senses, imagination, sensitive memory, and their presentations. For Lonergan this is self-evident and in need of little elaboration:

> There is an empirical consciousness characteristic of sensing, perceiving, imagining.. As the content of these acts is merely presented or represented, so the awareness immanent in the acts is the mere givenness of the acts ... Empirical consciousness needs, perhaps, no further comment, for by it we illustrated the difference between conscious and unconscious acts.[29]

The use of our senses and imagination is foundational in the dramatic situations of our daily living, which revolve around the house we live in, the family of which we are a part, the street on which we live, the place of our work, recreation, and leisure. They are involved in conversations, reading, and listening to music. They are involved in all scientific inquiry, be it in an archaeological site, DNA analysis, or brain scans. All happily affirm that they are aware of the sights and sounds of the street. Very many are at a loss when invited to identify themselves as the subject of the conscious activities of seeing and hearing. Where do seeing and hearing and imagining take place in us? What do they look like? The answer must be that they are not like anything that can be seen or heard or found and identified in our sensory world. In comparison with their content, the seen and heard, empirically conscious activities, such as seeing and hearing, are quite strange. To identify and describe ourselves as empirically conscious involves a whole sea change. Lonergan makes this move too quickly.

As well as the awareness of ourselves sensing and perceiving, there is also a conscious awareness of intelligence, of what in us strives to understand. At this point Lonergan introduces the terms 'obverse' and 'reverse' to describe both intelligence and rationality. Mental operations are like a two-sided coin. One side faces intelligible situations in the world; the other side is characterized by a conscious awareness of intelligence. The distinction parallels Cassirer's object consciousness and ego consciousnesss or awareness.

For a detective arriving at a crime scene, the state of affairs found there poses a whole series of questions. Who is the victim? Where is the weapon? Whose blood drops are those? What, precisely, is the relevant evidence? The detective's expectation is that each of the items at the crime scene is intelligible, fits into an intelligible pattern of events, relations, and causes. But as well as the intelligibility of the elements of the crime scene, there is also the conscious awareness of his or her intelligence operative when the detective performs at the crime scene as a detective. That self-awareness, which can vary in intensity and vividness, is no part of the crime scene but cannot occur without it. Involving the awareness of the awakening of one's questioning, of being stuck and frustrated, and at certain moments the enlightenment of insight, it is a kind of self-awareness that is qualitatively distinct from the empirical. Because it is different but always presupposes empirical consciousness or self-awareness, Lonergan relates the two in terms of levels.

If intelligibility and intelligence are the two dimensions of the second level, reasonableness and groundedness are the two dimensions of the third or rational level:

> Reasonableness is reflection inasmuch as it seeks groundedness for objects of thought; reasonableness discovers groundedness in its reflective grasp of the unconditioned; reasonableness exploits groundedness when it affirms objects because they are grounded.[30]

Reasonableness as experienced is ego-awareness, as making groundedness present is object awareness. As the detective assumes the elements of the crime scene are characterized by a certain chain of relations and causes, so the jury member assumes that the formulations of the prosecution and defence need to be critically grounded. Such critical groundedness will be provided by the sufficiency, or not, of the evidence. Because the conscious awareness of reasonableness seeking groundedness presupposes both the empirical and the intellectual, Lonergan again relates it to them in terms of levels of awareness. That conscious awareness of reasonableness again cannot be found in the world of the cognitional agent. It is no part of the evidence it scrutinizes but cannot arise without it.

Cognitional operations on different levels are characterized by different conscious qualities, empirical, intellectual, and rational. Different cognitional operations on the same level, seeing or hearing on the empirical level, questioning or understanding on the intellectual level, reflecting and judging on the rational level are characterized by the same kind of consciousness. The higher levels of consciousness presuppose and cannot arise without the lower.

There is a certain minimalism in Lonergan's account of consciousness as self-awareness. Nowhere does he undertake the challenge of narrating, descriptively, what on a particular occasion it is like to be aware of oneself listening to a symphony or awakening to a problem. Rather, he sets up a series of significant signposts that mark out the territory. Accordingly, the strangeness of the experiences he is addressing tends to be veiled.

Similarly, in his account of levels the main thrust is to affirm that there are different levels of consciousness. Only minimal remarks are made about how they differ. For many, one of the great unsolved scientific problems is the explanation of the chasm between unconscious neural activity and conscious sentience. Within the structure of consciousness itself, it could be argued that the transition from the perceptual to the intellectual level, from the non-linguistic to the linguistic, is much more perplexing and involves a much greater chasm! The same is the case for the transition from the intellectual to the rational. The differences differentiating the different activities on the different levels are huge. Still, if Lonergan's remarks are minimalist, they have laid down the groundwork for further descriptive explorations of this strange territory.

Self-affirmation: Affirming How in Fact I Know Something

And I had to have a *true* judgment, one true judgment at least, so I had to have chapter XI, 'I am a knower.'[31]

In their daily grind doctors have constantly to take responsibility for their medical diagnoses, in which they affirm certain matters of fact. In a criminal trial a group are selected and mandated to meet in order to determine a matter of fact: did *X* commit such and such a crime? The jury listens to the testimony of the witnesses and to the questions and arguments of the defence and prosecution. Eventually, the matter is handed over to them and it becomes their responsibility to determine the facts.

Philosophical analysis for Lonergan in certain respects is no different. As a jury trial sets out to resolve a question of fact, so too his philosophical quest and related problem solving has focused on the questions: what in fact is the structure of human knowing, how in fact does it transcend itself, what sort of a world does it in fact make known? No less than in the case of doctors or jury persons, it is Lonergan's position that philosophers have a responsibility to determine the facts of cognition. In the light of his long exploration and his articulated answer he now, at this point, invites his readers to evaluate the evidence and judge responsibly the correctness or not of that account. What, in fact, happens when one comes to know something?

His reflections on the self and on consciousness are an integral part of the build-up towards that invitation, which he presents somewhat brusquely:

> Do I see, or am I blind? Do I hear, or am I deaf? Do I try to understand or is the distinction between intelligence and stupidity no more applicable to me than to a stone? Have I any experience of insight, or is the story of Archimedes as strange to me as the account of Plotinus' vision of the One? Do I conceive, think, consider, suppose, define, formulate, or is my talking like the talking of a parrot? I reflect, for I ask whether I am a knower. Do I grasp the unconditioned, if not in other instances, then in this one?[32]

The concluding phrase suggests that we could come to understand how we know without first judging and knowing something other than ourselves. Seeming to absolve the reader from the burden of making or remembering other judgments, it is problematic. The theorem of duplication would suggest that until we have made and identified the direct judgment 'X is the case,' we cannot make sense of ourselves as knowers. A better phrasing at the end of the previously quoted paragraph would be: have I grasped the unconditioned in other instances, made other judgments? The remembered performance of what he terms, in chapter 9, *all* of the elements of the direct mode of knowing would seem to be a condition of possibility of self-affirmation.

A first task that the philosopher turned jury-person has to address is: do I clearly understand the question and the suggested answer on which I am being invited to pass judgment? It is a question whose meaning in the present context has been developing since Lonergan's first introduction to philosophy by Whiteside. It is not inviting us to affirm what we see, hear, wonder about, understand, think about, and judge. It is inviting us to wonder about, explore, and understand the related conscious thought processes involved. The goal is to affirm that in coming to know something we are consciously aware of ourselves perceiving, imagining, questioning, puzzling, suddenly understanding, articulating what we understand in propositions, questioning the evidence, and eventually judging. If the question is avoided because it has been found to be uninspiring or boring, we must acknowledge that we are neither interested in nor likely to understand how we know.

In filling out our passport forms we normally have no difficulty in answering questions about our date and place of birth, nationality, and related matters – in affirming facts about ourselves. Similarly, when we fill out our

CV we do not have difficulty listing the facts: places we have lived and worked in and the work experiences we have gained. The present question is an invitation to affirm certain facts about our mental processes, about how, as conscious, our minds work. The evidence relevant to our affirmation of our date of birth is based on our birth certificates and on the testimony of others rather than on direct or remembered experiences. The evidence relevant to the present judgment is accessible to all human beings every time they engage intellectually in direct mode problem-solving activities.

As Lonergan poses the question, it does not refer directly to a specific remembered or written account of the awakening of a question for intelligence and subsequent problem solving. His later genetic analysis of the problem of objectivity will offer some clarifications, including the suggestion that, genetically, the judgment of self-affirmation is not first. At this point, the invitation to self-affirmation needs to be more specifically related to a remembered or present direct mode problem-solving experience. Does one, for instance, have a memory of being puzzled by the question of the definition of probability or of a scientific law? Does one have a memory of being puzzled by the direction one's life seems to be taking or by an interpersonal situation in one's everyday world and how to deal with it? Does one have a memory of subsequent moments of insight as a result of which one could verbally frame a definition or articulate a possible way of dealing with the situation? Alternatively, one can test Lonergan's theory against one's experience of puzzling over the problems of emergent probability, the development of common sense, or the explanation of things Lonergan will shortly address in chapters 1–8 and that, in *Insight*, were intended as a prelude to that judgment.

There is no better preparation for the judgment of self-affirmation than actually being on a jury and having to make a judgment about a matter of fact in the world, '*X* is.' Spontaneously one finds oneself engaging with the question, what happened at such and such a time in a certain place? Witnesses are called to testify in response to the questions and cross-questions of the prosecution and defence. It is the responsibility of the jurors to follow that process of investigation until the time arrives when they have to depart and engage in their own deliberations about the truthfulness of not of the conclusions. Taking into account the positions of the defence and prosecution, their deliberations will be concerned with making a judgment: *X* is so, *X* is not so, or it cannot be determined whether *X* is so. The memory of that clear-cut experience of oneself as completing the cognitional process in relation to some to be determined and affirmed fact in the world provides vital evidence both for the question and for the judgment of self-affirmation, 'I am a knower.' The role in the judgment of self-affirmation of remembered specific cognitional events from the realms of mathematics, science, and common sense needs to be more adequately developed.

When in response to the question a case has been made, the philosopher, like the jury person, has to engage responsibly with it. As Lonergan puts it: 'for our self-affirmation is, as we have insisted and may be pardoned for repeating, primarily and ultimately a judgment of fact.'[33] Following a line started in 'Thought and Reality' and repeated in 'Intelligence and Reality,' Lonergan now points out that if you are meaningfully raising and engaging with the question for reflection, 'am I a knower?' that very performance becomes an essential element in the evidence. It presupposes that you understand something – the names of the different cognitional activities, sensing, perceiving, wondering, suddenly understanding, etc. – and the suggested structure of their relations. That understanding of cognitional structure is articulated in a proposition. The terms and relations involved also refer to activities and their relations that are experienced not in the world of sense but of consciousness. Is it the case that one does not find oneself passively entertaining the formulated understanding, but, like the jury person, attempts to critique it and find if there are further unanswered questions before passing a positive or negative judgment on it? Any deliberate and responsible critical effort to engage with the question shows that a negative judgment would be inconsistent with and would contradict what one is doing.

How we know is not necessarily in accordance with Lonergan's formulation. Neither is it arbitrary. The conditions of the conditioned reside in our performance. At this point a major development takes place in Lonergan's use of the term 'facts':

> Finally, fact is virtually unconditioned: it might not have been; it might have been other than it is; but as things stand, it possesses conditional necessity, and nothing can alter it now. Fact, then, combines the concreteness of experience, the determinateness of accurate intelligence, and the absoluteness of rational judgment. It is the natural objective of human cognitional process.[34]

The terms 'virtually unconditioned' were introduced by Lonergan in his analysis of reflective understanding and judgment. Here he is affirming that fact, the object of judgment, is virtually unconditioned. A definition of fact unique to Lonergan, it is, I believe, a profound clarification of the meaning of what might be termed 'cognitional facts' as contrasted with what in his earlier writings he referred to as 'brute facts.'

As jury members have the responsibility of determining a fact, so also in this case reason as judge has a similar responsibility. Lonergan repeats again and again that self-affirmation is a judgment of fact.[35] In a somewhat puzzling manner he now insists that there are two steps involved in the particular judgment of fact:

> We have distinguished two issues; there is the problem of objectivity, and from this we have carefully prescinded not only in the present section but also in all earlier sections; there is also the prior problem of determining just what activities are involved in knowing, and to this prior problem we have so far confined our efforts. Hence we asked, not for the conditions of knowing an object, but for the conditions of the possible occurrence of a judgment of fact. We have asked for the conditions of an absolute and rational 'Yes' or 'No' viewed simply as an act. We have not asked on what conditions there would be some fact that corresponded to the 'Yes'. We have not even asked what meaning such correspondence might have.[36]

At this point the judgment is about what in fact is involved in knowing as a performance.[37] Whether that performance makes something known is, for Lonergan, a further question. For this reason it is odd that part 2 of the book, entitled 'Insight as Knowledge,' begins at the chapter on self-affirmation.

Chapter 12: Judging Is Knowing Being

> In the eleventh chapter there occurs the first judgment of self-affirmation, but only in the twelfth chapter is it advanced that judgment is knowledge, and only in the thirteenth is it explained in what sense such knowledge is to be named objective.[38]

Chapter 11 of *Insight* invited its readers as jury-persons to pass judgment on whether or not they performed a certain structured group of cognitional activities. Whether anything became known through that patterned performance of activities was bracketed. As a preface to removing the brackets, Lonergan criticizes the mistreatment of the problem of fact by Kant and Hegel. Being as fact can only be reached to the extent that the virtually unconditioned is reached in judgment. This was ignored by Kant and not discovered by Hegel: 'The only objective Hegel can offer the pure desire is a universe of all-inclusive concreteness that is devoid of the existential, the factual, the virtually unconditioned.'[39] Hegel for him is a thinker who, like Kant, cannot acknowledge factually fixed points of reference and cannot advance by distinguishing what is certain from what is unknown or more or less probable. His range of vision is enormous, even unrestricted, 'but it is always restricted in content, for it views everything as it would be if there were no facts.' More tellingly:

> Why did Fichte, Schelling and Hegel write their enormous systems? Because for them the possibility of judgment was that you have to know everything about everything; that was the only possible unconditioned. They didn't have the idea of the virtually unconditioned.[40]

In his invitation to the judgment of self-affirmation Lonergan is inviting his reader to make a break with the systems of Hegel and Kant, although it also seems the case that any direct mode judgement would also make the point. On this point, Lonergan lives in a quite different philosophical world than Kant and Hegel.

Anyone who grasps the virtually unconditioned and makes a judgment, such as the judgment of self-affirmation, goes beyond the viewpoint of Hegel. With this in mind, the punchline of the chapter occurs on the very last page, where most readers are likely to miss it:

> For this reason, we place the discussion of Self-affirmation prior to the discussion of the Notion of Being. Self-affirmation is the affirmation of the knower, conscious empirically, intelligently, rationally. The pure desire to know is a constituent element both of the affirming and of the self that is affirmed. But the pure desire to know is the notion of being as it is spontaneously operative in cognitional process and being itself is the to-be-known towards which that process heads.[41]

In chapter 11 Lonergan invited a response to the question, do you in response to your desire to understand yourself in fact perform these mental activities? Now, he is removing the brackets and inviting us to discover that there is more to the activities than the performance. In the judgment of self-affirmation, an aspect of the cognitional self becomes affirmed and known. A philosophical fact is established. The reader is drawn further into the challenge to affirm the relation between intellectual desire and what exists.

Chapter 13: Objective Knowledge and Kant's Problem

> Sixthly, the principle notion of objectivity solves the problem of transcendence. How does the knower get beyond himself to a known?[42]

In 'Intelligence and Reality' Lonergan clarified what he meant by the problem of objectivity by contrasting his own view with that of relativist and empiricist theories of knowledge. He went on to address as the main problem the relation between the subject and object of knowledge. In chapter 13 of *Insight,* under the heading of the principal notion, he starts with the main problem. Subsequent sections deal with experiential, normative, and absolute objectivity. In lecture notes written shortly after he had completed the chapter on objectivity, he made it clear that the natural developmental order of the problem is the reverse:

> In knowledge as considered developmentally, first there is had
> material objectivity, next normative, thirdly absolute, and fourthly
> consequent objectivity. For first we sense, or experience, next we
> inquire and reflect, thirdly we judge, and fourthly through several
> judgments we contemplate the field of existence.[43]

This is corroborated by a phrase in chapter 14, written long after 13, where he follows the natural developmental order and uses the term 'consequent': 'and knowing being became objective knowing through a grasp of the nature of experiential, normative, absolute, and the consequent principal objectivity.'[44] This suggests that in order to engage with and enter into the development of the problem, chapter 13 should be first read in the reverse order, starting with experiential objectivity and concluding with the principal notion of objectivity. It also makes clear that in order to enter into Lonergan's foundations and distinguish between known objects and the knowing subject, several judgments of facts must be made. The judgment of self-affirmation is one of such a plurality and cannot be the first.

Objective knowledge requires a correct relation between the knower and what is known, the objective of the pure desire to know, on all levels of cognition, experiential, intellectual, and rational. In what consists an objective relation with the given of a problem? The clue is to be found in understanding the manner in which the given of a problem relates to our intellectual desire: 'There is a still deeper reason. Why is the given to be defined extrinsically? Because all objectivity rests upon the unrestricted, detached, disinterested desire to know.'[45] For our knowing to be objective, not just our senses but also our pure desire to know must relate correctly to the given as given.

In his later lectures on topics in education he draws an interesting contrast: 'the first spontaneous answer is that the objective is what is out there; and being objective is seeing what is out there, all of it, and not seeing anything that is not there. That is what objectivity is.'[46] That objective knowing is a matter of taking a good look is the notion of objectivity that runs through the empiricist, positivist, pragmatist, and sensist positions. If there is more to knowing than taking a good look, then the related theory of objectivity will be more complex.

The pure desire to know begins with experience, and so in objective knowledge it has to establish a right relation with experience. But there is all the difference in the world between the way in which our sensory and instinctive nature and our pure desire to know relates initially and directly to experience, to the given as given: 'Further, the given as given is unquestionable and indubitable.'[47] Experiences as such are unquestionable, but we might not be open to them. Accordingly, to be objective will demand a respect for all of the experiences that are relevant to any particular inquiry. There follows experiential or material objectivity:

> But counterfeit objectivity is a kind of actual objectivity; all that is required for it is sense perception itself. Again, material objectivity is had in true sensations and in illusions and hallucinations alike; all these things occur and all alike need explanation. But in illusions and hallucinations there is no counterfeit objectivity, since there is no similitude between such experiences and the field of existence.[48]

In *Insight* experiential objectivity pertains to the given of questioning. Questioning always presupposes a given, a residue, which is unquestioned and to which it is related. So the term 'given' is being used in a very wide sense, as effectively anything that is presupposed by questioning or inquiry. It includes not only what he terms the 'veridical deliverances of outer sense' but also images, dreams, illusions, hallucinations, personal equations, subjective bias, and so forth.[49]

There is the given not only of natural science but also of the psychologist, methodologist, and cultural historian. His concluding remark is puzzling: 'Experiential objectivity has to rest on the same basis, and so the given is defined, not by appealing to sensitive process, but to the pure desire regarding the flow of empirical consciousness as the materials for its operation.'[50] Does it address the problem of the objective relation between the pure desire to know and the data of sense and of consciousness, the data of the empirical scientist and of the cognitional theorist?

Under normative objectivity Lonergan treats of points raised in 'Intelligence and Reality' under the headings of 'inhibited,' 'reinforced,' and 'interested' as against disinterested. Again, as with experiential objectivity, normative objectivity is a form of relation between the pure desire to know and its objective: 'Hence, to be objective, in the normative sense of the term, is to give free rein to the pure desire, to its questions for intelligence, and to its questions for reflection.'[51] Of note in his treatment of normative objectivity is a reference to the classical and statistical phases of empirical method and an absence of reference to the four biases of common sense.

Absolute objectivity is related to what might be termed the 'absoluteness' of facts. If, in fact, Caesar crossed the Rubicon or a certain person shot President Kennedy, then that fact is an absolute and nothing in the history of the universe can change it. It is on the basis of this quality of objectivity that our knowledge becomes public:

> Hence, it is in virtue of absolute objectivity that our knowing acquires what had been named its publicity. For the same reason that the unconditioned is withdrawn from relativity to its source, it also is accessible not only to the knower that utters it but also to any other knower.[52]

Significant is his comment that absolute objectivity does not imply a subject/object relation. It constitutes the entry of our knowing into the realm of being but, by itself, does not suffice to posit, distinguish, and relate beings. Several judgments are needed in order to deal with the subject/object relation. The solution to the Kantian problem is beyond it.

It is with the treatment of the principal notion of objectivity and at no previous point that the problem-solving process running through chapters 9–13 finds its terminus. There Lonergan develops his theory of the mind-world relation, what he terms the 'epistemological problem,'[53] a step further. The problem of objectivity, taken to its limit, is a problem about how our knowing relates to being, about the relation of the subject and object of knowledge. It follows that inevitably it expands into the Kantian problem.

Lonergan's solution is given in the principal notion, the climax of these chapters: 'Principally the notion of objectivity is contained within a patterned context of judgments which serve as implicit definitions of the terms, object, subject.'[54] The subject is what becomes known in the judgment of self-affirmation. An object of knowledge is something that becomes known in a judgment other than the judgment of self-affirmation:

> Again, being is divided from within; apart from being there is nothing; it follows that there cannot be a subject that stands outside being and looks at it; the subject has to be before he can look; and, once he is, then he is not outside being but either the whole of it or some part. If he is the whole of it, then he is the sole object. If he is only a part, then he has to begin by knowing a multiplicity of parts (A is; B is; A is not B) and add that one part knows others ('I' am A). Sixthly, the principal notion of objectivity solves the problem of transcendence. How does the knower get beyond himself to a known?[55]

The principal notion of objectivity answers that question. In the judgment 'this is a wordprocessor,' an object of knowledge becomes known. In the judgment 'I am a knower,' the subject of knowledge becomes known as an object. Both become known in the same way. The judgments 'I am not this wordprocessor' and 'I know myself as the knower who knows this wordprocessor' follow. Once these judgments are made, an understanding of the relation between the subject and object of knowledge and between thought and reality follows. There is no bridge to cross. Needless to say, this problem does not surrender its mystery without a struggle.

The principal notion of objectivity builds on very many of Lonergan's earlier insights. These would include his insights into the key role of the pure desire to know and of judgment in the mind-world relation. To these we should add his distinction between the two interdependent modes of operation of cognitional structure, the direct and the introspective, and the need to make a plurality of judgments in order to distinguish between the subject and object of knowledge. Through the performance of the direct mode we come to know common-sense situations in the world, and the classical and statistical laws of the sciences and instances of the mind-world relation come into being. The subject of knowledge cannot become known through any such direct mode of operation.

In so coming to know that B is, C is, D is, and so forth, we are being presented with the conscious cognitional data of the introspective mode. The data of cognition as such are just as much an object of inquiry, of the pure desire to know, as the data of sense. The desire to know can wonder about itself. In the understanding of that data in the judgment of self-affirmation, the pattern of cognitional activities that is to be understood duplicates itself. Through that judgment 'A is,' the subject who knows that B is, C is, D is, etc., comes to be known. Through the above plurality of judgments, knowledge of the distinctions and relations within being of the subject and objects of knowledge is attained. Through the introspective mode, the subject and the relation between the subject and objects of knowledge become known. Mastering those distinctions and their relations does not arise without a struggle.

Although within being a fundamental given is the community of knowers, in 'Intelligence and Reality' and here Lonergan might be read as giving the impression that he is dealing with the relation of a single, solipsistic knower to the world. Alternatively, his analysis could be interpreted as articulating the cognitional relation to the world of any knower within the community of knowers. In a brief comment he gestures towards the possibility of developing out of his account of the notion of being and objectivity a philosophy of a community of such knowers. Among the objects that we can come to know are other knowing subjects: 'Again, one may define a subject as any object, say A, where it is true that A affirms himself as a knower in the sense explained in the chapter on Self-affirmation.'[56] The remark is problematic because clearly others in the world perform as knowers and are known as such whether or not they make the judgment of self-affirmation. It is provocative because his assertion that some known objects will also be knowing subjects suggests the possibility of developing his theory of objectivity into a theory of a community of knowers. Involved would be the affirmation of others as constituted by the pure desire to know, the pursuit of insights and related judgments. This would be in contrast with the reductionist view of the human in our culture.

Lonergan ended the second movement of the process of composition at the end of chapter 13 with a puzzling remark: has he really broken out of subjectivity?[57] He adds that a further complex analysis will be needed to address this criticism, suggesting that the highly generic nature of his account of the principal notion of objectivity needs, as was the case in 'Intelligence and Reality,' to be fleshed out. Almost the entire subsequent process of authoring will be concerned with that fleshing out. *Insight* could not have ended at chapter 13. It would have been essentially incomplete.

19

Insights into Emergent Probability

World process is the probable realization of possibilities.[1]

Early in 1952, having articulated his foundations, Lonergan began the third movement in the composition of *Insight*. A creative movement running through the first eight chapters, it would involve new insights into emergent probability, the development of common sense, and the explanation of things. Written from within the perspective of his foundations, those chapters fill out and develop the meaning of the relation of the subject and object of knowledge within his theory of objectivity. The emerging world view develops his reworking of Kant's Copernican revolution in a range of contexts.

For Lonergan mind, particularly as intellectual desire and as the power of insight, is constituted by emergent qualities. The recurrent emergence of intellectual desire is clearly conditioned by the stilling of other, competing desires. It is difficult to work on an intellectual problem if one is cold or hungry or in certain ways emotionally disturbed or extremely comfortable. His own performance illustrates that it is also conditioned in the sense that answers to later emergent questions depend on solutions to earlier.

From this point on, the recognition of emergent properties in both the questing desire and its quested object, the universe, becomes central. In this he was influenced by Shull, whose book *Evolution* he had read while composing 'Finality, Love, Marriage.' As well as making notes on chance and the statistical gene concept of species, he copied a chart from page 45 of the book sketching the various geological epochs of the universe: Archeozoic, Proterozoic, Paleozoic, Mesozoic, Cenozoic, and Psychozoic.

This related to Shull's discussion of the occurrence of life in terms of place and time on the earth. On the next page Lonergan noted the radical eruption of life during the Cambrian Outburst. That eruption could be considered a form of emergence.

Shull's final chapter is entitled 'Emergent Evolution,' an interesting spin on Bergson's *Creative Evolution*, not listed in his references. His review of various meanings of the word 'emergent' poses the question, what, if anything emerges in the universe? G.H. Lewes in his *Problems of Life and Mind*, published in 1875, discussed the emergence of conscious mental states from the unconscious. The title of C. Lloyd Morgan's book *Emergent Evolution*, published in 1923, suggests that emergence was central in evolution itself. H.S. Jennings, who in 1930 published *The Biological Basis of Human Nature*, was a firm advocate of emergence, hailing it as biology's declaration of independence. According to Shull, Jennings argued that 'there must once have been a time when sentience, feelings and ideas did not exist, and concludes that such new things must have "emerged."'[2]

McDougall's rejection of emergence in his *Modern Materialism and Emergent Evolution*, published in 1929, did not convince Shull. He was exercised by the manner in which subatomic particles would combine to allow for the emergence of chemical elements and compounds, of chemicals for the emergence of biological life, of biological life for the emergence of what he calls sentience, and of sentience for what he calls mind. There was a time when chemical elements, sentience, and mind did not exist. In order for them to come into existence there must have occurred some form of emergence. Out of this he poses the question, what is new in emergences? His response is of the form: new relations rather than individuals or species. These questions posed in chapter 18 of *Evolution* about emergence echo through chapters 4, 8, and 15 of *Insight*.

When Kierans asked Lonergan if economics was a context for emergent probability, Lonergan replied that it had come from evolution. Despite this, some of the images necessary to lead our questioning into the problem of explaining emergence and survival come from the field of economics, Schumpeter's book directly linking economics and its cycles to evolution.

In 1942 Lonergan described the economic process as a conditioned series of emergences. The existing level of technological and economic advances conditions the standard of living that can next be produced in an economy. Nonetheless each new emergent idea that shapes the products produced by an economy has its day. It has to die and be replaced by a more advanced idea. The stagecoach gives way to the train, the clipper to the steamer. In economics we get the idea, not only of emergence, but also of survival.

In his 1944 economics text Lonergan defined the phrase 'emergent standard of living' as the aggregate of rates at which goods and services pass from the productive process and enter into the standard of living. It was determined by the series of conditioned emergences in the production process. Emergent processes were at the heart of his view of the economic order in the world. In *Insight* he lists as examples of schemes of recurrence the repetitive economic rhythms of production and exchange.[3] This suggests an interplay in his mind between his uses of the term 'emergence' in economics and in evolution.

Emergence is a complex and interesting phenomena posing many questions. Where within them do Lonergan's interests lie? Between his 'Intelligence and Reality' lectures and the final text of *Insight*, Lonergan drafted some pages with the heading 'A Priori Categories.' On pages 9 and 10, which remain, we find the following:

> Such inter-dependent cycles may be the building-blocks for higher combinations, and in turn these open the way to further possibilities. From the simple rhythms, for example, that seem discerned in chemical elements, through the more complex combinations of the chemical compounds, a way is opened to the double stratagem of the organism, which draws sustenance by forming a cycle with its environment, which secures the perpetuity of its precarious system through the cycle of birth, growth, maturation, and reproduction, which finally reinforces this cycle by the statistical tactic of large numbers. The device admits enormous variations, and at their limit the organic underlies a new type of cycle of sensitive apprehension, anticipation, appetite, and action that transforms the technique of drawing nourishment from the environment and opens the way for the still further cycles of intelligence, will, and choice. There follows a new series of possible cycles: domestic, economic, political, religious, cultural, scientific, and philosophic; and again the later and more complex structures are conditioned in their possibility by the prior actuality of simpler and more rudimentary forms.[4]

The terms 'interdependent cycles' in the opening sentence underline a significant advance beyond the events of 'Intelligence and Reality.' A key element of world order for Lonergan is the emergence, not of solitary atomic cycles, but of an ordered sequence of sequentially interdependent cycles, a trend. The being-in-place of earlier cycles conditions and makes possible the emergence of later cycles. It is this given datum, described in the above quotation, that is the source of the question of emergent probability. That question asks about the kind of explanation of the phenomena that modern science, with its distinct classical and statistical methods of inquiry and related insights, has to offer. In *Insight* he approaches it differently, inferring the world order of emergent probability from those methods of inquiry.

Essential to the question is a sense of a temporal succession of interrelated cycles that have emerged in world order. The long-term and stable existence of the solar and lunar cycles of the earth makes possible the emergence of the water cycle over the earth's surface. The atmospheric oxygen cycle makes possible the later respiratory cycles of animals and humans, the nitrogen cycle making possible certain aspects of their growth. Seasonal agricultural cycles make possible a regular supply of food and lead to the cycles of barter and of the circulation of money and goods in later exchange economies. Agricultural and technological development makes possible the emergence of cultural and political cycles. Not only the standard of living but the world order of the entire universe is characterized for Lonergan by the qualities of possibilities and emergences. In *Insight* he will add the dimension of blind alleys and breakdowns, to which could be added false starts and precariousness. The trend that is in world order must be such that it allows both an emerging series of linked cycles and the possibility of the collapse and breakdown of the series. To what extent, if at all, can an understanding of the methods of questioning and insights of classical and statistical science explain this trend in world order?

On Linking Probability with Emergence

The problem of the meaning of probability for Lonergan goes back as far as his London University examination in 1928, with its question about the application of the laws of chance to single events. The notes taken at his grace course in 1947 by his student William Stewart show that Lonergan's grasp of its significance for a science of world order was developing. On page 6 of the 'Intelligence and Reality' notes Lonergan divided empirical method into a classical and a statistical phase.

The classical phase is characterized by questions of the form What is X? or Why is this an X? – an acceleration, mass, a gas, an eye or ear, an insight, judgment, courage, prudence, wisdom? That classical form of questioning anticipates an insight into the appropriate conjugate forms of acceleration, mass, a gas, sight, and so forth.

Statistical science has its genesis in the distinct but related question asking how often events such as defined movements, gases, plants or animals with particular attributes, instances of seeing, hearing, or questioning occur. Its concern is not with particular once-off events or occurrences, but populations whose members are random or non-systematic. There is no formula on the basis of which one can calculate and predict each outcome in response to the How often? question.

As classical insights are into conjugate forms or relations, statistical insights are into probabilities, which specify ideal frequencies of occurrence of the member events. Specifying how often, ideally, the initial and sustaining conditions of events occurs, those probabilities have a very direct connection with world order. Statistical science deals not with abstract theories but with the occurrence of frequencies of events that come under the theories. At least from the time of 'Intelligence and Reality' it was Lonergan's position that classical and statistical questions and insights, although irreducibly different, are complementary. The question he is now beginning to home in on is of the form, what kind of world order is proportionate to the combination of these two distinctive types of method of scientific inquiry?

In his pursuit of this agenda we can also see him filling out the definition of the subject and object of knowledge given in his principal notion of objectivity. Classical questions and insights presuppose a certain type of object of knowledge in the world. Statistical questions and insights presuppose a distinct but related type of object. Through objectifying systematic processes and their conjugate forms and non-systematic processes and their probabilities, we articulate certain attributes of the known. Through objectifying classical and statistical questions and insights, we articulate parallel attributes of the knowing subject.

If a first movement is concerned with differentiating the insights of classical and statistical science, a second has to do with distinguishing probability and emergent probability. What is meant normally by the word 'probability' has some degree of clarity, which Lonergan articulates in chapter 2 of the final text. What is meant by the terms 'emergent probability' is anything but clear. Why, in 1951, did Lonergan link 'emergent' with 'probability' in his statement that group form is emergent probability?

Firstly, emergent probability was predicated of group form, not of an individual member of a group. Secondly, the actual events that occur in the group are governed by probability laws. Thirdly, at this point he is talking about events rather than interdependent schemes of recurrence or species of things. It is not clear what precisely, within the context of world order, is meant by the remark that events that actually occur affect the expectations of what is to occur. I believe that just over a year later, in the process of composing chapters 2–4 of *Insight*, he made something of a breakthrough on *an aspect* of the relation between probability theory and emergences in world order. The biographical task will be to explore, to the extent that it is possible, what was involved in this breakthrough.

The discovery of the interdependent cycle as one possible answer to the question, What emerges? was first articulated in the Lapierre texts, written between 'Intelligence and Reality' and *Insight*. They also show his efforts to link emergence with probability. After our previous quote from the Lapierre fragments (note 4 above), the text on the rest of the page is crossed out. That text opens with a reference to a fourth step, the fragment unfortunately containing no information on the first three:

> The fourth step is the grasp of an idea. It may be named emergent probability. It involves two elements, first, the general idea of probability and, secondly, the combination of this idea with the seriation of possibilities.

On page 10 we find 'emergent probability' replaced by 'emergent potentiality' and 'the seriation of possibilities' by 'a series of conditioned possibilities.' Cycles are not mentioned.

Normally, 'probability' means the numerical value around which the relative frequencies of occurrence of types of events in a population oscillate. In its application to gaming and genetic populations, probabilities are normally thought of as constants. The value around which the relative frequencies of heads and tails fluctuate is assumed not to change. Although in such games there are series of possibilities, there are no transforming emergences. The series of outcomes in no way affects the probability of the next outcome. There is neither emergent probability nor, in Lonergan's sense, a seriation of possibilities.

By contrast, the economic process involves a series of transformations of the possibilities of nature into an emergent standard of living. Emergent evolution involves a series of transformations of the wider possibilities in the universe into an emerging trend of conditioned and conditioning cycles or schemes of recurrence. At any point in time there could be very many possibilities, fewer probabilities. Both differ from the actual course of events.[5] In both cases the seriation of possibilities is such that what has already emerged in the economic or evolutionary process modifies the possibilities of the next emergences in the series.

What Lonergan is trying to do is to work out an application of probability theory, not to single events in an aggregate or population, but to a series of conditioned possibilities. In contrast with the situation in gaming and genetics, the problem of the relation of probability to world order is extremely complex and puzzling. One can only presume that in the further lost pages Lonergan began this analysis.

Experience teaches us that it is reasonable to expect certain occurrences to be relatively frequent, others relatively rare. In a human population there will be a range of possible hair colours, some rarer than others. Because of this, it is reasonable to expect the occurrence of blonde or red hair among a human population to be relatively rare; brunettes will be relatively frequent. In a population of coin tosses it is reasonable to expect that, in a large enough population of events, the number of heads will not differ in any regular way from the number of tails. In these cases reasonable expectation, not of the next event but of frequencies of numbers of events in populations, is for Lonergan a knowledge of probability. Probability is a mean value about which the relative frequencies oscillate. It is neither a past nor a future fact. It does not predict what any event or outcome will be. It is a statement about a normative mean, a tendency.

Lonergan challenges us with the question, what reasonable expectations might we hold with respect to the universe as a whole?

> For that universe is what is to be known through true judgment; and true judgment is a product of reasonableness. If by reasonableness we can know what in fact is so, then by reasonableness we can also know what is to be expected to be so. I do not mean that such expectation is to be confused with knowledge of fact; I do not mean that such expectation is present knowledge of what will be fact. Probable expectation is neither knowledge of fact nor prediction of fact; it is, however, knowledge of an objective tendency, nisus, appetite, trend that corresponds to reasonable expectation as actual being corresponds to reasonable affirmation.[6]

This seems to suggest that the insight into emergent probability will be an insight that it is reasonable to expect a trend in probabilities relating to interdependent cycles in the world. As probability articulates what it is reasonable to expect in a random population of events, emergent probability articulates what it is reasonable to expect in the trend in the world. Involved is a trend in probabilities.

What Lonergan is suggesting is that just as it is reasonable to hold probability expectations with respect to particular classes of events within populations, so also it is reasonable to expect a trend in probabilities in the universe as a whole. The cycles that are functioning have a bearing on the cycles that could next function. As certain possibilities are realized, the probability of later dependent possibilities becoming actual changes. It may increase or decrease. In this sense there can emerge a trend in probabilities. That trend can in turn become a reasonable expectation. To those raised with the understanding that the probability of an event does not change, this is a line of analysis that poses a host of questions.

Knowledge of that trend or tendency, as with knowledge of probabilities, will not amount to knowledge of past or future events. But it will amount to an articulation of reasonable expectations, just as it is reasonable to expect blondes to be rare in a human population. This, I believe, is what Lonergan is up to in working out emergent probability. Within the framework of the question, What is probability? he discusses the relation between the possible and the actual for the universe as a whole. Knowledge of emergent probability is knowledge of a trend in the universe that is reflected in changing probabilities.

Emergent Probability in *Insight*

In chapter 2 of *Insight* Lonergan greatly expanded on his earlier treatment in 'Intelligence and Reality' of classical and statistical insights and related heuristic structures. Classical insights are related to what he terms 'systematic,' statistical to non-systematic processes. In 'Intelligence and Reality' Lonergan first posed the question, What is involved in applying classical laws (for which we could read the laws of motion) to particular situations? It was his conclusion that the initial conditions necessary in order for a particular event to follow could not be systematized. Probability theory is concerned with the frequencies with which events and their initial conditions, defined by classical laws, occur in the universe. In his later treatment in chapter 3 of *Insight* of the canon of statistical residues, he argues that classical insights take us so far and no further in our understanding of world order. There is always a statistical residue.

Chapter 4 is structured around two movements. In the first he explores the complementarity of classical and statistical knowing. In the second movement he explores the parallel complementarity in what is known. This objectification of the subject and object of knowledge invites us to recognize how Lonergan is writing the chapter out of his foundations, in particular his principal notion of objectivity. The knower is here the knowing scientific subject constituted by the skills of classical and statistical methods of questioning and insights. The known object is the world order of emergent probability. Both the knowing subject and the known world order become known through the operation of the pure desire to know.

Chapter 4 opens up the question, what sort of world order corresponds to the knowing of the classical and statistical subject of knowledge? He acknowledges that the question of species of things within world order, which was up for consideration in 'Intelligence and Reality,' is on hold in the first four chapters. In 'Intelligence and Reality' Lonergan also acknowledged that classical and statistical science dealt with complementary aspects of world order, but had not yet worked out what that entailed. The clues that prepare the way for his answer will be the notions of systematic and non-systematic processes, and the results of his explorations of elements of world order characterized by a linked series of conditioned and conditioning cycles. Are systematic and non-systematic processes independent or interdependent, separate and distinct or interwoven? Is there or is there not an interplay between them?

His manner of treatment, following 'Intelligence and Reality,' is to consider how we experience and understand systematic and non-systematic processes. The great proponent of systematic processes was Laplace, who claimed that any situation in world history could be deduced from any other. He affirmed that there was 'a single mathematical formula by which a suitably endowed intelligence might deduce any world situation from complete information on a single situation.'[7] Laplace's demon, Lonergan seems to suggest, could calculate even psychogenic health from the world distribution of atoms in any basic situation. What we have here is full-blown mechanist determinism, the thesis that world order in its entirety is basically systematic and predictable. It will not involve any surprising and unpredictable emergences.

This prompts Lonergan again to ask what possible concrete inferences in the domain of world order we could infer from a perfect knowledge of the totality of classical laws. Classical laws presuppose and apply to systematic processes. This invites us to explore the meaning of system and systematic processes and the place that systematic processes have within the universe as a whole. A definition of such a process follows. Although brief, it is the heart of the matter, and if missed in the details the analysis will be robbed of its heart. He sums up his analysis of concrete inferences from classical laws with a definition of systematic process as follows:

> (1) the whole of a systematic process and its every event possess but a single intelligibility that corresponds to a single insight or a single set of unified insights,
> (2) any situation can be deduced from any other without an explicit consideration of intervening situations, and
> (3) the empirical investigation of such processes is marked not only by a notable facility in ascertaining and checking abundant and significant data but also by a supreme moment when all data fall into a single perspective, sweeping deductions become possible, and subsequent exact predictions are fulfilled.[8]

Although illustrations are not offered, the kind of thing he has in mind would be Newton's prediction of the movement of the planets. Once certain parameters of the system are known, the masses and velocities at a particular point, *other things being equal* subsequent states of the system can be calculated directly from the initial state. It is, it must be admitted, a narrow meaning of the word 'system.' Whether it applies without qualification to the higher sciences is an open question.

Systematic processes have three characteristics: They are reversible, monotonous, and closed. In contrast, non-systematic processes are novel, irreversible, and open. Even though the same laws of motion govern every outcome in a series of sequences of coin tosses, every sequence in the series is different, novel, irreversible, and open. It is of the form of a random or coincidental aggregate of events or episodes that cannot be related by any single formula. Understanding the sequence requires multiple distinct insights. As systematic processes raise questions about classical laws, non-systematic processes raise questions about statistical laws or probabilities. Probabilities do not tell us how the sequence unfolds, but how often the conditions necessary for certain events occur. Probability laws explain the character of coincidental aggregates of tosses.

Once both a systematic and a non-systematic component are affirmed in the world, the question arises, how do they add up and relate in world order? The core of this problem is addressed in the canon of statistical residues. It begins by supposing full knowledge of abstract classical laws.[9] In order to apply such abstract laws to predicting particular events, certain initial conditions must be fulfilled, certain subsequent conditions must occur, and other interruptions not occur. Later in his analysis Lonergan argues that the prior conditions form a diverging series. In some limited situations the conditions conditioning the occurrence of an event, instead of diverging, in fact close on themselves. Following this line of inquiry, for the first time in print Lonergan uses the phrase 'schemes of recurrence':

> In fact, it can be shown that there do exist recurrent particular cases. For example, our planetary system is periodic; it is an individual set of masses; most of them are visible; and a relatively small number of concrete insights makes it possible to determine an indefinite sequence of particular cases.
>
> On the other hand, while such schemes of recurrence are many not only in number but also in kind, still each presupposes materials in a suitable constellation that the scheme did not bring about, and each survives only as long as extraneous disrupting factors do not intervene. The periodicity of the planetary system does not account for its origins and cannot guarantee survival.[10]

Appealing to the canon of statistical residues, Lonergan argues that the initial conditions determining any particular event defined by classical laws cannot be systematized. The occurrence of an event Z is conditioned by the occurrence of its series of initial conditions. Those initial conditions in turn are conditioned. It follows that for some event Z to occur, a diverging series of initial conditions must be in place. Most generally, that diverging series is a random or coincidental aggregate, a statistical residue. In a limited number of instances it closes on itself, and then we get a scheme of recurrence.

Lonergan's Insight into the Emergence of Schemes of Recurrence

It was from the above insights into schemes of recurrence as being constituted by a closed circle of initial conditions that Lonergan was led to his
insight into the interplay of the systematic and the non-systematic dimensions of world order. In the subsequent passage in *Insight* where Lonergan
describes the significance of the scheme of recurrence, one has the feeling
that he is describing a major insight of his own:

> Accordingly, our appeal will be to insight. We shall begin from the
> problem of showing how both classical and statistical laws can coa-
> lesce into a single, unified intelligibility commensurate with the
> universe of our experience. Against this problem we shall set our
> clue, namely, the scheme of recurrence. On the one hand, the world
> of our experience is full of continuities, oscillations, rhythms, rou-
> tines, alternations, circulations, regularities. On the other hand, the
> scheme of recurrence not only squares with this broad fact but also
> is related intimately both to classical and to statistical laws. For the
> notion of the scheme emerges in the very formulation of the canons
> of empirical method. Abstractly, the scheme itself is a combination
> of classical laws. Concretely, schemes begin, continue, and cease to
> function in accord with statistical probabilities. Such is our clue, our
> incipient insight.[11]

The phrase 'our incipient insight' has a personal ring about it. I believe that
he is talking here about his own insight, which solved for him the problem
that he had been groping with since 'Intelligence and Reality' and through
the intermediate fragments. It was a significant moment of clarification in his
search to understand how probability theory might apply to world order as a
whole. Not only has he now got the notion of a scheme of recurrence, but he
has also related it to both classical and statistical insights and related laws.

Reversing the order in which I believe he thought out the problem, at
this point Lonergan opens up the meaning of schemes of recurrence
through a list of illustrations:[12]

> the planetary system
> the circulation of water over the surface of the earth
> the nitrogen cycle
> the routines of animal life
> the repetitive economic rhythms of production and exchange
> defensive schemes involving generalized equilibria such as the
> health of a plant or animal or of an economy considered as a
> defensive scheme.

Again in the list there is a sense of a temporal series of conditioned and conditioning schemes. Unless the earlier are in place the later cannot emerge and function. The emphasis on economics is striking, challenging his remarks to Kierans.

World order is then characterized by the emergence and survival of schemes of recurrence. If a certain pattern of events and conditions is fulfilled, a series of events will close on itself. At this point, each event in the scheme ceases to be isolated or atomic but becomes a part of the system of relations that make up the scheme. The probability of emergence of the scheme at this point shifts from the product of the individual probabilities of each event to their sum. Once the sequence closes it will repeat itself until disrupting circumstances emerge that cause it to collapse.

Not all schemes are as stable and long lived as the solar and lunar. As well as the probability of emergence, there is also the probability of survival of a scheme. This implies that many emergent schemes will flourish for a time and then cease or be replaced. Illustrations are to hand in the field of economics, where new ideas render the older redundant: the train displaced the stagecoach, steamers displaced clipper ships, and banks replaced brokers who in turn had replaced money changers.

On the basis of his analysis of classical and statistical insights and related laws, Lonergan comes to formulate his understanding of the resultant world order. It is comprised of a linked series of conditioning and conditioned schemes of recurrence. In order for later schemes to emerge, the earlier have to be in place. Each of the emerging schemes is characterized by a distinct probability of emergence and of survival. It follows that world order is constituted by a schedule of probabilities of emergence and survival of a linked series of schemes of recurrence. In ordinary probability the events that have occurred have no bearing on the events that are yet to occur. In emergent probability the schemes that have emerged in the world determine the probabilities of what next might occur and emerge. The theory of emergent probability does not determine the schedule of those probabilities, but rather puts it before us in the form of a reasonable expectation.

If Lonergan's incipient insight has shown that in certain circumstances, events in an otherwise coincidental aggregate can form a closed cycle or scheme of recurrence, the crucial development involves enlarging this from a single such scheme to world order as a whole. How can one explain, not just the emergence of a particular scheme, but rather of a linked series of conditioned schemes P, Q, R, ... where in order for Q to emerge P must be in place, and for R to emerge P and Q must be in place? Following this line he makes a distinction between the possible seriation, the probable seriation, and the actual seriation.

The actual seriation is the unique series of actually occurring schemes in our universe emerging at particular places and times. The solar, lunar, and subsequent water and nitrogen cycles would be segments of that seriation.

The possible seriation is a pure theoretical construct based on the classical laws of our universe. Under this heading Lonergan again takes up the points he was thinking through in his 'Notes on Integration' (p. 217), though later he will further clarify it with respect to the initial or basic world situation, whose significance 'is limited to the possibilities it contains and to the probabilities it assigns its possibilities.'[13]

The problematic element that brings in the notion of probability is the probable seriation of schemes of recurrence:

> The probable seriation includes all that would occur without systematic divergence from the probabilities ... [it] depends on statistical as well as classical laws, and, indeed, on the statistical laws that arise from the initial or basic situation of our world. Still, if it is not as abstract as the possible seriation, none the less, it is ideal. For each moment of world history, it assigns a most probable future course. But it also assigns a series of less probable courses, and it has to acknowledge that any of these may prove to be the fact.[14]

If the possible seriation links possibilities with classical laws, 'the probable seriation depends on the classical and the statistical laws that arise from the initial situation of our world.'[15] This in turn poses the question, does emergent probability as Lonergan envisages it assume fixed statistical laws and not allow for the actual emergence of new statistical laws at later stages in the unfolding of the universe?

Classical laws for Lonergan cannot explain the number of instances to which they apply, their distributions and concentrations in world order. Statistical insights cannot explain why there are different families of events in the universe, each with its own distribution of frequencies. It is Lonergan's claim that emergent probability is an explanatory idea.[16] In its own way it enables us to explain, make sense of, the large numbers of events and the very long time intervals in the universe. The explanation of world order that emerges from the combination or sum of classical and statistical insights and laws is greater than the understanding that arises from either part considered on its own.

In chapter 15 Lonergan will introduce a process dimension to his metaphysics. Engaging with the problem of development, it takes us beyond the horizon of classical and statistical insights. With a backward reference to 'Finality, Love, Marriage,' he will suggest that cosmic processes are to be explained with reference to the notion of finality. How emergent probability and finality relate and whether emergent probability is to be thought of as an element within finality are some of the great puzzles with which the book *Insight* leaves us.

Explaining Space and Time

The insight into emergent probability is a high point of the first five chapters of *Insight*. It is followed by chapter 5, 'Space and Time,' for which two sources can be identified. Section 2.5 of the final text of chapter 2 is entitled 'Invariance,' and it signals that the matter will receive a fuller treatment in chapter 5. Section 2.5 of an earlier draft of chapter 2 was entitled 'Restricted Invariance' and made no reference to a later chapter 5. This suggests that chapter 5 was a later addition that grew out of the problem of invariance.[17] Only a minimal reference to absolute space occurs in the lectures on intelligence and reality. In an early table of contents the chapters on common sense are numbered 5 and 6. This suggests that chapter 5 on space and time, initially entitled 'Space, Time and Measurement,' grew out of his earlier treatment of invariance and equivalence. This would have been stimulated by his reading of Schilpp's volume on Einstein, which appeared at the time. His work on emergent probability in chapter 4 will constitute a second input and source of the problem.

A number of early drafts of the chapter are available, of two, three, and six pages, and show how much work was involved in developing them into the final version. The earlier, three-page version opens with the principle of exclusion. Central is the problem of the distinction between primary and secondary qualities and absolute and relative space and time. In contrast, Descartes considered the *res cogitans* was just as real as the *res extensa*. Lonergan briefly notes the subsequent movement through Hobbes, Berkeley, Spinoza, Leibnitz, and Hume. A primary source of his ideas was E.A. Burtt, *The Metaphysical Foundations of Modern Science*.[18] Newton's notion of absolute space and time as well as his bucket experiment are critiqued. Reference is also made to A143, B183 of Kant's *Critique of Pure Reason*, which describes the real as what fills the empty form of time. The later theme of positions and counterpositions is running through the treatment just as much as that of space and time.

The two-page summary again refers to Burt and opens with remarks on absolute and relative space and time in Newton. It concludes with a reference to Victor Lenzens' discussion of a stone dropped from a vehicle on a perpendicular line.[19] The description of its path relative to the vehicle is a perpendicular line, relative to the earth a parabola, relative to the sun a complicated curve determined by the earth's spin and orbital motion. This poses questions about the relation between the equations of motion in different frames of reference.

The six-page draft is clearly the latest in that it refers to Einstein and Lindsay and Margenau's *Foundations of Physics*. It opens, following on the two-page summary, with a discussion quite close to that in 2.3 of chapter 5 of *Insight*, of frames of reference and of relative and invariant statements. The question of transforming expressions from one reference system to another enters at the end of page 2. The fundamental rule is that such transformations must not involve any change in the expression of abstract truths. Needless to say, the geometrical transformations that relate a movement in one frame of reference to another are grasped by insights rather than some picturing of movements in a mythical absolute space and time. The intelligibility of space and time is given in the relations of a verified geometry rather than in such picturing.

This, Lonergan remarks, brings him within striking distance of Einstein's theory of relativity, whose basic postulate is the invariance of the mathematical expressions of the laws of physics when they are expressed in different frames of reference. For the sake of clarification I add Einstein's own formulation:

> Every general law of nature must be so constituted that it is transformed into a law of exactly the same form when, instead of the space-time variables x, y, z, t of the original co-ordinate system K, we introduce new space-time variables, x', y', z', t' of a co-ordinate system K'.[20]

Drawing a distinction, between abstract principles and their verbal or mathematical expression, Lonergan sees here a link between the postulate and cognitional theory. There must be no change in the meaning of the expression when it is recast relative to different frames of reference.

Building on these sources, chapter 5 of *Insight* opens up questions about the abstract intelligibility of space and time, that is, of extensions and durations. There is the primitive experience of time, of the slipping of our present into our past, and of our future into our present. There is also the primitive and given experience of extension, of things being in front and behind me, to the right and to the left. We can arrive at a certain kind of explanation of colours and sounds. What kind of explanation can we arrive at of extensions and durations? It will be concerned with the shift from experiential to pure conjugates, from description to explanation. Because this involves frames of reference, there arises the problem of the relativity of the frames and related expressions and the invariance of the abstract laws and their concepts. It expands into a demanding analysis of measurement that Lonergan claims overcomes Einstein's division of the universe into rods and clocks on the one hand and everything else on the other.[21]

The complexity of the tree that has grown out of the section on invariance in the first draft of chapter 2 is bewildering for the non-theorist.

As well as the abstract intelligibility of extensions and durations, there is also the question of the concrete intelligibility of space and time. The source of this question is chapter 4, and it brings statistical forms of questioning to bear on it. The question is answered, briefly, in terms of emergent probability. At the end of his earlier six-page draft Lonergan put it: 'Thirdly, since statistical thought deals with the concrete, it offers what intelligible account there is of space and time. For example, inasmuch as an emergent probability would explain the numbers, distributions, concentrations, and frequencies of things and events, it would reveal the intelligibility proper to space and time.' The point is repeated in a passage at the end of chapter 5 in *Insight*:

> It has been argued that a theory of emergent probability exhibits generically the intelligibility immanent in world process. Emergent probability is the successive realization of the possibilities of concrete situations in accord with probabilities. The concrete intelligibility of Space is that it grounds the possibility of those simultaneous multiplicities named situations. The concrete intelligibility of Time is that it grounds the possibility of successive realizations in accord with probabilities. In other words, concrete extensions and concrete durations are the field or matter or potency in which emergent probability is the immanent form or intelligibility.[22]

There is involved in this an expansion of the question of space and time over and above that of the classical approach that runs through Newton and Einstein. What puzzles the student of Lonergan is the replacement, reminiscent of his dialectical categories, of schemes of recurrence by situations. To the extent that they differ, do those differences call for an enlargement in the concept of emergent probability? As well as these more obvious themes, there is also running through the earlier drafts questions about realism in relation to space and time that were introduced by Newton and continued by Descartes. In them we get some glimmer of what later Lonergan will refer to as positions and counterpositions.

The Future Move to Rome Announced

In the spring semester of 1951-2, as he was working creatively on the early chapters of *Insight*, he also taught a theology course on faith in collaboration with Elmer O'Brien. For it he made out his own supplementary notes entitled 'The Analysis of Faith,' the final page being dated 8 March 1952.

Later these notes would come into play in section 4.2 of chapter 20 of *Insight*, entitled 'The Analysis of Belief.' That section opened up the question, what is involved in belief and under what circumstances is it reasonable to believe a truth revealed either by another human being or by God? Important is his differentiation in the notes of practical religious questions from those of science and philosophy. Faith seems to presuppose a religious question and arises out of it. There is a light of faith that illuminates our world in a manner that goes quite beyond the manner in which our agent intellect illuminates it.

In the midst of this burst of creativity, the question of his future transfer to Rome came to a head. In Rome in 1938 it had been decided that he would teach theology there after finishing his dissertation. The outbreak of the war changed that decision and returned him to Montreal. That change of plans, I believe, made possible the authoring of *Insight*. It is not the sort of book that would have emerged naturally in the Roman context. Towards the end of January 1950, Jannsens, the Jesuit General, some twelve years after Lonergan had initially been assigned to teach in Rome, now requested that he be transferred to the Gregorian as a professor. Initially the request was that he go there for the academic year 1952–3.

On 14 January 1951 J.L. Swain, the Canadian provincial, wrote a reply to Jannsens' request in which he was less than enthusiastic that Lonergan be transferred to Rome. This did not change the general's mind. On 12 May 1952 Robert Nunan wrote to Jannsens that they were upset at the thought of losing Lonergan to the Gregorian, he being 'the only theology professor of our Province who is truly outstanding, and he has been invaluable in the stimulus and assistance that he has given to the other members of the staff at the Scholasticate.' Nunan went on to say that they had no one ready at the time to teach 'On the Incarnate Word' and wondered if it would be possible for Lonergan to stay on until Christmas to do this. His plea was successful, and Lonergan was left in Toronto for another year. During the summer of 1952 he knew that he would be transferred to Rome in September 1953. A deadline now came into play, governing the final stages of the composition of *Insight*.

In a letter to Eric O'Connor on 23 July 1952 Lonergan remarked:

> The sum and substance of the matter is this. Fr. Nunan got leave to keep me for a semester next year to teach *de Verbo Incàrnato*. The Rector of the Gregorian, since their dogma courses do not divide with our semesters, decided to let me have the other semester to work at my book. But, according to the General, I am to be applied definitively to the Gregorian at the beginning of the scholastic year, 1953–4.

Now the Gregorian Press cannot set up type in English without a
diverging series of misprints: for every correction they make, they
add a few more misprints in handling the type. Hence, if I can
possibly do it, I must try to finish and arrange for publication of
a first part of my work before my departure. It would be entitled,
Insight, and the remainder could be named, Faith, or Insight and
Faith.

This leaves me with a long row to hoe yet. I shall be in Montreal
in the latter part of August, and then we can discuss matters. But as
things stand, you can see that if I am not to miss *my* boat, I shall have
to resist the attraction I feel for a month or so in Montreal next
winter or next spring.

Nunan's intervention earned an extra year in Toronto for Lonergan. It is
interesting to contemplate the fate of *Insight* if he had been moved to
Rome in the autumn of 1952, or if there had been no request for him to
transfer to Rome. His comments on a diverging series echo his work on
statistical residues in *Insight*. The remarks on insight and faith, clearly
related to the course he had taught, underline Lonergan's position that
Insight was a part of a wider project. In 1952 his first attempt at a title for
Method in Theology was 'Faith,' or 'Insight and Faith.' His interest in the
relation between faith and insight was not a casual one. It was one on which
his return to Rome would exert a decisive influence.

Insights into the Dialectical Development of Common Sense

The tension between incompletely developed intelligence and imperfectly adapted sensibility grounds the dialectics of individual and social history.[1]

In chapter 9 of the final draft of *Insight*, inspired by the challenge of exploring concrete judgments of facts, Lonergan first considered the question of common sense as a distinctive form of knowledge. Those judgments presupposed a common-sense culture that he began to differentiate from the scientific. In the final write-up of chapters 6 and 7 during the summer of 1952, he began to relate common sense to his earlier work on the dialectic of history. Initially a single chapter with the title 'Common Sense,'[2] it was later divided into two concerned, respectively, with objectifying the subject and object of common sense. Written out of his foundations, it again reflects his principal notion of objectivity.

The chapters are unusual in that prior to writing *Insight*, common sense was not a major preoccupation of Lonergan.[3] With dialectic it was different, his interest in it going back to his surd sermon in Heythrop in February 1927. There he came up against the fact that in many situations human beings are in flight from insights. As a result, they avoid allowing their understanding to develop in a manner appropriate for dealing with their situation. This insight informed his analysis of the themes of progress and decline, dialectic, and the differential equation of history in his writings in the late 1930s. Dialectic again surfaced in his essay 'The Role' in 1951. With the exception of its ethical context, the themes in that essay are close to the text of chapter 7.[4] Lonergan's path to chapters 6 and 7 was through ethical considerations of the good as well as the problem of concrete judgments of facts. He now brackets those ethical considerations.[5]

Running through the text, we find Lonergan addressing a series of questions of the form: What is common sense? How does it differ from science? Is it a form of knowledge that a fully developed science will eliminate? Has common-sense understanding its own field of specialization, its own responsibilities to the truth that no development of science or philosophy could ever override? There was involved in these questions a vast expansion of his horizon on insight and the agent of knowledge. That expansion involves exploring a mode of human knowing that is more extensive, comprehensive, differentiated, and nuanced than the scientific or the philosophical. Given the very complexity of common-sense knowledge, we should not expect from Lonergan an exhaustive treatment or a comprehensive theory. Rather, we should ask ourselves: precisely what was his focal concern, the important thing he was trying to draw to our attention about this complex field?

On 3 February 1953, shortly after the autograph of those chapters was typed up, he lectured in public on their content. In three points he summed up what he considered important in them:

1. Common sense as intellectual
2. Development of Common Sense in us and its aberrations – changes in us
3. Practical development of Common Sense and its aberrations – changes in things.[6]

Through his or her common-sense knowledge, the subject of common sense comes to know and relate to its object, the world of the common-sense community. Affirming that common sense involves the same intellectual powers as science, the focus of Lonergan's questions becomes, how do both the subject and object of that knowledge develop? His answer will be: dialectically. In this he is introducing a dialectical element into his reworking of Kant's Copernican revolution. It is in his analysis of the dialectical development of common sense, both subject and object, that his contribution to this complex field is to be found.

Common Sense as an Intellectual Development in its Subject

Common sense involves the same emergent intellectual operations – questioning, understanding, and judging – and the same structured problem solving as does science:

> Common sense, unlike the sciences, is a specialization of intelligence in the particular and in the concrete. It is common without being general, for it consists in a set of insights that remains incomplete, until there is added at least one further insight into the situation in hand; and, once that situation has passed, the insight is no longer relevant.[7]

Common-sense questions and insights arise from and are into specific, unique, concrete, and particular situations in which we, as common-sense subjects, participate and which address us in our lives. Whereas the insights of science are into relations in the data that are in a sense independent of how any individual relates to them, the insights of common sense directly relate us to those situations. Determining ways we can deal with and go on with them, they are of the form of relational skills or conjugates, a point not developed by Lonergan. Because human situations change, the insights of common sense are in a state of constant change.[8] In these features there is a certain affinity in his orientation and vocabulary with those of Dewey.[9]

It follows that the common-sense subject is a situation subject.[10] There cannot be a common-sense subject unless there is a proportionate human situation in the world in which that subject and others are involved. Subject and situation are correlatives, the situation constituting the phantasm of the questions and insights. Questions arise about the kind of changes that can occur in the subject, in the situation, and in the relation of the subject to the situation. It will be Lonergan's thesis that common-sense subjects can respond to or be in flight from the intellectual challenges of the situation. Because of these two possibilities, changes for him in any common-sense situation always involve a dialectical element. As a result of the dramatic and social dialectics, elements of the individual's biography and of the groups' social history take shape, posing the question, how?[11]

In contrast with scientific theory, every individual of every street, village, region, place and time in history will have his or her own unique and particular specialization of practical common-sense understanding and related language. Like the understanding involved in a criminal inquiry, it will concern specifically named people, places, dates, and events that are involved in the situation. Although there will obviously be some overlap at a certain point, my common sense by definition will be other, different from yours: our common sense other, different from theirs. Every distinct ethnic group will have its own distinct blend of common-sense knowledge. Communication between common senses is spontaneous and problematic because of the immense complexity of its concreteness.

The accumulation of changing common-sense insights cannot, as in a science, be articulated in a system of primitive and derived terms. If this is the case with common-sense knowledge, how can we engage with it philo-sophically? How can it be taught in a school or university? What are its text books and how is it to be examined? What precisely is the nature of the specializations of scientific and common-sense understanding? How do they relate to each other in a civilization where both exist at a sophisticated level of development?

The Many Patterns of Experience of the Common-Sense Subject

Up to this point in the composition of *Insight* the emphasis on the intellec-tual dimension of the person has been overwhelming. It now comes as a relief to discover that at last Lonergan begins to address the question, where does the intellectual fit into the overall experience of the human being? The judgment of self-affirmation discloses, not the totality, but rather the intellectual component of the person. How is that component involved when as human beings we engage with the people and situations of our world? How does it operate within the field of human self-awareness involved in the interactive drama of human living in the presence of others? For Jung, as interpreted by Jolan Jacobi, whom Lonergan read and on whom he made notes, the psyche was constituted by the intellect; by the spirit, which meant for him the artistic, ethical, and religious dimension; by the unformed instinctual biological nature, as well as the unconscious.

In response Lonergan now begins to address the question, what is the range of patterns of experience that make up the constitution of the subject (a term that made its appearance in the chapter on objectivity) rather than the self of common sense? Consciousness both has a bodily basis and is characterized by a stream. As bodily, it is restrained and in certain respects conditioned by our bodies. As stream, it is made up of directions or currents, of striving, effort, or, as I would prefer to put it, desires. Those directions or desires define the elements of a pattern. In this Lonergan's vocabulary of consciousness is expanding beyond that of chapter 11.

When lions are hungry they hunt, when in season they mate. When they hunt or mate, their individual sensory activities of listening and seeing and moving and smelling are not random or isolated. Rather, those activities are structured or patterned by the lions' instinctive biological desires for food and drink, for sexual union for the generation of offspring, and for the preservation of their lives when faced with a predator. Such instinctive biological desires run most of the non-human conscious universe. There are aesthetic desires that express themselves in play and artistic creation. In them there is a liberation from the narrow confines of the biological. There are intellectual desires whose pursuit is scientific or common-sense or philosophical truth. There are dramatic desires whose goal is the successful living out of the daily drama in the presence of the intersubjective community to which one belongs. When operative, those desires structure the elementary acts of our consciousness into patterns.

It is one thing to be engrossed intellectually in reading a text in a library or working on a technical problem in an office or on a newspaper report of a crime. It is another to be enveloped by the aroma of food and find one's intellectual concentration faltering until hunger begins to dominate. It is one thing to find oneself engaged in some high drama in one's family, it is quite another to detach oneself from it and settle down to paint a landscape or listen to a musical performance. We can lie on the beach enjoying the touch of the warm sun on our skin, but rather than becoming still, we might find our minds and imagination beginning to work in new ways. Eventually, in the night, our self-awareness lapses into sleep and, from time to time, the self-awareness of the dreamer.

At times one pattern of self-awareness slips easily into another. At other times there is involved the crossing of a chasm such as we experience when we walk through a peaceful garden into the casualty ward of a hospital. The quality of the awareness of ourselves involved in the different patterns is irreducibly distinct. The chasm can be such that when one pattern has ended, the vivid realism and presence of the present pattern could persuade us that the self of the other pattern was illusory and unreal. It is also the case that a stressful pattern, such as that involved in being in a hospital casualty ward, can cause ripples in our self-awareness that can surface long after we have left that scene and are engrossed in another.

Lonergan defines a pattern of experience as:

> In such an illustration insight grasps the biological pattern of experience. By such a pattern is not meant the visible or imaginative focus of attention offered by the characteristic shape and appearance of an animal ... Rather, the pattern is a set of intelligible relations that link together sequences of sensations, memories, images, conations, emotions, and bodily movements; and to name the pattern biological is simply to affirm that the sequences converge upon terminal activities of intussusception or reproduction or, when negative in scope, self-preservation. Accordingly, the notion of a pattern takes us beyond behaviourism.[12]

Greater emphasis is needed in the definition on the role of desires and fears.[13] Desires shape not merely patterns, but the pattern of patterns within the total life.

Focal in Lonergan's group is the dramatic pattern involving our awareness of ourselves and of our world in living out our lives and desires in the presence and company of others. That self-awareness is patterned by the unfolding of the dramatic plot that we happen to find ourselves living:

> But behind palpable activities, there are motives and purposes; and in them it is not difficult to discern an artistic or, more precisely, a dramatic component ... Not only, then, is man capable of aesthetic liberation and artistic creativity, but his first work of art is his own living. The fair, the beautiful, the admirable is embodied by man in his own body and actions before it is given a still freer realization in painting and sculpture, in music and poetry. Style is in the man before it appears in the artistic product.[14]

For Lonergan such living is artistic because, for all his mathematical style, he asserts, without explaining what he means, that a human person is an artist and his or her life work a work of art.

Lonergan now begins to address the role of understanding within that artistic and dramatic project:

> The characters in this drama of living are moulded by the drama itself. As other insights emerge and accumulate, so too do the insights that govern the imaginative projects of dramatic living. As other insights are corrected through trial and error that give rise to further questions and yield still further complementary insights, so too does each individual discover and develop the possible roles he might play ... Still there is no deliberation and choice about being stamped with some character.[15]

In contrast with the impersonal tone of scientific problem solving of the first five chapters, there emerges here the challenge to think out how common-sense insights into ways of dealing with the problems involved in the dramatic relations of which one is a part enable one to go on with the drama. The character and actions of the others in our lives and the events we share with them set problems for our practical problem-solving intelligence. If certain insights are forthcoming, they will enable us to go on with the drama in related ways. Avoiding the questions and related insights will in turn have consequences for the playing out of the drama. What precisely does it mean to suggest that insights and the flight from insights are elements in an artistic and dramatic project?

There follows an analysis of a sub-plot within the overall manner in which our insights shape the interpersonal drama of our lives. Inspired by his Heythrop sermon on the flight from understanding, Lonergan begins to examine the peculiar consequences of a flight from the appropriate insights needed to go on with a dramatic situation. Intellectual development assumes agents who love the light, but there are also those who love the dark: 'Just as insight can be desired, so too it can be unwanted.'[16] Without yet naming it as such, he is pointing towards the depths of the dialectic of mind. The human mind for most of the chapters that follow now becomes for him the theatre of a tension between the love of light and the love of darkness.

Parallels are to be found in Stekel, whose *Technique of Analytical Psychotherapy* Lonergan had read. For Stekel the patient in analysis is caught between the will to health and the will to illness.[17] Because a person can use illness as a controlling factor in his or her dramatic world, the will to illness can in many instances be the stronger. Central for Lonergan in controlling the interaction between the participants in the dramatic pattern of experience is the love of light and the love of darkness of the participants.

This controlling interaction is shown symbolically in Arthur Miller's *Death of a Salesman*.[18] After many years of drifting, the elder of two sons returns home to make his peace with his father. Willy, the father, a failure as both salesman and father, lives largely in his world of illusory dreams and fantasies. Significant is his dream that his eldest son Biff will be great. His presence poses the question for Biff: how does an ordinary son understand and deal with an authoritarian father living in a fantasy world and trying to live out his fantasies through his son? The son had shared in his father's dreams, in particular that he, the son, will one day be great. In this sense his self-understanding is stuck in an illusion. How is the son's self-awareness patterned by the presence of this father? How is the father's self-awareness patterned by the presence of his drifter son? What pain, joy, questions, and denials does the presence of the other evoke in each of them? How do those feelings influence the questions they ask and insights they seek?

There is, however, more to the drama than that fantasy. Just as Biff, at the start of his young adult life, was preparing to go to study at the University of Virginia, something came between father and son that has gone underground and become a blind spot in the father. Since that time their relationship and the related situation between them has been stuck. Because of this the son has been drifting. Their meetings have been characterized by an undercurrent of anger and tension. Biff's mother and brother are in the dark but childhood friend Bernard is more perceptive, at a crucial point in the drama posing the crucial question, 'What happened in Boston, Willy?'[19] Willy angrily rejects the question as totally meaningless. It has nothing to do with anything. His defence and denial mechanisms have repressed the question and cleverly keep it at bay. His blind spot is secure. If it is a significant question for his life and his relationship with his son, he cannot grow with it and is stuck.

Although the tensions remain, the father yet again persuades Biff of his greatness and that he just needs the right break for things to change for him. Inspired by this talk, the son goes for an interview for a job that is out of his league. As he is waiting to talk to the interviewer, he suddenly understands the truth about himself, understands his identity:

> And suddenly I stopped, you hear me? And in the middle of that office building ... I saw – the sky. I saw the things that I love in this world. The work and the food and time to sit and smoke. And I looked at the pen and said to myself, what the hell am I grabbing this for? Why am I trying to become what I don't want to be?[20]

He comes to understand that he is not in the image of his father's fantasy. He is just an ordinary individual who, despite his father's failings, loves him. On the basis of this dramatic insight he can now go on with his life and put an end to the drift and illusions. He is also able to forgive his father for what it was that came between them in Boston.

Willy and Biff, in their symbolic ways, are depth-images of the mixture in all of us of the pursuit of and the flight from insight, of the love of light and of the love of darkness that is at the heart of all our dramatic living. Biff has to come to understand the truth about himself, his character, talents, and possibilities. He has to understand the truth about his father's failures as a salesman, a husband, and a father. He has to understand his father's mistaken self-understanding of himself as a great salesman. Finally, he has to understand what his father mistakenly expects of him. On the basis of this understanding he will be able to go on with things. Willy, who loves the darkness, has to use his understanding to ensure that questions relevant to his illusions about himself and the episode in Boston are seen off. His understanding itself can work with almost diabolical skill and cunning to keep itself in the dark. These two tendencies are in all of us. It is because of this tension that our development as common-sense subjects is not that of a pure intellect, but dialectical. Introducing this dialectical dimension takes the analysis of the notion of the subject beyond that involved in self-affirmation and the principal notion of objectivity.

The recognition of the blind spots of dramatic bias draws Lonergan into the question, can they be explained? How does a blind spot arise and enlarge its impact on human living? Inspired by psychoanalytic discourse about scotosis rather than moral considerations, Lonergan focuses on the relation between the neural and the psychic in the dramatic performance: 'The first condition of drama is the possibility of acting it out, of the subordination of neural processes to psychic determinations.'[21]

The terms 'neural' and 'psychic' make a first and sudden entrance in the text at this point like unexpected strangers, posing the question, what are Lonergan's sources for these terms?[22] 'Neural' is not a word to be found in Jacobi or Stekel. Although Dalbiez, the teacher of Ricoeur, whom Lonergan read, hesitated to suggest that the neural could be the cause of psychic events, his discussion of those terms must have been suggestive for Lonergan. Of the two, 'psychic' is the one that will occur most frequently in the subsequent text of *Insight*.[23] Most significantly, it does not occur in chapters 9–13, again suggesting 6 and 7 were written later. What will become clear is that Lonergan will use the terms 'psyche' and 'psychic' in his own unique way, one quite different from that of Jacobi and Dalbiez. In chapters 8 and 15 he will more clearly differentiate the psychic from the intellectual. At this point in the composition of chapter 6 this differentiation does not yet seem clear.

'Scotoma' is a word that occurs in both Jacobi and Stekel, Stekel calling scotomization a form of repression. What seems to be involved is some form of unconscious repression of the memory of a highly significant dramatic event. What Lonergan now attempts to do is integrate his theory of insights into an explanation of the process of scotomization. Why are there blind spots in the field of our dramatic insights, our dramatic understanding? What is their root cause? Involved in the dramatic pattern of the common-sense subject is a neural and a psychic dimension. They are related at an unconscious and a conscious level. Still, those unconscious neural structures, what Lonergan calls neural demand functions, are demands for psychic representation. Corresponding to certain neural patterns will be correlative psychic states, images, phantasms. In response he introduces the notions of the repressive and constructive censorship:

> For the censorship and its aberration are operative prior to conscious advertence and they regard directly not how we are to behave but what we are to understand ... Accordingly, we are led to restrict the name, repression, to the exercise of the aberrant censorship that is engaged in preventing insights.[24]

The operation of the constructive and the repressive censorship is to be located in the interplay between the neural and the psychic levels. If certain images or phantasms are not forthcoming, then certain related insights will be blocked. It will follow that certain highly significant events fail to be assimilated in the life. Related to this there is the practical role of the psychotherapist.

For both Jacobi and Stekel the therapist has the task of disclosing the blind spot and its source to the analysand. Lonergan provides an insightful account of the task:

The analyst has to outwit the resistance. He has to discern the transference, to be able to make capital of it, and know when to end it. He has to be able to wait for favourable opportunities, ready to take the initiative when the occasion calls for it, capable of giving up when he is defeated, and ingenious in keeping things going when he sees he can win. In this complicated and dangerous chess-game, he is to be gaining insight into the patient's basic trouble, winning his confidence by the explanation and removal of superficial symptoms, and preparing the way for the discovery of the profound secret. Finally, he has to be able to end the analysis, stiffen the analysand to self-reliance, contribute what he can to the happy ending in which both need of the analyst and disturbing memories of the analysis pass away.[25]

Drawing on Stekel's insightful book, Lonergan is here making the point that psychoanalysis in one of its dimensions is a retrospective education of the imagination and understanding. Both Stekel and Jacobi agree that for a cure more than that is needed.

The affirmation of the neural and the psychic as distinct but related levels of activity now draws Lonergan back into the question of the manner in which levels of operation, in this instance conscious and unconscious, are related. As he was finishing chapter 6 he sketched out a possible explanation in terms of emergent probability. Clearly, learning a musical instrument will involve an interplay between motor schemes of recurrence in our limbs and psychic schemes of recurrence in our hearing. Lonergan suggests that the psychic are linked to related neural schemes of recurrence:

For the acknowledgement of statistical laws gives a new status to the science of psychogenic health and psychogenic illness. Neural determinants settle not unique psychic events but sets of psychic alternatives. Psychic determinants acquire an independent function of selecting between neurally determined alternatives. It becomes possible to conceive two distinct sets of schemes of recurrence, one conscious and the other non-conscious, where each set follows its own classical and statistical laws yet through its own laws is linked to the other set. Then, psychic health is the harmony of the two processes, conflict and breakdown are their incompatibility, psychogenic aberration is a direction of the stream of consciousness that heads towards breakdown, and analytic treatment is at once a reorientation of the stream of consciousness and a release from neural obstructions with a psychic origin.[26]

The passage is hugely significant in that it shows him beginning to search for an explanation of the link between levels of operation. That the classical and statistical laws on the different levels are linked is affirmed, but the way in which they are linked is not at this point explained. In this his writings here differ from his later account of the meshing of levels and schemes of recurrence in chapter 8. A key insight into the problem of levels that he developed when composing chapter 8 was not in place at this point. When he came to complete the book late in 1954, influenced by Godin, he took out this first account and replaced it with one based on the ideas later worked out in chapter 8.[27]

Chapter 7: The Object of the Common-Sense Subject

The object or world of the subject of common sense is for Lonergan largely a community of subjects, a social community made up of individuals and groups and related situations. The subject relates in many ways to that world: experientially, through feelings and spontaneity, cognitionally, and ethically. That constantly changing world is the product of the practical common sense of the community, which initially expresses itself in the manner in which primitive hunters take time out to make spears and nets. As it develops, practical common sense gives birth to the advanced technologies that come between the human community and the world of nature. The social world of practical common sense pulses in accordance with the rhythms of emergent probability. This in turn sets problems for the economy and the politicians.

No less than its individual members is the common-sense community in which·we live constituted by pure intellects. We are born into particular families in particular villages, towns, cities in particular countries at particular times in history. We are parts of a social history with its conflicts and related dramas:

> Thus, primitive community is intersubjective ... The bond of mother and child, man and wife, father and son, reaches into a past of ancestors to give meaning and cohesion to the clan or tribe or nation. A sense of belonging together provides the dynamic premise for common enterprise, for mutual aid and succour, for the sympathy that augments joys and divides sorrows.[28]

We belong, firstly, to the intersubjective community, which corresponds to experience and desire, presumably largely biological, instinctive, and aesthetic. It has its nucleus in the family and clan, its identity in its history. Within the same geographical region there can exist many such intersubjective communities. In Lonergan's case there was his own inter-subjective family, the Lonergans of Buckingham, with their particular traditions. There was the town into which he was born with its distinct ethnic and religious groupings and the social tensions caused by the strike in 1906.

Secondly, we belong to the world of the civil community, which corresponds to the constructions of intelligence. Through its operation there emerges the good of order that it invents: technological, economic, legal, and political. In these social orders the intellectual pattern of experience comes to be writ large.

Thirdly, there is the world of the cultural community, which transcends state boundaries and political epochs. Lonergan's earlier essay 'The Role' made clear that centrally the cultural community involves questions of values that are bracketed in the long section on cosmopolis in chapter 7.

As 'The Role' suggested, intersubjective, civil, and cultural communities are not geographically distinct and isolated, but more like different levels within one and the same community. Because of this, the manner in which an individual identifies with those levels can vary. For some their dominant world will be that of the intersubjective level. It will focus on their family, tribe, or nation with their symbols of group or national identity and resonances of feelings. For them the civil and cultural levels will have little appeal and might even be viewed with suspicion or hostility. For others it will be the civil level of community with its aspirations towards economic, legal, and political organization that dominates their interest. They could view the intersubjectivity level with its tribalism and, at times, naked nationalism with disdain. Yet others will make their home largely in the cultural level of cosmopolis. At different times in a person's life his or her bonding and feelings of loyalty or sense of being alienated from each of these levels in the human community will vary.

Dialectical Tensions and Biases in the Community

Intersubjective spontaneity and intelligently devised social order possess different properties and tendencies. Yet to both by his very nature man is committed.[29]

For Lonergan we are bonded to the intersubjective community through what he now variously terms our human sensitivity, human intersubjectivity, human spontaneity, or intersubjective spontaneity.[30] Human sensitivity is a complex notion. It involves a felt sense of group origins and identity as well as of present group feelings in relations to others. It is suggestive of the psyche in its social orientation. Spontaneity is a frequently occurring word in the chapter. As in chapter 6 he dealt with the neural basis of the psyche, so here he is dealing with its psychosocial orientation.

By contrast, we are connected with the civil community primarily through our intellect with its practical questions concerned with what is to be done. The implementation of new technological insights necessitates changes in the economic system. New economic insights in turn call for changes in the legal and political orders. In its technological, economic, educational, legal, and political dimensions that community is the expression of our practical insights, which become the basis of the laws that govern shared communal living. No less than the common-sense living of the individual, that of the civil community is characterized by a constant state of change. Elements of Schumpeter's analysis of technological innovation and economic evolution come to mind here.

Bracketing cosmopolis and the cultural level, Lonergan next considers the tensions between the intersubjective and civil levels of community. With a backward reference to dramatic bias, he now introduces the category of dialectic, like a new melody, into the text of the book. Tacit in chapter 6, it will feature centrally in chapter 7, followed by the dialectic of things and body in chapter 8. Chapter 14, written next, will introduce the dialectic of philosophy with its positions and counterpositions. Chapter 17 will open up the dialectic of metaphysics. In the order of composition, dialectic will run through those five chapters as a root notion.

In the notes taken by Thomas O'D. Hanley at Lonergan's lecture on common sense as social on 3 March 1953, we find the heading 'Political structures' with the subdivisions 'Social dialectic' and 'Notion of dialectic.' Lonergan introduces his notion of dialectic with reference to Plato, Aristotle, Hegel, Marx, and Bergson. From Bergson's name O'D. Hanley drew a line to what appears to be a definition of dialectic: 'two principles which account for a determinate field of events, where the events modify the principles cumulatively.'[31] The notes are ambiguous as to whether this is to be read as Bergson's definition or that of Lonergan.

In *Creative Evolution* Bergson's discussion is concerned with the meaning of the terms 'order' and 'disorder.' Central is the distinction between an automatic order, which seems largely biological and hereditary, and a willed order: 'Now, as soon as we have clearly distinguished between the order that is "willed" and the order that is "automatic," the ambiguity that underlies the idea of *disorder* is dissipated, and, with it, one of the principal difficulties of the problem of knowledge.'[32] Instead of speaking of order and disorder, Bergson seems now to speak of two orders in tension. Did this line of analysis suggest to Lonergan two principles at work in a determinate field of events, where the cumulative unfolding of the events modifies the relation of the principles?

Lonergan's definition of dialectic is straightforward: 'A dialectic is a concrete unfolding of linked but opposed principles of change.'[33] A dialectic occurs when there is an aggregate of events of a determinate character whose unfolding may be traced to either or both of two principles. The tension between the constructive or repressive censorship in dramatic bias and the tension between intersubjectivity and practical common sense in the social order are offered as examples of such principles. The principles are opposed but fatally linked, so that the overall changes they effect will be determined by the ratio of the balance or imbalance of the forces between them. The study of dialectical process is in part the study of the conflicts between the principles.

On page 60 of O'D. Hanley's notes we read, 'If no bias from intersubjectivity, no conflict, doctrine of progress would be true,' a development of the understanding in harmony with human sensitivity would take place. By way of contrast, if the tensions between the two principles become unbalanced in favour of human sensitivity, the inhibiting effect will result in a biased development. As a result the path of the individual or group, like that of the biased wheel, does not run true. In addition to dramatic bias, Lonergan now identifies three further types of biased developments of common sense, individual, group, and general. Biases are a measure of the imbalance of the forces between the principles.

Egoism for Lonergan 'is neither mere spontaneity nor pure intelligence but an interference of spontaneity with the development of intelligence.'[34] Individual bias occurs when the egoism of an individual interferes with his or her ability to understand and relate to the other as in any sense an end in themselves. As a result, the appropriate development of the individual's understanding of the human situation is inhibited. A probing image of individual bias is given in Ibsen's *A Doll's House.* Helmer's spontaneous psychosocial orientation in the world is proud, arrogant, and habitually self-centred. He understands himself as at the centre of that world, which is largely there to serve him. He understands individuals and things in that world as related to his needs and self-esteem. His wife's role is to massage his ego and entertain him, doll-like, when he emerges from the serious business of making a living. She is certainly not thought of as in any sense his equal. His spontaneous sensitivity directs his questions and insights rather than the contrary.

His wife, Nora, has a quite different spontaneous sensitivity and related responses to situations. She is sensitive, aware, other-orientated, concerned, and out to please her husband and others in her world. They, not she, are at its centre. This is in part a consequence of how she views the sacred duties of marriage. In the course of their marriage doctors inform her that

Helmer was suffering from a serious illness. A cure would necessitate a long holiday in a benevolent climate. It is also made clear to her that he should not be told about his illness. In response, her needs become secondary to his. She begs and borrows and, as a result, her husband's health is restored. Again we see how her spontaneous sensitivity directs her questions and insights.

The drama moves towards a crisis when Helmer discovers that Nora borrowed money behind his back. Instead of being lovingly sensitive to the fact that his wife saved his life, he retreats into an ocean of self-pity, accusing her of having violated his honour as a gentleman. His total self-absorption and self-centredness become transparently clear to her. She recognizes that he loves only himself and does not love and respect her at all. Helmer's spontaneous sensitivity has blocked the proper development of his understanding.

For Lonergan, group bias, like individual bias, 'rests on an interference with the development of practical common sense. But while individual bias has to overcome normal intersubjective feeling, group bias finds itself supported by such feeling.'[35] As individuals exist in a web of personal relations, groups exist in a pattern of intergroup relations. In the Buckingham of Lonergan's childhood there were different economic, ethnic, and religious groupings. In his Rome years the different nation states Italy, Germany, Spain, Austria, Russia, and the United Kingdom could be interpreted from a similar perspective. Like individuals, groups have their myths and realities that shape their sense of their history and their spontaneous sensitivity. All of these come into play when, through their representatives, they come to deal with other groups.

From this perspective the dialectical relations between Nora, Helmer, Krogstad, and Mrs Linde are images of the pattern of the relations among social groups writ small. The egotistical self of a powerful group interprets itself as at the centre of the universe, from which all its social relations radiate out. Other groups are there to serve its needs with no reference at all to a principle of reciprocity. A dominant group will view any efforts to construct a social order in which it is not at the centre of things as diabolical. When the territorial or ethnic ego of such a group is challenged the situation can become dangerous for others.

Group bias occurs when a group harbours feelings of superiority and of domination towards another group, or inversely, of inferiority and oppression. Much more dangerous than individual bias, it involves the interference of the intersubjective desires and fears of the group with its proper intellectual development. Those desires and fears control and reinforce the questions and insights that are allowed and ridicule every proposed development of social order that runs counter to their interests. In this way the bias of group egoism distorts the social order in a manner that can range from the subtle and invidious to the grotesque and absurd and, ultimately, lead to violence and war.

If initially the social distortions of the group's bias are hidden, as the social situation unfolds they become more and more noticeable. Despite the brilliant efforts of the group to argue their case, in time the challenge to them mounts. If some in the group are attentive to this trend, it can develop an ability to produce its own corrections. If not, the decline of the social situation into some form of conflict would seem inevitable.

The general bias of common sense is more complex. It 'cannot be corrected by common sense, for the bias is abstruse and general, and common sense deals with the particular.'[36] The insights of that common-sense of groups and nations and the courses of political and economic action that they propose and direct are a key factor in the shaping of history. Those insights cannot be replaced or eliminated by a scientific theory or a philosophical world view. Given that common sense is a particular specialization of human understanding, the question arises, what is its role and what are the limitations of its role within the historical process proper? In the long section that follows, entitled 'General Bias,' Lonergan explores some of the implications of his theory of the dialectical development of common sense for a philosophy of history.

Although it is difficult to establish what precisely Lonergan means by 'general bias,' a first statement would be to the effect that it involves a 'disregard of larger issues and an indifference to long-term results.'[37] General bias occurs when common sense rejects the criticism that there are problems beyond its competence. This leads Lonergan directly into considerations of history, which he considers to be in accord with emergent probability. The challenge to humankind is to become the facilitator of emergent probability in human affairs. The conclusion must be that common sense must be subordinated to a human science that 'is concerned, to adapt a phrase from Marx, not only with knowing history but also with directing it. For common sense is unequal to the task of thinking on the level of history.' There is needed a critique of history before there can be any intelligent direction of history. The opinions and attitudes of the present have to be traced to their origins, and the origins have to be critiqued in the light of dialectic. This leaves us with questions about the integration of emergent probability and dialectic in Lonergan's thought on history.

As every bias results in a distortion and decline in the social situation, general bias results in what Lonergan terms the 'longer cycle of decline.' Instead of the succession of social viewpoints increasing in intelligibility, the opposite occurs. By repeatedly compromising the demands of the pure desire freely to question and understand social and historical realities, general bias ensures that insights essential to the long-term unfolding of the social situation are absent. As a result, the social world becomes cumulatively incoherent. At a first level it is affirmed that intelligence simply cannot cope with the problems. At a second level detached and disinterested intelligence is dismissed as irrelevant to the problem of directing human history. Machiavelli and Hitler deal, not with the ideals of intelligence, but pragmatically with their immediate historical situation. With typical brevity, in his lectures on *Insight* Lonergan sketches a cycle of decline at work: 'So: Catholicism raised bias which led to Protestantism, whose inconsistencies led to Rationalism, whose insufficiency led to Tolerance, which couldn't handle situations and gave way to Totalitarianism.'[38]

There is needed a cosmopolitan community and viewpoint that transcends the nationalisms of nations and groups. Its relation with the general bias of common sense is for Lonergan not unlike the relation of the therapist to the dramatic bias of the analysand. As the therapist has to labour to determine what is the dramatic bias, so cosmopolis has to labour to establish what in any culture the general bias is:

> Beneath it lies the almost insoluble problem of settling clearly and
> exactly what the general bias is. It is not a culture but only a com-
> promise that results from taking the highest common factor on an
> aggregate of cultures. It is not a compromise that will check and
> reverse the longer cycle of decline. Nor is it unbiased intelligence
> that yields a welter of conflicting opinions. This is the problem. So
> far from solving it in this chapter, we do not hope to reach a full
> solution in this volume.[39]

As the proper unfolding of common-sense understanding is a principle and cause of progress, its biased unfolding is a principle of decline. There results the social surd, a distortion of the social and historical order that can be identified, described, and discussed. What is peculiar about that distortion is that, being unintelligible, it cannot be understood and explained in causal terms. It is not caused by intelligence and rationality, but rather the failure to be adequately intelligent and rational. As our spontaneous expectations are that the world is intelligible rather than unintelligible and irrational, there is needed a critical standpoint that moves beyond that perspective in dealing with such distortions.

Having introduced the notion of dialectic and the four related biases and cycles of decline, Lonergan now asks, How widely does this critical attitude apply? What is its field, over what realm does it, so to speak, range? It is a critical attitude that applies to all dramatic living with its tendency towards dramatic and individual bias. It applies to the life of all groups and their interaction with other groups. It applies to the manner in which politicians, in dealing with the political process, take shortcuts into the future and dismiss genuine long-term questions as irrelevant.

Related to this critical attitude is the question of a generalized empirical method appropriate for the study of the data of consciousness. In 'Intelligence and Reality' Lonergan was interested in the conscious dimension of the intellectual pattern of experience as it unfolded in, for instance, mathematics and empirical science. In chapter 6 on the subject of common sense he added the biological, aesthetic, and dramatic patterns of experience to the intellectual. In chapter 7 he has widened the field to include the conscious dimension of common-sense interpersonal and social living. That personal and social enterprise is marked by dramatic, individual, group, and general bias. Generalized method addresses that data of consciousness as shaped by its connections with and involvements in the totality of dramatic, social, and historical living. There is in this move an enormous expansion in his viewpoint on the data of consciousness.

It is his conclusion that 'dialectic stands to generalized method, as the differential equation to classical physics, or the operator equation to more recent physics.'[40] The differential equation enables us to envisage a whole host of solutions to problems of movement or of the organization of energy in chemical elements. Dialectic will provide us with a general critical attitude for addressing social and historical situations to the extent that they are consciously constituted.

Lonergan is yet again trying to come to terms with his problem in the 1930s of a differential equation for history. The wave equation of Schrödinger helps us to make sense of the periodic table of the chemical elements. Is there a comparable viewpoint in the field of history? It is a question that has been with Lonergan for over fifteen years. It is his thesis at this point that dialectic and dialectic method stand to huge aggregates of human experience and data as the wave equation does in physics and chemistry. It lifts his study of the data of consciousness right out of the horizon encountered in the chapter on self-affirmation. The fundamental frame of reference here is neurally, dramatically, socially, and historically interrelated patterns of conscious experience. Centrally Lonergan is proposing dialectic, not as a mechanical procedure, but as a highly intelligent personal critical stance and outlook. The critical attitude of dialectic may enable us to diagnose the biases of common sense, but how, it will be asked, are we to liberate ourselves from them?

The dialectical analysis of common sense in chapters 6 and 7 widens the definition of the subject and object that we find in chapters 13 and 4. The questions, how is the object known? how is the subject known? how is the object distinguished from and related to the subject? remain but now include a dialectical dimension.

21

Insights into the Irreducibility
of Things

But a species ... is an intelligible solution to a problem of living in a given environment.[1]

The lower viewpoint is insufficient for it has to regard as merely coincidental what in fact is regular ... Accordingly, if the laws of subatomic elements have to regard the regular behaviour of atoms as mere patterns of happy coincidences, then there is an autonomous science of chemistry. If the laws of chemistry have to regard the metabolism and division of cells as mere patterns of happy coincidences, then there is an autonomous science of biology.[2]

Towards the end of 1952, in the composition of chapter 8 on things, Lonergan completed the third act in his performance of authoring *Insight*. It addressed a topic that had for him a long history, going right back to his Heythrop days. It later featured in the Keeler 'Essay on Newman' and, largely inspired by Aristotle's writings on substance, in the 'Thought and Reality' and 'Intelligence and Reality' lectures. For over a year after the latter lectures the topic was bracketed while he composed chapters 9–13 on his foundations, followed by the first seven chapters. Chapter 8 incorporates and synthesizes that past, but it also throws up something new and surprising in the sections on explanatory genera and species. Significant also is the change in the title from Aristotle's 'substances' to the more Kantian 'things.' The thirteenth chapter within the movement of authoring *Insight*, it comes across as a profound crescendo but also as a bewildering confusion to non-theoretically minded readers. It also shows just how much the problem of explaining differences in things had matured for him.

A 'thing' is for Lonergan a concrete and intelligible unity-identity-whole. As Cassirer puts it: 'The individuality of an organism is not to be expressed in terms of any one special property, but depends on the correlation obtaining among all its parts.'[3] Lonergan tends to leave open the manner of the correlation between the conjugates and the statistics of their events within the intelligible unity. But he does make the countercultural remark that there are no things within things, electrons within atoms, atoms within plants, cells within animals. There are electron- and atom- and cell-like properties in the higher grade of things, but not lower grade things themselves. You cannot have an intelligible unity within an intelligible unity. The remark is minimal but its implications are wide ranging. In the light of his work on patterns of experience and dialectic, he now affirms that the way we relate to things stands within the dialectical polarities of the intellectual, biological, and aesthetic patterns of experience. Depending on which pattern we are in, a garden or vineyard or an orchard or 'the other' can take on an entirely different character.

The first ending of chapter 6 of the autograph of *Insight* also left him with the unresolved problem of explaining the relation between the neural and psychic levels of operation. A related problem had surfaced earlier in the notes for 'Intelligence and Reality,' where he picked up Kant's assertion that explanation in the life sciences was not necessarily based on mathematics. These now become elements of the problem of explaining how species and genera of things differ.

Genera and Species as Explanatory

The terms 'genus as explanatory' and 'species as explanatory' enter suddenly in chapter 8, inviting us to ponder their conjunction. By 'genus' and 'species' I take it that Lonergan means something like 'family' and 'family members': 'within each genus there can be different species.'[4] Hydrogen would then be a genus in the species element; a lion would be a species in the genus animal. What in this context does Lonergan mean by the term, 'explanatory'?

Classical insights explain data in terms of a system of conjugates. Statistical insights in a sense explain a coincidental aggregate of events in terms of a group of probabilities. Insights into higher viewpoints explain how mathematical understanding develops. Dialectical insights explain how common sense develops. Of significance, in the first version of chapter 6 of *Insight*, was his attempt to explain the interaction of different levels of operation, the neural and the psychic. When in chapter 8 Lonergan writes 'genus as explanatory' and 'species as explanatory,' does he have some of the above kinds of explanation in mind or something quite different, new? What exactly is it that he is trying to explain?

A first dimension of the problem has to do with explaining differences in the members of a particular family or genus. In what manner might the differences between a triangle and a circle, between an electron and a proton, between hydrogen and helium, an oak tree and a rosebush, a fish and a bird, a mathematician and a musician be explained? A second dimension of the problem, his main concern, involves the explanation of differences between the different families of things and related grades of being. How are the differences between the elementary particles and the chemical elements, between the chemical elements and the cellular life of plants, between the cellular life of plants and the conscious life of animals, and between the conscious life of animals and the intelligent life of humans to be explained? All such differences are to be explained.

There is involved in this enlargement important and wide-ranging questions about the nature and meaning of the universe as the objective of the pure desire to explain and know. These questions have been maturing in the broad movement of the empirical sciences throughout the twentieth century and it is to be expected that they will be further advanced by twenty-first-century science. It is only by locating chapter 8 within this wider movement that sense can be made of the insight and related explanation Lonergan is seeking. Although beyond the scope of a strict biographical narrative, by drawing on such clarifications I hope the following remarks facilitate an engagement with Lonergan's explanatory insights.

Chemical, Organic, Animal, and Human Differences

Both Newton in his *Opticks* (1704)[5] and Dalton in his *New System* (1808) addressed the problem of explaining differences in the family of material substances. Different material substances have different qualities or properties such as colour, weight, texture, and ability to combine. Initial classification based on sensible similarities and differences soon began to give way to an explanation of differences based on measurement of atomic weight. The development reached a turning point in the work of Mendeleyev. On 17 February 1869, while puzzling over the order in the elements, he wrote down all their known properties on cards. Inspired by the example of solitaire, he began to search for an order in them, but it eluded him. The insight eventually arrived in a dream and was communicated in his paper of the same year.[6] As atomic weight increased, a periodic repetition in the properties of the elements was found, but it took some time to determine the exact nature of the grouping. As late as 1894 they were grouped numerically as 1, 7, 7, 17, 17, 31. Only after the discovery of the inert gases did they settle down to their final grouping of 2, 8, 8, 18, 18, 32. The question now arises, what is the explanation of the grouping of their properties in this manner?

Late in the day, in 1897, Thomson discovered the electron, and in 1910 Rutherford conducted his famous scattering experiments on the nucleus. This posed fundamental questions concerning the nature of the relation of the newly discovered particles of physics and the periodic law of the elements and compounds. In this way the second of Lonergan's question began to take shape: how are the laws of the elementary particles related to the laws of the chemical elements? What is the explanation of the relation between the chemical family of things and the family of elementary particles?

The movement towards explanation found its fulfilment in the work of Niels Bohr, Heisenberg, Schrödinger, Pauli, and others. Starting with his classical paper on the hydrogen atom in 1913, Bohr and his later collaborators came progressively to understand the physical basis of the chemical elements. Each element has its own unique light spectrum, light-emitting and -absorbing properties, and energy structure, as well as the property of forming compounds with other elements. This poses the question, how are these related to the laws and properties of electrons and protons? Most significantly, Bohr, with the help of Stoner and Smith, developed a succession of mathematical images presenting the details of the problem.[7] (See Table 1.)

Table 1.

Element	Atomic No.	Group Size	Energy Levels
H	1	2	1
He	2		2
Li	3	8	2,1
Be	4		2,2
B	5		2,2,1
.			
Ne	10		2,2,6
Na	11	8	2,2,6,1
.			
.			
A	18		2,2,6,2,6
K	19	18	2,2,6,2,6,1
etc.	etc.	etc.	etc.

The energy levels are related to changing electron-like properties in the different chemical elements as the atomic number increases. This establishes the physical basis of the chemical elements.

In that imaginative presentation of the physical properties of the elements, Bohr and his collaborators eventually came to understand the periodic law of the chemical elements, the explanatory law of the genus. In the wave equation and theory of quantum numbers that followed, differences among the elements came to be explained in terms of different solutions to various energy-related problems on the level of physics. A periodic law of properties of one family of things, the chemical elements, came to be understood in terms of different solutions of the configurations of the physical laws defining electrons, protons, and neutrons. From the viewpoint of physics, those regular empirical configurations of the laws of physics are accidental.

In 1950, as Lonergan was getting into his stride in composing *Insight*, Cassirer's *The Problem of Knowledge* was published; Lonergan read it soon after.[8] According to Cassirer, Linnaeus was a brilliant observer with a logical mind and a mania for classification. In his passion to codify and arrange, he classified plants by their distinctive blossoms, insects by their wings, and fish by their scales. On this basis he assigned two Latin names to each organism, their genus and species. His advance was criticized as dealing merely with names rather than with things and their properties.[9] For Lonergan, an understanding of the use of names, involving an empirical knowledge of the matter of the thing, precedes scientific explanation proper.[10] How are such differences to be explained rather than merely described?

Within this movement in 1906 Thomas Morgan began to map specific organic traits, eye colour and wing formation in the fruitfly, to the location of genes in their chromosomes – this before it was clear what a gene was.[11] This would be followed decades later by the first edition of Victor McKusic's *Mendelian Inheritance* (1966), a book now in its twelfth edition.[12] Where the chemists were tracking the physical basis of the elements, the biochemists were tracking the chemical basis of organic traits and differences. In 1944 Avery suggested that the key to such differences was to be found in DNA. As the properties of different chemical elements seemed related to those of physics, so the different hereditary properties of plants, animals, and humans were anticipated as having a chemical basis and explanation.

At the time Lonergan was reading Cassirer, Crick and Watson were working on the problem of explaining the chemical basis of heredity. A first move was made in their insight into the chemical structure of DNA in 1953. There now arose the possibility of explaining differences in organic features in terms of variations in sequences of the base codes C, T, A, and G of genes. By 1960 the shy, secretive genius Marshall Nirenberg and his group at the National Institute of Health succeeded in cracking the genetic code.[13] Involved was an understanding of the link between DNA, RNA, and protein synthesis. With advances in biotechnology in the 1980s, there followed a period in which different biological properties of organisms began to be related to base code sequences in their chemical DNA. A milestone was reached with the articulation of the human genome. Again it was clearly anticipated that an explanation of differences in the higher grade organic properties would be related to different configurations of the lower. From the viewpoint of chemistry, the regular occurrences of those configurations are accidental.

In the 1920s and 1930s, in the work of Wilder Penfield and others, a further dimension of the problem opened up. Pioneers of the neurosciences, they began the work of mapping sensory and motor functions over all parts of the cerebral cortex.[14] Gene mapping, as was noted, was concerned with establishing a correlation between gene sequences in a chromosome and organic traits such as eye colour or wing formation. In a similar vein, sensory and motor mapping was concerned with establishing a correlation between the functioning of the neural structures in certain areas of the brain and sensory activities such as seeing, hearing, tasting, and remembering. What is distinctive in the present instance is that the higher traits, unlike the organic neural qualities, are also conscious.

From the perspective of neurobiology, recent work by Antonio Damasio identifies two core problems:

> The first is the problem of understanding how the brain inside the human organism engenders the mental patterns we call, for lack of a better term, the images of an object. By object I mean entities as diverse as a person, a place, a melody, a toothache, a state of bliss; by image I mean a mental pattern in any of the sensory modalities, e.g., a sound image, a tactile image, the image of a state of well-being.[15]

In his explorations of the relation between the psychic and the neural Damasio is not quite so reductionist as Crick, drawing a clear and irreducible distinction between a neural pattern or map and the activities of the conscious imagination.[16] He gives a profusion of illustrations of neural structures and patterns. He also clearly illustrates the correlation between neural disorders and behavioural defects on the level of feelings, sensory recognition, and the like. His goal is to explain the manner in which our perceptual activities are rooted in the neural.

Damasio's second problem has to do with understanding how, at the same time as forming images, the brain also forms a distinct sense of the psychic self (as opposed to the self of self-affirmation) as the owner of the mental processes. This in turn leads him to the question, how is the emergence of what he terms different 'autobiographical' selves from 'proto' and 'core' selves, and involving personal memories unique to each person, to be explained?[17] Involved is the formation of significant differences in the neural maps of the different selves. In this process it seems the memories of the conscious self, far from being determined by the neural, actually form the neural connections.

Lonergan addresses these questions in both an animal and human context. As the sensitive psyche or sensibility of the animal and human has a bodily basis, an explanation of conscious sensitivity will in certain respects be psychoneural. Significant differences in the neural structure will result in significant differences in the related animal sensitivity:

> For an animal to begin a new mode of living, there would be needed not only a new sensibility but also a new organism. An animal species is a solution to the problem of living, so that a new solution would be a new species; for an animal to begin to live in quite a new fashion, there would be required not only a modification of its sensibility but also a modification of the organism that the sensibility systematizes.[18]

Clearly, different neural structures of the eye and ear and the mobility of the organism will result in different sensibilities.

Unlike many who consider neural patterns as the single key to explaining animal behaviour and differences, he adds:

> An explanatory account of animal species will differentiate animals not by their organic but by their psychic differences. No doubt, there are many reasons for considering the study of animals to pertain not to psychology but to biology. In the first place, animal consciousness is not accessible to us. Secondly, an indirect study of an animal's psyche through its behaviour is difficult, for what is significant is not any instance of behaviour but the range of different modes of behaviour relative to another range of significantly different circumstances ... Against them stands a fact: the animal pertains to an explanatory genus beyond that of the plant; that explanatory genus turns on sensibility; its specific differences are differences of sensibility.[19]

Differences in animal behaviour and functioning are to be explained by differences in the conscious attributes of their sensitive psychology. The conscious psyche of the animal is psychosocial. This poses the question, In terms of the operation of their senses and instincts, how do they live in their environment? Young gull chicks respond instinctively to the red dot on the beak of the parent gull. Explaining animal behaviour and differences will involve two things: firstly, the web of psychosocial relations within which the animal psyche operates, and secondly, the neural basis of the animal psyche. Lonergan does not accept that the psychosocial dimension of the explanation can be reduced to the psychoneural.

Studies such as Howard Gardner's profile of the mentalities of Mozart, Freud, Virginia Woolf, and Gandhi in his book *Extraordinary Minds* pose for us the question, how are we to explain human differences?[20] For Lonergan humans differ in terms of their mathematical specializations, their scientific viewpoints, the civilization to which they belong, and their philosophy. Again there are two dimensions to the question, a first addressing the explanation of differences within the human family, a second addressing how that family differs from others. For Lonergan these questions cannot be answered in terms of our spontaneous psychic sensitivity alone. The key to the explanation of both kinds of human differences is in the higher level human activities:

> So inquiry and insight, reflection and judgment, deliberation and choice are a higher system of sensitive process. The content of images provides the materials of mathematical understanding and thought; the content of sensible data provides the materials of empirical method; the tension between incompletely developed intelligence and imperfectly adapted sensibility grounds the dialectics of individual and social history.[21]

For Lonergan these activities set the human family apart from others in their scientific and common-sense orientations. Human differences within the family are to be explained in terms of different contents to our questions, insights, judgments, and decisions. To state that inquiry and insight are a higher system to sensitive process is at this point to say something new about cognitional structure. The question about the precise nature of the interaction between our imagination and intellect, left open in his account of cognitional structure, is beginning to deepen.

As insights are into what is sensed or imagined, differences in what is sensed and imagined will give rise to different questions and insights. Different specializations of intelligence will be related to parallel specializations of the imagination. The mathematical imagination of a Hilbert, Nash, or Erdos runs through the images of geometry, algebraic and differential equations, group and game theory. The imagination of physicists such as Rutherford, Feynman, or Hawking ranges in its involvement from the images of particle tracks in bubble chambers to photographs of the distant stars and their related theoretical symbolisms. The imagination of physical chemists such as Mendeleyev, Bohr, Stoner, and Smith runs through imaginative presentations of the physical and chemical properties of the elements, their light spectra and periodic nature. The imagination of geneticists such as Morgan, Crick and Watson, and McKusic runs through images of chromosomes and related human hereditary traits. More recently, we are becoming familiar with the bar code images of the geneticists, which are making their entry in courts of law. The imagination of neuroscientists such as Penfield and Damasio runs through images of the neural structure of the brain and brain activity, and related human behaviour patterns. Novelists discover the features of characters in their novels in the verbal and imaginative behaviour of the characters in their own world. Historians, poets, and persons of common sense all have their own unique specializations of imagination and understanding. In this sense they all differ.

Insights into imaginative presentations on the level of physics are part and parcel of explaining the periodic law of the chemical elements. Insights into imaginative presentations on the level of chemistry, DNA and base codes, etc., are part and parcel of explaining the hereditary properties of living things. Insights into imaginative presentations on the neural/brain level are part and parcel of explaining the conscious properties of the life of the sensitive psyche.

Cognitional theory, recognizing that insights in all scientific disciplines are into the presentations of the imagination, sets out to find a general explanation of the nature of that relation. Unavoidably and intimately related to that explanation are the explanatory relations between the being of the genera or families of physics and chemistry, chemistry and biology, biology and the conscious psyche. The explanatory relation between the understanding and the imagination reflects fundamental structural relations between the different grades of being in the entire universe. It appears that we are back at a subset in the Kantian Copernican revolution. The structure of the relations within consciousness reflects the structure of the relations within the known world.

Just as the chemical elements are constrained by the laws of physics, plants by the laws of chemistry, animals by their neural laws, so insights are constrained by the laws of the senses and imagination, and their objects. What is imagined in the different fields is the source of ranges of problems that are set for our understanding. While they remain problems they remain constraints. The emergence of insights that solve those problems becomes the basis of liberating skills that enable us to go on with our lives in new ways: read music, play the violin, write a computer programme, navigate and fly an aircraft, author a book. Might the parallel hold for the emergent relations between the matter of physics and the higher forms of the chemical elements, and all along the line? Do the emergent insights of Bohr, Crick and Watson, Penfield, and others into the higher laws in the imaginative presentations on different levels reflect some likeness of what it was like, ontologically, for those higher levels to emerge in the cosmic process?

The profound implications of the final phrase in the previous quote on dialectic for understanding human differences also needs to be unpacked. The formation of our sensibility by our family circle, the local and national groups to which we belong, and our historical contexts stands in tension with the striving of our practical common sense and gives rise to differences in our common sense. Human differences also need to be understood dialectically.

Remarks such as 'inquiry and insight are not so much a higher system as a perennial source of higher systems' follow.[22] A page later we read: 'Intelligence is the source of a sequence of systems that unify and relate otherwise coincidental aggregates of sensible contents,' underlining the non-Cartesian nature of Lonergan's philosophy of mind. In this we see in him a contrast between intellect as systematizing sensory and imaginative processes in the self or subject, which he rarely develops, and their contents in the world, which he mainly considers.

Lonergan rounds off his discussion of explanatory species with an obscure but provocative remark that a human being

> is at once explanatory genus and explanatory species. He is explanatory genus, for he represents a higher system beyond sensibility. But that genus is coincident with species, for it is not just a higher system but a source of higher systems.[23]

Does this run contrary to our expectations that on the intellectual level every human being is a distinct species in the human genus, a distinct, unique, and unrepeatable solution to its problem of living in an environment?

Lonergan's Anti-reductionist Thesis Stated

For those like Edward Wilson for whom reductionism, the breaking apart of nature into its natural constituents, is the cutting edge of science,[24] the problem of explaining differences between different genera and species of things is simple. It is their thesis that there are no real ontological distinctions between any of the vast range of complex things that we encounter in our world. A human being and an atomic element are simply mechanical complexifications of the same microscopic things. A dog is a slightly more complex plant; a human is a slightly more complex dog. Once physics has explained those micro-things or tiny building blocks of which everything is constituted, then the problem of the explanation of the entire universe will fall into place. Equating knowing with taking a good look at what is out there in the world, reductionism entirely overlooks the implications of the nature of intellectual desire and of insight into phantasm for the way the world is.

Against reductionism, Lonergan affirms that the laws of the higher sciences cannot be reduced to the lower:

> Now it seems that such explanatory genera exist. The laws of physics hold for subatomic elements; the laws of physics and chemistry hold for chemical elements and compounds; the laws of physics, chemistry and biology hold for plants; the laws of physics, chemistry, biology and sensitive psychology hold for animals; the laws of physics, chemistry, biology, sensitive psychology, and rational psychology hold for men.[25]

He does not accept that macro-things are just complex micro-things. As we move up through the grades of being, irreducibly the complexity of the higher expands. As a consequence, he has to face up to the problem of explaining their irreducible distinctiveness, diversity, and complexity.

In section 3 of chapter 8 of *Insight*, entitled 'Genus as Explanatory,' Lonergan attempts to work out an answer to the question: how precisely do the laws of plants differ irreducibly from the laws of chemical elements, of animals from those of humans? In contrast with the reductionists, who anticipate a universal explanation in terms of the lowest level, he suggests that we relate to the series of grades in its upward rather than in its downward movement. From this perspective, the 'immanent intelligibility or constitutive design increases in significance as one mounts from higher to still higher systems.'[26] The higher up the grades one goes, the more complex and irreducible are the solutions to the problem of life. In this context Lonergan talks about four expanding degrees of freedom from limitation on the levels of chemical compounds, multicellular plants, animals, and finally the human being.[27] Through these freedoms from limitation the limitations of the lower levels are overcome, and there emerges the immense complexity we find in our universe. Clearly, this poses difficult questions about the meaning of the laws of nature.

Central in Lonergan's explanatory strategy is the notion that something like or parallel to the relation between the image and the emergent insight recurs at each new level of freedom. In 1943 in his early drafts on Aquinas, Lonergan arrived at the understanding that insights are into phantasms. At the time it was clearly a new point of departure whose possible significance was to some extent obscure. Few, then, could have anticipated the manner in which in 1952 he would explore the implications of that earlier insight for our understanding of the explanatory structure of the entire universe.

This, in turn, helps us to appreciate why he choose the phrase from Aristotle's *De Anima* for the title page of the book. Drawing out the full implications of that phrase is central to its movement and meaning.

Lonergan's New Explanatory Insights

With little introduction in the section on genus as explanatory, Lonergan presents his new insight into this problem. Again and again he refers to a species as a solution to the problem of life, the problem of living in an environment. This suggests that the explanation of the relations between the conjugates and related laws of a higher and a lower genus might be found on the analogy of the materials of a problem and the solution to a problem. Lower levels of activity/operation or life and the physical environment they give rise to comprise the materials of a problem whose solution gives rise to the emergence of a higher level of life:

> But a species is not conceived as ..., it is an intelligible solution to a problem of living in a given environment, ... still a solution is the sort of thing that insight hits upon and ...

> Thus biological species are a series of solutions to the problem of systematizing coincidental aggregates of chemical processes ...

> An animal species is a solution to the problem of living, so that a new solution would be a new species.[28]

This is borne out in Gerhard's Hertzberg's assertion in his *Atomic Spectra and Atomic Structure* that the hydrogen atom and the periodic law of the elements are, in part, of the form of solutions to the wave equation.[29] The materials of the solution are presented on the level of the matter and laws of physics. The structures of the chemical elements, both individually and as a genus, are of the form of solutions to the problem of establishing certain arrangements or distributions of energy in a particular physical environment. The same could be said for biological species of plants and animals. To suggest that genera on the different levels are like solutions to problems is to suggest that in some way they reflect a likeness to human insights. The environment of the genera will stand to the problem and the solution as the phantasm stands to the question and the insight.

Different species within a genus can then be thought of as distinct solutions of a similar kind to the problem of living in an environment. Differences in genera can be thought of as the emergence of solutions to problems of an entirely different kind. The analogies with the emergence of the higher viewpoints of algebra and group theory in relation to arithmetic are striking. The higher genera are like solutions to problems concerned with going beyond the limitations of the lower genus rather than to problems that arise within the lower genera. Because of this, Lonergan refers to them as a succession of higher integrations.

This in turn poses the question, what emerges and in what sort of a relation does it stand with the environment from which it emerged? In this context skills or algorithms can be thought of as solutions to particular problems presented by living in a world. At a certain point in word-processing, problems can arise about changing underlined text to italics in an entire document or converting a document from WordPerfect to Word. In each instance the problem is solved by the skill of composing a sequence of coded instructions that is named a macro. In the first instance, that sequence will search throughout the document for the instruction 'underline' and then, through a series of further instructions, change it to 'italics.' In the second, it will search through the codes in one word-processor programme and change them into those of another.

The materials of possible skills are given in the available instructions that can be written into a macro. These correspond to operations or activities on the lower level genus. The form of a skill or algorithm is the actual sequence or rule discovered though insights and written to solve a particular problem. In many situations this could extend to thousands and even millions of instructions involving nesting and chaining. What is distinct is the exercise or act of the skill in response to the problem for which it was written. Through the act of the skill the entire sequence of coded instructions is enacted.

To have a particular skill is to have an ability to bring about, on a regular basis or when appropriate or needed, such an entire sequence of activities. Each of those individual activities or events has its own particular laws and relational properties or meanings. The form of the skill can in no way violate them. What it adds is a particular sequencing of those events or activities. Through it an aggregate of events that otherwise would only occur by happy coincidence, as Lonergan puts it, can now be made to occur on a regular basis by the exercise of the skill. Clearly, the form of the skill cannot be reduced to any of the individual operations it manages.

The exercise of a skill is a single event that manages the sequence of other events or activities. In the formation of habits, skills can become routine or even, as Lonergan notes, inertial.[30] Differences in skills can be identified with differences in both the problems they address and the rules they apply to solve those problems. Such differences in skills suggest a basis for explaining differences in genera and species of things.

In the following passage in *Insight* Lonergan formulates his insight into the explanatory relation between genera. In a highly technical manner, he also redefines conjugates as skill-like or algorithmic:

> Consider, then, a genus of things, T_i, with explanatory conjugates, C_i, and a consequent list of possible schemes of recurrence, S_i. Suppose there occurs an aggregate of events, E_{ij}, that is merely coincidental when considered in the light of the laws of the things, T_i, and of all their possible schemes of recurrence, S_i. Then, if the aggregate of events, E_{ij}, occurs regularly, it is necessary to advance to the higher viewpoint of some genus of things, T_j, with conjugates C_i and C_j, and with schemes of recurrence S_j. The lower viewpoint is insufficient as it has to regard as merely coincidental what in fact is regular.[31]

The link or meshing between the conjugates C_i and C_j is given in the relation between the elements or matter of a skill or algorithm and its form. Like an algorithm, the higher conjugate C_j makes regular the occurrence of an aggregate of events that come under it and are defined by the lower conjugate C_i. He now has a line on the problem addressed in the first ending of chapter 6 on the relation between conjugates and schemes of recurrence on different levels.

The difficult technical notation used by Lonergan can be related to a skill or algorithm as follows:

1. The matter of skill or conjugate can be selected from an aggregate of possible events, E_{imj}. Although the skill is an attribute of the genus T_j, the materials of the skill are provided by aggregates of events that are the attributes of the genus T_i and its species T_{im}, T_{in}.
2. The form of skill is its intelligibility which is twofold:
   (a) its ability to order a number of the events E_{imj} in a particular temporal sequence, usually for a specific purpose
   (b) its ability to relate to a system of other skills in its own genus in terms of schemes of recurrence
3. The exercise of the skill is an act or operation that makes the sequences of events recur on a regular or irregular basis. Lonergan will address this, not in chapter 8, but in chapter 15 under the category of act.
4. A skill, like an algorithm, is usually a solution to some problem. Lonergan does not directly consider conjugates of species as solutions to problems, although it is implicit in his definition of an animal species as a solution to the problem of living.
5. Skills can be properties of genera and species, of families and their members. Within a family there can be distinctive skills, those for in-

stance of all the different sports in the human family, which can be the basis of the division of the family, the genus, into species. Different families will in turn be characterized by their different skills or families of skills. In this sense, differences in skills can be a basis for explaining differences in things.

On this technical level, different chemical elements have different skills in managing energy levels and related events such as light absorption and emission. Different plants will have different skills in organizing the chemical environment through their roots and leaves, by means of which that environment nourishes the plant. Higher skills can also become elements in schemes of recurrence or events in an aggregate of skills organized and made to recur regularly by yet a higher skill. In this way, there arises the possibility of explaining and linking distinct aggregates of events, the possibility of explanatory genera.

Lonergan's final point against reductionism has to do with the way in which the exercise of higher order skills makes regular the recurrence of aggregates of events on the lower level in a manner that from the viewpoint of the laws of the lower level, is accidental. This becomes a basis for explaining the enlargement of freedom from limitations in the higher grades of being. The following quotation, selected from many references given in the endnote, illustrates the point:

> Then, if the aggregate of events, E_{ij}, occurs regularly, it is necessary to advance to the higher viewpoint of some genus of things T_j, ...
> The lower viewpoint is insufficient for it has to regard as merely coincidental what in fact is regular ... for the higher enters into the field of the lower only in so far as it makes systematic on the lower level what would otherwise be merely coincidental.[32]

Through the regular exercise of the solution to the problem, of the conjugate or skill C_j, the aggregate of events E_{ij} can be made to occur regularly. Puzzling is Lonergan's interchange of the terms 'regular' and 'systematize' in the quotations. Higher skills involve a freedom from the limitations of the lower skills in that they can make regular the occurrence of aggregates of the lower skills in response to higher level problems of living in an environment.

The paradigm illustration of a conjugate as a skill is insight itself, whose materials can be the contents of what is imagined or perceived or the sensible activities themselves. In this sense, it could be argued that Lonergan is solving his problem of the terms that go into the laws of higher disciplines by an appeal, not to the terms and relations of mathematics, but rather to insight itself. Differences in genera are to be explained in terms of different but related higher and lower order skills. Differences in species are to be explained in terms of different internal skills.

The relation between our understanding and our imagination reflects a fundamental ontological structure in the universe as a whole. Lonergan frames this with a backward reference to the higher viewpoints of mathematics:

> Within this larger domain, the successive departments of science are related, for the laws of the lower order yield images in which insight grasps clues to the laws of the higher. In this fashion, the Bohr model of the atom is an image that is based on subatomic physics yet leads to insights into the nature of atoms. Again, the chemistry of the cell can yield an image of catalytic process in which insight can grasp biological laws. Again, an image of the eye, optic nerve, and cerebrum can lead to insights that grasp properties of the psychic event, seeing, and so the oculist can make one see better or more generally the surgeon can make one feel better ... This linking of the main departments of science runs parallel to the notion of successive viewpoints outlined in our first chapter.[33]

In 'Intelligence and Reality' that relation was articulated minimally in terms of the correspondence of the structure of the levels in the knowing and in the known. Here it is receiving a much more technical elaboration in terms of the matter and form of skills or higher forms. If we understand the structure of the relation between the understanding and the senses and imagination, we will understand in that structure something about the universe as a whole. If we misunderstand that relation, for instance deny the distinction between the imagination and the understanding, that misunderstanding will find expression in our ontology and cosmology. Affirming that the structure of the relation between insight and the imagination reflects the structure of the relations between the different genera in the universe further specifies the nature of the relation between the subject and object of knowledge. If Lonergan's point here is correct, there is a much greater chasm between the imagination and the understanding than between the unconscious neural and the conscious psychic levels. Unless one understands this isomorphism, one will have difficulty making sense of his full theorem of isomorphism in chapter 14.

In the three sections of chapter 8 dealing with genus and species as explanatory and emergent, Lonergan is searching for a comprehensive explanation of the explanations of the things in our universe. In this he is filling out details of his early dream when he began to compose *Insight*, and of the unspecified objective of the pure desire to know. All differences among and across families of things are to be explained. As insights are the basis of types of explanation, there is involved here an insights into the nature of insight as the basis of his explanation of the relations between distinct genera. As insights are into phantasms or sensible presentations, so different sensible presentations will give rise to different insights. The sensible presentations of things on the level of physics differ from those of chemistry, biology, sensitive and rational psychology. But insight into sensible presentations will be the basis of all explanation.

The dream of the explanatory goal is to unite the cognitional theorem with the details of the phantasms in the different sciences because the use of the imagination and the pursuit of insights is a recurrent feature. That dream is fleshed out and given shape in two visionary chapters in *Insight*, chapters 8 and 15, which should be read as a unity. Not to glimpse the vision taking shape in them is to do an injustice to Lonergan. In those chapters we see the profound depths of the implications of his choice, in 1943, of the phrase 'insight into phantasm' and the reason why he chose this phrase from Aristotle's *De Anima* for the title page of the book.

There is no chapter in *Insight* that more acutely than chapter 8 poses the problem of the competence needed in a multiplicity of sciences in order to work out a world view. Its strange technical vocabulary needs to be translated into the language of the empirical sciences. The effort to explain the emergence of things in terms of emergent probability opens up the question about the emergence of things but does not answer it. Neither does the chapter address the explanation of the growth and development of things, of changes in the skills of a plant, animal, or human. Rather, it assumed fixed conjugates or skills in the different genera. Nor is his analysis of higher conjugates adequately focused on the psychobiological and the psychosocial. Chapter 15 will further develop the intellectual vision.

Insights into Philosophical Method, Polymorphism, and Isomorphism

With chapter thirteen the book could end. The first eight chapters explore human understanding. The next five reveal how correct understanding can be discerned ... However ... if I went no further my work would be regarded as incapable of grounding a metaphysics. A metaphysics would be possible and yet an ethics impossible. An ethics could be possible and yet arguments for God's existence impossible. In that fashion seven more chapters came to be written.[1]

As a sense of Lonergan's work on the book became known, interest in what he was doing developed in the Jesuit community. In response he gave a series of sixteen evening lectures on Tuesdays between 11 November 1952 and 21 April, largely on the book. Notes taken by Thomas O'D. Hanley SJ at this series are extant and give us a window into the process of composition at this time. The first six lectures, up to the Christmas break on 16 December, dealt with material from the first three chapters, lectures on 20 and 27 January with emergent probability.[2]

Addressing a group educated in scholastic philosophy, he began by stressing his own scholastic roots. He recalled Hoenen's article in *Gregorianum* in 1933 and Trinitarian speculation in St Thomas, which inspired his *Verbum* articles. Aquinas, he holds, asserts that intellect grasps species in phantasms, the intelligible in the sensible. Unusually, he posed as his opening question, Is there insight? followed by his second question, What is insight?

Adopting a dialectical, synthetic, and critical approach, he intended to explore insights in mathematics, empirical science, common sense, and human science. Dialectically, he addresses the consequences of understanding or not understanding something. Analysis proceeds from the data of experience, searches for connections, and then aims at synthesis. In contrast, the synthetic approach starts from a root notion and proceeds to data in order to build up a total picture. In this we find echoes of his slogan in the introduction to *Insight* on understanding understanding. The notion of a moving viewpoint does not find mention in the notes.

Critically, the approach will not play down the difficulties posed by Augustine's admission that it took him years to discover that reality is not a body. As Augustine, so modern mathematics got off to a false start with Descartes, modern science with Galileo.[3] Although they did magnificent work in their fields, both had a false understanding of objectivity. These illustrations of the dialectic of objectivities suggest that Lonergan was working on chapter 14 with its positions and counterpositions as he opened the lectures.

A large crowd of students attended the opening lecture, at which Lonergan was remembered as pacing up and down. The lecture was proclaimed brilliant and masterly. Frederick Power, a Jesuit student at the time, remarked:

> I understood very little of the contents of the lectures but I felt that I was listening to someone who was giving the basic and even ultimate explanation of the various topics. I was entranced, as it were, by the experience. I have never had such an experience before or since.

Some of the students were put off by the mathematics and discontinued.

Crowe was in Rome at the time and wrote to Lonergan for information on what he was up to. On 23 December 1952 the latter replied, sketching the state of work in progress as follows:

> The lectures are the book. No reportatio available. About 12 chapters done. About 6 chapters to go. Will finish next September, if I do not have to do too much re-writing. Sheed of Sheed and Ward seems very interested. His comment on a list of chapters and a summary, sent him by a third party, was 'thrilling, love to see MS, love to see Fr. L.' Topics: insight in maths, empirical science, common sense, knowing things, judgment; objectivity of insight; nature of metaphysics; God; dialectic of individual consciousness (Freud) of community (Marx) of objectivity (philosophies), of religion. Had hoped to include theology, but impossible now that I am going to Rome in September. Boyer and Dezza both here last fall and both clear and definite on point that no writing done at Greg. Hope the *exinanitio* will not be permanent.[4]

Notable is the phrase 'the objectivity of insight' as well as the emphasis on different forms of dialectic, in particular the dialectic of the objectivity of philosophies.

In his lecture dealing with the patterns of experience on 13 February 1953, we find him using the phrase 'polymorphism of consciousness.' His first datable use of those terms, it suggests that at this point he had finished chapter 14 on the method of metaphysics. On 3 March Bergson is mentioned. Close to the time of composition of chapter 15 with its theme of finality, this mention suggests that Lonergan was influenced by Bergson's *Creative Evolution*. The phrase 'the dialectic of philosophy' occurs in Lonergan's last lecture on 21 April.

In his letter to Crowe, Lonergan talked about going out into the highways and byways to find someone to type up the book for him in a form suitable for a publisher. Beatrice Kelly did most of the typing, his brother Gregory helping with some of the later chapters.

The list of chapters and summary sent to Sheed by a third party has never been recovered. The earliest known outline available of the whole book contains eighteen chapters rather than the twenty of the final version. Given below, it is most likely his vision of the book in December of 1952:[5]

INSIGHT: A STUDY OF HUMAN INTELLIGENCE

Part I: Insight as Activity

Chapter

I:	The Elements of Insight
II:	The Heuristic Structures of Empirical Method
III:	The Canons of Empirical Method
IV:	The Complementarity of Classical and Statistical Investigations
V:	Space, Time and Measurement
VI:	Common Sense
VII:	Common Sense (contd)
VIII:	Things
IX:	The Notion of Judgment
X:	Reflective Understanding

Part II: Insight and Knowledge

I:	Self-Affirmation
II:	The Notion of Being
III:	The Notion of Objectivity
IV:	The Dialectic of Philosophy

V: Elements of Metaphysics
VI: Elements of Ethics
VII: Elements of Natural Theology
VIII: The Structure of History

For the first time the term 'insight' enters into the title of his work, replacing the earlier 'Thought and Reality' and 'Intelligence and Reality.' The preface will suggest that the division of the book into two parts ought to occur after chapter 11. Also to be noted is the difference in the order in which Lonergan expected a reader to read the sequence of chapters and the order in which he composed them. The book needs to be read in both orders.

Less dominant here than in the final list of chapter titles is the term 'metaphysics.' Initially the first three chapters had a common title, 'Elements of Insight,' which was later restricted to the first chapter. In his use of 'elements' in his metaphysics, he seems to be distancing himself from Kant's categories, with their purely mental associations. Notable are the titles of chapters 14, 16, and 18: 'The Dialectic of Philosophy,' 'Elements of Ethics,' and 'The Structure of History.' The last of these makes it clear that at this point Lonergan wished to incorporate an analysis of history into the work.

Composing Chapter 14: The Conflict of Philosophies

First, in any philosophy, it is possible to distinguish between its cognitional theory and, on the other hand, its pronouncements on metaphysical, ethical, and theological issues.[6]

Crowe's letter and O'D. Hanley's notes date chapter 14 between November 1952 and January 1953. Composed immediately after chapter 8, it also draws its inspiration from chapters 9–13, composed first. Time is needed to assimilate precisely how it relates to both of those sources. In the course of composition it had three successive titles: 'The Generalized Notion of Philosophy,' 'The Dialectic of Philosophy,' and 'The Method of Metaphysics.' Each title has its point, the succession indicating his changing focus when authoring.

Fifteen pages from a variety of early drafts of chapter 14 are extant and make interesting reading. Its earliest known title was 'The Generalized Notion of Philosophy,' illustrating the thrust of Lonergan's mind, his desire to explain from the most general of viewpoints. In one outline draft, responding tacitly to Hegel's challenge (a challenge that, as we shall see, he will address directly in chapter 17), he remarked that the study of insights has now to be extended to include philosophical insights and, it might be added, oversights:

> Some insights yield one philosophy; others yield another; and so a fully general study of insights leads to a generalized notion of philosophy that embraces in a single sweep all the schools despite their divisions, their contradictions, their mutual incomprehension ... In the present chapter our topic is this generalized notion.[7]

Differences in insights could arise from different answers to the same questions or from differences in the questions.

What precisely might philosophical insight be into? In the draft Lonergan asserts that the primitive object of philosophical analysis is the structure immanent in human knowing when the human subject is in the intellectual pattern of experience. It involves experience, intelligent inquiry, and rational reflection. But 'human knowing' is ambiguous. There is an instinctive knowing that we share with the animals, constituted by experience and extroversion alone and so independent of intelligent and reasonable questions. There are also the aesthetic, artistic, dramatic, mystical, and practical patterns of experience. The intellectual pattern is one among many, and its intensity can vary greatly.

The primitive object of philosophy, the structure of human cognitive knowing, exists in its pure form only when the human person is in the intellectual pattern of experience. At other times that structure gets perturbed by the other patterns. There results what Lonergan terms a 'series of perturbed objects.' Because of such perturbations, a person's questions about and insight into knowing itself as a conscious datum can become distorted. But because our knowing relates us to the known world, a distortion of our insight into knowing can result in a related distortion that can spread throughout the whole of our world view.[8] The positions of Scotus and Kant in relation to insight, judgment, and the virtually unconditioned come to mind. Clearly, the insights of some philosophers will misunderstand the intellectual pattern of experience; others will more correctly apprehend it. Conflicting viewpoints can develop. A generalized viewpoint is needed in philosophy that examines and critiques such insights.

Lonergan begins a second outline draft with remarks reminiscent of the opening of the A-Preface of Kant's *Critique of Pure Reason*. Despite two millennia of attention from profound minds, at the present time on almost every issue in philosophy there is the widest diversity of opinion. This fact, which he names the scandal of philosophy, is an expression of its dialectical

368 Composing Insight: The Artistry of Desire

problem. Why is there so much conflict and disagreement about what constitutes a philosophical question proper and about the answer to an agreed philosophical question?

The empirical sciences settle their disputes by an appeal to observation, experiment, and method. Philosophical disputes drag on for centuries and then are abandoned because the parties become jaded, again a Kantian theme.[9] Philosophers seem to have no effective criterion for resolving their disputes. Not only that, but after the mathematician, the scientist, and the experts in common sense have had their say, what, if anything, is left over for philosophers? If the object of philosophy is the same as that of science or common sense or mathematics, then it is superfluous. Because of its lack of an effective criterion, its very existence is to be doubted. What are the facts of philosophy and how do they relate to philosophical systems, well ordered or not? What is the structure of philosophy? If philosophy is articulated in a correct system, will it exclude progress? If it offers a wrong system, what is the good of it? All of this points to the need for a philosophical and metaphysical method.

Involved in Lonergan's explorations of the source of the conflicts in philosophy is a further deepening of his questions about the nature and content of consciousness. His earlier account of the intellectual pattern and related judgment of self-affirmation only dealt with a part of a whole. His later analysis of patterns of experience and dialectic in chapters 6 and 7 made it clear that self-awareness as conscious has many unfamiliar faces and uncharted moods. All existential cognitional subjects, be they philosophers, scientists, or persons of common sense, live initially in state of a radical but undiagnosed confusion as to the nature of their consciousness. Clearly understanding and differentiating the intellectual pattern of experience from the biological, aesthetic, and dramatic is no small task. Without it, confusion about the nature of mind and its relation with the known world is inevitable. Lonergan's long philosophical odyssey has taught him that a failure critically to understand the polymorphic nature of consciousness is a source of the conflicts in the philosophy of mind and world. [10]

Late in chapter 14 of *Insight*, Lonergan goes some way towards describing what is involved in overcoming this inherent confusion:

> Philosophic evidence is within the philosopher himself. It is his own inability to avoid experience, to renounce intelligence in inquiry, to desert reasonableness in reflection. It is his own detached, disinterested desire to know. It is his own advertence to the polymorphism of his own consciousness. It is his own insight into the manner in which insights accumulate in mathematics, in the empirical sciences,

> in the myriad of instances of common sense. It is his own grasp of
> the dialectical unfolding of his own desire to know in its conflict with
> other desires that provides the key to his own philosophic develop-
> ment and reveals his own potentialities to adopt the stand of any of
> the traditional or of the new philosophical schools. Philosophy is the
> flowering of the individual's rational consciousness in its coming to
> know and take possession of itself. To that event, its traditional
> schools, its treatises, and its history are but contributions; and with-
> out that event they are stripped of real significance.[11]

A focal passage, this gives autobiographical expression to the content of his
struggle to understand himself that was part and parcel of the process of
composing *Insight*. Self-affirmation is here being redefined and relocated
in a wider and richer dialectical context, with a resulting deepening in
meaning.

The path towards his foundations involves a fairly massive personal
development. In contrast with the methodology of Descartes, it requires
that we struggle with our mathematical and scientific and common sense
insights just as much as with the texts of the philosophers that we find in the
tradition. It also invites us to come to terms with and own the range of non-
intellectual desires and related patterns of experience that make up our
self-awareness. The emphasis in the quote on distinctive and irreducible
desires as the basis of patterns of experience is an advance over chapter 6.
The personal development involved in this expanded self-knowledge is not
straightforward, but involves, unavoidably, a crooked dialectical path. It
involves the achievement of a real rather than a notional openness to the
problem of the many forms of self-consciousness.

What is emerging is the notion of philosophy as a commitment to a
valued form of personal development involving a pedagogical and a methodical phase.[12] Contrary to what we might think, few can describe clearly
the intellectual pattern of experience and the related operations of the
human mind. The pedagogic challenge, which shaped the structure of
the first thirteen chapters of *Insight*, is to enable the reader to break out of
the confusion of desires and realisms in which we as humans are caught. In
this, the language of pedagogy has replaced that of intellectual conversion.

Within the dialectical context, the goal of the pedagogic phase becomes
that of adopting a position on knowing and reality in dialectical opposition
to other positions. Cognitional theory for Lonergan is the basis of a position in a philosophy. Its pronouncements on metaphysics, ethics, and
theological issues he names its 'expansion.'[13] At this point, to complete the
formulation of a cognitional theory a stance has to be taken on basic issues
in philosophy. That stance can be either a position or a counterposition:

It will be a basic position,

(1) if the real is the concrete universe of being and not a subdivision of the 'already out there now';

(2) if the subject becomes known when it affirms itself intelligently and reasonably and so is not known yet in any prior 'existential state'; and

(3) if objectivity is conceived as a consequence of intelligent inquiry and critical reflection, and not as a property of vital anticipation, extroversion, and satisfaction.

On the other hand, it will be a basic counterposition, if it contradicts one or more of the basis positions.[14]

Puzzling is his stance at this point on the relation between cognitional theory and epistemology. His language of pedagogy and of counterpositions contradicting positions is more suggestive of logic than of intellectual conversion.

Metaphysics as a Framework for Collaborative Creativity

The third and final title of chapter 14 was 'The Method in Metaphysics.' If the themes of the first two titles were concerned with philosophers putting the desires of their own house in order, the final is concerned with the resulting clear-sighted vision of the known world in which we live. The analysis moves from the form of the desire to the form of the desired, which, following 'Intelligence and Reality,' is to be articulated in terms of heuristic categories. Chapters 2 and 4 of *Insight* posed the question, how can the classical and statistical heuristic structures be integrated into a partial world view? Working out the world view of emergent probability was a first move in this programme.

Extrapolating from this beginning, Lonergan offers his definition of metaphysics: 'Now let us say that explicit metaphysics is the conception, affirmation, and implementation of the integral heuristic structure of proportionate being.'[15] In their search for a range of distinctive types of explanation scientists are filling out the currently unknown contents of various heuristic structures. By way of contrast, 'philosophy obtains its *integrated* view of a single universe, not by determining the contents that fill heuristic structures, but by relating the heuristic structures to one another.'[16] That integrated view is of a framework for collaborative creativity of the scientific community. In terms of the image at the heart of Lonergan's notes on order, the metaphysician is the master builder, not of the cathedral of knowledge, but of the framework by means of which it will be built up by the community. The metaphysical question is concerned with articulating the framework through which knowledge of the whole will become present. There is a need to think of it in terms of a community of metaphysicians constituted by a shared method rather than of a single imperial mind.

Metaphysics for Lonergan has the task of examining the search spaces of the questioning in each of the sciences of physics, chemistry, biology, and sensitive and rational psychology. Those different disciplines deal with different genera and species of things: particles, elements, plants, animals, and humans. Differences between the distinct genera and differences between species in each genera are to be explained. Through this pursuit, the elements of a prospective world view come to be assembled. Through its interest in that world view, metaphysics could also be interpreted as a discipline whose task is to encourage the unlocking in the community of all the questions relevant to an explanation of our universe.

The goal of metaphysics is an understanding of the explanatory structures of all of the different genera and species of things. Without some appreciation of the strategies of integration in chapters 4 and 8, it is a tough nut to crack. In what follows, Lonergan insists that what he is offering is an illustration aimed at testing a possible method.[17] Given the heavy emphasis on scientific explanation in the following text, the place and status of common sense and historical knowledge in his analysis are problematic.

Having clarified for oneself the nature and objective of the intellectual pattern, one can begin the second and metaphysical phase proper of the personal development, guided by methodological precepts. The goal of method, as Lonergan now defines it, is to facilitate an articulation of a clear and distinct notion of all that we can know, the form of the desired. Central to his method will be his own reformed version of Kant's Copernican revolution.[18] In 'Intelligence and Reality' Lonergan defined proportionate objects of knowledge as the range of beings with a structure that corresponds to our knowing. In chapter 8 on genera and species as explanatory, the relation between the imagination and understanding and the matter and form of things was further developed. In chapter 14 he begins to use the language of the isomorphism of mind and world.

The transition to explicit metaphysics is of the form of a deduction based on that isomorphism:

> Secondly, the major premise is the isomorphism that obtains between the structure of the knowing and the structure of the known. If the knowing consists of a related set of acts and the known is the related set of contents of these acts, then the pattern of the relations between the acts is similar in form to the pattern of relations between the contents. The premise is analytic.[19]

The things we know have the same structural relations as our knowing. It follows that Lonergan's metaphysical world view is really a filling out of his principal notion of objectivity. The relation between the knower and the known is given in the pure desire to know. The distinction between the subject and object is worked out in the principal notion of objectivity. The theorem of isomorphism has to be interpreted as a further filling out of that notion. Lonergan's world view is at its heart an objectification of the relation between the knowing subject and the known universe.

For Dewey the patterns of relations in a map and in the country mapped are isomorphic.[20] In Lonergan's use of the term, the structure of the relations between the different activities that make up our knowing are reflected in and reflect an isomorphic structure in everything that we come to know. The ontology of the human mind and the universe that it knows, towards which Kant was groping in his Copernican revolution, is in these chapters breaking further into the light of day. There is an uncanny likeness between the structure of our consciousness as cognitional and the structure of the beings of the universe.

Chapter 15: A New Definition of Conjugate Potency, Form, and Act

What we say about the things that we know, their intelligible unity and relational properties, must be in accordance with the manner in which we know them. There follows in chapter 15 an account of the metaphysical elements of central and conjugate potency, form, and act. What is new and quite unusual in it is his redefinition, drawing on chapter 8, of conjugate potency, form, and act.

In 'Intelligence and Reality' Lonergan defined potency, form, and act as divisions or lines of cleavage in the universe of being. Building on chapters 8 and 14, chapter 15 opens by articulating a new understanding of the metaphysical elements of potency, form, and act. In the light of his earlier suggestion of nine, his blunt assertion at this point that 'there are six of them,' central and conjugate potency, form, and act, is questionable.[21] In the light of his analysis of the relation between higher and lower conjugates or forms in chapter 8, a new element emerges in the definitions.

The fourth *Verbum* article acknowledged that tables and chairs and weights and measures are made up of matter. It then posed the question, can measures be endlessly divided, or is there some prime matter out of which all things are made? For Aristotle such matter was not defined in terms of its imagined or pictured divisibility, but rather in terms of its ability to take on all possible forms. It follows in chapter 15, where he starts to execute his programme, that coincidental aggregates of events are the matter for the higher conjugate forms:

> For coincidental manifolds of lower conjugate acts, say A_{ij}, can be imagined symbolically. Moreover as the coincidental manifolds are the conjugate potency for the higher conjugate forms, so the symbolic images provide the materials for insight into the laws relating the higher forms.[22]

Whereas in tables and chairs the form of the matter differs according to the structure and function, the conjugate forms of the things of the higher sciences differ in accordance with the manner in which they manage aggregates of events, the 'matter,' on the lower levels. This definition in 1953, a highly significant development, suggests a possible link between chaos theory and algorithms. Out of a coincidental sequence of possible events, an algorithm is a selection of a particular sequence in order to solve a particular problem. The coincidental aggregates are the matter, the sequencing of them is the form, their occurrence the act. The relations between conjugate potency, form, and act are isomorphic with the relations between our experiencing, understanding, and judging.

Because he holds that the relation between matter and form can recur on different levels, there arises a basis for summing up the relation between the insights of the different sciences.

> Images, apart from insight, are coincidental manifolds; but images under insight cease to be coincidental, for their elements become related intelligibly ... Such syntheses and unifications can rise and fall in endless succession without altering a single element in the fundamental properties of insight, for those fundamental properties are the principle whence the endless succession would spring.[23]

In chapter 1 of *Insight* Lonergan made it clear that there are no rules for the emergence of new insights. Now we can see why. New understanding always emerges from a base in an imaginative chaos. This relation between insight and the imagination/image reflects a fundamental relation between the different levels or grades of being in the universe. Chaotic or coincidental aggregates of events on the level of physics become the relational potency or 'matter' for the relational or conjugate forms of chemistry. Coincidental aggregates of events on the level of chemistry become the relational potency or matter for the higher conjugate forms (or algorithms) of biology, and so on.

There is a sense of Lonergan's revisiting this problem, with which he had long wrestled and to which he believed he had made a major contribution, for the last time.

Conjugates or relational potencies, forms, or skills and their exercise are not ultimates but the attributes of some unity, some thing. In chapter 8 it was his thesis that the laws of physics, chemistry, biology, sensitive and rational psychology hold for human beings. Although a human person is characterized by skills on all those levels or grades, 'still, man is not just an assemblage of conjugates; he is intelligibly one, and that unity has its metaphysical ground in his central form.'[24] What holds the whole series of aggregates together, gives them a unity? If Lonergan develops a new understanding of relational potency, form, and act, he leaves us with a range of related questions concerning unitary potency, form, and act. How are the skills parts of the unity? In what sense, if any, is the pure desire to know a skill or an organizer of the process of acquiring and developing skills? How do the metaphysical elements accommodate development?

Problematic is the question of the metaphysical status of desire. Where precisely does intellectual desire, the pure desire to know, fit into the scheme of the metaphysical elements? Is desire central or conjugate potency, form, or act? This question goes deeper than might seem evident at first encounter. The analysis of the metaphysical elements of a species of thing at this point does not explain either the emergence or the exercise of the skills. The question arises, what in a species of thing makes it act, moves it to use its skills in a certain situation? What is the objective counterpart in the known world to desire in the knowing?

If Lonergan suggests that the goal of metaphysics is to critically reorient scientific and common-sense knowledge, it must be admitted that he does not address the latter. Nor does he work out a metaphysics of history. Despite this, we should bear in mind that his desired goal was to work out such a metaphysics.

A methodical metaphysics will proceed on the basis of a clearly articulated understanding of the manner in which the mind mirrors the world and the world the mind. But the method, he suggests, is not essential:

> There is nothing to prevent an intelligent and reasonable man from beginning with the set of secondary minor premises, from discovering in them the structures they cannot escape, and from generalizing from the totality of the examined instances to the totality of possible instances. In fact, this has been the procedure of the Aristotelian and Thomist schools and, as will appear, their results largely anticipate our own.[25]

Clearly, the best method would be an intelligent and interactive use of both approaches.

23

Process Metaphysics: Finality, Development, the Human Image

The problem of the origin and development of organisms has occupied philosophy since its earliest beginnings.[1]

The life, for Lonergan, of a presently existing human being is a concrete and intelligible unity that integrates intellectual, psychic, neural, chemical, and physical levels of activities and related laws. As the imagination conditions the intellect, so, more generally, events and their laws on the lower levels condition the possibilities on the higher. The higher escape the limitations of the lower. Clearly, the downward series of levels of activity does not go on for ever, and so there arises the question, what is prime potency or prime matter? It is Lonergan's suggestion that the modern scientific concept of energy, framed by the Hamiltonian, is a possible candidate. All living things as well as all humanly invented artefacts need energy in order to sustain their life or activities.

It is also the case that modern science reveals that the higher levels of activity, such as consciousness and intellect, emerged in the universe only quite recently. The appearance of modern humans is currently dated at between 150,000 and 200,000 years ago. A common ancestor for the human and chimpanzee lines is dated at about seven million years ago. Some 500 million years ago conscious animal life peters out and we are left with largely underwater plants. Some three billion years ago we find on earth the first evidence of cellular life. There was a time before that when no organic life existed on the planet.

Before organic life could emerge, there had to exist the chemistry of life. On one estimate so common a compound as water, H_2O, could form only after the formation of the earth over four billions years ago.[2] The simplest chemical elements are dated at some fifty thousand years after the big bang.

In 1970 Hawking and Penrose succeeded in convincing the scientific community that the universe began with a big bang, a singular period of intense concentration of energy.[3] A very short time after the origin, the gravitation forces separated from the original unified force.[4] For up to the next three minutes the energy levels of electrons, protons, and neutrons were too high to form chemical elements. After three minutes protons and neutrons began to fuse into atomic nuclei. It took a further ten thousand years for the electrons to bind and start to form the chemical atoms. At a certain point the ratio of hydrogen and helium became established.

The question arises, how can this process/evolutionary viewpoint of the universe be linked with metaphysical analysis? The answer must be that in one of its dimensions, the question about prime potency is from a process point of view a question about the origins of the universe. Lonergan just about touches upon this in the following remarks:

> Finally, there has been suggested a correlation between the expanding universe and the emergence of additional energy. If this happens to become accepted, is it to be explained because prime potency grounds both the space-time continuum and the quantity of energy, so that an increase of one involves an increase of the other?[5]

Although the physics here might be questionable, the cosmic meaning of the problem of prime potency is on the agenda.

As one ponders the problem, the parallels in arithmetic stand out. Binary arithmetic is a self-contained system of terms, 1, 10, 11, 110, etc., and relations of addition, subtraction, and so forth. Through linking numbers with the symbols of an alphabet and introducing certain operations and their rules, there can emerge a solution to the problem of mapping binary symbols onto a linguistic system. On a higher level, sequences of instructions can be codified in algorithms, which bear some affinity with Lonergan's higher integrations, which can resolve recurring problems. At even higher levels, these can be integrated into word-processing programmes and the like. In this manner we can see that the relation between potency and limitation is not simple and straightforward, but highly creative. In this upward movement we can catch a glimpse of the converse problem, that of potency and finality. How do the higher levels of being emerge from the limitations of the potency of the lower levels?

Finality: The Dynamic Principle of Process in the Universe

As the question of potency and limitation was one about both downward and backward sequencing, so the question of the finality of the universe is one about understanding the upward and forward sequencing of processes in the universe as a whole.

Two meanings of 'finality' need to be distinguished. When someone says there was a finality about an event or passage, they mean an absolute and irreversible ending, a closure. Related is the meaning of being a finalist in a final. An exception to this mainstream use is given in the Oxford dictionary as 'the principle of final cause viewed as operative in the universe.' In this sense 'finality' means not something final, but the factors that are moving the universe from its beginning towards an assumed destiny or end.

Following this second sense, Lonergan defines 'finality' as the dynamism of reality. To assert finality 'is to deny that this universe is inert, static, finished, complete. It is to affirm movement, fluidity, tension, approximativeness, incompleteness.'[6] By 'finality' he means not the goal but the form of the process towards the goal in the universe. Although it is a directed dynamism, what it is directed towards is indeterminate: 'It is not headed to some determinate individual or species or genus of proportionate being,' a thesis that has something in common with Bergson's claims.[7]

Lonergan's sources for this and the related section that follow on development are Shull, Bergson, and Cassirer. The sense of the title of Bergson's book, *Creative Evolution*, comes close to what Lonergan means by 'finality.' Evolution for Bergson shows how the intellect has been formed by an uninterrupted progress along a line that ascends through the vertebrate series up to man. Reality is perpetual growth, a creation pursued without end. The idea of creation merges with that of growth.[8] The book is a debate about the merits and, largely, the demerits of mechanisms and of teleology. It contains an extensive discussion of finality and leans towards a version of it rather than of mechanism.

As noted, the final chapter in Shull's book *Evolution* is entitled 'Emergent Evolution.' There was a time, states Shull, when the chemical elements, sentience, feelings, and rationality did not exist. Earlier he had identified the significance of the emergence and role of ancestors in evolution: 'Individuals belonging to one species have sprung from a common ancestry, and they owe their similarities to inheritance of the ancestral qualities.'[9] The ancestor is the emergence of a new type of solution to the problem of living in an environment. The descendants share in that problem-solving skill. In terms of Lonergan's essay 'Finality, Love, Marriage,' influenced by Shull, such emergences would be instances of vertical finality.

Finality, the dynamic aspect of the real involves false starts and break-downs as well as stability and progress. It can result in the joy of success but also the sadness of failure. It is not apart from corruption and aberration:

> Effective probability makes no pretence to provide an aseptic universe of chrome and plastic. Its trials will far outnumber its successes, but the trials are no less part of the programme than its successes. Again, in human affairs, finality does not undertake to run the world along the lines of a kindergarten; it does undertake to enlighten men by allowing their actions to have consequences that by this cumulative heaping of evidence men may learn.[10]

Finality involves a realism that can be quite at odds with human dreams and fantasies, dreams of power and security, of the absence of death and disease, pain and violence, abuse and repression:

> But human utopias are paper schemes. They postulate in the universe more perfect materials than those with which it builds. They suppose that the building can be some extrinsic activity apart from the universe itself. They forget that they themselves and all their great achievements and all their still greater hopes and dreams are but the by-products of the universe in its proper expansion in accord with its proper intelligibility.[11]

Up to this point emergent probability held centre stage in Lonergan's world view. Through the fateful combination of classical and statistical laws, an emergent order of conditioning and conditioned schemes of recurrence becomes apparent in the universe. Behind the introduction of the term 'finality' is a different kind of emergence. That emergence results not just from 'the classical laws that rest on forms, from the statistical laws that rest on acts,' but also from 'the emergent process that rests on potency.'[12] What emerges through the process of finality are not just schemes of recurrence but, one might speculate, primordial ancestors, the ancestral chemical, plant, animal, human, the ancestor of a genus and of a species. This aspect of the question of finality was brought into focus for Lonergan by, I believe, Shull and Bergson.

A second kind of emergent process from potency to form occurs in living species in the course of their organic and instinctive and intellectual development. This dimension of the question was focused for him by Cassirer and Bergson. For Lonergan, it is a principle of finality operative in the universe that manages these emergent processes, including emergent probability. In this sense finality is a key to emergent probability. If understood, it would explain the emergence of new species of things with their classical and statistical laws and related possible schemes of recurrence.

Kant's notion of formal purpose in biology, for him a mental category rather than a property of the world, is to be contrasted with Lonergan's notion of finality. Finality, for Lonergan, is a property of the universe and as such can be empirically verified at work in the universe. He repeatedly insists that finality is a fact: 'our knowledge of finality is a knowledge of what in fact is so.'[13] Despite Lonergan's dismissal of Kantian purpose as a purely mental category, we can learn much about finality by considering it as a real verifiable property of living things in the world. Cassirer sees purpose at work in Darwin's theory of natural selection.

In drawing a parallel between intellectual desire, the notion of being in us, and finality, Lonergan advances his articulation of the kind of thing finality is:

> By finality we refer to a theorem of the same generality as the notion of being. This theorem affirms a parallelism between the dynamism of the mind and the dynamism of proportionate being. It affirms that the objective universe is not at rest, not static, not fixed in the present, but in process, in tension, fluid.[14]

Is he advocating a sort of isomorphism between intellectual desire as a notion of being and finality as the principle that manages the emerging structure of genera and species of things within the universe?

Within the universe the emergence of the level of physics, with its energy, particles, and their laws, poses problems that are resolved by the emergence of the chemical elements and compounds. The emergence of the chemical elements and compounds poses problems that are solved by the emergence of plants, that is to say, of biological life. The emergence of organic biological life poses further unanswerable questions that in turn are resolved by the emergence of the animals, with their distinctive life of psychic consciousness. Finally, the emergence of the animals posed further unanswerable questions that in turn are resolved by the emergence of humans with their intellectual desire to understand, make sense, and through insights and formulations engage in linguistic communication.

Human intellectual desire can respond to this dynamic principle at work in the universe and attempt to understand it. It can try to master the problem-solving sequence and so show the process of finality at work. In this and every other aspect of its activity, human intellectual desire itself is a participation in and extension of that very process. The present study, to the extent that it is attempting to understand the concrete unfolding of Lonergan's intellectual desire, is a study of cosmic finality at work in Lonergan's own life.

Though speculative, the affirmation of a parallel between the dynamic reality of the desire of the mind and the dynamic reality of the universe as a whole, its finality, is, for me, one of the more radical statements in the book. It resonates with the meaning of Bergson's *Creative Evolution*, with reality as growth. Lonergan is asserting that there is a creative process at work in the universe as a whole that is isomorphic with the performative nature of the notion of being, the intellectual desire of the human mind. In this sense intellectual desire is an extension of the principle of finality in the universe as a whole.

Deepening the Vision: Explaining the Development of Things

Chapter 8 bracketed the question of the development of things. The metaphysical elements as defined at the start of chapter 15 assume a hierarchic but non-developmental universe. This does not mean that Lonergan is insensitive to the question of development. On the contrary, his doctoral thesis involved a study of how Aquinas' ideas on the doctrine of grace developed. So far in *Insight* he has studied the development of the insights of mathematics as well as the dialectical development of common-sense and philosophical insights.

In the final sections of chapter 15 he explores genetic method, the method involved in the study of a development. In the background is the problem posed by Kant and enlarged by Cassirer about explanation in the life sciences. The things studied by physics and chemistry do not develop. Those studied in the life sciences do. There arises the question, what sort of understanding can we expect of living and developing things? Of note in this context is Lonergan's remark that 'we do not affirm that biology deals with the same type of conjugate forms as does chemistry or physics.'[15] No explanation of the difference is offered. The limited input in the section from Freud and Jung[16] suggests that at this point his main source of inspiration for the problem was Cassirer.

Chapter 10 of Cassirer's *The Problem of Knowledge* is entitled 'Developmental Mechanics and the Problem of Cause in Biology.' It addresses the questions of phylogeny and ontogenesis, of the relation between the developmental path towards the species as a whole in the universe and of a particular member of the species. The individual does not exactly repeat the history of the path. The precise manner of the relation between the two is disputed but is not unrelated to Lonergan's use of the term 'finality' in the context of both cosmic and individual development. Cassirer's reflections suggest that in time it came to be appreciated that the study of evolutionary origins in Darwin and others had little to say about the explanation of how a member of a species develops organically throughout its individual life cycle.

In order to avoid getting deadlocked by the dispute over phylogeny and ontogenesis, there were those who held that the causes of development were to be mastered through the study of physiology: 'and it would be understood in a causal sense only when each later stage could be connected with the next preceding one in accordance with definite laws.'[17] Central in the debate was the distinction between describing the stages of growth of an organism and explaining their relation. Historical description and experimental analysis has to be seen as the necessary preliminary move on the path to the causal laws.

Development entails a change. But is it the case that all changes could be described as developments? When the earth changes its orbital position in relation to the sun we would not normally refer to this as a development, but rather as a change of state. Similar considerations apply to other relational laws, such as the movement of a projectile or the expansion of a gas. One chemical element can change into another. Would this be considered as a development or as a change of state?

Students of elementary mathematics learn to master the addition, subtraction, multiplication, and division tables. In so doing they engage with and become familiar with particular numbers. Later they can engage with a problem that involves adding or multiplying previously unknown numbers. Is this a change in the state of their acquired skills or a development of their skills? When pupils go on to learn the laws of elementary algebra or of group theory, would we refer to that as a change in the state of their arithmetical skills or as a development of new skills? There follows the notion of levels of skills, with the higher level skills taking as their matter the manipulation of lower level skills. For Lonergan development involves the emergence of higher level skills. The new skills result in a new kind of mastery of the lower level skills. But how, precisely, do higher level skills relate to lower level?

These reflections help us to gain entry into Lonergan's definition of a development as 'a flexible, linked sequence of dynamic and increasingly differentiated higher integrations that meet the tension of successively transformed underlying manifolds through successive application of the principles of correspondence and emergence.'[18] By a 'higher integration' he means something like the acquisition of higher level skills or the emergence of higher level algorithms. These restructure events and materials to solve problems that are beyond the range of the previous stage. The level of the new skills is related to what Cassirer and others refer to as a 'distinct stage' in a development. In this sense a higher integration is not an abstraction or a correlation, but an actual management by an organism of its environment. Important is the fact that Lonergan's analysis of development seems to address 'a movement from the relative dependence of childhood to the relative autonomy of maturity.'[19] Like Erikson's writing on the life cycle, Lonergan's analysis will focus on normal and healthy rather than on abnormal or aberrant development. It also seems to exclude Heidegger's challenge to see human growth as a being-towards-death.

If one meaning of a development has to do with a change in skills, another has to do with a related change in laws:

> But there are also emergent processes and the classical laws that can be verified at their inception are not the classical laws that can be verified at their end. There are correlations that can be verified in the adult organism. There are correlations that can be verified in the fertilized ovum. But the two sets of correlations are not identical. In determinate materials, there has occurred a change in what can be grasped by insight, formulated as law, and affirmed as verified. One set of conjugate forms has given place to another. The process from one set to the other is regular. But this regular process is not in accord with classical law, for there are no classical laws about changes in classical laws.[20]

The claim is that the law of development cannot be a classical law. This poses the question, how can a sequence of stages be regular without being systematic? Lonergan suggests that it has the character of the manner in which a successive series of higher viewpoints such as arithmetic, algebra, and group theory are related and linked in terms of the cognitional 'law' of images and insight. This cognitional-like 'law' relating successive viewpoints in mathematics clearly differs from a classical law with its system of correlations. If distinct, then a solution to the Kant/Cassirer problem of law, causality, and purpose in the life sciences might be to hand.

Organic, Psychic, and Intellectual Development

Cassirer posed the question of the explanation or causes of development, but did not distinguish in it the distinct dimensions of plant, animal, and human development. For Bergson those dimensions were central to the problem:

> The cardinal error which, from Aristotle onward, has vitiated most of the philosophies of nature, is to see in vegetative, instinctive and

rational life, three successive degrees of the development of one and the same tendency, whereas they are three divergent directions of an activity that has split up as it grew.[21]

Not only do the bodies of animals grow; so also do their sensory perceptions and their instincts. Through the use of its senses, a dog can progressively learn much about its geographical environment and the persons it encounters. In the same way, a chimpanzee can learn much about the members of its troop and whether to relate to them as master or slave. Such learning involves a large element of instinct, of sensory stimulus and response. It involves a dimension of consciousness not found in plants. In humans there is also intellectual development, which expresses itself in the early linguistic abilities of the child.

For Lonergan, following Bergson, the vegetative/organic, the instinctive/psychic, and the intellectual are distinct and not to be confused. A full theory of the causes or explanation of development will have to address how those three distinct but interrelated dimensions are caused and interact with each other.

In their 'Homeo-Box Genes and the Vertebrate Body Plan,' Eddy M. De Robertis et al. illustrate the vast complexity of the problem of explaining organic development.[22] Central is the development from a single to billions of cells of the distinct spatially structured organism of a plant, an animal, or a human. Each organism has its own unique spatial arrangement, be it root, trunk, and branch structure, leaf shape and distribution, organ location and arrangement or manner of locomotion – wings or feet, all fours, upright walking. That structure defines the boundary between what is in and out,[23] and the way in which the organism functions in its environment. In the process of organic development that forms the spatial structure, biologists talk about certain genes being switched on and others switched off at certain points in the development. This in turn poses the question, what causes the genes to be so switched on and off?

Related to organ shape and function, there is also the question of the stages in the development of size, shape, structure, and function of the organism from conception to adulthood. A first stage for higher animals and humans runs from fertilization to gastrulation. Before gastrulation the cell mass grows without a well-defined body axis and shape. Early in this stage, prior to the formation of stem cells, cells are not committed to particular organs and their structures. The blastocyst can recover from extreme damage and produce an unharmed adult organism.

During the process of gastrulation a well-defined body axis emerges. It is followed by the embryo stage, in which the various organs begin to form in their appropriate places on that body axis – be it for a fish, a frog, a bird, a human. Any significant cell damage that takes place after this point will be irreversible throughout the rest of the life cycle. There follows the fetal stage proper, which runs from the end of the embryo stage until birth, and during which the different organs grow and become established in the body plan. For humans at a particular point of neural development in this stage, there emerges an awareness of the sensations of pain and possibly sound. There emerges the phenomenon of sensations, of the psychological.

Pregnancy as a whole ends with birth, when the respiratory system has to adjust quickly to an air environment rather than the liquid environment of the womb. In the first year after birth, massive and hugely complex brain growth takes place in the human. Present studies of how the various patterns of neural networks emerge and become established are in their infancy. Late in the first year the child begins to recognize and respond to particular words. During the second year it learns to name things, and sometime after can grasp the meaning of a two-word sentence. As well as organic and psychic development, intellectual development has begun.

Further stages in organic growth would involve the emergence of upright walking, of the maturing of the reproductive cycle during adolescence, of early adulthood, of mid-life and old age. It is the case that the human organism is all the time in process and never reaches some stable destination.

Clearly, the laws of the internal structures and the skills that relate to external functions that characterise pre-gastrulation, the embryo, the fetal and later stages of the developing organism differ. That series of linked stages is not logically related or related like the sequence of numbers in a mathematical series. What is happening is that through emergent processes the actual classical laws, as Lonergan calls them, the habits or skills that can form schemes of recurrence, change. In the early stage the possibilities of development are totipotential. As the process unfolds, the possibilities in an organic sense become more specific. How, within the categories of a metaphysics, do you explain the development and growth of an organism within which movement a spatial shape and structure with head, hands, and feet forms and an interconnected series of organs, eyes, ears, nose, mouth, backbone emerge? For Aristotle 'sight is the intelligibility grasped not only in the developed eye and optic nerve but also proleptically in the developing eye of the foetus.'[24] How do you explain the management by an organism of its life cycle?

Psychic development, although rooted in the organic, transcends it. Its autonomy is illustrated in the following remark:

Again, the initiatives may be psychic, for man's sensitivity not only reflects and integrates its biological basis but also is itself an entity, a value, a living and developing. Intersubjectivity, companionship, play and artistry, the idle hours spent with those with whom one feels at home, the common purpose, labour, achievement, failure, disaster, the sharing of feeling in laughter and lamenting, all are human things and in them man functions primarily in accord with the development of his perceptiveness, his emotional responses, his sentiments.[25]

This sits well with the general thrust of Erikson's writings at the time, his first paper on the life cycle and his book *Childhood and Society* both appearing in 1950. In them he was searching for an understanding of regularities in the sequence of stages of human development.[26] He was also sensitive to the interaction in human development of the organic and the psychic, the psychobiological or psychoneural and the psychosocial.[27] The initiatives for psychic development are both organic – changes in the size and function of the organism – and social – changes in the social world. In the developing life of the child, there is the experience of being born into a social world in which the centrality of the mother is displaced by the father, sibling rivalry, and participation in a playgroup.

Early initiatives for psychic development are provided by the experience of being born, of the transition from the world of the womb to the world of the mother, and of establishing a psychic relationship with the mother:

> The young infant established trust in the 'inner certainty' and the 'outer predictability' of his mother's existence and support when he could let her out of his sight without undue anxiety. He trusted that she would be constant and supportive. From this 'consistency, continuity, and sameness of experience,' the infant formed 'a rudimentary sense of ego identity.'[28]

Can there be a series of further initiatives in a life by means of which the primal instinctive skill of trust and mistrust formed so soon after birth becomes progressively transformed?

A second developmental challenge has to do with the entry of the father into the world of the child and, related, the sense of having to live according to laws. Of relevance is the psychobiological challenge of learning to control one's bowel movements, and of responding positively or negatively to the laws in the world.

A further developmental stage with its related initiatives arises with the emergence of the child's ability to enter into playgroups. Erikson quotes Friedrich Schiller to the effect that 'man is perfectly human only when he plays,' and William Blake: 'The child's toys and the old man's reasons are the fruits of the two seasons.'[29] Friedman sums up Erikson on play as follows:

> Play was far more than a particular to be considered by the analyst in order to compensate for children's verbal shortcomings. There was in fact a unique 'language of play with its various cultural and age dialectics.' It was no mere 'intermission or a vacation from urgent life.' The concept of 'repression' was inappropriate to the 'subverbal experience' of the play world. The conceptual baggage and the techniques that analysts customarily used with adults were not appropriate for children. The child should not be forced 'to adapt himself to the verbalized and classified world.' The wise analyst 'enters the child's world as a polite guest and studies play as a most serious occupation.'[30]

Erikson's scheme images out aspects of psychic development. Trust or mistrust, autonomy or shame, initiative or guilt are emotional rather than rational skills. The initiatives for learning those skills are changes both in one's body and in one's social world. Erikson will not allow the psychic to be reduced to the biological or neural.

In his study of the life cycle Erikson works with a heuristic structure or expectation of a regular sequence of developmental challenges, initiatives, and related developmental stages. Although he recognizes the organic, psychic, and intellectual dimensions, he does not consider them separately. His focal contribution was to locate the identity crisis in the stage of adolescence and to understand it in terms of generational tensions between children and parents rather than in terms of cultural repression. His ritualization of experience, of the daily greeting of the newborn infant by the mother, seem not unrelated to Lonergan's schemes of recurrence.[31] His scheme, simple though it is, is challenging to students of Lonergan in that it suggests that psychic development is always dialectical. It involves at every stage the mastery not simply of a psychic skill, but of dialectically opposed skills such as trust and mistrust. A regular sequence of new emergences in the process calls forth changes in skills. New psychic skills emerge, not necessarily in a rigid but in a flexible manner, in tandem with certain organic developments.

The study of intellectual development was also in the air at the time Lonergan was thinking out and composing *Insight*. Piaget had been publishing on the topic since the 1920s, aided in his researches by his wife and their observations of their children. Although Lonergan did not read him until after *Insight* was composed, it is interesting to note that in 1953 Piaget published an article in *Scientific American* entitled 'How Children Form Mathematical Concepts.'[32] In the same year he would publish in *Diogenes* an essay entitled 'Genetic Psychology and Epistemology.'

As the psychic emerges at a certain stage in pregnancy, the intellectual emerges early in infancy. Around eight months after birth the sounds a child makes change to a babble. At this point children can recognize some words but not form them. By eighteen months they can use words such as 'mama,' 'dada,' 'juice,' 'ball,' 'doggie,' 'gone,' and so forth. A new stage emerges around eighteen months when they respond with 'dog,' 'clock,' and so forth to the question 'what'sat?' Around two years they can work with two-word sentences: 'mommy gone' but not 'gone mommy,' 'more cookie' but not 'cookie more.'[33] There arises a stage of identifying words and objects, of naming. A second skill is that of understanding a sentence, of the nexus between the terms, the subject and the predicate.

Intellectual development, to the extent that it underpins linguistic development, expresses itself in the emergence of new linguistic skills and in changes in those skills. Piaget has analysed it in terms of a phase of concrete operations from the ages of about seven to eleven, which is succeeded by a phase of formal operations of a more logical or propositional or abstract nature.[34] Young children are intellectually comfortable in the world of immediacy with its concrete language and stories. There comes a point when there emerges a new linguistic skill that enables them to deal with the abstract symbols of arithmetic, algebra, physics, and chemistry. The image of development suggests a stage characterized by specific intellectual and linguistic skills that can range over a certain field. This in turn gives way to a later stage characterized by new insights and related skills that can range over a quite different field.

The initiative for change 'may be intellectual; its source is a problem, one is out to understand.'[35] In this context we can think about the various initiatives for development in Lonergan's own life, his philosophical confusion over cognition at Heythrop, the manner in which his experience of the Depression provoked him to search for its causes, his awakening in Rome and Amiens to the problem of a philosophy of history and to the need for a modern methodological theology. His awakening to each of these problems was the basis of an initiative for an intellectual development. To this one could add his present concern to understand development itself. This brings before us a distinction between a development viewed as a quest and understood from a pedagogical standpoint. In the former the development involves a journey into an unknown. In this sense its terminus is not a stage in a regular series of stages. When the term of such a quest has been reached, it can in turn become a stage in later educational pedagogy. How these two phases of development interact is left open in Lonergan's analysis.

Genetic Method: The Operators and Integrators of a Development

The goal of our descriptive detour was to bring into focus some partial elements of the materials that pose the question about the explanation of a development. The concern was to illustrate the meaning of Lonergan's remark:

> Comparative study of successive stages, of normal and abnormal successions, of similarities and differences of successions in different subspecies, species, and genera, and of the general economy of increasing psychic differentiation, would provide the materials to be understood in grasping the nature of the higher system as operator.[36]

Only by engaging in such a wider programme of reading, hinted at in the previous sections, does the interpreter of Lonergan become clear on the kind of thing that the latter's understanding of development is trying to explain. Such an explanation will have to address what it is that causes the changes from one stage to another in a development, be it organic, psychic, or intellectual.

Central to explaining development for Lonergan is a new type of insight into what he terms the 'operator' and 'integrator' of the development:

> On the one hand, there is the subject as he is functioning more or less successfully in a flexible circle of ranges of schemes of recurrence. On the other hand, there is the subject as a higher system on the move. One and the same reality is both integrator and operator; but the operator is relentless in transforming the integrator. The integrator resides in successive levels of interrelated conjugate forms that are more familiar under the common name of acquired habits. But habits are inertial.[37]

If we understand the operator and integrator, we will understand what causes the organism, animal, or human being to grow through the series of stages of development.

Lonergan's task is not directly to specify any particular operator, but to articulate the kind of things an operator and an integrator are. The ac-

count that he offers is as minimalist as his description of the different kinds
of development:

> The higher system as integrator corresponds to a set of conjugate
> forms, of laws of the classical type, of alternative ranges of schemes
> of recurrence; and the higher system as operator effects the transi-
> tion from one set of forms, laws, schemes to another set ... Still, what
> is the operator? In the general case, it is the upwardly directed
> dynamism of proportionate being that we have named finality.[38]

A clear enlargement is taking place. Initially Lonergan defined conjugate
forms in terms of mathematical-like systems of relations. Next he enlarged
the definition to allow higher conjugate forms to regularize coincidental
sequences of acts on a lower level. Now he is talking about operators that
can cause the emergence of a series of conjugate forms (or algorithms),
which in turn bring about different systematizations of the lower manifolds.
So the operator as constant of the development changes the conjugate
forms as the organism grows. It could do so by replacing them or by
integrating them into a higher integration or algorithm. The integrator is
the present set of forms that it has caused to emerge in the development.
Intellectual desire changes the understanding but is in a sense a constant of
intellectual growth.

A distinction has to be drawn between the orientation of the scientists
attempting to understand development and the orientation of the metaphysician, whose concern is to articulate the related heuristic structures. In
this instance the relevant heuristic structure is: specify the operator. It
becomes known by grasping the cause of the differences that appear in the
interrelated set of capacities to perform as the course of the development
moves on to the next stage. As classical method has the task of determining
the indeterminate function, so genetic method has the task of understanding the operator as the source of such differences.[39]

Intellectual desire, which expresses itself in the performance of questioning, is most suggestive of the operator of an intellectual development. The
set of insights emergent in response to it is equally suggestive of an integrator of development. Previous insights would be the basis of older skills, the
newly emergent of newer skills. Intellectual development in this sense
involves either a shift from one system of skills to another or an integration
of older skills into newer. The psychic and the organic operator, though
utterly different, would also reflect a certain likeness to the intellectual
operator. Biological desire would move organisms through a series of
organic stages, psychic desires through a series of psychic stages.

Formulating and systematizing a conceptual system is the work of the intellectual integrator. The emergence of a further unresolved question transforms it into the operator of an intellectual development.[40] Intellectual development for Lonergan at times seems to have greater implications for the universe as a whole than for the human person: 'Hence, the higher system of intellectual development is primarily the higher integration, not of the man in whom the development occurs, but of the universe that he inspects.'[41] This tends to play down the implications of intellectual desire as an operator of intellectual development and as a principle of the unity of the human person.

In a letter to Fred Crowe dated 5 May 1954, Lonergan wrote about his discovery of H.S. Sullivan's *The Interpersonal Theory of Psychiatry*,[42] which found mention in the final typescript. For Sullivan human development divides into the heuristic stages of infancy, childhood, the juvenile era, preadolescence, early adolescence, late adolescence, and adulthood or maturity. Unlike Erikson's, his concern as a psychiatrist is with explaining serious mental disorders and disturbed development. He is interested in explaining the manner in which anxiety in a mother is communicated to the infant. This can become the basis of an explanation of certain features of the later performance of the person. Events or circumstance in later life, a hint or something more can lead to the arousal of what he calls 'uncanny emotion,' of which the awe experienced on a first visit to the Grand Canyon would be an example. Among the genus of uncanny emotions he includes dread, horror, and loathing.

In his letter Lonergan speculates that the operator of development might be found in anxiety, uncanny emotion, awe, dread, horror, and loathing. As the pure desire to know can manage intellectual development through its stages, so anxiety through its social encounters can manage the emotions through their developmental stages. Through it, Sullivan, who threw out the 'Freudian myth of instincts, libido, death instinct,' was able to combine the psychoneuroses, schizophrenia, and paranoia in a single theory. The emphasis on abnormal psychic states is clear. The letter raises many questions, but does put before us the task of drawing on the work of professionals rather than solving metaphysical problems by some form in internal discourse.

Further questions arise.[43] Where do finality and the operator and integrator of a development fit into the metaphysical elements? Does the operator of a development have a role to play in understanding the intelligible unity of a developing being? Unlike a table or a chair, a watch or a computer, clearly the intelligible unity of that being changes as it develops. Would this in turn clarify the meaning of central form, of intelligible unity?

Related is the question, when does a development and its operators and integrators begin and end in a life? Is there one or many operators managing different aspects of organic development? Is there one operator of psychic development, anxiety? Or are there many, including trust, autonomy, shame, needed to explain different aspects of psychic development? Are intellectual developments in common sense, science, and philosophy a seamless garment managed by the same intellectual operator? Or does it weave a series of garments? Or is it a different desire weaving different garments? The questions extend to the unity of the human. How does the organic operator relate to the psychic and the intellectual? How do the operators and integrators on the different levels of development interact? Do they have their core autonomy but within the performance of the higher operators? Clearly, these questions are related to the meaning of the intelligible unity of a human person.

The Developmental Unity of the Human

Out of the affirmation of three levels of development, each involving its own level of operators and integrators, there begins to emerge an image of the human in terms of a developmental unity. If in the plant there is organic development alone, in the animal there is both organic and psychic development. Human development is more complex, involving the organic, psychic, and intellectual. These are not three independent processes, and it becomes Lonergan's task to articulate the heuristic structures that will promote an integrated knowledge of how these three processes interact in the process of human development. It is his suggestion that they are interlocking, 'the intellectual providing a higher integration of the psychic and the psychic providing a higher integration of the organic.'[44] As such, they are parts of the unity of the human being:

> Nor are the pure desire and the sensitive psyche two things, one of
> them 'I' and the other 'It'. They are the unfolding on different
> levels of a single, individual, unity, identity, whole. Both are I and
> neither is merely It. If my intelligence is mine, so also is my sexuality.
> If my reasonableness is mine, so also are my dreams ... The same 'I'
> on different and related levels of operation retains the opposed
> characters.[45]

If, in this, he related the different levels of development in terms of higher integrations, three pages later he draws attention to a fundamental dialectical tension in human development:

> For the self, as perceiving and feeling, as enjoying and suffering, functions as an animal in an environment, as a self-attached and self-interested centre within its own narrow world of stimuli and responses. But the same self, as inquiring and reflecting, as conceiving intelligently and judging reasonably, is carried by its own higher spontaneity to a quite different mode of operation with the opposite attributes of detachment and disinterestedness. It is confronted with a universe of being in which it finds itself, not the centre of reference, but an object co-ordinated with other objects and, with them, subordinated to some destiny to be discovered or invented, approved or disdained, accepted or repudiated.[46]

The relation between a higher integration and the manifold it integrates is not dialectical. Here the tension between organic and psychic development on the one hand and intellectual development on the other is dialectical. Human development cannot be explained simply in terms of genetic method. It inevitably involves a dialectical dimension.

There follows a further context for self-affirmation. A first was the narrow context of chapter 11 on self-affirmation. The second came in chapter 14 after he had added to his foundations in chapters 9–13 the chapters on maths, empirical science, common sense, and things. It clearly acknowledged the polymorphic nature of consciousness and the related dialectical dimension. A third context occurs at the end of chapter 15 on human development. Tacitly, the section on genetic method is inviting the reader to discover that the operations affirmed in self-affirmation are the constants that operate their intellectual development. To Lonergan's cognitional and dialectical self is now added the further dimension of the developmental self.

That intellectual desire is a constant of a development again poses questions about what constitutes the unity of the human person. Is it the operator or something other than the operator? Both here and in the end of the following chapter, which addresses the problem of the unity of a human being, the question of central forms is still left open. For Lonergan central potency, form, and act are constants throughout a development: 'and so development is to be formulated in terms of conjugate potency, form, and act.'[47] This suggests that an intelligible unity is an unchanging numerical entity. But it seems to overlook the fact that, as intelligible, it changes with every development in the individual, as in a symphony or story. Every change in the individual is a part of that intelligible unity. It cannot be understood as such apart from the totality of such changes.

For Lonergan, as for Sullivan, every development involves a starting point and a term. In the human subject there is for him some more or less conscious apprehension of both and of the process involved. If that apprehension is correct, then the unconscious and conscious elements of the development unfold in harmony. If incorrect, they can operate at cross purposes. There results what he terms the 'conditional law of genuineness': 'namely, that if a development is conscious, then its success demands correct apprehension of its starting point, its process, and its goal.'[48] What is interesting about the passage is the acknowledgement of the temporality of the subject. What is problematic is that it seems to suggest that we can understand or predict where finality is trying to take us in our lives as they develop.[49]

The following quote poses a question as to whether the tensions involved in the problem of genuineness introduce an inevitable dialectical element into genetic method:

> So there emerges into consciousness a concrete apprehension of an obviously practicable and proximate ideal self; but along with it there also emerges the tension between limitation in general and transcendence; and it is no vague tension between limitation in general and transcendence in general, but an unwelcome invasion of consciousness by opposed apprehensions of oneself as one concretely is and as one concretely is to be.[50]

The notion of an ideal self obviously raises a number of questions about the self and temporality and about the cognitional and the ethical. Is his theory of human development suggesting that the ideal or proper self resides in some future? Might not the developmental self be the intelligible unity of the totality of its temporal experiences past, present and future?

The emerging acknowledgement of an inevitable interplay between the genetic and dialectical in development leads to a further climax in the book. This finds expression in Lonergan's recognition and differentiation of four distinct and irreducible kinds of questions and related insights: classical, statistical, genetic, and dialectical.

> Accordingly, the anticipation of a constant system to be discovered grounds classical method; the anticipation of an intelligibly related sequence of systems grounds genetic method; the anticipation that data will not conform to system grounds statistical method; and the anticipation that the relations between the successive states of changing system will not be directly intelligible grounds dialectical method ... Accordingly, taken together, the four methods are relevant to any field of data; they do not dictate what data must be; they are able to cope with data no matter what they may prove to be.[51]

This statement implies that methods are really mental expectations and attitudes with which we approach the data of the universe. That data can be anticipated as systematic, coincidental, developmental, or conflicting. There is something of a climax in this statement in that it expresses the destination of his quest to understand different kinds of scientific insights as set forth in his vision statement in the notes on order. It is important to note that dialectic was thought out before genetic method. Because of this, there is a sense in which they are not at this point integrated into a related world view. Creative individuals do not leave everything neat and tidy.

Chapter 16: Metaphysics as Science

In chapter 16 the tone of the analysis changes. In the opening section on distinctions and relations and the metaphysical elements, finality and development are hardly mentioned. In July 1958 Lonergan wrote a letter in reply to a question from a Fr Gerard Smith about relations. Smith was writing a book on metaphysics, subsequently published as *The Philosophy of Being*.[52] In his letter Lonergan disagreed with the Thomistic division of relations into transcendentals and predicamentals. This he considered to be a classification rather than a causal understanding in terms of end, agent, matter, and form: 'Science is not knowledge of things through the ten predicaments but through causes, ... and the cause in every case is the primary relativity of *Insight* or the internal relation of *The Analogous Conception of the Divine Persons*.'[53] He concludes that the problem is neither clear nor simple.

It is not the business of the metaphysician to interfere with the direct work of the physicist, chemist, the biologist, or psychologist. But he or she does have the task of articulating the dynamic cognitional structure that initiates and controls their respective inquiries and the general characteristics of the goal towards which they head.[54] Section 4 of the chapter addresses questions of unity, the unity of the universe and the unity of a particular being, a fruit fly or a human. The section is problematic because, although the questions opened up are profound, it gives the impression that because of time limitations the treatment is hasty.

Hastily Lonergan attempts to relate the question of the unity of the universe to the categories of potency, form, and act. The potential unity is grounded in prime conjugate potency, posing questions about prime central potency. In chapter 5 emergent probability was identified as the form of space and time, of the totality of concrete extensions and durations. Here it is identified not as the form, but rather the actual unity of the universe. Without mention of finality, the form of the unity of the universe is now identified with the successive levels of conjugate forms that set up the fields of physics, chemistry, biology, the psychic, and, in the human being, the intellectual. It is left for us to speculate where Lonergan's desired metaphysics of history would fit into this unity.

There follows a provocative section on the unity of a concrete being whose real focus is on the unity of the human. In this he was inspired, I believe, by Bergson's treatment of the categories of the material and the spiritual in *Creative Evolution*. This posed the question, does the category of the spiritual, which is defined in contrast with the material, make sense? This would have provoked Lonergan into reflecting on the possibility that insight might belong to the category of spiritual; might be somehow quite distinct from the material objects it understands, the laws of gravity or the periodic law of the elements, and so forth. If so, in what sense might the human, constituted by both insights and the laws of gravity, be material or spiritual or a mixture of both? In what sense might the intelligible unity of the human, the central form, be constituted by the spiritual rather than the material?

We talk about matter and materialism, but what precisely do we mean by matter, and how might it be defined? The question challenges us to work out a definition of matter, firstly in relation to form, and secondly in relation to spirit. In Aristotle, Aquinas, and Lonergan matter is defined in relation to form as that which precisely has the capacity to become in-formed. The wood can take on the form of a table or chair, the aggregate of chemical events can take on the form of a cell. For Lonergan, when we understand we grasp a universal apart from its instances, the ideal frequency apart from the non-systematic divergence of actual frequencies. This opens up the possibility of defining matter in relation to spirit:

> But just as spiritual intelligibility is apart from the empirical residue, so material intelligibility is not without it. The universal can be thought but cannot be without the instance; ... ideal frequencies can be formulated but cannot be verified apart from actual frequencies. The empirical residue, then, is at once what spiritual intelligibility excludes and what material intelligibility includes.[55]

It is Lonergan's conclusion that human understanding is neither constituted by or intrinsically conditioned by the empirical residue, that is to say, by matter. Accordingly, in this sense, he designated it spirit.

This, for Lonergan, poses questions about the meaning of the intelligible unity of the human that is termed central form. Is that unity material or spiritual or a combination of both? It is his conclusion that because the spiritual in this technical sense can perform in a manner that transcends the material, the human central form must be spiritual. No doubt the discussion will make latter-day materialists highly uncomfortable. The response must be that in some sense intellectual desire and insight are different from the material entities in our universe. Once they have been identified and affirmed, then the question of those differences is up and can only be avoided by obscurantists.

In the course of composing chapters 15 and 16 there occurred an immense flowering of Lonergan's engagement with some of the questions of a metaphysics of nature, a challenge that could be traced back to his introduction to Kant. In 'Intelligence and Reality' he began his response in terms of isomorphism and heuristic categories. In chapter 4 of *Insight* he engaged in an exercise in working out how two distinct types of insights could be integrated into a world view. In chapter 8, probing the significance of isomorphism, he started to explore how the structure of consciousness contained clues about the structure of the universe. In chapter 15 he opened up surprising questions about potency and limitation, about finality and the operators and integrators of development. Chapter 16 asked about the meaning of matter and spirit.

At this point in his quest, having opened up these different windows on the problem, his questions about the metaphysics of nature begin to fade out. There will, from time to time, be future remarks on emergent probability or finality, little on potency, form, and act. At this juncture, though limited as are all things human, his real work was done on his dream of developing an integrated world view based on the distinct questions and insights of the sciences.[56] His metaphysical legacy is to be discovered in the searching questions and related clues that the present chapter has attempted to capture. As the next four chapters will show, he would now find himself drawn into a new agenda, the agenda of *Method in Theology*.

24

On Mythic and Philosophical Consciousness: Truth and Its Expression and Interpretation

Work on the final four chapters of *Insight* began during the spring of 1953. The last episodes of the last movement in the drama of composition, they are in many ways the expression of an aspiration or dream. Written in haste, they were finished towards the end of July. In them the book ends with a flourish.

Behind their dense prose, creative and challenging questions are taking shape. How does the advance of scientific and philosophical consciousness relate to mythical or what Lonergan would later term 'symbolic' consciousness? Would a fully explanatory account of the universe eliminate all sense of mystery, of the unknown? What is the distinction between truth and myth? How might the philosophical project address the way the mob can surrender its responsibility to the myth makers in the pursuit of the good? Can there be a science of the conflict of interpretations of the texts and truths of cultures? Is there a perspective from which the many distinct philosophies can be correctly interpreted? What is the meaning of freedom, and how does the ethical dimension of the human relate to the cognitional? Is knowledge of the existence of God within the compass of human cognition? How ought human beings, as cognitional and ethical, deal with the problem of evil? The breadth of the questions shows the character and vitality of the mind of the man. Given the time at his disposal, it would be foolish to expect a thorough analysis of the problems.

Although he is still working from his cognitional foundations, there is a certain change in direction. Chapters 14–16 were a natural ending of his philosophical explorations of a post-Kantian metaphysics of nature. In the remaining chapters his interests start to move to the human sciences, ethics, and religion. Containing the seeds of a new beginning, the concluding chapters of *Insight* are rehearsing some of the questions that will shape his later *Method in Theology*, and ought to be read as a link between the two works. Reading the two together shows where his questions in those concluding chapters were trying to go.

Teaching Christology: The Backdrop to the Problem of Interpretation

In the fall/spring semester of 1952/53, just before Lonergan began the composition of chapter 17, John Wickham attended his course on Christology. It was a course Lonergan had studied in Rome with Leeming in 1936, when it had so significantly shaped his stance on realism. He taught it for the first time in the 1948/9 semester in Toronto, following closely the 1930 text by D'Alès, *De Verbo Incarnato*. The need for him to teach it in Toronto during this semester was the reason he now had time to compose the final chapters of *Insight*. Addressing the question put by Christ to his disciples, 'who do men say that I am?' its material was at the heart of Lonergan's religious beliefs. Arguing from the New Testament, the first part of D'Alès' book treated Christ as truly God and truly man. The final thesis of this section on the question of Christ's knowledge and consciousness would come to interest Lonergan. Before Christmas 1952 he composed an eight-page supplement on the consciousness of Christ, a topic that related to his work on consciousness and objectivity in *Insight*. When he transferred to Rome in September 1953 he would enlarge it into a monograph that would be published before *Insight*.

The second part of the book addressed the manner of the hypostatic union of the humanity and divinity in Christ. The third part, not taken up by Lonergan, asked why Christ became man and answered in terms of the human need for redemption. Although he did not know it at the time, Lonergan would soon find himself teaching this course in the Gregorian University, where it would become a major part of his work for years to come. In this teaching assignment in Toronto, aspects of his life after *Insight* were beginning to take shape.

The first section of the course dealt with the New Testament interpretation of Christ as the fulfilment of the Old Testament prophesies. Teaching it for a second time caused Lonergan to start thinking about some of the methodological issues it raised, especially in the light of his recent insights into genetic and dialectical methods. In his critique of dialectical theology in 1947, Lonergan explicitly mentioned Bultmann. His reference on the second page of chapter 17 to the significance of myth in Bultmann's principles of New Testament interpretation links the Christology course to the chapter. In 1926 Bultmann composed his 'The New Approach to the

Synoptic Problem,' which laid down the principles of source, form, and redaction criticism. Redaction criticism is concerned with understanding the way in which a later editor redacted or modified an earlier text because of a later audience. Form criticism is concerned with distinguishing the various literary styles – psalms, prayers, stories, proclamations, and so forth – in the writings of a tradition. Source criticism is concerned with establishing the original text of an author redacted by a later series of authors. It is not unrelated to the functional specialty of research.

During the war years, at a time when Adolf Hitler was one of the most dangerous myth makers of the twentieth century, Bultmann composed his famous 'New Testament and Mythology.' It addressed the task of radically demythologizing the New Testament proclamation, most of which he considered to be myth. Through demythologization it would determine the pure *kerygma*, or core of truth, in the writings. The essay, first published in 1947 and in English translation in 1953, the year Lonergan was writing on myth, soon became the subject of considerable debate and criticism.[1] Central in both of Bultmann's writings were the methodological problems involved in understanding the reinterpretations of an original religious text.

Wickham remembered that at the time of the Christology course there was the sound of much typing coming from Lonergan's room, the audible expression of the final stages of his work of composition. Lonergan came across to him as quite engrossed in that work. He had little wish to engage with students in discussing their questions, tending on the whole to offer them a book instead. But Wickham did find that, unlike some of the other teachers, he was helpful in the exams. Lonergan, he felt, had an agreeable human side that came through to the students. In disputes with academics he could at times show a hostile face.

As well as opening up methodological questions about myth and truth, the course also put before Lonergan's mind the different symbolic interpretations of Christ in the New Testament. These range through Prophet, Son of Man, Son of David, to Son of God. There followed the more technical questions addressed by the early Church councils of the patristic period about the precise status of Christ. Was he a creature or the Son of God? In time answers were formulated in terms of the consubstantiality of the Father and Son. The medieval period inherited these developments. Under Aquinas' persistent questioning a further reinterpretation was worked out whose aim was to arrange the emerging questions in the tradition into a systematic viewpoint. This background of a succession of interpretations and reinterpretations of who Christ is by the authors of the gospels, of the patristic and the medieval texts, each composed for a quite distinctive culture, influenced the authoring of chapter 17. It must have stimulated

Lonergan to begin to think out the relation between genetic and dialectic methods and this process of interpretation.

The question, how do you understand the sequence of genetic and dialectically related interpretations of Christ and Christian truths? would occupy him for years to come. In 1972, the year after he had finished *Method in Theology,* he returned to it in his Harvard seminar on Christology, using R.H. Fuller's *The Foundations of New Testament Christology,* not without difficulty, to present the biblical dimension of the problem.[2]

With this move, quietly, the primary object of understanding in his study changes in chapter 17, the longest in the book, from nature to culture and its related meanings and values. With the exception of myth-making consciousness, which was signalled in 'Intelligence and Reality,' the topics that it treats were the last that Lonergan decided to include in the book. Before chapter 17 was drafted he had decided on chapters on ethics, natural theology, and redemption, but not on truth and interpretation.

Chapter 17: The Dialectic of Mythic and Philosophical Consciousness

Chapter 17 of *Insight,* Robert Doran has remarked, is like the content of a Hegelian sandwich, the opening and closing sentences containing significant references to Hegel. Lonergan begins by acknowledging Hegel's challenge to work out a philosophy of philosophies but, rather than engaging with the historical details of the problem, asks 'whether there exists a single base of operations from which any philosophy can be interpreted correctly.'[3] This leads to a difficult and, in many ways, obscure section entitled 'Metaphysics, Mystery and Myth.' The metaphysics dreamt of by Kant has been shown by Lonergan to be a possibility. Assuming it was to develop through its latency and problematic period and become established, the question arises 'whether mystery and myth are cognate to these earlier stages and whether they vanish in the measure that the earlier stages are transcended.'[4]

A significant related paragraph in 'Intelligence and Reality' provides a context for the opening discussion of the sense of the unknown.[5] The unrestrictedness of the pure desire to know introduces the unknown, in the guise of the infinite, into human life. It makes possible the unleashing of vast human energies in the execution of plans concerned with masterminding the human good in the universe. At the same time, it introduces an element of the terrifying and catastrophic into human desires and loves. Without a grounded self-knowledge, the self can become a self-regarding centre capable of ecstatic devotion to a cause or person, what Heidegger terms the hero. There can follow a dialectic of contempt of liberal bourgeoisie in tension with a materialist ideal fanned by a religious-like fanaticism. The officials of the new order are kept in line by delations and purges. This suggests that Lonergan's thought about the unknown at this point might have been more influenced by a Bolshevist or Marxist rather than a National Socialist historical context.

In chapter 13 of *Insight* a task of metaphysics for Lonergan was the articulation of the integral heuristic structure through whose filling out the unknown proportionate being comes to be known. Section 1.1 of chapter 17 addresses the question of the orientation of the pure and unrestricted human desire to know into the unknown. As we are not a pure intellect, this orientation has to find a psychic or sentient counterpart that intimates, harmoniously, the unplumbed depths of humankind's related feelings, emotions, and sentiments. Such feelings

> become integrated in the flow of psychic events inasmuch as they
> are preceded by distinctive sensible presentations or imaginative
> representations and inasmuch as they issue forth in exclamations
> and bodily movements, in rites and ceremonies, in song and
> speech.[6]

As a result, pragmatically, experience becomes divided into two spheres, the sphere of the familiar, the domestic, the common and the sphere of the strange, the unexplored and unknown. Of note is the fact that being-towards-death and death as a known unknown and the feelings it evokes do not enter into the analysis. The primary field 'of mystery and myth consists in the affect laden images and names that have to do with this second sphere.'[7] Echoing Cassirer, Lonergan distinguishes between the image as image, as symbol, and as sign.[8] The image as image is the sensible object that functions within a psychic context. As symbol, the image is related with the known unknown, as sign it is linked with some interpretation of the significance of the image.

The history of religions shows that interpretations that transform the image into a sign are an enormous and divergent series. In a difficult illustration of this point, there occurs one of the rare mentions of Hitler in Lonergan's writings:

> Moreover, precisely because of its relation to the known unknown,
> the image can be interpreted as a sign in manners that are as numer-
> ous and diverse as human ingenuity and human contrariness. So it
> is that the full range of interpretations includes not only the whole
> gamut of religions but also the opposite phenomena of anti-religious
> feeling and expression, not only anti-religious views but also the

intense humanistic idealism that characterized liberal display of detachment from all religious concern, not only elevated humanism but also the crudely naturalistic nationalism that exploded in Germany under the fascination exerted by a Hitler, not only such social aberrations but also the individual aberrations that led Jung to declare that very commonly psychoneural disorder is connected with problems of a basically 'religious' character.[9]

No attempt is made to enlarge upon this fleeting reference. Lonergan goes on to remark again that there is the familiar and domestic world in which a spade is a spade, and there is also our participation through our pure desire to know in the finality of the universe. Where finality is leading us receives pragmatic, conceptual, naturalistic, humanistic, or religious answers.

In 'Intelligence and Reality' the goal of self-knowledge was not simply self-affirmation. It also included an objective apprehension of the universe, of the self in the universe, and of the role of the self in the universe. Section 1.2 of chapter 17 does not articulate the goal of that project quite so succinctly. It does affirm that there is a long history involved in the genesis of humankind's self-knowledge and a parallel history in the genesis of metaphysics. In order to understand its own genesis, metaphysics has to address the historical phenomena of myths and mysteries.

Mythic Consciousness as Pejorative and Allegorical

Cassirer's *Substance and Function* and *The Problem of Knowledge* had influenced aspects of the composition of chapters 8, 13, and 15. Now volume 2 of his *Philosophy of Symbolic Forms*, entitled *Mythical Thought*, plays a final note of influence on the problem of relating scientific and philosophical with mythic consciousness.[10] Influenced by Kant's emphasis on critique, Cassirer attempted to write a critique of mythical consciousness. It was, as Lonergan later commented, a rationalist-based critique that would give way to a more benign view of myth later in the twentieth century. Comte and Schelling, mentioned at this point by Lonergan, are extensively discussed in the book.

Cassirer's question was concerned with the nature of the relation between modern theoretical or explanatory consciousness and mythical consciousness. Later, when Lonergan was questioned about his view of myth, he recalled Cassirer's illustration of how some people live with a fantastic notion of the world:

Cassirer talks about the tribe that – while they've never seen the villages that the tigers have, and the elephants have – they were quite certain that such superior beings would have enough sense to live in villages too. This construction of reality is something that goes on, that man spends millennia developing ... The process of education is maintaining the gains we've already made. .. you have the mythic consciousness of the primitive ... in the ancient high civilizations, in which the King was the god and the source of order in the universe.[11]

Cassirer concludes his critique with remarks on the religious dimension of the dialectic of mythical consciousness. It poses questions for us about the relation between mythic and symbolic consciousness.

Influenced by what he has read in Cassirer, Lonergan refers to the consciousness of the primitive as mythic. It could be a form of consciousness that lacks self-knowledge and whose view of reality is governed by the counterpositions.[12] What, perhaps, is not sufficiently emphasized is that mythic consciousness can inhabit advanced scientific and even philosophical thought. As Caputo has shown in his *Demythologising Heidegger*, an aura of myth can surround even the great philosophers.[13]

Pejoratively, mythical consciousness can be the consciousness of the myth maker, who could operate in the field of politics, science, or religion, or of the uncritical scientist who constructs a world of tiny unimaginable knobs or a sponge-vortex ether. More recently, there are the scientific myths that we can know the mind of God or myths that reduce the meaning of the human person to the chemical, DNA. There are medical personnel who affirm that DNA is the solution to all the illnesses in the world. The highly sophisticated philosopher or scientist who lacks self-knowledge can be just as much a myth maker as the primitive. There are also the politicians who resort to myths for reasons of power: 'Power in its highest form is power over men, and the successful maker of myths has that power within his reach and grasp.'[14]

The oblique references to Bolshevism in 'Intelligence and Reality' and Hitler in *Insight* show that lurking behind the engagement with myth is also a concern with a philosophy of history. Such a philosophy would have to address the problem of the manner in which the myth makers and magicians hijack the course of history. How mythic consciousness as such relates to what Lonergan had defined as the counterpositions in chapter 14 is a difficult question.[15]

Positively, there is a consciousness that employs an allegorical use of myth. Such would be Plato's use of the story of Gyges and the Ring, which expresses the core problem of the *Republic*. Around the time Lonergan was writing on myth, Tolkien was composing the first part of his *The Lord of the Rings*. To this we can add C.S. Lewis' *Till We Have Faces: A Myth Retold*, a reworking of the story of Psyche and Cupid. In 1949 Joseph Campbell published *The Hero with a Thousand Faces*, which claimed to discern a mono-myth of human journeying in all cultures. At the time of the writing of *Insight*, there was in these writers something of a renaissance in the allegorical sense of 'myth.'

Only later, when he was introduced by Eric O'Connor to the work of Northrop Frye, did Lonergan widen his sense of myth:

> But myth is also used in the sense of a narrative that embodies symbols, like Northrop Frye's *Fables of Identity*. There is a terminological difficulty with the usage in *Insight*, but I believe in the permanent necessity of the symbol for human living. You can't talk to your body without symbols, and you have to live with it.[16]

In what he considers to be the pejorative sense, myth makers are enemies of human truth and the human good. As mythic consciousness is an absence of self-knowledge, so metaphysics is the product of self-knowledge. Echoing the final section of Cassirer, he adds: 'As myth and metaphysics are opposed, so also they are related dialectically.'[17] As in 'Intelligence and Reality,' here the philosophical response to the myth makers is in terms of an effective philosophy of education. That education will have the task of exorcising 'the risk of adventurers climbing to power through sagacious myth-making,' surely a reference to Hitler.[18] Again themes of a projected philosophy of history rumble through the remarks.

From Metaphysics to Mystery Purified of Myth Making

Section 1.6 of chapter 17 articulates the core of the dialectical problem involving metaphysics, mystery, and myth. Mystery, he earlier acknowledged, is a fundamental category in the thought of Marcel. As for Lonergan being is intelligible, so for Marcel it is mysterious. Although in chapter 20 Lonergan twice remarks that the whole world of sense is a mystery that signifies God as we know him, nowhere, to my knowledge, does he refer to being as mysterious.[19] Although Lonergan does not name any of Marcel's works, presumably in mentioning him he has in mind *Mystery of Being, Volume 1: Reflection and Mystery* and *Volume 2: Faith and Reality*, published in English in 1950–1.[20] These contain Marcel's Gifford Lectures given in Aberdeen in 1949 and 1950. In chapter 8 of the first volume, Marcel poses questions about 'my life,' about who I am rather than what I am, questions that were ahead of their time and have profound implications for the project of self-affirmation. It is Marcel's thesis that, as it unfolds before them, a person's life is ungraspable and eludes them. This finds some resonances in Lonergan's later thesis that his philosophy is written from a moving viewpoint about a moving viewpoint. It would be Marcel's thesis that the advance of knowledge will never eliminate the elusiveness and ungraspability of my own future life. The advance of scientific explanation will never eliminate the element of the unknown.

In his own way Lonergan makes a parallel point. At the heart of our detached and disinterested desire to know is an unrestricted potential for openness to being. As knowledge grows, metaphysics engages with the task of articulating, heuristically, the features of the unknown. That development is not of a pure intellect, but of intellect inseparably caught up with and related with the sentient and organic dimension of the human. As our human intellectual potential advances in knowledge, there still remains the notion of the unknown. It follows that no matter how intellectually advanced humankind is in its pursuit of the unknown, it always stands in need of dynamic images that function on the sensitive level as symbols and as signs of that orientation.

> To such images, then, let us give the name of mysteries. For if that is
> an ambiguous name, if to some it recalls Eleusius and Samothrace
> and to others the centuries in which the sayings and deeds of Jesus
> were the object of preaching and of reverent contemplation, still
> that very ambiguity is extremely relevant to our topic.[21]

In Athens around the time of Socrates the Eleusinian mysteries were celebrated by the Archon-King and assistant priests as an official festival. The small mysteries were celebrated towards the end of February in honour of Persephone, the great mysteries around September in honour of Demeter. Regardless of status, any person could become an initiate, men and women, slaves and free, foreigners. A procession along the sacred way was part of the rite of initiation, in which an ear of wheat played a central symbolic role. It is disputed whether the ritual offered the *mystes* some sort of personal survival after death or just a better life.[22] Samothrace was also a centre of the Catabrian mysteries of Greek worship.

In the concluding pages of section 1.6 Lonergan brings into a focus his engagement with metaphysics, mystery, and myth. If metaphysics is based on self-knowledge and a progressive understanding of the relation between one's intellectual desire and its object, mythic consciousness in its pejorative sense is for him an absence of self-knowledge. As metaphysics cannot eliminate the sense of the known unknown, neither can it be integrated into human living without employing 'dynamic images which make sensible to human sensitivity what human intelligence reaches for or grasps.'[23] A permanent dialectical tension is involved in the subsequent problem of integrating the intellectual and the sensitive levels of the human. Lonergan sums up that core dialectic in two points:

(1) that the intellectual activities are either the proper unfolding of the detached and disinterested desire to know or else a distorted unfolding due to the interference of other desire, and

(2) that the sensitive activities, from which intellectual contents emerge and in which they are represented, expressed, and applied, either are involved in the mysteries of the proper unfolding or distort these mysteries into myths.[24]

In order for the self-knowledge and world views of philosophy to direct human living, there is needed dynamic images that communicate to human sensitivity what it is towards which intelligence is reaching. Part of the development is a clarification of the interaction of human intelligence and sensitivity in such development, 'and so [a person's] advance in self-knowledge implies an increasing consciousness and deliberateness and effectiveness in his choice and use of dynamic images, of mottoes and slogans.'[25] The representation of the intellectual strivings on the level of human sensitivity can involve the proper unfolding of the mysteries or can distort them into myths. Hand in hand with advanced self-knowledge and science will be a more conscious and controlled use of mystery purified of myth. This is an analysis that leaves us with questions about Lonergan's particular use of the terms 'known unknown' and 'mysteries.'

Lonergan is critical of the naive hope that through the advancement of knowledge progress, devoid of decline, will result. It is an attitude that results in a fundamental disillusionment, the discovery that

the advance of human knowledge is ambivalent, that it places in man's hands stupendous power without necessarily adding proportionate wisdom and virtue, that the fact of advance and the evidence of power are not guarantees of truth, that myth is the permanent alternative to mystery and mystery is what his hubris rejected.[26]

Similar themes, including a link between mystery and symbol, are to be found in Eliade's *Images and Symbols* (1952) and *Traité d'histoire des religions* (1948, 1953), to which Lonergan refers. In the preface to the former, Eliade makes clear that although the course of human development may cause symbols to change or their new masks to be uncovered, they will never disappear from the psychic dimension of the spiritual life of man. In this he differs from Levy-Bruhl's tendency to think of the primitive imagination as something that would eventually be overcome. A mythological rubbish heap lives in ill-controlled zones of human life, offering a possible starting point for spiritual renewal. This rubbish heap does not belong only to a superstitious past that lives on, so to speak, in children and poets. It has not been overcome by modern people with their efforts to separate serious things from dreams and dream life. Disdaining mythologies will not prevent modern man from feeding on discarded myths and degraded images. The Second World War, the most terrible historical crisis of the twentieth century, demonstrated that the rooting out of the mythical is an illusion.[27]

In 'An Interview with Fr. Bernard Lonergan, S.J.' Lonergan drew attention to a terminological difficulty with his use of the word 'myth' in *Insight*.[28] 'Mystery' and 'myth' could both be included in the meaning of the word 'symbol.' In contrast, Northrop Frye's *Fables of Identity* uses 'myth' in the sense of a narrative that incorporates symbols. In his reflections in '*Insight* Revisited' Lonergan remarks that in chapter 17 'my use of the word, "myth" is out of line with current usage. My contrast of mystery and myth was between symbolic expression of positions and counterpositions.'[29]

In one of his later essays, 'Reality, Myth, Symbol,' Lonergan recalled that Plato composed myths. In a late letter Aristotle confessed that as he grew older he became less a philosopher, less a friend of wisdom and more a friend of myths. It is innate in us as humans to desire to understand the world, but there is much that is obscure about it. In the face of such obscurity, we form hunches that find their expression in stories:

> Stories, as is being currently affirmed, are existential: there are true stories that reveal the life that we are really leading, and there are cover stories that make out our lives to be somewhat better than they are in reality. So stories today and myths of yesterday suffer from a basic ambiguity. They can bring to light what is truly human. But they can also propagate an apparently naive view of human aspiration and human destiny ... So we are led from myth to symbols, for there, it would seem, lie the roots of the hunches that myths delineate.[30]

The passage, like that in *Second Collection* on myth, clearly shows that symbols rather than myth or narratives are his passion.

In this late essay he also acknowledges a lacuna in his work in relation to the symbolic and the feeling dimension. He had articulated an intellectual, moral, and religious conversion. Bob Doran convinced him that he needed a psychic conversion, which occurs within ourselves when we uncover the workings of our own psyches. At this point Lonergan drew attention to Progoff's distinction between dynatypes and cognitypes. The dynatypes ground our basic lifestyles and are for me rooted in our core desires. The cognitypes are the symbols that release the vital energies contained in our dynatypes.[31] With the rider that we need to think in terms of social as well as personal cognitypes, it is a fitting reflection, late in Lonergan's life, on the role of the symbolic in a human life.

On Truth and Its Linguistic Expression

At the centre of the dialectic of the pejorative sense of myth and metaphysics is the question of truth. Strangely, the word 'truth' has hardly appeared up to this point in the text of *Insight*. In chapter 9 on the notion of judgment he stated, fleetingly, that it is on the level of judgment that questions about truth and falsity arise. Despite this rare use of the word, Lonergan boldly asserts that it has been his concern all along, and now he sets out to gather together different points made in different chapters. Under the criterion of truth he refers obliquely to absolute objectivity, the publicity of knowledge, and the conditions of the virtually unconditioned being independent of the judging subject. The remote criterion is the proper unfolding of the pure desire to know. In different inquiries the terms 'infallibility,' 'certitude,' 'certainty,' 'probability,' 'ideal,' and 'actual frequency' are involved. These are different qualities of judgments.

Truth was implicitly defined by Lonergan in his definition of being. Being is what is known by the totality of reasonable or true affirmations. Knowing is true by its relation to being, and truth is a relation of knowing to being. The chapter on objectivity was concerned precisely with the nature of the right relation of knowing with being. When knowing becomes properly self-transcending, it is true. Within this context meaning can be given to 'truth as the conformity or correspondence of the subject's affirmations and negations to what is and is not.'[32] The remarks are easily read and seem obvious. What can be overlooked is the sense of the startling strangeness of the pure desire to know and its relation to its object in the definition. It puts Lonergan's theory of truth outside the horizon of the philosophy of Kant and most subsequent propositional theories of truth. It is only within the context and framework of the performance of the pure desire to know that the truth or falsity of propositions makes sense.[33] Without engaging with that ungraspable desire in us and how it generates propositions in its unfolding, the definition of truth seems trite.

Typically brief notes follow on infallibility, certitude, certainty, probability, ideal and actual frequency as attributes of judgment. An ontological dimension to truth is identified because what is, being, the object of knowledge, is intelligible. These preface the chapter's final section on the relation between cognitional activities and linguistic expression. Again

Cassirer's *Philosophy of Symbolic Forms* hovers. Lonergan's prose is dense, but if we want to see where he is trying to go we should turn to the section on early language in chapter 3, 'Meaning,' in *Method in Theology*. Also significant is the concluding section of the chapter entitled 'Interpretation' in that work, where a tribute is paid to Cassirer and Snell. Lonergan concludes the latter chapter with remarks on the possibilities of coupling transcendental method with the work of exegetes.

If there is something of a new departure at this point in his thought, it has to do with the relation between truth and its linguistic expression. In his analysis of acts of meaning in the chapter on the notion of being, Lonergan did not attach much significance to the instrumental nature of language: 'Ordinary instrumental acts, such as spoken or written words or symbols, offer no special interest.'[34] Language is at this point instrumental in cognition rather than constitutive. This overlooks the fact that it is in communication that cognition is properly completed and that language as written and spoken is constitutive of communication.

Although in chapter 17 of *Insight* Lonergan continues to distinguish the cognitional from the linguistic, he is more accommodating of their interpenetration:

> The interpenetration of knowledge and expression implies solidarity, almost a fusion, of the development of knowledge and the development of language. Words are sensible: they support and heighten the resonance of human intersubjectivity; the mere presence of another releases in the dynamism of sensitive consciousness a modification of the flow of feelings and emotions, image and memories, attitudes and sentiments; but words possess their own retinues of associated representations and affects, and so the addition of speech to presence brings about a specialized, directed modification of intersubjective reaction and response. Still, beyond the psychology of words, there is their meaning. They belong together in typical patterns and learning a language is a matter, first, of grasping such patterns and, secondly, of gradually allowing the insights, by which the patterns are grasped, to be shortcircuited by a sensitive routine that permits the attention of intelligence to concentrate on higher-level controls.[35]

Insights are moments in the process of cognition, which is not completed until the thoughts that express them find linguistic expression. That expression can happen just as much in solitude as in community. New and original insights give birth to new and original uses of language. Still, if expression is an integral element in cognition, it is also a flexible or fluid one. Lonergan is now ready to engage with the core problem, 'namely, the relation between truth and expression.'[36]

A central problem Lonergan now addresses is that of how a tradition, be it religious or philosophical or more generally cultural, originally expresses itself, interprets and subsequently re-expresses its interpretation and the truths it accumulates in the tradition as time goes by. An illustration here would be a teacher introducing a class to a Socratic dialogue concerned with a question such as, what is virtue and can it be taught? There are the foundational social experiences, such as that of a virtuous parent trying to pass on his or her virtue to a wild child. The questions that those original experiences provoked can become a constitutive element in the tradition. There are the insights that caused the original author to arrive at a certain understanding of an original problem and wish to communicate them in a certain literary form. One could go back to the Greek dramatists and apply the same consideration to their analysis of social justice, to Plato's *Republic* on the good, and to Aristotle's psychology in the *De Anima*. Similar considerations apply to the encounter with God that is expressed in the Christian Gospels or in the Koran. The classics of a tradition express certain key human experiences and the questions and insights that surround them.

The Greek and Christian authors express their understanding for their contemporaries. Socrates has certain insights into the problem of defining a virtue, Aristotle into the psychological faculties. Those insights are expressed in their texts, which are written for their contemporaries. To them we could apply Lonergan's remarks:

> an expression is a verbal flow governed by a practical insight (F) that depends on a principal insight (A) to be communicated, upon a grasp (B) of the anticipated audience's habitual intellectual development (C), and upon a grasp (D) of the deficiencies in insight (E) that have to be overcome if the insight (A) is to be communicated.[37]

What is significant here is how he is now extending the analysis of insight from the natural sciences to its role in forming linguistic expression and related communication. But because illustrations are thin on the ground, it is difficult to get a grip on that role.

Once the experience and related questions and insights are articulated in a text, that text in turn becomes an object of analysis and of interpretation. There could be deficiencies in the wonder of those addressed, in that their wonder, their capacity to question, might need to be awakened. And so in history there emerges a historical sequence of commentaries on the *Republic*, the *De Anima*, the *Metaphysics*, the Gospels. But those later commentators do not live in ancient Greece or Palestine. They could be patristic, medieval, or modern. They could also be literary or technologically minded. They could be addressing an audience for whom certain aspects of Greek or Hebrew culture are extremely remote and strange. Some elements of the text will not be interesting or significant and will be neglected. Others will be deemed highly significant and will resonate with readers. What is found to be very significant will vary greatly from generation to generation of interpreters.

The teacher as an interpreter and communicator has, for Lonergan, to assess the state of intellectual development of pupils and bring it into play in his or her communication. To the teacher we can apply Lonergan's further remarks:

> By an interpretation will be meant a second expression addressed to a different audience. Hence, since it is an expression, it will be guided by a practical insight (F') that depends on the principal insight (A') to be communicated, upon a grasp (B') of the anticipated audience's habitual intellectual development (C'), and upon a grasp (D') of the deficiencies in insight (E') that have to be overcome if the principal insight (A') is to be communicated.[38]

As stated, this seems to presuppose a correct understanding of the original author. Unless we are simply to repeat the original expression, the expression of a truth is relative to a particular audience. An image here would be Sorabji's effort to articulate all the commentaries on Aristotle's *Metaphysics* in history. There we have an image of a series of interpretations addressing quite different audiences than did the original text. So we do not get a single interpretation of a text, but an emerging historical series. That series could be random or genetically related. It would be random if the authors did not know and did not consult any of the earlier interpretations. It would be genetic if they did so consult and if their interpretation developed some points in the earlier interpretations.

For Lonergan a reflective interpretation arises when we begin self-consciously to appreciate the real differences in context between a series of interpretations of an initial truth and its expression. A first illustration here might be ancient (Aristotle and Cicero) and modern (Burnet, Cushman, and Voegelin) readings and interpretations of Plato's *Republic*. A second illustration would be interpretations of who Christ is in the Gospels and early Christian tradition.[39] In the Gospels there is offered an interpretation in terms of a series of symbolic expressions: Son of Man, Son of David, Son of God. The early tradition in the Council of Chalcedon interprets Christ as the one who is *homoousios*, of one substance with the Father. This technical expression is not found in the Gospels and poses a profound question about the continuity of truth in the sequence of interpretations.

Given that all specific interpretations are relative to a particular audience, if interpretation is to become a science

> then it has to discover some method of conceiving and determining the habitual development of all audiences and it has to invent some technique by which its expression escapes relativity to particular and incidental audiences.[40]

A science of interpretation must be able to rise above the almost accidental relativity of an interpretation to a particular audience. As he makes clear in the 'Epilogue,' Lonergan is here articulating a core element of the problem of method in theology as he understands it at this point in his life. For a theology has to study the series of interpretations of the basic texts of a religion and add its own interpretation of them for its own audience and culture. At this point Lonergan seems to assume that interpretation can be scientific in a manner that parallels the natural sciences. Not all would agree.

Interpreters are never pure intellects who always infallibly understand the meaning of the original text. They are flesh-and-blood, historically situated human beings who, like all persons of common sense, suffer from bias. Bias adds to the complexity of the relativity of an interpretation to a particular audience. Lonergan compares contemporary common sense with historical sense. Our contemporary accumulation of common sense enables us to anticipate how others in our worlds would speak or act in typical situations. The scholar, by long learning about the documents and life of another age and insights into those documents, develops a historical sense. By that sense he or she can anticipate how men and women of the time would act in certain kinds of situations:

> However, just as our common sense is open to individual, group, and general bias, so also is historical sense. Moreover, just as our common sense cannot analyze itself or criticize itself or arrive at an abstract formulation of its central nucleus, so also the historical sense is limited in a similar fashion; both are far more likely to be correct in pronouncing verdicts than in assigning exact and convincing reasons for them. But if interpretation is to be scientific, then the grounds for the interpretation have to be assignable; if interpretation is to be scientific, then there will not be a range of different interpretations due to the individual, group, and general bias of the historical sense of different experts; if interpretation is to be scien-

tific, then it has to discover some method of conceiving and determining the habitual development of all audiences and it has to
invent some technique by which its expression escapes relativity to
particular and incidental audiences.[41]

It follows that the members within a sequence of interpretations can be
both genetically and dialectically related. The dialectical relations involved
contribute to the schisms and conflicts and even wars that are so evident in
the histories of the various cultural traditions. In this Lonergan is moving
towards a more general view of dialectic than the dialectic of philosophy in
chapter 14. Genetic and dialectic dimensions are an essential element in
questions of interpretation. Resolving those questions will involve genetic
and dialectic methods.

The introduction of genetically and dialectically related interpretations
opens up for him the question of a science of interpretation, with all the
technical meaning that that entails. For many, interpretation is more of an
art than a science. A hallmark of scientific explanation for Lonergan is that
it rises, in its viewpoint, beyond a relativity to a particular individual or
group. A scientific interpretation would, by implication, have to transcend
its relativity to a particular interpreter and audience with their limited
viewpoint and biases. It is in this context that Lonergan introduces the
notion of a universal viewpoint: 'By a universal viewpoint will be meant a
potential totality of genetically and dialectically ordered viewpoints.'[42] By
'viewpoint' he does not mean a visual perspective on a landscape, but an
intellectual perspective based on sets of questions and insights into a
related set of truths. The significance of the same truth will be different for
every different interpreter of that truth.

Imaginative illustrations are needed of the sort of thing that a universal
viewpoint might be in order to determine whether it makes any sense at all.
First of all, there is the notion of an ordered set of viewpoints. Every
biography of the same subject, Luther or Darwin or Freud, is different.
There follows the possibility of a genetic sequence of biographies emerging
in history of one and the same subject. As access to sources grows, later
biographers will know more about a particular subject than their predecessors. They might also know more about the kind of insights involved in
biographical truth than their predecessors. In this sense we can envisage a
genetic sequence of viewpoints on the truth of a particular life. Some
subjects, such as Luther, will stand in a dialectical relationship with potential biographers from different religious traditions. There follows the possibility of a genetic and dialectically ordered series of biographies concerned
with the truth of a life.

In this way the writing and rewriting of biographies of Luther, Freud, and

Darwin is an ongoing process. But after six or seven biographies of an author have been written, they begin to reveal just as much about the viewpoint and values of the biographers and their audiences as about their subject, about the interpreter as well as the interpreted. Following this line, Lonergan suggests that the universal viewpoint has as much to do with the interpreter's capacity to grasp meanings as with the meanings grasped. Involved is a new variation in Kant's Copernican revolution concerning the relation between the human mind and its objects in the world. This particular variation applies specifically to the task of interpretation:

> There are the external sources of historical interpretation and, in the main, they consist in spatially ordered marks on paper or parchment, papyrus or stone. But there are also sources of interpretation immanent in the historiographer himself, in his ability to distinguish and recombine elements in his own experience, in his ability to work backwards from contemporary to earlier accumulations of insights in human development, in his ability to envisage the protean possibilities of the notion of being, the core of all meaning, which varies in content with the experience, the insights and the judgments, and the habitual orientation of each individual.[43]

As through a glass darkly, we get a glimpse here of the outline of a response to Hegel's challenge at the opening of the chapter to develop a philosophy of philosophies.

A final element in chapter 17 has to do with the implications of positions and counterpositions on knowing, objectivity, and being in the realm of interpretation. The goal of interpretation is to understand the universe of being, not to construct a cinema-like fantasy of what was done. In interpretation reality becomes known and present in true judgments.[44] At its end the chapter leaves us with a sense of the challenging profundity of the issues raised matched by a frustration at the abstractness of their treatment.

25

The Cognitional and the Ethical

But good will is never better than the intelligence and reasonableness that it implements.[1]

Up to this point, Lonergan's intellectual probings have disclosed a universe of species of things emerging in accordance with the principle of finality and continuing in accordance with emergent probability. They reveal a cognitional subject who develops organically, psychically, and intellectually but who also has to struggle with the burden and blindness of bias in the common-sense world as well as with the counterpositions in philosophy. Culturally, that subject lives in a world of symbols, art works and texts, and experiences a conflict of interpretations and reinterpretations.

In chapter 18, entitled 'The Possibility of Ethics,' Lonergan enlarges his interests into some searching questions about the relation between the ethical and the cognitional. How do human beings as ethical agents participate in the finality and emergent probability of the universe? How is willing the good limited by or dependent on cognition? How does it transcend cognition? How does the method of ethics relate to that of metaphysics? Are there ethical equivalents of the cognitional, epistemological, and metaphysical questions, of the Kantian Copernican revolution, of the theorem of isomorphism, and of positions and counterpositions? Does bias enter into ethical choices? Despite the fact that in 1965 he will modify his understanding of the relation between the cognitional and the ethical, the questions posed in this chapter will not lose their validity.[2] They show us the state of the question for him at this point in his life. Is it possible to connect and integrate an ethics with all that has gone before?

Addressing the notion of the good, the opening section of the chapter made its first appearance as section 5 of an early version of chapter 16, 'Metaphysics as Science.' This metaphysical context of its genesis explains the emphasis on the ontology of the good and on the parallels between metaphysics and ethics.[3] Later, chapter 18 became a separate chapter entitled 'Elements of Ethics' before it found its final title, 'The Possibility of Ethics.' Against scientific determinism and reductionism he will argue for the possibility of ethics within his foundations. If the possibility is established, the details will be left to others to work out. Significant in that narrowing down is a neglect of the dialectical partner of the human good, evil, the term being rarely mentioned in the chapter.[4] Only in his lectures on topics in education and in an unpublished preface to his *Christology* in 1964 will Lonergan begin to address that further question. In those later works he will explore the notions of particular evils, evils of disorder, and cultural evils, the evil counterparts to the elements of the good. He has to deal with one issue at a time.

In the second part of chapter 16, written later, Lonergan explores the peculiar contingency involved in the freedom of the will. In placing it beyond the cognitional, he begins to sound the autonomy of the ethical, and the ethical dimension of the self or subject starts to come into view. A third and final part opens up the problem of ethical development, which includes the need for us to be liberated from the unfreedoms of our will. That liberation, he argues, cannot come from within the cognitional or ethical spheres of experience. Reminiscent of Kierkegaard, Lonergan will suggest that we project ourselves on the ethical level but come to realize ourselves on the religious. What is being offered is a hasty sketch. Its significance for our understanding of Lonergan as an author lies in its future implications. It is of the form of a beginning rather than an ending. Ethics and religion are topics that will engage him on the further journey through his lectures on topics in education to *Method in Theology*.

The Ontology of the Good

Ethical theory and its related notion of the human good are, in certain respects, concerned with understanding human persons as ethical agents. Through that direct mode agency persons participate, individually and collaboratively, through their desires, insights, and decisions in the advancement or decline of the processes and order in the universe. The discoveries of hydrogen fusion and of DNA have faced us with all kinds of ethical questions about their use in the world. Is the human good that, ethically, we pursue unrelated to the more general order in the universe disclosed by scientific and metaphysical analysis? Are there ethical parallels of the project of the self-affirmation of the knower? How does ethical development relate to organic, psychic, and intellectual development? It is questions such as these, rather than the details of particular moral dilemmas or imaginative explorations of particular decisions, with which the first section of the chapter is concerned.

Lonergan's illustrative basis of particular goods, the good of order and values in response to his analysis of deliberation and decision, is minimalist. That is not where his question is. In order to image out the issues we need to ask ourselves, How does an educational, agricultural, technological, economic, legal, or political system and related communities emerge in world history, develop, sustain itself, and struggle with its survival? How do human groups choose, realize, and sustain in the world such instances of the human good? In need of greater emphasis is the place of life choices or even choices of ethical foundations or of the good and valuable self in the account of the good.

An educational system is not something that we find in the world like mountains, seas, forests, and primates. It is something that comes into being through our response to the practical problem of educating an up-and-coming generation of human beings to the level of the culture in which they are to participate. The overall problem breaks down into problems about needed particular skills or goods to be communicated through the education system, be they in numeracy or literacy. Those needs will not be once off, but recurring in successive years as each new class takes the place of its predecessor. That recurrence is not written in stone but governed by probabilities of survival. The system recognizes that those skills are not static but developing. Accordingly, as well as the need to develop skills at a certain level, there also arises a need for a genetic sequence of educational inputs to address changing levels of skills, the need for a good of order. Finally, questions arise about values, about tradition and innovation. How is an educational system to be structured in relation to the sciences, technology, and the humanities? Is the school or system to be secular, denominational or interdenominational, nationalist or cosmopolitan in its outlook? It is through practical problem solving and related practical insights and reflection that we engage ethically with these issues.

Parallel questions can be addressed to agricultural, economic, and legal systems. Economies and legal systems are not entities that we find by accident in our world. Again, it is through our deliberations and decisions that they come to exist. This poses for Lonergan a question about the relation between being and the good. Is the same system of intelligible order that is discovered through inquiry into the pre-human universe to be found in its prolongation through our ethical participation and projects? Lonergan argues that this is the case:

> Again, the intelligible orders that are invented, implemented,
> adjusted and improved by men, are but further exploitations of
> prehuman, intelligible orders; moreover, they fall within the univer-
> sal order of generalized emergent probability, both as consequents
> of its fertility, and as ruled by its more inclusive sweep.[5]

What Lonergan is affirming at this point is that the good is identical with
the intelligibility of being. Although they are the fruit of human choices,
the intelligibility of educational, agricultural, economic, and political systems is an integral element of the intelligibility of the universe. Their
emergence and survival will, for instance, exhibit the features of finality and
emergent probability.

This invites us to pose the question, to what extent is the human good as
much an object of intellectual desire and understanding as well as of
human choice? Only by excluding questions for intelligence can the he-
donist claim that the good and its opposite, evil, are to be settled on the
level of experience as such.[6] It seems that the ways in which we understand
the human good are the same as the ways in which we understand the
overall intelligibility of the universe. Does this mean that the good is good
because of its intelligibility, that the intelligible and the good are identical?
The critic might object that this rules out the possibility of insights into evil
orders in the universe. Despite its absurdity, there was an intelligibility
involved in the Holocaust. It involved planning and ordering, insights into
strategies and structures. What is the difference between that kind of
intelligibility and the intelligibility of a hospital or a school? In one the
finality was promoting the good, in the other evil.

A final point has to do with community. Being, which is the objective of
the pure desire to know, is not known by any individual. Rather, it is the
objective of the collaborative striving of the community of knowers. Similarly, the human good is not realized by or for a single individual; it is
realized by a community and for a community.

Willing the Good

As through human knowing we come to know what exists, so through
human willing we will the good. Human goods such as a career choice or an
educational or political system are not realized by the judgments of cognition, but by willing them. As willing is not an element in cognitional
structure, the further question about the nature of their relation begins to
appear. Echoing his thought in the 1930s on the interdependence of the
intellect and will, Lonergan now goes on to define the will:

> Will, then, is the intellectual or spiritual appetite. As capacity for
> sensitive hunger stands to sensible food, so will stands to objects
> presented by intellect.[7]

A number of points arise. Firstly, the intellect and will are not separate
faculties that operate in isolation from each other. They are interrelated
and interdependent. Enlargements in the field of understanding result in
an enlarged field of ethical choice. Secondly, at this point the will for him
has the character of an appetite or desire. Thirdly, questions about the
good and the evil will and the goodness of the objects presented to the will
by the intellect at this point are bracketed. The goodness of the intellect
and will and of the intelligibility of being is assumed. It is one thing, for
instance, to choose to build a bridge across a river in a situation of agreement. It is another to decide to declare war or to execute, violently if
necessary, a robbery.

Lonergan's assertion of the interdependence of intellect and will has to
be read in the context of the fact that most of his analysis of insight had to
do with formal causes. In ethical action the intellect becomes an element in
the efficient causality of the action. This suggests that in order to clarify the
relation between intellect and will, further analysis of insight in its efficient
mode is necessary. How insights into correlations, the statistics of events,
intelligible unities, emergent probability, and finality open up the field of
possible decisions needs to be explored.

There follows Lonergan's basic ethical precept at this point in his explorations: to act morally is to act in accordance with reason. Cognitionally, a
judgment is reasonable or rational if it is moved by relevant and significant
evidence. Ethically, a decision is rational if it is moved by the demand for
consistency between what one understands and what one does:

> So it is that the empirically, intelligently, rationally conscious subject
> of self-affirmation becomes a morally self-conscious subject. Man is
> not only a knower but also a doer; the same intelligent and rational
> consciousness grounds the doing as well as the knowing; and from
> that identity of consciousness there springs inevitably an exigence
> for self-consistency in knowing and doing.[8]

The knowing that Lonergan is talking about is not just knowledge of the
proposed course of action, but also knowledge of the proposed course of
action as good or bad, right or wrong. This requires the rider of right
reason; otherwise it does not make sense. In order to make this clear, there
is a need to introduce into the analysis judgments of value. It comes as a

surprise to those familiar with the later Lonergan that what he refers to in *Method* as judgments of value that affirm or deny that some *X* is truly or only apparently good are not treated in *Insight*.[9] It was a point that he had not yet worked out. This limitation does not necessarily invalidate the ethical precept; rather, it invites its enlargement to accommodate judgments of value.

There will be those who do not want to know this precept and its implications. There will be those who rationalize their knowing so that it becomes consistent with their doing. There will be those who simply renounce the moral imperative. For different reasons Lonergan is in agreement with Kant that there is a moral imperative, a meaning to the word 'ought.'

There follows on page 624 (600) one of the rare mentions in the book of the word 'conscience.' Before he could publish his *Traumdetung*, Freud had to overcome his emotions and sentiments and follow an intelligent and reasonable course of action. What is clear is that at this point ethical action for Lonergan is to be directed by understanding and reason rather than, in any sense, feelings or emotions. The contrast with *Method in Theology* is stark: 'Intermediate between judgments of fact and judgments in value lie apprehensions of value. Such apprehensions are given of feelings.'[10] Voegelin identifies a similar shift in the transition from Plato's *Republic* to the *Laws*.[11] Feelings have an essential role to play in decision making and in willing the good.

The human will for Lonergan is the spiritual appetite that finds its satisfaction, not directly in food and drink or beauty, but in objects of choice presented by intellect. Such objects could be particular goods, a good of order and values. This entails an ordering of particular goods and orders of particular good in some evaluative scheme. Involved is the problem of ethical responsibility. At this point (as contrasted with his later view in *Method*), being ethically responsible means for Lonergan choosing in such a manner that one's choices are consistent with one's knowing.

Individuals make ethical choices and then give reasons for making them and for acting as they act. And since the case of Eichman, who reasoned that his evil actions were simply an acting out of the Kantian imperative to do one's duty, it must be obvious that the rationalization of one's choices is one of the central dilemmas of ethics. The analysis at this point needs to be enlarged to include the possibility of good and evil orientations within the intellect and will.

Value is the good as a possible object of choice of rational, moral self-consciousness. As objects of desire fall under schemes of recurrence to give rise to the good of order, the good of order is a possible object of rational choice. By 'rational choice' Lonergan means willing that is consistent with what one knows. Despite the fact that values may be true or false rather than good or bad, he had not at this point worked out the role of the judgment of value in the ethical process. False values are the result of a flight from the moral precept; true values are the object of rational choice. Values as choices are terminal, but originating in that their implementation involves changes in our orientation in the universe.

As surprising as the absence of the phrase 'judgments of value' in his analysis of the ethical process is the definition of the notion of value in relation to choice and willing. It is not being defined in relation to the heart's desire, the transcendental notion that we find in *Method in Theology*. That had not yet been worked out. In the early 1960s Lonergan remarked to Fred Lawrence, Conn O'Donovan, and others that what was holding up his work on *Method in Theology* at the time was the problem of the notion of value. These sections in *Insight* were a stage on the way to the fuller position in *Method*.

Ethical Finality, Freedom, and Consciousness

The dynamic structure that is involved in the enlargement from knowing to doing is for Lonergan the basis of an ethics through which the human person participates in the finality of the universe:

> Just as the heuristic structure of our knowing couples with the gener-
> alized emergent probability of the proportionate universe, to reveal
> an upwardly directed dynamism of finality towards ever fuller being,
> so the obligatory structure of our rational self-consciousness
> (1) finds its materials and its basis in the products of universal
>   finality,
> (2) is itself finality on the level of intelligent and rational conscious-
>   ness, and
> (3) is finality confronted with the alternative of choosing either
>   development and progress or decline and extinction.[12]

It is through our ethical agency that as human beings we participate at the deepest human level in the finality of the universe.

Acknowledging the ethical dimension of consciousness leads to the further question, under what circumstances do the decisions we make emerge freely in our lives? Negatively, they are not caused by activities on the level of the sensitive psyche or the lower levels of biology, chemistry, or physics. In two places Lonergan turns to his canon of statistical residues to suggest such a negative argument.[13] The occurrence of any event, Z, in space and time requires a diverging series of scattered antecedents, $P, Q, R, ...$ The existence of such statistical residues is the condition of possibility of higher sciences. He suggests that it is not impossible to make 'accurate predictions of the distant future when schemes of recurrence exist and their survival is supposed.'[14] The significance of statistical residues for him is not that it implies freedom, but that it opens up the possibility of distinct and autonomous sciences. This means that in certain respects the higher will not be determined by the lower.

Positively, there are antecedents on the level of intelligence and reflection. There is the underlying sensible flow, what he calls 'coincidental manifolds of sensible presentations,' which may involve a dimension of affective and aggressive feelings. A sensitive psychologist could discern various laws at work in the process, understand the operators of sensible and psychic development, and infer consequent schemes of recurrence. The implication is that our activities on the sensitive level, including our feelings, are in this sense not free but determined. What does not seem to be envisaged is that there might be a quality of feelings whose appropriate place was on the different levels, feelings associated with the beauty of nature, with the excitement of problem solving, the joy of insight, the anxiety of judgment and decision making. If acts of willing can be free, other human acts are not. Being in prison is a state of unfreedom, which poses the question, is freedom something we attribute only to the human act of willing?

Lonergan accordingly narrows down the study of freedom to the human intellect and will:

> In this process there is to be discerned the emergence of the elements of higher integration. For the higher integration effected on the level of human living consists of sets of courses of action, and these actions emerge inasmuch as they are understood by intelligent consciousness.[15]

The description of the practical insights of the ethical agent is again minimal. Lonergan does not address questions about a personal vocation, about career choices, or about deciding how to deal with biases. In such cases there might be little intellectual clarity about the future course of action and its consequences. The decision might involve a leap of faith. Although he talks about the practical questions, he does not at this stage associate it with an ethical desire that parallels the pure desire of cognition. Ethical insights, just like the insights of the empirical sciences and common sense, are a dime a dozen. Most of them are vain ideas, bad life or business proposals, whose futility only comes to light in the subsequent collapse of the related venture. At this level no question about correctness arises. What would we mean by a correct ethical insight? How do correct and incorrect in the ethical process relate to true and false, good and bad, right and wrong?

As the preliminary to the cognitional judgment is reflection on the relevant evidence, so prior to the decision there is practical reflection on the proposed course of action and on the motives of the actor. Will the course of action be satisfying, agreeable or disagreeable, result in an improvement of the situation in the world? Significant is Lonergan's observation:

> Thirdly, the reflection has no internal term, no capacity of its own to come to an end ... Fourthly, because the reflection has no internal term it can expand more or less indefinitely.[16]

It is the decision, rather than a judgment of value, that brings the process of reflection to an end.

At this point Lonergan's vocabulary changes. His thesis has been that cognitional theory was the foundation for ethics and religion. He now begins to talk about the ethical dimension's involving an enlargement of consciousness, from empirical, intellectual, and rational consciousness to moral self-consciousness. In a new use of terminology, he employs the term 'self-consciousness' for the type of consciousness involved in decision making:

> In other words, there is a succession of enlargements of consciousness, a succession of transformations of what consciousness means. Waking replaces dreaming. Intelligent inquiry emerges in waking to compound intelligent with empirical consciousness. Critical reflection follows understanding and formulation to add rational consciousness to intelligent and empirical consciousness. But the final enlargement and transformation of consciousness consists in the empirically, intelligently, and rationally conscious subject
> 1) demanding conformity of his doing and his knowing, and
> 2) acceding to that demand by deciding reasonably.[17]

Elsewhere he names the consciousness involved in ethical decision making as rational, moral self-consciousness.[18]

In the enlargement of consciousness that occurs in ethical agency the term is not 'judgment' but 'decision.' It is in the peculiar kind of contingency involved in the act of deciding and effecting a course of action that the meaning of its freedom is to be located:

> The decision, then, is not a consequent but a new emergence that both realizes the course of action or rejects it, and realizes an effec-

tively rational self-consciousness or fails to do so. None the less, though the act of will is a contingent emergence, it also is an act of the subject; the measure of the freedom with which the act occurs is also the measure of his responsibility for it.[19]

In his analysis Lonergan made it clear that rational reflection did not determine the decision, the act of will. Decisions or acts of willing are free in the sense that they are not necessitated by reflection. The agent is free to make or not make the decision and could in fact fail to do so. This does not mean that in any instance making the decision is arbitrary. Decisions are also intelligible in that they complete the ethical enlargement and intelligibility of the ethical agent, their absence unintelligible in that that enlargement is absent or frustrated. The suggestion that taking responsibility for one's decisions is an essential element in one's freedom is also provoking. It suggests that there is an element of unfreedom involved in making a decision and then renouncing one's responsibilities in relation to it.

In Lonergan's emphasis on the decision being an act of the subject we find an enlargement in his meaning of the self or subject and a related enlargement in the project of self-affirmation. As on the cognitional level we can pursue questions and experience our insights without noticing what is going on, so also on the ethical. In his later writings Lonergan would talk about the existential discovery 'of oneself as a moral being, the realization that one not only chooses between courses of action but also thereby makes oneself an authentic human being or an unauthentic one.'[20] Related, there is his change in vocabulary from self-consciousness of the cognitional to the rational moral self-consciousness of the ethical subject.

Lonergan sums up the relation between the knower and the known world and the ethical agent and the human good in terms of an enlargement of the theorem of isomorphism:

> As metaphysics is a corollary to the structure of knowing, so ethics is a corollary to the structure of knowing and doing; and as ethics resides in the structure, so the concrete applications of ethics are worked out by spirit inasmuch as it operates with the structure to reflect and decide upon possible courses of action that it grasps.[21]

A key element in the possibility of ethics within his world view has been established. But as our comments on the role of feelings, the judgment of value, and the notion of value make clear, other key elements that define the structure of the relation between the ethical agent and the good that comes to be constructed are missing. In this sense, Lonergan's analysis of the problem stands to his later thought in *Method in Theology* and after as 'Thought and Reality' stands to *Insight*.

Effective Freedom: The Developmental Problem

The concrete being of man, then, is being in process. His existing lies in developing ... For complete self-development is a long and difficult process.[22]

As there is organic, psychic, and intellectual development, so also there is ethical development. Central in it is the development of one's freedom and related sense of responsibility. In our infancy others make decisions for us. The range of our freedom and of our responsibility is zero. There comes the time in adolescence or early adulthood when we have to make our own life decisions and accept the responsibilities they impose. The range of our freedom and responsibility is enlarging, opening up. How is this development of freedom to be measured, and what problems are peculiar to it? As he does not have a transcendental notion of value, at this point Lonergan cannot approach the task from the standpoint of operators and integrators.

Lonergan's illustration of the distinction between essential and effective freedom in terms of giving up smoking, he being a quite heavy smoker while writing *Insight*, needs to be expanded. Alcohol taken in moderation is a good. Taken to excess it is bad. To become addicted to it is to lose control over one's willing. To the extent that alcohol addiction leads to violence and abuse it becomes destructive, and in the limit, evil. There is the compulsion of the alcoholic and of the drug addict. All therapies work on the basis that addicts might be essentially free to give up their compulsions but recognize that, through their addictions, they have effectively lost control over their willing. Winning back effective freedom is no easy matter. Not until five years after the actor Anthony Hopkins had made the break with alcohol did he began to feel he had regained his freedom, his control over his willing. All therapy for those addicted to drugs or alcohol is based on the presupposition that human beings are essentially but not necessarily effectively free. As the statistical nature of the results illustrates, only a small percentage regain effective freedom.

Our effective freedom is, for Lonergan, constrained by external circumstances, our sensitivity, intellectual development, and antecedent willingness. Clearly, it is limited because of our external circumstances, which Lonergan tries to capture in his illustrations of a prisoner and an Eskimo. The early existentialists thought about freedom as the attainment of unlimited power to do what one wanted in the world without any external constraints. Later de Beauvoir came to appreciate that freedom could never be detached from the force of circumstances in a life, from 'one's place, one's body, one's past, one's general environment, other human beings, and one's death.'[23] The external circumstances of our birth, the family we are born into, the setting in history, all limit our freedom. The body that destiny has endowed us with may limit our freedom to be an athlete, musician, or explorer. In what sense are we free to go against our circumstances or fate? Some will no doubt exclaim that they have risen above their circumstances and that all should do likewise. As in many cases, the exception proves the rule.

There are also limitations in our freedom that arise because of our psychoneural state and our character. Persons may suffer from a condition such as manic depression or autism, which may restrict the range of their freedom. They may have had an upbringing in early childhood that so imprinted on their psyches that it restricts the range of their freedom. As a result they may suffer from certain compulsions and have an almost addiction-forming psyche. As our freedom is embodied, so the decisions that we make have to find their psychic and bodily attunement.

As knowledge is power, the historical context of our intellectual development also places limits on our freedom. Before penicillin or antibiotics or various vaccines were discovered, we were not free to cure certain illnesses. Accordingly, at every stage of intellectual development there is a limit to the possible interventions we can make in the world. Different individuals also have different intellectual capabilities. Some are good at mathematics, others at language, and others at communication and diplomacy. The greater the development of one's practical intelligence, the greater the range of one's freedom. Intellectual development is moved by an unrestricted intellectual desire, the pure desire to know: 'But to reach the universal willingness that matches the unrestricted desire to know is indeed a high achievement.'[24]

There follows a reference to Kierkegaard on the function of irony and satire in effecting the transition from the aesthetic to the ethical state and on humour in the transition to the religious stage:

> The aesthetic and ethical spheres would seem to stand to the whole man, to the existential subject, as the counter-positions and positions stand to the cognitional subject. ... on the counterpositions the good is identified with objects of desire while the intelligible good of order and the rational good of value are regarded as so much ideological superstructure.[25]

The remark is of considerable interest. It makes a clear statement that the cognitional subject of self-affirmation and of intellectual development is not a concrete intelligible unity, identity, whole, but a part of the whole person. Suggesting that there are positions and counterpositions in ethics as in cognitional theory relates to what Lonergan will later refer to as moral conversion. For the movement from a counterposition to a position is not a matter of logic and argument, but of conversion through which the norms of rational self-consciousness, rather than pleasure or pain, become the basis of the ethical life.[26]

As his interest is in the relation between the intellect and the will, it should not surprise us that Lonergan focuses on limitations in the essential freedom of the will that have a basis in the understanding. It is one thing not to be able to cure an illness because one does not understand the function of a drug such as penicillin. It is another not to be able to will a particular course of action because of an intellectual scotosis such as we find in Willy Loman. By the rather harsh phrase 'moral impotence,' which has its source in his doctoral dissertation on grace and freedom, Lonergan means the limitations in our freedom to will that result from the lack of intellectual and volitional development.

It is in this context that Lonergan introduces the element of bias in willing. As common sense is subject to bias, so

> we can expect that individual decisions will be likely to suffer from
> individual bias, that common decisions will be likely to suffer
> from the various types of group bias, and that all decisions will be
> likely to suffer from general bias.[27]

Because the biases inhibit the proper development of the common-sense understanding of the individual, group, or society, the related decision making will, to that extent, be unfree and biased. The biases of understanding condition the freedom of our willing. This in turn poses the question, how do we liberate ourselves from our biases?

Willy Loman is essentially free to change his understanding of himself and of his son, but he is not effectively free to do so. Helmer is essentially free to change his understanding of himself in relation to his wife, but again is not effectively free to do so. Groups with racial or ethnic biases, as the history of Alabahma and Bosnia and Northern Ireland illustrate, are essentially free to change their understanding of the other in relation to themselves, but not effectively free to do so. Any occasion where one person refuses to sit down and converse with another on a matter of common importance is an expression of the absence of effective freedom. The recourse to violence of all kinds and, ultimately, war is an expression of the failure of humankind to achieve effective freedom, for violence is not a rational basis on which to conduct our lives, ethical or otherwise.

Similarly, philosophers are essentially free to develop their understanding of themselves in accordance with the dictates of the pure desire to know. Still, few make it central in their philosophy, and fewer still objectify it and give it the significance it merits. The desire for truth and the appropriation of truth may not be the central motive of many individuals, even philosophers. They are essentially free to undertake that path; but they must win effective freedom.

Many will feel quite comfortable with the affirmation that the achievement of effective freedom is hard for those with addictions or certain personality disorders. They will not be so welcoming of the claim that all human beings, to the extent that they are intellectual and ethical, are involved in a drama whose plot centres on achieving or avoiding effective freedom. Parents, educators, doctors, workers, managers, counsellors, priests, policemen, and politicians are all confronted with the task of achieving effective freedom in their own interpersonal worlds. It might involve the undoing of biases, of bigotry, racist attitudes, hatreds, the prisons of our minds and hearts that lock up our essential freedom to grasp the truth and pursue values. It might involve letting go outdated ways of understanding and teaching or might demand forgiveness, a change of heart. The illustrations, though limited, point to the extensiveness of the limitations on our effective freedom.

Taken to its limits the question asks, is it possible for human beings naturally to achieve the effective freedom that is necessary in order to live ethically? As such, it clarifies an aspect of the meaning of the title of the chapter, 'The Possibility of Ethics.' It is Lonergan's conclusion at this point that, internally, there is a darkness in the human intellect illustrated by its biases and the counterpositions, and a related weakness in the human will. At the heart of Lonergan's quest was the anticipation that through the insights of our intellect the problems that the world brings to us, economic, historical, interhuman, philosophical, or whatever, can be resolved. Given that stance, it comes as a shock to discover his diagnosis that at the heart of both the human intellect and will is a problem for which he holds there is no human solution.

26

Questions and Insights in Religion

Our subject has been the act of insight or understanding, and God is the unrestricted act of understanding, the eternal rapture glimpsed in every Archimedean cry of Eureka.[1]

In his *I and Thou* Martin Buber remarked that in every particular human encounter with a Thou there is a glimpse through to the eternal Thou.[2] If we extend the lines of human relations, it is Buber's view that they meet in the eternal Thou. In his concluding chapters Lonergan attempts to explore a parallel possibility. It arises, not from the experience of friendship and love in the field of personal relations, in which he acknowledges his treatment is skimpy, but from the aspirations of modern science and a related metaphysics. These are particular expressions of the desire of the human mind to understand the universe. As they progressively disclose to us more about that peculiar desire and the world it makes known, they pose the question, Would a complete scientific explanation of the universe be sufficient to satisfy us? Or is it the case that if we extend the lines of the intellectual desire and insights of modern empirical scientists they point beyond themselves to an eternal Thou? Are there further depths to the form of the desired that are strangely present through their absence in the desire?

Chapters 19 and 20 were rapidly composed during the summer of 1953. At Christmas 1952 he listed them as chapters 17 and 18 with the titles 'Elements of Natural Theology' and 'The Structure of History.'[3] As 1953 unfolded, his metaphysical explorations expanded and new chapters were added. As a result, in the final months of composition they became chapters 19 and 20, their titles being changed to the more opaque 'General Transcendent Knowledge' and 'Special Transcendent Knowledge.' In them he was attempting to see if our questioning spirit can take us beyond the questions and knowledge of the empirical sciences, common sense, and a proportionate metaphysics and into the realm of religion. As he put it later, 'before we can grasp transcendent being intelligently, we have to extrapolate from proportionate being.'[4]

In this extrapolation chapter 19, which he declares on its opening page is concerned with determining whether we can know, not what God is, but that God is, sits closer to 15 and 16 in movement, style, and development. In this one is reminded that Cantor, the mathematician, succeeded in proving that there exists a set of transcendental numbers too big to count without identifying any existing number.[5] Following on from this, chapter 20 explores the extent to which we can know about a divinely inspired solution to the otherwise humanly irresolvable problem of evil. With its emphasis on the liberation of mind and will, it connects more directly with the third section of chapter 18 on the liberation of the will. With the epilogue, it deals with a religious anthropology, suggesting, in addition to the organic, psychic, and intellectual, a further level of development, the religious.[6]

Why Does Something Exist Rather than Nothing?

Only if Lonergan can show that there is an ultimate limit to the kind of explanation of the universe that science and a related proportionate metaphysics can offer would the further question of knowledge of God's existence begin to make sense. But how can it possibly be shown that there are aspects of the universe that science cannot and never could explain? In his treatment of existence in section 8 of chapter 19 dealing with causality, an entry into the problem can be gained.

Lonergan's intellectual conversion in 1935 involved the insight that it is through judgment alone that what exists becomes known. In 'Intelligence and Reality,' he predicated existence of substances and of acts or operations. Through our judgments we come to know that Darwin existed and wrote the *Origin of the Species*. Existence can also be considered an attribute of events, situations, and indeed of the entire universe that comes to be known through our judgments. 'Intelligence and Reality,' in its discussion of Newman, also introduced the vocabulary of concrete judgments of facts. To the extent that cognitional facts and existence are proportionate to our judgment, they share a common meaning and can, I believe, be interchanged in what follows. Both become known, not by mere gaping, but

through our assent to a proposition in a judgment with its grasp of the
virtually unconditioned. Fading out after its emergence in chapters 10–12
of *Insight*, the term 'facts' now reappears.[7]

In order to engage with the problem, it is important to have moved from
a notional to a real grasp of what he means by 'existence.' Under what
circumstances would one assent to the following propositions?

> Newman wrote the *Grammar of Assent.*
> Darwin wrote *The Origin of the Species.*
> Crick and Watson discovered the structure of DNA.
> Lonergan wrote *Insight.*
> I am a knower in the sense in which Lonergan defines knowing.

On one level, the answers to the first four are self-evident in the sense that
there is a widespread social consensus about them. Why should one assent
to the social consensus?

There follows the possibility of appealing, critically, to the relevant evidence that experts in the fields of studies dealing with Newman, Darwin,
Lonergan, and Crick and Watson can place on the table. The typescript of
the autograph of *Insight* can be inspected and compared with other related
typescripts that Lonergan authored at the time. The evidence of those who
attended his courses 'Thought and Reality,' 'Intelligence and Reality,' and
on *Insight*, of the reviewers who knew him, can be accumulated. Eventually
one arrives at the position that, on the basis of the evidence, it would be
irrational not to make a positive judgment in relation to the proposition. A
similar piece of research could be pursued in relation to Newman, Darwin,
and Crick and Watson. One comes to understand who it is the names refer
to, the meaning of the works and their relation to their authors. These
intellectual pursuits could in turn provide one with the evidence for the
further question about knowing. Before one can reflect on and judge the
truth of the proposition, one has to understand what it means.

In each instance the judgment is neither necessary nor arbitrary. Only if
all the significant relevant questions are articulated and related evidence
forthcoming in which the conditions of the conditioned judgment are
fulfilled would one's assent be rational. Through that assent to the proposition one makes the move from the realm of thought to the realm of some
known existence in the world. That known existence is neither necessary
nor arbitrary, but conditioned.

The above propositions can be enlarged to include scientific explanations. The physical world presents us with questions such as: what are the
laws governing movement, the properties of the chemical elements and

compounds, the laws governing the hereditary properties of organisms, the laws governing evolution? There emerge scientific explanations of the form:

> The chemical elements and compounds can be explained in terms of a periodic law of the form X.
> Certain aspects of the hereditary properties of living organisms can be explained in terms of their DNA.
> The evolutionary laws explain the relations between genera and species in the universe.

Through the self-correcting process of scientific inquiry and research in history, a process that involves many false starts, errors, and dead ends, the laws of nature slowly come to disclose themselves to our understanding. Other laws might govern our universe, but through the process of verification the intelligible conditions of the laws that exist come to be progressively identified. The revisions of history do not eliminate the expectation of the existence of contingent scientific laws that govern our universe. As the laws of nature that govern our universe become disclosed to us, there again arises the further question, why do the laws of physics, chemistry, biology, and evolution exist? It is Lonergan's claim that empirical scientists progressively show the laws of nature, but that is as far as they go. Why there exist laws of nature and beings such as ourselves who can attempt to understand and think them is for him a question that empirical science cannot resolve.

Lonergan sums up the consequences of this as follows:

> Thus, every judgement raises a further question; it reveals a conditioned to be virtually unconditioned and by that very stroke it reveals conditions that happen to be fulfilled; that happening is a matter of fact and, if it is not to be a mere matter of fact without explanation, a further question arises.[8]

How, precisely, his use of the term 'fact' in the phrase 'mere matter of fact' relates to his earlier position on concrete judgments of fact and brute facts is a puzzling question. The existence of Darwin, of his authoring of *The Origin of the Species*, or of the relation between DNA and hereditary properties, as known, are intelligible. There is the intelligibility of the meaning of the propositions and of the fulfilment of the conditioned, the sufficient evidence. It is in the matter-of-fact fulfilment of the conditions that Lonergan finds the source of a further question:

If nothing existed, there would be no one to ask questions and nothing to ask questions about. The most fundamental of all questions, then, asks about existence yet neither empirical science nor a methodically restricted philosophy can have an adequate answer ... Again, in particular cases, the scientist can deduce one existent from others, but not even in particular cases can he account for the existence of the others to which he appeals for his premises ... For every proportionate being that exists, exists conditionally; it exists inasmuch as the conditions of its existence happen to be fulfilled; and the contingence of that happening cannot be eliminated by appealing to another happening that is equally contingent.[9]

Startling is Lonergan's claim that neither science nor philosophy, nor, one could add, common sense, can answer the question. Effectively, Lonergan is saying here that the question has no human answer. The explanation of existence is in a real sense beyond our comprehension.

This, in turn, draws our attention to the mysterious and unfathomable face of existence. In our normal discourse we frequently make assertions of the form, 'Newman existed and wrote his *Apologia*.' That every such affirmation can in turn pose the question, Why are there such facts or existences rather than nothing? is largely missed or dismissed. In chapter 20 we find Lonergan remarking that 'the whole world of sense is to be, then, a token, a mystery of God,' a mystery that 'symbolizes the further depths that lie beyond our comprehension.'[10] Could it be argued that the mystery that is to be associated with the world of sense is an element in the wider mystery that is to be associated with existence and facts?

Lonergan now takes the analysis a step further. Acknowledging that the explanation of existence is in a sense beyond our comprehension, that is to say mysterious, he goes on to ask, Is existence itself intelligible or unintelligible? Is what exists intelligible but existence itself unintelligible? With little elaboration he responds that being, the objective of the pure desire to know, which becomes known in the totality of true judgments, is intelligible. For him only what is intelligible can be; the unintelligible cannot be. The conclusion, 'If existence is mere matter of fact, it is nothing. If occurrence is mere matter of fact, it is nothing,' follows.[11] Existence and occurrence cannot be unintelligible.

The results of the analysis are twofold. Firstly, it affirms that there is no human answer to the question, 'Why is there something rather than nothing?' within the realms of empirical science, common sense, and metaphysics. Secondly, it affirms that despite this, there must be an explanation of the mystery of existence. In this sense the question, 'Why something rather than nothing?' is a source of the question of God. To probe the question of God's existence is to explore the possibility that what we encounter as the mystery of natural existence might be intelligible and have an explanation even though the human mind can never directly comprehend it.

On Causality and the Mind's Desire

Two further preliminaries have to be negotiated before the question of a proof of God's existence arises. Firstly, the meaning and significance of efficient, exemplary, and final causality have to be reviewed. Secondly, we will examine the question, does an exploration of what is it we can desire to know take us from the realm of finite insights to unrestricted understanding? Both have a bearing on the difficult question of the referent of the word 'God.'

For Aristotle material, formal, exemplary, efficient, and final causality are modes of explanation. When we ask, Why is this a car rather than a house? an explanation can be given in terms of its matter, idea/structure and function, manner of manufacturing and, finally, what it is used for. Acknowledging that humanly, we cannot understand the explanation of existence, can we show that existence has a cause, that is to say an explanation? To pose this question is, for Lonergan, to address an aspect of the question of God.

Lonergan's section on causality in chapter 19 has to be read in this context. Can it be argued that to ask why things or cognitional facts exist is to ask about an efficient, exemplary, or final cause? The possibilities for explanation contained in the notion of causality need to be examined.

In certain crime situations where there are no witnesses, the questions, analysis, and arguments have to be based on circumstantial evidence. In many of those situations the manner in which the crime was caused can be understood even though the agent is neither known nor named. In such cases the unknown agent or cause of the crime, who can be designated by X, is in principle knowable. In the present case the agent or cause is in principle unknowable.

Slightly different is the case of coming across a book that exhibits a clear style and intelligible content but with no named author on its title page or within its text. Here the cause is not a direct part of and is nowhere present in its product, the given data. Under what circumstances would it make sense to say: 'I know that X was the author of the text'; 'There is clearly an author Y who will never be named and known'; and, 'There is no author'? To say that Y could never be known is not to say that he or she does not exist, but that necessary data and evidence have been irreversibly destroyed. Involved in composing the text we can identify an element of efficient causality, in deciding to author it of final causality, of choosing it as worthwhile.

At this point, the analysis of causality invites us to reflect on the referent of the word 'God.' Ordinary names such as 'John' and 'Mary' arise from ostensive or what Lonergan calls nominal definitions based on the given of our senses. We experience John and Mary before we name them and affirm their existence. Of the many uses of the name 'God,' its use to denote a cause or explanation of existence or facts does not arise in this manner. It is singular in that it is the name of an unknowable and hence mysterious being, because by definition God cannot be known directly through experiencing, questioning, understanding, and judging. In the ordinary course of events, we can only affirm what we experience and understand. How could we possibly affirm the existence of a being that cannot be directly experienced or understood within parameters of the known universe?[12] Lonergan is now asking whether existence can be explained in terms of the causality of a being, the explanation of whose nature is beyond our power of insight.

A further dimension of the question takes us beyond the anthropomorphic turn. All cosmic and human agency and patienthood involves some form of causality. In contrast, if there is to be an adequate explanation of why things and facts exist, the causality that explains them must itself be uncaused. For if the cause of existence had itself a cause, then we would be involved in an infinite regress of explanations. No doubt there will be those who hold that the evolutionary laws of the universe are the uncaused causes that cause the emergence of all the grades of beings that we find. But no sooner have we asserted the existence of such laws than the question arises, why do such evolutionary laws exist rather than nothing?

Accordingly, there arises the notion of an uncaused cause or an unmoved mover. What is significant about this notion is that it can only be defined negatively, as a being that itself has not been caused. What, positively, this means cannot be comprehended. It is in fact mysterious. Clearly, that uncaused cause will not be any part of the circumstantial evidence itself, will not be directly present in the known universe. Can we reach a judgment, 'X is the cause of Y' where, unlike in the crime scene, we could never directly understand and know who or what X is? By means of the circumstantial evidence, that is, the existing and known universe, can the existence of a mysterious unknowable uncaused cause be affirmed?

It must be acknowledged that Lonergan does not help in clarifying certain radical differences in the meaning of causality as it applies to a creator and a creature. The intelligibility of creature causality helps to focus the question only by way of analogy rather than of similitude. Our causality always presupposes that certain material things and qualities exist from which we can manufacture other things. To explain human causality involves mastering the manner in which human insights are the efficient causes of the new things that come to exist. To design and make a computer presupposes a whole dimension of chemical things as well as the laws of physics and chemistry. After we make the computer it can take on a life of its own.

In contrast, the causality involved in explaining the existence of the universe is an ultimately mysterious causality that can create from nothing and sustain existence. Although the human mind can comprehend the manner in which human beings are the efficient causes of new things, it cannot comprehend or explain why anything exists. It can intimate that a form of causality is involved, but the nature of that causality is incomprehensible. In the face of such an ungraspable mystery, the analogy of human creativity takes us so far and no further.

A universe brought into existence cannot remain in existence without the continuing relation of dependence on its creator. For no creature that exists has within itself the power to remain in existence. Only the creator has that power. It follows that the continuing existence of all created things is permanently dependent on the will of the creator. Although the phenomenon of human causality can direct us to the question of the existence of a creator, at a certain point the mysterious nature of the causal relation between a creator and creation must be expressed. This Lonergan does not do adequately.

I begin in the middle of chapter 19 by exploring a possible limit in the scientific search for explanation. Lonergan begins that chapter by asking a more difficult question: what is being? As being is the objective of the desire of the human mind, the question can be recast as: what is the goal of our intellectual desire? What knowledge would truly satisfy the desire of the minds of mathematicians, empirical scientists, biographers, and persons of common sense individually and collectively to understand, explain, and know? If Lonergan's earlier focus on self-affirmation was on how in any instance we know, his present focus is on what it is we can desire to know.

In the restricted inquiries of the empirical scientists, persons of common sense, biographers, and philosophers, their intellectual desire is satisfied and stilled by correct but finite insights and knowledge. The insights of Pythagoras into his theorem and of Wiles into a proof for Fermat's theorem satisfy their intellectual desires in particular mathematical inquiries. The insights of Einstein into special and general relativity theories and of Crick and Watson into the chemical structure of DNA satisfy and still their intellectual desires in particular empirical enquiries. The insights of persons of common sense into their dramatic interhuman situation or of biographers into aspects of the plot of the life of their subjects satisfy their intellectual desire in relation to determining a particular matter of fact.

It is a common experience that no sooner has one problem been solved in these situations than the next one emerges and greets us. Clearly, the outcome of all particular investigations only partially satisfies human intellectual desire. Despite our best efforts as adults to convince ourselves that we know everything that it is worthwhile knowing, recurrently we are confronted with our wide-ranging ignorance. Cracks and crevices and chasms emerge in our view of the world. The discomfort we experience when faced with what we cannot comprehend or explain can act as a spur for further intellectual development. As that experience repeats itself over time, it can also lead to the personal discovery that there will always be more to one's intellectual desire than can be satisfied by the limited finite insights that it is one's good fortune to accumulate.

Only if one has the memory of such a succession of experiences will one feel the impact of the further question, in what would my or our intellectual desire find its complete satisfaction? Where do the extended lines of my unresolved intellectual desire point, direct me? Classically, mathematicians extrapolate from a finite number of terms in a series, 1, 4, 9, 16, 25, ... to an infinity of further terms. Lonergan's extrapolation from a series of finite insights to an unrestricted insight differs. Every term in the mathematical series is a part of its infinity. Within its indivisible unity the unrestricted act of understanding will have to grasp all of our finite insights, but it will not be made up of them. It will be distinct.

Two points arise. Firstly, does the outcome of the extrapolation from finite insights to an unrestricted insight make sense? Secondly, assuming it does, the question arises, is there any sense in which we could understand anything about an unrestricted act of understanding?

In human insights a distinction has to be drawn between the act and its content or object. At this point, reverting to the terminology of *Verbum: Word and Idea*, Lonergan renames the content or object of an insight an 'idea.' It is a term involved in a Platonic-Cartesian/Aristotelian-Thomist dialectic and a whole host of similar problems concerning the mind-world relation. The idea of a circle is the set of terms and relations grasped in the image and articulated in the definition. Idea in this sense is a property or quality of the object of knowledge, not of the activity.

Following this line, Lonergan develops his extrapolation. As a finite and restricted human insight grasps the idea of a circle, gravity, or DNA, so an unrestricted insight would grasp the idea of being, of everything that exists. Again, the idea of being would not be a property of the understanding, but of what it understood.

Scientists and historians will object, How could any understanding, restricted or unrestricted, know the future course of evolution and of human history? The next steps in human history are only a small fraction of all the possibilities. These in turn shape the possibilities that are to follow. The finality of the universe is indeterminate, and the future course of history is determined by present contingent acts of human willing. These are precisely the questions Lonergan addressed in his notes 'On God's Knowledge and Will.' He answered that whereas with human insights things exist before we know them, from the point of view of God's understanding nothing exists unless it has been understood and willed to exist by God. Nothing exists before God understands and wills it. The past, present, and future of cosmic evolution and human history exist because God unrestrictedly understands and wills them. Central to an unrestricted act of understanding would be its self-knowledge. From that self-knowledge knowledge of everything else would arise.

Augustine, C.S. Lewis, Thomas Merton, Melanie Griffin, and others recognized at the heart of the desire of their minds a longing that cannot be satisfied by a knowledge of the world and all within it. It is a longing that cannot find rest because it is all the time being drawn out of itself and beyond itself by an eternal Thou.[13] Is there in the depths of the desire of the human mind a largely unrecognized dimension that seeks a more direct form of knowledge of the transcendent and divine?

The Notion and Existence of God

Our concept of an unrestricted act of understanding has a number of implications and, when they are worked out, it becomes manifest that it is one thing to understand what being is and to understand what God is.[14]

Lonergan next connects his notion of unrestricted understanding worked out in his extrapolation with the classical notion of God. That equating does not come out of thin air. That God is unrestricted understanding was a position he found in Aquinas as interpreted in the fifth *Verbum* article. It is also the notion of God that pervades his notes 'On God's Knowledge and Will,' which was inspired by, among others, Lennerz's *De Deo Uno*, a classical traditional text of the time.[15] There follows his analysis of the notion of God, in which he simply selects points from those fuller notes. In articulating the notion of God, he is showing that it is one and the same thing as an unrestricted act of understanding. The traditional divine attributes of classical theodicy can all be grasped in such an infinite act of understanding. It is Lonergan's conclusion that, beginning with the highly impersonal question 'What is being?' he arrives at the notion of a personal God.[16]

The further task that Lonergan has to address is the manner in which an unrestricted act of understanding can become an element in the solution of the problem of existence:

> In the third place, then, a transcendent being relevant to our problem must possess two basic attributes. On the one hand, it must not be contingent in any respect, for if it were, once more we would be confronted with the mere matter of fact that we have to avoid. One the other hand, besides being self-explanatory, the transcendent being must be capable of grounding the explanation of everything about everything else; for without this second attribute, the transcendent being would leave unsolved our problem of contingence in proportionate being.[17]

Unlike the virtually unconditioned of what we know through judgment, God's existence is formally unconditioned. It is not conditioned by or dependent on anything else. It is either necessary or impossible but cannot be contingent. Through our dependent existence we stand all the time in a relation of dependence on a creator. What applies to the individual also applies to the entire universe.

To affirm that being becomes known through an infinite insight is to affirm that to us it is a mystery that in itself is completely intelligible. One of the problems is that at times Lonergan tends to lose sight of the dimension of mystery. He makes misleading remarks like, 'If God is a being he will be known through intelligent grasp and reasonable affirmation,'[18] suggesting that God can be known in much the same way as general relativity or evolution theory. Despite what follows, the opening phrase in the quote below is unfortunate:

> For when we grasp what God is, our grasp is not an unrestricted act of understanding but a restricted understanding that extrapolates from itself to an unrestricted act and by asking ever further questions arrives as a list of attributes of the unrestricted act.[19]

We might grasp an analogical likeness of God, but that is never a grasp of what God is.

Again the question arises, does this mean anything at all? Is anything of a positive nature or meaning being said? Or is it simply saying that God cannot be contingent, non-self-explanatory, caused? What a non-contingent self-explanatory uncaused being might be like is something quite beyond the range of our understanding. We point to a human attribute and declare that God must not suffer from this limitation. But what, positively, that would mean we could never in this life know. We might be able to point at the issue by way of analogies, but ultimately what we are talking about here is mystery. Might it be the case that we could never understand the non-contingent and we might never understand the self-explanatory? At this point the critic will say: does this make sense at all?

So far we have been in the realm of speculation. Eventually the question of the grounds of the speculation arises.

> But can you prove the existence of God? Vatican 1 defines that you can. So I added another chapter on that.[20]

For Lonergan, to prove that God exists involves showing that there are reasonable grounds for affirming the existence of an unknown unrestricted act of understanding. Related is the question, under what circumstances could one affirm the existence of finite understanding, of insights other than one's own? – a question Lonergan does not raise. In science it would come through a communication of a discovery such as the double helix structure of DNA. In industry it would come through the communication of an innovative product. The grounds for the existence of finite insights are to be deduced through the communication of finite intelligibilities. The grounds for the existence of unrestricted understanding would be that the real is completely intelligible. Inversely, if reality is completely intelligible then unrestricted understanding exists.

In his notes for the lecture 'The General Character of the Natural Theology of Insight,' delivered at the Divinity School of the University of Chicago in 1967, Lonergan recalled that in chapter 19 of *Insight* he had worked out an argument for the existence of God. His seventh point was that the realities of this world are not of themselves completely intelligible. By the use of the method of empirical science, one event or existence can be accounted for by appealing to other events or existences: 'But no attempt is made or can be made to meet the questions, Why does anything exist? Why does anything occur?' He concludes that if reality is to be completely intelligible, there is need for a completely intelligible being that can account for the existences and occurrences of this world. Such a being would be an unrestricted act of understanding that can be shown to have the properties traditionally associated with God. It would also be open to further determinations from the field of revelation, a Trinitarian nature.

The argument he considered to constitute any natural theology that he happened to have is as follows:[21]

If the real is completely intelligible, God exists.
But the real is completely intelligible.
Therefore, God exists.

Recalling his childhood sense of realism and sibling rivalry, previously noted in chapter 2, he went on to clarify the premise that the real is completely intelligible by introducing a middle term: Being is completely intelligible. Equating the real with being leads to the conclusion that the real must be completely intelligible. His proof requires that we once and for all break out of the Greek *mythos* and into the *logos*, out of the bounds of a Kantianism, idealism, existentialism, or a positivism.[22]

If reality or being is completely intelligible, then the idea of being exists. The idea of being, of everything that is, is what would be known by an unrestricted act of understanding. In Lonergan's use of the word 'idea,' the idea of gravity or DNA or evolution can exist before it is humanly understood. Clearly, Lonergan is being guided by his affirmation in 'On God's Knowledge and Will' that contingent things can only exist because God knows and wills them.

It follows that every perceived incomplete aspect of the universe, existence, illness, and evil, all have to be understood as part of something greater. It would be incomprehensible for a God of infinite understanding to create a universe in which illness, evil, and existence were ends in themselves. In themselves existence, evil, and illness are, from a human perspective, all defective in their intelligibility.

Lonergan went on to make clear that his proof stands outside the Kantian horizon, which holds that speculative reason has only three possible ways of proving the existence of God: physico-theological, cosmological, and ontological. For Lonergan:

> One cannot prove the existence of God to a Kantian without first
> breaking his allegiance to Kant. One cannot prove the existence of
> God to a positivist without first converting him from positivism. A
> valid proof has philosophic presuppositions, and the presuppositions
> of the argument set forth in *Insight* are indicated in the antecedent,
> 'the real is completely intelligible.'[23]

Lonergan's thesis that being is the objective of the pure desire to know and that its intended object becomes known in the totality of true judgments has no place within the Kantian philosophy. Sala's account of his discovery of the strangeness of their differences makes the point well.[24]

Clearly, Lonergan's own personal affirmation that there is a God is not dependent on philosophical analysis and proof. His commitment to his religious vocation came about by the quite different route of his upbringing in the faith community of his family and culture and his personal experience of a vocational calling in his teens. In chapter 19 Lonergan, who is committed to his religious beliefs and vocational calling, is effectively posing the question, can the existence of the God of my religious beliefs be known through natural cognitional processes and proofs?

At the start of the 1960s Matt Torpey, a student in Rome, used to talk to Lonergan before his lectures. On one occasion Torpey said that he was just beginning to see the point of the *Quid sit* and the *An sit* questions, but added, 'when a man is in love, he is always asking WHO are you?' Lonergan replied, his voice rising and falling, 'That just illustrates the limitations of the scientific method,'[25] that is to say, of the style of questioning used in chapter 19 of *Insight*.

In 1970 at a conference on Lonergan's thought in Florida chapter 19 was critiqued as a ghost of an earlier age. Lonergan was defensive, holding that it was part of the process of rounding things off because of his immanent transfer to Rome. But he did add that while his cognitional theory was based on a long apprenticeship in the realm of cognitional experience, his account of God's existence made no appeal to religious experience. Treating God's existence and attributes in an objective fashion,

> it made no effort to deal with the subject's religious horizon. It failed to acknowledge that the traditional viewpoint made sense only if one accepted first principles on the ground that they were intrinsically necessary and if one added the assumptions that there is one right culture so that differences in subjectivity are irrelevant.[26]

All proof presupposes a horizon or framework, a viewpoint, world view, differentiation of consciousness.

Two years later, in the fall of 1972, he enlarged the point in his lectures on the *Philosophy of God, and Theology*. The source of the question of God is not just the contingency of existence, but also God's gift of his love: 'In both disciplines man is seeking to know whom he is in love with.'[27] Religious experience, experienced as a call by Augustine, Merton, Lewis, or Lonergan himself, involves an awareness of a mysterious object of wonder that goes beyond the domain of what Lonergan calls 'proportionate being.' Part of the religious quest is to make sense of that experience and of the desires it opens up and awakens. How chapter 19 will survive in such a future development is an open question. There are those who maintain that, rather than rejecting the structure of the argument, we should recast it in the wider framework that acknowledges the intellectually, morally, and religiously converted subject.[28]

Chapter 20: Finally, the Problem of Evil

Still, there is a fact of evil and man is inclined to argue from that fact to a denial of the intelligence or power or goodness of God ... since God is the first agent of every event and emergence and development, the question really is what God is or has been doing about the fact of evil.[29]

Lonergan began *Insight* with a dream of working out a world view based on an integration of the different kinds of questions and insights that have emerged largely in the modern scientific and philosophical experience. The focus of his exploration was on the natural power of the human mind to master its natural environment, the entire universe. Well into the summer of 1953, as the September deadline approached, he began to compose the final chapter of the book. We have to imagine him, possibly as late as June 1953, in haste thinking it out. Addressing the problem of evil, it somewhat surprises the reader. Why is Lonergan treating this as his final question? Is it an afterthought? Or are there hints in his work to date that suggest it might really be the final and true destination of the journey of his mind-quest in the process of authoring and composition? In what sense is that problem and its assumed solution transcendent, beyond the comprehension of scientific and common-sense and philosophical knowledge?

Two sources feed into the problem. Firstly, there is an input from his recent theological teaching, especially from his 1951 course notes 'On God's Knowledge and Will.' Secondly, there is the theme of the flight from insight or understanding that originated in his Heythrop days. In the 1930s it found expression in his explorations of progress and decline, of the dialectic or conflicts of history, a theme continued in composing chapter 7 of *Insight*. In chapter 20 he attempts to relate it to the problem of evil. Not unrelated is the fact that his first title for this chapter was 'The Structure of History.'

Within the movement of composing *Insight*, the word 'evil' was rarely used and there was little direct reference to a problem of evil. Chapter 18 on the good made only a fleeting reference to the category of evil as experience.[30] The problem of the liberation of the effective freedom of the will was one of moral impotence rather than of moral evil. In chapter 19 the problem of evil was treated fleetingly in the context of the classical problem in theodicy on the causality of sin. As God is in some sense the cause of everything that happens, a disturbing question is to what extent, if at all, God is the cause of human sins and their consequent moral evils. Needless to say, Lonergan was a strong defender of the position that God could not in any direct sense be the efficient cause of human sins and the consequent moral evils that are to be found in world order.

Now, for the first time in the book, Lonergan discusses as sinful the failure of a being with free will to choose a morally obligatory course of action or to reject a morally reprehensible one. These involve a sin against oneself and against the order in the universe. Moral evils for him are the consequences both in the world and in the agent or subject of basic sins. Lonergan also acknowledges, in a manner not to be found in his chapter on ethics, that the understanding can propose morally reprehensible courses of action and collaborate with our disordered moral inclinations. In terms of the earlier ethical analysis, moral evils do not seem to be the same thing as bias. He does not at this point suggest that morally evil acts cause physical harm and suffering to others. Physical evils are simply the shortcomings of an evolving world. Whether God is to any extent the cause of human suffering through the physical evils in the world, such as natural disasters, epidemics that are not the result of human agency, and inherited illnesses, is left an open question.

The slightness of the references to and engagement with the problem of evil in the build-up to chapter 20 might suggest that it was something of an afterthought. It is one thing to suggest that the human will is morally impotent, incapable of achieving sustained development and effective freedom. It is quite another to link or even equate that with moral evil and harmful physical evils of deprivation. Very many human beings fail to develop in an appropriate manner, and we don't necessarily equate that failure to develop with evil behaviour. The question arises, what failures in development, if any, are to be equated with the problem of evil?

The opening treatment of the problem of evil in chapter 20 was prefaced by points made at greater length in his 1951 course notes 'On God's Knowledge and Will.' There he taught that evil is a privation of the good. There is assumed some intelligible unity or whole, say, a human person or the unity of the universe. The whole ought to exist, but some complement of the existing parts is missing. Moral evil, the formal part of a formal sin, is constituted by an unreasonable deficiency in a moral action. It is not something that is, has being as such, but an absence of being. Moral evil amounts to action against the intelligible ordination or direction of the universe, an order willed by God. It is a defect in the will itself from which physical evils, such as the harm caused by a knife wound to a person, follow. In one of his rare references to harm, Lonergan adds that the harm caused is not a moral but rather a physical evil.

This leads to the question whether God wills the moral evils that are experienced in the universe:

Moral evil does not belong inasmuch as God does not plan how
affairs might be ordered so that some people merit reward and
others in like manner merit punishment; God's plan is that all be
saved, and moral evil happens contrary to the order of things conceived and planned by God ... However moral evil does pertain to
the order in the universe inasmuch as God through the denial of its
intelligibility anticipates (preconceives) moral evil, and through the
permission of the malice of the creature, by a kind of consequent
willing he wills moral evil.[31]

A distinction is drawn between various senses of God's will, directly by pure
dominion, indirectly through secondary causes, and antecedent and consequent. As well as acting directly, God also acts in the world through creatures. Permitting evil and permitting innocent persons to suffer the harm
caused to them by morally evil persons amounts to a process of governing
by secondary causes. Lonergan gives the illustration of the death of the
lions' prey being necessary in order that the higher animal form might
continue. He does not address the case of God permitting the murderer,
through the perverse causality of his evil will, to bring about not just harm
but the death of another human being.

Why does the omnipotent God permit such malice or evil? Lonergan
puts it more specifically:

Thus there is no reason why the order of the universe might not by
the divine wisdom exhibit both concepts of divine dominion, both
the pure use of divine dominion shown in physical and moral miracles according to a special economy of divine wisdom, and also the
conjoined use of the same divine dominion by which God produces
his own justice and the truth of things by acting through secondary
causes.[32]

Lonergan is stating that God's justice rules through permitting the evil
actions of creatures to cause harm to others. How can this be known?
Providence or fate can appear to be a friend or an enemy, be good or bad
luck.

We are here in the depths of religious mystery which, somewhat uncomfortably, he acknowledges:

h)   Once these things are established, it is clear what the mystery of
this tractate is. It is especially the mystery of divine transcendence;
nothing in this world can happen unless the omniscient God knows

it and God the almighty Lord wills or allows it; but there are formal elements of sin in the world; therefore God permits them.

There is then, the mystery of iniquity; there are formal elements of sin which can be understood neither in themselves nor in another.

The first mystery by an excess of intelligibility exceeds the finite intellect. The second mystery by a defect of intelligibility admits of no understanding.[33]

There is an echo of acts above and acts below nature in his 1938 analysis of history. God does not will sins and related evils, but wills to permit them. The insights of the human mind can never understand the reasons why this is so. They are above our nature. God's ways are simply beyond and above our ways. This acknowledgement of mystery is marginal in the notes and almost non-existent in the concluding chapters of Insight.

It has to be admitted that, on a casual reading, chapter 20 of Insight does not seem to present itself as directly addressing the structure of history, the second source. The few occurrences in it of the word 'history' do not illuminate its structure.[34] Against this there is the fact that in 'Insight Revisited' Lonergan explicitly linked chapter 20 to his analysis of history in 1937–8.[35] There he had analysed the course of history in terms of an ideal line of progress resulting from acts according to nature, decline resulting from acts contrary to nature, and renaissance as the result of supernatural virtues. In 'Insight Revisited' he repeats that line of analysis, adding that 'the whole idea was presented in chapter twenty of Insight.' It has to be acknowledged that its presence is not as clear as in the 1937–8 notes or in the remarks in 'Insight Revisited.' In that essay he makes it clear that chapter 20 presupposes as its context the analysis of bias in chapters 6 and 7, and moral impotence in 17.

The section in chapter 20 headed 'The Problem' opens with the phrase, 'The cult of progress has suffered an eclipse.' The term 'progress' directly connects the diagnosis of the problem with chapter 7 on common sense[36] and with his earlier work on history in the 1930s. We have seen that in order to make sense of chapter 15, one has to read as a continuation of chapter 8. In order to make sense of the diagnosis of 'the problem,' one has to read it directly as a continuation of chapter 7 and remotely of his earlier work on history. This links it directly to the problem of the structure of history. Problematic in his opening remark is the utopian-like statement that development entails that perfection belongs to the future.

In his popular Ten Theories of Human Nature, Leslie Stephenson holds that every theory has to address the question, what is wrong with the human being and how might the resulting disfigurements be addressed?[37] As well as addressing the problem of progress, Lonergan now has to articulate what his philosophy says is wrong with the human being and its implications for human progress. The section on intellectual and moral development implies that the problem arises because decisions are made before humans have the responsibility and maturity to make them. There results the social surd, and a related succession of ever less comprehensive social syntheses. The root of the problem is the failure of the human to achieve a dialectical understanding. There arises the need for a cosmopolis, but a cosmopolis requires for its success a critical human science and related correct philosophy.

In one of its dimensions as Lonergan conceives it, the problem of evil equates with the imprisonment of the human mind in the biases of common sense, dramatic, individual, group, and general. In a second dimension it amounts to an imprisonment of the human mind in the counterpositions of philosophy. In its third dimension it amounts to the imprisonment of the human will by the absence of effective freedom, the problem of moral impotence, even though the term 'moral impotence' is not used.

Clearly, in his intention to write a chapter on the structure of history, Lonergan intended to connect these problems in human nature with problems in the philosophy of history. At the heart of the human mind and will, those qualities on which we rely to solve the problems of living in our environment and, hopefully, of progress in history, there is an unsolvable problem of evil. The conclusion of Lonergan's prolonged analysis of the structure of human knowing and willing is that inherent in that structure is an intractable problem of evil whose solution is beyond the natural powers of the mind and will. The problem of evil is not out there in our world. It is potentially in all of us.

God's Solution to the Problem of Evil: The Religious Subject

No matter how one cares to phrase it, the point seems to remain that evil is, not a mere fact, but a problem, only if one attempts to reconcile it with the goodness of God, and, if God is good, then there is not only a problem of evil, but also a solution.[38]

As in chapter 19 for existence, so in chapter 20 evil cannot for Lonergan be a mere matter of fact. The unintelligible cannot be. Assuming that the universe is the product of unrestricted understanding, what sense is to be made of the fact of evil, granted that there can be no divine afterthoughts? Perhaps inspired by this thought at this point, on page 717 (694), without any real explanation of its meaning, Lonergan remarks that his book has been written from a moving viewpoint. It is a notion that he will develop in the introduction, written later. It captures, I believe, something of huge importance about his experience of composing *Insight* and about the task of understanding human understanding.

In contrast, God does not create a universe in which an unanticipated problem of evil arises for which he then has to work out a solution. For some mysterious reason God thought it good to create a universe in which the possibility of evil and of a solution to the problem of evil are part and parcel of its order. An enormous problem for us humans, it is a primary religious mystery. Assuming the existence of a God who is infinite in his understanding and love, the question arises, what response does God make to the problem? Acknowledging that evil remains in abundance, what sort of a solution to the problem of evil might it be possible for us to identify? Clearly, it must be a solution that changes the meaning of evil and the suffering it gives rise to. It must also be of the form of a solution that creates in us attitudes and dispositions to the permanent scar that evil is on the human and historical horizon.

As there are many experiences of the fact of evil, so there are many senses in which we can refer to it as a problem. Clearly, to live in an evil political regime is to find oneself confronted with the problem, how do I manage my life in this situation? To live in a violent and evil family environment or neighbourhood will again pose problems for the members: how do I conduct myself in this dangerous environment? Such responses are dealing with a pragmatic solution: how do I relate to and live out my life in a situation that contains evil people and their related evil actions? They are not addressing the problem of purging the violence from a violent situation or the corruption from a corrupt political regime.

A second level of the problem of evil arises for victims of an evil action or crime. In the aftermath of the crime, they have the problem of managing their lives. It is a profound human problem involving the adjustment of our sensitivity and feelings towards the one who has harmed us, and the pursuit of insights and decisions in the realms of healing, justice, and forgiveness in order to redirect our lives.

Problem-solving scientists or political reformers, while they might acknowledge the problem of finding pragmatic solutions to the evils of particular situations, will want more. To talk about evil as a problem suggests that it enters into the problem-solving frameworks of the sciences or technology or of political and law reform. After all, problem solving is the lifeblood of the work of mathematicians and empirical scientists. Cannot the methodology of the empirical sciences be adjusted and extended to resolve the problem of evil in a manner similar to that involved in solving the genome project? Against this, there is the fact that acts of violence against persons can result in loss of life or life-long suffering and disability for which there is no human compensation. Our problem solving cannot undo the consequences of such acts.

Lonergan's approach has to do with God's response to the core disorders in the human mind and will, which for him have no human solution. It will be continuous with the actual order in the universe, emerging in accordance with emergent probability, finality not being mentioned:

> Fifthly, the solution can consist in the introduction of new conjugate
> forms in man's intellect, will, and sensitivity. For such forms are
> habits. But man's intellect is an unrestricted potency, and so it can
> receive habits of any kind; man's will is good insofar as it follows
> intellect ... Moreover, the higher conjugate forms have to meet a
> problem that varies as man develops and declines, and so they too
> must be capable of some development and adaptation ... the appro-
> priate willingness will be some type of species of charity.[39]

Faith and charity are the conjugate forms in humankind's intellect and will. Only in the epilogue will he affirm that it is a part of the unfolding structure of human history.

These proposals, like almost everything else in *Insight*, did not come out of thin air. In 1947–8 he taught a course on faith and the virtues using Lennerz's *De Virtutibus* as his text. The long first section on the analysis of faith, a heading in Lennerz's text, prepared the way for the parallel section in chapter 20 of *Insight*. Significant in that treatment was the light of faith, the manner in which religious faith could enlighten the human mind in its darkness, be, as Newman called it, a kindly leading light. After a long and intellectualist treatment of faith, there follows a shorter section on the love of God and charity and a quite short section on hope. Later, he prepared his own supplementary course notes on the analysis of faith, whose influence can be discerned in chapter 20.[40]

In 'Finality, Love, Marriage' Lonergan had attempted to relate the traditional teaching on grace to more recent reflections on the ends of marriage within an evolutionary world view. Central there was the distinction between natural friendship and charity. In proposing his heuristic structures to the solution to the problem of evil as he has diagnosed it on the intellectual and ethical level, he is attempting to relate the traditional teaching on the theological virtues, on faith, hope, and charity, to the problem. Charity transforms the will, faith transforms the intellect. His treatment of the love of God before the light of faith points towards *Method in Theology*, where faith will be defined as the knowledge born of being in love with God.

The solution to the problem of evil involves not a withdrawal but an engagement with the dialectic of good and evil in our world. Apart from the surd of sin, the universe, and in particular the person of good will, is in love with God: 'But to will the good of a person is to love the person; and so to will the order of the universe because of one's love of God is to love all persons in the universe because of one's love of God.'[41] That love of God will be self-sacrificing, repentant, dialectical – returning evil with good – and joyful.

Lonergan opened his analysis of charity with the remark that good will follows intellect. The liberation of the intellect will come through hope that the will will will to make it good. In this respect, the liberation of the intellect would seem to follow the will. That hope will overcome the despair of the imprisonment of the counterpositions and the presumption that the objective of our human desire can be attained by human striving rather than by the gift of God. The advancement and dissemination of knowledge always requires social collaboration and belief. Religious faith becomes 'a transcendent belief operative within a new and higher collaboration of man with God.'[42] The motive of faith will be God's omnipotence and omniscience. The object of faith includes an affirmation of man's spiritual nature, freedom, responsibility, and of the existence of God's solution to the human problem of evil. The nature of that solution will in many ways remain a mystery beyond our comprehension. The human collaboration with God in addressing the problem of evil will also exhibit failures that can be traced to their human origin in dramatic, individual, group, and general bias.[43]

The treatment also poses some problems. In chapter 15 Lonergan had explored organic, psychic, and intellectual levels of development, adding an ethical level in chapter 18. In the final chapter ethical development either gets contracted to the intellectual or gets written out, as in his remarks about four levels of development, organic, psychic, intellectual, and religious, in the epilogue. The question also arises, ought not religious development to be analysed in terms of operators and integrators rather than simply in terms of the conjugate forms of faith, hope, and charity?

The Ending

As the character of a story can be profoundly anticipated in its beginning, so it can be recollected in the ending. Lonergan began *Insight* with a dream of an integrated understanding of the universe and of our place in it. His opening story of Archimedes' struggle to understand and related eureka experience is representative of the desire in us all to bring forth our own creative insights and experience the joy they bring. Lonergan ends the book with a paragraph about the collaboration of the mind and heart of the human individual with the love of God in the pursuit of the solution to the problem of evil:

> Nor will he labour alone in the purification of his own mind, for the realization of the solution and its development in each of us is principally the work of God who illuminates our intellects to understand what we had not understood and to grasp as unconditioned what we had reputed error, who breaks the bonds of our habitual unwillingness to be utterly genuine in intelligent inquiry and critical reflection by inspiring the hope that reinforces the detached, disinterested desire to know and by infusing the charity, the love, that bestows on intelligence the fullness of life.[44]

Despite Lonergan's desire to distance himself from the text, there is to this closing remark a personal ring. Throughout the performance of authoring *Insight* the dark presence of the source of all questions, who for the most part quietly and unperceived unlocks them for us and leads us towards their solutions, can be dimly discerned. Recognized or not, there is involved in the quest of the human mind and its participation in the finality of the universe through its problem-solving activity a profound religious spirituality. It is through the gift of God's love and light that human understanding achieves its fullness of life.

27

Introduction, Epilogue, Prefaces, Publication

In other words, not only are we writing from a moving viewpoint but also we are writing about a moving viewpoint.[1]

At the start of his doctoral studies in 1938 Lonergan was assigned, on their completion, to become a teacher of theology in the Gregorian. Because of the outbreak of the war, he returned to Montreal in 1940 on the assumption that, at a later date, he would be recalled to Rome. As things turned out, that recall was delayed until 1953, providing him with exactly the circumstances he needed in order to research and compose *Insight*. In September 1953 he returned to Rome and was appointed a professor in the theology faculty of the Gregorian University, where he would teach until 1965. There, shortly, a new chapter in his life would begin that would take him on the road to his later *Method in Theology*. On any reckoning, composing the last seven chapters of *Insight* in the time available before the move was just short of miraculous. According to Crowe, the introduction and the first preface were not in place in August and so could have been composed during the transition.[2] A reference to the introduction in the last paragraph of the epilogue suggests the former was written first. A year later the published preface was composed as the result of a conversation with his publisher. Each of these elements had a different purpose and are in their own ways revealing.

The Introduction

In his introduction Lonergan addresses prospective readers about what they might expect to find in the book. Its themes give us clues as to how he viewed it around the time it was finished. Four such themes stand out.

Firstly, a personal invitation is addressed to the reader: 'more than all else, the aim of the book is to issue an invitation to a personal decisive act.'[3] Where Kant called upon reason 'to undertake anew the most difficult of all its tasks, namely, that of self-knowledge, and to institute a tribunal which will assure reason its lawful claims,'[4] Lonergan calls on rational self-consciousness to take possession of itself. Central to the path on which one is being invited to journey by the author is an invitation to make certain discoveries about one's own cognitive desires and powers. The invitation to take a stance on a basic fact and the form of analysis involved in it come across as strangely disturbing in the culture of modern philosophy. Added to this is the fact that as it is written, *Insight* is a quite impersonal book. Lonergan never disclosed the details of his own personal struggles and his own experiences of insight in his journey towards self-appropriation.

The second and by far the most prominent theme is his thesis about the dualism in human consciousness and in human knowing. Starting on the very first page of the introduction it recurs frequently, the following string of quotations speaking for themselves: 'in each of us there exist two different kinds of knowledge' (11, xvii); 'For the present enterprise is concerned to unravel an ambiguity and to eliminate an ambivalence. Augustine of Hippo narrates that it took him years to make the discovery that the name, real, might have different connotations from the name, body' (15, xx); 'Clearly in a contemporary effort to resolve the duality in man's knowledge it would be foolhardy to ignore, if not the most striking, at least the most precise element in the evidence' (15–6, xxi); 'But the hard fact is that the psychological problem exists, that there exist in man two diverse kinds of knowing, that they exist without differentiation and in an ambivalent confusion until they are distinguished explicitly' (17, xxii); 'To conclude, our aim regards: (1) not the fact of knowledge but a discrimination between two facts of knowledge' (22, xxviii).

This theme, clearly on his mind as he finished the book, dominates the introduction as nowhere else in *Insight* or in his other writings. Although addressed to the reader, his remarks that 'from the horns of that dilemma one escapes only through the discovery (and one had not made it yet if one has no memory of its startling strangeness) that there are two quite different realisms,'[5] are clearly autobiographical. The language is strong. He is saying that he was startled by the strangeness of the vision of reality that his vision quest had disclosed. Widespread is the myth, even in the scientific community, that knowing is a matter of picturing what is out there now to be observed. Startlingly different is the reality made present by the strange cognitive powers of intellectual desire, insights, and related judgments. The transition from the one to the other involves a Platonic-like journey out of the cave of the dominance of the senses, instincts, and imagination. This has to be read in the context of his remark that through our senses there is made present to us empirical knowledge of reality, of brute facts.

The third theme has to do with his slogan about understanding understanding: '*Thoroughly understand what it is to understand, and not only will you understand the broad lines of all that there is to be understood but also you will possess a fixed base, an invariant pattern, opening upon all further developments of understanding.*'[6] His goal, through insight into a range of types of insights into phantasms, is to work out a world view. The theme restates what he had said in his notes on order at the start of the process of composition. The structure of human knowing that Lonergan is inviting the reader to take possession of is a constant, an invariant of human development. It is the unchanging cause of the process of intellectual development.

The fourth topic has to do with the fact that the book is written from and about a moving viewpoint, a theme first stated in chapter 20.[7] It sets down an initial minimal viewpoint with respect to insight, cognitional structure, the self, and so forth. As the book develops, the viewpoint within which those notions are to be interpreted enlarges to the point when at times the initial viewpoint is incorporated into later, higher viewpoints. To the cognitional self the moving viewpoint adds the subject of common sense, the ethical self, and finally the religious self. The viewpoint of the philosopher of mind changes. The viewpoint of what is being written about is also something that changes. There is also the distinction between the moving viewpoint of the manner in which *Insight* was authored and the manner in which Lonergan intended it to be read. The indications are that Lonergan's interest in Gödel's theorem, mentioned in this context and in chapter 17, came late in the process of composition.[8]

One cannot overemphasize the significance of the present point. In it Lonergan is articulating a profound insight into his experience of composing the book. It contrasts with his efforts as recently as in the O'D. Hanley lectures to present a systematic approach to the study of human understanding. Much philosophical analysis has been concerned with logical consistency and clarity of meaning within a system of thinking. Problems arise where both the meanings being analysed in a text and the standpoint of the interpreter of those meanings change. To deal with them, a paradigm of analysis that accepts the reality of human development is needed. The successive viewpoints are of course related and linked, but not in terms of logic.

In his later years Lonergan frequently summed up his philosophical project in terms of three questions: 'What am I doing when I am knowing? Why is doing that knowing? What do I know when I do it?'[9] First articulated in his grace course in 1947, they are the questions that for him constitute cogni-

tional theory, epistemology, and metaphysics. Little information on their
background is to be found in the introduction. There, on the evidence
available, he seems to contract them into two questions:

> The first part deals with the question, What is happening when we
> are knowing? The second part moves to the question, What is known
> when that is happening?[10]

The first part of the book ends with the chapter on reflective understanding placed prior to that on self-affirmation. In tension with this, two pages
later we read:

> In the eleventh chapter there occurs the first judgment of self-
> affirmation but only in the twelfth chapter is it advanced that judg-
> ment is knowledge and only in the thirteenth is it explained in what
> sense such knowledge can be named objective.

This seems to imply that the chapter on self-affirmation should be in the
first part of the book. A second part should run through chapters 12 and 13
addressing the epistemological question, and a third concerned with what
is known should begin at chapter 14.

Lonergan concludes the introduction by recalling Hume's advice that
one does not conquer a territory piecemeal by taking a village or an outpost
here and there. Rather, one has to march on the capital and conquer the
citadel. Even after one has gotten one's strategy right and successfully taken
the territory, there remains a vast amount of mopping up and consolidat-
ing to be done. His contribution is that of a single individual marching on
the citadel of rational self-consciousness. In the preface he states that no
doubt he will be accused of trying to operate on too broad a front. He
replies that one has to construct a whole ship, as a part of a ship is no good
at all.[11]

The Epilogue

In the introduction Lonergan articulated his dream of grounding an understanding of the broad lines of all that is to be understood by an understanding of understanding. In the epilogue he reviews the journey of his
reader through the text and reflects on what he hopes it has achieved. Here
he expresses himself more personally, reveals more of himself to the reader
than in any other place. Exclaiming that the long-suffering reader is entitled to a summing up, he is frank about his limitations: 'For many matters
have been treated in isolation; others have been handled in a series of

disparate contexts; still others have been partly developed but left unfinished.'[12] This is not false modesty, but a truthful expression of the problem
of the competence required in order to integrate the insights from a wide
range of disciplines into a world view.

In many ways *Insight* is a series of suggestions of possibilities in need of
enlargement. In this sense, what Lonergan said about Aquinas in a letter in
1958 can be applied to his own work:

> St Thomas dealt with questions at a determinate stage of their devel-
> opment and, in a large number of instances, contributed to their
> advance. Hence his thinking is on a moving front, and the front is
> not a single straight line but rather a jagged line with outposts and
> delayed sectors ... Accordingly I contend that interpretation by
> deduction from the text of St Thomas is a merely subjective projec-
> tion of one's own logical ideal on the text, that correct interpreta-
> tion has to take into account the tensions created by advance that is
> not always complete, and that Thomism, as distinct from a historical
> account of St Thomas, has to complete such advance.[13]

With this in mind, we should not skip lightly over his asterisked footnote on
the first page of the epilogue acknowledging the skimpy treatment ac-
corded to personal relations in his work. Developing an I–Thou based
metaphysics of communicative acts within the horizon of critical realism
remains an urgent future task. He did not address it.

Recalling his remarks in the introduction on writing from a moving
viewpoint, he continues with some frank comments on his motivation for
the whole project:

> If I have written as a humanist, as one dominated by the desire not
> only to understand but also, through understanding, to reach a
> grasp of the main lines of all there is to be understood, still the very
> shape of things as they are has compelled me to end with a question
> at once too basic and too detailed to admit a brief answer. The self-
> appropriation of one's own intellectual and rational self-conscious-
> ness begins as cognitional theory, expands into a metaphysics and an
> ethics, mounts to a conception and an affirmation of God, only to
> be confronted with a problem of evil that demands the transforma-
> tion of self-reliant intelligence into an *intellectus quaerens fidem*. Only
> at the term of that search for faith, for the new and higher collabo-
> ration of minds that has God as its author and its guide could the
> desired summary and completion be undertaken.[14]

It was his wish to write the first eighteen chapters solely in the light of human intelligence and reasonableness in order to express Catholic thought's affirmation of the essential independence of other fields.[15] On this matter I would not doubt his sincerity. The commitment in those eighteen chapters towards understanding the natural capabilities of human insight and the ideal of humanism, the complete flowering of the potentialities of the natural human mind and human nature, is total.[16] Nonetheless it is his inevitable conclusion that there are inherent limitations in the humanistic ideal in relation to the problem of evil.

There follows in the opening of the epilogue a highly focused summary of the project of *Insight*. It unfolds in five movements. The first is concerned with affirming the invariant structures of human knowing. The second has to do with understanding the isomorphic structures of all that there is to be known. The third adds the ethical, the dimension of reasonable choice, to human knowing. The fourth envisages the profounder structure of the relation of knowing and the known that arises in general transcendent knowledge. The fifth addresses the question of human knowing and doing collaborating with God in addressing the problem of evil. Much of the epilogue will be concerned with the possible contribution of his work to that further higher collaboration that it envisages and to which it leads. This should not be seen as an afterthought, but as an expression of his core desires. He is now writing from his terminal viewpoint as 'a believer, a Catholic, and it happens, a professor of dogmatic theology.'[17]

Within this framework the book can be read as a contribution to an introduction to theology, or apologetics as it was known. Theology for him would be an intellectual discipline that has key responsibilities in the realm of understanding the human participation in God's solution to the problem of evil.[18] Apologetics will have to deal with the relation between faith and reason, so he outlines the challenge to faith of the new and modern empirical sciences and their domains. One of the striking things about *Insight* is how immersed its author was in the scientific culture of the time.[19]

Next, for the first time in public, at this point in the epilogue he discusses how the work could be considered a contribution to the method of theology. The (first) Vatican Council in successive statements has insisted:[20]

(1) that divine revelation was to be regarded, not as a human invention to be perfected by human ingenuity, but as a permanent deposit confided to the Church and by the Church to be preserved and defended, and

(2) that every group and every period should advance in the un-

derstanding, knowledge, and wisdom, by which the same
doctrine with the same meaning was to be apprehended ever
more fully.

He considers that this affirmation of identity in difference and development illustrates the relevance of his analysis of development and of interpretation that envisaged:

(1) initial statements addressed to particular audiences,
(2) their successive recasting for sequences of other particular
audiences,
(3) the ascent to a universal viewpoint to express the initial statements in a form accessible to any sufficiently cultured audience,
and
(4) the explanatory unification from the universal viewpoint of the
initial statements and all their subsequent re-expressions.

But isomorphic with this interpretative process there is the Catholic
fact of

(1) an initial divine revelation,
(2) the work of teachers and preachers communicating and applying the initial message to a succession of different audiences,
(3) the work of the speculative theologian seeking a universal formulation of the truths of faith, and
(4) the work of the historical theologian revealing the doctrinal
identity in the verbal and conceptual differences of (1), (2),
and (3).

Within the movement of his desire *Insight* is of the nature of a preface to
that future work.

The method of a modern theology will for Lonergan have to articulate
categories that will enable theologians to interpret modes of religious
expression of different places and times. Reflecting his Christology course
of 1952, these will span the early symbolic cultures of the New Testament,
the process or developmental culture of the patristic era, the systematic
modes of thinking of the medieval universities, and the modern scientific
and historically conscious cultures of the present time. A problem that will
be addressed under the heading 'differentiations of consciousness' in his
later work is taking shape here. A methodical theology will both understand
the universal operations of the human mind and relate them to significant
transformations of one and the same message as the human story unfolds
along and across cultures.

The question now arises, where does the actual participation of human beings with God in addressing the solution to the problem of evil fit within Lonergan's scheme of things? For theology, which presupposes some form of faith or beliefs, takes us beyond the domain of reason or cognition. Responding to this, he recalls his thought on biological, psychic, and intellectual development as set forth in chapter 15, glossing over, it seems, the ethical development of chapter 18. From the standpoint of those earlier remarks on development, he goes on:

> The advent of the absolutely supernatural solution to man's problem of evil adds to man's biological, psychic, and intellectual levels of development a fourth level that includes the higher conjugate forms of faith, hope, and charity.[21]

This would necessitate the recontextualization of his thought so far on the subject of consciousness within the framework of a religious anthropology. It is yet a further illustration of the moving viewpoint. In his later thought the question of the relation between the ethical and the religious level would become problematic.

The Prefaces, Title, Publication

The final elements in the composition of *Insight* were the prefaces. Again there was involved an amount of writing and rewriting, some fragments from the earlier drafts being extant. On a folded page headed 'Preface' in which text of the original preface was contained, we find: 'A study of human understanding is primarily a study of methods. Its bearing on concrete policies is by implication rather than by direct pronouncement.'[22] In the first sentence it is inferred that classical, statistical, genetic, and dialectical insights are to be understood as methods. In the second sentence we find Lonergan struggling to articulate the usefulness of his study of insight. What power does it bestow on us, and how would it enable us to go on with things in the world?

> Knowledge is power. It is power to do and power to control. As natural science yields power over nature, so human science yields power over men. But if philosophy exists, if an organization of all knowledge exists, then it must be the basic and immanent source of the direction and control of power. Are we to say philosophy does not exist? Or are we to acknowledge that philosophy is the most significant of all practical pursuits?[23]

In these fragments we find Lonergan struggling with the question, what is the good of philosophy, in particular of a philosophy of insight and knowledge? What he did not succeed in articulating was the light that insights into the pure cycle of the economic process, into emergent probability, cosmic finality, and the biases of common sense, especially general bias, contribute to our understanding of the historical process. To this we could add the light that an understanding of the pure desire to know and related insights contributes to our understanding of the meaning of the human person.

Two quite different prefaces were composed, an unpublished one at the end of his work in 1953 and the one published in the book, which was composed a year later.[24] Both are somewhat toned down from what we find in the fragments. The original preface seems more rushed and less focused than the final one. It sets out an invitation to scale the summit of one's interiority as constituted by rational self-consciousness. The book is not an argument, but rather a programme. It presumes not premises but readers. It does not deduce conclusions from a religious faith or the principles of a philosophy. It invites readers to bring into focus their own intelligence and reasonableness. To do this is to gain insight into insight, the event that lies behind the verbal exterior of mathematics, science, and common sense. In this, 'one has to strive to mount to the level of one's time,' a phrase, according to Crowe, that Lonergan borrowed from Ortega y Gasset.[25] The manner of engagement with the cultural advances of one's time reflects his concern in the notes on order with achieving competence in the range of disciplines necessary in order to work out his world view.

According to Crowe the origin of the final version of the preface, the one published in the book, was in a lunch conversation between Lonergan and T. Michael Longman in the summer of 1954. During the meal Longman 'kept pumping Lonergan on his reasons for writing, his hopes for the book, etc. At the end of the meal he said very simply, "Why don't you put all that in your Preface?"' Lonergan went to work on it, and completed it by 26 August.[26]

Prefaces are usually brief and refer to those who have assisted the author on his or her journey, and end with a statement of gratitude. In contrast, the majority of Lonergan's final preface is more like a second introduction. After introducing the meaning of an insight with reference to the ideal detective story, it goes on to sketch the place of an analysis of insight within philosophy as Lonergan conceives it. It next poses the question, what would be the good of such a philosophy, the use, the cash value? It proposes that a philosophy based on insight into insight will be a philosophy of true progress. A philosophy based on an oversight of insight or of a flight from insight will be a philosophy of decline. Striking is this desire to link his study of insight with his long interest in the problem of progress and decline in culture, the problem that had engaged him in the 1930s. On a deep level, Lonergan wanted to work out an understanding of understanding that would bestow on us some power or control over progress and decline, that is to say, over history. Here, at the end, in the final preface he is pointing towards a link between his work and a major unresolved question. As Crowe points out, the book is essentially unfinished.[27]

More recently, in two important articles, Crowe has drawn attention to some further unfinished business, recognized by Lonergan shortly after completing the text.[28] In the introduction we find a twofold occurrence of the phrase 'insight into insight.' In the preface it occurs some fifteen times. After the book was published, the question arose for Lonergan: how can this phrase be reconciled with the thesis of Aquinas that insights are always into phantasms, that is to say, sensible or imaginable presentations? In the direct mode of cognitional operation in mathematics, science, and common sense, insights in their object or intentional dimension involve an engagement with the imaginative presentations of problems in our world and the related linguistic expressions involved in their solutions. In their conscious dimension they are experienced as a related real but unimaginable awareness. This seems to suggest, following Aquinas, that in a sense there can be no insights into insights themselves. Significant in this context is the point that was made in the fourth *Verbum* article that the intellect knows directly, not the phantasm, but the thing that the phantasm represents, the rule of the circle, law, probability, and so forth. This suggests that the task of the introspective mode is to have an insight into the 'insights into the phantasms' of the direct mode.

In his articles Crowe charts the stages in Lonergan's further reflections on the problem up to an interview the latter gave in 1981 to Luis Morfin that, for Crowe, suggests that he had worked out his own resolution of the problem.

> So what are you going to do? You set up dummies: the language
> symbols, linguistic symbols; you relate the linguistic symbols to one
> another: sensation, imagination, feeling, inquiry, understanding,
> judgment, judgment of value and decision, being in love with God ...
> But you have to have all these things on their different levels, and
> their relations to one another, each on its own level. So you create
> the phantasm, just as the mathematician does.[29]

For their insights to emerge mathematicians need images of geometrical shapes or the symbols of their equations, scientists need imaginative representations of the data, persons of common sense an imaginative engagement with their situation in the world. The parallel question here is: what image or phantasm is necessary in and through which we can arrive at an understanding of the insights of classical and statistical science or the insights of common sense? What sort of a phantasm is necessary in order for us to arrive at an understanding of cognitional structure? In each instance the intellect again knows directly, not the phantasm or image, but the thing that the phantasm represents, classical, statistical, and common-sense insights or cognitional structure.

The performance of the direct mode of cognition in science and common sense provides the conscious data for the introspective mode. It follows that the analysis of the data of consciousness as cognitional can never be direct. It is always derivative of linguistic descriptions of the performance of the direct mode. What it seems is being called for is the addition of a more descriptive linguistic account of the phenomena of the direct mode of cognitional operation in mathematics, science, and common sense than has been the case. This linguistic account will, in turn, provide elements of the required phantasms. The subsequent insights will not be into the phantasm in itself, but into what it represents. The first thirteen chapters of *Insight* will be a starting point of this development, which will result in a deeper understanding of the nature of our access to the data of cognition as conscious.

Before ending the preface with an acknowledgement of those who had supported him since he was introduced to philosophy twenty-eight years earlier, Lonergan adds a biographical passage detailing how he personally experienced his quest, his prolonged search, his dark struggle, half lights and detours in his slow development.[30] Some will dismiss remarks like this as a form of false modesty. On the contrary, it articulates compactly what the present biographical narrative has attempted to communicate.

Illuminating is the sequence of titles used by Lonergan in the course of the *Insight* project. During the course of the *Verbum* studies the word 'insight' began to grow in significance for him but did not appear in the titles of either the articles or the book: *The Concept of* Verbum *in the Writing of St Thomas*, and Verbum: *Word and Idea in Aquinas*. His first title for the *Insight* project was 'Thought and Reality,' followed later by 'Intelligence and Reality.' Common to both was the word 'reality' and the absence of the word 'insight.' During the process of composing the book, the earliest title he used (close to December 1952) was *Insight: A Study of Human Intelligence*. A middle revision entitled it *Insight: An Essay in Aid of Personal Appropriation of One's Rational Self-Consciousness*. Finally it became *Insight: A Study of Human Understanding*. Clearly, the word 'insight' grew in significance for him and became the anchor word in the title, and indeed in the whole project.

In contrast, 'reality' faded out of the titles, although not out of the problem. The titles in this sense reflect Lonergan's preoccupations.

Below the title there is the quotation, which can be traced through Hoenen to Aquinas, on insight grasping the forms in the images. It reminds us that in his first essay in Heythrop Lonergan posed the question, how do we make intelligent inferences directly from sense data rather than from primitive propositions? Truly, the quote on the title page reminds us that in our beginning is our ending. It also warns us that Lonergan's philosophy of insight cannot be integrated with the Kantian view of mind. Insights are *into* qualities of the world.

The first typescript was completed during the summer of 1953.[31] With almost no emotion, he announced to Crowe: 'It is done. It has been a long haul.' Leaving the manuscript with Crowe, he went for a holiday to Moncton. Instead of using the time to prepare his classes, Crowe spent most of the next three weeks reading the text, fascinated by what he read. Lonergan returned, did his packing, and moved to Rome. With the exception of some revisions during the summer of 1954 brought on largely but not totally by the reader, his work on *Insight* was over. An unusual period in his personal intellectual history was winding down. But it would not be properly ended until he had found a publisher.

In April 1954, three years after *Humani Generis*, the text was passed by the ecclesiastical censors in Rome, and the search for a publisher began. In a letter to Crowe on 5 May, Lonergan wrote about his discovery of H.S. Sullivan. Mircea Eliade was also stimulating his interest in symbols. Influenced by comments by André Godin, mentioned in the preface, he revised the sections on Freud at the end of chapter 6. A reference to Susanne Langer also made an appearance at this point.[32]

He initially approached Oxford University Press in New York, who replied that the work was too technical for them and advised him to try their press in England. In June he wrote to Crowe that he was tired of waiting on the Clarendon Press and had approached T. Michael Longman. On 26 October, after Longman had got his report from a Professor George Temple FRS, Sedelian Professor of Natural Philosophy in the Mathematical Institute at Oxford, Lonergan wrote that *Insight* had hit a snag.

Temple disliked the first five chapters, but his criticisms were vague and thin on specific points. He advocated a series of volumes, metaphysics first, then ethics, then psychology. Lonergan at first considered this impossible, but was prepared to revise or scuttle chapters 1–5. Before he had time to seek advice from his mathematical friends, Eric O'Connor and Phil Leah, it became clear that Longmans were not taking Temple's criticisms too seriously. He made some revisions to parts of the first two chapters, specifically clarifying the notion of inverse insight to make it 'plain as a pikestaff.' As a result, he felt that the two chapters were now much better from the viewpoint of the specialist reader. Later, Lonergan was open to Longmans proposal of a number of volumes on the condition that they all share the same title and advertising.[33] Longmans clearly recognized *Insight* as a work of exceptional significance and wanted to publish it. But they also recognized that from a publisher's viewpoint it was risky, suggesting that Lonergan approach the Compton Trust Fund, which supports such works. As things turned out, that was not necessary.

As the drama of negotiating with publishers continued, Lonergan began his second year of teaching. In the first semester he taught a course on *Insight* entitled '*De Methodis Universim Inquisito Theoretica.*' Interesting is the occurrence in the title of the term 'method.' For his Trinity course in the second semester he prepared some notes that would appear as Appendices 1 and 2 in *The Analogous Conception of the Divine Persons*. He complained of rotten health from November through to January, suffering from colds and an ear infection, and generally feeling miserable.

His anxieties were eased when at the end of the teaching year he signed a contract with Longmans, on 25 June 1955, and another with The Philosophical Library on 22 September.[34] According to Lonergan, Wynn-Lewis was the 'reader who sold the book to Longmans.'[35] In *Caring About Meaning* he remarked, 'The publisher's reader of *Insight*, the one who really knows his stuff, said, "The only thing on scientific method is Mill, and no one pays any attention to that."'[36]

From mid-June he was involved in several weeks of oral examinations of large numbers of students, which drained him. On 7 July he set off by land and sea for Canada. In a letter to Eric O'Connor, he said that since arriving in Montreal two months earlier he had been hanging on the ropes, so tired that he was unable to visit. He escaped the torrid Montreal summer by spending a month in the cooler climate of Halifax.

On 21 September Lonergan wrote to Courtney Murray, including in his letter a copy of a reader's report. Acknowledging that philosophy was tending to be analytic, with less and less positive content, overall the report welcomed the breadth of Lonergan's project. Over against analytic philosophy stood existentialism, scholasticism – usually viewed as outdated – and Marxism. Lonergan's study is a thoroughly modern treatment of the question, 'what is understanding?' The basic criticism in the report is worth quoting:

> I cannot accept the intellectualism of Professor Lonergan's approach to the nature of human life and the understanding of the Universe. I do not believe in the pure, disinterested desire to know

which he postulates: I think he has rightly argued that man has (or is?) a principle which is not purely reactive, purely determined by circumstances, but I do not believe enquiry is that principle. Similarly, I think there is a fallacy in holding that Being can be defined as 'that which is known by intelligence' – as if the law of falling bodies were part of the real world and not a human invention: I think he is right in criticising the ordinary theory of abstract knowledge as a sort of impoverished copy of the real world (chapter 3, section 6.2 – the real core of his whole case), but I think he has put over a fast one in his own theory of the process. This objection determined my reaction to his whole case (e.g., to his suggestion that good behaviour means reasonable behaviour, sin irrationality). However, that is his case and I cannot see any easy refutation.

Given the then prevailing accusations of Catholicism as being anti-intellectualist, it is ironic that the work should be critiqued for being too intellectualist.[37]

On 23 September Lonergan set sail for Rome and his class of seven hundred. In November he came down with some kind of ulcer, fortunately not a long-term health problem. Some revisions of the typescript were suggested, in which the considerable help provided by Crowe and O'Connor eased the tedium of proof reading and correcting typing errors. In his letter of 27 December he reassured Crowe that he had mastered *Insight* on the theory of knowledge to such an extent that he was creatively extending it. He commented on complacence as an antidote to anxiety, a possible reference to a study of complacency and concern in Aquinas that Crowe was embarking on.[98] He also remarked that the Freudian superego was the same as Aquinas' *cogitativa* that children develop about what is good and bad. The galleys arrived in the middle of January and absorbed him to the end of March.

As he was correcting the galleys and teaching *On the Incarnate Word*, he composed in Latin, a language he considered clipped his lyric wings, a difficult but probing monograph on Christology. It was a supplement to the course text and dealt with the specialized question of Christ's constitution and consciousness, the development of the question that Leeming had introduced him to in 1935 and that had brought about his intellectual conversion. In April 1956 he wrote to Crowe that he had 224 typed pages with parts crossed out here and there. To get there he had slugged his way through two or three times that amount. He thought he could try again, addressing the chief points more heavily and omitting more. His ulcer, though needing diet and pills, had been trouble free for the past months. He was back on the dawn patrol, teaching his first class at 8:30 a.m., and found himself going to bed wondering what he was going to say the next morning, which caused him stress.[39]

The page proofs of *Insight* started to arrive in July as he was leaving Rome for Halifax, where he spent the summer. Soon after, Crowe took on the hugely demanding task of preparing an index. In July Lonergan was given a thorough medical examination that revealed that, rather than having an ulcer, he was just working too hard. He was told not to work so hard and to avoid certain foods. Much of the summer was spent on corrections and problems associated with the table of contents, the corrected page proofs being returned to Longmans on 24 August. Crowe was at this time busy at work on the index, proofs of which arrived in Rome in November.

Insight was published in March 1957, 2030 copies being printed. Within a year a second edition was in print. Soon 101 reviews had appeared, largely of the first edition. It was a significant publishing event in mid-twentieth-century Catholic intellectual history. It emerged in a Catholic world that, as Peter McDonough has pointed out in his *Men Astutely Trained*, was just beginning to become bored with the prevailing scholasticism: 'By the end of the fifties the deposit of faith, as expressed in neo-Thomism, suffered from a surfeit of stability. The outcome of the debate was certain, and the game lost interest ... The dynamics of cultural transmission pitted new Jesuits against "the venerable fathers," practically regardless of their views.'[40] *Insight* was published at a time when, in America and elsewhere, there were the seeds of an intellectual restlessness among the new generation of students, a restlessness that would become more pronounced and widespread throughout the 1960s. The reception of *Insight* in some Catholic circles was determined by the fact that it presented philosophers with a bridge from the scholastic to the modern world.

Not only did Crowe compile the index, an arduous task; he also wrote an introduction entitled 'The Origin and Scope of Bernard Lonergan's *Insight*,' which was published in *Sciences Ecclesiastique* in 1957.[41] Acknowledging that he was writing it as a student of Lonergan's thought rather than as a critic, he divided it into three parts. The first part was on understanding understanding, the second on insight in Aquinas, and the third on its implications for theology. Lonergan received a copy in March and on 14 May wrote to Crowe that 'Part I of *Insight* is an approach to metaphysics through subjectivity; it appeals to subjectivity to settle what the true proposition means (xxiii 1–6).' There is involved in it a quiet despoiling of the Egyptians, by whom he meant the existentialists, but he does not put it this way because he would be misunderstood.[42] He was more impressed with parts 1 and 2 of Crowe's article, the third part being too determined by his local situation.[43]

In May Lonergan wrote to O'Connor that he was having quite a time swotting up on his lectures to be given at Boston College in July. They had requested lectures on mathematical logic and existentialism rather than insight, but his treatment would lead towards the latter.[44] The section on truth in the logic lectures again addresses the question of the virtually unconditioned. The lectures on existentialism explore themes such as the subject, conversion, horizon, time, and history. In them there was the genesis of an attempt to relate his viewpoint to those of Husserl, Heidegger, Marcel, Jaspers, and Sartre. This was to be the first of very many summer institutes Lonergan would give in the United States, Canada, and else-where, for the duration of his years in Rome. The list is impressive, generating an image of the energy of the person and the dynamism of his mind. They include St Mary's University Halifax lectures (1958); Xavier Cincinnati Philosophy of Education (1959); 'Critical Realism and the Integration of the Sciences,' University College Dublin 1961; forty lectures on *Insight*, Moraga, California, 10 July–4 August 1961; 'Method in Theology,' Regis College, Toronto, 1962; and 'Method in Theology,' Georgetown University, Washington, 1964. In these institutes we do not find him simply repeating what he had worked out in *Insight*. His ideas were evolving all the time on the path that would eventually lead him to the later work *Method in Theology*.

In October Lonergan had a long talk with Michael Longman about possible future books. Longman said that as a publisher he was interested in the one Lonergan thought to be the most important. This Lonergan stated to be *Method in Theology*. The conversation, Lonergan remarked, 'helped me to clarify my mind on the issue and at the same time put me at ease re future plans.'[45] In and through this conversation the decision to write *Method in Theology* crystallized. Being moved from Rome to Canada in 1940 because of the outbreak of the war had facilitated the *Verbum* articles and *Insight*. His return to Rome would now facilitate work on the question about the method of theology that was posed there in the course of his doctoral studies in 1938. The transition to that research programme was beginning to take place. The next chapter in the journey of his desire was beginning to announce itself.

In letters to Crowe and O'Connor towards the end of 1957 and into the New Year, Lonergan noted that Crowe's 'Origin and Scope of Insight' had made a very considerable impression in the Gregorian. John Dunne CSC, the later well known author, was in Rome and reading *Insight* with interest. Lonergan noted reviews by Copleston, De Finance, O'Doherty, Dawson, Murray, Wesley, Wynn-Lewis, Mascall, Lotz, and Norris Clarke. Sebastian Moore thought the book was epoch making and wrote for a review copy for the *Downside Review*. Norris Clark seemed to Lonergan to make a considerable concession by accepting that *intelligere* meant 'understanding.' Albertson in the *Modern Schoolman* review did not notice that Lonergan's definition of probability, dealing with real events, was scientific rather than mathematical. For his discussion paper '*Insight*: Preface to a Discussion,' which Crowe had agreed to read, Lonergan remarked that the book was trying to make the fact of understanding and its centrality in our knowledge an issue. If that is overlooked, then the contributions of Aristotle and Aquinas will be lost.

A letter to Eric O'Connor on 26 March 1958 opens with some remarks on James Collins' review in *Cross Currents* on Hegel and Kant. Lonergan's account of Hegel's dialectic as conceptualist, closed, and necessitarian in contrast with the intellectualism and openness of his own position is for Collins a problem. Lonergan next turns to the relation between Kant's schematism and the virtually unconditioned:[46]

> The question here is not one of a formula, but of the implications of a fact. Because there is a grasp of the virtually unconditioned, there is a third cognitional level supervening on sense and understanding and going beyond them. Because the resultant judgment rests on the unconditioned, it is rational; this rationality summons reason and its ideals from its Kantian supervisory role (with a transcendental illusion) to make it part and parcel of all human knowing. Because the judgment is factual (*virtually* unconditioned), there are excluded both post-Kantian idealism and pre-Kantian rationalism; moreover this factual aspect of judgment selects what is correct in Kant's empiricist tendency. Because the judgment is the decisive issue, because it effects and it alone effects the promotion from 'I feel' and 'I think' to 'I know,' it alone is the criterion of knowing, and this eliminates what is wrong in Kant's empiricist tendency; Kant says categories validly used if empirical reference; but this is a further criterion besides the judgment; and cannot be justified by analysis of judgment. Finally, because judgment rests on unconditioned, it is absolute, independent of subject; hence I know means 'I know being' (Chap XII) and 'I know being' includes 'I know subjects and objects' (chapter XIII). Moreover this is immediate realism of judgment: the foregoing argument is needed, not that I may know, but that I may know that I know.

He continues with remarks on the distinction between scientific and mathematical probability, which seem to be in response to Albertson in the *Modern Schoolman* review and would be one of a number of revisions in the second edition.[47]

His letter of 4 April 1958 to O'Connor adds that he considers his metaphysics to be 'a scheme with a fairly detailed account on a number of issues;

it bears comparison with the alleged non-schematic metaphysics; it offers a scheme because a scheme is both all-embracing and concrete, while mere generality is abstract.' He goes on to worry about the formation of a clique against the book, similar to that which killed Murray on church and state.

By May 1958 the question of French and Italian translations was in the air. During the summer he loafed for a while in St Mary's Halifax, working on the relations between *Insight* and Kant's *Critique of Pure Reason.* In August he gave ten lectures there on *Insight* entitled 'Understanding and Being,' in which the focus was on self-appropriation.[48] The second edition of *Insight* was published on 24 November. On 29 December he replied in detail to the questions of a number of students attempting to study *Insight* in Innsbruck. By this time in his work on his courses, '*De Intellectu et Methodo*' (1958–9) and 'On System and History' (1959–60), the project of the method of theology was becoming established in his life.

Epilogue: Recollecting the Human Mystery

In order fully to know a road one must walk it in both directions. In the same way it is sometimes said that we live our lives forwards but understand them, to the limited extent that we do, backwards. The forwards experience can be like groping our way with difficulty down a dark and unpredictable passageway whose light switch is there to be discovered at the far end. Acknowledging our current familiarity with the biographical details of the life, what illumination, it might be asked, should we expect to discover through recollection in the backwards reading of the narrative? In his book *Life Study*, Ira Progoff suggests that it is one thing to become familiar with the biographical experiences in a life; it is another to understand in them an emergent work of art.[1] For him the artistry of the life is revealed in the inner movement of that life through its stepping stones from a beginning to a later destination.

The epilogue, which should now be read as a continuation of the introduction, addresses this task. From the perspective of the authored text of *Insight*, can we identify the stepping stones of Lonergan's desire through which the movement of his quest and the subsequent authoring of *Insight* were forged? In broad outline, the following moods and phases in the journey, which are couched in the first person to identify Lonergan as the subject of the desire, suggest themselves.

1. During my philosophical studies, my desire was awakened by exposure to certain unsolved problems in philosophy concerning the mind and its relation to reality. Newman's notion of the illative sense eased my confusion at the time.
2. During the 1930s I struggled with those problems and the intellectual

conversion they necessitated, but in 1935 I made a breakthrough on the relation between judgment and existence.

3. Direct work on these problems paused from 1935 until 1943 while I worked on the philosophy of history, theology, and economics.

4. In 1943 I resumed work on them through my researches in the *Verbum* articles and my course in 1946 on the problem of thought and reality. This was a time of intensive research, during which Aquinas taught me a great deal and my understanding of and focus on the problems deepened.

5. Inspired by some unsolved problems raised by the content of the *Verbum* articles, I made a series of breakthroughs on cognitional structure and on the notions of being and objectivity that were articulated in my course on the problem of intelligence and reality in 1951.

6. Between 1951 and 1953 I composed the autograph of *Insight* out of the foundations in my work on intelligence and reality. It was an intense period in which there occurred an explosive growth in my understanding. Significant new developments occurred in the realms of common-sense knowledge, consciousness, and self-affirmation.

7. I wrote the early chapters on scientific method and the subject and world of common sense out of the foundations, in particular the principal notion of objectivity.

8. Chapters 14–20 were written hurriedly but contained an agenda for enlarging implications of the mind-world problem into the realms of process metaphysics and interpretation. My explorations in ethics and religion as well as the need to address the issue of interpersonal relations would eventually convince me of the need to enlarge the framework of the mind-world problem itself into those realms.

9. With the completion of *Insight*, my desire in relation to certain aspects of the problems was stilled, in others opened up to a further agenda that would eventually lead me to my later work on *Method in Theology*.

The stepping stones and related chapters are the events and phases though which the life quest moves. Like the chapters in a book, the meaning of each and the mood and phase of the quest it establishes are related to the unity of meaning of the whole work. They invite us to bring into focus the emergent architecture and artistry of Lonergan's intellectual desire and the related emerging clarification of the structure of the philosophical problem it is addressing.

Firstly, there is the highly dramatic event of the beginning of a quest. Such a vocational awakening is not something that is defined internally. On the contrary, in many lives, such as Darwin's with his voyage of the Beagle, Wittgenstein's with his meetings with Frege and Russell, or Jacqueline Du

Pre's with her first experience of the sound of a cello shortly before her fifth birthday, it involves one's potential desires being called forth by an appropriate constellation of events and circumstances in the world. The recurrence of this fit in many creative lives is highly mysterious. Lonergan's quest, which ultimately would result in the authoring of *Insight*, began at Heythrop in 1926 with the awakening of his passion for a particular group of the questions of philosophy. How in that beginning the shape and course and destination of the quest is present and anticipated, and when achieved, recognized, is an interesting question. But the fact of the beginning and its significance as a directing presence in everything that follows is beyond dispute. Without it, there would be no destination.

Secondly, that awakening/discovery of the path of his desire was followed by a succession of enlargements and refigurations of his initial interests and inspiration. Significant in that enlargement is the role of persons and accidents in his life, of apparent good luck and bad luck.[2] In Heythrop there was the accident of picking up Newman's *Grammar of Assent*, in Montreal of reading J.A. Stewart's *Plato's Doctrine of Ideas* and Hoenen's essay. The unexpected move to Rome in 1933 brought him into contact with Leo Keeler, Stefanu, and Leeming. Had the war not broken out and had he remained teaching theology in Rome, I doubt *Insight* would ever have been written. Instrumental in the decision to write it was the founding of the Thomas More Institute at just the right time to invite him to lecture on the problem of thought and reality. As it unfolds with its twists and turns, the movement of Lonergan's intellectual desire might at certain points within the journey seem arbitrary, accidental, even chaotic. But from a later perspective we can glimpse in those accidents in his life a trend that opens up and develops his desire as well as the elements of the problem. Again notable in this expansion is the impact of these events and persons in the world on his personal desire and its related quest.

After his breakthrough in 1935 on judgment and existence, inspired by Hoenen, he returned in 1943 to the question of the mind-world relation in earnest, convinced that Aquinas had something significant to offer. In contrast with Kant and the scholastics, he began to use the phrase 'insight into phantasm' to characterize understanding. He replaced Plato's theory of ideas with Aristotle's and began to see the desire of the mind, self-knowledge, and insight into phantasm as key elements in the Kantian problem. From Aquinas he began to appreciate that the subject and object of knowledge would be known in essentially the same way, through the appropriate operation of the desire of the mind, thus eliminating the myth of the chasm.

After he moved to Toronto in 1947, Lonergan articulated for the first time in public the three basic disciplines and their related questions that are involved in the mind-world relation: cognitional theory, epistemology, and metaphysics. In the fall of that year, he articulated the insight that transcending immanentism required not a single but three distinct concrete judgments: I'm real, You're real, I'm not you.

Although the *Verbum* articles brought into focus for him the range of activities involved in our thought processes, they left him with significant unsolved questions concerning their interrelation and the related problem of the nature of consciousness. In his review of Dom Illtwd Trethowan in 1949, for the first time he began to talk about three levels of cognitional operations. There followed a series of breakthroughs on intellectual desire as a notion of being, and thus the key to the mind-world relation; on cognitional structure; and on the principle notion of objectivity with its plurality of judgments. All of these were articulated in his 1951 course on the mind-world relation entitled 'Intelligence and Reality.' In these developments he found himself becoming progressively startled by the strangeness of the pure desire of the mind to know and its objective and related realism.

That course also articulated his insights into higher viewpoints in mathematics and went on to explore the classical and statistical insights of the scientists. In this he began to draw a fundamental distinction between two modes of knowing, the direct and the introspective. Through the direct mode we operate as mathematicians, scientists, or persons of common sense in our worlds and related communities. The introspective mode takes the data of the direct mode as its object of analysis, a connection that it should never break. Its project is to understand the mind-world relation as it emerges in the direct mode, a project that is defined by the questions of the three disciplines cognitional theory, epistemology, and metaphysics. Strategically, he began with the cognitional question, but all three must be addressed in order to understand the mind-world relation as it is posed by the direct mode.

There followed in the course notes a metaphysical sketch, an exploratory analysis of the relation between the knower and the known, drawing on the categories of Aristotle. Here the later theorem of *Insight* on the isomorphism of knowing and known was nascent. The relations between what we know in the world by our senses, understanding, and judgment are isomorphic with the relations between those cognitional activities. In this, the third of the three questions was addressed.

Lonergan began composition of the autograph of *Insight* in the summer of 1951 with chapters 9–13. To the core insights of 'Intelligence and Reality' he added an analysis of the notion of consciousness, an invitation to self-affirmation, and the genesis of his work on common sense.

From the horizon of chapters 9–13, especially the principal notion of objectivity, which defines and distinguishes the subject and object of knowledge, he began to write the first eight chapters, which could be considered as a filling out of those insights. In response to questions about the subject and object/world of scientific method, he articulated in great detail classical and statistical questioning and insights, and a proportionate world order of emergent probability forged by the interplay of classical and statistical laws in the world. In his analysis of the subject and object of common sense he articulated his understanding of the dialectical development of the subject, and of the world of common sense as characterized by dramatic, individual, group, and general bias. When composing chapter 8 of *Insight* on things, drawing on his insight into higher viewpoints, he explored in the most comprehensive manner the implications of his theory of insight for our understanding of genera and species of things. His position there is strongly anti–reductionist.

Chapters 14–20 were written hurriedly from January to July of 1953. Lonergan recognized that his insight into the polymorphism of common-sense consciousness also applied to philosophers, and so he recast his foundations to include a dialectical context. There followed chapters sketching a metaphysics, related to that of 'Intelligence and Reality,' but in which he began to replace the static view there and in chapter 8 with a process view inspired to some extent by Bergson's *Creative Evolution*. Involved was a sketch of the significance of the notion of finality and of the structure of genetic method. His course on Christology in 1952 inspired him to write a chapter on the interpretation and reinterpretation of the major texts of a culture. All of these developments were explorations within the foundations of the mind-world problem as he had articulated it.

The last chapters addressed questions in the realms of ethics and religion. Although they dealt with the enlargement of consciousness into the ethical subject and the human good, and the enigmas of existence and evil, they were not integrated into the framework of an enlarged Kantian Copernican revolution, which would include, in addition to the mind-world relation, the ethical and religious subject-world relation.

In the introduction, his *Insight* quest completed, Lonergan found himself again struck by his discovery that there are two realisms in the human, an animal and an intellectual/rational. His objectification of the intellectual/rational realism is massive, not so that of the animal realism. In the epilogue he invites us to extend his analysis of the mind-world relation into the field of interpersonal relations, of the self and the other.

Through its interaction with its historicity, traditions – philosophical, scientific and religious – and fate, the cumulative problems that were presented to Lonergan's intellectual desire came be forged into the intellectual plot in his life. The unity of meaning that is the plot is that of an emergent work of art rather than of a life plan. It is music-like rather than law-like, the subproblems emerging like melodies in a symphonic work. As that plot unfolds, its future is always ungraspable. Only in the actual writing of *Insight* did Lonergan become clear on what he was trying to do. But the longer intellectual desire unfolds the more focused it becomes on the problems, and the more clearly the subject comes to be aware of what it is that is being sought. Significant also are the moments of major decisions, in 1943 to research *Verbum* and in 1946 to compose *Insight,* in which those works are chosen as his values. In these decisions we see elements of the ethical responsibility of the agent for his or her life quest. The analysis of the successive transformations in the relation between the agent's desire and world also suggests the possibility of transforming the problem of the subject-object relation and Kant's Copernican revolution into a narrative/ historical context.

Thirdly, to show the emergence, development, formation, and maturing of Lonergan's basic set of philosophical questions and related insights is to situate the book *Insight* firmly within the philosophical tradition. It reveals his creative enlargement and clarification of the structure of the mind-world problem, and his subsequent insights into a possible solution to that restructured problem. It also shows something central to the process of his authoring. The authored text in its linguistic and meaningful dimension is the expression and product of those insights. Authoring is the effort of the desire of the author to articulate and publicly express that vision in order to communicate it to others. That sought communication is articulated in the original sense or meaning of the words of the text that come to be chosen by the author through a process of at times extensive rewriting and revision. Authoring entails working out an appropriate linguistic expression in the text that the author feels does justice to his or her desire and understanding. In many instances, that desire is only stilled at the term of many refinements of an initial draft. It follows that, in a sense, intellectual desire and the insights it seeks are the core language-forming powers involved in the process of authoring. In this sense a distinction can be drawn between the original meaning of an author and the later derived meanings of a text by interpreters.

Fourthly, there arises the notion of personal identity in its intellectual and ethical dimensions. A person's intellectual identity is related to the path of their intellectual desire in their life, the directions that it establishes, and the set of questions it addresses, insights and related intellectual and linguistic skills that it seeks. There arises the question, who is Bernard Lonergan? He is the subject of the stepping stones, indeed of the whole narrative, the one whose intellectual desire was awakened by the questions of thought and reality, of the economic cycle, philosophy of history, world views. Ethically, he is the one who made the decisions to author the *Verbum* articles, *Insight* and, later, *Method in Theology* and who took upon himself the responsibility of seeing those decisions through. He is the one who had insights into cognitional structure, the notion of being, and the principal notion of objectivity. These were followed by his insights into emergent probability, the dialectical development of common sense, and a possible explanation of genera and species of things. To understand the emergent unity of the path of his desire in the relation between the subproblems and the basic problems in the overall plot is, with hindsight, to understand a unity in what seems, as it is experienced, a fragmented series of cognitional activities. A sense of personal intellectual identity replaces fragmentation. The growth of his intellectual desire and of his intellectual identity are seen to go hand in hand.

Fifthly, there is a dialectic of familiarity and strangeness involved in our understanding of intellectual desire.[3] As we begin to identify and become familiar with the fact of intellectual desire in ourselves and others, the question arises, what is this desire, intentionally and consciously, like? How well can we understand and enter into our own intellectual desire and that of another person? How deeply has Lonergan's desire been shown and probed? What is it like to be the subject of this desire, to experience it opening up from the initial nothingness of a seed-potential in problem solving and subtly establishing growth directions in our life? What sort of a desire awakens in someone when they are twenty-one and motivates them to strive in search of a vision for twenty-eight years? How well can we come to describe and know what it was like for Lonergan, day after day over the course of the twenty-eight years involved, to be in that state of the tension of inquiry? How well can we understand and master the creative processes that were involved in composing *Insight*? What sort of a desire finds its satisfaction not in food or drink or money or power but in the sense or meaning of the words that make up the text of *Insight*, to which it has given birth? Can we explain why Lonergan's desire directed him to this work rather than to some other? Or is the best we can do simply to show the path of his desire? Can we explain why it is that there is always more in the desire of an author than can find an expression in his or her authored texts? What, if anything, do the extended lines of the desires that are in us and that motivate our quests point towards? What is the beyond that our desire seeks?

The books read, the lectures attended and given, the authored drafts and texts produced on the road to *Insight* are the public expression of the journey of the mind of the author. They express the engagement of the desire of the mind with the problems that moved it. The linguistic narrative that is the present texts shows the long, slow build-up of twenty-six years with its emergent basic and subquestions and scattered moments of insight. This leads into an account of the explosive finale between 1951 and 1953 that involved thinking out and composing the MSA autograph.

That linguistic narrative also constitutes a phantasm that can be the source of further questions about the phenomena of the desire of the mind as conscious, and that in turn can move our insights in response to them. For as well as the problems that the desire of the mind engages with, there is also the self-conscious awareness of being in intellectual desire that all the time accompanies the problem solving. What has to be discovered is that the entire linguistic narrative has been building up a descriptive familiarity with the historicity of an essential conscious and intentional human quality of Lonergan that is inherently and irreducibly strange. What sort of a vocabulary do we need in order to describe to ourselves the moods and phases of the kinds of consciousness, of self-awareness, involved in it? At this point there is needed the discovery that much more is concealed by the language of desire and its resolution than is revealed.

If I have succeeded in getting some form of glimpse into the structure of the creative processes involved in puzzling out and composing *Insight*, it remains a glimpse into fragments of an intense conscious and intentional intellectual life. There is much more to the conscious life of the mind of Lonergan as author than finds expression in those sources. Still, this should not distract us from appreciating that what is grasped of the mind of the author in and through the images of the public sources is remarkably strange. It is a strangeness that will not be eliminated by adding more and more texts and so expanding our sense of more of the details of the conscious life of the author. It is a strangeness that is not the result of our ignorance, an ignorance that one might expect to be overcome by further information gathering and insights. The familiarity of the public face of the authored text masks the strangeness of the conscious and intentional awarenesses involved in the processes that gave birth to it. The goal of the present study is not to make the desire of the mind familiar. Rather, it is to make the strangeness of that desire as involved in problem solving and authoring familiar. The narrative of our entire study is like a signpost that points to the conscious and intentional life of Lonergan's intellectual desire as involved in authoring *Insight*. What, it asks, was that desire like, and how well can we comprehend it? To some extent we can show what it does: moves a vision quest and, in the process of authoring, shapes the identity and self-consciousness of the author as agent. As, slowly, our attunement to it grows, it leaves us, progressively, with a sense of a startlingly strange and irreducibly mysterious dimension to the desire at the heart of the human, the desire that quests and authors.

Notes

Numbers in brackets are the pagination in the original version of *Insight*, etc.
Abbreviations: LRIT – Lonergan Research Institute, Toronto; LB – Library; File – L;
Archive – A; *CWL X – Collected Works of Bernard Lonergan, Vol. X*

1 Alasdair Macintyre, *After Virtue: A Study in Moral Theory* (London: Duckworth, 1985), 219.
2 Paul Ricoeur, *Critique and Conviction* (London: Polity Press, 1998), 89.
3 For a highlight of the later journey see Mathews, 'A Biographical Perspective on Conversion and the Functional Specialties,' *Method: Journal of Lonergan Studies*, 16 (1998) 133–60.
4 References throughout the text to authors not listed in the bibliography of works read by Lonergan indicate this interactive dimension.

Chapter 1. Introduction: Desire and the Shaping of an Author

1 Stephen Coote, *John Keats, A Life* (London: Hodder and Stoughton, 1995), 172.
2 Pedro Arupe SJ, *One Jesuit's Spiritual Journey: Autobiographical Conversations with Jean-Claude Dietsch, S.J.*, trans. by Ruth Bradley (St. Louis: The Institute of Jesuit Sources, 1986), 102.
3 *CWL 3 Insight*, 28–9 (4).
4 Ibid., 9 (xv); 210 (186).
5 For comments by Lonergan on the manner in which the imagination gives one the big leads in one's life, see Elaine Cahn and Cathleen Going, eds., *The Question as Commitment: A Symposium*, Thomas More Institute Papers/77 (Montreal: Thomas More Institute, 1977), 110; see also 19. For comments on recognizing a direction in his life and the two related pulls, see Pierrot

Lambert, Charlotte Tansey, and Cathleen Going, eds., *Caring about Meaning: Patterns in the Life of Bernard Lonergan*, Thomas More Institute Papers/82 (Montreal: Thomas More Institute, 1982), 147 (hereafter *CAM*). On the big questions in his life, see *The Question as Commitment*, 9; on following his dynatype 'Reality, Myth, Symbol,' *CWL 17 Philosophical and Theological Papers 1965–1980*, chap. 20; on his attitude to auto/biography, see *CAM*, 131, 197–8.

6 Macintyre, *After Virtue: A Study in Moral Theory* (London: Duckworth, 1985), 219.

7 Chapter 5 of his *The Hero's Journey: Joseph Campbell on his Life and Work* (San Francisco: Harper and Row, 1990) is titled 'The Vision Quest.'

8 *Critique and Conviction: Paul Ricoeur – Conversations with Francois Azouvi and Marc de Launay* (Cambridge: Polity Press, 1998), 80–2.

9 Robert Cushman, *Therapeia: Plato's Conception of Philosophy* (Westport, CT: Greenwood Press, 1958) 139–50.

10 Ingmar Bergman, *Images: My Life in Film* (London: Bloomsbury, 1994). The remark is printed on the dust cover of the hardback version.

11 Edgar Schein, 'The Academic as Artist,' in A.G. Bedeian, ed., *Management Laureates* (Cambridge, MA: JAI Press, 1991), 50–2. See also the account by Simon Singh and Kenneth Ribet of Andrew Wiles' insight in 'Fermat's Last Stand,' *Scientific American* (November 1997), 36–41. The proof as written demands logical rigour; the process of discovering it is artistic and cannot be reduced to rules or logic.

12 See *CWL 3 Insight*, 210 (187) on one's life as a work of art; see also 237 (212).

13 Ibid., 372 (348); also 399–400 (375) on the notion of objectivity.

Chapter 2. Quebec Origins: A Classic Student, an Illness, and a Surprising Vocation

1 *CAM*, 41.

2 Pierre Louis Lapointe, *Buckingham: In the Heart of the Lower Lievre District* (City of Buckingham: 1990), 108–9.

3 Ibid., 224–6.

4 *CAM*, 41.

5 *CAM*, 195.

6 'The General Character of the Natural Theology of *Insight*,' *CWL 17 Philosophical and Theological Papers 1965–1980*, 8–9.

7 *CAM*, 12.

8 For the origin of the name and its Trinitarian connotations, see Lapoint, 60.

9 *CAM*, 138; Lapointe, 298, 306.

10 Lapointe, 199–200, 292–3.

11 *CAM*, vii. For further details, see Crowe, *Lonergan* (London: Chapman, 1992), 3–4; Richard M. Liddy, *Transforming Light – Intellectual Conversion in the Early Lonergan* (Collegeville, MN: Liturgical Press, 1993), 4.

12 *CAM*, 15, Cahn and Going, *The Question as Commitment*, Thomas More Institute Papers/77 (Montreal: Thomas More Institute, 1977), 10; *CAM*, 217.

13 *CAM*, 132, where he also comments on his kindergarten experience.

14 No information on the academic programme in the school during Lonergan's years could be found in the archives in Buckingham or La Prairie.

15 *CAM*, 2, 50.

16 *CAM*, 141.

17 'The General Character of the Natural Theology of *Insight*,' 8.

18 *CAM*, 133.

19 *CWL 3 Insight*, 549 (526).

20 H.G. Gadamer, *Truth and Method* (London: Sheed and Ward, 1975) 5ff., especially 8. Mill would also exert a profound influence on Lonergan.

21 Peter Gay, *Freud: A Life for Our Time* (London: Dent, 1988), 64.

22 William McNeill, *Arnold Toynbee: A Life* (Oxford: Oxford University Press 1989), 29.

23 Ibid., 29.

24 Carlen, Claudia, IHM, eds., *Papal Encyclicals 1903–1939* (Ann Arbor, MI: Pierian Press, 1981), 76.

25 Jesuit Curia, 'The Pontifical Biblical Institute,' in *The Jesuits: Yearbook of the Society of Jesus 1990* (Rome: Jesuit Curia, 1990), 30.

26 G.P. Fogarthy SJ, *American Catholic Biblical Scholarship: A History from the Early Republic to Vatican II* (San Francisco: Harper and Row, 1989), 166–8.

27 Ibid., 185.

28 Slattery, *Loyola and Montreal* (Montreal: Palm, 1962), 9–10; *CAM*, 131, on the choice.

29 Slattery, 272.

30 *A Second Collection*, 210; *CAM*, 152.

31 *CAM*, 134.

32 *CAM*, 135.

33 *Loyola College Review*, 1918–9, no. 5, 91; on his medal, see *General Prospectus of Loyola College*, 1918–9, 2.

34 *CAM*, *138*. Lonergan's aunt Mary on his father's side was a religious sister. James and Simon Lonergan were ordained priests in 1857 and 1871.

35 *CAM*, 138; on the illness see 136.

36 *CAM*, 137. For further related details, see 136–8, 141.

37 *CAM*, 131; on commitment see 138–9.

38 C.S. Lewis, *Surprised by Joy* (Glasgow: Collins Fontana, 1955), 182; see also Emilie Griffin, *How God Became Real* (London: Sheldon Press, 1981), for an insightful account of responses to the intervention of God in human lives.

39 New York: Allyn and Bacon, 1916, 1919.

40 Joseph Deharbe SJ, *A Complete Catechism of the Catholic Religion*, 6th American ed., trans. Rev. John Fander (New York: Schwartz, Kirwin and Fauss, 1908).

41 W. Devivier, SJ, *Christian Apologetics, or Rational Exposition of the Foundations of*

Faith, Vols. 1 and 2, trans. and with an introduction by L. Peeters SJ; ed., augmented, and adapted by Joseph C. Sasia SJ (San Jose: Popp and Hogan, 1903, 1924). The two volumnes contain a definition of religion, a significant discussion of faith and reason, and reflections on Roman Catholicism in relation to other Churches and cultures.

42 On apologetics see *CWL 3 Insight,* 754 (732).

43 *CAM,* 21.

44 *CAM,* 137.

45 *CAM,* 142.

46 In a taped interview (available at the LRIT) with Ray Phelan SJ in 1973, when asked about McCaffray Lonergan described him as 'magnificent.' For an assessment of McCaffray, see the tribute by F.X. Curran in *Woodstock Letters* 89, no. 2 (April 1960).

47 *Woodstock Letters* 89, no. 2 (April 1960), 169.

48 According to Harvey Egan, Lonergan grew up with the notion that the superior almost defined your life, told you where to go, what to do, what your life's work was going to be. As his personal dream flowered between 1933 and 1938, this left him with the question, how do you reconcile a personal dream with the role of superiors in your life? After he went to Boston College in 1975, it was brought to his attention that the role of the superior for Ignatius was that of benevolently facilitating the apostolic work that the subject came to be enthusiastically engaged in. According to Egan, this discovery was extremely liberating and meant a great deal to Lonergan.

49 See Paddy Kitchen, *Gerald Manley Hopkins: A Life* (Manchester: Carcanet, 1989), 116ff for comments on the composition of place and the use of the senses in the exercises, and their impact on Hopkins.

50 Louis J. Puhl SJ, *The Spiritual Exercises of St. Ignatius* (Chicago: Loyola University Press, 1951), 12.

51 *CAM,* 145. The retreat notes are available at the LRIT.

52 *CAM,* 22–3. For a further discussion of conscience, see 155–6. It is my judgment that, despite a perceptive article he wrote on the feeling dimension of the spiritual exercises for the *Loyola College Review* (1940/1; reprinted in *Loyola Today,* 1991, 3–4), as a vehicle for religious growth they did not really take in his experience. This is confirmed by remarks in a letter he wrote in Boston in 1975; see note 36, chap. 6 below.

53 *Curiosity at the Centre of One's Life: Statements and Questions of R. Eric O'Connor,* Thomas More Papers/84, ed. Martin O'Hara (Montreal: Thomas More Institute, 1987), 391.

54 *CAM,* 217.

55 *Curiosity at the Centre of One's Life,* 421.

56 Letters of 5–9 August 1925 and 20 June 1927, LRIT. All letters can be found in this archive; hereafter I omit reference to it.

Chapter 3. Heythrop: Awakening to the Problem of Knowledge

1 Not until 1969, when the faculties moved to London and became integrated into London University, was that desire fulfilled.

2 *Curiosity at the Centre of One's Life*, Thomas More Papers/84, ed. Martin O'Hara (Montreal: Thomas More Institute, 1987), 413.

3 Carolus Frick SJ, *Logica* (Freibourg: Herder, 1924), 2.

4 'Insight Revisited,' in *A Second Collection* (London: Darton, Longman and Todd, 1974), 263. In the preface to his *Ontologia* (Freiburg: Herder, 1928), Frick lists a series of texts developed by Jesuits for use in their philosophy studies. These included *Philosophia Naturalis* by Hahn and *Theologia Naturalis* by Boedder, who also published in English in the Stonyhurst Series. According to Paul Kennedy, Whiteside used Frick's *Logica* and Bolland used the text by Hahn.

5 For an obituary, see *Letters and Notices* (British Jesuits) 79 (1974) 362–8.

6 See *Lonergan Studies Newsletter* (LRIT, February 1985), 2.

7 *CAM*, 45. On the absence of metaphysics at Heythrop, see 43. See also 15, 47, 129.

8 Richard M. Liddy, *Transforming Light: Intellectual Conversion in the Early Lonergan* (Collegeville, MN: Liturgical Press, 1993), 102–3, 175.

9 T.Z. Lavine, *From Socrates to Sartre: The Philosophic Quest* (New York: Bantham, 1984), 197.

10 F.H. Bradley, *Appearance and Reality: A Metaphysical Essay* (Oxford: Clarendon Press, 1978 [1893]), 147–8, 159.

11 Letter 6 to Henry Smeaton, 11 December 1926.

12 *The Question as Commitment*, 10, where Lonergan describes how questions arose for him in his life. In a gem of a letter to Lemieux on 31 December 1976 he commented that out of his philosophy studies in the twenties he took away two convictions, '(1) that what is significant is not the abstract universal but the concrete act of understanding; and (2) Acts 28, 26f,' the passage for the sermon.

13 Theodore Kisiel opened chap. 1 of his book *The Genesis of Heidegger's* Being and Time (Berkeley: University of California Press, 1995) with the question, Where does *Being and Time* really begin? He argues that Heidegger first found the path that would result, many years later, in the book in a course he gave in 1919 on phenomenology. See *CWL 3 Insight* 9 (xv) for the acknowledgment by Lonergan of the beginning.

14 G.H. Joyce, *Principles of Logic* (London: Longmans, Green, 1908), 7–8, 132–3; H.W.B. Joseph, *An Introduction to Logic* (Oxford: Clarendon Press, 1906), 20–4, 40–1, 56, 93, 278 on names and universal terms of concepts.

15 Joseph, 56; Joyce, 133.

16 In his Blandyke essays, 'The Form of Mathematical Inference' (*Blandyke*

Papers 283 [January 1928], 127) and 'The Syllogism' (ibid. 285 [March 1928], 1, 3), Lonergan comments that Moncel had an abhorrence of the term 'universal,' which the latter felt implied a misleading notion of concepts. Moncel also held that inferential judgments differ from others in following, not from experience, but from previous judgments. He also rejected the definition of a judgment as the identification of two concepts, for psychological reasons among others. See also *Curiosity at the Center of One's Life, Statements and Questions of R. Eric O'Connor*, Thomas More Papers/84, ed. Martin O'Hara (Montreal: Thomas More Institute, 1987), 413.

17 For an amusing anecdote on Bolland, Suarez, and Thomas, see *CAM*, 28–9.

18 *CAM*, 10; *The Question as Commitment*, 10.

19 *CAM*, 137.

20 *CAM*, 16.

21 *A System of Logic*, in *Collected Works*, Vol. 7 (Toronto: University of Toronto Press, 1973). For an expanded account of what follows, see my 'On Lonergan and John Stuart Mill,' *Milltown Studies*, 35 (1995), 39–50.

22 See Joseph, 171, for a clarification of these points.

23 *Truth and Method* (London: Sheed and Ward, 1975), 8.

24 *A System of Logic*, 12.

25 Joyce, 39–40, 111–13, 298; Joseph, 146–9; Lonergan, 'The Form of Mathematical Inference,' 128.

26 Joseph, 514.

27 Peter Coffey, *The Science of Logic*, Vol. 2 (London: Longman, Green, 1912), 1.

28 Joyce, 370; *CWL 3 Insight*, 72, 74 (48, 51).

29 Joyce, 370; Coffey, Vol. 2, 268ff.

30 Joyce, 371; *CWL 3 Insight*, 672–4, 688.

31 Joyce, 121. 'Predicables' was a topic on the syllabus. Porphyry's tree will shortly find mention in an essay by Lonergan entitled 'The Syllogism.' See also Mill, *A System of Logic*, Vol. 1, 56. On categories in general, consult chapters 3 and 7.

32 Ibid., 123.

33 Joseph, 58n.1. Interesting is Mill's treatment of the definition of the circle: see *A System of Logic*, volume 1, book I, chap. 8, paras. 5, 143–5; Lonergan, *CWL 3 Insight*, 31–2, 35 (7, 10).

34 'The Form of Mathematical Inference,' 134–5. To illustrate the role of the image in algebraic inference, he poses a typical algebraic puzzle: 'A dealer buys a number of horses for $280.00. If he bought 4 less he would have paid $8.00 more for each. How many did he buy?' In response we say: let x be the unknown, and ask what can be said about x even though we don't know what it is. The equation $280/x + 8 = 280/(x - 4)$ is the result of a simple concrete inference. In *Insight* this strategy will become the basis of heuristic structures.

35   Ibid., 131–2. For later related remarks, see *CAM*, 230; *CWL 3 Insight* 329, sec.
     7 (304).
36   'The Form of Mathematical Inference,' 136–7.
37   *CAM*, 13. Frick's *Logica* is mentioned in the opening paragraph.
38   'The Syllogism,' 4.
39   Liddy, 23.
40   'The Syllogism,' 2; Joseph, 307. On page 356, in a chapter entitled 'Induc-
     tion,' Joseph talks about numerical or spatial relations being apprehended
     by intellectual insight. The term 'insight' also occurs in Joyce, 337, 339.
     Discussing the 'explanations which are given to children by way of illustra-
     tions and analogies of matters beyond their experience,' Joyce suggests that
     explanation may give us a real insight into the nature of the fact it explains,
     new light into the thing itself. On page 397 he remarks that the nature of
     spatial extension and figure is given to us by insight.
41   *CAM*, 30–1, 80–6, 225–6.
42   The quote is from page 29 of Nassan's notebook. The bibliography included
     M. Bober, *Karl Marx's Interpretation of History* (1927); Bernadetto Croce,
     Historical Materialism and the Economics of Karl Marx; Max Beer, *The Life and
     Teaching of Karl Marx* (1921); and Karl Koutsky, *The Economic Doctrine of Karl
     Marx*.
43   Lonergan, *Philosophy of God, and Theology* (London: Darton, Longman and
     Todd, 1973), 62.
44   The sources for the points in the following paragraphs are *CAM*, 13–15,
     110–11. He had read Newman's *The Idea of a University* in the Juniorate and
     The Present Position of Catholics in Loyola in his first or second arts year, and
     will refer to *The University Sermons* and *The Arians of the Fourth Century* in his
     Blandyke paper on Newman. He was impressed by Newman's distinction
     between doubts and difficulties, which helped him to feel free to look
     difficulties in the eye without having them unsettle his faith or vocation.
45   Page references in what follows are to John Henry Cardinal Newman, *An
     Essay in Aid of a Grammar of Assent* (Westminster, MD: Christian Classics,
     1973): 295, 316 on evidence; 321–9 on the further illustrations. See also 344
     on certitude.
46   'True Judgment and Science,' 195. LRIT transcript, 1.
47   Newman, 361–2.
48   Ibid., 345.
49   *CAM*, 14; see also '*Insight* Revisited,' in *A Second Collection*, 263, where a
     parallel comment is made.
50   *CAM*, 111. Frick in his *Logica*, 163, labelled Kant a transcendental idealist and
     Fichte, Schelling, and Hegel absolute idealists. Fichte's idealism was subjec-
     tive, Schellings' objective, and Hegel's logical.
51   *CAM*, 109.

52 'True Judgment and Science,' LRIT transcript, 6.

53 Edward Sillem, ed., *Philosophical Notebook of John Henry Newman*, Vol. 1 (Louvain: Nauwelaerts, 1970), 187.

54 Newman, chap. 9, 346. Newman also talks about matters of fact (343), taking the facts by themselves (367), incredible facts (376), and 'facts cannot be proved by presumptions' (383). How, precisely, the use of the illative sense relates to the determination of the facts seems to be left open by Newman. Only when Lonergan came to write *Insight* did he affirm that facts are known in true judgments.

55 *CAM*, 184; *CWL* 10, 34, 237. Nassan, McCauley, and Kennedy seemed to think that the students did not read the newspapers or listen to a radio, but they were not certain.

56 Cyril Barrett, *Wittgenstein on Ethics and Religious Belief* (Oxford: Blackwell, 1991), 188ff.

57 *CAM*, 2, 9.

58 O'Hara, and Ward, *An Introduction to Projective Geometry* (Oxford: Clarendon Press, 1937) 27–8, for a basic statement on points, lines, and planes; 292–5 on relativity.

59 '*Insight* Revisited' in *A Second Collection*, 263–4; Letter to provincial, 1935.

60 *CAM*, 2. Questions on the first paper dealt with functions, infinite series, the roots of equations, exponentials, Demoivre's theorem, and complex variables. The second paper dealt with coordinate geometry and the ellipse and hyperbola, as well as differentiation and integration.

Chapter 4. Puzzled in Montreal by the Depression and Plato's Ideas

1 *CAM*, 31.

2 Ibid., 32.

3 Conversation with Eric Kierans.

4 Dawson, *The Age of the Gods* (London: Sheed and Ward, 1933). Lonergan's comments are in LRIT Library File 745. See also '*Insight* Revisited,' in *A Second Collection*, 264; *CAM*, 9, 37; *CWL 10 Topics in Education*, 234, 251–4.

5 Dawson, xii–xvi, are central.

6 Ibid., 3–4.

7 Ibid., 4.

8 For a resonance in *Insight*, see CWL 3 *Insight*, 233 (207).

9 Sources for the present paragraph are Dawson, 92–3, 130; *CWL 21 Political Economy*, 11, 21, 23 (for references to the ox and plough), 24–5, 30, 133.

10 'Gilbert Keith Chesterton,' *Loyola College Review* 17 (1931), 8.

11 *CAM*, 31, 225ff., for an important discussion; see also Cahn and Going, *The Question as Commitment*, 32.

12 Fallon., SJ, *The Principles of Social Economy* (New York: Benziger Brothers,

1934). The original was published in French in 1929; the first English edition arrived in 1934. Kierans maintains that William Bryan was using it in Loyola in 1931. In the forties Lonergan remarked to Kierans that he thought the book was a pretty good overview.

13 Thompson, *Calculus Made Easy* (London: Macmillan, 1910; rev. and enlarged 2nd ed. 1910, 3rd ed. 1946).

14 Arthur Kimball, *Elements of Physics*, 4th rev. ed. (New York: Henry Holt, 1929).

15 *CWL 4 Collection*, 129–30 (138–9); Michael Shute, *The Origins of Lonergan's Notion of the Dialectic of History* (Lanham: University Press of America, 1993), 32, 87; see also Lonergan's 'Essay in Fundamental Sociology,' LRIT Archives, 100.

16 J.A. Stewart, *Plato's Doctrine of Ideas* (Oxford: Clarendon Press, 1909); *CAM*, 48. For context see Mark Morelli, 'At the Threshold of the Halfway House: An Investigation of the Lonergan/Stewart Encounter,' paper presented at the Lonergan Workshop, Boston College, June 2000.

17 '*Insight* Revisited' in *A Second Collection*, 264–5, where he remarked that Stewart cured him of his nominalism. In a letter to his provincial written 22 January 1935, he remarked that reading Stewart left his nominalism intact.

18 Stewart, 2.

19 Ibid., 68.

20 Ibid., 47.

21 Ibid., 58.

22 Ibid., 103.

23 Ibid., 118–19.

24 Ibid., 23; see also 40–1 for, among other things, a discussion of abstraction.

25 Ibid., 74.

26 See page 4 of the Boston Workshop transcript for 19 June 1979, LRIT Archives; see also *CAM*, 44. The insight comes between the datum and the concept expressed in the equation.

27 Crowe, *Lonergan*, 17; see also 33n.41.

28 Ludwig Schopp, ed., *Fathers of the Church: A New Translation*, Vol. 1, *Writings of Saint Augustine* (New York: Cima, 1948).

29 Peter Brown, *Augustine of Hippo: A Biography* (London: Faber and Faber, 1967), 110.

30 *Answer to Skeptics* 2, 5, 12; 2, 7, 16; 2, 11, 25; 3, 18, 40; on 'truth-like'; 2, 9, 23 for Augustine's position.

31 Brown, 120; Augustine, *Answer to Skeptics*, 2,7,17; *Divine Providence and the Problem of Evil*, 1, 11, 31.

32 *The Happy Life*, chap. 1, 4.

33 *CWL 3 Insight*, 15 (xx–xxi). See also Liddy, *Transforming Light* (Collegeville, MN: Liturgical Press, 1993), 54ff.

34 *A Third Collection*, 193.
35 *Divine Providence and the Problem of Evil* 1, 1, 1–3; 1, 4, 11; 1, 8, 26; 1, 10, 29.
36 Ibid., 2, 3, 10; 2, 4, 11–12.
37 Ibid., 2, 7, 23.
38 Ibid., 2, 18, 47; *Soliloquies*, 1, 2, 7.
39 *Soliloquies*, 2, 2, 2.
40 Ibid., 2, 5, 8.
41 Ibid., 2, 7, 14
42 Crowe, obituary, *Newsletter: Upper Canada Province* 60:3 (May–June 1985), 15–18.
43 Letter to provincial, January 1935.
44 Hoenen, 'De Origine Primorum Principiorum Scientiae,' *Gregorianum*, 14 (1933), 153–84. A rough translation of Hoenan's articles is available at the Lonergan Centre, Milltown Park, Dublin.
45 '*Insight* Revisited,' in *A Second Collection*, 266–7. Whether he read Hoenen's article in Montreal or shortly after he moved to Rome is an open question.
46 Hoenen, 154 (3). Numbers in parenthesis indicate the pagination in the English translation.
47 Ibid., 155 (3).
48 *CAM*, 10–11, a most crucial text; see also *CWL 3 Insight*, 36 (12), on a circle of terms and relations.
49 Hoenen, 162 (11).
50 Ibid., 166 (16).
51 Ibid., 166–8 (16–18) for points made in *Questiones Disputate, De Anima*, a. 5; *Questiones Disputate, De Ver.*, q. 11, a.1; *Questiones Disputate, de Ver.*, 2.3 a. 2.
52 Ibid., 170(21) in *Posteria Analytica*, book 1, lecture 30, n.4.
53 Hoenen, 172 (22).
54 Ibid., 176 (28) from *De Memoria et Reminiscentia*, lect. 2.
55 Ibid., 176 (28) from *Summa Theological*, I, q. 84, a. 7.
56 The remark was made in an interview that I recorded on 19 May 1988. See also *CWL 3, Insight*, 776.
57 *CAM*, 9.
58 Letter to provincial, January 1935.

Chapter 5. Struggling with History and Reality in Rome before the War

1 Crowe, *Lonergan*, 19, 34n50; Letter of Hingston to the Assistant, 5 December 1933, in which he suggests that Lonergan specialize in fundamental theology.
2 *CAM*, 237.
3 The Quirinale, where Hitler would have been received, is at the rear of the Gregorian University. Hitler is mentioned in *CWL* 3, 557 (534); the Nazis in *CWL* 21, 4; Nazism and Hitler on pages 61–2 of O'D. Hanley's notes taken at Lonergan's course on *Insight* in 1952–3.

4 Rudiger Safranski, *Martin Heidegger: Between Good and Evil* (Cambridge, MA: Harvard University Press, 1998), chaps. 13–14.

5 Maurice Friedmann, *Martin Buber's Life and Work: The Middle Years, 1932–1945* (Detroit, MI: Wayne State University Press, 1988), chap. 9, esp. 159.

6 R. Overy and A. Wheatcroft, *The Road to War* (London: Macmillan, 1989), 32.

7 A. Bea, 'The Apostolic Constitution, *Deus Scientiarum Dominus*, Its Origin and Spirit,' *Theological Studies* 4, no. 1 (March 1943), 34–52.

8 Ibid., 38.

9 'Theology in Its New Context' in *A Second Collection*, 57.

10 *CAM*, 73. On 261ff., in the context of a remark by David Tracy, Lonergan comments that the manual theology as developed at the Gregorian provided a sound basis for postgraduate research.

11 Letter to provincial, 22 January 1935.

12 *CAM*, 103–4.

13 Pages 7–9, 13, 23, 24, 27, 28, and 32–36 are extant, LRIT Archives A14–237 (hereafter entitled 'Essay for Keeler on Newman')

14 Crowe, *Lonergan*, 34n.49 and page 13 of the fragments.

15 Liddy, *Transforming Light* (Collegeville, MN: Liturgical Press, 1993), 76–84, esp. 84.

16 'Essay for Keeler on Newman,' 7, para. 4.

17 Ibid., 13.

18 Ibid., 8.

19 Ibid., 8.

20 Ibid., 9, confirms the suggestion of Crowe and Liddy that in the notes Lonergan is more in favour of Plato than Aristotle. In *CWL 2 Verbum*, 155 (114) we find: 'It corrects the misguided intellectualism of Plato for whom the intelligible was real but not of this world.'

21 'Essay for Keeler on Newman,' 24.

22 Ibid., 13, 23, 24 for the points dealt with in the present paragraph.

23 Ibid., 23.

24 Ibid., 27–8 for text quoted in this paragraph.

25 Ibid., 33–4.

26 Komomchak, 'Lonergan's Early Essays on the Redemption of History,' in *Lonergan Workshop*, Vol. 10, *The Legacy of Lonergan* (Boston: Boston College, 1994), 159–77. The term metaphysics of history occurs on 171, note 20, in a reference to Peter Wust, '*Crisis in the West.*' This essay, which also deals with dialectic, was published as the second of the *Essays in Order*, 95–152, edited by Christopher Dawson and T.F. Burns (London: Sheed and Ward, 1931).

27 LRIT Archives File 713, History. The typescript 'Philosophy of History' runs from pages 95 to 130.

28 Safranski, 282ff.

29 'Philosophy of History,' 96; 97ff on matter and material differences.

30 'Philosophy of History,' 99–100. In *CWL 3 Insight,* 268–9 (244), Lonergan talks about dialectic standing to generalised method as the differential equation to classical physics, or the operator equation to more recent physics.

31 'Philosophy of History,' 100ff. on sound philosophy, matter, and contingence.

32 Ibid., 103–4.

33 Ibid., 129; see also 121.

34 Liddy, 96–100. Keeler's *The Problem of Error from Plato to Kant* was published in Rome (Analecta Gregoriana, Issue 6, 1934). The review appeared in *Gregorianum* 16 (1935), 156–60.

35 Liddy, 98n.24.

36 Ibid., 99–100.

37 '*Insight* Revisited,' in *A Second Collection,* 265; *CAM,* 107–9.

38 *CAM,* 268.

39 Page 4 of the LRIT typescript version of the letter to the provincial.

40 '*Insight* Revisited,' in *A Second Collection,* 266.

41 It is preceded by five pages of notes entitled '*Pantôn Anakephalaiôsis*' and a two-page outline entitled 'Sketch for a Metaphysics of Human Solidarity.' Appended to it are two pages of notes on *Philosophy and History: Essays to Ernst Cassirer* (Oxford: 1938), in which he notes a definition of the concept of history given by J. Huizinga: 'History is the intellectual form in which a civilization renders account to itself of its past.' As every civilization holds its own history to be the true history, there will inevitably be a plurality of forms of history.

42 '*Pantôn Anakephalaiôsis,*' 17–19. The exhortation is given in *Quadragesimo Anno* in *Papal Encyclicals 1903–1939,* edited by Claudia Carlen IHM (Ann Arbor, MI: Pierian Press, 1981), 76.

43 In Edmund Husserl, *The Crisis of the European Sciences,* transl. with an introduction by David Carr (Evanston, IL: Northwestern University Press, 1970), 269–99.

44 Ibid., 299.

45 Heidegger, *An Introduction to Metaphysics* (New York: Anchor Doubleday, 1961). The quotations that follow are from 31–41, on the greatness of National Socialism 166.

46 See *CWL 3 Insight,* 688 (665) on the transformation of metaphysics.

47 *CAM,* 258.

48 '*Insight* Revisited,' in *A Second Collection,* 265; see also *CAM,* 21, on Augustine on *veritas* and Aquinas on *esse.*

49 The quotation is from a transcript by Nicholas Graham of discussions at the Lonergan Workshop, Boston, 13 June 1978, available in the LRIT.

50 *CAM,* 21.

51 Sala, *Lonergan and Kant: Five Essays on Human Knowledge* (Toronto: University

of Toronto Press, 1994), xvi–xvii. See Thomas Kuhn, *The Structure of Scientific Revolution* (Chicago: University of Chicago Press, 1962), 204, for intellectual conversion in paradigm shifts in science.

52 Sala, xvi.

53 'An Interview with Fr. Bernard Lonergan,' in *A Second Collection*, 222.

54 G. Passelecq and B. Suchecky, *The Hidden Encyclical of Pius XI* (New York: Harcourt Brace, 1997), 101–10, discuss *Mit Brennender Sorge*.

Chapter 6. Postgraduate Studies in Theology: A New Road Taken

1 See Lonergan's Tertianship Retreat Notebook, LRIT Archives, 20 for Christ and the meaning of history, 53 for God in history.

2 William A. Barry and William J. Connolly, *The Practice of Spiritual Direction* (New York: Seabury Press, 1982).

3 R.P. Aurel, *La Vie Chretienne: Conferences Troisième An 1937–8*. A text is available in the Jesuit Archives in Paris and in Milltown Park, Dublin.

4 Ibid., page 6 of the text of the last lecture: see also 'Finality, Love, Marriage,' in *CWL* 4, 25 (24).

5 '*Insight* Revisited,' in *A Second Collection*, 265.

6 LRIT Archives File 713, History. There are five texts in all. The first three are on analytic concepts of history, and the fourth deals with a theory of history from a theological perspective. The final text is a series of notes he made on Vols. 1–3 of Toynbee's *A Study of History* (Oxford: Oxford University Press, 1934). In what follows I specify location by title and page number.

7 'Outline of an Analytic Concept of History,' 6.

8 Ibid., 4.

9 Ibid., 5.

10 Ibid., 8.

11 'Analytic Concepts of History in Blurred Outline,' 11.

12 'Outline of an Analytic Concept of History,' 10.

13 Ibid., 12.

14 'Analytic Concepts of History in Blurred Outline,' 13.

15 Passelecq and Suchecky, *The Hidden Encyclical of Pius XI* (New York: Harcourt Brace, 1997), 1.

16 '*Insight* Revisited,' in *A Second Collection*, 266.

17 On the genesis see Crowe, 'A Note on Lonergan's Dissertation and Its Introductory Pages,' *Method: Journal of Lonergan Studies* (October 1985), 1–9. For his own account of researching the thesis, see *Curiosity at the Centre of One's Life*, 375–6, 405ff, and defence notes, 15 where Lonergan narrates the story. For summaries of the material, see *CWL 1 Grace and Freedom*, 66 (63), 171, and the introduction to his thesis, 25–6.

18 See *The New Catholic Encyclopedia* (New York: McGraw Hill, 1966–7) Vol. 2, under 'Domingo Bañez'; Vol. 9, under 'Luis de Molina.'

19 Ibid., 48.
20 *CWL 1 Grace and Freedom*, 155. Not all quotes from this text have counterparts in the earlier book version, *Grace and Freedom*.
21 Ibid., 156.
22 Ibid. Implicitly, Lonergan is employing a genetic method.
23 As his study is of a development, the works of Aquinas must be accurately dated. For details see James A. Weisheipl OP, *Friar Thomas D'Aquion: His Life, Thought, and Word* (New York: Doubleday, 1974), x for comments on Aquinas' intellectual development, 70 for remarks on the *Sentences*, 125 for a chronology of the disputed questions, 126 for an account of the *De Veritate*, 129 ff., for remarks on the *Contra Gentiles*, and 220ff. for remarks on the chronology of the *Summa*. Weisheipl's comments on Aquinas' intellectual development lack depth. See also Terry L. Miethe and Vernon J. Bourke, *Thomistic Bibliography 1940–1978* (Westport, CT: Greenwood Press, 1980), xix–xxii.
24 *CWL 1 Grace and Freedom*, 159–60.
25 *CAM*, 4–5, see also 91–4 for an important discussion.
26 *CAM*, 5.
27 *CAM*, 92.
28 *CWL 1 Grace and Freedom*, 171; 6 (4).
29 Ibid., 7–8 (6).
30 Ibid., 10 (8)
31 Ibid., 10 (8).
32 Ibid., 14–15.
33 'Method in Catholic Theology,' in *CWL 6 Philosophical and Theological Papers 1958–1964*, 21.
34 *CAM*, 5–6. On page 6 Lonergan contrasts Scotus with Aquinas, showing how Aquinas was thinking things out: 'Thomas was the intelligent man.'
35 The text quoted is preceded by the following: 'I had been hearing these words (Consolation without a previous cause) since 1922 at the annual retreats made by Jesuits preparing for the priesthood. They occur in St. Ignatius's "Rules for the Discernment of Spirits in the Second Week of the Exercises." But now, after fifty-three years, I began for the first time to grasp what they meant. What had intervened was what Rahner describes as the anthropological turn, the turn from metaphysical objects to conscious subjects. What I was learning was that the Ignatian *"examen conscientiae"* might mean not an examination of conscience but an examination of consciousness: after all in the romance languages the same word is used to denote both conscience and consciousness, both *Gewissen* and *Bewusstsein*. I was seeing that "consolation" and "desolation" named opposite answers to the question, How do you feel when you pray? Are you absorbed or are you blocked?' Letter to Thomas O'Malley, Dean of Arts and Sciences, Boston College, LRIT, Archives, 1979.

36 *CWL* 1, *Grace and Freedom* 79ff. (76ff.).

37 Ibid., 86 (84).

38 Ibid., 83–4 (81).

39 Ibid., 86 (84).

Chapter 7. Economics or Cognitional Theory: Towards Desire's Decisions

1 Because none of his letters to his mother have survived, the present treatment of his bereavement might appear to lack depth and sensitivity, but that is not my intention.

2 '*Insight* Revisited,' in *A Second Collection*, 267.

3 *Curiosity at the Center of One's Life*, 118–19.

4 '*Insight* Revisited,' in *A Second Collection*, 266; *CAM*, 93.

5 *CAM*, 88–9. According to Jack Belair, in the summer of 1941 he went down to New York and came back with his own set of six volumes, as well as the Sorokin volumes.

6 *A Third Collection*, 103; *CWL 10 Topics in Education*, index under Withdrawal-and-return (Toynbee), 308.

7 LRIT A23.

8 *The Question as Commitment*, 110; see also 32, where in 1977 he remarks that the question is still genuine.

9 *CAM*, 183–4.

10 The quote is from page 5 of the 1978 typescript. See *CWL 15 Circulation Analysis*, 19. Lonergan makes the same point about constantly revising his insights in *CAM*, 251.

11 Notable is the fact that Lonergan did not involve statistics in his economic quest. Many of Lonergan's casual reviews and lectures in the period from 1940 to about 1945, ending with his 'The Trend towards Economic Centralization' in 1945, had to do with economics and the response to the anticipated end of the war. He wrote short popular pieces such as 'Saving Certificates and Catholic Action,' in which his theory of the interrelation of prices, savings, and production is evident; 'Democracy's Second Chance,' which refers to Toynbee on withdrawal and return; 'Is Modern Culture Doomed?' in which both Toynbee and Sorokin are mentioned; and 'Social Security and Reconstruction in Canada.'

12 *CWL 21 Political Economy*, 322.

13 Ibid., 9–10, where the classical economists, Marxists, and Keynesians are acknowledged. See also 80ff. for references to Major Douglas (and his writings); 51–2 to Walras; 89 to Stalin's five-year plan; 127 for a critique of rate of gold production, mercantilism, systematic deflation, or more efficient use of money. On Pesch see *CWL 15 Circulation Analysis*, xxxi. On the question of his relation to Joseph Schumpeter's *Business Cycles* (New York:

McGraw Hill, 1939), which uses the terms 'cycles,' 'waves' and 'rhythms,' see xxv,n.10. On page 11 the terms 'production,' 'distribution' and 'consumption,' reminiscent of Fallon, occur.

14 *CWL 21 Political Economy*, 7, 26.

15 Philip McShane *Economics for Everyone: Das Jus Kapital* (Halifax: Axial Press, 1998), chap. 2 on the production process, chap. 3 on the circulation of money.

16 *CWL 21 Political Economy*, 23.

17 Ibid., 27.

18 Ibid., 27.

19 Ibid., 19. Nowhere in his early economic analysis do probability considerations enter. The analysis of the conjunction of 'emergent' and 'probability' will only occur between 1951 and 1952. See *CWL 15 Circulation Analysis*, 28, para. 8, for the 1944 definition of the term 'emergent standard of living.'

20 *CWL 21 Political Economy*, 20.

21 Ibid., 31, on normative, probable, and actual exchange values. This needs to be related to Marx on surplus value, which Lonergan consistently dismisses as a blunder. See also pages 5 and 9 of his notes on Robbins, LRIT Archives File 60.

22 *CWL 21 Political Economy*, 38.

23 Ibid., 33.

24 Ibid., 34.

25 Ibid., 28.

26 *CAM*, 85. This in turn poses questions about remembering moments of insight. Gerald McGuigan remembered that Lonergan was using flow diagrams in 1940.

27 *CWL 21 Political Economy*, 42.

28 Ibid., 41; see also 100–6.

29 Ibid., 100; see also 60–1.

30 Ibid., 56.

31 *CWL 4 Collection*, 4 (2).

32 'The Forms of Inference,' *CWL 4 Collection*, 7 (5). The phrase 'an intellectual insight into arithmetical operations' occurs on page 6 (4). 'Intellectual insight' occurs in Kant's *Critique of Pure Reason*, A134, B173, and 'intellectual intuition' in B xl, note a.

33 *CWL 4 Collection*, 16 (15).

34 *Ibid.*, 20 (19).

35 Ibid., 21–2 (21), where God is referred to as the 'divine artisan.'

36 A. Franklin Shull, *Evolution* (New York: McGraw Hill, 1936), 281. Lonergan made notes on the text, LRIT Archives A22, dealing with evolution, chance, and the statistical concept of species. See *CWL 4 Collection*, 43n.67 (44n.67), for Lonergan's reference to Shull.

37 *CWL 4 Collection*, 20 (20).

38 Ibid., 22 (21–2).

39 Ibid., 24 (23).

40 Ibid., 27 (26).

41 Ibid., 31–2 (31); see also 36, 43–4 (36, 44–5), where the movement from *eros* through friendship to charity is again traced.

42 In *Insight* self/subject-object rather than the me-other relationship is the dominant one. On this see Jo-Ann Pilardy, *Simone de Beauvoir: Writing the Self* (Westport, CT: Praeger, 1999), 16.

43 *CWL 4 Collection*, 28 (27).

44 *Ibid.*, 30 (29).

45 Ibid., 38 (38).

46 *CAM*, 264.

47 *CWL 15 Circulation Analysis*, 161–2; *CAM*, 183 on reading J.A. Schumpeter's *Business Cycles*.

48 *CWL 15 Circulation Analysis*, 28.

49 See O'Hara and Ward, *An Introduction to Projective Geometry* (Oxford: Clarendon Press, 1937), 27–8; *CAM*, 183. Notable also was Watt's use of the term 'rising standard of comfort.' The term 'aggregates' occurs in Shull, *Evolution*, 269, 279.

50 1944 typescript, 23; *CWL 15 Circulation Analysis*, 35 adds 'wave or.'

51 *CAM*, 182, 165ff.

Chapter 8. Insights into Phantasms as the Origins of Words

1 See *CWL 4 Collection*, 257 for details.

2 '*Insight* Revisited,' 266–7. He repeats the account of Hoenen's influence in one of his late works, 'Reality, Myth, Symbol,' *CWL 17 Philosophical and Theological Papers 1965–1980*, 388.

3 Hoenen, 'De Philosophia Scholastics Cognitionis Geometricae,' *Gregorianum* 19 (1938), 508. Cantor's insights into aleph-one, discussed in Paul Hoffmann, *The Man Who Loved Only Numbers* (London: Fourth Estate, 1998), 219–25, do not seem to be reconcilable with the claims of naive realism or intuitionism. Hoenen also explores (510–11) the imaginative basis of Euclid's fifth axiom concerning the exact number of lines that can be drawn through an external point parallel to a given line. A third illustration (511ff.) comes from the field of axiomatics, with special reference to Hilbert's use of implicit definition. Hilbert does not give nominal definitions of points, lines, and planes, as did Euclid. Any object that can be identified as having the pattern of relations in the implicit definitions will fall under the definition. It was a style that inspired Lonergan.

4 For the mathematical details see Hoffman, 219–23, for the diagonal image

necessary for the insight. Lonergan's account is given on pages 15–17 of the original MSA autograph.

5 'De problemate necessitatis geometricae,' *Gregorianum* 20 (1939), 19–54. The discussion of Plato's number starts at page 20.

6 Ibid., 39; see also 41.

7 *CAM*, 52–3.

8 'Reality, Myth, Symbol,' *CWL 17 Philosophical and Theological Papers 1965–1980*, 388.

9 His decisions in Montreal at the start of the 1930s to devote his spare time to economics, and later in Rome to explore elements of a philosophy of history, were earlier but not as significant for his intellectual career at the time.

10 This was the title he wrote on the earliest known draft. Later he renamed the book version *Verbum: Word and Idea in Aquinas*.

11 That Aquinas' mind had changed and developed was news to many in the manual tradition of Thomism, as the hostile reaction to Bouillard's *Conversion et grace chez Thomas d'Aquin: Etude historique* (Paris: Aubier, 1944) shows.

12 *CWL 3 Insight*, 769 (747–8).

13 *CWL 2 Verbum*, 230–50 (A 85). Page 76 of the second is missing. The collected works volume identifies the page numbers of the original text, which I am using. A remark on the endnote number sequence (ibid., xvii) indicates the editors hold that the typescript is a single work. My own opinion that there might be two distinct texts is based on the fact that, as a typescript, pages 60–77 have a quite different style. The header is different, and the endnote numbers are typed in rather than manually inserted. The matter is open, but does not greatly influence the points I am exploring in my text.

14 *De Anima*, 431a–b.

15 On the significance of the word for him, see *CAM*, 52–3.

16 *CWL 2 Verbum*, 232 (20).

17 Ibid., 230 (16).

18 Ibid., 232 (19–20).

19 Ibid., 239 (69).

20 Ibid., 245 (92).

21 *De Anima*, 429a15, 430a20. See also 429b5, 20, 431a1.

22 *CWL 2 Verbum*, 245 (92).

23 Ibid., 245 (93).

24 Ibid., 245–6 (92).

25 Ibid., 249 (101).

26 Ibid., 249 (100).

27 *CWL 2 Verbum*, 250 (102). The term 'rational consciousness' also occurs on 232 (20), 245, 246 (94), 248 (98), and 249 (100). 'Intellectual consciousness' occurs on 230 (1), 'psychological consciousness' on 248 (99), 'data of con-

sciousness' on 235 (61), 237 (65), and 239 (68), and 'unity of consciousness' on 239 (68).

28 Annie Cohen-Solal, *Sartre: A Life* (London: Heinemann, 1987), 249–53. See also James Miller, *The Passion of Michel Foucault* (London: Harper, 1993), 42ff.

29 Rudiger Safranski, *Martin Heidegger: Between Good and Evil* (Cambridge, MA: Harvard University Press, 1998), 347ff.

30 George Steiner, *In Bluebeard's Castle* (London: Faber, 1971), 34.

31 *CAM*, 103–4. See also Letter 2 to Crowe, 1953.

32 *De Trinitate*, XV, xii, 22, in Whitney Oats, ed., *Basic Writings of Saint Augustine*, Vol. 2 (New York: Random House 1948), 846.

33 See *CWL 2 Verbum*, 205 (198), for matters dealt with in this paragraph.

Chapter 9. Thought and Reality: Measuring the Kantian Bridge

1 '*Insight* Revisited,' in *A Second Collection*, 268.

2 The chapter deals with the contrast between facts and thought, truth, and the relation between thought and the Other of thought. According to the library cards at Regis, Lonergan twice borrowed the text but, when questioned about its possible influence on him in Boston in 1979, remarked that he had not studied it.

3 He made the decision to compose *Method in Theology* in December 1958 and to return to his research on economics in 1975.

4 The notes, hereafter referred to as 'Thought and Reality,' are comprised of thirty pages of notes in a ring-bound folder, numbered on one side up to page 13. An indexed typescript, running to thirty pages, has been prepared by Tom Daly, LRIT L File 31. Page references are to that text.

5 'Thought and Reality,' 27, following the *Verbum* fragment, repeatedly emphasizes that thought is a process but is distinct from the processes of nature.

6 *CWL 3 Insight*, 32 (xxviii).

7 He remarked to Philip McShane that when the problem opened up for him, he had to go and talk with someone about it. As we have seen, his experiences with Keeler, Maréchal, and Leeming were a part of his own struggle.

8 Kristana Arp, *The Bonds of Freedom: Simone de Beauvoir's Existentialist Ethics* (Chicago: Open Court, 2001), 48.

9 *CWL 4 Collection*, 39 (39).

10 *Curiosity at the Center of One's Life*, 381. Lonergan is here applying his later precepts of interpretation in *Method in Theology* to reading *Insight*. A precondition is that one knows what the word 'insight' refers to.

11 'Thought and Reality,' 4, sec. 3b. The term 'consciousness' also occurs on page 7, and 'supervenes' in the preface to *Insight: CWL 3 Insight*, 3 (ix).

12 *CWL 2 Verbum*, 193 (185), on *nous, epistemene, sophia, phronesis*, and *techkne*.

13. Ibid., 50 (36).

14 *CWL*, 5 *Understanding and Being*, discussion 1, 258.
15 Excerpt from questions at the Lonergan Workshop, Boston, 19 June 1979: transcript of the archive file, 7.
16 Lewis, *Surprised by Joy* (Glasgow: Fount, 1977), 20.
17 'Thought and Reality,' 6.
18 Ibid., 10.
19 Ibid., 12.
20 Ibid., 13.
21 *CAM*, 21.
22 The term 'genus' occurs on pages 6, 15, and 23 of 'Thought and Reality.' Its one occurrence in the later 'Intelligence and Reality' course has to do with being.
23 *CWL 3 Insight*, 545 (521). On Porphyry's Tree see H.W.B. Joseph, *An Introduction to Logic* (Oxford: Clarendon Press, 1906), 115; G.H. Joyce, *Principles of Logic* (London: Longmans, Green, 1908), 129ff.
24 'Thought and Reality,' 21.
25 Ibid., 26.
26 Melbourne Mason and Thérèse Mason, Eds., *Inquiry and Attunement* Thomas More Institute Papers/81, (Montreal: Thomas More Institute, 1981), 1, 13, 15.
27 In his convocation address at Concordia University on 9 June 1980, O'Connor remarks that in his education he was never taught to ask the questions that were answered by what he was learning: *Curiosity at the Center of One's Life*, 561.
28 The term 'fact' occurs in the notes on 3 and 16, 'brute facts' on 3 and 4. 'Experiential consciousness' occurs on 4, 'consciousness' on 7, the 'subconscious' on 8. On 22 we find the remark that thought moves on another level, but this refers to development in viewpoint rather than levels of consciousness. Page 27 is very strong on thought as a process.
29 From a two-page communication from Charlotte Tansey entitled '1939–1945' and dated 19 May 1994. It contains a reflection on the people involved and the circumstances out of which the Thomas More Institute was formed.
30 In a phone conversation on 10 September 1996, Peter White remarked that Lonergan had stayed with them for two or three days in the summer of 1957. White found him pleasant but almost impossible to converse with.

Chapter 10. Aquinas on Cognition and Its Transcendence

1 Michael Vertin, 'Remembering Bernard Lonergan,' *Bulletin* (The Lonergan Research Institute), 13 (November 1998), 3–4. This is one of Lonergan's few remarks on a moment of insight in his own life. On page 41 of Thomas Daly's notes taken at Lonergan's course 'Method in Theology' in Rome 1963–4, Daly writes: 'first year on the first article after all material was col-

lected with indices. Where should he begin? The second in two weeks. It follows the understanding of the first question.'

2 *CWL 2 Verbum*, 15 (2).

3 William Allman, 'The Mother Tongue,' *Mysteries of Science, U.S. News and World Report* (Special Collectors Edition), 1 July 2002, 50–1.

4 *CWL 2 Verbum*, 17 (4).

5 Ibid., 20 (7).

6 Ibid., 25 (12). Is this an expression of the insight by means of which he was able to make it all hang together? Note 48 suggests that for Lonergan Aquinas' thought on the distinction between understanding and inner word developed from the *Sentences* through the *De Veritate* and the *Contra Gentiles* to the *Summa*.

7 Ibid., 24 (11) on introspection; 18, 22, 38, 46 (5, 9, 25, 33) on process.

8 Chapter 5 of Collingwood's *Autobiography*, entitled 'Question and Answer,' makes the same point.

9 *CWL 2 Verbum*, 26 (12).

10 *CWL 4 Collection*, 82 (85). His next essay, 'A Note on Geometrical Possibility,' ibid., 93ff. (99–101), discusses in detail the division of definitions into nominal and essential.

11 *CWL 2 Verbum*, 31 (18) on *morphe*. He is unusually insistent in note 58, page 28 (note 54, page 14), that for Aristotle understanding is firstly a matter of knowing a cause and secondly of its expression in a scientific syllogism. To miss this, he maintains, is to miss almost everything.

12 Ibid., 38 (25). See also 76 (64) on the different role of sense and imagination in science, mathematics, and metaphysics. Mathematical judgments are based not on the evidence of the senses but of the imagination.

13 Ibid., 42 (29).

14 *CAM*, 19; see also *CWL 3 Insight* 28–9 (4); Paul Strathern, *Mendeleyev's Dream* (London: Penguin, 2001), 286; D.L. Hurd and J.J. Kipling, eds., *The Origins and Growth of Physical Science* (Harmondsworth, U.K.: Penguin, 1964), 123–4 on Kukulé.

15 *CWL 2 Verbum*, 40–1 (27–8). There is a need to engage in the same exercise with a range of different mathematical problems.

16 Ibid., 39–40 (25).

17 Ibid., 47–8 (34).

18 *CWL 3 Insight*, 36 (12).

19 *CWL 2 Verbum*, 60 (47). The fourth article is difficult to locate within this plan, a point that will be addressed later.

20 *CWL 2 Verbum*, 60 (47). This is the only reference to Newman on the illative sense in *Verbum*. There are none in *Insight*.

21 Ibid., 70–1 (58–9); see also 64–5 (51–2).

22 Ibid., 62 (49).

23 Ibid., 63 (50).
24 Ibid., 72 (59).
25 Ibid., 75 (63); see also 77 (65) on coercion.
26 Ibid., 77 (65).
27 Ibid., 77 (65).
28 Ibid., 79 (67).
29 Ibid., 80 (68).
30 Ibid., 80 (69).
31 Ibid., 80–1 (69).
32 Ibid., 83 (71).
33 Ibid., 83 (71). On page 84 (72) there is the puzzling remark, 'Only by reflection on act can one arrive at the difference of potency.' Does this refer to the different potencies of the knower and the known?
34 Ibid., 83–7 (72–4).
35 Ibid., 86–7 (74–5).
36 Ibid., 88 (76).
37 Ibid., 88 (77).
38 Ibid., 90 (79).
39 Ibid., 90ff. (79ff.).
40 Ibid., 95n.176 (84.n.175).
41 Ibid., 94 (82–3).
42 Ibid., 95 (84).
43 Ibid., 96 (85).
44 Ibid., 97–8 (86–7).
45 Stephen Coote's narration in his *John Keats: A Life* (London: Houghton and Stodder, 1995) of how Keats' impending death started to extinguish his unfulfilled desires for poetic creativity and love brings into focus the problem of the measure of our desires.
46 *CWL 4 Collection*, 186–7 (199–201).
47 *CWL 2 Verbum*, 97 (86).
48 Ibid., index under 'concept of being,' for a list of locations where the phrase occurs.
49 Ibid., 98–9 (88).
50 Ibid., 99 (88–9). This anticipates his two modes of operation in *CWL 3 Insight*, 299 (274).
51 Ibid., 100 (90).
52 Ibid., 101 (91).

Chapter 11. Toronto, the Operations of the Mind, and a Creative Illness

1 Letter to provincial, 5 May 1946.
2 *CAM*, 158–9.
3 From a recorded interview with Fred Crowe, 26 April 1988.

4 W. Terrance Gordon, *Marshall McLuhan: Escape into Understanding, A Biography* (New York: Basic Books, 1997), 135.

5 From course notes made available to me by Walter Principe. Fr Nikolaus Haring, whose name occurs in the third *Verbum* article, also participated in the course.

6 *CWL 3 Verbum*, 107–8 (98–9).

7 Ibid., 118 (109).

8 Ibid., 140 (130).

9 Ibid., 149–50 (139–40). Note the occurrence of the terms 'level' and 'empirical consciousness' in this and the following quotation.

10 Ibid., 148 (137–8).

11 *CAM*, 51.

12 *The Modern Schoolman* (1946–7), 224. The accusation of idealism could have been related to Lonergan's review of Keeler's book in *Gregorianum* in 1935. On idealists, see *CWL 2 Verbum*, 164 (153), 166 (155), 186 (176), 189n.199 (179n.200). Note 199 opens with the remark, 'This is the critical point in philosophy.'

13 Ibid., 225.

14 *CWL 2 Verbum*, 49n.163 (34–5n.159).

15 O'Connell, 227.

16 Ibid., 228.

17 *CWL 2 Verbum*, 166 (155).

18 Ibid., 189n.199 (179n.200) The points need to be thought out in a non-mathematical context.

19 Ibid., 172 (161).

20 O'Connell, 230–1.

21 Ibid., 233.

22 Recorded interview with Crowe, 30 April 1988.

23 Crowe's 'Notes for Lonergan's Course on Faith and Charity, 1947–8' are available in the LRIT.

24 *CWL 3 Insight*, 400 (376).

25 They need to be read in the context of the treatment of love in 'Finality, Love, Marriage.' *CWL 4 Collection*, chap. 2.

26 Crowe's 'Notes for Lonergan's Course on Faith and Charity, 1947–8,' 28.

27 William Stewart's 'Notes Taken at Lonergan's Grace Course, 1947–8' are available in the LRIT.

28 The three terms 'gnoseology,' 'epistemology' and 'metaphysics' will be used in the *Verbum* articles. The three key questions that define *Verbum* and *Insight* – What am I doing when I am knowing? Why is doing that knowing? What do I know when I do it? – run through *A Second Collection*, 37, 86, 138, 203, and 241.

29 *CWL 3 Insight*, 51 (27). Whether emergent probability or contemporary cosmology takes the problem a step further is an open question.

30 From a recorded interview with Crowe, 30 April 1988.
31 See Anthony Stevens, *On Jung* (London: Routledge, 1990), 7, 19, 161–2, 178–80.
32 Crowe, *Lonergan*, 43ff.
33 *CWL 4 Collection*, chap. 5.

Chapter 12. Human Insights as Reflections of the Divine Nature

1   Lauer, 'Comment on "An Interpretation,"' *The Modern Schoolman* 25 (1947–8), 251–9, 259n.38. When the reviews of *Insight* came out, Lonergan would remark in a letter to Fred Crowe (Letter 34, 21 February 1958) that Norris Clark made a big concession in acknowledging that *intelligere* meant understanding.
2   *CWL 2 Verbum*, 153 (142).
3   Ibid., 155 (144). The letters *a, b, c*, are material; their shapes, location and arrangement are known by our senses. Their combination in words, sentences, paragraphs, and books involves a material dimension known by our senses and a meaningful dimension known by our understanding. Certain combinations generate certain meanings, other combinations other meanings. The manner in which the material dimension of all alphabets can be reduced to a binary system is suggestive of prime matter.
4   Ibid., 155 (144).
5   Again the parallels with language are striking. Textbooks on the eye and sight involve a unique and precise conjunction of letters in words that one would not find in a textbook on the ear. Particular forms or laws require related conjunctions of matter.
6   *CWL 2 Verbum*, 157 (146).
7   Ibid., 159 (148).
8   Ibid., 160–1 (149).
9   Ibid., 164 (153).
10 Ibid., 166 (155). See O'Connell, 'St. Thomas and the *Verbum*: An Interpretation,' *The Modern Schoolman* 24 (1946–7), 228.
11 *CWL 2 Verbum*, 174 (163–4).
12 Ibid., 169 (158).
13 Ibid., 174–5 (164).
14 Ibid., 174 (163).
15 Ibid., 177 (166).
16 Ibid., 178 (167–8).
17 '*Insight* Revisited,' 266–7. See chap. 8, note 3 for the full quote.
18 See A.W. More, ed., *Meaning and Reference* (Oxford: Oxford University Press, 1992), 260.

19 *CWL 2 Verbum*, 184–5 (174).
20 Interview with Crowe.
21 *CWL 2 Verbum*, 195 (186–7); see also 193ff., 183ff.; 84–5 (72–3), 195 (187); Plato, *Sophistes*, 248e; Aquinas, *Contra Gentiles*, II, 98ff.
22 *CWL 2 Verbum*, 193 (184).
23 Ibid., 192–3 (184–5).
24 Ibid., 196 (188).
25 Ibid., 196 (190).
26 Ibid., 209 (201).
27 Ibid., 209 (201).
28 'A Personal Memoir on the Origins of the Catholic Theological Society of America,' *Proceedings of the Catholic Theological Society of America* 35 (1980), 337–45.
28 From a recorded interview with Crowe, 30 April 1988.
30 Letter to Crowe, 3 March 1980. Contrast with *CAM*, 98.
31 *Method in Theology*, 352.
32 *CWL 3 Insight*, 769–70 (747–8).
33 'Notes taken by Crowe on Lonergan's Course on Christology, 1948–9,' thesis V, 23.
34 Ibid., thesis XVIII, 65.
35 Ibid., 67–9. Crowe writes 'Greg 1945' after the title. He is referring to Alois Mager, *Mystik als seelische Wirklichkeit. Eine Psychologie de Mystic* (Graz: Puset, 1945).
36 'Notes taken by Crowe at Lonergan's Course on the Trinity, 1949–50,' 16.

Chapter 13. The Vision of the First Beginning

1 *Curiosity at the Center of One's Life*, 389; *CAM*, 236.
2 In Letter 27 to Fred Crowe, Lonergan remarked that 'I began *Insight* in 1949. Longmans first received the MS in May, 1954.'
3 For a wider sense of the textual phantasm, consult the bibliography on the chronology of texts Lonergan composed during the years of thinking out *Insight*.
4 See the bibliography list of books Lonergan borrowed/read while composing *Insight*.
5 P.A. Schilpp, *The Philosophy of Ernst Cassirer* (Illinois: Open Court, 1949), contains a chapter by Susanne Langer entitled 'On Cassirer's Theory of Language and Myth.' The influence of Cassirer will weave through *Insight*.
6 *Modern Schoolman* 27 (1949–50), 152–5.
7 *CWL 4 Collection*, chap. 6. Hoenen's remark is on page 92 (97).
8 The editors' note 'b' on the text (*CWL 4 Collection*, 271–2) refers back to the

problem of integration with reference to *Acta Apostolicae Sedis* 23 (1931) on 'Quaestiones scientific cum Philosophia conjuncta.'

9 *CWL 4 Collection*, 93–4 (98).

10 These illustrations are my own. A brief description of the discovery is offered in Simon Singh and Kenneth Ribert, eds., 'Fermat's Last Stand,' *Scientific American*, November 1997, 36–41. I am using Watson, Wiles, and, in the next paragraph, Rothstein, to illustrate Lonergan's point.

11 Edward Rothstein, *Emblems of Mind: The Inner Life of Music and Mathematics* (New York: Avon Books, 1995), 38; see also 136, 143.

12 *CWL 4 Collection*, 94 (98). There are for him many more than two kinds.

13 Ibid., 94 (99).

14 Ibid., 94 (99).

15 Ibid., 94 (99). The link between this and the empirical residue in *Insight* is clear from the text: 'It follows from the priority of the sensible that there will be an inevitable residue of sensible elements that are not themselves unifications of lower elements, but only the common matter of all higher unifications.'

16 Ibid., 94 (99).

17 Ibid., 97 (101). Definitions and propositions are for Lonergan the same kind of things.

18 *CWL 3 Insight*, 36 (12)

19 *CWL 4 Collection*, 102 (107).

20 'On God's Knowledge and Will' (LRIT Archives LB 130), chap. 13, 24ff., of English version.

21 LRIT Archives, A 197.

22 LRIT Archives, A 324, with the headers of 'Order,' 'A Note on Integration,' 'Nature and Grace,' 'The Elimination of Order.'

23 Ibid., 'A Note on Integration,' 1–2.

24 Ibid., 'Order,' 21.

25 Ibid., 'The Elimination of Order,' 1. Lonergan is critical of Scotus' view of the contingent and nominalism but does not provide textual references. The term 'insight' occurs four times in the notes, 'intellectual' occurring in three of them, on this single page and on pages 22 and 24 of the notes on 'Order.'

26 Ibid., 'Order,' 22.

27 For a helpful interpretation of Archimedes, see John Philips Jr, *The Origins of Intellect: Piaget's Theory* (San Francisco: Freeman, 1975), 121ff., D.N. Perkins, *The Mind's Best Work* (Cambridge, MA: Harvard University Press, 1990), chap. 2. Being Lonergan's only account in the book of the insight experience, this needs to be complemented by others.

28 28 *CWL 3 Insight*, 28.

29 See C.S. Lewis, *Surprised by Joy* (Glasgow: Fount, 1977), 20.

Chapter 14. Experimenting with the Insights of Mathematicians and Scientists

1 'Intelligence and Reality,' 9, para. 5 (LRIT LB 131.5). The whole of the following chapter has to be read from this perspective.

2 *The Question as Commitment*, 33.

3 A familiarity with a text such as chap. 4 of C. Lanczos's book, *Numbers without End* (Edinburgh: Oliver and Boyd, 1968), entitled 'Evolution of the Number Field,' is essential in order to follow Lonergan's treatment of higher viewpoints.

4 I am slightly recasting the imagery of his account but not, I hope, the substance.

5 Cassirer, *Substance and Function* (Chicago: Open Court, 1923), 54ff.

6 *CWL 3 Insight*, 41 (16).

7 C. Lanczos, *Numbers without End* (Edinburgh: Oliver and Boyd, 1968), 90ff.

8 Cassirer, *The Problem of Knowledge* (New Haven, MA: Yale University Press, 1966), 42–3, a book named in *Insight*, 504 (479).

9 'Intelligence and Reality,' 3; see also *CWL 5 Understanding and Being*, 358; Liddy, *Transforming Light* (Collegeville, MN: Liturgical Press, 1993), 95–6.

10 'Intelligence and Reality,' 27. He also addressed this question in his grace course in 1947, at which William Stewart took notes.

11 Cassirer, *The Problem of Knowledge*, 118.

12 Dava Sobel, *Galileo's Daughter: A Drama of Science, Faith and Love* (London: Fourth Estate, 1999), 347ff. This is not a Lonergan source, but I am drawing on it to make the same point.

13 Lonergan did not read Lindsay and Margenau's *Foundations of Physics* until quite close to writing the final version of chap. 2 of *Insight*. An early extant text, composed after 'Intelligence and Reality,' has no reference to it.

14 LRIT A 276–80, Empirical Method, page 4.

15 Jo Ann Boydston, ed., *John Dewey: The Later Works, 1925–1953*, Volume 12, *1938, Logic: The Theory of Inquiry* (Carbondale: Southern Illinois University Press, 1986), 336, equates functional correspondence with conjugate relations. The discussion of conjugate relations of data on 477 refers specifically to mass, length, and time, all of which Lonergan refers to as conjugates in *Insight*. Dewey also uses 'isomorphism' on 398ff.; 'primitive terms and relations in a science' on 403, and 'probability as a frequency' on 465–73. He has an extensive treatment of the canons of modern science, and chapter 18 is entitled 'Terms of Meaning.' The term 'cultural matrix' (which occurs in the introduction to *Method in Theology*) is central in chapters 3 and 24. On page 481 he remarks that 'all inquiry proceeds within a cultural matrix which is ultimately determined by the social relations.'

16 James Watson, *The Double Helix* (Harmondsworth, U.K.: Penguin, 1968), 141–55, esp. 152.

17 *CWL 3 Insight*, 522 (498).

18 'Intelligence and Reality,' 5.

19 *CWL 3 Insight*, 505 (480).

20 'Intelligence and Reality,' 8.

21 Ibid., 8, *b* and *c.*

22 Ibid., 8, *c.*

23 Ibid., 9, 1. It is clear that Lonergan made his breakthrough to cognitional structure before he composed these notes.

24 'Intelligence and Reality,' 9. For parallels see *CWL 3 Insight*, 95–6, 299 (72–3, 274).

25 Cassirer, *Substance and Function*, 156–62.

Chapter 15. The Breakthrough to Cognitional Structure

1 This remark was carefully copied by me onto a disk from a small note-sized piece of paper on which Tom Daly had written it, and which has since gone missing from my files.

2 *CWL 4 Collection*, 20 (20).

3 References to Kant, the most frequently quoted author in the notes, occur on pages 12–13, 16, 19, 23, and 28–9. See the bibliography for details of the Kantian texts Lonergan was reading at the time.

4 *Critique of Pure Reason*, A299-3012, B 355-9: 'Reason is never in immediate relation to an object, but only to the understanding' (A643, B671).

5 *CWL 3 Insight*, 299–300 (274).

6 Ibid., 412 (387), affirms that cognitional theory is basic to metaphysical, ethical, and theological issues. In *Method in Theology* Lonergan will revise that relation but not the content of his cognitional theory.

7 *CAM*, 14. For Newman in chapter 4 of the *Grammar of Assent*, inference and assent are primarily related to propositions. Through them real assent is related to objects or things 'represented by the impressions which they have left in the imagination' (75). He also relates assent to facts: 'Thus, whereas no one could possibly confuse the real assent of a Christian to the fact of our Lord's crucifixion ...' (38); and facts to inference: 'Thus, did the Stoic infer the fact of our Lord's death instead of assenting to it?' (39). Most significantly, we find: 'An act of assent, it seems, is the most perfect and highest of its kind, when it is exercised on propositions, which are apprehended as experiences and images, that is, which stand for things' (40). Assents for Newman deal with the concrete. There is in all of this the problem of the ontological status of the things and facts assented to.

8 Lonergan's course notes do not, on page 11, elaborate on the meaning of

the absolutely unconditioned. On Kant, see *Critique of Pure Reason*, A579ff., B607ff. In A584, B612 Kant discusses 'the regress from the conditioned, which is given, to the unconditioned.' Kant, for Lonergan, did not have the notion of the *virtually* unconditioned. See also Newman, *Grammar of Assent* (Westminster, MD: Christian Classics, 1973), chap. 8, part 2, 'Informal Inference,' sec. 3, where the problem of the sufficiency of the evidence is addressed.

9 Because at this point Lonergan is focusing on the judgment and not on the fact that it makes known, he relates the 'virtually unconditioned' to the judgment. In the final write-up of *Insight* he will hold that facts are virtually unconditioned.

10 *Critique of Pure Reason*, A304, B361. The whole of the section from A299, B355 to A309, B366 should be read on this. See also the discussion of the Kantian unconditioned in Giovanni Sala, *Lonergan and Kant*, 22ff.

11 *Critique of Pure Reason*, A308.

12 *Grammar of Assent*, chap. 9, 345f.; 157–8, 189 on inference and assent; chap. 1 on modes of holding a proposition, which, I believe, influenced the opening section of chap. 9 of *Insight*.

13 'Intelligence and Reality,' 12, para. 5.

14 Ibid., 12, para. 4.

15 *Grammar of Assent*, chap. 363, discusses legends and facts and the problem of discriminating facts from fictions. Page 367 discusses tradition in terms of 'a tale descriptive of some real matter of fact.' On pages 326–7 we find 'take the facts which are proved before you' and 'or of the fact of his guilt.'

16 'Fact' does not occur in the index of the more recent translation of the *Critique of Pure Reason* by Werner S. Pluhar (Indianapolis: Hackett, 1996), but '*einsicht*' (insight) does.

17 'Intelligence and Reality,' 11, 2c; 12, 2; 13, 11. Assent being the dominant issue, Newman rarely uses 'judgment.' In chap. 9, sec. 3, part 1 we find him using 'facts' and 'judgment' in the same paragraph. Chap. 1, secs. 2 and 3 links judgments, propositions, assent, and concrete matters.

Chapter 16. The Mind's Desire as the Key to the Relation of Thought and Reality

1 William Stewart, 'Notes on Lonergan's Grace Course,' 32; Cassirer, *Substance and Function* (Chicago: Open Court, 1923), 271.

2 'Intelligence and Reality,' 13, 2; 9, 3.

3 See *CAM*, 145, where the question of Ignatian influences was put to him.

4 Although Kant acknowledges intellectual desire, it does not for him have the same status as understanding, judgment, and reasoning. Human reason for him finds itself burdened with questions it is not able to answer: 'the ques-

tions, never ceasing, its work must always remain incomplete' (A, viii); see also B xv, 426. An element of his philosophy has to do with removing our illusions about what we can desire to know.

5 In 'Openness and Religious Experience,' *CWL 4 Collection*, 186–7 (199–200), he makes a distinction between openness as an achievement and as a gift.

6 'Intelligence and Reality,' 27, 1.

7 See *CWL 3 Insight*, 433 (408) for a link with chap. 14.

8 'Intelligence and Reality' 14, sec. 5.

9 LRIT Archives, A268–71. The quotations are from an unnumbered page with the heading 'Intellectual Conversion.'

10 R.E. Cushman, *Therapeia: Plato's Conception of Philosophy* (Westport, CT: Greenwood Press, 1958), 46.

11 *Gorgias* 481c; *Republic* 519b.

12 Cushman, 45; John Wild, *Plato's Theory of Man* (Cambridge, MA: Harvard University Press, 1949).

13 LRIT Archives A268–71.

14 'Intelligence and Reality,' 14. In notes drafted after 'Intelligence and Reality' (LRIT Archives A268–71) he comments that a systematic conversion is 'not from a particular error to a particular though strange truth, but from one general orientation to another general orientation ... For intellectual conversion is from an orientation that arises spontaneously and remains in possession by sheer inertia; and it is to an orientation that can have no other motivation than mere reasons.'

15 LRIT Archives A268–71.

16 *CWL 3 Insight*, 422 (397), discusses the starting point of prospective metaphysicians; 423 (398) refers to its method as pedagogical. In the introduction he refers to the problem of realism as psychological.

17 R.M. Liddy, *Transforming Light* (Collegeville, MN: Liturgical Press, 1993), chap. 4.

18 Cushman, 44; see also 143f on knowledge by conversion.

19 'Intelligence and Reality,' 16, sec. 7: see also 15, sec. 1 and CWL 2 Verbum, 95(84), 96(85) on the link between intellectual light and judgment in Aquinas.

20 *Critique of Pure Reason*, B75, A51.

21 C.S. Lewis, *Surprised by Joy* (Glasgow: Fount, 1977), 176–7.

22 *CAM*, 116.

23 'Intelligence and Reality,' 16, 7.

24 Ibid., 16, 9.

25 Ibid., 18, 3*d*.

26 *CWL 3 Insight*, 279 (254).

27 'Intelligence and Reality,' 17, 1*d*.

28 Ibid., 17, 2*e*.

29 Cassirer, *Substance and Function*, 278; see also 271 on the two distinct spheres
of things and mind, 278 on the problem of transcendence, 297 on the
epistemological gap (where Cassirer, echoing Lonergan, remarks: 'we find
there is no epistemological gap to be laboriously spanned by some authorita-
tive decree'); 298 on the problem of the definition of an object.

30 'Intelligence and Reality,' 18, 3*c*, *e*.

31 Ibid., 18, 3*c*.

32 In the fall of 1947 he articulated it in terms of three judgments: I'm real,
you're real, I'm not you; then we are out of immanence (see note 24, chap.
11 of the present work). In *CWL 3 Insight*, 400 (376) he varies the content: I
am a knower, this is a typewriter, I am not this typewriter. Significantly, on
401 (377) he adds that one part, *A*, knows others.

33 'Intelligence and Reality,' 18, 3*e*.

34 *CWL 3 Insight*, 401 (377).

35 Cassirer, *The Problem of Knowledge*, (New Haven: Yale University Press, 1940),
115.

36 'Intelligence and Reality,' 20, 3*a*.

Chapter 17. Exploring the Real Known World: A Metaphysical Beginning

1 'Intelligence and Reality,' 23, 1*a*.

2 B Preface, xvi–xvii.

3 'Intelligence and Reality,' 23, 1; 25, 1.

4 Ibid., 26, 7*c*.

5 Ibid., 24, 6*f*.

6 Ibid., 24, 5*b*.

7 Ibid., 26, 6*d*.

8 Ibid., 24, c; see also notes for 'Thought and Reality' on the same point.

9 Jo Ann Pilardy, *Simone de Beauvoir: Writing the Self, Philosophy Becomes Autobiography* (Westport, CT: Praeger, 1999), 16. Lonergan's analysis is concerned
with objectifying how the subject is a member of a scientific, economic, or
theological community.

10 In the B-Preface to the *Critique of Pure Reason*, xvf., which I maintain
Lonergan had in mind when working on these notes, Kant posed these
questions. Here, after his exploration of the categories of metaphysics,
Lonergan asks, Can philosophy become a science? In *Insight* he will revise it
to ask about metaphysics as a science.

11 'Intelligence and Reality,' 28.

12 Ibid., 27–8.

13 Ibid., 16, 7.

14 Ibid., 29, 3.

15 *CWL 4 Collection*, 275 for the editors' introduction to the text.

16 Ibid., 110 (116). See 'Intelligence and Reality,' 61, where he adds that
    Catholicism raised up bias.
17 *CWL 4 Collection*, 112 (118).
18 Ibid., 111–12 (118–19).
19 'The Mystical Body,' Domestic exhortation, Jesuit Seminary, Toronto,
    November 1951, 1 (LRIT LB 159).

**Chapter 18. Beginning in the Middle: Common Sense, Consciousness,
and Self-Affirmation**

1 *Curiosity at the Centre of One's Life*, 389.
2 The entire text is available at the LRIT; see *CWL 3 Insight*, xviii–xix for the
   distinction between MSA, Lonergan's own typescript; MSB, the edition typed
   by Beatrice White for the publishers; and PT.
3 The page, reproduced on page xxvii of *CWL 3 Insight*, is found in an autograph file that contains chapters 9–11. Although not dated, it is clearly post–
   'Intelligence and Reality.'
4 The texts associated with the headings 'Forms of Experience' and 'Critical
   Enlightenment' are missing. See *Insight*, 268 (243) on the intellectual form
   of experience; 269 (244) on dialectic as a form of critical attitude. The
   ninety-two pages, also missing, could refer to an earlier version of the first
   five chapters, the first three of which were initially a single chapter of sixty-
   seven pages with the title 'Elements.'
5 Their favoured account of the order of composition is stated initially in *CWL
   3 Insight*, xx and repeated on xxii. Reasons given include the change in the
   line spacing from single to double in the middle of chapter 6, it being single
   in 9–13 and 1–6. There is also the remark Lonergan made in a letter to
   Crowe on 24 September 1954 from Southwell House to the effect that the
   poorest part of the carbon version was done first, namely chapters 9–13. In
   his last years, when his memory was suspect, Lonergan remarked to Tom
   Daly that he wrote the final version of the chapters on science last and to
   Robert Doran that chapters 6 and 7 came before 1–5 (*CWL 3 Insight*, xxii).
   Internal and external evidence supports the proposal that they were written
   after 9–13 but before 6–8, which presuppose emergent probability. It is also
   possible that he was referring to work he did on the dialectic of history in the
   1930s.
6 *CWL 3 Insight*, 300 (275).
7 Ibid., 298 (273).
8 It is interesting to read his analysis of common-sense judgments in chap. 10
   in tandem with the opening of chap. 6 on common sense.
9 *CWL 3 Insight*, 317 (291–2), where we find: 'The relations of things among
   themselves are, in general, a different field from the relations of things to us.

There is an apparent overlapping only when we consider the relations of
men among themselves; and then the different procedures of description
and explanation prevent the overlapping from being more than apparent,
for description is in terms of the given while explanation is in terms of the
ultimate reached by analysis.'

10 Ibid., 308 (283).

11 Ibid., 311 (286).

12 Ibid., 318 (293).

13 *CWL 2 Verbum*, 101 (90–1).

14 'Intelligence and Reality,' 26, 29.

15 *CWL 3 Insight*, 647 (624), where Lonergan uses the term 'the whole man,' by
which he designates the existential subject in contrast with the cognitional
subject.

16 *CWL 3 Insight*, 343 (319).

17 Ibid., 350 (326).

18 Ibid., 352 (328).

19 *CWL 7 On the Ontological and Psychological Constitution of Christ*, part 5, secs. 1
(on consciousness) and 2 (on 'I'), especially para. 77f. Lonergan offers five
rather complex meanings of the referent of 'I' and poses the question, What
does 'I' refer to in Christ's statement 'Before Abraham was, I am'?

20 *CWL 3 Insight*, 345 (321).

21 *CWL 7 On the Ontological and Psychological Constitution of Christ*, 173.

22 *CWL 3 Insight*, 346 (321).

23 Cassirer, *Substance and Function* (Chicago: Open Court, 1923), 295. For the
influence of Bergson on Lonergan's thought on consciousness as a datum,
see *CAM*, 256–7.

24 *CWL 7 On the Ontological and Psychological Constitution of Christ*, 159. The
parallels with Cassirer should be obvious.

25 Ibid., 161.

26 'The aim of the book is to raise consciousness. It draws attention to operations of which, in a technical sense, readers are already conscious. But that
consciousness is not yet knowledge but rather, as it were, the raw materials
for knowledge. To advance from the materials to the finished product, one
must attend to conscious operations, distinguish different kinds, compare
them and relate them to one another, grasp the various dynamic patterns in
which they occur, and discover in such patterns the ground and source of
methods ... To raise consciousness one proceeds obliquely. So the book
begins with a long series of five-finger exercises for the reader to perform
and thereby raise his own consciousness of his own operations.' *Lonergan
Studies Newsletter* 12 (1991), 23.

27 Liddy, *Transforming Light* (MN: Liturgical Press, 1993), 206.

28 *CWL 3 Insight*, 346 (322).

29 Ibid., 346 (322).
30 Ibid., 347 (323).
31 'An Interview with Fr. Bernard Lonergan,' in *A Second Collection*, 222.
32 *CWL 3 Insight*, 352–3 (328).
33 Ibid., 365 (342).
34 Ibid., 355 (331).
35 Ibid., 365 (342).
36 Ibid., 363 (339); see also 343 (319).
37 Ibid., 343 (319): 'The affirmation to be made is a judgment of fact. It is not that I exist necessarily, but merely that in fact I do. It is not that of necessity that I am a knower, but merely that in fact I am. It is not that an individual performing the listed acts really does know. But merely that I perform them and that by 'knowing' I mean no more than such a performance.'
38 Ibid., 18–19 (xxiv). The question arises, was this something he felt he needed to point out with hindsight as he was writing the preface rather than something he was in control of when writing chapters 9–13? Also, by 'first' does he mean first in general or first philosophical judgment?
38 Ibid., 397 (372–3). The next quote in the paragraph is from the same section.
40 *CAM*, 110–11.
41 *CWL 3 Insight*, 398 (374). The quote, coming right at the end of chapter 12, poses the question, was chapter 12 written before 11?
42 Ibid., 401 (377).
43 'Consciousness of Christ,' point 8 (Course Notes 1952, LRIT LB 138).
44 *CWL 3 Insight*, 411 (386).
45 Ibid., 407 (383).
46 *CWL 10 Topics in Education*, 175 (234).
47 *CWL 3 Insight*, 406 (381).
48 'Consciousness of Christ,' point 9.
49 *CWL 3 Insight*, 406 (382).
50 Ibid., 407 (383).
51 Ibid., 404 (380).
52 Ibid., 402 (378).
53 Rarely in *Insight* does Lonergan use the term 'epistemology.' The index refers one to pages 401–2 (377), but 'epistemology' does not occur there. In a remark on page 412 (387) ('Firstly, in any philosophy, it is possible to distinguish between its cognitional theory and, on the other hand, its pronouncements on metaphysical, ethical and theological issues') epistemology seems to have been incorporated into cognitional theory.
54 Ibid., 398 (375). I would frame it in terms of a patterned set of questions and related judgments.
55 Ibid., 401 (377). The phrase 'the problem of transcendence' occurs in

Cassirer's *Substance and Function*, 278, the text continuing: 'If we have once enclosed ourselves in the circle of "self-consciousness," no labour on the part of thought (which itself belongs wholly to this circle) can lead us out again.'

56 Ibid., 400 (375).

57 Ibid., 408 (383–4).

Chapter 19. Insights into Emergent Probability

1   *CWL 3 Insight*, 149 (126).

2   Shull, *Evolution*, 281. Works by Jennings are listed on 292.

3   *CWL 3 Insight*, 141–2 (118).

4   Lapierre 'Insight Drafts,' A Priori Categories, 9; see also A273–5, where page 7 is on *a priori* categories.

5   *CWL 4 Insight*, 142 (119).

6   Lapierre, 'Insight Drafts,' A Priori Categories, 9. Although crossed out this text gives us a valuable insight into what Lonergan was thinking.

7   *CWL 3 Insight*, 155 (132); see also 79, 228 (56, 204) for references related to the present paragraph. Laplace is mentioned once in 'Intelligence and Reality' but not in the context of the question of determinism. He is mentioned eight times in *Insight*, all in the context of determinism.

8   *CWL 3 Insight*, 71 (48).

9   When Lonergan was composing chapter 4 he had not worked out the problem posed in 'Intelligence and Reality' about the nature of the relation between higher and lower conjugates.

10   *CWL 3 Insight*, 110 (87).

11   Ibid., 140–1 (117).

12   Ibid., 141–2 (118).

13   Ibid., 149 (126).

14   Ibid., 142–3 (119–20).

15   Ibid., 143 (120).

16   *CWL 3 Insight*, 147 (124).

17   In an earlier version of chap. 2, page 29 (LRIT Archives), section 2.5 is headed 'Restricted Invariance,' and Section 2.6 deals with equivalence. There is no mention in this version of a chapter 5 on space and time. It seems that the early chapters were written as a unit with the single title 'Elements.' In this version 'Elements' is crossed out and replaced by 'Heuristic Structures.'

18   Burtt, *The Metaphysical Foundations of Modern Science* (New Jersey: Humanities Press, 1925).

19   Lenzen, *Nature of Physical Theory* (New York: 1931), 85.

20   Albert Einstein, *Relativity: The Special and General Theory* (London: Methuen, 1960 [1920]), 42–3. Einstein's account up to this point is surprisingly read-

able and is essential if one is to grasp what Lonergan is up to. See also Lindsay and Margenau, *Foundations of Physics* (New York: Dover, 1957), 356f.

21 *CWL 3 Insight*, 194 (170), including the footnote.

22 Ibid., 195 (171–2).

Chapter 20. Insights into the Dialectical Development of Common Sense

1 *CWL 3 Insight*, 291 (266).

2 The typescript ran to 114 pages, the line spacing changing from single to double at section 2, 'The Subjective Field of Common Sense.' Later he renamed the section starting at page 52 'Chapter VII, Common Sense (contd).' Clearly, we should read them as a single chapter. The extension of emergent probability to the human world suggests that the final version was written after chapter 4.

3 Possibly relevant would be his 'The National Mentalities of Europe,' a talk given at St Anthony's Parish, Montreal, in 1941 (LRIT A20). For earlier remarks on common sense see *CWL 2 Verbum*, 249 (101); 'Thought and Reality' 10, 20; 'Intelligence and Reality,' 24; and *Insight*, chap. 9, sec. 5.

4 See *CWL 3 Insight*, 238 (212–13) for an analysis of the intersubjective and civil communities, 242 (217) for the introduction of dialectic. All of these concepts were included in 'The Role.'

5 Ibid., 268 (243).

6 Thomas O'D. Hanley, 'Notes Taken at Lonergan's *Insight* Lectures,' Toronto, 1953 (LRIT Archives File 79), 43. *Insight*, 557 (534) refers to German nationalism under Hitler as an aberration, linking it with Lonergan's analysis of dialectic.

7 *CWL 3 Insight*, 198–9 (175). The emphasis on the passing of situations seems to overlook their significance in narrative of a human person's life and of memory.

8 *CWL 3 Insight*, 204 (181).

9 Chapter 4 of Dewey's *Logic: A Theory of Inquiry* (Vol. 12 of *John Dewey: The Later Works*, 1925–1953, ed. Jo Ann Boydston [Carbondale, IL: Southern Illinois University Press, 1986), is entitled 'Common Sense and Scientific Inquiry.' For him common sense is constantly changing; intellectually, it regards the same experiences or situations as science but from a different perspective. Lonergan is distinctive in his emphasis on the dialectical nature of changes in common sense and related social aberrations.

10 Theodore Kisiel, *The Genesis of Heidegger's Being and Time* (Berkeley: UCLA Press, 1995), 62–5, suggests that Heidegger's use of the term 'situation' amounts to a paradigm shift in philosophy, his 'historical ego' and the 'ego of the situation' later becoming *Dasein*. In his 'Reading a Life: Heidegger

and Hard Times,' Thomas Sheehan remarks: 'For Heidegger the theoretical orientation of the pure ego of Husserlian phenomenology sucks the blood out of the richly textured *Umwelt*, the firsthand world of lived experience (Erleben) in which one primarly exists and carries out practical tasks': *The Cambridge Companion to Heidegger*, ed. Charles Guignon (Cambridge: Cambridge University Press, 1993), 78f.

11   *CWL 3 Insight*, 243 (218).

12   *CWL 3 Insight*, 206 (183).

13   The form of the desired is in the desire. The aesthetic desires of a van Gogh or Matisse, the intellectual desires of a Newton, Einstein or Freud structure not simply casual patterns of experience from time to time in their lives, but the core pattern of their life structures over its lifetime.

14   *Insight*, 210–11 (187). The categories of plot, character, falling in love, and being in love need to be added to Lonergan's analysis of the dramatic pattern and the notion that a human life is a work of art unpacked.

15   Ibid., 211–12 (188).

16   Ibid., 214 (191).

17   Wilhelm Stekel, *Technique of Analytical Psychotherapy* (London: The Bodley Head, 1939), xxi, 2–3.

18   The illustrations from *Death of a Salesman* (London: Penguin, 1976) and Henrik Ibsen's *A Doll's House* (in *A Doll's House and Other Plays* [Harmondsworth, U.K.: Penguin, 1965]) that follow, not in Lonergan's text, are offered in the hope that they will illuminate the points he is making.

19   Miller, 74.

20   Ibid., 105.

21   *CWL 3 Insight*, 212 (189). In certain respects, in chapter 6 Lonergan is concerned with the psychoneural and in chapter 7 with the psychosocial.

22   Lonergan's own card index contains a reference to Roland Dalbiez (the teacher of Ricoeur), *Psychoanalytic Method and the Doctrines of Freud*, Vol. 1, *Exposition*, Vol. 2, *Discussion* (London: Longmans, Green, 1941, 1948). A much-used textbook at the time in third-level education, it opens with a discussion of the metaphysics of consciousness, in particular the relation between the unconscious and the psychic or conscious. Dalbiez accepts that in the universe the higher is conditioned by the lower but is dubious that a psychic event can be caused by a solely material cause (Vol. 1, 8–9). Lonergan made handwritten notes on Jolan Jacobi's *The Psychology of Jung*, 5th ed. (London: Routledge, Kegan and Paul, 1949) on pages on one side of which he had previously typed an early draft of chapter 2 of *Insight* (LRIT Archives, A 276–80.) Jacobi discusses the static and dynamic laws of the psyche. Lonergan's notes include remarks on the Jungian scheme of introvert, extrovert, etc., as well as on the persona, ego, shadow, anima, and on the mediators

between conscious and unconscious activities. Although influenced by these authors, his use of the terms 'psyche' and 'psychic' is not necessarily identical with that of either Dalbiez or Jacobi.

23 See *CWL 3 Insight*, 481 (455–6) for a further occurrence of the term 'neural.'

24 Ibid., 216 (192–3).

25 Ibid., 225–6 (202).

26 Original MSA autograph text (LRIT Archives), sec. 2.7, p. 49.

27 *CWL 3 Insight*, 229 (205); see also note *w*, p. 793. The paragraphs starting, 'Still, whatever may have been Freud's involvement in mechanist determinism ...' assume the reader is already familiar with the ideas developed in chap. 8.

28 Ibid., 237 (212).

29 Ibid., 241 (215).

30 Ibid., 248, 243, 239 (223, 217, 214).

31 O'D. Hanley notes (LRIT Archives), 59; see also *CAM*, 256–7.

32 Henri Bergson, *Creative Evolution*, transl. Arthur Mitchell (London: Macmillan, 1911), 244. The term 'dialectic' is discussed on 251.

33 *CWL 3 Insight*, 242–3 (217). In *Method in Theology* dialectic will have ethical roots.

34 *CWL 3 Insight*, 245 (219).

35 Ibid., 247 (222).

36 Ibid., 258 (233).

37 Ibid., 251, 252 (226, 227) for the points dealt with in the present paragraph.

38 O'D. Hanley notes, 62.

39 *CWL 3 Insight*, 266–7 (242).

40 Ibid., 268 (244).

Chapter 21. Insights into the Irreducibility of Things

1 *CWL 3 Insight*, 290 (265).

2 Ibid., 281 (256).

3 Cassirer, *The Problem of Knowledge* (New Haven: Yale University Press, 1940), 131.

4 *CWL3 Insight*, 464 (438). Only in chap. 15 does he make this relation clear.

5 Newton, *Opticks* (New York: Dover, 1952), 375, 388–9.

6 Paul Strathern, *Mendeleyev's Dream: The Quest for the Elements* (London: Penguin, 2001), 286.

7 Gerhard Herzberg, *Atomic Spectra and Atomic Structure* (New York: Dover, 1944), 13–54 on Bohr and the hydrogen atom, 120f. for the explanation of the periodic table of the elements. That the energy structure of the hydrogen atom is a solution to the wave equation (38) supports Lonergan's thesis that a species is a solution to the problem of existing in an environment. The

code of the four quantum numbers, n, l, m, (39), and later spin (124), define the relational properties of the chemical genus.

8 *The Problem of Knowledge* is mentioned on page 504 (479) of *CWL 3 Insight.*

9 Cassirer, 127.

10 'A Note on Geometrical Possibility,' *CWL 4 Collection*, 93f. (98f.).

11 Jeff Lyon and Pewter Gorner, *Altered Fates: Gene Therapy and the Retooling of Human Life* (New York: Norton, 1996), 40. Schrödinger's 1946 lectures 'What Is Life? further advanced the question of the chemical basis of life.

12 Jeff Wheelright, 'Reading the Language of Our Ancestors: Getting Up to Speed on Medical Genetics through the Vision of Victor McKusic,' *Discover,* February 2002, 70–7.

13 Lyon and Gorner, 45.

14 E.D. Wilson, *Consilience* (London: Abacus, 1999), 111; see also Wilder Penfield, *No Man Alone: A Neurosurgeon's Life* (Boston: Little, Brown, 1977).

15 Antonio Damasio, *The Feeling of What Happens: Body, Emotion and the Making of Consciousness* (London: Heinemann, 2000), 9. In 317f. he again addresses the questions, what is an image and what is a mental pattern?

16 Ibid., 317.

17 Ibid., 198–9. See also Rita Carter, *Mapping the Mind* (London: Weidenfeld and Nicolson, 1998), 265f., on the neural basis of personal memories that gives rise to differences in the self. In *The Private Life of the Brain* (London: Penguin, 2000), 61–4, Susan Greenfield asserts that the number of neurons in the brain of the newly born does not increase greatly. What changes in development are the connections. Through stimulation by unique experiences and conversations the generic brain becomes, through its connections, personalized. This suggests distinctive neural connections emerging in every individual brain.

18 *CWL 3 Insight*, 291–2 (266).

19 Ibid., 290–1 (265–6).

20 Howard Gardner, *Extraordinary Minds* (London: Weidenfeld and Nicolson, 1997).

21 *CWL 3 Insight*, 291 (266). At this point the problem of explaining the development of things begins to be posed. The subsequent treatment of genetic method in chap. 15 leaves open the extent to which dialectic should be considered as a basis for explaining species differences.

22 Ibid., 291 (266). His remarks on the famous experiments on sea urchins link his work at this point to Cassirer's *The Problem of Knowledge*, 195ff., and Bergson's *Creative Evolution* (trans. Arthur Mitchell [London: Macmillan, 1911]), 44–5.

23 *CWL 3 Insight*, 292 (267).

24 Wilson, 58.

25 *CWL 3 Insight*, 280–1 (255).

26 Ibid., 289 (264).

27 Ibid., 289–91 (264–6).

28 Ibid., 290 (265); 288–9 (263); 291–2 (266).

29 Hertzberg, 38ff. On the role of the Pauli exclusion principle in explaining the periodic law of the chemical elements, see chap. 3.

30 *CWL 3 Insight,* 501 (477) refers to conjugates as acquired habits.

31 Ibid., 281 (255–6). My suggestion that what Lonergan means by 'higher conjugates' and 'higher integrations' has something in common with the meaning of an algorithm is speculative. Algorithms and higher integrations can occur on ever higher levels, possible events on one level, becoming the materials for a higher level algorithm or integration. Both are of the form of solutions to problems on the higher level. Both are relevant to the problems of complexity and of reductionism.

32 Ibid., 281 (256). For further related passages, consult 283 (257), 288–9 (263), 289 (264), 292 (267). Lonergan's most forceful statement of this point occurs on pages 465–6 (440) of chap. 15.

33 Ibid., 282 (256–7).

Chapter 22. Insights into Philosophical Method, Polymorphism, and Isomorphism

1 '*Insight* Revisited,' in *A Second Collection,* 275; see also 222 and *CAM,* 70. The structure of the course notes for 'Intelligence and Reality' makes it difficult to conclude that the book could have ended at chapter 13.

2 LRIT, File 79. No lectures were given on space and time. On 3 February he began chapter 5 containing four lectures on common sense as subject and object, his first public statement on these matters. A digression on Aristotle's notion of substance and its relation to thing included reflections on development related to the discussion of genetic method in chap. 16 of *Insight*. On 10 March he began lectures on the notions of judgment and reflective understanding, followed by lecture 14 on self-affirmation. The final lectures on 14 and 21 April on the notions of being and objectivity express a distinction between the notion and the idea of being.

3 This relates to comments on Galileo, Descartes, and objectivity in the context of primary and secondary properties on the opening page of a three-page draft on space and time from the Lapierre *Insight* residue.

4 Letter 1 to Crowe. Notable is the absence of any reference to self-affirmation or space and time.

5 LRIT Archives, A379.

6 *CWL 3 Insight,* 412 (387).

7 The remarks come on one of the several pages numbered '2' in the fifteen pages still extent of the Lapierre *Insight* residue (LRIT). They invite us to

identify the questions and insights grounding the philosophies of, for instance, Wittgenstein, Heidegger, Hannah Arendt, and Simone de Beauvoir.

8 Lapierre *Insight* residue, Philosophy 4.

9 'And now, after all methods, so it is believed, have been tried and found wanting, the prevailing mood is that of weariness': *Critique of Pure Reason* Aix.

10 The term 'polymorphism' was used at his *Insight* lecture on 16 February 1953, suggesting that he was at that point thinking out chap. 14.

11 *CWL Insight,* 429. The remarks do not extend to the moral or religious spheres.

12 Ibid., 20, 423, 426 (xxvi, 398, 401) on pedagogy; on method 426 (401). Both are part of his philosophical method. On commitment see *Method in Theology,* chap. 10, 'Foundations.'

13 *CWL Insight,* 412 (387) omits epistemology from the list, 413 (388) includes it. After February 1965 he will come to affirm that ethical and religious attitudes and choices can guide and direct the cognitional. In this change in his viewpoint on relations between the cognitional, ethical, and religious, the content of his cognitional structure will remain constant.

14 Ibid., 413 (388).

15 *CWL 3 Insight,* 416 (391).

16 Ibid., 451, 495 (426, 470).

17 Ibid., 512 (488): 545 (521).

18 Ibid., 438 (413) on the 'Copernican revolution.'

19 Ibid., 424f. (399f.). For a statement on isomorphism as a mapped pattern of relations, see 'Isomorphism of Thomist and Scientific Thought,' *CWL 4 Collection* 133ff. (149ff.). Earlier Lonergan defined 'metaphysics' as the science that relates heuristic structures to one another. How the theorem of isomorphism comes into play in this is left open.

20 'Isomorphic' is a term that occurs in Dewey's *Logic of Inquiry* (Vol. 12 of *John Dewey: The Later Works,* 1925–1953, ed. Jo Ann Boydston [Carbondale, IL: Southern Illinois University Press, 1986]), 396–99, 407.

21 As in 'Thought and Reality' Lonergan did not yet have a cognitional theory, his parallel probings of the related metaphysical elements of potency and act were unfocused. After his breakthrough to a theory of cognitional structure in 'Intelligence and Reality,' potency, form, and act were defined by the same set of relations as experiencing, understanding, and judging. There resulted three different kinds of potency, form, and act – individual, conjugate, and group – and nine different elements. Different kinds of questions are related to differences in potency, form, and act. This suggests that there might be more than nine metaphysical elements, not fewer.

22 *CWL 3 Insight,* 465 (439).

23 Ibid., 466 (440–1). A problem arises about the distinction between a coinci-

dental aggregate of events and a coincidental manifold such as a structure, which might not be of events.

24 Ibid., 270, 542 (245, 518); see also 484 (459) 7.1 on central form as a constant and invariant of a development. Does this seem consistent with the changes in the intelligibility of the unity that takes place in a development?

25 *CWL 3 Insight*, 425 (400).

Chapter 23. Process Metaphysics: Finality, Development, the Human Image

1 Cassirer, *The Problem of Knowledge*, 151.

2 Philip Ball, *A Biography of Water* (New York: Farrer, Straus and Giroux, 2000).

3 Stephen W. Hawking, *A Brief History of Time* (London: Bantam Press, 1988), 50.

4 Rick Gore, 'The Once and Future Universe,' *National Geographic,* June 1983, 740–8.

5 *CWL 3 Insight*, 469 (444).

6 *CWL 3 Insight*, 472, 474, 476 (446, 448, 451). In the context of finality Lonergan will also use the phrase 'emergent process.'

7 *CWL 3 Insight*, 473 (447). On this see Bergson, *Creative Evolution*, trans. Arthur Mitchell (London: Macmillan, 1911), 195, 173.

8 Bergson, ix, 252, 254. Worth quoting is one of Lonergan's last remarks on finality in 'Reality, Myth, Symbol' (*CWL 17 Philosophical and Theological Papers 1965–1980*, 387) that the *elan vital* is 'the formative power that underpins the evolution of atomic elements and compounds, of the genera and species of plant and animal life, of the spontaneous attractions and repulsions of human consciousness that, when followed, produce the charismatic leaders of social groups, the artists who catch and form the spirit of the progressive age, the scientists who chance upon the key paradigms that open new vistas upon world process, the scholars who recapture past human achievement and reconstitute for our contemplation the ongoing march of human history, the saints and mystics who, like the statue of Buddha, place before our eyes the spirit of prayer and adoration, and I would add, the Christ, the Son of God, whose story is to be read in the Gospels and the significance of that story in the Old Testament and the New Testament.'

9 Shull, *Evolution* (New York: McGraw Hill, 1936), 8–9 on ancestors and ancestry.

10 *CWL 3 Insight*, 474 (448–9).

11 Ibid., 473–4 (448).

12 Ibid., 473 (448).

13 Ibid., 472 (446). The next sentence continues: 'Accordingly, our question of finality is simply a question of correctly understanding a fact.'

14 Ibid., 470 (445).

15 Ibid., 505 (480). A possible candidate would be the integrator of genetic method. On 501 (477) he talks about habits as conjugate forms, so clearly he is enlarging the meaning of the term.

16 Ibid., 482–3 (456–7).

17 Cassirer, *The Problem of Knowledge*, 179.

18 *CWL 3 Insight*, 479 (454).

19 Ibid. (478).

20 Ibid., 506 (481–2).

21 Bergson, 142.

22 *Scientific American*, July 1990, 26–32. In what follows I am describing some modern developments of the problem in order to illuminate Lonergan's meaning.

23 Antonio Damasio, *The Feeling of What Happens: Body, Emotion and the Making of Consciousness* (London: Heineman, 2000), 135f. Significant here is the problem of how, through managing aggregates of biological events in a development, the operator forms a spatial structure such as an eye. Lonergan does not seem to address this question directly.

24 *CWL 3 Insight*, 507 (482).

25 Ibid., 496 (471). Strange is the absence of dialectic, of conflict, in the account.

26 'Essentially, he felt that he was only beginning to get a sense of the vast complexity of the human life cycle, and he was irritated by popularizers who cast it in overly finite form': Lawrence Friedman, *Identity's Architect: A Biography of Erik H. Erikson* (London: Free Association Books, 1999), 221–2; see also 236. On 201 he outlines the three coexisting processes the relations between which he was trying to understand: '(1) the biological (the process of organismic organization); (2) the psychological (an individual's capacity for ego synthesis); (3) the social organization of ego organisms in geographic-historic units.' Although Erikson's psychological also includes the intellectual, there is involved a large element of what Lonergan would term the psychic.

27 Ibid., 202–3: Erikson was more attentive to the psychological than the organic roots of his patient Sam's outbreaks. The latter's defences were characteristic of a fragile sense of ego identity that made it difficult for him to anticipate inner as well as outer dangers.

28 Ibid., 220. Erikson was dealing with normal rather than pathological development. See also *CAM*, 244–6 for remarks on Erikson.

28 Friedman, 201f.

30 Ibid., 200–1.

31 See Erikson, *Toys and Reasons* (New York: Norton, 1977), 85f. for illustrations of ritualization in everyday life. For Lonergan such schemes of recurrence would reveal the higher system as integrator at any given stage: 'The study of

animal behaviour, of stimulus and response, would reveal at any stage of development a flexible circle of ranges of schemes of recurrence': *CWL 3 Insight*, 493 (468).

32 *Scientific American* 189, no. 5 (1953).

33 Alison Gopnik, Andrew Meltzoff, and Patricia Kuhl, *How Babies Think: The Science of Childhood* (London: Weidenfeld and Nicolson, 1999), 111f.

34 J.H. Flavell, *The Developmental Psychology of Jean Piaget* (London: Van Nostrand, 1963) chaps. 5, 6.

35 *CWL 3 Insight*, 496 (471–2).

36 Ibid., 493 (468).

37 Ibid., 501 (476–7).

38 Ibid., 490 (465).

39 Ibid., 491, 495 (466–7, 470).

40 Ibid., 493–4 (469).

41 Ibid., 494 (469).

42 Sullivan, *The Interpersonal Theory of Psychiatry* (New York: Norton, 1953).

43 Lonergan seems to be using the notion of higher integrations to explain both the emergence of higher genera from lower and the succession of developmental stages in a species. In the former case new genera emerge. In the latter case new conjugates emerge in one and the same thing or species. Can both of these be explained on the same basis?

44 *CWL 3 Insight*, 494 (470).

45 Ibid., 499 (474–5). Related is his remark: 'What the existentialist discovers and talks about, what the ascetic attempts to achieve in himself, what the psychiatrist endeavours to foster in another, what the psychologist aims at understanding completely, the metaphysician outlines in heuristic categories': ibid., 495 (470).

46 Ibid., 498 (473).

47 Ibid., 484 (459).

48 Ibid., 500 (476). Does 'goal' suggest ethical aims and choices?

49 Because our life dreams always contain core truths and core illusions, development for Daniel Levinson is always a dialectical interaction between reality and illusion, see his *The Seasons of a Man's Life* (New York: Ballantine, 1978), 90–3. In contrast, we can never apprehend the way in which a plot will unfold and end in our lives.

50 *CWL 3 Insight*, 501–2 (477).

51 Ibid., 509–10 (485).

52 Smith, *The Philosophy of Being* (New York: Macmillan, 1961).

53 On primary relativity see *CWL 3 Insight*, 517–8 (494); on internal relations see *De Deo Trino II Pars Systematica: The Analagous Conception of the Divine Persons* (Rome: Gregorian University Press, 1964), 291–315.

54 *CWL 3 Insight*, 522 (498).

55 Ibid., 540 (516).
56 His course notes on his *Insight* lectures at Morega in 1961, with few exceptions, follow closely the text of *Insight.*

Chapter 24. On Mythic and Philosophical Consciousness: Truth and Its Expression and Interpretation

1 *CWL 3 Insight,* 554 (531) mentions Bultman's principles of New Testament interpretation.
2 Normin Perrin's 'Recent Trends in Research in the Christology of the NT,' *Essays in Divinity* 6 (1968), 217–35, is also mentioned. On page 6 of a section entitled '*Homoousion*' of the notes Lonergan made for the course (available at the LRIT) we find:

> What we have been endeavouring all along to achieve is not a notional but a real apprehension of a development in doctrine:
> We have considered Christology:
> in the mind of Jesus as implicit in his words and works
> in the earliest Palestinian community
> in the minds of Greek speaking Jewish converts
> in the mind of mission to the Gentiles
> in the mind of Jewish Christians
> in the convictions of Tertullian
> in the Platonist interpretations of Origen
> in the contentions of the Arians
> in the doubts and confusions that followed
> in the clarifications of Nicea and Athanasius

3 *CWL 3 Insight,* 554 (530)
4 *CWL 3 Insight,* 555 (531).
5 'Intelligence and Reality,' 29.
6 *CWL 3 Insight,* 556 (532).
7 *CWL 3 Insight,* 556 (533).
8 Cassirer, *The Philosophy of Symbolic Forms,* Vol. 2: *Mythical Thought* (New Haven: Yale University Press, 1955), 23f.
9 *CWL 3 Insight,* 557 (534). See also chap. 5, note 3 of the present work. No reference is given for the remark on Jung. Presumably Lonergan is referring to Jung's remark that, of the hundreds of patients that passed through his hands, there was hardly one whose problem was not that of finding a religious outlook on life, and that none of them had been healed who did not regain their religious outlook: 'Psychotherapists or the Clergy,' in his *Collected Works,* Vol. 11 (1932), 334.
10 In *Mythical Thought* we find sections entitled 'The Mythical Consciousness of the Object' and 'The Dialectic of Mythical Consciousness.' Also of interest is

the mythic perspective (159f.) that death is not the end of the self of soul but simply a transition. This book was initially published in German in 1925 and reprinted in 1953. The first English translation came out in 1954, after Lonergan had composed the basic text of *Insight.* In contains an extensive discussion of Schelling's thought on the matter as well as brief remarks on Comte. Schilpp's 1949 work *The Philosophy of Ernst Cassirer* (Chicago: Open Court, 1949) contains a number of essays on mythical thought, one of them by Susanne Langer.

11 'An Interview with Fr. Bernard Lonergan, S.J.,' in *A Second Collection*, 225–6. The tigers-and-elephants reference can be found in Cassirer, *The Philosophy of Symbolic Form*, 179.

12 *Insight*, 564, 566–7 (541, 543, 544) on myth and counterpositions.

13 Caputo, *Demythologizing Heidegger* (Bloomington: Indiana University Press, 1993).

14 *Insight*, 567 (543).

15 See note 12 above and section 3.7 of chap. 17 of *Insight.*

16 *A Second Collection*, 225. The quote poses questions about the relation between myth and symbol.

17 *CWL 3 Insight*, 566 (543).

18 Ibid., 567 (543).

19 Ibid., 711, 714 (689, 692).

20 London: Harvill Press.

21 *CWL 3 Insight*, 571 (547).

22 *Encyclopedia Britannica*, Vol. 16 (London: 1957), under 'Mystery.'

23 *CWL 3 Insight*, 571 (548).

24 Ibid., 572 (548).

25 Ibid., 572 (548).

26 Ibid., 572 (549).

27 Eliade, *Images and Symbols* (Paris: Gallimard, 1952), 22. I am indebted to Garrett Barden for drawing my attention to these themes in Eliade.

28 *A Second Collection*, 225. He adds: 'but I believe in the permanent necessity of the symbol for human living. You can't talk to your body without symbols, and you have to live with it.'

28 '*Insight* Revisited,' in *A Second Collection*, 275.

30 'Reality, Myth, Symbol,' in *CWL 17 Philosophical and Theological Papers 1965–1980*, 386. Lonergan seems to be suggesting here that stories are on the way to understanding and theories; see *CAM*, 197–9.

31 'Reality, Myth, Symbol,' in *CWL 17 Philosophical and Theological Papers 1965–1980*, 390; Ira Progoff, *Depth Psychology and Modern Man* (New York: McGraw Hill, 1959), 182f.

32 *CWL 3 Insight*, 575 (552).

33 In this sense Lonergan would agree with Collingwood's critique of truth as a property of propositions with no reference to the questions they answer. See R.G. Collingwood, *An Autobiography* (Oxford: Oxford University Press, 1970), chap. 5.

34 *CWL 3 Insight*, 383, 576f. (359, 553). In the later pages Lonergan affirms an isomorphism between knowing and its linguistic expression. Corresponding to the multiplicity of the experiential there is the multiplicity of the linguistic. The structure of the combination of the words corresponds to insight and formulation. Linguistically, to affirm or deny corresponds to judgment or negation.

35 Ibid., 577 (554).

36 Ibid., 578 (555).

37 Ibid., 585 (562).

38 Ibid., 585 (562).

39 See R.H. Fuller's *The Foundation of New Testament Christology* (New York: Scribner's, 1965) and reference to Perrin in note 2 of the present chapter.

40 *CWL 3 Insight*, 587 (564). One wonders if the thesis of general relativity theory that the laws of gravity must be independent of any particular frame of reference influenced Lonergan's thought here.

41 Ibid., 587 (564).

42 Ibid., 586 (564).

43 Ibid., 588 (565).

44 *A Second Collection*, 275–6. Chapters 7–11 deal with research, interpretation, history, and dialectic.

Chapter 25. The Cognitional and the Ethical

1 *CWL 3 Insight*, 652 (629).

2 See Adrian Theodore Peperzak, *Beyond: The Philosophy of Emmanual Levinas* (Evanston, IL: Northwestern University Press, 1997), 111–12, 118, 221–3, for a discussion of the claims of ethics or ontology to be the first philosophy.

3 His first analysis of the human good in terms of the particular good, the good of order and values, came in his essay 'The Role of the Catholic University in the Modern World,' written just after his metaphysical explorations of potency, form, and act in 'Intelligence and Reality.'

4 It occurs in *CWL 3 Insight*, 629 (606), in the section on the ontology of the good. Pages 633–4 (610–11) talk about willingness being right or wrong, good or bad. The problem of evil is addressed in chapter 20.

5 Ibid., 628 (605).

6 Ibid., 629 (606).

7 Ibid., 621 (598).

8 Ibid., 622 (599).

9 Ibid., chap. 20, 730 (708–9). Judgments on the value of beliefs are discussed, but judgments of value as such are not discussed in the chapter on ethics.

10 *Method in Theology*, 37.

11 Eric Voegelin, *Plato* (Baton Rouge: Louisiana State University, 1957), 231–6. In the *Laws* discernment of feelings, as in Ignatian spirituality, becomes a central event in decision making.

12 *CWL 3 Insight*, 626 (603).

13 Ibid., 631, 640 (608, 617). It is helpful to read together 631ff. (607ff.) on the notion of freedom with 639ff. (616ff.) on freedom, as they deal with the same themes from slightly different perspectives.

14 Ibid., 640 (617).

15 Ibid., 640 (617).

16 Ibid., 634–5 (611).

17 Ibid., 636–7 (613).

18 Ibid., 624 (601), on rational, moral self-consciousness; 634 (611) where rational self-conscious occurs. See also 622 (599) on the shift from consciousness to self-consciousness.

19 *CWL 3 Insight*, 642 (619).

20 *Method in Theology*, 38. For many this discovery comes not within the parameters of their own selfhood, but in terms of the manner in which as an individual they relate to others.

21 *CWL 3 Insight*, 641 (618).

22 Ibid., 648, 650 (625, 627). Interesting is the use of the term 'man' rather than 'self' or 'subject.' The notion that self-development is complete at any point in a life is questionable, even mythical.

23 Jo-Ann Pilardy, *Simone de Beauvoir: Writing the Self, Philosophy Becomes Autobiography* (Westport, CT: Praeger, 1999), 17.

24 *CWL 3 Insight*, 647 (624).

25 Ibid., 647 (624).

26 At this point the implication of positions and counterpositions in ethics is not worked out. The distinction between the instinctive will, concerned with controlling others in one's world, and the spiritual will, concerned with practical insights, deliberation, and decision, needs to be acknowledged. Chapter 4 of Kristina Arp's *The Bonds of Freedom: Simone de Beauvoir's Existentialist Ethics* (Chicago: Open Court, 2001) is also to the point.

27 Ibid., 651 (628).

Chapter 26. Questions and Insights in Religion

1 *CWL 3 Insight*, 706 (684). The big question here is the meaning of the word 'glimpsed.'

2 Buber, *I and Thou* (Edinburgh: T & T Clark, 1966), 75. In note 1, 754 (731n.)
   in the epilogue, added at the proofreading stage, Lonergan remarks that his
   treatment of personal relations in *Insight* was skimpy. In fact, it was non-
   existent. It follows that his extrapolation to the eternal is from the aspirations of the scientific rather than the interpersonal.

3 By 'natural theology' Lonergan would have understood a movement in
   Catholic theology whose roots go back to Anselm and Aquinas and are
   modified by Descartes and Kant. More recently, the First Vatican Council
   held that human reason could prove the existence of God. For Kant's sense
   of natural theology, see *Critique of Pure Reason*, A632, B660.

4 *CWL 3 Insight*, 664 (641).

5 Paul Hoffmann, *The Man Who Loved Only Numbers* (London: Fourth Estate,
   1999), 229.

6 *CWL 3 Insight*, 762 (740–1). Of note is his omission of the ethical level of
   development in his thinking at this point.

7 Ibid., 662–3 (639–41), 675–6, 678–9 (652–3, 655–6).

8 Ibid., 676 (653).

9 Ibid., 676–7 (653–4).

10 Ibid., 711 (689), 714 (692).

11 Ibid., 675 (652).

12 Whether God can be experienced and in a sense known through 'religious
    experience' is a further and open question involving a quite different sense
    of the word 'experience' than that used in the empirical sciences.

13 Lonergan largely considers the pure desire to know in its scientific orienta-
    tion, in relation to the universe as stimulus and terminus. But Augustine,
    C.S. Lewis, Emilie Griffin, Thomas Merton, and others have found their
    desire to know being awakened and led by a source or power beyond the
    empirical universe. This poses wider questions about intellectual desire.
    There are also the related questions about the openness of that desire as
    a gift.

14 *CWL 3 Insight*, 680 (657–8).

15 'On God's Knowledge and Will,' sec. 11*e*, 19 of the current English transla-
    tion (LRIT Archives) refers to Lennerz's *De Deo Uno* (Rome: Gregorian
    University Press, 1948), 254ff., 364f., Lonergan adding that he was a very
    brilliant author.

16 *CWL 3 Insight*, 691 (668).

17 Ibid., 678 (655).

18 Ibid., 680 (657).

19 Ibid., 693 (670).

20 *CAM*, 70.

21 'The General Character of the Natural Theology of Insight,' *CWL 17 Philo-
    sophical and Theological Papers 1965–1980*, 5.

22 Ibid., 9f.

23 Ibid., 6; see also Kant, *Critique of Pure Reason*, A591, B619.

24 Sala, *Lonergan and Kant: Five Essays on Human Knowledge* (Toronto: University of Toronto Press, 1994), xvi–xvii.

25 Letter from Matt Torpey to Crowe dated 17 August 1996.

26 *Philosophy of God, and Theology* (London: Darton, Longman and Todd, 1973), 13. Reprinted in *CWL 17*, 172 (13).

27 Ibid., 52. There is a shift here from the divine nature to the divine 'who.' To ask, what is God? is to search for a common answer. To ask, who is your God? is to pose a question that will be answered in as many different ways as different persons experience the presence of God in their lives.

28 Ibid., 11–13, on the significance of the horizon of the subject and the relevance of intellectual, moral, and religious conversion.

29 *CWL 3 Insight*, 709 (687), and 'An Interview with Fr. Bernard Lonergan,' in *A Second Collection*, 222.

30 *CWL 3 Insight*, 629 (606). This is one of the rare occasions when the term 'evil' occurs prior to chap. 20.

31 'On God's Knowledge and Will,' 29–30. The affirmation that God wills all men to be saved is a central belief of Lonergan's, one he repeated again and again throughout his life.

32 Ibid., 69f.; see also sec. 23, 68, *e.*

33 Ibid., 58, *h.*

34 *Insight*, 712 (2 occurrences) (690); 742 (1 occurrence) (721). On 749 (728) he talks about a dialectical succession of situations. The main category in the chapter seems to be a world order, characterized by an emergent probability rather than by finality.

35 '*Insight* Revisited,' in *A Second Collection*, 271–2.

36 *CWL 3 Insight*, 259 (234), sec. 8.4.

37 Leslie Stevenson and David Haberman, *Ten Theories of Human Nature* (Oxford: Oxford University Press, 1998), 9.

38 *CWL 3 Insight*, 716 (694).

39 Ibid., 718–20 (696–8). On the structure of history, see 763 (742).

40 'The Analysis of Faith,' LRIT LB 136.

41 *CWL 3 Insight*, 720 (699).

42 Ibid., 741–2 (720).

43 Ibid., 743 (722).

44 Ibid., 750 (730).

Chapter 27. Introduction, Epilogue, Prefaces, Publication

1 *CWL 3 Insight*, 20 (xxvi).

2 Crowe, *Lonergan*, 72.

3 *CWL 3 Insight*, 13 (xix).

4 *Critique of Pure Reason* Axi.

5 *CWL 3 Insight*, 22 (xxviii).

6 Ibid., 22 (xxviii).

7 Ibid., 717 (694).

18 His card index system at the LRIT archives shows that as he was finishing *Insight* he began to read about Gödel's theorem, making various notes.

9 'Theories of Inquiry: A Response to a Symposion,' in *A Second Collection*, 37, where he comments that in *Insight* he was treating three linked questions. See also 'Philosophy and Theology,' ibid., 203.

10 *CWL 3 Insight*, 16 (xxii).

11 Ibid., 7 (xiii).

12 Ibid., 753 (731).

13 Letter to Fr Gerard Smith, 13 July 1958. In a similar vein, Theodore Kisiel has remarked that his study, *The Genesis of Heidegger's Being and Time* (Berkeley, CA: University of California Press, 1993), 3–6, allows us to jettison the stale view of *Being and Time* as a great book 'frozen in time' and instead to appreciate the erratic starts, finite high points, and tentative conclusions of what remains a challenging philosophical path.

14 *CWL 3 Insight*, 754 (731). This should be read in the context of his remarks on humanism in chapter 20, 747–50 (726–9).

15 Ibid., 765 (744).

16 Because God is the source and author, the one who unlocks in us all the questions relevant to our circumstances, there is, I believe, an implicit religious dimension to the humanist ideal. On this see 'Openness and Religious Experience,' in *CWL 4 Collection*.

17 *CWL 3 Insight*, 754 (732). Here we find Lonergan adding a terminal viewpoint to his earlier higher, universal, and moving viewpoints. What precisely it means is in need of careful clarification.

18 This is made clear by the fact that in 1964, when revising his Christology course, he added a long introduction that addressed the problem of good and evil.

19 It is interesting to speculate how Lonergan would have drawn on later developments in the sciences, such as in anthropology, cosmology, and the neurosciences, if he was to compose the book in 2049.

20 The following remarks are to be found in *CWL 3 Insight*, 761–2 (739–40).

21 *CWL 3 Insight*, 762 (741).

22 LRIT A351, *Insight*, Preface (drafts), xi. Three pages from that earlier draft, numbered x, xi, xi, survive.

23 Draft prefaces, x–xi. The three pages contain remarks on the impact of philosophy with reference to Marx and the Kremlin, again indicating his desire to develop a philosophy of history.

24 See F.E. Crowe, 'A Note on the Prefaces of *Insight,' Method: Journal of Lonergan Studies* 3, no. 1 (March 1985), 1–3. The text of the original preface is published on pages 3–7.

25 Crowe, *Lonergan,* 58. The phrase occurs on page 4 of the preface text.

26 Crowe, 'A Note on the Prefaces of *Insight*,' 2.

27 Crowe, *Lonergan,* 73.

28 Crowe, 'For a Phenomenology of Rational Consciousness,' *Method: Journal of Lonergan Studies* 18 (2000), 67–90 (see esp. 70–83); and 'The Puzzle of the Subject as Subject in Lonergan,' *International Philosophical Quarterly* 43, no. 2, issue 170 (2003), 187–205 (see esp. 195–200). I am also indebted to Daniel Monsour's 'Imaginable Date for Understanding What It Is to Understand' (draft version), paper presented at the 2004 Lonergan Workshop, Toronto, August 2004.

29 Bernard Lonergan, interview given to Luis Morfin, 11 July 1981, as transcribed by Frederick Crowe in 'For a Phenomenology of Rational Consciousness,' 78.

30 *CWL 3 Insight,* 9 (xv). The text is given in chapter 1 of the present work. The passage that follows in the preface refers to Joseph Wolftange, Norris Clarke, and Joseph Clark. Most probably during the summer of 1952 (but possibly 1953) Lonergan retired with them to the Jesuit house of philosophy in Plattsburg. Each morning, on their own, they read a section of the text; each evening, refreshed by an afternoon swim, they met to discuss it. Lonergan was anxious to listen to the responses to his work on a private level before he exposed it to a wider public.

31 *CWL 3 Insight,* xviii–xix on the three texts: Lonergan's typescript, MSA; that produced by Beatrice Kelly and Lonergan's brother Gregory, MSB; and PT, the published text. See also notes 10 and 11 on p. xvii; *CAM,* 124.

32 *CWL 3 Insight,* 208n.1 (184n.) The editorial note *g*208 states that this note was added to the MSB in Rome.

33 Letters 6–9 to Crowe, *CWL 3 Insight,* xx, n. 19. In his revisions he removed the account of Cantor's proof of the non-countability of the irrational numbers. On the suggestion of multiple volumes, see Letter 7 to Crowe, 26 October 1954.

34 For publication details consult 'Bernard Lonergan's *Insight*: A Publishing History' by Joseph E.E. Robidoux, 11 April 1986, LRIT.

35 Letters to Crowe: Letter 25, 24 December 1956, Letter 34, 21 February 1958.

36 *CAM,* 211.

37 In Letter 13 to Crowe on 27 December 1955 Lonergan refers to Bishop Wright's article in *Commonweal,* 16 December 1955, on Catholics and anti-intellectualism as good propaganda for *Insight.*

38 Crowe published three essays on the topic in *Theological Studies* in 1959.

39 L14, 11 April 1956; see also Letter to Longman, 20 April 1956.

40 Peter McDonough, *Men Astutely Trained* (Toronto: Macmillan, 1992), chap. 12, 379.

41 *Sciences Ecclesiastiques* 9, no. 3 (1957), 263–95. A copy of it had arrived in Rome by 28 March.

42 Letter 27; see also Letter 26.

43 In Letter 28, 17 July, he asks Crowe not to take so seriously his reservations.

44 Letter 26, FC, 28 March. The lectures have been published in *CWL 18 Phenomenology and Logic.*

45 Letter to O'Connor, 3 October 1957.

46 *CWL 3 Insight,* 446 (421) on Hegel, 364 (340) on Kant.

47 *Modern Schoolman* 35 (1957–8), 236–44.

48 Later published as *CWL 5 Understanding and Being.*

Chapter 28. Epilogue: Recollecting the Human Mystery

1 Progoff, *Life-Study: Experiencing Creative Lives by the Intensive Journal Method* (New York: Dialogue House Library, 1983), 13f.

2 Schopenhauer has speculated that with hindsight the apparently arbitrary accidents of good and bad luck can be understood as contributing to the epic that is the life: 'Transcendent Speculation on the Apparent Deliberateness in the Fate of an Individual,' published in *Arthur Schopenhauer, Parega and Parlipomena: Short Philosophical Essays,* trans. E.F.J. Payne (Oxford: Clarendon Press, 1974), 204.

3 A similar dialectic is involved in the familiarity and strangeness of facts. As known in true judgments, facts are familiar. But when they are known as virtually unconditioned, they point beyond themselves to an ultimate mystery

Bibliography

1. Basic Works by Lonergan

Collected Works of Bernard Lonergan (hereafter *CWL*), Vol.1, *Grace and Freedom: Operative Grace in the Thought of St Thomas Aquinas*. Edited by Frederick Crowe and Robert Doran. Toronto: University of Toronto Press, 2000.

CWL, Vol. 2, *Verbum: Word and Idea in Aquinas*. Edited by Frederick Crowe and Robert Doran. Toronto: University of Toronto Press, 1997.

CWL, Vol. 3, *Insight*. Edited by Frederick Crowe and Robert Doran. Toronto: University of Toronto Press, 1992.

CWL, Vol. 4, *Collection*. Edited by Frederick Crowe and Robert Doran. Toronto: University of Toronto Press 1988.

CWL, Vol. 5, *Understanding and Being*. Edited by Elizabeth Morelli and Mark Morelli, revised and augmented by Frederick Crowe. Toronto. University of Toronto Press, 1990.

CWL, Vol. 6, *Philosophical and Theological Papers 1958–1964*, Edited by Frederick Crowe and Robert Doran. Toronto: University of Toronto Press, 1996.

CWL, Vol. 7, *The Ontological and Psychological Constitution of Christ*. Edited by Michael Shields, Frederick Crowe, and Robert Doran. Toronto: University of Toronto Press, 2002.

CWL, Vol. 10, *Topics in Education*. Edited by Frederick Crowe and Robert Doran. Toronto: University of Toronto Press, 1993.

CWL, Vol.15, *Macroeconomic Dynamics: An Essay in Circulation Analysis*. Edited by Frederick Lawrence, Patrick H. Byrne, and Charles C. Hefling. Toronto: University of Toronto Press, 1993.

CWL, Vol. 17, *Philosophical and Theological Papers 1965–1980*. Edited by Robert Doran and Robert Croken. Toronto: University of Toronto Press, 2004.

CWL, Vol. 18, *Phenomenology and Logic: The Boston College Lectures on Mathematical Logic and Existentialism.* Edited by Philip McShane. Toronto: University of Toronto Press, 2001.

CWL, Vol. 21, *For a New Political Economy.* Edited by Philip McShane. Toronto: University of Toronto Press, 1998.

The Lonergan Reader. Edited by Mark D. Morelli and Elizabeth A. Morelli. Toronto: University of Toronto Press, 1997.

Method in Theology. London: Darton, Longman and Todd, 1971.

A Second Collection. London: Darton, Longman and Todd, 1974.

A Third Collection. Papers by Bernard Lonergan SJ, edited by Frederick E. Crowe SJ. New York: Paulist 1985.

The Way to Nicea: The Dialectical Development of Trinitarian Theology. London: Darton, Longman and Todd 1976.

2. A chronology of relevant texts/talks Lonergan composed up to and during the *Insight* years (including some relevant notes taken at his courses by students)

1927
16 February 1927: text of his surd sermon *The Acts of the Apostles* 28, 26; since destroyed.

1928
'The Form of Mathematical Inference.' *Blandyke Papers,* Heythrop College, Oxon; no. 283, January, 126–37, LB 101.

'The Syllogism.' (*Blandyke Papers,* no. 285, March, 33–64), LB 102.

1929
'True Judgement and Science,' *Blandyke Papers,* no 291, February, 195–216, LB 103.

'Infinite Multitude.' *Blandyke Papers,* no. 291, February, 217–20, LB 104.

Letter on 'Creation from Eternity.' *Blandyke Papers,* no. 292, Easter, 313–15, LB 105.

1931
'Gilbert Keith Chesterton.' *Loyola College Review* 17, 7–10.

1933
25,000-word essay on the act of faith for Henry Smeaton, text lost.

1934
30,000-word essay on Newman for Leo Keeler. Pages 7, 8, 9, 13, 23, 24, 27, 28, 32, 33, 34, 35, and 36 are extant, distributed between A14–237.

'Essay in Fundamental Sociology.' Pages 95–130 of a chapter entitled 'Philosophy of History' survive. Archives File 713, History.

1935–8

Review of L.W. Keeler, 'The Problem of Error from Plato to Kant: A Historical and Critical Study,' *Gregorianum* 16, 156–60.

Notes on Kant's *Metaphysics of Morals* (Italian translation), precise date unknown. A 12, 11 pages, A 13, 5 pages.

LTIT Archives File 713 (History) contains a wide range of texts Lonergan composed on history between 1934–5 and 1938. Included in the earlier phase are: Essay on Fundamental Sociology, front page with quote from Plato's *Republic* V, 473d, followed by a chapter entitled 'The Philosophy of History,' running from page 95 to 130; a seven-page typescript entitled *Pantôn Anakephaliôsis* that contains a subsection entitled 'Sketch for a Metaphysics of Solidarity,' leads into a twenty-five-page typescript, again entitled *Pantôn Anakephaliôsis*, subtitled 'A Theology for the Social Order.' From the later phase of his work there are three texts on analytic concepts of history, and a fourth dealing with a theory of history from a theological perspective. There are also notes he made on Volumes 1–3 of Toynbee's *A Study of History* (Oxford: Oxford University Press, 1934) and *Philosophy and History: Essays to Ernst Cassirer* (Oxford: 1938).

1939–41

Gratia Operans: *A Study of the Speculative Development in the Writings of St. Thomas of Aquin*. Doctoral thesis, Gregorian University, 1940, 338 pages

1941

'St. Thomas' Thought on *Gratia Operans*.' *Theological Studies* 2 (1941), 289–324.

The Italian Mentality, notes made for the talk, A 20.

National Mentalities of Europe, A 21.

'Savings Certificates and Catholic Action.' *The Montreal Beacon*, 7 February 1941.

'National Mentalities of Europe.' Lecture at St. Anthony's Parish, Montreal, 24 February 1941.

1942

'St. Thomas' Thought on *Gratia Operans*.' *Theological Studies* 3, 69–88, 375–402, 533–78.

Review of Dietrich von Hildebrand, 'Marriage.' *The Canadian Register*, Quebec edition, 23 May, 5.

Letter on Marriage, *The Canadian Register*, 6 June, 9.

Letter on Marriage, *The Canadian Register*, June 20, 1942, 9.

Notes made by Lonergan on Shull's *Evolution*, A 22.

Notes made by Lonergan for a talk on progress and decline with reference to economics, A 23.

'For a New Political Economy.' Typescript, later published in *CWL* 21.

1943–4

'The Form of Inference.' *Thought* 18, 277–92 (1943), *CWL 4*.

'Finality, Love, Marriage.' *Theological Studies* 4 (1943), 477–510.

Fragments of early *Verbum* drafts: Title, headers, etc., pages 1, 16–22, 60–77 (which may be a distinct draft), and 90–102 of early work on the *Verbum* articles are extant. *CWL 2*, 230–50, A 85.

Review of Harry M. Cassidy, 'Social Security and Reconstruction in Canada.' *The Canadian Register*, Quebec Edition, 10 April 1943, 5.

'A Theory of Circulation Analysis,' Typescript, later published in *CWL* 15.

1945–6

'The Trend to Economic Centralization.' Talk at Regiopolis College, 8 April.

'Thought and Reality.' Weekly lectures given at the Thomas More Institute, Montreal, from mid–November 1945 to May 1946.

Notes taken by J. Martin O'Hara at Lonergan's course 'Thought and Reality,' LB 31.

'The Concept of *Verbum* in the Writings of St. Thomas Aquinas.' *Theological Studies* 7, 349–92.

'On Supernatural Being.' 83-page supplement for his course on grace given 1946–7, LB 132.

1947–50

'The Concept of *Verbum* in the Writings of St. Thomas Aquinas.' *Theological Studies* 8 (1947), 35–79, 4404–44.

Notes taken by Crowe at Lonergan's courses on grace and on faith and the virtues, 1947–8, LRIT.

Notes taken by William Stewart at Lonergan's course on grace, 1947–8, LRIT.

Notes taken by Crowe at Lonergan's course on Christology, 1948–9, LRIT.

'A Note on Geometrical Possibility.' *The Modern Schoolman* 27, (1949–50), 124–38.

'The Natural Desire to See God.' In *Proceedings of the Eleventh Annual Convention of the Jesuit Philosophical Association*. Boston College, 18 April 18 1949, 31–43.

'The Concept of *Verbum* in the Writings of St. Thomas Aquinas.' *Theological Studies* 10 (1949), 3–40, 359–93.

Review of Dom Illtyd Trethowan, 'Certainty: Philosophical and Theological.' *The Modern Schoolman* 27 (1949–50), 153–5.

Notes taken by Crowe at Lonergan's course on the Trinity, 1949–50, LRIT.

'On God's Knowledge and Will,' course supplement, March 1950, LB 130.

1951

'The Mystical Body of Christ.' A domestic exhortation, Regis College, Toronto, November, LB 159.

'Le Role de l'universite catholique dans le monde modern'/ 'The Role of the Catholic University in the Modern World.' *Relations* 11, 263–5.

Archive references to possible notes, drafts, etc., of the pre-MSA autograph of Insight.

A 104, LB 131.5. 'Intelligence and Reality.' Lonergan's notes for his course at the Thomas More Institute, Montreal, March–May 1951.

A108. Twenty-nine pages of rough notes, handwritten, dealing with notions of being and objectivity, common sense, patterns of experience, statistical science, and canons.

A 109. Fragments of chapters 15, 14 ('The Dialectic of Philosophy'), and 6 Common Sense of *Insight*, written on the reverse side of A 108.

A 197. Notes on integration, order, etc.

A 268–71. Notes on intellectual conversion, fragments of early drafts of *Insight.*

A 273–5. Notes on *a priori* categories.

A 276–80. Notes on empirical method, Jolan Jacobi on Jung, etc., early drafts of *Insight.*

A 324. Notes on order and integration.

Michael Lapierre, '*Insight* Residue,' fragments of early drafts of *Insight*, including chapters 5 (Space and Time) and 14. LRIT Archives.

A 99. Lists revisions and excisions from the original manuscript of *Insight*, MSA.

1951–3

The autograph of *Insight*, MSA, composed largely during this time, after the lecture course 'Intelligence and Reality,' A 346–A 373.

'Analysis of Faith.' Supplementary notes for his course, 1952, LB 136.

'Insight.' A series of lectures from 11 November 1952 to 21 April 1953.

Notes taken by Thomas O'D. Hanley at Lonergan's *Insight* course, LB 79.

'De Conscientia Christi.' Supplementary notes for his course 'De Verbo Incarnato,' 1952–3, LB 138.

3. A chronology of some texts Lonergan read up to and during the *Insight* years

1918–22 Montreal

Betten, Francis S. *The Ancient World.* New York: Allyn and Bacon, 1919.

Betten, Francis S., and Alfred Kaufmann. *The Modern World.* New York: Allyn and Bacon, 1919.

Deharbe, Joseph, SJ. *A Complete Catechism of the Catholic Religion.* 6th American Edition. Translated from the German by Rev. John Fander. New York: Schwartz, Kirwin and Fauss, 1908.

Devivier, W., SJ. *Christian Apologetics, or Rational Exposition of the Foundations of Faith,* Vols. 1 and 2. Translated from the 16th ed. of the original French, with an introduction ('The Existence and Attributes of God') and a treatise ('The Human Soul: Its Liberty, Spirituality, Immortality and Destiny'), by L. Peeters SJ;

edited, augmented, and adapted to English readers by Joseph C. Sasia SJ. San Jose: Popp and Hogan, 1903, 1924.

1924–6 Pickering, Ontario
Plato's *Crito* in Greek.
Homer, *The Illiad.*
Historia Thucydio.
Thackeray, texts not specified.

1926–30 Heythrop, Oxfordshire
Frick, Carolus, SJ. *Logica.* Freiburg: Herder, 1924.
– *Ontologia.* Freiburg: Herder, 1928.
Hahn, Henrico. *Philosophia Naturalis.* Freiburg: Herder, 1906.
Boedder, Bernardo. *Theologia Naturalis.* Freiburg: Herder, 1911.
Coffey, Peter. *The Science of Logic: An Inquiry into the Principles of Accurate Thought and Scientific Method*, Vol. 1, *Conception, Judgement, and Inference*; Vol. 2, *Method, Science and Certitude.* London: Longman, Green, 1912.
Bradley, F.H. *Appearance and Reality: A Metaphysical Essay.* Oxford: Clarendon Press, 1978 [1893].
Joyce, G.H. *Principles of Logic.* London: Longman, Green, 1908.
Joseph, H.W.B. *An Introduction to Logic.* Oxford: Clarendon Press, 1906.
Mill, John Stuart. *Collected Works*, Vol. 7, *A System of Logic.* Toronto: University of Toronto Press, 1973.
Newman, John Henry. *An Essay in Aid of a Grammar of Assent.* Westminster, MD: Christian Classics, 1973.
Watt, Lewis. *Capitalism and Morality.* Oxford: Oxford University Press, 1928.

1930–3 Montreal
Douglas, Major. Texts unspecified. See *CWL* 21 80 for details of some of his writings.
Dawson, Christopher. *The Age of the Gods.* London: Sheed and Ward, 1933.
Fallon, Valere, SJ. *The Principles of Social Economy.* New York: Benziger Brothers, 1934. Lonergan would have read the French edition, published in 1930.
Thompson, Silvanus. *Calculus Made Easy.* London: Macmillan, rev. and enlarged 2nd ed. 1910.
Kimball, Arthur. *Elements of Physics.* New York: Henry Holt, 4th rev. ed. 1929.
Stewart, J.A. *Plato's Doctrine of Ideas.* Oxford: Clarendon Press, 1909.
Schopp, Ludwig, ed. *The Fathers of the Church*, Vol. 2, *Saint Augustine.* Washington, DC: Catholic University of America Press, 1948. On page 96 the translator, Denis Kavanagh OSA, comments on Augustine's nearness to the Cartesian *Cogito.* Texts quoted are *De Trinitate*, 10, 10, 14; *De Vera Religione*, 73; *De Civ. Dei*, 11, 26 as well as *De Lib. Arb.* 2, 12, 33; *De Beata Vita*, 2, 7; and *Sol*, 2, 11.

Hoenen, Petrus. 'De Origine Primorum Principiorum Scientiae.' *Gregorianum* 14 (1933), 153–84.

1933–40 Rome/Amiens

The Apostolic Constitution, *Deus Scientiarum Dominus* (God, the Lord of the Sciences).

Keeler, Leo. *The Problem of Error from Plato to Kant.* Rome: Analecta Gregoriana 6 (1934).

Aquinas,Thomas. *Summa Theologica*, I, qq. 27–43, complemented by Billot, *De Deo Uno et Trino.*

Wust, Peter. '*Crisis in the West.*' In *Essays in Order*, Vol. 2, edited by Christopher Dawson and T.F. Burns (London: Sheed and Ward, 1931).

Lennerz, H. *De Virtutibus Theologis.* Rome: Gregorian University Press, 1938.

D'Alès A. *De Verbo Incarnato.* Paris: Beauchesne, 1930.

Leeming, B. *Adnotations de Verbo Incarnato.* Rome: Gregorian University Press, 1936.

Kant, Immanuel. *Fondamenti della Metaphysics dei Costumi.* Translated by Giacomo Perticone. Edited by Signorelli. Rome: 1926.

Billot, L. *De Deo Uno et Trino.* Rome: Gregorian University Press, 1920.

Aurel, R.P. *La Vie Chretienne: Conferences Troisième An 1937–8.*

Toynbee, Arnold. *A Study of History*, Vol. 1–3. Oxford: Oxford University Press, 1934. The year 1934 is the earliest possible dating of these notes, but they could be later.

Landgraf, Arthur M. 'Die Erkenntnis der helfenden Gnode in der Fruscholastik.' Zeitscrift für Katholische Theologie 55 (1931), 177–238, 403–37, 562–91, 179–81.

For details of the texts of Aquinas studied, see references in *CWL* 1.

1940–7 Montreal

Toynbee, Arnold. *A Study of History*, Vol. 1, *Introduction: The Genesis of Civilizations*; Vol. 2, *The Genesis of Civilizations (cont.);* Vol. 3, *The Growth of Civilizations* (Oxford: Oxford University Press, 1934); Vol. 4, *The Breakdown of Civilizations;* Vol. 5, *The Disintegration of Civilizations;* Vol. 6, *The Disintgegration of Civilizations (cont.)* (Oxford: Oxford University Press, 1939).

Ford, John. 'Marriage, Its Meaning and Purposes.' *Theological Studies* 3, no. 3 (1942), 333–74.

Doms, H. *Du sens de las fin du marriage.* Paris: 1937.

Shull, A. Franklin. *Evolution.* New York: McGraw Hill, 1936.

Aristotle. *Nichomachean Ethics*, Bks. 8, 9.

1943–4

Hoenen, Petrus. 'De Philosophia Scholastics Cognitionis Geometricae.' *Gregorianum* 19 (1938) 508.

– 'De problemate necessitatis geometricae.' *Gregorianum*, 20 (1939), 41, 52.
Aquinas, Thomas. See *CW 2 Verbum* for details of the texts of Aquinas he began to
   read.

1944

CWL 15, Part 3, 161–2, indicates some of his reading for his work on economics.
   Works by Keynes and Schumpeter are mentioned, as well as the cycles associated
   with Juggler, Kitchen, and Kondratieff and a theory of history. Related are the
   notes Lonergan made on Schumpeter, the trade cycle, echoes of F. Hayeck,
   Monetary Theory and the Trade Cycle (1933), and, finally, mercantilism and gold,
   p. 120 – echoes of Pesch.
Schumpeter, Joseph. *Business Cycles*. New York: McGraw Hill, 1939. *CWL 15*, Part 3,
   161–2, indicates the influence of this work on Lonergan, the economic cycles
   associated with Juglar, Kitchin, and Kordratieff being, for him, an element in a
   philosophical theory of history.
O'Hara, C., and D. Ward. *An Introduction to Projective Geometry*. Oxford: Clarendon
   Press, 1937.

1945–6

Aristotle's general analysis of the relation between being and substance at the start
   of Book 7 of his *Metaphysics* for Lonergan's course 'Thought and Reality.'

1947

O'Connell, Matthew J. 'St Thomas and the *Verbum.*' *The Modern Schoolman* 24
   (1946–7) (224–34).
De Lubac, Henri. *Surnaturel* (etudes historiques), Coll. 'Theologie' 8. Edited by
   Aubier-Montaigne. Paris: 1946.

1948–53 Toronto

Mager, Alois. *Mystik als seelische Wirklichkeit. Eine Psychologie der Mystik*. Graz: Puset,
   1945.

Some books borrowed from the Regis Library

The date borrowed is indicated in the left column.

early   Jolivet, Régis. *La Notion de Substance: Essai historique et critique sur le dévelopment
         des doctrines d'Aristotle à nos jours*. Paris: G. Beauchesne, 1929.
1947   Jeans, James, Sir. *Physics and Philosophy*. Cambridge: The University Press,
         1943.
1948   Leibnitz, G.W. *The Monadology*. Oxford: Oxford University Press, 1948.
n.d.   Lenzen, V. *The Nature of Physical Theory*. New York, 1931.
1948   van Riet, G. *L'Epistemologie Thomiste*. Louvain: Editions de L'Institut súperior
         de philosophie, 1946.

1949   Hegel, G.W.F. *Phänomenologie des Geists.* Leipzig: Felix Meinar, 1949.

1950   Kant, Immanuel. *Critique de la Raison Pure.* Paris: Presses Universitaires de France, 1927.

– *Critique de la Raison Practique.* 5th ed. Paris: F. Alcan, 1921.

n.d.   Smith, A.H. *Kantian Studies.* Oxford: Clarendon Press, 1947.

n.d.   Smith, Norman K. *A Commentary to Kant's Critique of Pure Reason.* New York: Humanities Press, 1950.

n.d.   Bradley, F.H. *Appearance and Reality: A Metaphysical Essay.* Oxford: Clarendon Press, 1897.

n.d.   Kojève, Alexandre. *Introduction à la lecture de Hegel.* Paris: Gallimard, 1947.

1950   Marechal, Joseph. *Point de Depart de la Metaphysics.* 5 vols. Brussels: *L'Edition Universelle, 1944–9.* (Vol. 1, 29 January; vols. 2–5, 16 October).

Mure, G. *A Study of Hegel's Thought. (Logic).* Oxford: Clarendon Press, 1950. The Regis Library has holdings by Mure with the titles *An Introduction to Hegel* and *A Study of Hegel's Logic.*

Wittels, Fritz. *Sigmund Freud.* London: Allen and Unwin, 1924.

Other material read during the composition of *Insight*

Burtt, E.A. *The Metaphysical Foundations of Modern Science.* New Jersey: Humanities Press. (Trench, Trubner, 1925).

– *Philosophy of Symbolic Forms,* vol. 2, *Mythic Thought.* New Haven: Yale, 1955.

– *The Problem of Knowledge.* New Haven: Yale University Press, 1940.

Cassirer, Ernst. *Substance and Function: Einstein's Theory of Relativity.* Chicago: Open Court, 1923.

Dalbiez, Roland (the teacher of Ricoeur. *Psychoanalytic Method and the Doctrines of Freud,* Vol. 1, *Exposition;* Vol. 2, *Discussion.* London: Longman, Green, 1941, 1948.

Freud, S. *Wit and Its Relation to The Unconscious.* New York: Moffat, Yard, 1916.

Jacobi, Jolan. *The Psychology of Jung.* 5th ed. London: Routledge, Kegan and Paul, 1949.

The Journal of Nervous and Mental Disease, Vol 112, no. 1 (July 1950).

Kant, Immanuel. *Critique of Pure Reason.* Translated by Norman Kemp Smith, London: Macmillan 1933. This text was named in his 'Intelligence and Reality' notes.

Langer, Susanne. *Feeling and Form.* London: Routledge and Kegan Paul, 1953 (New York edition in 1942).

Lindsay, Robert, and Henry Margenau. *Foundations of Physics.* New York: John Wiley and Sons, 1947.

Schilpp, P.A. *Albert Einstein, Philosopher-Scientist.* New York: Tudor, 1951.

– *The Philosophy of Ernst Cassirer.* Chicago: Open Court, 1949.

4. Lonergan's lectures on *Insight* after 1957

For details see *CW* 3, 811–12.

5. General bibliographies

Comprehensive updated primary and secondary bibliographies of works by and on Lonergan can be found by searching under 'Lonergan bibliographies' on Google. Hopefully, the very comprehensive bibliographies of Terry Tekippe, missing from the web since his recent death, will soon find their way back.

Bernard Lonergan Index

This item is indexed in a developmental/thematic order. It locates in the narrative page references to significant events and themes in Lonergan's life. For further details of those themes, consult the particular entry in the general index.

1. Background

Family, origins: Father Gerald 15–19; death of 109; Mother Josephine 17–18; death of 104; Aunt Minnie 17–20, 109; brothers Gregory and Mark, 17–18, 104

Educated at: St Michael's College, Buckingham 16, 19; Loyola College, Montreal 24–5; Heythrop College, Oxon 32ff.; London University 36ff.; Imaculée, Montreal 61; Gregorian University, Rome 65ff.

Taught at: Loyola, Montreal 49; Imaculée, Montreal 109; Thomas More Institute 146; Regis, Toronto 177; Gregorian University, Rome 326, 452

Decisions made by him: to attend Loyola, Montreal 25; to enter the Jesuits 26; to end work on 'Finality, Love, Marriage' 128; and on the economics 130; to research *Verbum* 131–2; to write *Insight* 146–7; to write *Method in Theology* 467

Decisions made for him: to study classics rather than methodology 37; to study theology in Rome 65; to change from philosophy to theology 92–3; about thesis content 94; about move to Toronto 177; about move to Rome 326

Some significant authors who influenced his quest: Frick 33; Kant (through Whiteside and Frick) 34 (*see also* 539 for the Italian text of Kant he read in Rome); Mill 36; Aristotle, *de Anima* 36, 139; Marx 43; Newman 43; Dawson 50; Stewart on Plato 54; Augustine 58; Hoenen on Aquinas 61, 131; Lennerz 69; Philip the Chancellor 99–100; Aquinas: on moral impotence 100; on theory of operation 100; Toynbee 110–11; Bergson 123, 340; Shull 124; Schumpeter 129;

Aristotle: *Physics* 139, *Metaphysics* 154, categories of 154; d'Alès 203; Cassirer 212; Cassirer, *Substance and Function* 224; Einstein 324; Lindsay and Margenau 324; Cassirer, *The Problem of Knowledge* 350; Freud 364; Bultmann 398; Cassirer *Mythical Thought* 402; Langer 463

Some significant courses/seminars: Sacraments (including 'Finality, Love, Marriage') 123; On the Trinity 142; Thought and Reality 146; The Divine Processions 178; Grace 185; Christology 203, 242, 398; On God's Knowledge and Will 216; Intelligence and Reality 219; Analysis of Faith 325–6; Lectures on *Insight* 363

Some significant friends: Lucia Vallillee 19; Henry Smeaton 28; Eric O'Connor 110; Frederick Crowe 110, 178; Martin O'Hara 147; Patricia Coonan 158; Eric Kierans 158; Beatrice White (née Kelly) 159; Charlotte Tansey 159; Stanley Machnik 159; Phil Leah 463

Some significant illnesses: at Loyola 26; creative illness 188; cancer 479n.3

Some significant letters to: Smeaton 36; Keane 77; O'Malley 101, 492n.35; Louis Roy 189; Crowe 364; Smith 456; O'Connor 468; Lemieux 483n.12. *Note also* Mark Lonergan's letter to his brother Gregory on the death of their mother 105

Some significant notes taken by students at his courses: Thought and Reality 147; Grace 185–6; Christology 203; The Trinity 205; Lectures on *Insight* 363

Some significant persons who influenced the path of his life: Father, taught him mathematics 17; mother, loved by 18; cousin (possibly Lucia Vallillee), told him to read a book 19–20;

Whiteside 33; Bolland 31, 48; MacMahon 57; Swain 65; Hingston 65; Keeler 69; Leeming 82; Stefanu 83; Desbuquois 87; Keane 92; McCormick 92; Boyer 94; O'Connor 110; Crowe 110, 178; Nunan 326; Beatrice White (née Kelly) 365; Longman 460, 467

Some significant world events that affected on him: Depression 49; decline and disintegration of Europe in 1930s 66–7; Second World War and *Insight* 105, 326

Some significant writings: Blandyke Papers 41ff.; essay on Newman for Keeler 69ff., 'Philosophy of History' 73ff.; Analytic Concept of History 88ff.; *Gratia Operans: A Study of the Speculative Development in the Writings of St. Thomas Aquinas* 94; *For a New Political Economy* 113; 'Finality; Love, Marriage' 123; *An Essay in Circulation Analysis* 129; 'A Note on Geometrical Possibility.' 213; 'On God's Knowledge and Will' 216; 'Forms of Inference' 221; 'Openness and Religious Experience' 254; 'Role of the Catholic University in the Modern World' 281; *On the Ontological and Psychological Constitution of Christ* 465

2. Lonergan's quest

Awakenings of Lonergan's desire to know to its path: early interest in understanding 28; memory of noticing the involvement of insight in the translation process during his classical education 31; exposure to Kantian problem of thought and reality 34; surd sermon and dialectic 36; interest in theory of knowledge 36; interest in methodology 37; problem of progress 50; problem of

the economic cycle 51; philosophy/
metaphysics of history 73; interpreting Aquinas on operative and
cooperative grace and freedom,
which raised the problem of method
in theology 94

Some early quest stepping stones: exposure
to Mill on methodology 36; his
nominalism 36; problem of inferences from the data of sense 41;
Newman and the illative sense 45–6;
Stewart on Plato's Ideas 54; insight
into the role of understanding in the
definition of the circle 56; his early
Platonism/idealism in his essay for
Keeler 69; Stefanu/Maréchal on
judgment 83; Leeming and Aquinas
on existence 83; his intellectual
conversion 82–4 (*see also* 123, 131,
137); writes about intellectual conversion as a topic 254–7; startling
strangeness of intellectual conversion 147–8, 254–5; 'Forms of Inference' and his dream of an
empirically grounded theory of the
human mind as conscious 122;
Hoenen and Aquinas on phantasm
and understanding 131

3. Authoring *Verbum*
senses of *verbum mentis* 33, 133; early
uses of 'insight' 122, 135; insight into
phantasm 135; intellect as process
136; rational consciousness 136; on
brute fact 137; realism 137; Cajetan's
intellectual conversion 139; rational
and animal realism 137, 147, 162; the
objective reference of inner words
or thoughts 161; understanding and
defining 163; understanding and
quiddity 166; composition or synthesis
of insights and related thoughts and
language 167; the standard of judg-

ment 168; two levels of operation
169; the transcendence of thought/
cognition 170; wisdom 170; intellectual light as the measure of reality
174; distinguishing within what we
know by intellectual light between
an object and subject of knowledge
175; self-knowledge and duplication
175; processions, activity, operations
179; agent and patient 180; empirical
consciousness 181; intellectual consciousness, 496nn.2, 6; breaking out
of immanentism through three
judgments 184; the three disciplines
(cognitional theory, epistemology,
metaphysics) 186; creative illness
188; subsequent consolation 189;
matter and knowing 191–2; critique
of conceptualism 194–5; the change
in his position on idea (*eidos*, species) from Plato to Aristotle 198;
Platonic, Aristotelian, conceptualist,
and intellectualist accounts of
human knowing 199

4. Authoring *Insight*
The first movement – composing the proto-
Insight: review of Trethowan and
levels in knowing 212; 'A Note on
Geometrical Possibility' and his first
vision statement 213; notes on integration, possibility, and order 217;
world order and his second vision
statement 219; 'Intelligence and
Reality' and story of Archimedes'
eureka experience 220; higher
viewpoints 222; classical insights 230;
statistical insights and probability
aggregates 234–5; puzzling over the
data of consciousness 236; insights
into intelligible unities 239; the
breakthrough to cognitional structure 242–3; reflective understanding

and judgment 246; concrete judgments of facts 250; writes about intellectual conversion 254; startling strangeness of conversion 254 (*see also* 147); understanding the pure desire to know as a notion of being 257; objectivity 259; principal notion of objectivity – involves understanding solution to Kant's problem of subject and object of knowledge 261, 264; the object of knowledge 268; Kant's Copernican revolution reviewed 269; the categories of the known 270; potency, form and act 271; world order as an emergent probability 275; dialectical categories 277; the good of philosophy 280; 'The Role of the Catholic University in the Modern World' 281; levels in the good 281; parallels in society, intersubjective, civil and cultural 281; moral impotence, integration 282

The second movement, composing chapters 9–13: begins MSA with chapters 9–13 287; common sense enters 289; the conscious cognitional self 290; levels of cognitional operations/consciousness 296; empirical consciousness 296; intellectual consciousness 296; rational consciousness (differs from use of in *Verbum*) 296; self-affirmation 300; cognitional facts 302; judging as knowing being 303; from self affirmation as a mental performance to knowledge of a fact 304; the principal notion of objectivity as solution to Kant's problem of subject-object or mind-world relation 304–5

The third movement, composing chapters 1–8: final version of chapters 1–8

written out of the foundations of chapters 9–13 310; emergence 310; emergent evolution 311; emergent probability between 'Intelligence and Reality' and *Insight* 312ff.; on probability and classical science 313; linking probability and emergence 314–15; knower (subject) and known (object) of emergent probability 317; interplay of systematic and non-systematic processes 317; insights into emergent probability 320; what emergent probability explains 322; explaining space and time 323; the chapters on common sense and principal notion of objectivity 328; entry of dialectical element into that problem 328–9; common sense as intellectual development in its subject 329; patterns of experience 331; explaining dramatic bias 335; the neural and the psychic 335–6; the object of the common-sense subject 338; dialectic in the object 339; individual bias 341; group bias 342; general bias 343; cosmopolis 344; dialectic, generalized empirical method, differential equation of history 345; genera and species of things 347; explaining chemical, organic, animal and human differences 348; relation between image and insight as the key 356; Lonergan's alternative to reductionism 357; link between higher and lower conjugates 359; parallel with higher viewpoints in mathematics 361

The fourth movement, composing chapters 13 to the end

    A. *Philosophical method, the metaphysics of nature*: lectures on *Insight* 363; dialetic/conflict of philosophies 366;

polymorphism of philosophical consciousness 368–9; positions and counterpositions 370; isomorphism of knowing and known 371; a new definition of conjugate potency, form, and act 372–3; finality and process 377; a parallel between finality and the notion of being 379; organic, psychic and intellectual development 380, 382; genetic method, the operators and integrators of a development 388; human development 391; the material and spiritual unity of the human 395

B. *Metaphysics of culture, ethics, and religion:* Bultmann and Christology 398; Hegel, mythic and philosophical consciousness 400; Cassirer and mythical thought 402; metaphysics and myth 404; on truth and its linguistic expression 408; expression, interpretation, and re-interpretation 410; bias in interpretation 412; genetically and dialectically related interpretations 413; the universal viewpoint and the subject and object of interpretation 414; ontology of the good 416; willing the good 418; ethical finality, freedom, and consciousness 421; counterpositions, effective freedom, and bias in ethics 426–7; moral impotence 427; the enigma of existence 432; neither science nor philosophy can explain existence 433; causality of creature and creator 434; what is the desire of the mind ultimately in pursuit of? 436; the notion and existence of God 438; finally the problem of evil 443; input from 'On God's Knowledge and Will' 443; different senses of God's will 445; evil as mystery 445–6; evil and problem of structure of human history 446; God's solution to the problem and the religious subject 447; writing from a moving viewpoint 447–8; new higher conjugate forms of faith, hope and charity in the human person's intellect and will 449–50; ending of the book 451; a religious dimension to human quests 451; Introduction 452; invitation to master the confusion of realisms at the heart of human consciousness 453; slogan on understanding understanding, moving viewpoint, the three basic questions 454; Epilogue 455; limitations in his achievement 456; written as a humanist 456; apologetics, development, method in theology 457–8; Prefaces 459; unfinished aspects of *Insight* 461; the problem of insight into insight 461; publisher's readers' reports 463; publication 46; response to Collin's review with reference to Kant and Hegel 468

C. *Recollecting the life:* reading the life forwards and backwards 470; movement of Lonergan's desire through his stepping stones 471–2; the narrative as disclosing the question/intellectual plot structure of the quest 474; situating *Insight* in the wider philosophical tradition 475; related growth of the desire that authors and of identity of the author 475; dialectic of the familiarity and strangeness of intellectual desire 476; mysterious strangeness of the desire that quests and authors 477

General Index

abstraction 55, 62–3, 182–4, 191–2, 195–8, 229, 233, 291, 381, 487n.24

act: central 372 (*see also* existence; metaphysics: elements of); conjugate 276, 372 (*see also* conjugate; operation); group 276

action 42, 89, 103, 139, 149, 153, 171, 181–2, 248, 270, 277, 333, 348, 378, 419–20, 422–4, 427, 448; and art work of a life 348; controlled by understanding 153; ethical/moral 419–20, 422–4; evil 448; of God 70, 103, 444–5; *intelligere* and *dicere* 248; and knowledge by identity 171; as motion in the agent, passion in the patient, 149, 153 (*see also* operation); in social/historical situations, 73–4, 89; substance as cause of 73–4

affirmation: of fact 40, 99, 111, 139, 161, 204, 212, 264, 289, 316, 370, 379, 408, 428, 433, 439, 441, 450, 456, 458; of self 263–4, 279, 287, 291–305, 307–9, 331, 335, 345, 351, 368–9, 392, 393, 402, 404, 417, 419, 424, 426, 455, 471, 473

agent 50, 73, 79, 101, 125, 134, 139, 171–3, 180–2, 193, 199, 241, 260, 274, 291–2, 295, 298, 329, 334, 415–16, 422–4, 434, 443–4; intellect 62–3, 78, 173, 181, 183–4, 196–7, 204, 326 (*see also* intellectual: light; desire to know, pure); as operator 101, 139; as operated/acted on, 101, 139

aggregates. *See* coincidental aggregates

algorithm 358–9, 373, 376, 381, 389, 518n.31

Ambrose 59

application: of laws to data 39, 79, 196–8, 234–6, 315, 381, 424; premotion 101, 103–5 (*see also* cause: secondary; fate; God)

apprehension 33–4, 45, 54, 64, 70–1, 76–7, 90, 167, 169, 173, 175, 181, 212, 246, 280, 393, 420. *See also* value; existence

Aquinas. *See* Thomas Aquinas

Archimedes 3, 150, 162, 220, 300, 451, 504n.27

Aristotle viii, 11, 36, 46, 56, 62–3, 76, 82, 84, 101–2, 127, 132, 135–6, 139, 154–5, 163–4, 170–3, 188, 192–4, 197–200, 216, 221, 239, 270–1, 274–5, 277, 340, 346, 357, 362, 372, 382, 384, 395,

407, 410–11, 434, 468, 472–3; idea, eidos, 63–4, 135–6; identity of knower and known 194, 199, 212–3; *Metaphysics* 154, 239, 411 (*see under* Lonergan *for further titles*); method of study of psyche 221; and quiddity, or the 'what is it?' question 41, 197 and substance 41, 154–5, 216, 239, 270, 275, 346

artist in life vii, 9–12, 113, 144, 173, 281, 331, 333, 367, 385, 470–1, 480n.11, 520n.8

assent 44–46, 72–3, 77, 84, 134, 136, 139, 167, 169, 174, 176, 244, 246–8, 431; as act of judgment 246; notional and real 44, 246; unconditional to propositions 45, 248

Augustine 27, 54, 58–61, 78, 83–5, 98–9, 131, 143–4, 157, 176, 179, 200, 253, 256–7, 364, 438, 442, 453; conversion as clarifying 58–9; early dialogues at Cassiacacum 54, 58; inflamed by love of philosophy 59; *On Grace and Free Will* 98; the Trinity and the mind's word 43; pursuit of truth 58, 61, 83

Aurel, Leontius 86–7, 491n.3, 539

author vii–ix, 3–6, 8–13, 133–4, 167, 176, 211–12, 222, 326, 346, 354, 366, 399–400, 410–11, 414, 416, 431–2, 434–5, 443, 451, 453–4, 456–7, 460, 470, 472, 474–7; artistry of 9–12, 113, 471; desire of vii, 4–5, 8–9, 12, 134, 176, 399–400, 410, 451, 453, 456, 470, 472, 475–7; identity viii, 5, 8, 12, 246, 391, 475–7; presence of desire in text 12

awareness 149, 172, 174, 200, 219, 238–9, 252, 272, 291, 293–9, 331–4, 368–9, 384, 442, 477; of insight unimaginable 238, 461; of intentional object 294–6, 477; of self 149, 239, 252, 293–8, 331–4, 368–9, 477

Bañez, Domingo 95, 103, 491n.18

Begin, J. 30

being viii, 12, 55, 62, 70, 77, 82–4, 103, 124–5, 136, 140, 155–7, 163, 168, 174–5, 180, 182, 184, 186, 199, 203, 216, 241, 247, 250–1, 255–71, 273, 287–8, 303–5, 307–8, 316, 348, 354–6, 360, 365, 369–73, 376–7, 379–80, 382, 389–92, 394, 401, 404, 408–9, 414, 417, 425, 430, 433, 435–44, 465, 468–9, 471, 473, 476; apart from, is nothing 307; concrete universe of 369; grades of 156, 164, 348, 354, 356, 360, 373, 435; identified with reality 369, 441; intelligibility of 404, 418, 419; mysterious 404; can't be unintelligible 216, 407

Bergson, Henri 11, 123, 260, 311, 340, 364, 377–8, 380, 382–3, 395, 474, 511n.23, 516n.32, 517n.22, 520n.8

bias 7, 11, 89, 151, 163, 282, 290, 306–7, 341, 412–13, 415, 422, 427–8, 447, 450, 460, 474; dramatic 10, 335, 340; ethical 427; general 343–4, 412, 427, 450, 460, 474; group 90, 342; individual 90–1, 341–4, 427; in interpreter 412

Billot, Louis 69, 143, 160, 539

biological 50, 55, 124, 189, 192, 230, 241, 245, 311, 331–2, 338, 340, 345, 347, 350, 357, 361–2, 368, 379, 385–6, 389, 459, 521n.23, 521n.26

Bleau, Paulin 129, 142, 144

blind spot (scotosis) 10, 334–6, 427

Bohr, Niels 22, 229, 233, 349, 353, 361, 516n.7

bolshevism 68, 75, 79, 403

Bremond, A. 154

Bryan, William 26, 61, 486–7n.12

Bultmann, Rudolf 184, 398–9, 523n.1

Cajetan, Tommaso 61–2, 139–40, 186

Cano, Melchior: and manual tradition of Thomism 98, 202; paradigm of dogmatic theology 67–8

canon(s) 317, 319–20, 365, 421, 505n.15, 537; statistical residues 317, 319–20, 422

Casey, Bridget 15

Cassirer, Ernest 212, 224, 228, 230–1, 239, 260–1, 265, 294, 298, 347, 350, 377–82, 401–4, 409, 490n.41. *See also under* Lonergan

cause: efficient 12, 161, 436, 444; final 377, 434; formal 187, 419 (*see also* conjugate); secondary 102, 445

Charbonneau 26, 177

Chesterton, G.K. 51, 486n.10

Christ 29, 80–3, 95, 158, 203–5, 281, 283, 398–400, 411; consciousness of 87, 398; in creation 80; in history 81; hypostatic union in 203; Lonergan and 158, 283; mystical body of 73, 79–81, 92, 283; two natures and operations in 203

Christian 19, 23, 27–8, 30, 51, 72, 76, 80, 82, 92, 95, 98, 100, 127, 143, 150, 400, 410–11, 506n.7, 523n.2

Christology 203, 242, 398–400, 416, 458, 465, 474, 503n.33, 523n.2, 529n.18, 536

Cicero 19, 23, 58, 411

Clarke, Norris 467, 501

Classical: culture, education, economics, etc. 25, 29, 31, 69, 110, 135, 239, 438, 493n.13; method 389, 393 (*see also* method: statistical); and statistical laws 10, 150, 155, 240, 252, 255, 307–8, 312–14, 317–18, 320–3, 338, 370, 378, 462, 473–4

Coffey, Peter 39–41, 44, 484n.27, 538

cognition, thought, intellect as process 123, 136. *See also* thought: as process

cognitional structure 200, 216, 237,

241–5, 251, 262–3, 268–9, 272, 274, 288, 302, 308, 353, 394, 418, 454, 462, 471, 473, 476, 506n.23, 519n. 13, 519n.21; direct vs. introspective 221–2, 237–8, 240, 243–4, 262, 267–8, 270, 288, 295, 300–1, 304, 308, 416, 461–2, 473; isomorphic with universe of proportionate being 264, 274, 279, 371–2, 473; and three basic disciplines/questions of philosophy 140, 171, 186, 454, 501n.28

coincidental aggregates 235, 319, 321, 347, 355, 357, 372–3, 519n.23; regular recurrence of 346, 358–60

common sense 4, 7–12, 44, 116, 140, 151, 154, 156, 187, 240, 246, 250, 255, 257, 259, 267–8, 271, 278, 280–2, 288–93, 301–2, 307–8, 310, 328–331, 335–6, 338, 340–7, 353–5, 363–5, 368–9, 371, 380, 392, 412, 427, 433, 436, 443, 446–7, 454, 460–2, 471, 473–6; dialectical development of 328–9, 343, 380, 476; object of 328, 474; and principal notion of objectivity 328, 345; subject of 10, 292, 329, 331, 338, 345, 454

conceptualism 34, 36–7, 191

conjugate 222, 231–4, 239, 245, 274–8, 314, 324, 330, 347, 357, 359–62, 372–4, 382, 389, 392, 394, 449–50, 459 (*see also* form: conjugate); experiential 324; form as general name of scientific laws 154–5; higher 359, 362, 372–3, 389, 449, 459, 518n.31; potency, form, and act 274, 372–4; pure 324

conscience 78, 91, 420, 482n.52, 492n.35

consciousness vii, 4, 6–8, 11–12, 59, 74, 82, 87, 109, 136, 140–2, 148–50, 153, 158, 166, 171, 174, 181, 192, 196, 198, 200–1, 203, 205, 220, 222, 236–245, 261, 282, 290–300, 302, 306, 331–2,

337, 345, 352, 354, 364, 368, 372, 375,
379, 383, 392–3, 396–8, 400, 402–6,
409, 419, 421–4, 427, 442, 453, 455–6,
458–62, 465, 471, 473–4, 477; data of
165, 171, 201, 222, 236–42, 244,
293–6, 345, 462, 496n.27; empirical
306, 423; enlargements of 423; intellectual 205, 496n.27; isomorphism
(*see* isomorphism); levels of 12, 158,
205, 242–4, 282, 299 (*see also* CWL 3
*Insight 14 (xx) for the only two explicit
occurrences of the phrase in the book*);
mythic 280, 402–5; polymorphic 365,
368; rational 136, 140–1, 166, 174,
198, 203, 242, 296, 369, 419, 421, 423;
rational self 455, 462; stream of 337
contingent 70, 74, 103, 153, 187–8, 195,
219, 247, 264, 416, 423–4, 432–3,
438–42, 489n.31, 504n.25
cosmopolis 281, 339–40, 344, 447
Crick, Francis 152, 168, 213, 230, 350–1,
354, 431, 436
Crowe, Frederick ix, 57, 64, 69, 113,
128, 188, 191, 199, 364–6, 452, 460,
463–8; Christology course 203, 205;
early meetings with Lonergan 110;
grace course 184; *Insight* index 466;
letter from Lonergan about mother's death 104; 'The Origin and
Scope of Lonergan's Insight' 466–7;
problem of insight into insight 461;
Spellman medal 202; student of
Lonergan 178, 184
culture 8, 25, 27, 29, 50–1, 75, 81, 90–1,
110–11, 124, 129, 142, 282, 295, 309,
328, 344, 397, 399, 404, 411–12, 417,
442, 453, 457–8, 461, 474, 481,
493n.11

Dalbiez, Roland 336, 515–16n.22, 541
Daly, Thomas 241, 497n.4, 498n.1, 506
n.1, 509n.5

Darwin, Charles 111, 238, 379, 381,
413–14, 430–2, 471
Dawson, Christopher 20, 50–1, 74,
78–9, 89, 486nn.4–7, 489n.26, 538–9
decline 7, 54, 66, 75, 80, 88–92, 110–11,
114, 121, 124, 267, 277, 282, 328,
343–4, 406, 416, 421, 443, 446, 449,
460–1, 536. *See also* progress
definition: descriptive, nominal,
ostensive 89, 130, 214–15, 237, 294,
435, 495n.3; explanatory, essential
163, 214–15; implicit 12, 130, 230,
307, 495n.3
depression (economic) 6, 47, 49–51,
66, 111–12, 116, 387
Desbuquois, Gustave 85, 87
Descartes, René 34, 55, 57, 76, 78, 111,
172, 265, 323, 325, 364, 369, 518n.3,
527n.3
desire, form of desired in the desire
258, 269, 370–1, 429, 515n.13
desire to know, pure viii, 11–12, 137,
175, 254, 258–69, 280, 304–9, 317,
348, 362, 372, 374, 390, 400, 402,
405–8, 418, 426–9, 433, 441, 460,
527n.13 (*see also* agent: intellect;
intellectual: light); as notion of
being 175, 251, 257–9, 262, 269, 304,
379, 474; as unrestricted notion, 174,
251, 253–4, 257–8, 280, 305, 400–1,
426; protean nature of 258, 268, 414
determinism 38, 188, 217, 233–4, 318,
416
development 4, 8, 11–12, 22, 31, 50, 60,
74–8, 81, 83, 90–8, 110, 127, 129,
134–6, 153, 165, 167, 170, 173, 179,
186, 202–3, 216, 218, 220, 222–9, 239,
254, 272, 276–8, 282, 287, 289, 292,
297, 301–2, 305, 321–2, 328–9, 331,
333, 335, 341–3, 362, 368–9, 371,
373–5, 377–8, 380–96, 399, 405–6,
409–14, 416–17, 421–2, 425–7, 430,

437, 442–51, 454, 456, 458–9, 462, 465, 471, 473–6 (*see also* genetic method: operator *and* integrator); common sense 341; ethical 416–17, 425, 450, 459; intellectual 11, 76, 78, 90, 98, 220, 329, 342, 378, 383–92, 410–11, 417, 426–7, 437, 454, 459; mathematical insights 222ff.; organic 378, 382–4; philosophical 97–8, 147, 213, 292, 369, 392; psychic 384–6, 390–2, 422; regular sequence in a development not in accord with classical law 382; religious 450; theological 94, 96, 98

Dialectic, 8, 11, 36, 73, 76, 79–80, 88–90, 99, 125–6, 148, 153, 169, 176, 184, 246, 252–5, 265, 270, 276–8, 282, 325, 328–30, 334–5, 339–45, 347, 353, 363–9, 380, 386, 391–4, 400–8, 413, 417, 443, 447, 450, 459, 468, 474, 476; ascent, descent of love 126; of common sense, development (*see under* common sense); of interpretations 413; method 393, 398; of myth and metaphysics 403–4, 408; of things and body 148

Dilthey, Wilhelm 22, 39

Dobson, William 16, 18, 20–1

dog, knowledge/realism of 147, 153, 161, 295, 356, 382

dogmatic: and critical metaphysics 70; datum 100; and Kantian bridge 35; presuppositions 95; realism 184

Doran, Robert ix, 258, 400, 407, 510n.5, 533–4

Douglas, Major C. 51, 112, 493n.13, 538

duplication 175, 221, 244, 264, 288, 300

economy viii, 43, 51–4, 66, 75, 112–18, 120–1, 128, 130, 311, 320, 338, 486n.9, 486n.12, 488n.3, 493n.12ff., 534 (*see also* exchange; finance;

production); pure cycle, wave 115, 120–1, 130, 460; trade cycle 112, 115, 121, 130, 540

Einstein, Albert 21–2, 66, 229, 233, 324–5, 436, 513n.20, 515n.13, 541

Eliade, Mircea 406, 463, 524n.27

emergent: probability 6, 8, 10, 115, 129–30, 274–8, 301, 310–17, 321–5, 337–8, 343, 362–3, 370, 378, 394, 396, 415, 418–9, 421, 449, 460, 474, 476 (*see also* probability); standard of living 117, 129, 311–12, 315, 494n.19

epistemology 18, 33–4, 76, 93, 105, 140, 171, 173, 175, 186, 251, 267, 281, 370, 387, 455, 473 (*see also* objectivity, principal notion: and Kantian problem); and problem of Kantian bridge, 261–5; and three basic questions of philosophy (*see under* cognitional structure)

Erikson, Erik 382, 385–6, 390, 521n.26, 521n.31

ethics 11, 33, 43, 55, 72, 130, 201, 280, 282, 291, 328–9, 331, 338, 363, 365–6, 393, 397, 400, 415–28, 444, 449–50, 454, 456, 457, 459, 463, 471, 474–6

Euclid 22, 27, 136, 164, 213, 229, 495n.3

event 3, 24, 29, 41, 43, 66, 86, 93–4, 102–3, 141, 155, 168, 188–9, 202, 234–8, 246, 262, 269, 271, 273, 275–7, 292–3, 298, 302, 312–22, 325, 330, 333, 336–7, 340, 347, 358–61, 369, 372–3, 381, 390, 395, 401, 421, 430, 440, 443, 460, 466, 468, 471–2 (*see also* coincidental aggregates; probability); relation, in statistics, to metaphysical category of act 155

evil 12, 29–30, 58–60, 75–6, 90–1, 98–9, 217, 397, 416–20, 425, 430, 441, 443–51, 456–7, 459, 474, 487n.31, 488n.35, 489n.4, 496n.29, 525n.4, 528n.30, 529n.18; fact of 443, 447–8; God's solution to problem of 447, 450, 457; moral 444–5, 456; physical 217, 444–5; problem of 59–60, 397, 430, 443–4, 447–51, 456–7, 459

exchange (economic) 43, 51–3, 57, 113, 115–18, 120–1, 130, 229, 312–13, 320, 494n.21

exchange value 43, 53, 115

existence 4, 6–8, 12, 22, 34–7, 40, 43, 46–7, 69–71, 74, 77, 82–4, 94, 102, 125, 144, 155, 157, 165, 171–2, 181, 183–4, 187, 216, 247, 249–50, 256, 258, 265, 270–1, 276, 288, 294–5, 305–6, 311, 363, 422, 430–6, 439–42, 447–8, 471; affirming 430 (*see also* affirmation: fact); apprehension of 71, 77, 169, 173, 213, 246; and essence 34, 71, 83, 94; of God 43, 157, 165, 397, 440, 441

expectations 132, 235–6, 271, 290, 298 (*see also* possibility); emergent probability as reasonable expectation 275, 314–6, 321; mistaken and inverse insights 132; and probability 290; of 'what?' question 163

experience: aesthetic pattern 347; dramatic pattern 332–6, 345; intellectual pattern 4, 11, 80, 339, 345, 367–9, 371; patterns of 237, 239, 331, 345, 347, 365, 367–9, 515n.13, 537

Fact 3, 6, 10, 11–12, 22, 40–2, 45–7, 56, 71–2, 80, 84, 90, 137, 140, 147, 149, 150, 154, 157–8, 161, 184, 196, 218, 247–50, 252–3, 257, 261–4, 269–71, 289, 299–307, 316, 328, 359–60, 368, 379, 420–1, 430–5, 439, 443, 447–8, 453–4, 458, 468, 472, 476; brute 137, 147, 149, 150, 158, 204, 250, 302, 432, 454, 498n.28; cognitional 42, 47, 84, 250, 302, 430–1, 434; of evil 443, 447–8; mere matters of 432–3,

439, 447; as virtually unconditioned 468

Fallon, Valere 52–3, 486n.12, 494n.13, 538

fate 16, 29–30, 66, 94, 102, 241, 327, 378, 426, 445, 474; and God's application, causality 102; and providence 102

finality 8, 87, 100, 103, 123–8, 190, 241, 323, 365, 375–80, 389–90, 393–4, 396, 402, 415, 418–19, 421, 438, 449, 451, 460, 474; as educator 377; and emergent probability 378; horizontal 124, 128; parallel between dynamism of mind and 379; vertical 124–6, 241, 377

'Finality, Love, Marriage' 123, 128, 146, 148, 156, 164, 241, 291, 310, 323, 377, 449

Finance 44, 52–3, 121, 130, 229

Flanagan, Joseph ix, 31

form: central 82, 240, 374, 390, 392, 395; central and human unity, matter or spirit 395; conjugate 232–3, 274–8, 313–14, 372–3, 380, 382, 388–9, 449–50, 521n.15; conjugate, as instanced in scientific laws, related propositions 154–5; group 275–7, 314

freedom viii, 7, 29–30, 36, 80, 89, 92, 94–5, 98–103, 150, 185, 200, 219, 356, 360, 397, 416, 421–8, 443–4, 447, 450. *See also* will

Freud, Sigmund 22, 66, 188, 353, 364, 380, 390, 413, 420, 463, 465, 481, 515n.13, 515n.22

Frick, Carolus 33–5, 44, 62, 483n.3, 485n.37, 485n.50, 538

Frye, Northrop 404, 407

Fuller, Reginald 400, 525n.39

Gadamer, Hans-Georg 39, 481n.20, 484n.23

Galilei, Galileo 100, 230–3, 238–40, 265, 364, 505n.12, 518n.3

Garriou-Lagrange, Réginald 97

genera and species viii, 11, 34, 155, 275, 346–7, 356, 358–60, 371, 379, 432, 474, 476, 520n.8; as explanatory 346

genetic 96, 135, 230, 264, 278, 283, 292, 301, 380, 386–9, 392–4, 398–400, 411–4, 474; method 96, 135, 278, 283, 292, 380, 388–389, 392–4, 474; method, integrator 388–91, 396, 425, 450, 521n.15, 521n.31; method, operator 388–92, 396, 422

Gilson, Etienne 178

gnoseology 140, 171, 186, 501n.28. *See also* cognitional structure; knowledge; thought; understanding

God 3, 18, 21, 27–30, 42–3, 50, 55, 59–60, 67, 69, 73, 75, 80, 82, 86–7, 89, 94–104, 124–6, 138, 140, 142–4, 157, 160, 163, 174, 176, 179, 185, 189–91, 199, 201, 203–5, 216–18, 253, 258, 264, 283, 326, 363–4, 398–9, 403–4, 429–30, 433–5, 438–451, 456–7, 459, 461 (*see also* 'On God's Knowledge and Will'); existence of 43, 157, 165, 397, 440, 441; as Father 144; as love 442; human desire to know 174, 442 (*see also* 'Natural Desire to See God'); personal 439; persons and relations in 142; processions in 69, 142–5, 160, 178–9, 201; and secondary causes, fate and providence 102, 445; Son of 399, 411; Spirit of 143–4, 179, 201, 281, 283; as transcendental artisan planning history 102; as Trinity 142–3, 160, 176, 202, 205, 464; as unrestricted understanding 201, 434, 438, 440; Word of 82, 143

good 56, 73, 80, 117, 126–7, 185, 201, 217, 242, 280–1, 291, 328–9, 339, 368, 410, 415–21, 425–6, 443–4, 447, 450,

460; general 216–7, 242; levels of 281; of order 91, 281, 339, 417, 420, 427, 525n.3; 17, particular 216–7, 281, 417, 420; and values 281, 417, 420, 427, 525n.3

Gorman, Francis 15

grace 7, 27, 36, 84, 87, 89, 94–101, 123, 126–31, 158, 174, 184–5, 190, 202, 205, 278, 281, 313, 380, 427, 449, 454; actual 28, 94, 97, 101, 129; cooperative 94, 98; and freedom 100, 131, 202, 427; operative 94, 97–8, 101; sanctifying 27, 97, 100

Graham, Nicholas 116, 490n.49

Grammar of Assent 20, 44–5, 250, 431, 472, 485n.45, 485n.47, 485n.48, 486n.55, 506n.7, 506n.8, 507n.12, 507n.15, 538

Hanley, T. O'D 340–1, 363, 366, 454, 488n.3, 514n.6, 516n.31, 516n.38, 537

Hegel, G.W.F. 34, 46, 71, 73, 154, 187, 200, 249, 259, 303–4, 340, 366, 400, 414, 468, 485n.50, 531n.46, 541

Heidegger, Martin 66, 73, 81, 141–2, 382, 400, 467, 483n.13, 489n.4, 490n.45, 497n.29, 514n.10, 519 n.7, 522n.13, 529n.13

Heisenberg, Werner 233, 349

Hertzberg, Gerhard 357, 518n.29

Hilbert, David 12, 47, 130, 279, 353, 495n.3

Hingston, W. 7

history. *See under* philosophy; metaphysics

Hitler, Adolf 66–7, 73, 93, 104, 344, 399, 401–4

Hoenen, Petrus 61–4, 131–4, 241, 363, 463, 472, 487n.44, 488n.46f, 488n.47, 495n.2, 503n.7, 539

Homer 30, 538

Hume, David 69, 76, 78, 323, 455

Husserl, Edmund 81, 467, 490n.43,
515n.10

'I' 291–2, 391, 511n.19
idea ix, 20, 22, 28, 34, 36, 38–9, 46,
54–7, 69, 70–5, 79–81, 90, 96–7, 102,
110–11, 115, 136, 153, 157, 183, 189,
198–9, 219, 229, 239, 272, 304, 311,
315, 321–2, 340, 377, 380, 422, 437,
441, 446, 467, 472; of being 154, 199,
437, 441, 518n.2; as content of an
insight, act of understanding 57, 72,
437; as objective, and Lonergan's
option for Aristotle on, 198; for
Plato 55–6
idealism 34, 69, 72, 137, 147, 154, 162,
182–3, 187, 204, 402, 441, 468,
485n.50, 501n.12; between materialism and critical realism 69, 72; in
Kant, Fichte, Schelling, Hegel 34
identity: of author viii, 5, 8, 12, 246,
391, 475–7; knowledge by 139, 171
Ignatius of Loyola 29–30, 66, 71, 85,
101, 482n.48, 492n.35
immanence 24, 184, 265, 509n.32;
breaking out of, and three judgments 184
immanentism 34, 77, 147, 184, 473
inference 41–6, 122, 170, 200, 221, 239,
244, 248–9, 318, 463, 484n.16,
484n.25
insight: act of an unimaginable awareness 238, 461; classical and statistical
150, 230, 240, 274, 317, 314, 320–22,
347, 473; into cognitional structure
200, 243, 251, 272; common sense
330, 333, 343, 369, 461–2; into
concrete situations 289; early use of
the word, 135; into emergent probability 316, 323; into insight, 461;
and personal identity viii; into

phantasm 11, 64, 135–6, 140–1, 145,
164, 166–7, 182–3, 192, 196–7, 200,
250, 266, 289, 356, 362, 472; philosophical viii, 5, 367, 380
integrations, higher 358, 376, 381, 391.
See also algorithm; viewpoint: higher
intellectual: conversion 7, 58–9, 81,
83–4, 122, 131, 137, 139, 162, 244,
254–7, 261, 265–6, 268, 278, 280,
369–70, 430, 470–1; conversion as
starting point of philosophy 254;
light 173–6, 183, 186, 252, 254,
508n.19; pattern of experience 4, 11,
80, 339, 345, 367–9, 371
Intelligence and Reality 8, 55, 57, 71–2,
150, 173, 186–7, 216, 218–19, 221,
231, 242, 245, 250–5, 276, 281–2,
287–93, 305–6, 308–9, 312–14, 317,
320, 323, 345, 346–7, 361, 365, 370–2,
396, 400, 402–4, 430–1, 462, 471,
473–4
interpretation: 11, 22, 24, 59, 78, 87,
94–5, 140, 150, 182, 191, 201, 264,
280, 397–401, 409–415, 456, 458, 474,
474; bias and counterpositions in
413–14; and Christology 398–400;
conceptualist and intellectualist of
Aquinas 182; conflict of 11, 78, 397;
and conversion 280; genetically and
dialectically linked series of 398, 400,
411, 413; misinterpretation, traditions of 78, 87; original expression
and reinterpretation 409ff.; universal
viewpoint in 413
intuition 42, 59, 64, 77, 83–4, 122,
132–4, 136, 150, 212–13, 241, 254,
257, 265, 269, 494n.32
isomorphism 264, 274, 279, 290, 362–3,
371–2, 379, 396, 415, 424, 473,
505n.15, 519n.19, 525n.34. See also
cognitional structure: isomorphic

with universe of proportionate
being

Jacobi, Jolan 331, 336–7, 515n.22, 537 A
    276, 541
Jaspers, Karl 141, 467
Joseph, W.H. 39–44, 48, 483n.14,
    484n.22, 484n.26, 484n.33, 498n.23,
    538
Joyce, George Hayward 39–41, 44,
    483n.14, 483n.15, 497n.23, 538
judgment: concrete, of fact 248, 250,
    260, 289, 328, 430, 432; and existence
    40, 46–7, 71, 77, 83–4, 181, 184, 250,
    258, 270, 294, 305, 430–6, 440–2,
    471–2; and 'is' of predication 40;
    standard of 168; of value 201, 281,
    420–1; and virtually unconditioned
    45–6, 247–9, 260, 289, 302–4, 367,
    408, 431–2, 468
Juglar, Clément 129, 540
Jung, Carl G. 22, 188, 331, 380, 402,
    502n.31, 515n.22, 523n.9, 537 A 276,
    541

Kant, Immanuel viii, 4, 6–7, 10–11, 22,
    33–35, 39, 41, 54–5, 57, 62, 69–72,
    76–8, 84, 90, 111, 135–6, 141, 146,
    154, 165, 167–8, 175, 203, 212, 215,
    230, 242–3, 247–50, 253, 257–9, 261,
    263, 265–6, 268–71, 274–5, 277–8,
    288, 291, 303–4, 307, 310, 323, 329,
    346–7, 354, 366–8, 371–2, 379–80,
    382, 396–7, 400, 420, 441, 453, 463,
    468–9, 472, 474–5, 485n.50, 490n.34
    490n.51, 494n.32, 497, 506n.3,
    497n.4, 507n.8, 507n.10, 16, 509n.10,
    527n.3, 528n.23, 528n.24, 535, 539,
    541; on Copernican revolution viii,
    4, 34, 269–71, 274, 277, 310, 329, 354,
    371–2, 414–15, 474–5

Keane, Henry 88, 92, 94
Keating, Joseph 26, 28.
Keeler, Leo 69, 76–7, 105, 137, 158, 186,
    346, 472, 488n.13, 488n.16, 488n.21,
    490n.34, 497n.7, 535, 539
Kelly, Beatrice. See White, Beatrice
Kennedy, Paul 33, 86, 88, 483n.4,
    486n.55
Keynes, John Maynard 129, 493n.13,
    540
Kierkegaard, Søren 416, 426
Kitchin, Joseph 129, 540
knowledge vii, 4, 5, 8, 10–11, 18, 30,
    35–6, 40, 42, 44–6, 59–64, 69–71, 74,
    77–8, 81, 83–4, 95, 116, 122, 126,
    131–4, 137–40, 143–4, 147, 150–4,
    161–2, 167–8, 170–6, 182, 185–6, 190,
    192–5, 199, 203–5, 212–14, 216, 219,
    223, 242–5, 247–8, 251, 253–69,
    272–3, 277, 279–82, 288, 294–5, 302–
    8, 310, 314, 316–18, 328–30, 340, 350,
    362, 365, 370–1, 374, 379–80, 391,
    397–8, 405–6, 408–9, 419, 426, 430,
    436–8, 441, 443–4, 449–50, 453–5,
    457–60, 465, 468, 471, 472, 474;
    common sense 8, 329–30, 374, 471;
    as confrontation 199, 212, 265–6; by
    identity 139, 171; by intentionality
    140, 171; philosophical 74, 443; Plato
    and Aristotle, conceptualist and
    intellectualist positions on 199; as
    power 426, 459; scientific 172; sub-
    ject and object of 8, 11, 35, 140–1,
    162, 168, 175–6, 203, 251, 258, 261–6,
    269, 279, 305, 307–8, 310, 314, 317,
    362, 472, 474; — , common-sense
    328; — , scientific 314, 317; — ,
    interpretive 414; — , philosophical
    372; transcendent 282, 430, 457; two
    modes of (see cognitional structure:
    direct vs. introspective)

Kojève, Andre 541
Kondratieff, Nikolai 129, 540

Lagrange, Marie Joseph 24
Lambert, Pierrot 479
Landgraf, Arthur 539
Langer, Susanne 463, 503n.5, 524n.10, 541
Lapointe, Pierre Louis 15, 480
Lawrence, Frederick ix, 421, 533–4
Leeming, Bernard 7, 75, 82–4, 105, 131, 134, 162, 204, 398, 465, 472, 497n.7, 539
Lenzen, Victor 230, 233, 323, 512n.19
levels 4, 7, 8, 9, 12, 42, 75, 99, 101, 111, 114, 118, 120, 123–7, 130, 141, 158, 181, 197, 200, 205–13, 224–5, 228, 237, 241–2, 243–5, 253–4, 265, 271, 274, 276, 281, 296–9, 331, 336–8, 399, 347, 357–62, 374ff., 391, 416–17, 421, 423, 430, 459, 468; absent from 'Forms of Inference' 123; of being 374ff.; civilizational 111; in cognitional structure (see cognitional structure); of consciousness (see under consciousness); of development (see under development: organic, psychic, intellectual, ethical, and religious); of economic production 114, 119, 130; ethical 416, 449; faith, hope, and charity as fourth level 459; in the good 281; higher viewpoints in mathematics 224–5, 228; in knowing 216, 241, 243–5; of life in 'Finality, Love, Marriage 124–7; Lonergan's use of the term 241–2; neural and psychic 347; of operation (see under operation); relation between levels of operation, activity, being 357–62; in 'Thought and Reality' 158; three cognitional levels in Trethowan 213; in Verbum 169,

174, 181, 197, 200, 203; in Verbum draft 141
Liddy, Richard ix, 35, 42, 46, 59, 69, 76–7, 296, 480n.11, 483n.8, 485n.39, 489n.15, 490n.34, 505n.9, 511n.27
Lieber, Robert 67–8, 73
Lonergan, Ann 17, 159
Lonergan, Bernard. See Bernard Lonergan Index
Lonergan, Gerald 15, 17, 19
Lonergan, Gregory 17–19, 104, 365, 530n.31
Lonergan, Josephene (née Wood) 17–18
Lonergan, Mark 17
Longman, Michael 460, 463, 467
Longmans (publishers) 464, 466, 503n.2
love 18, 26–7, 30, 61, 69, 87, 100, 104, 109, 123, 125–28, 144, 156, 160, 176, 179, 182, 185, 189–90, 201–2, 216–17, 241, 280–3, 334–5, 342, 442, 448–51, 461; dialectical ascent/descent of 126; and erôs 126; and friendship 126; and grace 126; levels in 126

MacMahon, Thomas 57, 65, 92
Mager, Alois 205, 540
Maréchal, Joseph 7, 77–8, 83, 541
Margenau, Henry, 231, 324, 505n.13, 514n.20, 542
marriage 43, 123, 127–8, 158 See also 'Finality, Love, Marriage'
Martin, L. 23–4
Marx, Karl 43, 73, 111, 129, 340, 343, 364, 464, 485n.42, 494n.21, 529n.23
Marxist 51, 79, 401, 493n.13
materialism 69, 72, 137, 147, 162, 395
Mathews, William 479n.3
McCaffray, Arthur 28, 482n.46
McCormick, Vincent 92–4, 98, 104
McKusic, Victor 350, 354, 517n.12

McShane, Philip ix, 113, 212, 494n.15, 497n.7, 534
Mendeleyev, Dmitri 164, 238, 348, 354, 499n.14, 516n.5
metaphysics viii, 8, 11, 18, 34, 71, 72, 81, 154–5, 171, 175, 179, 186, 197, 239, 267–71, 274, 277–8, 281, 288, 322, 340, 363–6, 369–71, 374–5, 384, 393–7, 400–5, 408, 411, 416, 424, 429–30, 433, 455–6, 463, 466, 468–9, 471, 473–4, 483n.7, 489n.26, 490n.41, 490n.45, 46, 499n.12, 509n.10, 515n.22, 519n.19, 535, 539–41; Aristotle's 154, 197, 239, 270–1, 271, 411; elements of 230, 277, 372, 374, 380, 390, 394, 519n.21; Heidegger 81, 490n.45; of history 72–3, 79, 276–7, 374, 395, 489n.26 (see also philosophy: of history) process viii, 11, 375ff., 471
method(s) viii, 4, 7, 12, 22, 24, 27, 30, 37–40, 47, 52, 53–6, 67, 79, 84, 93, 95–6, 98, 122, 135–6, 153–4, 172, 218, 221, 235, 239–40, 306–7, 317, 320, 344–5, 353, 363–4, 366–71, 374, 380, 387, 392–3, 398–400, 412–13, 415, 432, 440, 457–9, 464, 471, 474; classical 389, 393; dialectical 393, 398; four 393; genetic 96, 135, 278, 283, 292, 380, 389, 392–3; Kant on 39; Mill, Joseph, Joyce, and Coffey on 39–41; problem of 36, 79, 93, 98, 176, 187, 201–3, 246, 396, 398–400, 409, 412, 420–1, 424, 450, 452, 457–8, 467, 471, 476; statistical 53, 312, 317, 393; and study of understanding (insights) 459; in theology viii; transcendental 409
Mill, John Stuart 4, 22, 36, 38–40, 50, 53, 74, 153, 464, 484n.21, 538
mind-world relation 7–8, 10, 146, 240, 251–2, 257–8, 267–8, 288, 307–8, 437,

471–5. See also cognitional structure: direct vs. introspective; immanence; 'Intelligence and Reality;' Thought and Reality; Kant: on Copernican revolution; knowledge: subject and object of, common-sense/scientific/interpretative/philosophical; objectivity: principal notion; philosophy: Lonergan's three basic questions
Molina, Luis de 95, 101, 103, 491n.18
Moncel, V. 33, 37, 42, 484n.16
money 51–3, 115–18, 120–1, 313, 321, 493n.13, 494n.15; circuits 116–20; circulation 116–21, 129, 229, 313, 494n.15
Moral: consistency 419; impotence 100, 282, 427, 443, 446–7
Morelli, Mark ix, 54, 487n.16, 533–4
Mussolini, Benito 7, 66–7
mystery 23, 27, 51, 97–9, 103, 142, 144, 150, 205, 230, 308, 397, 400–1, 404–7, 433, 436, 439–40, 445–6, 448, 450, 470, 524n.22, 531n.3
mystic 72, 150, 155–6, 176, 204–6
mysticism 70, 91
myth 10, 21, 56–7, 71, 258, 342, 390, 397–408, 441, 453, 472, 480n.5, 495n.2, 496n.8, 503n.5, 520n.8, 523–4n.10, 524n.12, 524n.13, 523n.30, 523n.31, 526n.22, 541

narrative viii, 5–6, 8, 12, 35, 241, 246, 292, 348, 404, 407, 462, 470, 475–7; identity viii; intellectual viii, 241; quest vii, 5; self 8
Nassan, Maurice 33, 43, 485n.42, 486n.55
National Socialism 7, 66, 79, 81, 280, 490n.45
'Natural Desire to See God' 163, 189–90, 536
nature 10–11, 21–3, 28, 35, 37, 39, 52,

62, 73, 82–4, 89–92, 99–100, 110, 112,
113, 115–17, 122, 126–7, 131, 133–4,
139–40, 148–9, 154–6, 162, 169,
171–3, 185, 189–91, 203

neural 244, 272, 294, 299, 336–7, 340,
347, 351–4, 361, 375, 384–6, 402, 426,
515n.21, 516n.23, 517n.17

Newman, John Henry 20, 42, 44–8, 69,
72, 78, 84, 90, 122, 137–8, 156, 158,
166, 169, 186, 189, 241, 243, 246–50,
253, 260, 289, 346, 430–1, 433, 449,
470, 472, 486n.53, 486n.54, 489n.13,
489n.16, 489n.21, 499n.20, 506–7,
535, 538

Newton, Isaac 22, 35, 39, 53, 71, 89,
100, 113, 229, 232–3, 265, 269, 318,
323, 325, 348, 515n.13, 516n.5

nexus: and judgment 76–7, 139; terms
and relations, substance and attributes 62, 76–9, 132–3, 139, 198,
387

nominalism 34, 36–7, 48, 54, 57, 78–9

objectivity: absolute 261, 305, 307, 408;
consequent 305; experiential 305–6;
material 305–6; normative 253, 260,
306–7

Objectivity, principal notion: and
interpreting subject and object, 414;
and Kantian problem 184, 261, 264,
288, 304–8, 314, 317, 328, 335, 372,
471; and knower and known of
emergent probability 314, 317; and
subject/object of common sense
328, 345

O'Connor, Eric 50, 109–10, 146, 157–8,
326, 404, 463–5, 467–8, 482n.53,
498n.27, 531n.45

O'Dea, Br Michael 20

O'Donovan, Conn ix, 421

O'Hara, Charles 33, 47–8, 130, 495n.49,
540

O'Hara, Martin 146, 482n.2, 536

'On God's Knowledge and Will' 216,
242, 281, 438, 441, 443–4, 449,
504n.20

'Openness and Religious Experience'
174, 254

operation 101–3, 129, 145, 174, 238,
243–4, 269ff., 473; of agent 101;
agent cooperative with God's grace
87; cognitional operations as conscious 292ff.; contingency of 187–8;
exercise of a faculty 82; existence
predicated of 430; explaining levels
of operation 337–8, 347ff.; God's
grace as operative and cooperative
in willing 94, 97; interdependence of
mind/intellect and will 419; levels
174, 197, 199 (two), 200, 203 (three),
243–4; mathematical 186, 222ff.; of
mind 33, 39–40, 45, 63–4, 74, 78, 80,
82–3, 122, 138–9, 164–6, 173, 176,
179–82, 187–8, 195, 238, 242–4,
252–3, 269ff., 317, 473; of mind and
will 80, 126, 430; operating, being
operated on 101; two modes of 222,
240, 288, 308

order. See world order

Origen 523n.2

Ortega y Gasset, José 460

pedagogy 68, 101, 369–70, 387–8,
519n.12

Penfield, Wilder 351, 354, 515n.14

Phelan, Ray 31–2, 39, 482n.46

Philip the Chancellor 99

philosophy 4, 6–7, 11–12, 24, 31–8, 43–
4, 48, 58, 60, 63, 66–7, 69–71, 73–9,
81, 83, 92–3, 105, 110–11, 131–2, 134,
148, 154, 160, 170, 177, 182–3, 187,
200, 204, 218–19, 229, 234, 239, 249,
254–8, 261, 264, 267, 278–82, 291,
300, 308, 340, 343, 365–70, 375, 387,

391, 400, 405, 414, 427–8, 433, 441, 447, 459–60, 464, 470, 472 (*see also* development); dialectic of 340, 365–8, 413; good of 280–1, 291, 460; and Hegel's philosophy of philosophies 400, 414; of history 7, 73, 88, 92, 93, 111, 343, 387, 403–4, 447, 471, 475; limits of 281; Lonergan's three basic questions in 186, 454–5; as moving viewpoint 405, 448, 452, 454; positions and counterpositions 265, 323, 325, 340, 364, 370, 403, 407, 414–15, 426, 428, 447, 450, 526n.26; starting point of 31, 140, 254, 278, 393, 407, 462

Piaget, Jean 386–7, 504n.27

Pius X 24, 34

Pius XI 79, 85, 92

Pius XII 104, 218

Planck, Max 21–2

Plato 7, 20, 30–1, 49, 54–7, 59, 64, 69, 71–2, 75–7, 97, 101, 132, 154, 161, 193, 197–200, 212, 254–7, 265, 278, 340, 403, 407, 410, 411, 420, 437, 453, 472, 479, 487n.16, 489n.20, 490n.34, 495, 503n.21, 508, 523n.2, 526n.11, 535, 538–39

Plotinus 300

Poincaré, Henri 132

polymorphism 363, 365, 368, 474, 519n.10

Porphyry 34, 41, 156, 484n.31, 498n.23

positions and counterpositions. *See under* philosophy

possibility 130, 132, 137, 213, 216–18, 221–2, 233, 254, 262, 265, 275, 282, 290, 312–13, 325, 335, 395, 415–18, 420, 422 (*see also* world order); of ethics 201, 282, 415–16, 424

possible intellect 62–3, 172, 180–1, 183, 194, 197, 200

potency 74, 135, 137, 145, 154, 157, 180–1, 187, 190, 196, 271–7, 325, 372–8, 392, 394, 396, 449, 500n.33, 519n.21, 525n.3; central 392, 394; conjugate 274, 372–4, 392; prime 375–6

prayer 25, 29, 86, 185, 205, 399, 520n.8; mental lights in 70; use of senses and imagination in Ignatian contemplation 29

probability 38–40, 45, 58–9, 188, 217, 235–6, 274–7, 290, 301, 313–7, 319–22, 408, 461, 468, 494n.19, 505n.15. *See also* emergent probability

production (economics) 49, 51–3, 101, 113–18, 120–1, 129–30, 229, 312, 321

progress 7, 25, 39, 50–1, 54, 73–5, 89–92, 110–11, 114–15, 149, 267, 277, 282, 328, 341, 344, 368, 377, 406, 443, 446–7, 460–1, 536. *See also* decline

proposition 24, 30, 34, 39–40, 44–6, 62, 76–7, 95, 128, 133, 141, 144, 154, 162–3, 166, 168–9, 184, 188, 192, 195, 198, 222, 242–3, 247–9, 273, 300, 302, 408, 431–2, 463, 466; analytic vs. synthetic 62; formulations of content of insights 134, 141, 162–3, 169, 184, 192, 195, 198, 222, 242, 247, 302; reality and truth 154, 273, 466

providence 20, 29, 58–9, 79, 95, 101–3, 129, 445, 487n.31, 488n.35

psychic 272, 336–7, 347, 351–3, 361–2, 375, 379, 383–6, 388–92, 394, 401, 406–7, 415, 417, 422, 425–6, 430, 450, 459, 515n.22

quest vii–ix, 4–10, 23, 36, 45, 68, 79, 84, 129, 246, 299, 387–8, 394, 428, 442–3, 451, 453, 470–2, 474–7

Rahner, Karl 142, 492n.35

realism: critical 69, 72, 184–5, 204, 456, 467; two kinds of 140, 147–8, 157,

474 (*see also* materialism; idealism);
and problem of method in theology
187

reality 6–8, 16, 22, 35, 37, 51, 55–7, 59,
61, 63, 65, 69–74, 82, 86, 90, 125,
136–7, 140, 145–7, 153–8, 161–2,
170–1, 173–5, 183–8, 191–5, 204, 212,
214, 239, 247, 249, 251–7, 260–1, 270,
278–80, 308, 364, 369, 377, 380, 388,
403, 414, 440–1, 453–4, 462–3, 470,
475; equated with being 369, 441. *See
also* 'Intelligence and Reality';
'Thought and Reality'

reductionism, Lonergan's response to
355–6, 360, 416

regular: occurrence of a coincidental
aggregate 346, 358–60; sequence
in a development is not classical law
382

religion 11–12, 23–4, 27, 50–1, 67–8, 72,
91, 184–5, 204, 218, 292, 364, 397,
401–3, 406, 412, 416, 423, 429–30,
450, 471, 474. *See also* 'Openness and
Religious Experience'

Roy, Louis 189

Sala, Giovanni 84, 441, 491n.52,
507n.10

Schelling, Friedrich 34, 46, 304, 402,
485n.50, 524n.10

scholastic 33, 35–6, 59, 61–2, 67–8, 70–
2, 76, 124, 131–6, 218, 269, 277, 363,
464, 466, 472

Schopenhauer, Arthur 531

Schrödinger, Erwin 345, 349, 515n.11

Schumpeter, Joseph 129, 311, 340,
493n.13, 495n.47, 540

Scotus, Duns 33–4, 62, 76, 78, 139–40,
179, 219, 266, 367, 492n.34, 504n.25

self. *See under* affirmation; awareness

Sheridan, Edward 53

Shull, A. Franklin 20, 124–5, 129, 156,

275, 310–11, 377–8, 494n.36, 513n.2,
520n.9, 539

Shute, Michael ix, 487n.15

situation 6, 10, 30, 41, 54–5, 74–5, 90–1,
101–4, 152–3, 157, 167, 172, 177, 185,
198, 218, 233–4, 236, 250, 253, 262–4,
267, 270, 277, 289, 292, 297, 301, 308,
317–19, 322, 325, 328, 330–4, 338,
341–5, 358, 412, 430, 434, 436–7,
448, 466; and common sense 267,
308, 330

skills 223, 317, 330, 354, 358–62, 373–4,
381–2, 384, 386–7, 389, 417, 475

Smeaton, Henry 28, 31, 36, 61, 68,
483n.11, 535

Socrates 35, 55, 62, 72, 163, 197, 256–7,
405, 410, 483n.9

Sorokin, Pitirim A. 110, 493n.5,
493n.11

Spinoza, Baruch 55, 78, 323

Stalin, Joseph 67, 111, 141, 493n.13

standard of living 51–2, 112, 114–15,
117, 121, 129–30, 311–13, 315,
494n.19

statistical 53, 74, 112, 129, 155, 234–6,
239–40, 275, 310–14, 317–23, 325–7,
337–8, 347, 393, 421–2, 459; method
53, 312, 317, 393; residues 234, 317,
319, 327, 421

Stefanu, S. 83–4, 472

Stekel, Wilhelm 334, 336–7, 515n.17

Stewart, John A. 20, 54–7, 64, 78, 97,
198, 241, 254, 472, 487n.16, 539

Stewart, William 178, 185–9, 217, 245,
251, 278, 313, 500n.27, 505n.10,
507n.1, 536

Stoic 72, 506n.7

strange vii–viii, 6, 11, 144, 147–8, 161,
181, 221, 238, 242, 254–5, 257, 267–8,
295–7, 299, 401, 429, 441, 453, 473;
startling 11, 147, 257, 408, 453, 476–7;
unimaginable 238

Suárez, Francisco 33–7, 44, 76, 78, 94, 241, 484n.17
subject. See knowledge: subject and object of
subjective 35, 137, 156–7, 162, 168–9, 183, 195–6, 204, 250, 253, 256, 260–2, 280, 282, 294, 306, 456, 485n.50
substance 41, 47, 55, 62, 70, 78, 102–3, 138, 154–7, 216, 224, 239, 270–1, 273–7, 346, 348, 411, 430. See also thing; genera and species
Sullivan, Harry Stack 390, 392, 463, 522n.42
supernatural 80, 89, 99–100, 536, 540
Swain, John 61, 65, 326

Tansey, Charlotte ix, 28, 159, 256, 479, 497n.29
Teresa of Avila 176
Thackeray, William 30, 538
theology: Christology 82–3, 203, 242, 398, 400, 416, 458, 466, 474; dogmatic 67–8, 457; fundamental 68; grace (see grace); Lonergan as professor of 457; manual tradition 67, 98, 142, 202, 488n.10; method of viii, 7, 96, 457, 468–9; moral 67, 128; speculative development in 94; systematic 94, 96; Trinity 21, 69, 87, 142–3, 160, 176, 202, 205, 464 (see also God: processions in, persons and relations in)
thing viii, 6, 11, 34, 37, 42, 46–7, 63, 70, 79–80, 102, 131, 138, 144–5, 147, 152, 155, 161, 163, 171, 186, 193–8, 205, 216, 239–40, 251, 267, 294, 311, 347–62, 364, 371–5, 380, 385, 391, 394, 434–8, 441, 461–2 (see also substance; genera and species); contingent 441; species of viii, 149, 267, 274–5, 314, 317, 355, 358, 371, 374, 379, 415, 474, 476

Thing-in-itself 34–5, 42, 70, 78, 154, 168, 260–1
Thomas Aquinas viii, 4, 7, 10, 33, 37, 57, 61–4, 65, 76–9, 83, 94–8, 100, 102–3, 105, 128–9, 131–5, 138–41, 143–5, 158, 160–1, 163, 165–76, 178–80, 182, 184–8, 191–2, 194, 196–203, 216, 219, 252, 254, 271, 283, 296, 356, 363, 395, 399, 438, 456, 461–3, 465, 466–8, 471–2, 492n.23, 492n.34, 496n.10, 498, 503n.21, 508n.19, 527n.3, 533, 536, 539–40
thought: as process 242, 498n.28 (see also cognition; experience: intellectual pattern of; gnoseology); and reality 6, 8, 35, 146, 150, 155, 157–8, 161–2, 168, 175, 183, 186–8, 245, 251, 261–4, 270–2, 302, 308, 346, 366, 424, 431, 462, 471–2, 475
Thought and Reality (course) 146, 150, 158
Toynbee, Arnold 23, 110–11, 480, 491n.6, 493n.5, 493n.6, 11, 535, 539
Trethowen, Dom Illtyd 212, 242, 245, 473, 536
truth vii, 23, 34, 40, 42, 44, 46, 55, 58, 60–1, 68, 70, 72, 74, 76, 80, 83, 90, 99, 103, 136–8, 154–7, 167–73, 242, 252, 255, 326, 329, 331, 397–400, 404, 406, 408–13, 427–8, 458, 467
Tyrrell, Bernard 83

unconditioned: in Fichte, Schelling, Hegel 304; in Kant 247–9; virtually (see under judgment)
unconscious 164, 195, 244, 293–4, 297, 299, 311, 331, 336–7, 393, 515n.22, 541
understanding 4, 6–11, 16, 28, 36, 38, 40–1, 46, 50, 54–60, 62–4, 68–72, 74–5, 79, 81, 84, 89, 96–7, 99, 101, 103, 112, 120–2, 125, 131–9, 141–5,

147–50, 152–8, 160, 162–75, 180–7,
190–204, 211, 213–219, 221–2, 225–
30, 233–49, 252–3, 256–60, 262–3,
267–8, 270, 272–4, 276–80, 287–8,
290–5, 297, 299–302, 304–5, 308, 313,
316–17, 319, 321–2, 328–37, 341–4,
347, 350–5, 357, 361–9, 371–4, 376,
378–80, 385–90, 393–5, 399–400, 402,
405, 407, 410–12, 414–16, 418–20,
422–3, 427–9, 431–2, 434–41, 443–4,
445–8, 450–1, 454–62, 464, 466–476
(*see also* insight); and Archimedes'
eureka 162; direct, developments in
170; direct, and definition, proposition, thought, *verbum mentis* 163;
direct vs. reflective 169; and *entendement, verstand, intus-legere, epistemi*, 70;
and immoral action 444; reflective,
and illative sense 246–7; reflective,
vs. judgment or assent 247; of understanding (slogan of *Insight*) 454;
unrestricted (*see under* God)
unimaginable, data of consciousness
165, 238, 296, 403, 461
unmoved mover 199, 435

Vallillee, Lucia 19
Vallillee, Rupert 17
value vii, 12, 43, 98–9, 110, 123, 201,
202, 256, 281, 339, 385, 400, 414, 417,
420, 421, 423, 425, 427–8, 460, 461,
475, 525n.3; apprehensions of 420
Vertin, Michael 498n.1
viewpoint 4, 153, 222–3, 228–30, 240,
252, 278, 343, 347, 353, 358, 361, 362,
367, 382, 413, 454, 473–4, 505n.3,
529n.17; conflicting 367; higher 56,

153, 222, 224–8, 240, 252, 278, 347,
358–61, 382, 454, 473–4; moving 212,
292, 364, 405, 448, 452, 454, 456, 459,
529n.17; terminal 457, 529n.17;
universal 413, 458 (*see also* interpretation)
Virgil 23, 102
Voegelin, Eric 30, 411, 420, 526n.11

Watt, Lewis 33, 43, 495n.49, 538
White, Beatrice (née Kelly) 159, 365,
530n.31
Whiteside, Philip 6, 32–4, 98, 300,
482n.4
Wickham, John 211, 398–9
will 72–3, 77, 80, 95, 97–9, 103, 153, 179,
182, 185, 201–2, 334, 416, 418–19,
427, 430, 436, 443–50; freedom of 99,
416, 427, 443; intellect and 80, 126,
179, 201, 427, 430
wisdom 45, 58, 170–1, 176, 219, 249,
406, 445, 458; divine 458; and knowledge, power 406; and order of
objective reality 170; and and transition from thought to reality 170–1;
and world order 219
Wittgenstein, Ludwig 47, 142, 198, 471,
486n.56, 519n.7
Wood, Josephine 17–18
Wood, Mary A. (Minnie) 17–20, 109
world order 8, 10–11, 50, 188, 213,
217–19, 221, 234, 273–6, 313–22, 444,
474
world view 6, 8, 74, 343, 362, 378, 394,
396, 406, 424, 442–3, 449, 456, 460,
475–6. *See also* emergent: probability;
finality